A HISTORY OF THE
OXFORD UNIVERSITY
PRESS

The Delegates' Room in the Clarendon Building

A HISTORY OF THE OXFORD UNIVERSITY PRESS

BY HARRY CARTER

VOLUME I

TO THE YEAR 1780

WITH AN APPENDIX
LISTING THE TITLES OF BOOKS PRINTED THERE
1690–1780

OXFORD
AT THE CLARENDON PRESS
1975

Oxford University Press, Ely House, London W.1

GLASGOW NEW YORK TORONTO MELBOURNE WELLINGTON
CAPE TOWN IBADAN NAIROBI DAR ES SALAAM LUSAKA ADDIS ABABA
DELHI BOMBAY CALCUTTA MADRAS KARACHI LAHORE DACCA
KUALA LUMPUR SINGAPORE HONG KONG TOKYO

ISBN 0 19 951032 6

ⓒ *Oxford University Press 1975*

*Printed in Great Britain
at the University Press, Oxford
by Vivian Ridler
Printer to the University*

Preface

THIS is intended to be the first of two or three volumes dealing for the first time comprehensively and in detail with the history of the University Press from its origin up to the present time. The records of the Press in its own archives, in the archives of the University, or at the Public Record Office, and in the collections of manuscripts at the Bodleian Library, the British Library, and elsewhere can make a substantial, and in some ways unique, contribution to the history of publishing and printing, as, indeed, of scholarship, over a long time. They needed gathering up and digesting into narrative form with the necessary explanation and commentary.

That was the task given to me, and this book is my partial acquittance of it. The remaining parts of the history have yet to be written, and they are beset by all the uncertainties of futurity, except where a will to persist is concerned.

It was the Delegates' wish that a history of the Press should be printed, and they chose to entrust the writing of it to one who is primarily a printer. Their Secretary favoured an approach to the subject of a broadly bibliographical kind, so that the book would supplement more than it would overlap the history of the University, which, as some readers will know, is a work of collaboration still at an early stage.

That the Press has a history of its own so largely separable from that of the University to which it belongs is an indication of something more than the average academic man's reluctance to involve himself in business and his consequent willingness to give free rein to the few who consented to do so. The Delegates of the Press have been recruited from the most eminent scholars in their different fields among the senior members of the University and presided over by its Vice-Chancellor. Experience showed that they and their officers made good use of their liberty. Whilst it is true that for a hundred years or more past the Delegates and their Secretaries have set great store by independence, they could claim it because of the very high standing which the Press achieved in the worlds of learning and literature, and perhaps not less because for nearly two hundred years the Press has been financially self-sufficient. In modern times it has been allowed to devote its profits to subsidizing learned works and research projects. It is this policy that has given the University Press its peculiar character and greatly enhanced its prestige in the world.

The near-autonomy of publishing and printing as distinct from the University's other affairs is reflected in the scant appearances that the Press makes in the University's written constitution. Commenting on this the Committee under Professor Sir Humphrey Waldock wrote in its *Report on the University Press* in 1970:

The Statutes, in short, give the impression to the uninstructed reader that the Press is a minor side of the University and the Secretary to the Delegates merely one of the more senior University officials. The reality is entirely different.

The Press in its own sphere is comparable in importance to the University itself, and the Secretary to the Delegates is the executive head of a publishing organization of national—indeed world-wide—importance.

This was no exaggeration: there is truth in the claim often made for the Oxford University Press that it is familiar to people in many parts of the world who know nothing else about the University of Oxford, and its books have a prominent part in the esteem for Oxford in the world outside.

The Press has, indeed, 'its own sphere', and its history has been the subject of a number of books aimed, like this one, at an unlimited readership. Of them the most informative and the greatest work of scholarship is *Oxford Books*, three volumes published in 1895, 1912, and 1931, compiled by Falconer Madan, one-time Bodley's Librarian. Madan's work is a bibliography, a catalogue of books printed in or relating to Oxford from the beginning of printing here in 1478 until 1680. It is not a history, nor is it confined to publications of a university press, but the very full annotation includes annals of printing in Oxford and reproduces significant documents. Its value to a historian of the University Press is immense. Madan also left in manuscript a list of short titles of Oxford books extending to 1850, a basis for a continuation of his bibliography. Without recourse to Madan this volume, if it had been feasible, would have been the work of a lifetime.

Madan denied that a history of the University Press was needed; and indeed all that matters about it—or almost all—as far as 1680 can be found in his pages by taking trouble. Nevertheless he was persuaded to write a popular summary of his unique knowledge, *The Oxford University Press, a Brief Account*, and it was published by the Delegates in 1908. It brought the history up to that date, and the later part, written from the author's own knowledge, is particularly valuable. Sir Charles Firth, the eminent historian, greeted this *Brief Account* warmly, complaining only that it was 40, not 400, pages.

Madan's booklet was followed in 1922 by another, *Some Account of the Oxford University Press, 1468–1921*, anonymous but by R. W. Chapman, the Delegates' Secretary. That, again, is valuable evidence where it is contemporary history.

In 1943 the Oxford Bibliographical Society printed for its members *The First Minute Book of the Delegates of the Oxford University Press, 1668–1756*, edited with useful notes by Strickland Gibson and John Johnson. It has since been added to the list of the Oxford University Press, London.

These editors, in reverse order, were authors of *Print and Privilege at Oxford to the Year 1700*, printed in 1946 for the same Society and put on general sale by the O.U.P. It covers much of the ground covered by the present volume, the early years only in the briefest outline, and it stops eighty years earlier than this. The writing of the book is attributable to the late Dr. John Johnson, Printer to the University 1925–46. Accurate and scholarly as his account is, some readers find that his love of drama and the elaborateness of his style militate against clarity. This book attempts a more sober and orderly statement of the facts.

For the contribution to *Print and Privilege* of the late Mr. Strickland Gibson, Keeper of the University Archives, that is to say the collection of material and the documentation of the text with footnotes, there can be nothing but praise and, on my part especially, gratitude. He had at his command not only the archives but the Bodleian collection of manuscripts, an advantage not easily gained unless by having care of them.

Last in order of date is *William Blackstone and the Reform of the Oxford University Press in the Eighteenth Century* by Mr. I. G. Philip, now Deputy Librarian at the Bodleian Library, published in 1957. To a much greater extent than the authors noticed above Mr. Philip made use of records at the Press, and I cannot claim that my account of the same subject, though it differs from his in the importance attached to the various parts of Blackstone's work for the Press, by any means displaces his as an indispensable authority.

However, with that exception, the unlimited access that I have enjoyed to the archive of the Delegates and of the Printer to the University has given me an advantage over previous historians of the Press and made it possible to add substantially to the information hitherto printed. The most notable accessions come, I think, from 'The Account for Printing', three manuscript volumes ranging in date from 1690 until 1780, and a fourth, a record of stock and sales from 1785 until 1804. The accounts, not used before for histories of the Press, show how many of the books printed here at that time were paid for by the Delegates and of those usually how many were sold and their prices. A good many books bearing only the imprint of the University are revealed by the accounts as publications by authors or booksellers. Names of authors of anonymous books and dates of those that are not dated are in some instances brought to light.

This press has older records than any other in England. I have done my best to extract from them what is of economic, social, or technical interest. Evidently a review of the work of this organization might make a serious contribution to the history of learning, and I have made some attempt to estimate the value of our records for that purpose also.

The rich collection of old typefaces, some of them still in constant use, for which the Press has matrices made in the sixteenth and seventeenth centuries and casts in its own small typefoundry, was dealt with in Horace Hart's *Notes on a Century of Typography at the University Press, Oxford, 1693–1794* of 1900 (reprinted with additional notes in 1970) and in the splendid folio book by Stanley Morison, *John Fell, the University Press, and the 'Fell' Types* (Oxford, 1967). I have not thought it necessary to dwell once more on the antiquities at the Press of special interest to typographers.

For two reasons 1780 seemed a suitable date for an end to Volume I. In that year the University was unable any longer to find a lessee for its privilege of printing the Bible and went into partnership with master printers in setting up a Bible Press. The prodigious expansion of Bible-printing thereafter altered the character of the business of the Delegates of the Press profoundly. From 1780, also, there ceases to be a complete record of books printed here other than those paid for out of University funds and issued with the authority of the Delegates of the Press. Books printed at the Press under contracts with other publishers, usually in early days the authors or enterprising booksellers, will have, for lack of a continuous record and because of their mounting number, to be more sparingly noticed in a future volume.

The Appendix giving the titles of books printed at the Press in the years 1690–1780 was undertaken as groundwork for the history and is printed as a contribution to a bibliography. Oxford books from 1681 onwards await a bibliographer: I hope that my transcripts of title-pages, references to the Press accounts, and slight annotation will simplify his task. My assignment was limited to the University Press, therefore I have omitted books with Oxford imprints that professedly were, or by relying mainly on typographical criteria I judged to have been, printed at other presses in the city. Bibles and prayer books in English or Welsh are not included in the Appendix. We have no record of those issued in 1678–1780 by lessees of the University's privilege of printing them, and so I could not better the list in Darlow and Moule's *Historical Catalogue of English Bibles* where editions from Oxford are concerned. My references to Donald G. Wing's *Short-Title Catalogue* are to the first edition.

I shall be grateful for additions and corrections to the Appendix relating to books from the University Press that I can hold in trust for an eventual bibliographer.

As a rule I have avoided troubling busier people with my difficulties; but I made exceptions. Miss M. M. Eady most kindly gave me the benefit of her knowledge of the University's constitution and some needed encouragement; Miss H. M. Petter generously kept me informed of her discoveries about the *Oxford Almanack*; Mr. Paul Morgan was my learned and friendly guide to college libraries and Dr. R. A. Sayce hunted for me (and found) rare items at Worcester College. At Cambridge Mr. J. C. T. Oates and Dr. Philip Gaskell were equally kind. Dr. Sten G. Lindberg, of the Royal Library, Stockholm, digested for me the learning about Erik Benzelius and *Codex Argenteus*. Mr. J. P. Chalmers helped me to information in American publications; Mr. R. Jeffery corrected my draft about books in Welsh.

It was fortunate for me that the publishers sent my manuscript to Dame Lucy Sutherland for criticism. I owe a good deal to her suggestions.

The Governors of Guy's Hospital were so generous as to photograph their portrait of Guy and give me a print.

I am conscious of having tried the patience of the staff of the Bodleian Library near to a reasonable limit; but they, from the Keepers of Manuscripts and of Printed Books *usque ad inferos*, treated me with their unvarying understanding and good humour, and I thank them all for it. So do I Mr. David Vaisey for his help with the Archives.

The Printer to the University, my employer and old friend, sustained and advised me throughout.

University Press
Oxford

Contents

PART I

INTRODUCTORY

PART II

THE AUGUSTAN AGE 1690–1713

PART III

THE BAD TIME 1713–1755

PART IV

THE ERA OF BLACKSTONE 1755–1780

List of Illustrations

Portraits and pages of books in the Bodleian Library are reproduced by permission of the Curators of the Bodleian Library

Abbreviations

A/cs.: Accounts.

1st A/cs.: 'The Account for Printing 1691–1708'. A manuscript book in the archive of the Delegates of the Press in which are copied the accounts rendered yearly to the Vice-Chancellor by the man in charge of printing.

2nd A/cs.: 'The Account for Printing 1708–47', similar to the first.

3rd A/cs.: 'The Account for Printing 1747–80'.

Arber, *Transcript*: *A Transcript of the Registers of the Company of Stationers of London*, ed. E. Arber (1875–7), 4 vols.

Blagden: Cyprian Blagden, *The Stationers' Company, a History 1403–1959* (1960).

B.M.: British Library (London).

Bodl.: Bodleian Library (Oxford).

Boswell: *Boswell's Life of Johnson, including the Tour to the Hebrides*, ed. by G. Birkbeck Hill, revised and enlarged by L. F. Powell (Oxford, 1934–64), 6 vols.

Burton: John Burton, *The Genuineness of Lord Clarendon's History of the Rebellion printed at Oxford vindicated* (Oxford, 1744).

Carter, *Wolvercote Mill*: Harry Carter, *Wolvercote Mill, a Study of Paper-Making at Oxford* (Oxford, 1957).

Chancellor's Court Acta: Entries in the manuscript Act Book of the Court of the Chancellor of the University of Oxford, in the University Archives.

Chancellor's Court Cause Papers: Documents relating to causes in the Chancellor's Court preserved in the University Archives.

Darlow and Moule: *Historical Catalogue of Printed Editions of the English Bible 1525–1961, revised and expanded from the Edition of T. H. Darlow and H. F. Moule, 1903, by A. S. Herbert* (London and New York, 1968).

'Delegates' Book': A manuscript register-book given to the Delegacy by William Blackstone in 1758, in which he had copied 'Extracts from Charters, Statutes, and other records relating to the University Press' up to 1658. Additions were made up to 1692 by the University Registrars. In the Delegates' archive.

D.N.B.: *Dictionary of National Biography*.

D.O.: Orders of the Delegates of the Press, a series of manuscript volumes at the Clarendon Press containing minutes of the Delegates' meetings from 1668 until the present.

dues: amounts charged by the University to outside customers of the Press in addition to the printers' bills to cover profit and overhead expenses.

First Minute Book: *The First Minute Book of the Delegates of the Oxford University Press, 1668–1756*, ed. Strickland Gibson and John Johnson (Oxford, 1943).

Gent. Mag.: *The Gentleman's Magazine* (Annual volumes, 1731–1858).

Greg, *Companion to Arber*: W. W. Greg, *A Companion to Arber, being a Calendar of Documents in Edward Arber's Transcript* [&c.] (Oxford, 1967).

Griffiths, *Laudian Code*: *Statutes of the University of Oxford Codified in the Year 1636 under the Authority of Archbishop Laud*, ed. John Griffiths (Oxford, 1888).

Gunther, *Early Science in Oxford*: R. T. Gunther, *Early Science in Oxford* (Oxford, 1923–67), 15 vols.

Hart: Horace Hart, *Notes on a Century of Typography at the University Press, Oxford, 1693–1794* (Oxford, 1900, reprinted in facsimile, 1970).

Hearne: *Remarks and Collections of Thomas Hearne*, ed. C. E. Doble, D. W. Rannie, H. E. Salter, and others. Oxford Historical Society (Oxford, 1885–1918), 11 vols.

Hist. MSS. Comm.: Historical Manuscripts Commission.

Imp.: Imprimatur. The Vice-Chancellor's (or Chancellor's) permission to publish signified by the word 'Imprimatur', his name, and the date, in a book printed in Oxford.

J.J. Coll.: The J.J. Collection, mainly of printed ephemera, made by the late Dr. John Johnson, kept in the Bodleian Library.

Johnson, *Letters*: *Letters of Samuel Johnson, LL.D.*, ed. G. Birkbeck Hill (Oxford, 1892), 2 vols.

Journeys of Celia Fiennes: *The Journeys of Celia Fiennes*, ed. C. Morris (1949).

Laud's 'Account relating to the U. of Oxford': 'An Historical Account relating to the University of Oxford', in *The Second Volume of the Remains of the Most Reverend Father in God William Laud, Lord Archbishop of Canterbury, written by Himself*, collected by Henry Wharton (1700).

Lee, *Memorial*: [John Lee] *Memorial for the Bible Societies in Scotland, containing Remarks on the Complaint of His Majesty's Printers against the Marquis of Huntly and others* (Edinburgh, 1824).

Lives of the Norths: Roger North, *The Lives of the Rt. Hon. Francis North, Baron Guilford; the Hon. Sir Dudley North; and the Hon. and Rev. Dr. John North*, ed. A. Jessop (1890), 2 vols.

LP: Large Paper. Copies of a book printed on bigger sheets than those used for the rest of the edition.

McKenzie: D. F. McKenzie, *The Cambridge University Press 1696–1712, a Bibliographical Study* (Cambridge, 1966), 2 vols.

Macray, *Annals*: W. D. Macray, *Annals of the Bodleian Library, Oxford*, 2nd ed. (Oxford, 1890).

Madan: Notebooks compiled by Falconer Madan giving brief and tentative particulars of books printed at, or relating to, Oxford between 1680 and 1851 (Bodl. MSS. Dep. e. 12, 13).

 References to these notebooks are given by years and Madan's numbers within years, thus 1691:15.

Madan, *Oxford Books*: Falconer Madan, *Oxford Books, a Bibliography of Printed Works relating to the University and City of Oxford or Printed or Published there* (Oxford, 1895, 1912, 1931), 3 vols. Stops at 1680.

ABBREVIATIONS xxi

Morison, *Fell*: Stanley Morison, *John Fell, the University Press, and the 'Fell' Types* (Oxford, 1967).

Moxon, *Mech. Ex.*: Joseph Moxon, *Mechanick Exercises on the Whole Art of Printing*, ed. Herbert Davis and Harry Carter, 2nd ed. (Oxford, 1962).

Newdigate Papers: Documents formerly belonging to the Newdigate family in the County Record Office, Warwick (Class CR 136).

Nichols, *Illus.*: John Nichols, *Illustrations of the Literary History of the Eighteenth Century* (1817–31), 6 vols.

Nichols, *Lit. An.*: John Nichols, *Literary Anecdotes of the Eighteenth Century, comprizing Biographical Memoirs of William Bowyer, Printer, F.S.A.* (1812–15), 9 vols.

O.E.D.: *The Oxford English Dictionary* (Oxford, 1884–1928), 13 vols. with Supplements of 1933 and 1972.

O.H.S.: Oxford Historical Society.

Philip: I. G. Philip, *William Blackstone and the Reform of the Oxford University Press in the Eighteenth Century* (Oxford, 1957).

Plomer, *Dictionary 1668–1725*: Henry R. Plomer and others, *A Dictionary of the Printers and Booksellers who were at Work in England, Scotland, and Ireland from 1668 to 1725*, ed. Arundell Esdaile (1922).

Prideaux: *Letters of Humphrey Prideaux, sometime Dean of Norwich, to John Ellis, sometime Under-Secretary of State, 1674–1722*, ed. E. M. Thompson. Camden Society Publications, 2nd series 15 (1875).

Print and Privilege: John Johnson and Strickland Gibson, *Print and Privilege at Oxford to the Year 1700* (1946).

P.R.O.: Public Record Office (London).

Reed, *Old English Letter Foundries*: T. B. Reed, *A History of the Old English Letter Foundries*, 2nd ed., revised by A. F. Johnson (1952).

Ruffhead: *The Statutes at Large from Magna Charta to 1763*, ed. Owen Ruffhead (1762–5), 9 vols.

s. sh.: single sheet.

S.P. (Dom.): State Papers, Domestic Series, at the Public Record Office, London.

Stationers' records: Documents in the custody of the Worshipful Company of Stationers of London.

S.T.C.: *A Short-Title Catalogue of Books printed in England, Scotland, and Ireland and of English Books printed Abroad, 1475–1640*, compiled by A. W. Pollard and G. R. Redgrave (1946).

Steele: Robert Steele, *Bibliotheca Lindesiana, Vol. v: a Bibliography of Royal Proclamations of the Tudor and Stuart Sovereigns and of Others printed under Authority, 1483–1714* (Oxford, 1910–13), 3 vols.

T.C.: *The Term Catalogues, 1668–1709 A.D.; with a Number for Easter Term 1711 A.D.*, ed. Edward Arber (1903–6), 3 vols.

Th. Sh.: Theatro Sheldoniano.

Timperley: C. H. Timperley, *Encyclopaedia of Literary and Typographical Anecdote*, 2nd ed. (1842).

Twells, *Life of Pococke*: [Leonard] Twells, 'The Life of the Rev. and most Learned Dr. Edward Pocock' in *The Lives of Dr. Edward Pocock by Dr. Twells, of Dr. Zachary Pierce . . . and of Dr. Thomas Newton, by themselves and of the Rev. Philip Skelton, by Mr. Burdy*, vol. i (1816).

Typ. Clar.: Typographeo Clarendoniano.

Univ. Arch.: University Archives.

V.-C.'s Computus: Accounts for the University's receipts and expenditure rendered annually to Convocation by the Vice-Chancellor, written in books preserved in the University Archives.

V.C.H.: *Victoria County History.*

Wing: Donald G. Wing, *Short-Title Catalogue of Books printed in England, Scotland, Ireland, Wales, and British America, and of English Books printed in Other Countries, 1641–1700* (New York, 1945–51), 3 vols.

Wood, *Ath.*: Anthony Wood, *Athenae Oxonienses, an exact History of all the Writers and Bishops who have had their Education in the University of Oxford*, 3rd ed. with additions by Philip Bliss (1813–20), 5 vols. References are to numbered columns.

Wood, *Fasti*: *Fasti Oxonienses, or Annals of the University of Oxford, by Anthony a Wood, M.A.*, ed. by Philip Bliss. Part i, 1500–1640 (1815); Part ii, 1641–91 (1820).

Wood's Life and Times: *The Life and Times of Anthony Wood, Antiquary, of Oxford, 1632–1695, described by Himself*, collected by Andrew Clark. Oxford Historical Society (Oxford, 1891–1900), 5 vols.

Retrospect

To the question, What is the Oxford University Press? history returns a long and rambling answer. A reader may reasonably ask to be satisfied on the point and to be given some definitions of terms before embarking on this volume.

In its wider sense, and the sense in which it is used in the title of this book, the Oxford University Press is an organization maintained by the University for producing and selling books. The University is incorporated by Act of Parliament with the legal style of the Chancellor, Masters, and Scholars of the University of Oxford. Whoever signs a contract for a book to be published by the Press is bound by mutual obligations to the Chancellor, Masters, and Scholars, and copyright in the published book, if the author parts with it, belongs to them (an exception must be made for the O.U.P., New York, which is a company and contracts as such).

For the past three hundred years and more the supreme authority in the University has entrusted Delegates of the Press with the printing, publishing, and selling of books, these being considered as necessary objects of its endeavours. The Delegacy, at present of nineteen senior graduates, always including the Vice-Chancellor, the two Proctors, and the University's Assessor, has the duty of deliberating on how best to achieve these objects, authorizing expenditure on them, and accounting for them to the delegating body.

During the time with which this volume deals the University was governed and delegations of its powers were made by Convocation, an assembly of graduates, masters of arts, and those of higher or equivalent degree (and until 1760 not only those who had kept up their membership of a college). Those who live away from Oxford are nevertheless entitled to attend meetings of Convocation and vote. Reforms since 1852 have transferred the effective control of the University's affairs to Congregation, a body whose membership is restricted to those resident in Oxford, in effect to the University's teaching and research staff. Both bodies have existed side by side since a remote time, and it would be difficult, as it would be needless for a history of the Press, to delimit their functions at any given time. In the seventeenth and eighteenth

centuries vacancies in the Delegacy of the Press were filled by appointments made by the Proctors with the assent of the Vice-Chancellor
exercising powers given them by Convocation: now the appointments
are made by a committee elected by the Hebdomadal Council of
Congregation and the General Board of Faculties.

The Delegates transact their business at periodical meetings convened
by the Vice-Chancellor, at which he presides as chairman. At one time—
and well into the nineteenth century—the whole work of publishing was
done by the Delegates unaided, apart from the secretarial help of the
University Registrar, who attended their meetings and recorded the
minutes. If a letter had to be written, the Vice-Chancellor would write
it or ask another Delegate to do so; if a report were wanted, he would
find a suitable person to draw it up. In recent times, owing to a great
increase in business, much of the work of the board has been done in
standing committees of its members reporting to the full sessions on
such matters as finance, recommendations on proposed publications,
religious books, and school books.

In the course of its growth the Press, that is to say the business controlled by the Delegates, has divided into departments with specialized
functions. When the first Delegacy was appointed in 1633 the University had no printing press: it had royal licence to appoint a printer, with
whom it dealt by contract. By pure chance the Delegates found themselves
directly engaged in printing for a brief spell in 1669–70, and in 1690
they took charge of a printing-office equipped for the University's service by Bishop Fell and his three partners.

Of the two divisions of the Press that have existed since 1690 it will be
best to consider first the publishing business, as being older than the
printing. The Clarendon Press, the publishing office at Oxford, has
developed from secretarial assistance given to the Delegates. In 1866
they appointed a salaried full-time Secretary, whose duties were at first
to record their resolutions and see that they were carried out, to keep
accounts and look after the finances, and to act as general manager of
publishing. It was found necessary in 1879 to add an Assistant Secretary
to conduct the whole business of a modern publisher's staff, as the
Secretary came to be increasingly concerned with bringing matters of
policy to the attention of the Delegates and co-ordinating the activities
of a growing number of committees, departments, and branches. There
is now an Oxford Publisher with a staff of more than 200; but besides
deciding matters of policy and those involving large sums of money

Ely House, Dover Street. The head office of the Oxford University Press, London. Built in 1772–6 as the town house of the bishops of Ely

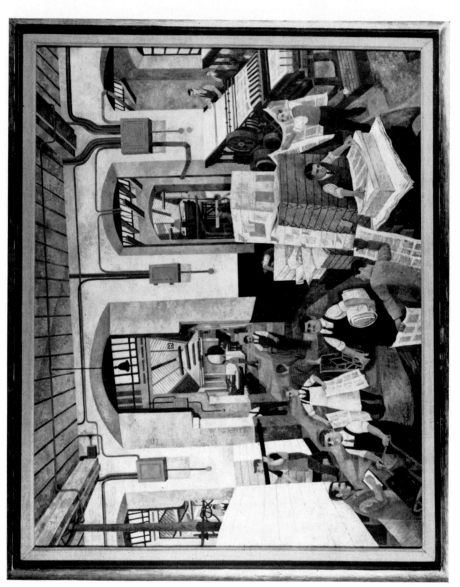

Part of the Machine Room at the University Press, Oxford. From a painting by Alfred Daniels (1959)

the Delegates in full session continue to accept or reject every proposal for a new book to be issued from the Clarendon Press.

The Clarendon Press was the name given to the building put up in 1712–13 to house the University's printing works, where there is a fine room still used for Delegates' meetings. Until 1780 the imprint 'at the Clarendon Press' was put on books printed there, whether for the University or for private customers, but in that year the Delegates decided to restrict that imprint to their publications. The name was transferred to the bigger building in Walton Street to which the printing works were moved in 1829, where accommodation has since been found for the Secretary and the publishing staff. In recent years the name 'Clarendon Press' has been confined to the publishing office in Oxford, and the printing department is distinguished as 'the University Press, Oxford'.

Selling books was for a long time the hardest and the least satisfactory of the activities of the Press. In the eighteenth century books were sold retail at the door and certain booksellers in London were persuaded to hold stocks of Oxford publications 'on sale or return'; but the discounts allowed them were less than was customary in the trade, so that sales were slow. From 1810 an Oxford bookseller, Joseph Parker, and after him his son, John Henry Parker, acted as sole wholesalers of Clarendon Press books, and being allowed by the Delegates the usual discount of 33⅓ per cent from 1838, did good business. The Delegates ended their agreement with Parker in 1861, and in 1863 they contracted with a London publisher, Alexander Macmillan, to act as their adviser and to promote the sale and distribution of their secular books.

Arrangements for selling Bibles were different. After a hundred years of letting to London booksellers the right to print the Bible at Oxford, the University was unable to find a lessee for the privilege in 1780, and took two printers into partnership to conduct the business and share the profit. One of the partners had a warehouse in London where he sold the Bibles wholesale at discounts acceptable to the trade. It was sold to the partnership in 1812. It was agreed in 1832 that Clarendon Press books should also be sold at the Bible Warehouse in London. In the early part of the nineteenth century the Bible Press managed by the partners made large profits and more partners were admitted to cope with the work. One of them set up a bindery in London on his own account in or before 1859 and began selling Oxford Bibles bound (until then all the books from the Press had been sold as folded and gathered sheets: editions stitched and covered in stiff boards at the Clarendon Press are first mentioned in 1863). In 1867 the Bible Press partnership bought the business in selling bound books and put a salaried manager in charge of it. The partnership bought the bindery in 1870. When the agreement with Macmillan came to an end in 1880, the manager of the Bible Warehouse was entrusted with the bound stock, the sale, and the distribution of all the books of the Press.

The bindery in London, moved from the Barbican to Aldersgate Street in 1878, was for many years the only one that the Press had, and it was equipped specially for binding Bibles. About 1890 a beginning was made with binding secular books at the printing works at Oxford, and in 1922 a large new bindery was opened there capable of dealing with most of the output of the Press. The bindery in London closed in 1934.

The London Manager in 1880 was Henry Frowde. Before his appointment in 1874 he was in business on his own selling Bibles and prayer books, and after it he was encouraged to undertake the production of some of the University's publications, especially hymn-books for the Anglican and Presbyterian Churches, medical books, and music, as well as reprints of the English classics at reasonable prices, printed some at Oxford and some elsewhere. That was the beginning of a separate publishing business controlled by the Delegates but managed in London, whose main function is to sell and distribute all the books of the Press, whether they originate in Oxford or in London, and secondarily to promote publications of its own. Frowde was given the more honorific title of Publisher to the University in 1896 in recognition of his great services. When he retired in 1913 and was succeeded by H. S. (afterwards Sir Humphrey) Milford, the output of books from the London office much increased and reflected the Publisher's scholarly and literary taste. Publications originating in London, bearing the imprint of the 'Oxford University Press, London', now roughly equal in number those from the Clarendon Press.

The publications of the two houses differ to some extent in character. The Clarendon Press may produce works that are not expected to make a profit, or even to cover their cost, if the Delegates consider it incumbent on the University to do so: the Oxford University Press is required to publish profitable books. Proposals to publish at the Clarendon Press are considered individually at Delegates' meetings and must be recommended to them by the opinions of specialists: the London Publisher submits a list of his proposed new books, and the Delegates normally accept it entire on his recommendation. The books of the Clarendon Press are, as a rule, learned in a narrower sense than those with the London imprint, which are calculated for a bigger class of readers.

From its beginning the Press has had aims that are extra-mural. It is true that it has always produced what the University needed in the way of statutes and notices, and in modern times examination papers; but these were never a large part of its business. Its texts have been designed for use in the world at large. Since most of the books until the end of the eighteenth century were in Latin, they achieved a certain currency abroad, and as commerce between countries became easier Oxford books were exported increasingly. The Delegates have always employed foreign scholars as readily as they employed Englishmen as authors and editors.

The aim of the Press as publisher is, broadly, the advancement of knowledge and religion, though excluding religious controversy. To this must be added the service of education at all levels. Attempts by the precursors of the Press in the seventeenth century to enter the market for school books were fought off or bought off by the London Company of Stationers, which claimed it as a monopoly; but the University sponsored a series of editions of the best Latin grammar and of an explanation of the Church Catechism. In 1863 the Delegates set up a Committee to advise on educational books, and have since made them an important part of their publishing. School books intended for English-speaking countries issue from the Clarendon Press, while the Oxford University Press in London and the Branches overseas deal with lesson books in the English language and those in vernacular languages for the rest of the world.

The third main department of the Press, to which we come after considering the two publishing houses, is the printing business. It may be said to owe its origin to Archbishop Laud, who presided over the University as its Chancellor from 1629 until 1641. Laud was intent upon publishing early Christian texts emanating from the Eastern Churches in their original languages, Greek, Hebrew, Arabic, and Syriac, and he thought Oxford the best place in which to found a press to print them. He induced the University to agree to set up a printing office under its common ownership and to equip it with a typefoundry where the type for learned texts could be cast. Laud's fall from power and the Civil Wars put off the realization of his plan, but after the Restoration in 1660 and the return to power of his admirers it was revived. John Fell, Dean of

Christ Church from 1662 until his death in 1686 and Bishop of Oxford from 1676, secured an allocation of space for printing in the Theatre given to the University by Archbishop Sheldon, finished in 1669.

The intention of the Delegates of the Press to contract with master printers for a supply of skilled labour to the printing house and let them sell the product proved unequal to the demands of learned printing. Fell resolved to finance it himself with help from Thomas Yate, Principal of Brasenose College. They persuaded a judge and a civil servant of high standing to lend their names to the enterprise, and in 1672 the partnership of four took a lease from the Chancellor, Masters, and Scholars of the right to exercise their privilege of printing and the use of such premises and equipment as they had for the purpose. They employed journeymen printers and a typefounder.

Liberty to print was a privilege conferred by grant from the Crown until ideas of constitutional law changed after the Revolution of 1688. Fortunately the University of Cambridge had secured it by a charter from King Henry VIII in 1534, giving it the right to have three printers and to print and sell 'all manner of books'. In 1557 King Philip and Queen Mary incorporated the Worshipful Company of Stationers of London and gave its freemen the sole right to print in the kingdom and power forcibly to prevent printing by others. The conflict of rights between Cambridge and the Stationers was resolved, in principle, by an opinion of the judges in 1629 that the University had power to print and might override monopolies of printing particular books or classes of books that Tudor and Stuart sovereigns had bestowed liberally since 1534. Of these the most profitable was the exclusive right to the Bible in English, the Book of Common Prayer, and the services of the Church of England, granted by Queen Elizabeth I to Christopher Barker in 1577 with the title of Queen's Printer. When Laud got from Charles I in 1632 a charter giving the University of Oxford a power of printing in the same terms as that possessed by Cambridge, the Stationer's Company on behalf of the monopolists bought off competition from the Universities by paying them an annual rent to forbear printing the numerous books which were the subject of royal patents.

When the agreement with Oxford was due for renewal in 1672 the Stationers were willing to buy forbearance for a further period, but the King's Printers were not, believing that the University had not resources enough to compete in the market for Bibles; so Fell and his partners entered upon their lease at Lady Day in that year intending to put an end to forbearance. They undertook to pay the University annually what it had been receiving from the monopolists.

In expecting to be able to defy the Stationers' Company and the King's Printers the Oxford partners were too sanguine. During their eighteen years' tenure they were obliged by a prospect of heavy loss to sublet to the Stationers almost continuously their right to print the so-called 'scheduled books'. Only where the Bible was concerned Fell refused to give in. He sublet to a consortium of four London Stationers who were willing to compete with the King's Printers by exploiting the University's privilege. Since the charter confined the privilege to printing in the University's precinct, the four Stationers had to set up their presses in Oxford. This sublease, granted in 1678, was the beginning of a separate Oxford Bible Press which continued as an organization distinct from the Learned Press until modern times, and in the nineteenth century it far exceeded the other in the bulk and value of its production.

When Fell's executors in 1690 surrendered the last lease held by him and his partners the Bible Press, like the Learned Press, came under the direct control of the University's Delegates. It was let to a succession of London Stationers at increasingly high rents until, in 1780, no one was found willing to take a new lease. It was then that the University took master printers into partnership with it for conducting the Bible Press, a system which lasted until 1881, when the last of the 'Managing Partners' were bought out. In 1883 a salaried Controller of the united Bible and Learned Presses was appointed; but separate accounts were kept for the two departments until 1906, and each had its own composing room until 1916. The title of Controller was superseded in 1927 by that of Printer to the University.

About 70 per cent of the capacity of the printing works is taken up by the two publishing houses, the percentage of Clarendon Press books printed there being roughly 60, and of London books 40. The Printer accepts work from other publishers, from private individuals, and from all the departments of the University.

The 'Bible privilege' of the two old Universities of sharing with the King's Printer the kinds of work reserved to him by his patent has not been challenged in a court of law since 1758, and it has in the past been a substantial source of profit to them, enabling the Universities to undertake unremunerative learned work. Restriction to these three presses of the right to print the Scripture in English has been the subject of complaint from time to time, and to mitigate the objection to it the three printers have let it be known for the past hundred-and-fifty years and more that they reserve to themselves by virtue of the privilege only the Authorized Version of the Bible printed entire without notes or illustrations, the Book of Common Prayer, and the services of the Church of England. The two Universities own copyright of the ordinary kind in the *New English Bible.*

Wolvercote Paper-Mill. From a wood-engraving of about 1890.

A fourth main division of the Delegates' business is paper-making. The senior Managing Partner in the Bible Press bought a long-disused paper-mill at Wolvercote on the Thames just above Oxford in 1855. It was pulled down and a new mill was built on the site at the expense of the Bible Press partnership. It has since been managed by a Controller responsible to the Delegates. The legal title of the mill was conveyed to the Chancellor, Masters, and Scholars in 1872. Wolvercote Mill, enlarged and modernized twenty years ago, is a large supplier of paper to the publishing and printing businesses besides serving outside customers.

The fifth part of the organization that is directly answerable to the Delegates is the New York Business. The Oxford University Press, New York, incorporated in the United States, was founded in 1896 primarily to sell the University's Bibles and other publications in that country. At one time the Branch was of service to the parent house by securing American copyrights for Oxford books by promoting editions of them printed in America. It has developed a large publishing business in books designed for sale there.

In 1872 the Delegates decided to buy No. 116 High Street, Oxford, as a repository for the sale of their Bibles and learned books. They must have been sold unbound until the London bindery was acquired two years later. As part of the 'Bound Book Business' it was put under the care of the London Manager in 1901, and the shop has since been a dependency of the Publisher in London.

Those are the ramifications and attributes of the Press which history can help to explain. The opening of branches overseas in the present century, offshoots of the London office and supervised by it, can be left for a later page.

CHAPTER I

Manuscript Books and the First Two Presses

THE existing printing business owned by the University goes back to 1690. A false start was made in 1669, when for a few months the Delegates took charge of printing and then gave it up.

It is more difficult to date the beginning of the University's publishing. In 1633 Delegates were appointed to decide, among other things relating to printing, which manuscripts in the Bodleian Library should be put to press in the coming years. The agreement with an Oxford printer for the first of them, the chronicle of Malalas, reserved to the Vice-Chancellor the fixing of the price of the book.

In 1634 the University's Chancellor, Archbishop William Laud, bound it by a statute to set up a corporately-owned printing office for producing learned books.

Further back, from 1584 onwards, there was a printer in Oxford licensed and subsidized by the University, whose appointment was justified by a need to print in the city books which would do honour to the famous academy.

The Oxford University Press is the present embodiment of an idea as old as the University. It has always used texts and edited them; it has always needed the multiplication of books under its supervision. The working of the idea until something recognizable as a university press emerges is admittedly prehistory. Therefore A. W. Pollard rightly objected to the title given to a brief history of the institution, *The Oxford University Press 1468–1921*. The difficulty of settling on a date to separate history from prehistory arises from a practical impossibility of separating them at all. Threads run from one into the other, and if it had no introductory prehistory, the history would have, in order to make itself understood, constantly to hark back to earlier times to pick up the threads.

In this book the division is made at 1690. The introductory part tracing the gradual approximation to a university press is a summary, for the most part of information previously available, becoming more detailed and better documented as it nears the end.

'These Defendants believe,' wrote the pleader for the University in 1684, 'and doubt not but to make it appeare, that before the Invention of Printing . . . the publishing and encreasing of all manner of Bookes was a very antient Privilege enjoyed by these Defendants Predecessors.'[1] Of the presence of men engaged in making books there is early evidence: a transfer of property in Catte Street about 1215 is witnessed by a *scriptor*, a bookbinder, two parchmenters, and three illuminators;[2] a stationer's widow is mentioned about 1250.[3] By 1290 the Chancellor had won from the magistrates of the city an admission that scribes, parchmenters, and illuminators came within his jurisdiction.[4] Royal confirmation of the arrangement was given by a charter of Edward III of 1355.[5] In a deed of 1346 the Chancellor's jurisdiction over four stationers is acknowledged by the Archdeacon.[6] These makers and sellers of books were servants of the University and, in the language of later times, 'privileged persons'.

In Oxford records the stationers (men who had a stance, stall, or shop) appear most often as valuers of personal effects of all kinds, and their especial concern with books is due to their being the commonest objects to be pledged in return for loans of money from the University's chests. The books, if not reclaimed, were sold by a stationer for the benefit of the chest. Nevertheless, a statute passed by Congregation in 1374[7] makes it clear that the stationers had a right to profit by the sale of

[1] The University's Case in the suit against it by Henry Hills and others. Blackstone's transcript in the Delegates' records.

[2] H. E. Salter, *The Mediaeval Archives of the University of Oxford*, i, O.H.S. lxx (Oxford, 1920), pp. 291–2.

[3] Ibid., p. 320.

[4] *Munimenta Academica Oxon.*, i, ed. H. Anstey, Rolls Series 50 (1868), p. 150.

[5] Salter, *Mediaeval Archives*, i, p. 155.

[6] *Munimenta Academica*, pp. 149–50.

[7] *Statuta antiqua Universitatis Oxoniensis*, ed. S. Gibson (Oxford, 1931), pp. 167–8. *Congregatio plena* was at that time equivalent to the modern Convocation.

books within the University's precinct in the ordinary course of business. The statute recites that there were too many sellers of books not sworn to the University and many valuable manuscript books were being sold out of Oxford, the owners being induced to agree to it by subtle arguments, so that the regular stationers were deprived of an accustomed profit; Congregation, therefore, orders that only the public stationers may sell books at a price of more than half a mark within the University's jurisdiction.

The stationers, sworn servants of the University, elected by Convocation, kept master copies of texts for hire and displayed them in their shops. So much may be gathered from a statute passed before 1380 requiring stationers and others who hired out *exemplars* to exhibit only such as were complete and accurate, on pain of forfeiting any that were faulty.[1] There is some evidence that the quires of the master copies were hired out separately: there are instances of books written at Oxford in the thirteenth century being made up of quires—of six, eight, or twelve leaves—numbered as *peciae* (*prima pecia, secunda pecia*, and so on). There are marginal notes such as 'peciam sequentem habet Cancellar. Oxoni.' and 'T. Suttune habet i peciam'. These notes are taken to mean that 'the separate quires were lent by the owner to other students or teachers, primarily to copy out',[2] as they were in Paris and in some other universities.[3]

Wills and inventories copied in the fifteenth-century register of the Chancellor show that not seldom the deceased had besides complete volumes quaternions of others.[4] People of modest means were content to economize in that way: a wealthy man might keep a scribe permanently employed. Richard Brown, archdeacon of Rochester, canon of York, Wells, and St. Asaph, gave directions in his will for the return to Glastonbury Abbey of a manuscript which was being copied for him by Matthew, his scribe at Oxford.[5]

Books brought in from abroad supplemented the stocks of the University's stationers; witness the list of those left with one of them, Thomas Hunt, in 1483 by two foreign merchants on sale or return.[6] Some of them

[1] Ibid., p. 186.
[2] A. G. Little and F. Pelster, *Oxford Theology and Theologians*, c. *A.D. 1282–1302*, O.H.S. xcvi (Oxford, 1934), p. 63.
[3] *The English Library before 1700*, ed. F. Wormald and C. E. Wright (1958), p. 69.
[4] *Registrum Cancellarii Oxon.*, ed. Salter, i, O.H.S. xciii (Oxford, 1932), pp. 111, 163, 164, 238; ii, O.H.S. xciv (1932) p. 232.   [5] Ibid. i, p. 232.
[6] Appended to F. Madan, 'The Daily Ledger of John Dorne', in *Collectanea*, i, O.H.S. v (Oxford, 1885), pp. 142–3.

were printed books, and they had not taken longer than one or two years to reach Oxford from Venice, Louvain, or Cologne.

To that extent the buying and selling of books was organized in Oxford before the first printer came, and was organized by the University. There were tradesmen competent to handle the output of the press, and the University (if we only knew it) must have taken printing, as it had taken manuscript, under its protection and surveillance.

THE FIRST OXFORD PRESS

For a knowledge of this press we are wholly dependent on the work of bibliographers.[1] Seventeen books from it are known in a perfect state or are believed to be represented by existing fragments. They have been arranged in a succession suggested by their typefaces and given tentative dates within the limits set by the first and last dated books. The three books in Type 1 do not give the name of a printer; of the four books in Types 2 and 3 one has a colophon giving the Printer's name as Theodoricus Rood of Cologne;[2] of the third group, set in Types 3, 4, 5, 6, and 7, one book gives the names of Teodericus Rood of Cologne and an Englishman, Thomas Hunt, as partners in the printing. Only five of the books give the place of printing, Oxford, and only eight are dated. All bibliographers are agreed on these tentative attributions and datings, and in believing that the first book in the series is wrongly dated 1468 in the colophon owing to the accidental omission of an x from the Roman numerals for 1478.

These assumptions are obviously fragile but defensible as convenient for librarians and others who have to catalogue the books. They must be accepted in the absence of evidence to the contrary. Similarly, it is convenient to assume that Theodoric Rood printed the books in Type 1.

Even if the printer had not described himself as coming from Cologne, so much could have been deduced from his type. His Type 1 shares most of its letters with the contemporary press at Cologne which goes by the name of Gerardus ten Raem[3] and some with the presses of Cologne's first printer, Ulrich Zel, and Richard Pafraet at Deventer, who came

---

[1] E. Gordon Duff, *Early Printed Books* (1893), pp. 147–55; and his *Fifteenth Century English Books* (1917), *passsim*; F. Madan, *Oxford Books*, i (Oxford, 1895), pp. 1–4, 237–62; Duff, *The English Provincial Printers, Stationers and Bookbinders to 1557* (Cambridge, 1912), pp. 1–22; D. E. Rhodes, 'Variants in the 1479 Oxford edition of Aristotle's Ethics', *Studies in Bibliography*, viii (Charlottesville, 1956), pp. 209–12.

[2] 'Rood', meaning red in Low German, may have been a nickname.

[3] Severin Corsten thinks that Ten Raem was a learned bibliophile who employed a printer: *Die Anfänge des Kölner Buchdrucks* (Cologne, 1935), pp. 50–2.

tat Augustinus de Ciuitate Dei, cū comentarijs Thomae de
lois et Nicolai Triuetth Professorum Ordinis Praedicatorum,
cujus p~ ~ot~ Schoffer Moguntiae. 1473. folio.

raaomis assignet Si inquam hec secundū
tradicionis supra expposite regulam con
sequantur aduertimus deprecemur vt
nobis et ommibus qui hoc audiunt conce
dat dominus fide quam suscepimus custo
dia curfu consumato expectare iusticie
repositam coronam : et inueniri inter eos
qui resurgunt in vitam eternam. liberari
vero a confusione et obprobrio eterno •
per custum dominum nostrum per quem
ē deo patri ommipotēti cū spiritu sancto
gloria et imperium in. secula seculorum
amen .

Explicit exposicio sancti Jeronimi in
simbolo apostolorum ad papam laurē
cium Impressa Oxonie Et finita An
no domini • M • cccc • lxviij • xvij • die
decembris •

(handwritten margin:) Rufini, is enim huj expositionē Author.

(handwritten lower half:)

... Nouam Rhetoricā fratris Laurentij
Guilielmi de Saona, impssā in Villā
St Albani. Anno. 1480. 4° g. 46. consul:
etiam Joh. Arnoldū de Chalcogra
phiae Inuentione, et Ber: Malinckrot
de Ortu, et progressu Typographiae
4°. H. 3. bid: Opinionum de Jmpssn: pg. 440.
441. ubi opinionem Jacobi Wimpsl: infe citat
et apprbat, qd Ars Typographica inuenta est
a Joh: Gutenberg. Anno Xī: 1440.

---

last page of the exposition of the Apostles' Creed wrongly attributed to St. Jerome, believed to be
the first book printed at Oxford.

from Cologne. All seven of Rood's types have characteristics of the Lower Rhenish school of lettering centred on Cologne.

That was the place from which printing might be expected to spread to England. By 1478 the practice of the art in that city had 12 years of experience behind it and at least a dozen master printers were working there. Caxton learned to print at Cologne, and it was from there that the first Cambridge printer came.[1]

Knowledge of this first Oxford press gained from a study of its books can be supplemented hardly at all from other sources. The University's records that might have thrown some light on it have been lost. The Chancellor's Register for the years between 1470 and 1497 is missing. It is mainly a record of convictions for breaches of the peace and other minor offences and compositions between contending parties subject to the Chancellor's jurisdiction. It may well be that the missing part, if it were found, would throw no light on the printing press. The Register of Convocation for the years between 1463 and 1505 is also lost; but that, being almost entirely concerned with the grant of degrees, is unlikely to have mentioned the printer.

There is a trace of Theodoric in the Accounts of the Proctors, where he is recorded as doing goldsmith's work, repairing and gilding a bedel's staff in the year 1481–2;[2] so he is likely to have been one of many men trained as goldsmiths who turned their hands to engraving the punches for making type, in his case with indifferent success. He is traceable, also, in the accounts of his landlords: in 1480 the Hospital of St. John received 26s. 8d. in respect of a house in the northern part of the parish of St. Peter-in-the-East 'in which Dyryke Dowcheman lives' (no doubt he worked there too);[3] and Magdalen College was paid in 1482–3 for repairs to a tenement where Dedyck Teutonicus formerly lived.[4]

What induced Theodoric to come to Oxford is quite obscure. In the colophon to the Phalaris of 1485 there is a Latin poem describing him as 'sent by Cologne'. That is one possibility; there were substantial business

[1] E. P. Goldschmidt, *The First Cambridge Press in its European Setting* (Cambridge, 1955); Otto Treptow, *Johann Lair von Siegburg* (Siegburg, 1964).

[2] Item solutum est pro tribus unciis argenti emptis ad reparacionem baculi bidelli inferioris in sacra theologia, ixs.

Item solutum est Dydycke pro factura et deauracione eiusdem baculi, xxiijs. iiijd.
> *Mediaeval Archives of the University of Oxford*, ed. Salter, ii, O.H.S. lxxiii (Oxford, 1921), p. 333.

[3] *Cartulary of the Hospital of St. John the Baptist*, ed. H. E. Salter, iii, O.H.S. lxix (Oxford, 1917), p. 272.

[4] *Register of Magdalen College*, ed. W. D. Macray, i (Oxford, 1894), p. 10.

men in Cologne who invested in the printing trade and reduced several of the independent craftsmen of its earliest days to the position of a contractor taking none of the risk.[1] One such capitalist or a consortium may have financed a mission of printing to Oxford. Alternatively, the printer may have been invited to Oxford by members of the University conscious of the need for reduplicating certain kinds of books by a means quicker and cheaper than handwriting. The fact that Thomas Hunt, a sworn stationer of the University, was in partnership in 1485 with Theodoric for the production of a book might seem to favour this view. Collective ownership, or even support, of a press by the University would, however, be out of accord with the ways of thinking at that time, even if the money had been there.

What makes this first Oxford press most nearly germane to the subject of this book is its connection with a revolution in the teaching of Latin grammar. The first grammar book written in English was printed on it. That would have been about the year 1481. Only two of its leaves are known, but they are proof enough of a will to leave behind the medieval school books, the Donatus *Ars minor* and the *Doctrinale* of Alexander Gallus. The fragment is part of a grammar book attributed to John Stanbridge, usher under Anwykyll at Magdalen College School when it was founded about 1478;[2] and entitled the *Long Parvula*. That was discovered in 1906, when a later edition of the work was reprinted in Germany.[3] When the school attached to Magdalen College opened its doors most of the colleges and halls in Oxford taught Latin to boys, and in 1466 there was dissatisfaction with the standard of attainment. A letter was sent in the name of the University to John Chedworth, bishop of Lincoln, in whose diocese Oxford was, begging his intervention to improve it.[4] Another sign of concern with the problem is a statute passed by Congregation in April 1478: If any venerable man is willing to found grammar schools where all who wish to come will be taught free, the teachers in the schools shall not be obliged to pay anything to the University, and the fee hitherto customarily paid may be recovered by any other teachers of grammar that there may be.[5]

[1] Severin Corsten, 'Ulrich Zells deutschsprachige Drucke', *Gutenberg Jahrbuch 1965* (Mainz), pp. 110–17; and the same author's 'Köln und die Ausbreitung der Buchdruckerkunst in den Niederlanden', *Quaerendo*, i (Amsterdam, 1971), pp. 5–17 (i.e. 81–93), 182–90.

[2] R. S. Stanier, *Magdalen School*, O.H.S., N.S. iii (Oxford, 1940), pp. 12–15.

[3] Hermann Varnhagen, *Libellus grammaticus latinus Longe Parvula* (Erlangen, 1906).

[4] Anstey, *Epistolae academicae Oxon.*, O.H.S. xxxvi (Oxford, 1898), ii, p. 381.

[5] Gibson, *Statuta antiqua*, p. 291.

The stirrings of an appetite for the New Learning were being felt here: bad Latin was ceasing to be a second language, and good Latin was becoming a school subject. Obviously a printing press could help, and one set up in such circumstances, though not of the University, was for the University. Given enlightened authors, Anwykyll the master, or Stanbridge the usher, of Magdalen's school, there could have been no better remedy than a press for unsatisfactory Latin. It was to provide models for the language that a press was brought to the Sorbonne in 1470, the first in France,[1] and the first presses in the eastern Netherlands, most subject to the influence of Cologne, were associated with high schools and printed grammars.[2]

As to the second Oxford grammar, finished probably in 1483, we are rather better informed. The fragments are of two editions, six leaves of one and about half the original 84 of the other. The work as a whole is known by an edition printed a little later, in 1489, at Deventer, no doubt for export to this country.[3] It had a long but revealing title: *Compendium totius grammatice ex variis autoribus, Laurentio, Servio, Perotto, diligenter collectum et versibus cum eorum interpretatione conscriptum, totius barbariei destructorium, et latine lingue ornamentum non minus preceptoribus quam pueris necessarium.*

Verses at the beginning of the book commending the author enjoin tender youth to praise John, who taught it well, and more at the end commending William Waynflete, founder of Magdalen College, convey that John wrote the book at that prelate's persuasion. Henry Bradshaw, the Cambridge librarian, suggested that John was Anwykyll,[4] and the book has come to be known by his name.

This grammar is written in Latin, but the verses referred to in the title had English translations. Appended to one of the editions printed at Oxford, but also sold separately, was a collection of sentences from the plays of Terence with English translations selected to make a phrase-book of conversational yet classical Latin. This collection, several times reprinted in London and entitled *Vulgaria Terentii*, was evidently useful when undergraduates in hall and boys in school had to speak that language.

[1] A. Claudin, *Origines de l'imprimerie à Paris* (Paris, 1899); D. C. McMurtrie, *The Fichet Letter* (New York, 1926).

[2] *Catalogue of Books printed in the XVth. Century now in the British Museum*, Part ix (Holland), p. ix.

[3] Ibid., p. 51.

[4] In a letter to the Dutch bibliographer J.-W. Holtrop, one of a number which will be published shortly, edited by Professor W. Gs. Hellinga.

It is significant that the *Compendium*, though it was based partly on the work of early post-classical grammarians, drew largely on that of Nicholas

They say or men say my son is a luffer
Meum gnatum rumor est amare
Men say the kyng shall com hydrr.
Aiunt regem huc esse venturum
They sey kynge alexander cōqueryd all t x worlde
Fama ē alexandrū regē totū orbem sub-
iugasse .
I haue suffryd or latt hym haue all his wyll.
Siui ammium vt expleret suum
If he espy that j go aboute to discepse hȳm j am loste
ottirly.
Si senserit quicꝗ me fallacie conari pe
rco funditus .
Thou must wedd a wife to day
Dxor tibi ducenda ē hodie inquit .
Trowpst or wenyst thou that j coure speke ony word
Cēsen me vbū vllū potuisse proloqui
wolde good I hadd known it be fore
Vtinam id rescissem prius
I am sory or heuy of this daye
Ex hoc sollicitus sum die · Hec diee me
multum sollicitat
This oon thynge j know we le she hath afecuryd that
thou shuldyst remēbyt hyt
n iiij

A page of Anwykyll's Grammar, printed at Oxford about 1483.

Perotti, first printed in 1473, an author still living when the Oxford book was compiled. Perotti's was the humanist's grammar, founded on the best classical writers, and reliance on it is a sign that Oxford was open to modern influences.

Another of the 17 books ascribable to this press, Cicero's speech *Pro T. Milone*, can be accounted for by the same desire for the destruction of barbarism. Every press in Europe was printing a work by Cicero, regarded as the pattern for prose-style and rhetoric. Oxford's was the first in England to issue one of his works, or, for the matter of that, any text by a classical Latin author.

Books from the first press at Oxford of which complete or nearly complete copies exist

Year	Short title	State	Imprint	No. of existing leaves	Type
1478	[Rufinus of Aquileia.] Expositio Sancti Hieronymi in Symbolum Apostolorum	Complete	Impressa Oxonie Et finita Anno domini. M.cccc.lxviij. xvij die decembris	42	1
1479	Aristotle. Nicomachean Ethics translated into Latin by Leonardo Aretino	Complete	Impressus Oxoniis. Anno domini M.cccc.lxxix	174	1
1480	Aegidius de Columna. De peccato originali	Complete	Impresso et finito Oxonie. A nativitate domini. M.cccc.lxxix. xiiij. die mensis marcij.	24	1
1481	Alexander de Hales. Expositio super libris Aristotelis de anima	Complete	Impressum per me Theodoricum rood de Colonia in alma universitate Oxon. Anno incarnacionis dominice M.cccc.lxxxi. xi. die mensis Octobris	240	2, 3
1482	Lattebury, John. Liber moralium super trenis Jheremie prophete	Complete	Anno domini M.cccc.lxxxij ultima die mensis Julii	292	2, 3
—	Terence. Vulgaria Terentii	Complete	—	32	4, 5
—	Rolle, Richard, of Hampole. Explanationes in Job	Complete	—	64	4, 6
—	Logic	Imperfect	—	162	4, 6
—	Lyndewood, William. Constitutiones provinciales	Complete	—	342	3, 4, 5, 6
1485	Pseudo-Phalaris. Epistolae	Complete	. . . in alma universitate Oxonie. A Natali christiano Ducentesima et nonagesima septima. Olimpiade foeliciter impressum est.	88	3, 5

Hoc Teodericus rood
quem collonia misit
Sanguine Germanus
nobile pressit opus
Atque sibi socius thomas
fuit anglicus hunte . . .

| 1486 | Mirk, John. Liber festivalis | Imperfect | . . . the yere of oure lord M.cccc.lxxxvj. the day after seint Edward the kyng | 174 | 5, 7 |

Fragments of books attributed to the first press at Oxford because of the type in which they are set

Short title	No. of existing leaves	Type
Latin grammar	2	2
Cicero. Oratio pro T. Milone	8	2
Anwykyll, John (?). Compendium totius grammaticae. With the Vulgaria Terentii	44(?)	4, 5
Anwykyll, John (?). Compendium totius grammaticae	6	4, 5, 6
St. Augustine. Excitatio ad elemosynam faciendam	8	4, 5, 6
Alexander de Villa Dei. Doctrinale	2	3, 5, 7

The first press disappeared as mysteriously as it came. There must be a presumption that it did not pay its way. The course of trade was against it; merchants brought to England goods that could be exchanged for money and went away with wool. Books were a traditional import, and concessions were made to aliens who would bring them in. Far from protecting the small home-production, King and parliament encouraged foreigners to sell their books here as well as to engage in the book crafts in this country.[1] This policy was in full force until 1523, when alien apprentices were barred, but had weakened very much by 1534, when an Act forbade the sale of bound printed books from abroad and the sale retail of imported books by undenizened aliens. By that time Luther had profoundly changed the attitude of governments towards printing.

Oxford, until very recent times, has found it easier to print books than to sell them. Its press began to flourish when London booksellers were given enough inducement to work with it. So, in the closing years of the fifteenth century and the first half of the next London was better able than Oxford to withstand competition from abroad. Of the books that Rood printed several were successfully reprinted during the following half-century in London: Mirk's *Festial* 15 times, Lyndewood's

[1] E. Gordon Duff, *A Century of the English Book Trade* (1905), pp. ix–xiii.

Constitutions 6 times, Alexander Grammaticus 5 times, the *Vulgaria* 3 times, and Stanbridge's *Accidence*, a development of Anwykyll's *Compendium*, some 40 times. There was nothing amiss with Rood's choice of titles.

This press made little impression on Oxford memories. When, about 1585, a committee of Convocation begged the intervention of the Earl of Leicester with the Queen to allow a press here, one of the grounds for the request was that: 'Fifty years since, more or less, there lived a man in this place who printed books, and they are still to be seen in the possession of some people. If, then,' the petitioners added, 'the University had its printer in that ruder age, how much more is such a man needed in the present abundance of learning?'[1]

Only one Oxford book of the *incunabula*, the Lattebury, is in the Bodleian *Catalogus* of 1620 or its supplement of 1635. The earliest historian of the University, Brian Twyne, makes a muddled reference to the press in his book published in 1608. He believed that the art of printing when it reached England was first settled at Oxford and thence, by the exertions of William Caxton, was carried to London; but he supposed that the first Oxford printer was John Scolar, who (as we shall see) printed a book here in 1518.[2] Anthony Wood gave an account of it in his *History and Antiquities of the University of Oxford* (1674),[3] but it is an unhistorical account because he accepted as true the fabrication by Richard Atkyns of an introduction of printing to this country in the reign of Henry VI by Frederick Corsellis, who, according to Atkyns, set up his press at Oxford. The imaginary Corsellis haunted our histories of printing, in the face of mounting disbelief, until he was dismissed as 'pure invention' by A. C. Ducarel, who had failed to find in Lambeth Palace the supporting documents alleged by Atkyns to be there.[4] Joseph Ames, in his *Typographical Antiquities* of 1749, laid a basis for the scientific study of the earliest Oxford printing.

THE EARLY-SIXTEENTH-CENTURY PRESS

The second press, which worked at Oxford for little more than six months in 1517–18 and was revived to the extent of issuing a booklet in 1519 or

[1] S. Gibson and D. M. Rogers, 'The Earl of Leicester and Printing at Oxford', *Bodleian Library Record*, ii (Oxford, 1949), pp. 240–5.

[2] *Antiquitatis academiae Oxoniensis apologia* (Oxford, 1608), leaf 3D3^v.

[3] Ed. J. Gutch (Oxford, 1792), i, pp. 623–5. It was first published in a Latin translation in 1674.

[4] 'Epistola ad auctorem' in Gerard Meerman's *Origines typographicae* (The Hague, 1765), ii, pp. 3–14; Duff, *English Provincial Printers*, pp. 3–7.

1520, has as much mystery about it as the first. The Chancellor's Register for the years 1515–26 no longer exists, and no Oxford record refers to John Scolar, whose name is given as the printer in four of the books, or to Charles Kyrfoth, his successor in 1519/20.

Books of the Early-Sixteenth-Century Press at Oxford

Author	Title	Imprint	No. of pages
Walter Burley	Tractatus expositorius super libros posteriorum Arestotilis	Impressum in academia Oxonie anno dominice incarnacionis M.CCCC. xvii. Die vero decembris quarto	20
Joannes Dedicus	Questiones moralissime super libros Ethicorum	Impressumque in celeberima vniuersitate Oxoniensi per me Iohannem Scolar in viculo sancti Ioannis Baptiste moram trahentem, Anno domini M.CCCC. decimooctauo. Mensis vero Maij die decimoquinto	152
Walter Burley	Compendium questionum de luce et lumine	Impressumque in celeberima vniuersitate Oxoniensi per me Ioannem Scolar in viculo diui Ioannis baptiste moram trahentem Anno domini M.CCCC. decimooctauo. Mensis vero Junij die quinto	16
—	Tractatus perbrevis de materia et forma	Impressum . . . in celeberima vniuersitate Oxoniensi per me Ioannem Scolar in viculo diui Ioannis baptiste moram trahentem Anno domini M.CCCC. decimooctauo. Mensis vero Iunij die septimo	16
Rob.–Whittington	De heteroclitis nominibus	. . . impressa per me Ioannem Scolar in viculo diui Ioannis baptiste moram trahentem Anno domini M.CCCC. decimooctauo Mensis vero Iunij, die vicesimoseptimo	20
—	Opusculum insolubilium	—	4
Jaspar Laet	Prenostica	In celeberima oxoniensi academia impressa	broad side
—	Compotus manualis ad usum Oxoniensium	Impressum est presens opusculum in celeberrima vniuersitate Oxoniensi per me Carolum Kyrfoth. In vico diui Joannis baptiste moram trahentem. Anno domini M.D.xix. Mensis vero Februarij die v.	16

Seven books and a broadside prognostical almanac are ascribed to this press.[1] Only one of the volumes is of a considerable bulk—152 pages— the others being booklets of eight or ten leaves. It is hard to believe that a press with so little employment was set up to supply a need of the University or had much encouragement from it.

With nothing but the printed matter to enlighten us, we must conclude tentatively that this press was an offshoot of that of Wynkyn de Worde, the industrious printer in London. The three typefaces in which the books of Scolar and Kyrfoth were set were being used at the same time by De Worde, and so were their type ornament, their woodcut initial letters, and device of the royal arms. The types were French of the fifteenth century; other London printers had one or other of them but not all three. The Oxford founts look fresher than De Worde's did in 1517, and Scolar used only an s with curls at the ends of the diagonal while De Worde was using it sparingly mixed with an older s with no curls. The types by themselves might not be enough to associate this press with De Worde's, but the types and the woodcuts are. The Oxford printer got his material from De Worde or had the same supplier as he.

A contention that this second Oxford press did not exist, because of a rule among bibliographers that identity of typographical equipment indicates a single press,[2] is unlikely to command general assent. Plausible as the presumption may be in dealing with the early *incunabula*, it loses its force with the development of typefounding and has no legitimate application to the state of affairs in 1518. Moreover, *expressum facit tacere tacitum*: Scolar's colophons assert emphatically that he printed in St. John the Baptist Lane within the University of Oxford, and in three instances that his editions were protected by privileges granted by its Chancellor. A vague recollection later in the century that a man had printed in Oxford some fifty years since[3] was probably founded in fact.

The contents of the books contribute surprisingly little to a history of this brief spell of printing. There is little pleasure to be got from trying to read them, for the texts are set in a very small rotunda with abundant marks of contraction. It is certain, though, that they are scholastic philosophy, if not medieval, then medieval in character. There is no trace of New Learning, no attempt to emulate Cicero's Latin.

---

[1] Duff, *English Provincial Printers*, pp. 67–70; Madan, *Oxford Books*, i, 5–7, 263–5; A. W. Pollard, 'A New Oxford Book of 1517', *The Library*, 2nd ser. x (1909), pp. 212–13.

[2] E. P. Goldschmidt, *The First Cambridge Press in its European Setting* (Cambridge, 1955), p. 61.

[3] Above, p. 12.

Burley, the author of two of the tracts, flourished in the early part of the fourteenth century; Dedicus, who wrote the only substantial work issued by the press, has not been identified. Madan's description of the tract on light as scientific can hardly be justified if 'science' is experimental. These are appendages to the works of Aristotle of the kind taught then in the Parvise at Oxford and not wholly superseded in the Schools there more than a hundred years later. The *Compotus manualis* printed by Kyrfoth is arithmetic in the days of Roman numerals: it expounds a method of calculating the dates of movable feasts by attaching numerical values to different parts of the hand.[1] Earlier editions had appeared in various countries. Whittington's little grammatical treatise was nearest to being contemporary in spirit. The author, admitted to the degree of B.A. in 1513, was a pupil of Stanbridge at Magdalen School. The conservative character of these books is in strong contrast to the output of the short-lived press at Cambridge in 1521-2, Greek and elegant Latin in Roman type.[2]

With all that, it must be allowed that the University by this time showed some awareness of the advantages of a printing press. Scolar's statement that three of his books were protected by a privilege from the University's Chancellor, forbidding others to print them in Oxford, is evidence that his press had something more than tolerance from the academic body. In the Dedicus he sets out in Latin the terms of the grant: 'It is forbidden by an edict under the seal of the chancery for anyone during seven years to print this excellent work, or sell it in a form paid for by another in the University of Oxford or within its precinct, on pain of losing all the books and five pounds sterling for every copy sold, wherever the books were printed, in addition to the other penalty provided by the edict. Don't think you can blind the crows.' The University was abreast of the times in making this grant: another six months were to pass before the earliest exclusive privilege for a book was granted by the king of England, though the king of France had adopted the practice in 1507, and the Emperor by 1512.[3] Both Scolar and Kyrfoth ornamented their books with a cut of the University's arms, a sign that they pretended to act for the academy; and the *incipit* of Burley's *Tractatus expositorius*, like those of the Dedicus and the *Opusculum*

[1] Christopher Wordsworth, *The Ancient Kalendar of the University of Oxford*, O.H.S. xlv (Oxford, 1904), pp. 110-94.
[2] E. P. Goldschmidt, loc. cit.; Duff, *English Provincial Printers*, pp. 73-84.
[3] Duff, *English Provincial Printers*, p. 68; P. Mellottée, *Histoire économique de l'imprimerie* (Paris, 1905), p. 80; O. Hase, *Die Koberger* (Leipzig, 1885), p. 229.

insolubilium, stresses the usefulness of the book to Oxford students. The *Compotus* is professedly designed specially for them.

No explanation for the silence of this press after February 1519/20 can be found. The memory of it soon vanished or became very indistinct. Brian Twyne in 1608 confused it with its forerunner of 1478–87. He wrote:

> The art of printing newly brought to England came first of all to Oxford, and thence by the exertions of William Caxton was carried to London also. That is proved not only by ancient documents but also by the fact that John Scolar, the first Oxford printer, set up a printing office here and in 1518 issued the commentaries of that most sharp-witted of Oxonians, Joannes Dedicus, on the *Moralia*.[1]

Anthony Wood, chronicling the introduction of printing to Oxford by Corsellis, which he dates in 1464, includes a description of three of Scolar's books in the Bodleian in his day: Burley's two tracts and the *Compendium questionum de luce et lumine*.[2]

---

[1] *Antiquitatis academiae Oxoniensis apologia*, leaf 3D3ᵛ.
[2] *History and Antiquities of the University of Oxford*, ed. J. Gutch, i (1791), p. 625.

Robert Dudley, Earl of Leicester (d. 1588), Chancellor of the University of Oxford from 1564. National Portrait Gallery

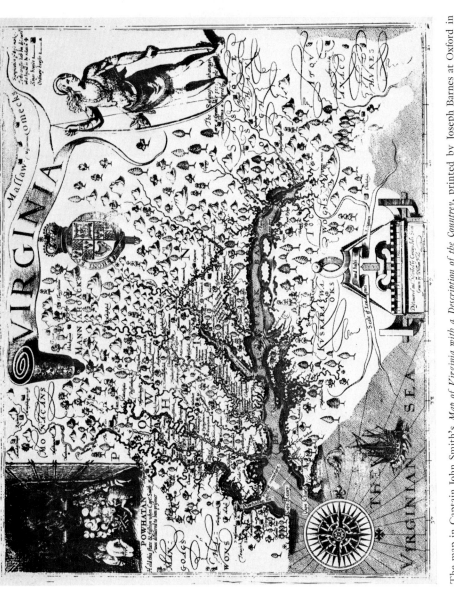

The map in Captain John Smith's *Map of Virginia with a Description of the Countrey*, printed by Joseph Barnes at Oxford in 1612. Reduced

CHAPTER II

Restraint of Printing and the Allowance of a Press at Oxford

A PRUDENT SILENCE

OXFORD made shift to do without a press for fifty years. No doubt the explanation is to be found in the unsettlement of religion. After 1520 for more than a century the history of printing is little more than a history of censorship, and the temper of our Henry VIII made this especially true of England. His proclamations of 1530 and 1538 imposing censorship by the ordinary of the diocese would not seriously have affected Oxford, for they related to 'bokes in englysshe tong, concerninge holy scripture';[1] but it may be noted that the Bishop of Lincoln, ordinary in this diocese, appointed commissioners to search the stalls at St. Frideswide's fair for heretical literature in 1531.[2]

The field was left open for Latin books, for logic, Aristotle, and grammar. While there was no press at Oxford a few of such were specially printed in London for Oxford stationers: De Lugo's *Principia seu introductiones in via doctoris subtilis* by Pynson for George Chastelain (*c.* 1508), *Formalitates de mente magistri Johannis Duns Scoti* about 1513 by De Worde for Henry Jacobi, a *Tractatus secundarum intentionum logicalium* and an *Opusculum insolubilium* by Peter Treveris for John Thorne or Dorne in or about 1527. The London printers brought out a great many grammars by Stanbridge and Whittington.

At some time in the second half of the sixteenth century (it is difficult to tell how or when) it came to be accepted that not only must books pass the censor but presses must be licensed, and, further, that the prerogative of the Crown extended to granting the licence. The first sign that printing without leave from the sovereign would be dangerous is a grant to Cambridge University of 1534. In this instance the King was evidently moved by a desire to entrust a reliable body with the means of combating heresy. The University had petitioned Cardinal Wolsey in

---

[1] A. W. Pollard, *Records of the English Bible* (1911), pp. 163–9, 240–2.
[2] Madan, *Oxford Books*, i, p. 273.

1529 'for the suppression of error' that there should be three booksellers allowed in Cambridge by the King, who should be sworn not to bring in uncensored books.[1] The charter of 1534 enlarged the privileges of the University by a right to have within its precinct three stationers and printers or vendors of books, who might lawfully print there all manner of books approved by the Chancellor or his vicegerent and three doctors, and to sell these books and others printed within this kingdom in any place within the realm.[2] Oxford took no action to secure the same favour. Geography made it less exposed to contamination from Germany and the Low Countries.

Possessing the right, Cambridge did not exercise it until 1583. Meanwhile the Crown asserted its prerogative affecting printing in the most positive manner. The charter of Philip and Mary to the Company of Stationers of London, granted in 1557, after reciting the mischief done by pernicious and heretical books, provides that:

no person within this our kingdom of England or dominions thereof, either by himself, or by his journeymen, servants, or by any other person, shall practise the art or mystery of printing or stamping any book, or anything to be sold, unless the same person is or shall be one of the society of the foresaid art or mystery of a stationer of the city aforesaid . . .

The Master and Wardens of the Company were given by this charter power to search for, and if it were found, to destroy any press not so authorized. There is no exception of the Universities.[3]

No more effective form of censorship could have been devised. A printers' protection society was vested with the power of the state to prevent competition with its members and to make sure that the profitable books that its members might not print others could not. Queen Elizabeth I in her *Injunctions* to the printers and publishers of 1559[4] relaxed none of the rigour of her predecessors, exempting only the profane authors previously printed and customarily read in schools and universities.

As the law stood a London Stationer might put up his press anywhere in the kingdom. Cambridge appointed John Kingston, a member of the Company, to be its first printer in 1576, and was only prevented from beginning to print by dissuasion from Lord Burghley. He thought it

[1] S. C. Roberts, *A History of the Cambridge University Press 1521–1921* (Cambridge, 1921), p. 19.

[2] Ibid., pp. 19–20.　　　　　　　　　　　　[3] Arber, *Transcript*, i, pp. xxviii–xxxii.

[4] *Injunctions given by her Majestie* 1559, c. 51; Arber, i, p. xxxviii.

would be undesirable for them to infringe the Queen's Printer's patent by producing psalters and prayer books, but he thought they might safely print 'matters pertaining to the schools &c.'.[1] When, in 1583, Thomas Thomas, who was no Stationer, was next appointed, the Stationers' Court sent a party to Cambridge to break up his press.

The University prevailed because of its charter of 1534. Oxford had no such protection; nevertheless it can only have been the example set by Cambridge that moved Convocation in 1584 to lend Joseph Barnes £100 'that he might have a press in the University for printing books the more easily',[2] and four months later to appoint a committee of doctors to reach conclusions on printing.[3]

To this time, roughly, belongs an undated document arguing a case for the press, *Supplicatio ad illustrissimum comitem Leicestriae summum Oxoniensis academiae cancellarium pro Typographia Oxoniae erigenda*. It is a brief for the University's Chancellor, Robert Dudley, first Earl of Leicester, to plead with the Queen for her leave to print at Oxford.[4] The drafting is anonymous, but academic in tone. Because of its apparent effect the *Supplicatio* may be said to begin a new stage of the advance of Oxford printing towards a true university press. The Latin may be translated as follows:

A prayer to the very illustrious Earl of Leicester, most high Chancellor of the University of Oxford, for the setting up of a printing press there and for the grant of a number of privileges for books not now privileged [to be printed] there as a help towards defraying the cost of a printing office.

Seeing that no university, however small, in Germany and France is without its press, foreigners find it as good as a marvel that in this whole realm of England printers are to be met with only in one city, and that, having no university, prints in virtually nothing but English. Therefore, he will be extremely serviceable to learning who can persuade the Queen's majesty, in accordance with her accustomed generosity, graciously to favour and firmly establish a printing office in the University of Oxford; for it surpasses all the universities of Europe in the grandeur of its colleges and the amount of their yearly incomes and yet is behindhand of every one of them in having no press.

---

[1] Roberts, *History of the Cambridge University Press*, p. 22.

[2] Reg. Conv. L 10, fol. 281 (15 Aug. 1584).

[3] Ibid., fol. 282* (23 Dec. 1584). A second committee with the same reference was appointed in January 1586: ibid., fol. 283.

[4] S. Gibson and D. M. Rogers, 'The Earl of Leicester and Printing at Oxford', *Bodleian Library Record*, ii (1949), pp. 240–5. Dr. Rogers had lately found the manuscript in the Bibliothèque Nationale in Paris.

Considerations bearing on the matter can be put thus or likewise.

First point. First of all: hidden away in the libraries of the University there are many very important manuscripts foully beset by dust and rubbish, and these could by means of a press set up in this city be rescued from vanishing for ever and spread over all Europe doing credit to our nation.

Second. Besides that, there are men in the place extremely skilled in all manner of languages and liberal arts, who as things are now are prevented by the slenderness of their means from staying in London while their works are being printed; consequently these men are overlooked and unknown among foreigners and barely known to their own countrymen, but given the convenience of this press they could very easily and swiftly refute and blot out the charge of laziness daily brought against them by foreigners.

Third: Foreigners have always thought it self-evident that where there is a settlement of scholars, there should be printers, so that books can be printed most correctly and texts most carefully collated. A university cannot be deprived of printers without loss to literature.

Fourth. There was a man living in Oxford fifty years ago, more or less, who used to print books, and they are still to be seen in the possession of certain people. If at that time, in a ruder age, the University had its printer, how much more is he needed in the present abundance of learning?

Fifth. Moreover, there is at present a substantial bookseller of Oxford, commonly called Joseph Barnes, who would willingly print books if he were given privileges for four or five of his choice not now covered by privileges and for any other works in Oxford libraries recommended to him by those men of learning, and if any who import books of all kinds from the Frankfurt fairs to this realm in exceedingly large numbers were obliged, as is fair, to export a moderate number of the Latin and Greek books to be produced by our printer.

Sixth. Furthermore, if a printer were settled in Oxford, the western parts of England, Wales, and the hitherto barbarous realm of Ireland would in course of time be watered with happier effect and more abundantly with pure streams of improved literature.

Last. Finally, whereas nearly the whole of the kingdom abounds in frivolous trifles written in English, tending rather to a corrupt morality than to any sound and serious education, the young might by these means be attracted to something healthier and more advanced.

God prosper it!

It is a rather conventional essay, and what must have been uppermost in the mind of the writer, the fear of being left behind by the other

University, is left out. That consideration would surely have affected
Queen Elizabeth in assenting to the proposal. She must have done so,
though no writing attests the fact, for Barnes had begun printing by
January 1585,[1] and the dedication to Leicester of the *Speculum moralium
quaestionum* by John Case, dated 1585, refers to 'this new advantage of
having a press, which by your means our University has lately obtained'
and calls the book the first fruits of it.

Joseph Barnes had been admitted to the number of Oxford booksellers
licensed by the Vice-Chancellor in 1573.[2] He was licensed to sell wine
two years later—the combination of the callings of bookseller and
taverner was not uncommon.[3] From the start of his exercise of the craft
he was an excellent printer, or else, as seems likely, he employed an
experienced and skilful journeyman. His stock of type for letters and
flowers was the best that the French typefounders working in London
could supply, mainly the big capital letters, Italics, and flowers of Robert
Granjon and Roman text typefaces by Pierre Haultin. Oxford could not
again until very recent times boast such a beautiful equipment of type,
and from the first it included Greek. The presswork was never bad.

Barnes had no Black Letter: his press belonged to a new age that had
begun since there had last been printing in this city. English books,
thanks largely to Huguenot refugees, reflected the face of humanism.
Since about 1535 Oxford colleges had been buying printed books,[4] and
the users of their libraries had grown accustomed to reading the Latin
classics as they were printed in Venice, Antwerp, and Paris, and the
Bible and Calvin in Roman type from Geneva.

The liberty of freemen of the Company of Stationers to print where
they pleased came to an end in June 1586 with the publication of a decree
of the Star Chamber confining the craft to London.[5] The decree is,
incidentally, the earliest act of state to recognize the existence of a press
at Oxford.

[Article 2] *Item* that noe Prynter of Bookes, nor any other person or
persons whatsoever shall sett up, keepe, or mayneteyne any Presse or
Presses, or anye other Instrument or Instrumentes for ympryntinge of
Bookes, ballads, Chartes, Portraictures, or any other thinge or thinges

[1] *In adventum illustrissimi Lecestrensis comitis ad collegium Lincolniense*, a single leaf dated
11 Jan. 1585.
[2] A. Clarke, *Register of the University of Oxford*, ii, O.H.S. x (Oxford, 1887), p. 321.
[3] F. Wormald and C. E. Wright, *The English Library before 1700* (1958), p. 71.
[4] *Oxford College Libraries in 1556* (Oxford, Bodleian Library, 1956), Preface.
[5] Arber, ii, pp. 807–12.

whatsoever, But onelye in the Cyttie of London, or the Subburbes thereof, and excepte one presse in the universitye of Cambridge, and another presse in the universitie of Oxforde, and no moe . . .

[Article 5] *Item* that none of the Prynters in Cambridge or Oxford for the tyme beinge shalbe suffered to have any more apprentices then one at one tyme at the most, But yt is and shalbe lawful to and for the sayd Prynters and eyther of them and their Successors to have and use the helpe of any Journeyman beinge freeman of the cyttye of London without contradic[tion] Any Lawe, statute, or Commaundment contrarye to the meaninge and due execuc[ion] of these Ordynaunces or any of them in any wyse notwithstandinge.

This exception from a prohibition was the nearest thing to a royal permission to print that our University, basing itself on a document, could claim until Laud in 1632 got a charter from Charles I expressly to that effect. It is true that the same monarch had referred to the press in a proclamation of 1625, reciting that 'for the publike advancement of Religion, and Learning, in our Universities of Oxford and Cambridge, there hath been for many yeeres a speciall Printer allowed and authorised at either of Our said Universities.'[1] It is not surprising that Chief Justice Hyde and Mr. Justice Richardson, deputed by the Privy Council to investigate the legal rights of Cambridge in this respect, had to report in 1629 'And touching the clauses in the Order of Referrence whereby wee are required to consider alsoe of the Charter of the University of Oxford, if they would attend with the same, wee were not attended with the charter of that University of Oxford neither with any members of that body.'[2] Sir Edward Coke, a Cambridge man, wrote in the Fourth Part of his *Institutes*, first published in 1644, 'This University of Cambridge hath power to print within the same *omnes et omnimodos libros*, which the University of Oxford hath not'[3]—a statement no longer true when it was first published but repeated in subsequent editions.

From 1586 until 1632 the law as to printing at Oxford was in an untidy state, doing no credit to the government or the University. A press was allowed, but the University's right to spend money on it or authorize its publications was doubtful.

There is no sign of uneasiness about the legality of his press in the work of Joseph Barnes. He printed some 300 books before retiring in

[1] *To inhibite the sale of Latine Bookes reprinted beyond the Seas, having been first Printed in Oxford and Cambridge*, 1 Apr. 1625: Bibliotheca Lindesiana, ed. Steele, i, No. 1401.
[2] *Acts of the Privy Council of England, 1628 July–1629 April* (H.M.S.O., 1958), p. 409.
[3] 6th ed. (1681), p. 228.

1617, and in them he regularly put the arms of the University as his printer's mark and described himself as Printer to the University. The business was his own and the profit or loss was his. In a letter from him read to Convocation in 1590 he refers to his loan from the chest: 'Whereas I hadde lent unto mee one hundred powndes by the decree of this howse that I might be the better able thereby to erecte a printing howse which I didde accordingly, although to my farre greater charge'.[1] All but £20 of his loan was repaid before he gave up work.[2]

Barnes's press was used chiefly for tracts and sermons on the Protestant, at first Calvinistic, side of religious controversy. Greek and Latin classical authors account for half a dozen of his total, and logic and philosophy based on Aristotle for as many. A long and rather frequent series of volumes of poems in learned languages by members of the University lamenting the deaths of prominent men or honouring royal births and marriages began in his time with a collection for the death of Sir Philip Sidney in 1587. That he did jobbing to the Vice-Chancellor's order is proved by surviving copies of orders for the Oxford market of 1602 and 1606.[3] The books of his that are most prized and consulted now are Captain John Smith's *Map of Virginia with a Description of the Countrey* (1612), Charles Butler's *Feminine Monarchie, or a Treatise concerning Bees* (1609), and the first *Catalogus* of the Bodleian Library of 1605.

Joseph Barnes was not a Stationer of London, but his son, John, was admitted to the freedom of that Company in 1601 and from then onwards is named in many of his father's imprints as stocking the Oxford editions in London, an arrangement that must have helped the press to pay its way. No doubt it was owing to the younger Barnes that two at least of Joseph's books were offered for sale at Frankfurt fairs by London Stationers.[4] Moreover by assigning his copy in his books to his son Barnes could make sure that the property in them would be respected

---

[1] Chancellor's Register 1582–94 (L 10), fol. 246. Oxford records contain nothing as revealing about the relation of a Printer to the University to the parent body as a letter to Lord Burghley from the Vice-Chancellor and Heads of Colleges at Cambridge of 1583, quoted by Sir Sydney Roberts: 'We dare undertake, in the behalf of Mr. Thomas whom we know to be a very godly and honest man, that the press shall not be abused, either in publishing things prohibited, or otherwise inconvenient for the church and state of this realm. And this we promise the rather, for that his grace [i.e. authority from the Senate] . . . was granted to him upon condition that he should stand bound from time to time to such articles as your honour and the greatest part of the heads of colleges should ty him unto.' S. C. Roberts, *A History of the Cambridge University Press* (Cambridge, 1921), p. 24.

[2] *Print and Privilege*, p. 6n.

[3] Madan, *Oxford Books*, i, pp. 53, 65.

[4] The Bodleian *Catalogus* of 1605 and Nicholas Fuller's *Miscellanea theologica* (1616) are in official Catalogues of the fairs in the name of Joseph Barnes.

by members of the Company.[1] In one instance Joseph had to complain of competition from abroad: in his petition to Convocation of 1590 he alleged that 'Doctor Case his Politiques' [*Sphaera civitatis* by John Case, printed by Barnes in 1588] have binne ofte printed beyonde the Seas to my great hinderance';[2] therefore he humbly entreated 'that yow would now decret by the authoritie of this howse that hereafter everie determining Baccheler should buye one of them off mee'. *Legati* were deputed to consider his request, but no action is reported.

A PLURALITY OF PRINTERS 1618–40

Barnes retired in 1617, the year before his death leaving goods valued at £1,128.[3] The imprints of Oxford books of 1617 give the names of John Lichfield and William Wrench as printers to the University. So long as they shared a press there was no contravention of the Star Chamber's decree of 1586. Wrench's name occurs in only one year: Lichfield's recurs constantly in records of Oxford printing until the end of the eighteenth century. John continued to print for the University until 1635 and had James Short as his partner from 1618 until 1624; William Turner succeeded Short and lasted until 1640. In 1627, however, Lichfield and Short parted company. In 1626 there was the first of 'diverse variances controversies and differences' between them, and in 1628 Turner brought a suit in the Chancellor's Court against Lichfield, claiming the recovery of equipment and stock worth £100.[4] Whatever the outcome, the two carried on separate businesses thereafter, each calling himself 'Printer to the University'. By having more than one press the University was defying the decree of the Star Chamber.

This was the state of affairs when William Laud, then Bishop of London and a Privy Councillor, was elected Chancellor of the University.

In the interval between the retirement of Joseph Barnes and the accession to the chancellorship of William Laud some notable books came from the Oxford presses: three editions of Burton's *Anatomy of Melancholy*, 'from my Studie in Christchurch, Oxon. Decemb. 5. 1620', Peter Heylin's *Microcosmus, or a little Description of the Great World*,

---

[1] *S.T.C.* 4754–65; *Records of the Court of the Stationers' Company 1602 to 1640*, ed. W. A. Jackson (1957), pp. 104–5, 245n.

[2] Chancellor's Register 1582–94, fol. 246. The Bodleian has a copy of an edition from Frankfurt am Main of 1589.

[3] Strickland Gibson, *Abstracts from the Wills and Testamentary Documents of Binders, Printers, and Stationers of Oxford from 1493 to 1638* (1907), pp. 26–8.

[4] *Print and Privilege*, p. 11n.

a modern political and historical geography, and the first novel printed here, *Guzman de Alfarache* in an admirable English translation. Robert Sanderson's *Logicae artis compendium* (1619), Thomas James's Bodleian *Catalogus* of 1620, and Bishop Thornborough's alchemical treatise, Λιθοθεωρικός, were offered at Frankfurt fairs.

The University was brought a step nearer to a printing business of its own by an acquisition of printing type in 1619. The Vice-Chancellor entered in his accounts for the year ending 21 July 1620 two items for 'carriage to Oxford of the Greek types given to the University by Sir Henry Savile'. The compiler of a list of Savile's benefactions writes in 1622, as though the University already owned a press: 'Officinam Universitatis Typographicam literis graecis innumeris, literarumque matricibus (monimento insigni) ditavit.'[1] The fount, it is easy to see, is one with which Savile printed the works of St. Chrysostom at Eton in 1610–13 in six folio volumes. It is a big type, suitable for texts, whereas Barnes and his successors had only a small Greek, fit for footnotes. The matrices, in number 319, of which 153 are for ligatured letters and contractions, are still at the Press with added ligatured sorts made to the order of Fell.[2] Cambridge University borrowed them in 1629 and had type cast for printing a Testament.[3]

[1] *Ultima linea Savilii* (Oxford, 1622), p. [iii].
[2] Morison, *Fell*, pp. 102–3.
[3] Madan, *Oxford Books*, ii, pp. 517–20.

CHAPTER III

Archbishop Laud's Plans for a University Press

LAUD'S VISION OF A LEARNED PRESS

LAUD began his term as Chancellor in 1629, determined to be more than a figurehead to the University, rather to put some order into its constitution and to see that it was maintained. Items in his list of 'Things which I have projected to do, if God bless me in them' are these:

vi. To collect the broken, crossing, and imperfect Statutes of the University of Oxford; which had lain in a confused Heap some Hundreds of Years. Done.

xii. To set up a Greek Press in London and Oxford, for Printing of the Library Manuscripts; and to get Letters and Matrices. Done for London.

xiv. To procure a large Charter for Oxford, to confirm their ancient Priviledges, and obtain new for them, as large as those of Cambridge, which they had gotten since Hen. 8. which Oxford had not. Done.[1]

Laud was thoroughly at home in the University; he had been a fellow of St. John's College from 1593 to 1610, served for a year as proctor, and was President of the college from 1611 until 1621. His ecclesiastical preferments and the large part that he played in affairs of state still left him time to intervene constantly in academical government. Even before he was Chancellor he drew up, in 1628, a new statute to remedy the time-honoured 'factious and tumultuous' election of proctors.[2] As the breeding-ground of clergy with a great influence on opinion in the Church, Oxford was of great moment to him.

The 'Library Manuscripts' which Laud thought called for printing by a reformed press were the Barocci Collection of 240 Greek manuscripts assembled in Venice which he had secured and persuaded the previous Chancellor, the 3rd Earl of Pembroke to give to the Bodleian Library in 1628.[3] His own gifts of some 1,300 manuscripts came later, in 1636–41.

[1] pp. 68–9 of 'The Diary of the Life of Arch-Bishop Laud' in *The History of the Troubles and Tryal of the Most Reverend Father in God, and Blessed Martyr, William Laud*, ed. H. Wharton (1695).

[2] Ibid., pp. 43–4.

[3] Ibid., p. 44.

The irregularity of Oxford printing in the eyes of the law was cured by Letters Patent dated 12 November 1632 got by Laud from King Charles I. They give the Chancellor, Masters, and Scholars a right to appoint three *typographi*, printers of books, and booksellers, any act or ordinance to the contrary notwithstanding. The terms of the grant were similar to those of the charter to Cambridge of 1534, allowing the sale of the product anywhere in the King's dominions but requiring approval of the content by the Chancellor or his vicegerent and three doctors, one being a doctor of divinity.[1] There was a technical defect in the charter, and Laud took the opportunity of securing ampler powers for the University by another, dated 13 March 1632/3. It allowed each of the three printers to have two presses and two apprentices notwithstanding the decree of the Star Chamber of 1586; it forbade others to reprint for twenty years any edition that the *typographi* printed from a manuscript in an Oxford library or any other of their books for ten years on pain of confiscation, and gave to the University authorities a power to search for and seize offending reprints. The two instruments were consolidated in the so-called Great Charter to the University of 1636, which also contained declaratory clauses confirming the King's intention that liberty to print 'all manner of books' included such as were the subject of exclusive patents to other printers.[2]

These royal grants and those to the like effect given to Cambridge still have force in them inasmuch as the courts of law, even in times when the royal prerogative was least considered by them, have held that they warrant the two Universities in disregarding the King's Printer's otherwise exclusive right to print and sell (in England) the Bible in English, the Book of Common Prayer, and the services of the Church of England. Their freedom to do so, the Universities' 'privilege' of Bible-printing, will often be referred to in the pages that follow. The salient facts about its origin are these.

THE ORIGIN OF THE BIBLE PRIVILEGE

Henry VIII, having in 1530 forbidden the printing of books of Holy Scripture in English, unless licensed by a bishop, empowered the University of Cambridge in 1534 to print all manner of books not publicly

[1] Madan, *Oxford Books*, i, pp. 281–3.
[2] Ibid., pp. 283–5; pp. 58–60 of Laud's 'Account relating to the U. of Oxford'; *The Great Charter of Charles I to the University of Oxford, 3 March 1636*, ed. S. Gibson, with an opinion by Sir William Holdsworth (Oxford, 1935).

prohibited that had been approved by its Chancellor or Vice-Chancellor and three doctors. In 1577 Queen Elizabeth I issued a patent to Christopher Barker appointing him her printer of all statutes, books, bills, acts of Parliament, proclamations, Bibles, and New Testaments, in the English tongue of any translation, with or without notes, and of all services ordered to be used in churches, forbidding any other of her subjects to print any of these things under severe penalties.[1]

This first grant to Barker was for life, but patents repeating its words have since been granted for terms of years until 1882 and thereafter at the sovereign's will and pleasure.[2] The successive patents and the reversions to them have been bought from the Crown or the patentees for big sums of money.

In 1591 a Bible in the Genevan English translation was printed at Cambridge. The London Stationers petitioned Lord Burghley, High Treasurer of the realm and Chancellor of the University of Cambridge, to stop the press there until the following law term. The University appointed an advocate for its case,[3] but if there was a hearing its outcome is unknown. However, no more Bibles were printed at Cambridge until 1629.

Meanwhile, in 1623, the conflict between these parties came once more before the Privy Council, and King James was pleased to take its advice 'that the University should comprint with the Stationers and Printers of London in all Bookes whatsoever, as well priveledged as others, save only the Bibles, Bookes of Common Prayer, Grammers, Psalmes, Psalters, Primers, and Bookes of common Lawe, or any parte of them; with this Limitation neverthelesse, that they shall sett at Worke but one Presse only, for the printing of all or any the said priveledged Books. . . .'[4]

The fresh start of Bible-printing at Cambridge in 1629 was the result of a charter to the University from Charles I, dated 6 February 1628 (N.S.) declaring that the class of books it might print included those particularly expressed in any Letters Patent to any other person or persons.[5] Nevertheless, the King's Printer and the Stationers still contested the right where the Bible and the metrical psalms were concerned.

---

[1] A. W. Pollard, *Records of the English Bible* (1911), pp. 322–6.

[2] *Universities of Oxford and Cambridge* v. *Eyre & Spottiswoode Ltd.*, [1964] Ch., p. 736.

[3] Burghley's son, Robert Cecil, was thanked for undertaking the defence: J. Ward, *The Lives of the Professors of Gresham College* (1740), pp. 59, 60.

[4] *Acts of the Privy Council June 1623–March 1625* (H.M.S.O., 1933), pp. 141–2.

[5] Cited by the judges in their report to the Privy Council in 1629: *Acts of the Privy Council 1628–9*, p. 406; Greg, *Companion to Arber*, pp. 199–203.

On the same 6 February Thomas and John Buck, Printers to the University, were summoned to the Star Chamber to answer a complaint by the Stationers that they flouted that court's decree of 1586 'by useinge 4. presses and keepinge 5. Apprentices, & three or fower Workemen not Freemen of London, besides other Journeymen'. Roger Daniel was cited also for selling psalm-books printed at Cambridge.[1] The whole matter of the legality of printing by the University was referred to the judges, and possessed of their opinion[2] the Privy Council on 16 April 1629 decreed a compromise: the University was permitted to print any number of Bibles in quarto and Medium folio, with or without the liturgy and the singing psalms to form part of the same volume, while the Bible in other formats was reserved to the King's Printer.[3] The folio Bibles issued from Cambridge in 1629 and 1638 are distinguished by great improvements to the text of the Authorized Version.

Oxford was put on the same footing as Cambridge on 9 March 1636 (N.S.), when an Order in Council declared that 'the Universitie of Oxforde and their Printers shall for the time to come enjoye the benefit of all the Articles and Clauses in the said Orders of the 10th of December 1623, and of the 16th of Aprill 1629.'[4] Apart from the restriction on the formats of the Bibles that the Universities might print, the King in Council was at length reconciled with the King as he expressed himself in Letters Patent.

LAUD'S OVERSIGHT OF THE PRESS

Having secured for his University a firm legal warrant for its printing, Laud advised it to use the new powers warily, so as not to antagonize the Stationers or the King's Printer.

Though your Patents be large, yet coming over the Heads of the King's Printers and other Stationers here in London, I shall advise you not to suffer any of your Printers as yet to print Bibles, Service Books, Grammars, Primers, &c. (which caused the late and chargable Controversy betwixt Cambridge and them); but let your Privilege settle a while, and gather strength quietly. Lastly, such Orders as shall be thought fit to be made for the limiting of your Printers, and keeping them in due Obedience to the

[1] Blackstone's transcript in the Delegates' archive.
[2] The judges considered that the charters permitting Cambridge to print *omnimodos libros* were effective in law: S.P. (Dom.), Car. I, vol. 139, No. 4.
[3] Privy Council Register, vol. 39, pp. 200–2, printed in Greg, *Companion to Arber*, pp. 203–5.
[4] Blackstone's transcript from a copy in the University Archives.

University upon all occasions (which may be best advised on by you, that are upon the place), I think, may now very fitly be inserted into a Chapter by themselves among the Statutes, that so they may have the more binding Authority over them.[1]

He would not commit himself as to the fitness of the two printers in Oxford, Lichfield and Turner, to exercise the new powers. 'Confirm not either of the two Printers which you now have, in any of the Rights of these Patents till all Orders concerning them be settled. Secondly, that you name as yet no third Printer, but keep the place empty, that you may get an able man, if it be possible, for the Printing of Greek, when you shall be ready for it.'[2]

This was Laud writing in 1633, and already parts of his plan for the press at Oxford are apparent. It was to be a University printing by contract, the agents being tightly controlled tradesmen, who were bound, at least part of their time, to produce what they were told and run the risk of selling it. It was to publish manuscripts. More than once Laud expressed a hope that he might live to see some of his gifts to the Bodleian multiplied in print.[3] Like the petitioners of c. 1584,[4] and other propagandists of printing in early days, he regarded the capacity of the craft to preserve texts previously available only in writing as its chief recommendation. He would have been disappointed by the number of Bodleian codices that have served as copy, however many have provided footnotes. Thirdly, this was to be a Greek press. Laud put among his ambitions the setting up in London and Oxford of presses equipped for work in that language.[5] Three books printed in London in Greek were the penalty that he exacted from the King's Printers for the blasphemies and obscenities of the 'Wicked' Bible of 1631.[6] That experiment in royal learned printing in England came to an end for good and all in 1638.

At Oxford the resolve taken in Convocation, on hearing the new charters read, to proceed with printing the chronicle of John Malalas, using the Greek type given by Sir Henry Savile[7] had evaporated by 1636, overcome by 'the peevishness, or extreme sottishness' of the printer, William Turner, who accepted the commission and the loan of the University's type, but did nothing.[8]

In 1633–4 Laud's spare time was taken up with revising new statutes for the University drawn up by a delegacy of Convocation. The draft

[1] Laud's 'Account relating to the U. of Oxford', pp. 59–60.
[2] Ibid.   [3] Ibid., pp. 58, 130.   [4] Above, pp. 19–20.   [5] Above, p. 26.
[6] Reed, *Old English Letter Foundries*, pp. 130–2.
[7] *Print and Privilege*, p. 12.   [8] Madan, *Oxford Books*, ii, pp. 524–5.

was sent to him for approval; and 'this act of the University appears to have been understood by the Chancellor as committing to him an absolute authority to settle the Statutes according to his own mind.'[1] Tit. xviii, Sect. v, *De typographis Universitatis*, bears all the marks of his authorship. It begins with a mention of the recently-granted charters and continues (in Latin), 'Lest mean and narrow-minded tradesmen should misuse the indulgence of a most gracious king for their private advantage, it is decreed' etc. Nobody in future was to use the style of Printer to the University unless he submitted to the rules and regulations of Convocation relating to printers.

The bishop had a poor opinion of the printing trade.[2] The section goes on with reflections on printers and puts a check on those of Oxford:

Since experience of the trade shows that these mechanic craftsmen for the most part look for profit and saving of labour, caring not at all for beauty of letters or good and seemly workmanship, and bundle out any kind of rough and incorrect productions to the light of day, be it provided by this statute that an Architypographus shall preside over the University's public printing office, which is to be established in a building specially devoted to this purpose. He shall be a man thoroughly acquainted with Greek and Latin literature and deeply learned in philological studies. His functions shall be to superintend the printing done in that place and to see that the material and equipment, that is to say the paper, presses, type, and other implements of this workshop shall be the best of their kind. In all work that comes from the University's public printing office he shall determine size of type, quality of paper, and width of margins, correct correctors' mistakes, and take unremitting care of the good appearance and fine workmanship of the product.

To his post, so that he may be the more promptly and readily available for it, be it provided by this statute that the office of Superior Bedel of Civil Law (as being the least busy of the bedelships) as soon as it next becomes vacant shall be for ever annexed, and besides that a fixed share of the profit from the printing proportioned to his contribution to the funds or capital of the printing office shall hereafter be assigned to him by the delegates of Convocation for framing statutes for printing.

It is a proof of the extreme formality of Laud's mind that he foisted this scheme in all its rigidity and untried upon the University. Paper work had gone far ahead of real life, particularly where the unpaid contractors

---

[1] Griffiths, *Laudian Code*, p. x.
[2] See his tirade against it in *Reports of Cases in the Star Chamber and High Commission*, Camden Soc., 2nd ser. 39 (1886), p. 305.

were concerned; and it is difficult to imagine the Architypographus com-
bining the higher literacy with technical competence, designing books
and correcting proofs in the intervals of minding the business of the Law
Faculty, and keeping accounts in both his capacities. Laud's scheme, and
his code of university statutes as a whole, were unalterable after royal
approval in 1636, until in 1856 a new royal charter gave the University
power to repeal or alter its old statutes and frame new ones,[1] and the plan
for printing caused trouble in times to come. However, its coming into
operation depended on two conditions being fulfilled; a building for the
press was not found until 1669, and the bedelship of Civil Law did not
fall vacant until 1656.

A university press existed in Laud's brain when he framed the statutes
in 1634. Of the things needed to make it a reality money was one.
Evidence of the want of it at the time can be found in the coupling of the
office of Architypographus with that of Superior Bedel of Civil Law, so
that the stipend attached to the bedelship might pay for both. It is
equally evident in an agreement made in the same year between the
University and William Turner whereby Turner would print the
Chronicle of Malalas, paying the editor and providing some of the type
in return for liberty to print three almanacs a year for seven years under
the protection of the University's charters.[2]

Learned publishing does not pay. The Laudian Code took the first
step towards subsidizing it by providing that if there were a surplus in
the fund for building and maintaining the Schools Quadrangle (begun in
1613) it should be devoted to the learned press.[3] The fund, fed by
exactions on matriculation and admissions to degrees, has since 1656
been accounted for separately in the annual Computus of the Vice-
Chancellor. Expenditure on the building was so heavy that no surplus
occurred until 1650, and after that when there was a balance in the fund
it was used in many years to make up for a deficit in the University's
general account.[4] Blackstone in 1758 reckoned that if this direction in the
Laudian statutes had been obeyed the amount paid to the Press in the
years 1656–97 would have been £15,674, while he had only been able to
find that £240 and some smaller sums for the purchase of type had been
spent on editing and printing.[5]

---

[1] Griffiths, *Laudian Code*, pp. xxv–xxvii.   [2] *Print and Privilege*, p. 13.
[3] Tit. XX, s. 4; Griffiths, *Laudian Code*, p. 196.
[4] Madan, *Oxford Books*, iii, p. xvi; but further investigation is needed.
[5] Bodl. MS. Top. Oxon. d. 387, fols. 34–6; *To the Reverend Doctor Randolph* (Oxford, 1757),
pp. 20–1.

William Laud, Archbishop of Canterbury, Chancellor of the University of Oxford 1629–41. By Sir Anthony Van Dyck. Dated 1636

Gerard Langbaine (1609–58). Provost of Queen's College and Keeper of the University Archives

Edward Pococke (1604–91). Oriental scholar

A second step was taken three years later when the University sealed the first of its agreements, dated 12 March 1637 (N.S.), with the Company of Stationers not to print books for which the Company had exclusive patents and to forbear printing Bibles and certain other books 'now used to be printed by the King's Majesties Printer' and Lily's grammar in consideration of an annual payment of £200. It was the first of a series of 'Covenants of Forbearance' lasting until 1780, though with interruptions during the Commonwealth.[1] Laud wholly approved the compact of 1637: 'For certainly it will be more beneficial to the University for the Advance of a learned Press to receive £200 a Year, than to print Grammars, and Almanacks, &c., and more Honour too.... Now I shall require this of You and your Successors, that this Money which You yearly receive may be kept safe, as a Stock apart, and put to no other Use, than the Settling of a learned Press.'[2]

As soon as this source of revenue was assured the University made a move towards a printing business of its own by equipping itself with type for Hebrew and Arabic. Samuel Brown, a London bookseller and brother to one of the University's proctors for the year, went to Leyden and negotiated early in 1637 a sale of type, matrices, and punches from the stock of a typefounder, Arend Cornelisz. van Hoogenacker, lately deceased.[3] The collection brought back by Brown, still recognizable in the equipment of the Press, includes a number of incomplete sets of

برای خَیْر مِلت خُون اَخْن وَ اِجرَی نُمَایَد – لِهُنَا اَز صَمِیم

قَلْبِ بَا شَعْف تَمَام خُونرَا تَهْنِیت مِیکُونَیم کَه چُنِین مِهْمَان

جَلِیلی بَا مَلکَه نِیشَوْکَت خَویش دَر مَوقَعی کَه دَروَاقَع

בְּרָא אֱלֹהִים אֵת הַשָּׁמַיִם וְאֵת הָאָרֶץ: וְהָאָרֶץ הָיְתָה תֹהוּ

וָבֹהוּ וְחֹשֶׁךְ עַל פְּנֵי תְהוֹם וְרוּחַ אֱלֹהִים מְרַחֶפֶת עַל פְּנֵי

הַמָּיִם: וַיֹּאמֶר אֱלֹהִים יְהִי אוֹר וַיְהִי אוֹר: וַיַּרְא אֱלֹהִים

אֶת הָאוֹר כִּי טוֹב וַיַּבְדֵּל אֱלֹהִים בֵּין הָאוֹר וּבֵין הַחֹשֶׁךְ:

The Arabic and one of the Hebrews got from Leyden in 1637. Cast in the matrices kept at the Press.

---

[1] *To the Reverend Doctor Randolph*, pp. 17–18; Madan, *Oxford Books*, iii, pp. 406–7. Agreements since 1744 were made in 1765 and 1779.
[2] Laud's 'Account relating to the U. of Oxford', p. 126.
[3] Univ. Arch. S.E.P. P17ᵇ(3), fol. 3.

matrices for the Greek, Hebrew, Syriac, and Arabic scripts, which the
University, for want of a skilled man to cut the missing letters, has
never completed and made serviceable, but it did provide matrices
enough for casting Arabic type of a convenient size and square Hebrew
in four sizes. Besides these there are matrices for a Rabbinical Hebrew,
used in recent times to supply enough type for examination papers, the
Press having no other for that script.[1] The cost of the acquisition and
Brown's expenses about it came to £293.11s. 6d.[2] John Greaves, oriental
scholar, wrote approvingly of the transactions and thought the University had good value for its money.[3] A less complacent critic would have
said that Brown was a bad judge of typefounder's material.

Doubtless the arrival of the oriental types gratified Archbishop Laud
as bringing nearer the time when he might see some of his gift of manuscripts put to press. He writes on 5 May 1637 to the Vice-Chancellor:
'You are now upon a very good Way towards the setting up of a learned
Press, and I like your Proposal well to keep your Matrices and your
Letters safe; and in the mean time to provide all other Necessaries that
so You may be ready for that Work. For since it hath pleased God so to
bless me, as that I have procured You both Privilege and Means for that
Work, I should be very glad to see it begun in my own Lifetime, if it
might be.'[4]

Laud knew that the public printing office must wait for the completion
of the Schools, when money might become available. He urged the
Vice-Chancellor in September 1637 to finish building the extended
Bodleian 'that so the learned Press may really and heartily be set upon'.[5]
Also his thoughts had turned now and again to making the necessary
appointments. 'And because the Beginning of such a Work will be very
difficult, as also the procuring of a sufficient Composer and Corrector for
the Eastern Languages, You have done exceeding well to think of him at
Leyden, and to get him over upon as good Terms as You can, and to
give him an annual Pension in the mean time, that he may not be tempted
from your Service.'[6] He applauds the prospective choice of William
Cartwright as Architypographus and Law Bedel, 'when the Voydance
shall come'; and, reminded of bedels, ''tis come into my Head to ask

---

[1] The material got from Leyden is fully described in Morison, *Fell*, pp. 233–43.
[2] V.-C.'s Computus 1592–1650, fol. 124.
[3] S.P. (Dom.) Car. I, vol. 331, No. 75 (Feb. 1638).
[4] Laud's 'Account relating to the U. of Oxford', p. 130.
[5] Ibid., p. 141.
[6] Ibid., p. 130.

this Question, Why may not all three Esquire Bedels join in the learned Press, tho' perhaps but one of them need be the chief Manager.'[1]

A week later he comes back to the subject in a letter of 26 May 1637:

But indeed, if the University would set sadly to it, and bring in some Batchelors of Art to be Yeomen Bedells, which are wellgrounded and towardly, to serve that Press as Composers or otherwise, it would in time be of excellent Use. And they which thrived well and did good service, might after be preferred to be Esquire Bedells, and so that Press would ever train up able Men for itself. And though there be time enough to think of this Business, yet certainly it would not be amiss, now while 'tis res integra, to propose it (in general at least) to the Heads, that every Man may have his Eyes upon, and help to perfect, so good a Business . . .

Moreover, reading a letter about filling the place of Clerk to St. Mary's Church had made him think 'that such a Man might be chosen Clerk, as may be serviceable to the learned Press, either as a Founder of Letters, or as a Pressman'.[2]

It would have been interesting to see how this idea of a printing and publishing business, so unlike capitalist industrial organization, would have worked; but the clouds were gathering about Laud and when his admiring followers regained power after the Restoration they had to abandon the letter of Laud's instructions. He resigned the Chancellorship of the University on 25 June 1641[3] and was succeeded by an enemy of his, the Earl of Pembroke.

Even when Laud's power was at its height his influence on the choice of books to be printed at Oxford does not seem to have been strong. The two printers, Lichfield and Turner, printed mainly Protestant theology of a Calvinist or near-Calvinist kind: the Heidelberg Catechism was printed at Oxford in 1629 and works by the Presbyterians William Ames and Festus Hommius, in 1630. When these two books were reprinted nine years later Laud protested strongly to the Vice-Chancellor and threatened to 'suppress' the two printers if they published books without an imprimatur.[4] In the case of William Page's *Treatise of Bowing at the Name of Jesus* (an observance by which Laud set great store) he went over the head of his archbishop and got a command from the King that the book, printed by Lichfield in 1631, should be put on sale. Abbot had advised suppressing it and letting the controversy started by William

[1] Ibid., p. 131.   [2] Ibid., p. 138.
[3] 'Diary' in the *History of the Troubles and Tryal*, p. 61.
[4] 'Account relating to the U. of Oxford', p. 185.

Prynne on its subject die down.[1] Oxford was not by any means solidly Laudian: there were old scores with him on personal grounds besides opposition to his 'Arminianism'.[2]

To Laud's credit be it said that he had a hand in directing to Lichfield's press at Oxford a work of genuinely modern scholarship, perhaps the first to come from here, the *Epistola ad Corinthios* of Pope Clement I, printed for the first time in the original Greek.[3] The text was present on some tattered leaves at the end of *Codex Alexandrinus*, the gift to Charles I of the Patriarch Cyril Lukaris in 1628. Patrick Young, the King's librarian, transcribed it and edited it with notes and a Latin translation. A peculiarity of the edition was the use of red ink for words and letters supplied by the editor to fill up lacunae.

This book, published in 1633, was the learned press in being. The necessary constituents were there: a scholar-editor with uncommercial motives, a printer equipped with uncommon type (Savile's Greek), a competent corrector, and someone willing to pay the cost with little prospect of recovering it. It was not, however, a university press. The University contributed the type and perhaps the corrector; who paid for the printing is not known, but there is no sign of expenditure on it in the accounts of the Vice-Chancellor; there are acknowledgements in the preface and in Young's correspondence of royal munificence.[4]

[1] Laud's 'Account relating to the U. of Oxford', pp. 24-5.
[2] Ibid., pp. 33-43.
[3] The first of the two epistles is printed entire with a fragment of the other. Laud's responsibility for getting the work done at Oxford is not, I believe, documented, but a likely guess: cf. H. R. Trevor-Roper, *Archbishop Laud, 1573-1645*, 2nd ed. (1965), pp. 274-5.
[4] Bodl. MS. Smith 75, fols. 82, 197. The printers were accused of *inclementia*: MS. Smith 76, fol. 51.

CHAPTER IV

Learned Printing during the Interregnum

CIVIL war, breaking out in 1642, overwhelmed the little presses at Oxford with orders for royalist propaganda and jobbing, but not quite to the exclusion of learned printing. That this was kept in some sort alive is owing to James Ussher, the erudite Archbishop of Armagh, and to Gerard Langbaine the elder, Provost of Queen's College. Work began on Ussher's *Epistles of Ignatius, Polycarp, and Barnabas* in 1640 before the resort to arms. The archbishop was thereafter, when not in Oxford, not inaccessible from it, and besides two books of his own he put to press one by Thomas Morton in 1644 and persuaded John Greaves to finish Bainbridge's *Canicularia* and get it published in 1648. Ussher's edition of the *Epistles* was finished in 1644 but was destroyed in a fire at the printer's so that it had to be done again four years later.[1] The texts, like the Clement of 1633, are pseudonymous but none the less valuable authorities for the early history of Christianity, and the one attributed to Barnabas had not previously been printed in the original Greek. The text was the result of collating several manuscripts, two of them in Oxford colleges. The Greek when it varied from the accepted Latin version was printed in red. Savile's fount of type was still in excellent condition, but the Roman, not renewed since Barnes's day, was not. An edition of Longinus in Greek and Latin in the care of Langbaine was done in 1644.

The period of Oxford printing after the Royalists' surrender of the city in 1647 until the Restoration is remarkable for publications in the 'oriental' languages and in mathematics, Edward Pococke dominating the former field and John Wallis the other. The University can claim little credit for these books, for it had no money, so that the finance had to be provided by booksellers in London and Oxford. A small surplus in the Schools Account in some years was enough to pay for the purchase of type, but other money there was none. The principal support of learned printing, the £200 a year promised by the Stationers' Company for the University's forbearance to print books covered by patents

[1] Madan, *Oxford Books*, ii, Nos. 1685, 1739.

granted to members of the Company was not paid regularly after 1642 until a new agreement was reached in 1661.[1]

What the University could contribute to oriental printing is due to the munificence of Archbishop Laud. We owe to him not only the nucleus for the Bodleian's wonderful holding of manuscripts in the languages of the Middle East but the endowment in 1636 of a chair of Arabic and the choice of Edward Pococke to fill it. The first use of the matrices bought from Leyden in 1637 was in 1652 to cast the Hebrew for Pococke's edition of the *Porta Mosis* of Maimonides, but it seems probable that a small amount of type as well as matrices was included in the purchase of 1637, and that it was used to print a sheet of paradigms, *Tabula directoria*, by Victorinus Bythner, a teacher of Hebrew in Oxford, in 1637 and his grammar, *Lingua eruditorum*, in 1638.[2] The existence of an imported fount would also account for quotations in Hebrew in Pococke's *Specimen historiae Arabum* of 1648–50.

Some 'small Arabick letter' figures in the payment by the Vice-Chancellor for the purchase from Leyden in 1637. Probably it is this fount that is to be seen in two works printed at Oxford before a large supply was cast in the University's matrices in 1654–5. One of these was *Canicularia* by John Bainbridge dated 1648,[3] where Arabic type is used to print the astronomical tables of Ulugh Beg written in Persian. This essay on the Dog Star was left incomplete by Bainbridge, the first Savilian Professor of Astronomy, and finished, at Ussher's request, by his successor John Greaves. In the same year, 1648, was printed the greater part of Edward Pococke's *Specimen historiae Arabum*, in which there are very substantial passages in Arabic and quotations in Hebrew.

This part of a book, to be regarded as an earnest of Pococke's intentions in the way of publishing, was a collection of notes on a brief description of the rise, manners, language, and religion of the Arab people by Gregorius bar Hebraeus, a Jacobite Christian bishop, styled in Arabic Abu al-Faraj, who died in 1286. Pococke's voluminous annotations, drawn from more than a hundred manuscript sources, established his reputation as the foremost Arabic scholar in western Europe.[4] The text by Gregorius with a Latin translation by Pococke was added to the notes and published with them in 1650. It is an extract, making 15 pages, from Gregorius's history of the world which Pococke afterwards published entire.[5]

[1] Univ. Arch. S.E.P. 9(5), 9(7).
[2] Madan, *Oxford Books*, i, pp. 197, 204.
[3] Ibid. ii, No. 2002.
[4] Twells, *Life of Pococke*, p. 149.
[5] Madan, *Oxford Books*, ii, No. 2034.

The professor evidently thought it was time for him to justify his appointment and provide students with a text by a publication such as the distractions of the time (from which he suffered severely) and the limited supply of exotic types permitted.

Before more substantial works in the oriental scripts could be undertaken type would have to be cast in the University's matrices. They were in the safe hands of Gerard Langbaine, confided to him in 1644 when he became the University's Keeper of the Archives. Finding himself in charge of a fund of printing equipment whose history he did not know and difficult to classify without a technical training, he set himself to inventory the punches and matrices, noting missing and defective characters.[1] He showed good judgement in confining himself to the Hebrew and Arabic, for which the sets of matrices were virtually complete. His patient survey was a necessary preliminary to setting a typefounder to work.

The first call for the Arabic came from John Greaves, ejected by the Parliamentary Visitors from his chair at Oxford, who wanted type for two books partly in Persian which he proposed to get printed in London.[2] He borrowed the matrices in 1648 and had a fount cast by a London typefounder who added matrices for numerals and other defective sorts. A year later he returned the matrices to Oxford, where it was considered that some of them had been damaged.[3]

By 1652 the University, though it had little in the way of type or apparatus for making it, felt a need for a place to keep it in. Convocation noted that some of the University's type was on loan to printers and other typographical equipment had been allowed to be kept in places not very convenient, and resolved to devote the Old Congregation House, an annexe of the University Church, as a store for these things and to rename it *Domus typographica Universitatis publica*.[4] This was the name given in the statutes to the proposed University Press, so the first step in Laud's programme for printing had been made—but in name only. Nevertheless, the appropriation of this room was a presage of a university press: the need for common ownership of type for learned works had been formally recognized.

Preparations for producing Pococke's *Porta Mosis*, a selection from Maimonides' commentaries on the Mishnah, began in 1652. Expenditure

---

[1] Univ. Arch. S.E.P. P17ᵇ(3), fols. 43, 47.
[2] *Elementa linguae Persicae* and *Anonymus Persa de siglis astronomicis* (1649).
[3] Univ. Arch. S.E.P. P17ᵇ(7).
[4] Reg. Conv. T, p. 164; Madan, *Oxford Books*, iii, p. 409.

on the Hebrew type for it was agreed to by the Vice-Chancellor on the strength of an assurance by Langbaine that 'something of Dr. Pococke's would speedily be printed with [it]'.[1] Maimonides wrote Arabic but in Hebrew script, and Pococke decided to print with Hebrew type (though of the square kind, not the Rashi that was usual for commentaries).

The Old Congregation House, which Convocation in 1653 voted to use as a storehouse for type. (From James Ingram's *Memorials of Oxford*, 1837.)

Langbaine summoned a typefounder from London to inspect the University's matrices and on 31 March 1652 an agreement was signed for the casting of 200 lb. of Hebrew with points and the supply of additional matrices as necessary.[2] After much grumbling by the typefounder and long delay the type reached Oxford by the end of November.

Porta Mosis in Arabic and Latin with bulky annotations, relating especially to the Messianic prophecies, was published in 1655. In the mean time Pococke was engaged in getting ready an edition of the annals of Eutychius, a tenth-century Melchite patriarch of Alexandria, with a translation into Latin.[3] This he did 'upon the persuasion and importunity

---

[1] Twells, *Life of Pococke*, p. 186; C. Roth, 'Edward Pococke and the first Hebrew Printing in Oxford', *Bodleian Library Record*, ii (1948), pp. 215–19.

[2] Univ. Arch. S.E.P. P17ᵇ(11).

[3] Madan, *Oxford Books*, iii, Nos. 2297, 2385.

of Mr. Selden'[1] who left money by his will to pay for the printing. The book was published in 1656, by which time Pococke had lost faith in the author and grudged the time he had to spend on it out of respect for Selden's memory. For this book Arabic type was cast in London in the University's matrices in 1654–5.[2]

While Pococke was making Oxford known to the literate world as a centre of oriental studies John Wallis was laying a foundation for its position of eminence during a hundred years in mathematics. A fellow of Queens' College, Cambridge, he was chosen by Oliver Cromwell to succeed Peter Turner as Savilian Professor of Geometry at Oxford in 1649. His deserts were respected at the Restoration, and he remained in the chair until he died in 1703. In his later years he was also Keeper of the University Archives, and in that capacity he did notable services to the Press.

Wallis was a polymath, but primarily a mathematician. As such he was foremost in Great Britain between the death of William Oughtred and the rise to fame of Isaac Newton. His mathematical publications at Oxford during the Interregnum were an edition of Oughtred's *Clavis mathematica* (1652) and his own *Opera mathematica* (1656 and 1657), solutions of problems *De cycloide* (1659), besides polemics against Thomas Hobbes about geometry. He also published his English grammar (in Latin) here in 1653 and a sermon.[3]

The congeries of learned editors of the *Biblia Sacra Polyglotta* or London Polyglot Bible must be considered as ancestors of the English university presses of later times. Their Bible in nine languages and six folio volumes was generally accepted as surpassing in scope and exactness the famous polyglot editions of the Scriptures from Alcalá, Antwerp, and Paris. It set a standard in textual criticism which would in future be demanded of learned publishing,[4] a standard which only institutional presses could hope to reach and maintain. It was the co-operative achievement of scholars among the Anglican clergy, conceived at a time when many of them had been deprived of their benefices and had taken refuge in

---

[1] Twells, *Life of Pococke*, p. 225.   [2] V.-C.'s Computus 1650–4, fol. 150.

[3] For progress in the natural sciences at Oxford at this time, see M. Purver, *The Royal Society: Concept and Creation* (1967), part i, ch. 4; R. G. Frank, Jr., 'John Aubrey, F.R.S., John Lydall, and Science at Commonwealth Oxford', *Notes and Records of the Royal Society of London*, vol. 27 (1973), pp. 193–218.

[4] 'Effective awareness of the significance of textual criticism for the ancient versions of the biblical text may be said to begin only with the *Biblia Polyglotta* of Bishop Walton in 1657': Basil Hall in *The Cambridge History of the Bible*, ed. S. L. Greenslade (Cambridge, 1963), p. 64.

Royalist Oxford. When they dispersed after the surrender of the city and work on the book came to be controlled from London the two seminaries of the English Church were left with an enhanced confidence in the potentialities of Anglican scholarship.

Production of the Bible occupied the years 1652–7, and several of the most learned men in Oxford devoted themselves to it. Pococke was in great demand as adviser and supplier of manuscripts, but preoccupied as he was with *Porta Mosis* and the annals of Eutychius he had to decline most of the tasks that the editor, Brian Walton, would have liked to commit to him. Other Oxford men, Thomas Greaves, Samuel Clarke, Thomas Hyde, Alexander Huish, Thomas Pierce, Henry Hammond, were among the collaborators.[1]

THE FIRST ARCHITYPOGRAPHUS

In May 1658, the Superior Bedel of Law having died, Samuel Clarke was appointed in pursuance of Laud's provisions in the statutes to the combined posts of Architypographus and Law Bedel. He was an Arabic and Hebrew scholar and had been employed as translator and corrector on the London Polyglot Bible. At the outset of his career as supervisor of printing and publishing for the University he was compiling a seventh volume for the Polyglot. It was to contain a Targum on the Books of Chronicles, the Gospels in Syriac, the Pentateuch, Psalms, and lesser Prophets in Arabic, and, if possible, a supplement to the Old Testament previously published in Ethiopic. The printed prospectus[2] goes so far as to announce that 'the charge of the Impression will be borne by the University of Oxon.', but Clarke was expected to repay it out of the proceeds of sale and had to deposit the lease of his house as security.[3] The volume was never printed and remains in manuscript,[4] though Fell in 1669 wrote of it as being 'in hand' at the Press.[5]

There is a draft in Clarke's hand for a prospectus of a *Lexicon* in seven of the languages of the Polyglot to be compiled by Edmund Castell, Samuel Clarke, and Alexander Huish.[6] It is not dated, but the project

---

[1] H. J. Todd, *Memoirs of the Life of the Right Rev. Brian Walton* (1821), ch. 5; Twells, *Life of Pococke*, pp. 193 ff.

[2] The Bodleian copy (Fol. Θ. 663, fol. 36) has manuscript additions by Clarke.

[3] D.O. 17 Oct. 1668; *First Minute Book*, p. 4.

[4] Some leaves of the Targum on Chronicles were printed, presumably as specimens: Madan, *Oxford Books*, iii, No. 2763*.

[5] In a letter to Joseph Williamson of 12 Apr. [1669]: P.R.O. S.P. (Dom.), Car. II, 258, No. 168.   [6] Bodl. MS. Rawl. D. 897, fol. 155.

is the one that Castell unaided and after fearful sufferings finally brought to the birth in 1666, the famous *Lexicon Heptaglotton*.

Clarke contributed the preface, vocabulary, and treatise on Arabic prosody to the volume *Carmen Tograi* printed at Oxford in 1661 at the expense of Richard Davis, the main part being an Arabic poem with Pococke's Latin translation and notes intended for students of the language.

Until 1669 there is no instance of the University paying a printer for anything but jobbing (notices, lists, programmes, and stationery), except the books of occasional verses by several hands honouring state occasions. It would advance the cost of printing if private benefactors undertook to repay it. That was the case with Pococke's Arabic version of Grotius *De veritate religionis Christianae* published in 1660 at the expense of Robert Boyle,[1] and with William Seaman's New Testament in Turkish of 1664, paid for by Boyle and the Levant Company.[2] Clarke's account book[3] shows that the Architypographus was allowed to draw on University funds for books sanctioned by the Delegates but was responsible for seeing it repaid. In other words, the sums that Convocation had allocated for the support of a learned press, the Schools Money surplus, and the Stationers' payments for forbearance, were regarded as loans for printing. This meant that Clarke, who was a poor man, had to make sure that if the University's money was involved a financially reliable publisher would pay it back. If he failed to do so, the University would doubtless claim the books; therefore Clarke kept an account of unsold stock in the publisher's hands.

Clarke had funds at his disposal from which he made advances to the publisher (in all cases Richard Davis of Oxford) or to the printer and paid for paper for Malalas. In January 1660 Davis owed him £250. Most of this money must have come from the Schools Account, but in 1658 Clarke received £60 from the Stationers of London and £80 from the Bible-printers. In 1660, just before the return of King Charles, Convocation confirmed an allocation from the Schools Account of £40 for printing the Chronicle of Malalas and £140 for Pococke's complete Gregorius bar Hebraeus, on condition that security were given by the Architypographus and Richard Davis the publisher.[4] Clarke and Davis sealed a bond to the University for £240 and Davis gave bond to Clarke to save him harmless.[5]

[1] Madan, *Oxford Books*, iii, No. 2498.   [2] Ibid., No. 2727.
[3] Bodl. MS. Rawl. D. 1188.
[4] Reg. Conv. Ta, p. 16; *Print and Privilege*, pp. 37–8.
[5] Clarke's Account Book, 30 May 1660.

Clarke lists in his accounts the books for which he and Davis were jointly responsible to the University in 1664 and 1669. They were the *Statuta selecta* (1661), for the use of undergraduates, Pococke's Gregorius (1663), Thomas Jones's *Prolusiones academicae* (1660), *Carmen Tograi* (1661), and Grotius *De veritate* (probably the Latin edition of 1660).

The University's participation in this publishing and printing extended to choosing books for which its money might be lent and for which it would allow the use of its Greek, Hebrew, and Arabic type. It was guarded against loss, but could not profit.

Gerard Langbaine died in 1658 and custody of the academic stock of type and matrices was transferred to the Architypographus. He added to the inventory that Langbaine had begun a record of the Greek matrices got from Leyden in 1637—two sets so defective that his pains with them were ill bestowed.[1] More Hebrew and Arabic type was cast in London in 1655–7 at the expense of the Schools Account, and in 1656 the University bought a large fount of Anglo-Saxon from Nicholas Nicholls[2] for use in the *Dictionarium Saxonico-Latino-Anglicum* by William Somner. The book, completed in 1659 and published to subscribers at the initial expense of the author, was the foundation for Oxford studies in the northern languages.

---

[1] Bodl. MS. Rawl. D. 317, fol. 53; Univ. Arch. S.E.P. P17ᵇ(3), fol. 36ᵛ.
[2] A London typefounder, for whom see Reed, pp. 163–7.

CHAPTER V

The Gift of a Printing House

THUS far Samuel Clarke as Architypographus had played a humble part circumscribed by the University's timid attitude towards book-production. By 1668 the situation had altered, and Clarke found himself empowered to equip a printing house. Letters addressed to him in the last two years of his life, 1668–9, convey by inference that the academic body foresaw an acquisition of premises for printing and had decided on a modest provision of plant for it. There is no specific record of a resolve to take this step, but it had been under consideration for several years. Gerard Langbaine had written to Clarke on 7 December 1657 that the Vice-Chancellor had promised to call a meeting to discuss setting up a learned press and that he meant to argue strongly for it.[1] Langbaine died a month later, and the matter had to wait until Oxford settled down after the restoration of Charles and Church.

In June 1668 Clarke was offered a printing press,[2] and it was bought out of the Schools money. In August he was considering Joseph Moxon as a possible cutter of new typefaces.[3] In November Thomas Marshall, fellow of Lincoln College, then living in Holland, promised 'Specimina of the best Letter-founders' in Amsterdam and had searched in vain for 'a Letter-cutter for your new intended Presse'.[4]

What had brought about the determination to achieve the public academic printing-house that Laud prescribed? A delegacy for printing constituted in 1653 was regarded as having an unlawful origin and was superseded in 1662 by a new one which included the Dean of Christ Church, John Fell. During its first six years this delegacy, so far as is known, did nothing, but by September 1668 it had contracted with a London bookseller to produce a large learned book in its own printing-house and began to keep minutes of its conclusions. Doubtless the obligation to carry out the programme laid down by the martyred arch-bishop was on the consciences of the High Churchmen who had been

---

[1] B.M. MS. Add. 22905, fol. 9.
[2] Bodl. MS. Rawl. D. 398, fol. 145, printed in Hart, *A Century*, p. 157.
[3] B.M. MS. Add. 22905, fol. 81.   [4] Ibid., fol. 84.

restored to power at Oxford, and Fell by 1668 was sufficiently freed from his more urgent cares as Dean and Vice-Chancellor to be able to turn his thoughts to printing. The decisive step was taken when he persuaded Gilbert Sheldon, since 1663 Archbishop of Canterbury, to express a desire that the theatre, his gift to the University, should, when not in use for solemnities, accommodate the printers. Presses and furniture for

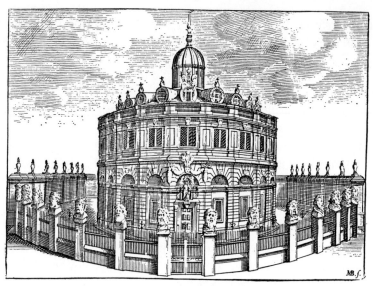

A publisher's device of the Sheldonian Theatre in use by 1699. The copper plate, engraved by Michael Burghers, is kept at the Press.

compositors were moved into the Theatre in 1668, or early in 1669, before the builders had done with it.[1]

It was a most unlikely solution to the problem, for hardly could a building be less suitable for a printing-office than Wren's Sheldonian Theatre. The presses were put in the cellar, where daylight scarcely penetrates, and the compositors worked in the passage-way beneath the first tier of seating in spaces which they had to clear when the Theatre was needed for a solemn act, lecture, or concert. Fire, needed by pressmen and compositors, was inaccessible.

Anthony Wood describes the arrangements.[2] The cellar had presses

[1] The first payment for printing in the Theatre entered in Clarke's accounts is dated 11 March 1669. The typefounder, Joseph Leigh, wrote on 4 Feb. 1668/9 that the printers were not ready to set presses to work: Bodl. MS. Rawl. D. 398, fol. 141; Hart, p. 156.

[2] *Historia et antiquitates Universitatis Oxoniensis* (Oxford, 1674), Liber ii, p. 25.

at the south end, the central area held white paper, and printed sheets were kept in the semicircular north end. The compositors had little rooms or cupboards under the stairs to the gallery above them where they kept their type and tools.[1] Handsome frames, of oak with turned legs and panelled backs, were made by John Rainsford, an Oxford joiner, to support the cases of type at which the compositors worked. Thirteen of these frames were in constant use at the Press until the early years of this century: five are there still and several grace museums in various parts of the world. Rainsford also made presses and cases for type. His work was paid for by the Vice-Chancellor in 1668–9 out of the Schools money. David Loggan, the engraver, sold the University a rolling press for printing copperplate.[2]

In 1669, therefore, the Chancellor, Masters, and Scholars of the University of Oxford had their own premises for printing and a minimum of equipment; but to do the work and sell it they had still to rely on contractors. Laud's plan, enjoined on his academic posterity by immutable statutes, contemplated that the *typographi Universitatis*, who in 1669 were Anne and Leonard Lichfield and Henry Hall, would do the printing under the supervision of the Architypographus and, presumably (though the Laudian plan is silent about this) make arrangements for sale and distribution recouping their costs from the proceeds.

The earliest minute of a meeting of the Delegates for Printing, as they called themselves then, records their decision to entrust Robert Scott, a prominent London bookseller, with the printing of the *Synodicon*, a collection of the canons of the Eastern Church in Greek and Latin. It was a task far beyond the means of the Oxford *typographi*, but Scott 'was in his time the greatest librarian in Europe; for besides his stock in England he had warehouses at Frankfort, Paris, and other places, and dealt by factors'.[3] Nevertheless, the *Synodicon* nearly broke him.

Fell's protégé and friend, John Mill, attributed to the Dean the choice of this very large and learned work to be the first book to be put in hand at the University's own presses. 'He set his heart', Mill wrote, 'on printing

[1] William Beveridge gave an elegant account of these dispositions in the Prolegomena to the *Synodicon* (Oxford, 1672), p. xxiv: Intra hoc illustre admodum aedificium, praeter amplissimum illius sinum publicis celebrandis comitiis destinatum, spatia quaedam circumcirca relinquuntur, operibus Typographicis affabre accommodata. Quaecunque autem Chalcographi, per aeneos suos literarum Typos ex innumeris repositoriorum loculamentis celerrima manu raptos, ibi composuerunt, e praelis subtus ordine dispositis, in Charta subdita exprimuntur.
[2] Extracts from the Vice-Chancellor's Computus are printed in *Print and Privilege*, p. 41.
[3] Roger North, *Lives of the Norths*, iii, pp. 290–1; Plomer, *Dictionary*, 1668–1725, pp. 264–5.

the synodical canons of the ancient Church; and when that was done he thought it appropriate to dedicate the book, as the first-fruits of the Sheldonian press, to its famous founder' (meaning Sheldon).[1] The editor, William Beveridge, considered the earliest canons and decrees of the Eastern Church as having apostolic sanction, a view which Fell perhaps shared and consequently thought it an honour for the English Church to make them accessible in a good edition.

The two folio volumes of the *Synodicon* make 1,588 pages of Greek, Latin, and a good deal of Arabic set in two columns in medium-sized type. The University lent Scott what it had in the way of presses, type, and other equipment, but he had to provide 400 lb. of Greek and more than 500 lb. of Roman and Italic, besides all the paper. The contributions of the University and Scott to this great undertaking are hard to define. It may be assumed that Oxford funds met the cost of editing, translating, and correcting. Scott brought over from Paris compositors experienced in setting Greek—John Bagford, writing about 1714, said there were four of them.[2] Anthony Izard, a freeman of the Stationers' Company, was in charge of Scott's workmen; John Hall was probably the senior of men employed by the University. Obadiah Walker, fellow of University College and a friend of Fell, was involved in the management, probably instructed by the Delegates of the Press. Thomas Bennett, M.A. of Christ Church, whom Fell liked to employ, was corrector and made translations. Samuel Clarke as Architypographus ought, according to the Laudian statute, to have been in general charge, but he is not known to have done more than pay out small sums for materials.

Responsibilities for the joint enterprise became worse confused after six months, when Scott had to ask the University to relieve him of supervising and paying for the printing. The reason given in the Delegates' minute was Scott's need to attend to his foreign business, but there are indications in subsequent events that the financial burden had proved too heavy for him. The minute reads:

At the request of Mr Scott Bookseller of London that by reason of his Occasions to goe beyond the Seas he cannot attend in person the impression of the Canons of the ancient Church &c formerly decreed to be printed here, that the University would be pleased to defray the charges of Printing and correcting the said Impression as from time to time they shall grow due; He providing all the Paper, and assigning for security the whole

---

[1] John Mill, *Novum Testamentum cum lectionibus variantibus* (Oxford, 1707), Prolegomena, p. clxv (in Latin).   [2] B.M. MS. Harl. 5901, fol. 85.

John Fell (left) with John Dolben and Richard Allestree. By Sir Godfrey Kneller

Thomas Yate (d. 1681), Principal of Brasenose College, Fell's most   Sir Joseph Williamson (1623–1701), Secretary of State, one of Fell's

Impression to the University, till whatt shall be soe expended, be by him reimbursed to the University. It was agreed upon That his request should be granted accordingly.[1] (13 March 1669)

A printed prospectus of unknown date is reason to think that at one time the University did not expect to be repaid; for the imprint of the *Synodicon* was to be 'Oxoniae, Typis Universitatis in Theatro Sheldoniano; Prostabunt apud Robertum Scott, Londini',[2] reducing Scott to the position of a mere agent for the sale.

Scott's incapacity may not have lasted long. By January 1670 the Vice-Chancellor had spent £200 on the book on his behalf.[3] In August he wrote to Fell as though the edition belonged to him: 'Sir I [. . .] oblieged to your great care of my booke att the Theatre, and y[. . .] begg the favour of the Continuance of itt, for I intend god willing [. . .] beyond sea in the Spring, and if my booke bee not finished abou[. . .] itt will bee a great prejudice to mee, for my whole voyage w[. . .] concerne that booke.'[4] In the event Scott with help from his brother-in-law paid off his debt, and the imprint of the volumes issued in 1672 is 'Oxonii, e Theatro Sheldoniano. Sumptibus Gulielmi Wells et Roberti Scott, bibliop. Lond.'.

For a matter of months the University had proved its capacity to manage an impression, had directly employed printers' labour, and faced the prospect of disposing of the result at its own risk. For this brief spell of time the conditions for the existence of a true university press may be said to have been fulfilled. Yes: but the book was a very special one: Fell had set his heart on it. No general disposition to go beyond Laud's provisions for a printing house where work was done by contract can be attributed to the Delegates.

The first book to be completed in the Theatre was a collection of verses lamenting the death of the Queen's mother.[5] It came out in 1669, bearing the imprint 'E Typographia Sheldoniana'. Anne Lichfield, alone or with her son Leonard, was paid to print it. It was one of a number of books printed on the University's presses by the *typographi*.[6]

JOHN FELL

In December 1669 Samuel Clarke died. George Hickes thought he died of the cold in the Bodleian Library, like Gerard Langbaine and many

---

[1] *First Minute Book*, p. 5.   [2] Bodl. MS. Junius 7, fol. 1.
[3] Bodl. MS. Rawl. D. 398, fol. 124.   [4] Ibid.
[5] Madan, *Oxford Books*, iii, No. 2814.
[6] e.g. Madan, ibid., Nos. 2869, 2875, 2878, 2914, 2927 in 1670–2.

brave men before him.[1] That autumn Fell ended a term of three years as Vice-Chancellor and had the more leisure to turn his attention to printing, 'our new trade', as he called it in a letter of April 1669.

His character as drawn by Gilbert Burnet will serve as background to the record of his achievement as printer and publisher.

Fell, Bishop of Oxford, was a man of great strictness in the course of his life, and of much devotion. His learning appears in that noble edition of St. Cyprian, that he published. He had made great beginnings in learning before the restoration: but his continued application to his employments after that, stopt the progress that otherwise he might have made. He was made soon after Dean of Christ's church, and afterwards Bishop of Oxford. He set himself to promote learning in the University, but most particularly in his own college, which he governed with great care: and was indeed, in all respects, a most exemplary man, tho' a little too much heated, in the matter of our disputes with the Dissenters. But, as he was among the first of our Clergy, that apprehended the design of bringing in Popery, so he was one of the most zealous against it. He had much zeal for reforming abuses; and managed it, perhaps, with too much heat, and in too peremptory a way. But we have so little of that among us, that 'tis no wonder if such men are censured by those, who love not such patterns, nor such severe taskmasters.[2]

By 1669 he was the most powerful man in the University, having the ear of the King and of the Chancellor, the Duke of Ormonde, besides generally being able to sway the votes of Christ Church men in Convocation. He did not hesitate to use his power to dispose of patronage to promote those who would work with or for him or to keep others from obstructing his designs.

John Mill's testimony that it was Fell who persuaded Archbishop Sheldon to provide for printing in the Theatre and that he procured the *Synodicon* to be the first of the books undertaken there is convincing. These were great achievements, and the Dean looked forward with confidence to more. He writes in April 1669 to his friend Joseph Williamson,

---

[1] Bodl. MS. Ballard xii, fol. 125.

[2] *Bishop Burnet's History of his Own Times*, ed. G. Burnet and others (1724, 1734), i, p. 695. The cap in the last sentence fits Tom Brown, to whom is attributed the epigram inseparable from the memory of Fell. It has been traced back to 1715 in the 3rd ed. of *The Works of Mr. Thomas Brown*, iv, p. 113, in the form:

> I do not love you, Dr. Fell;
> But why I cannot tell;
> But this I know full well,
> I do not love you, Dr. Fell.

secretary to the powerful Lord Arlington and clearly a rising man in the public service, about the new learned press 'which I hope by God's blessing may not only prove usefull to us poor Scholars but reflect some reputation and advantage on the Publick' and announces that 'besides this present Work [the *Synodicon*], we have in hand a Seventh volume to be added to the Polyglott bible: and a new Catalogue of the books in our Library; and shall by God's assistance and the Patronage of our Friends go on to greater things.'[1]

He suffered a reverse when his nomination of Thomas Bennett to succeed Clarke as Architypographus was outvoted in a rebellious Convocation in December 1669 and Norton Bold was elected. Bennett was a useful drudge as corrector, translator, and editor and could be trusted to know his place: Bold was unfit for the post and might be a hindrance. That was a serious discouragement; and the two books that Fell cited were not proceeded with, the Catalogue not being finished until 1674. The chronicle of Malalas, decided on in 1633, for which paper was bought in 1661, was dropped. Fell doubted the will of the Delegacy and the University as a whole to print and publish. To his friend Sir Leoline Jenkins, Judge of Admiralty and Principal of Jesus College, the Dean wrote in July 1671, 'It is certain that while the Charge of the Presse lyes at large in the hands of the University, it can never be lookt after, or managed to advantage.'[2]

At Oxford he had a staunch ally in Thomas Yate, D.D., Principal of Brasenose, and with him he concerted a plan to form a private company to undertake printing and publishing in the University, exploiting the privilege granted by its charters instead of forbearing to do so in return for a rent. Of this project they had 'frequently discourst' with Jenkins. The three knew that to carry it out meant supplanting the Company of Stationers and the King's Printers as lessees of the privilege at a rent at least equal to the £200 a year that they were paying.

The imminent expiry of the Stationers' lease or covenant of forbearance, due to take place on Lady Day 1672, and the certainty that in the mean time Convocation would vote for its renewal unless a better offer could be got, decided Fell and Yate to act. On 27 August Fell wrote to Jenkins:

Mr. Principal and myself last week reminded the Vicechancellor of the speedy expiration of our bargain with the Stationers. The Principal

---

[1] P.R.O. S.P. (Dom.) Car. II, 258, No. 168.
[2] S.P. (Dom.), Car. II, 291, No. 230.

proposed finding persons to undertake the whole affair of printing here, and to secure the interest of the University, which being now left to a general care, is wretchedly neglected.[1]

An invitation was sent to Williamson on the same day 'to joyn with Sir Leoline Jenkins and some other of your friends in a Delegacy which will want your Countenance and interest'.[2]

[1] S.P. (Dom.), Car. II, 292, No. 116.   [2] Ibid., No. 115.

CHAPTER VI

Fell's Press

THE FOUR UNDERTAKERS FOR PRINTING

THE partnership effectively headed by Fell did not exceed the number of four. Barlow, Provost of Queen's and a Delegate of the Press, and some others declined to join it.[1] A meeting of the Delegates on 22 August 1671 agreed to recommend to Convocation a draft lease of the University's privilege of printing to Fell, Yate, Jenkins, and Williamson to take effect from Lady Day 1672 for three years at a rent of £200 a year.[2] The Heads of Houses approved the letting early in October, only Barlow objecting. He thought the rent not enough to cover the use of premises and presses. For the same reason Convocation refused its consent in October, but Fell and Yate reasoned with the malcontents, and on 16 November the decision was reversed.[3]

The two partners in Oxford made it clear to the other two that they wanted from them advice, patronage, and protection, but not contributions in money. Leoline Jenkins, knighted in 1670, was judge in the Court of Admiralty and in the Prerogative Court of Canterbury. He lived in London, paying an occasional visit to Oxford, where until 1673 he kept the headship of Jesus College.[4] Joseph Williamson, besides being secretary to Arlington, who 'loving his ease more than businesse . . . remitted all to him', edited the *London Gazette* and was a member of Parliament. He was knighted in 1672, and in 1674 he succeeded Arlington as Secretary of State.[5] 'Now in truth we apprehend', Fell wrote in August 1671, 'that besides Mr. Principals and my industry here, it will be necessary that we have yours and Mr. Williamsons countenance in London.'[6] 'It is neyther Mr. Deanes intencion nor myne', Yate assured Jenkins a month later, 'to draw you to any hazard or adventure more than you are free and ready to undergoe, and therefore wee must secure you from the £200 per annum that you covenant with us to pay.'[7] Fell was nervous lest the

---

[1] Ibid. 293, No. 95.
[2] *First Minute Book*, pp. 8, 9.
[3] S.P. (Dom.), Car. II, 293, No. 152, 294, No. 49.
[4] William Wynne, *Life of Sir Leoline Jenkins* (1724).
[5] J. R. Magrath, *The Queen's College* (Oxford, 1921), ii, pp. 43–50; *D.N.B.*
[6] S.P. (Dom.), Car. II, 292, No. 116 to Jenkins. [7] Ibid., No. 164.

University's right by prescription and charters to comprint on the
patent-holders would be rejected by the common lawyers in Westminster
Hall, and Yate asked Jenkins to get counsel's opinion on the point.[1]
Possibly Jenkins, though strictly a civilian, was able to reassure them, for
no opinion can be found. Over a period of thirteen years it seems that the

Sir Leoline Jenkins.
From an Original by H. Tuer.

London partners were able to do little to relieve the other two of their
burden, and as time went on and they came to be employed in business of
great moment in the public service they were consulted less often.

   For money the partners expected to have to rely mainly on their own
resources. 'Wee foresee the bussinesse cannot be caryed on with any
credit, or to any advantage without a great stock of money', Yate wrote
in September 1671, 'and wee hope by our selves and our friendes to bring
in a very considerable summe of money to make provision for necessary

[1] S.P. (Dom.), Car. II, 292, No. 164.

thinges to set us on workeing.'[1] There were hopes of the Oxford book-sellers: 'The Stacioners of this Towne talke of bringing in £500 or £600',[2] and these tradesmen 'make no doubt of vending whatever proportions of Priviledged bookes . . . in all the Parts of England; without ever hazarding seizures at London'.[3] Complaints made later of lack of financial support and broken promises are grounds for thinking that expenditure by the partnership came largely out of the pockets of Fell and Yate. In August 1672 Jenkins perceived that the Dean and the Principal had laid out more than £200 on building 'Conveniencies for Printing',[4] and by October they had spent about £1,500.[5]

It might have been expected that the revenues of the University that were earmarked for the support of a learned press would be paid to the partners; and a third of these funds came into being in 1669 as part of Sheldon's benefaction. In his deed of gift of the Theatre and an endow-ment for its upkeep he had declared: 'What shall every year be remaining of the Rents, over and above the Charge of Repayres, I desire may be imployed for the best advantage and encouragement of the Learned Presse there designed, and allready sett at Worke.'[6] The annual payments from the Stationers' Company ceased at Lady Day 1672, when the lease to Fell and his associates took effect and the partners began paying an equivalent amount for the privilege. The surplus of Sheldon's fund accumulated during Fell's tenure of the press until in 1686 it amounted to £475, but none of it had been spent on printing. The third source of revenue allocated to the press, the surplus of the Schools Money, was used to pay the partners for printing the few books sponsored by the Delegates of the Press. So there was a distinction between 'Delegates' books' and 'Partners' books', the University having no financial responsi-bility for the latter.

Payments to Fell and Yate appear in the accounts of the Vice-Chancellors: £305 'towards printing the Catalogue' of the Bodleian printed books in 1673, £245 and the cost of paper for Josephus in 1684–5, £200 for Morison's Herbal in 1678–9, £40 in 1674 and in 1685 for 3,000 extracts from the statutes. The Delegates made small contributions to authors' fees and editing: to Hyde for the Catalogue £80, to Wood for the *Historia* £150. They bought copies of the partners' editions to give away; as many as 1,000 of the Catalogue and 117 of the *Historia*.

---

[1] Ibid.   [2] Ibid.   [3] Ibid. 294, No. 49, 19 Nov. 1671.
[4] Ibid. 314, No. 16.   [5] Ibid. 316, No. 167.
[6] Printed in Madan, *Oxford Books*, iii, p. 410.

Yate played his subordinate part in the enterprise most honourably. It included the finances and the dealings with booksellers, and besides that he drafted the lease from the University to the partners and a case for counsel's opinion on the legality of the privilege; he made a list of books affected by exclusive patents. 'The manage of the mony Affair is Mr. Principal's province', Fell wrote, 'I concerne my selfe only in Letters.'[1] By 'Letters' he meant type.

FELL'S TYPEFOUNDRY AND THE IMPORTED 'FELL' TYPES

When Clarke died at the end of 1669 Fell took upon himself the search for good type and, if not a letter-cutter, a typefounder, and he continued negotiations through the agency of Thomas Marshall in Holland.

In October 1670 Marshall announced the dispatch from Amsterdam of matrices for Roman and Italic type of two sizes, Small Pica and Brevier.[2] That was the first instalment of the equipment still kept at the Press for casting the so-called 'Fell' type. The Small Pica and Brevier were the work of Christoffel van Dijck (1601–69), a famous letter-cutter, and they are very good typefaces; Van Dijck's son sold the matrices to Marshall, who, ending his long exile, thereupon came back to Oxford. Fell had to make do with the other sizes of type that he could get from the type-founders in London; and in 1668–9 Nicholas Nicholls sold the University some 'Latin letters', probably the undistinguished Romans and Italics used in the *Synodicon*, of which one is described, fairly, in the Oxford *Specimen* of 1693 as 'not good'.

Fell was reasonably dissatisfied with the state of typefounding in this country, and convinced by Dutch books and the specimens that Marshall had sent of the great superiority of the art as practised in Holland. 'The foundation of all successe', he wrote in December 1671, 'must be layd in doing things well, and I am sure that will not be don with English Letters.'[3] He was impatient to add more to the matrices that Marshall had sent the year before and a typefounder, for without such a man the matrices must lie idle. He thought he could not plan ahead without knowing what his supplies of type would be. He confided to Jenkins, 'It has always bin my opinion, that we must first secure to our selves a

[1] S.P. (Dom.), Car. II, 302, No. 28, 7 Jan. [1671/2].
[2] Bodl. MS. Rawl. D. 398, fol. 138; Hart, p. 163. A full account of the 'Fell' types and their acquisition is given in Morison, *Fell*.
[3] S.P. (Dom.), Car. II, 294, No. 206.

good founder, and a good stock of Letters; and then it will be seasonable to resolve of what and how much we should set in hand with.'[1]

The indispensable middleman, Thomas Marshall, D.D., was in 1670 in a hurry to get back to Oxford. Fell said that his dealings in Holland on behalf of the University's press were such that 'no English-man besides himself is in any degree qualified to undertake'.[2] In 1647 Marshall had quit Oxford to escape the attention of the Parliamentary Visitors, and soon afterwards found employment in Holland as chaplain to the English Merchant Adventurers. There he had worked with Francis Junius the younger and been joint editor with him of the Gospels in Gothic and Anglo-Saxon (Dordrecht, 1665). The making of the exotic types for that book would have brought him acquaintance with typefounding. He also learned Coptic. Elected to a fellowship of Lincoln College in 1668, he was afraid of being absent when the headship of the college fell vacant. It did so in June 1672, and Marshall was made Rector.

Fell, who did not spare himself, expected a like devotion to what he thought was their duty in others. He tells Jenkins in December 1671 'of my agency with Dr. Marshall, with whom I think I have prevaild to adventure himself, notwithstanding his ill health, upon the journey into Holland'.[3] The Rector of Lincoln, experiencing the rigours of a Dutch winter and discouragement at the hands of the typefounders, stayed until February 1672, when the imminence of war between that country and this obliged him to come home.[4] He was constrained to leave behind a part of his purchase, the matrices which are the most precious of the collection that Fell bequeathed to the University for Greek, Roman, and Italic typefaces and flowers. The captain of the Harwich packet, which went on plying for some time after the outbreak of war for the convenience of the belligerents, managed to smuggle out what had been left behind in money-bags.[5] A quantity of cast type, consigned to an English merchant at Antwerp, reached Oxford in mid-August 1672.[6] Moreover, Marshall had persuaded a Dutch journeyman typefounder to come here. He was Harman Harmansz., a workman in Van Dijck's foundry, and he reached Oxford by 1 August 1672.[7] At this happy outcome of Marshall's mission Fell rejoiced: 'We are now in hopes to go forward.'[8]

[1] S.P. (Dom.), Car. II, 294, No. 81, 27 Nov. 1671.
[2] Ibid., No. 130.   [3] Ibid.
[4] Fell–Marshall correspondence printed in Hart, pp. 161–72.
[5] S.P. (Dom.), Car. II, 304, No. 153.
[6] All Souls MS. 239, fol. 667, printed in Madan, Oxford Books, iii, p. 413.
[7] S.P. (Dom.), Car. II, 313, No. 117.   [8] Ibid.

There was reason to be pleased. A typefoundry under his control stocked with matrices for typefaces of excellent design would be enough to raise Oxford printing above the prevailing English level; for the standard of typefounding in London was low.[1] The typefaces were common in continental, and to some extent in English, printing, and in no way distinctive: they became peculiarly 'Fell' types by effluxion of time as other printers discarded them. Their origins are various, some being the work of famous French letter-cutters of the sixteenth century,

ΑΒΓΔΕΖΗΘΙΚΛΜΝΞΟΠΡΣΤΥΦΧΨΩ

αβϐγΓδδϵζη θϑι κλμνξοπϖρ σϛς τυϡφ φχψω

The biggest of the Greek types got by Fell from Holland in 1672.
It was originally made for Plantin by Robert Granjon in 1565.

while others were Dutch of a later time. They are all good, the Greeks by Robert Granjon, imitating the beautiful *Grecs du roi* by Claude Garamond for King Francis I, especially so. 'Such Greeks as I despaird of', Fell wrote.[2]

The grounds for rejoicing had limits. Fell had asked for a typefounder, 'an able workman, and if such a one may be had, one who can also cut letters'.[3] Harmansz. was of the humble kind who do no more than cast and dress type, and so long as he was depended on the Oxford foundry must be stocked with second-hand matrices. To cut the punches and with them strike the matrices for new typefaces called for talents that only three or four men then living in Europe possessed. In England one man, Joseph Moxon, practised the art with mediocre results, but he practised other more lucrative arts and trades as well; moreover he had been considered for the post.[4] Besides that, Marshall had been able to get matrices only for the smaller sizes of type, suitable for the texts of most books but not for headings and titles or for grandiose pages and broadsides. For those Fell had to buy from the London houses and from Moxon. Marshall's attempt to find Coptic and Syriac matrices in Holland had failed.[5] 'I se', he reported to Fell, 'we English must learn to use our own hands at last to cut Letters as well as print with them.'[6]

[1] Marshall wrote, 'The typefounders in Amsterdam would perswade me, that, had you their Formes or Matrices, your Founders would miscast the Types or Letters': B.M. MS. Add. 22905, fol. 85. [2] S.P. (Dom.), Car. II, 303, No. 18.
[3] Bodl. MS. Rawl. D. 317, fol. 263; Hart, p. 168.
[4] B.M. MS. Add. 22905. fol. 81, 17 Aug. 1668. See above, p. 45.
[5] Bodl. MS. Rawl. D. 317, fols. 264, 270; Hart, pp. 166, 167.
[6] Bodl. MS. Rawl. D. 317, fol. 270ᵛ.

THE FIRST BOOKS OF FELL'S PRESS

Fell and Yate laid their plans assuming that the University's privilege would shield them effectively while they trespassed on the cherished monopolies of the Stationers' Company and its members. This assumption alone offered their undertaking a prospect of financial success or at worst acceptable loss. The sale of school books must subsidize the learned press. Fell opened his mind to Jenkins: 'It is evident that both in point of honour and interest, it imports the University that the gainful priviledged books by being printed here, should enable us for the Edition of those other Authors which will afford no pecuniary advantage.'[1] Yate professed to be confident that 'wee shall not be restrayned by those Patentes of that nature that have beene granted to the Kinges Printers, to the Stationers and others, but shalbe at liberty to comprint with them all their Bookes (which is all wee shall desire), for wee are resolved to print better and with more care then those that now print have done, and to sell cheaper, and this is the proper and best use wee can make of such a Privileige.'[2] A measure of optimism is needed on setting out, but this was an excess of it.

A list of proposed titles was ready in October;[3] Yate drew up a schedule of works that were the subjects of exclusive patents for printing, beginning with those granted to the Stationers for primers, psalters, metrical psalms, and almanacs, then their texts for schools from Aesop to Virgil; the King's Printer's for statutes, proclamations, and Bibles and Testaments in English; Roger Norton's for the Bible in Latin and the Grammar; lastly Edward Atkyns's for law books.[4] In August 1672 Jenkins on a visit to Oxford noted that his partners had printed several school books and were going on to more.[5] The books, *Sententiae pueriles*, *Pueriles confabulatiunculae*, Cato's distichs, Corderius, Aesop, and the works of Ovid,[6] are not to be found in a bibliography of Oxford printing for reasons to be explained later. The *Brevissima institutio*, normally printed with the Grammar in one volume, was published by the partners in 1672, but it was newly edited and so outside the terms of Norton's patent.[7]

As for the Bible Fell was in doubt. 'I have a great mind', he wrote in

[1] S.P. (Dom.), Car. II, 291, No. 230. [2] Ibid. 292, No. 98.
[3] Ibid. 293, No. 123.
[4] S.P. (Dom.), Car. II, 292, No. 164(V). Monopolies of printing were excepted from the general avoidance of perpetual monopolies by the Statute of Monopolies, 1623/4: 21 Jac. I, c. 3, sect. 10.
[5] Ibid. 314, No. 16. [6] Univ. Arch. S.E.P. P17ᵇ(1)ᶜ.
[6] Madan, *Oxford Books*, iii, No. 2929.

November 1671, 'if it be possible, that we may be benefactors to the Nation in the matter of bibles; but if we are tied up to the Quartoes and folioes, 'twill not be worth our while to meddle with them.'[1] The allusion was to the Order in Council of 9 March 1636 restricting the sizes of the Bibles that the Universities might print.[2] Jenkins advised keeping close to the Order.[3] However, hearing that Archbishop Sheldon approved of 'an attempt of an Edition of the Bible', Fell writes, 'we shall think upon it with more courage then we did.'[4] What he favoured was an annotated Bible edited by six doctors of divinity under the general management of the Regius Professor, Richard Allestree. He drafted proposals for the work in detail,[5] but for some reason went no further.

In general, Fell thought 'it will be convenient to apply our Stock to the books of trade that will return to account. Larger Works for the dignity, as well as the use of learning, we must proceed upon by the help of subscriptions.'[6]

He mentions in a letter of 11 January 1671/2 a paper to be issued for the information of patrons of learning. It exists in draft in the Library of All Souls;[7] and it is a document of prime value for revealing the extent of Fell's ambition as publisher, for the methods he preferred for achieving it, and by allowing a comparison with accomplished fact for measuring his success. As a list of the subjects on which a learned man in that age wished to be informed, in the opinion of one good judge, it merits setting out in full.[8]

The manifesto begins by announcing the publications already in hand by the Delegates of the Press when the partners took charge.

The Councils gr: l. 2 Vol: fol. [the *Synodicon*]:
The history of the University in Latin fol: with cuts [Wood's *Historia*]
Catalogue of the Bodley-library fol:
Catalogue of the MS. fol:
Dr: Morison's herbal in latin fol: with cutts
The Arundel Marbles with their Explication in fol: together with a Discourse of Mr: Lidiats upon the Epocha, and others of like nature with cutts
A treatise concerning the Soul, Latin in 4° by Dr: Willis [*De anima brutorum*]
Aratus with the Scholia of Theon, Eratosthen: etc. 8°.

1 S.P. (Dom.), Car. II, 294, No. 49.   2 Above, p. 29.
3 S.P. (Dom.), Car. II, 302, No. 8.   4 Ibid. 305, No. 117.
5 Madan, *Oxford Books*, iii, pp. 413–14.   6 S.P. (Dom.), Car. II, 302, No. 46.
7 MS. 239, fol. 641; Madan, *Oxford Books*, iii, pp. 410–12.
8 On p. 63.

The *Synodicon*, discussed on an earlier page, was published by Robert Scott and his brother-in-law in London; the other books, excepting the catalogue of Bodleian manuscripts, were issued by Fell's partnership in the years 1672–6. What arrangements for distribution and sale were foreseen by the Delegates when they sanctioned the printing of these books is a matter for speculation.

The choice of these titles, one may be sure, was Fell's. He paid most of the cost of Wood's *Historia*, author's fee, translating, and printing. Willis was Fell's brother-in-law. Fell himself edited Aratus: it was one of the series of his 'New-Year Books' destined primarily to be presents for his pupils at Christ Church but also put on sale.[1]

FELL'S CONCEPTION OF A LEARNED PRESS

Like Laud, Fell had a low opinion of the printing trade, and of booksellers too. To Isaac Vossius in Holland he wrote in Latin on 17 March 1670/1: 'We have it in mind, provided the Vice-Chancellor agrees, and all goes well, to set up in this place a press freed from mercenary artifices, which will serve not so much to make profits for the booksellers as to further the interests and convenience of scholars.'[2] His panegyrist, John Mill, credits him with recalling printing, 'before his time carried on in the houses of small tradesmen and there to devoted to I know not what trifles in the semblance of books, to its proper dignity'.[3] Where booksellers were concerned it was a frame of mind as unwise as it was ungenerous, and handed down to later generations of Delegates did more than anything else to hinder the progress of the University's press for a hundred years. 'The vending of books we never could compasse'; one of them wrote, 'the want of vent broke Bp. Fell's body, public spirit, courage, purse and presse.'[4]

The model of a press that printed only the best books in the best style and was directed by scholars without a view to profit had been provided by Richelieu in his foundation of the French king's printing-office, the *Imprimerie royale du Louvre*. Dating from 1640, it had by 1670 issued noble editions. Fell's references to it show that it impressed him. On a more mundane level, he was familiar with learned books printed in Holland in good style during half a century by the Raphelengii, Blaeus, Elseviers,

[1] Madan gives a list of them in *Oxford Books*, iii, p. 521; and see the list of Fell's writings by J. S. G. Simmons in Morison, *Fell*, App. I.
[2] Leyden, Universiteitsbibliotheek, MS. Burm. Cod. Fol. No. 11, ii, fol. 62.
[3] *Novum Testamentum cum lect. var.*, p. clxv.
[4] Arthur Charlett in 1718: Hist. MSS. Comm., 2nd *Report*, p. 254b.

and Wetsteins. This was Holland's Golden Age in scholarship as in the fine and the decorative and useful arts. His recourse to Holland for matrices is a testimonial to Fell's regard for it, notwithstanding its abhorred Calvinism. By their copper-engraved frontispieces (many by a Dutchman), their manner of display of titles and headings, their unpretentious but purposeful make-up the books that he printed betray Dutch antecedents. 'I may possibly overvalue a designe which I have had long in my thoughts; but when I consider how much the Hollanders have added to their esteem in the World, by Printing well: as also that the King of France himself, receives an addition from his Louvre presse: I may hope that our Endeavors here may produce somewhat, which the publick may reap advantage from, and be concerned to encourage.' So Fell expressed himself to Williamson in April 1672.[1]

What he meant by a learned press is disclosed by the list of works that he purposed to print, drawn up at the beginning of 1672 (printed on p. 63). It is irrelevant but irresistible to comment that of the editions that he had in mind only two, Cyprian and Josephus (partly), saw the light, though other editions of several of the named authors or works followed in the next century. Failure to carry out the programme was due not so much to the want of sufficient and willing editors or authors as to a growing awareness that the books, if published, would not be bought.

At this press, naturally, scholarship would be directed to maintaining Fell's particular kind of Protestant churchmanship, a blend of Anglicanism with Cavalier politics, typified by the small military moustache which he wore with clerical attire. As one justification for his enterprise he saw 'preventing foraign Universities, and Cities; such as are Lions, Paris, Geneva, Antwerp, Bruxels, Leiden, Amsterdam, &c. to impose their Wares upon us, and oblige us to receive not only Books at their prizes [i.e. prices], but opinions from their dictates'.[2]

It would be a press that learned men and men of high rank and public spirit would want to support with gifts and interest-free loans of money. Others could invest capital sums in the confident expectation of dividends. Books would be published by subscription if the undertakers could be sure of 300 subscribers.[3]

---

[1] S.P. (Dom.), Car. II, 305, No. 98.
[2] *An Account of the state of the Press in the University of Oxford as it now stands, January 9. 1679 [1680]*, broadside, of which the Printer to the University has a copy.
[3] Advertisement of January 1671/2; Madan, *Oxford Books*, iii, pp. 411–12.

We purpose to Print, if we may be encouraged.

1. The greek Bible in a royal folio, to w^{ch}: purpose we haue procurd the vse of the Alexandrian MS. out of his Maties: library, with others of good note from diuerse Places; & haue of our own seueral copies of Venerable Antiquity neuer yet collated.

2. The Targum on the books of Chronicles, as also the Comments of R. Tanchum & other learned Rabbins on seueral parts of the Old Testament neuer yet printed, both in Heb: & Arab.

3. The Coptick Gospels neuer yet extant, out of a copy of Venerable antiquity in the hands of D^r: Marshall, & by him fitted for the presse.

4. The Coptick Psalter from a MS. in the Same hands, together with the Ancient Latin Psalter of the Western church.

5. The liturgicks & homilies of the Ancient English-saxons church, from MS. of venerable Antiquity, neuer yet Extant.

6. The Canons of the English Saxon church, far more perfect & correct, then the Edition of S^r: H. Spelman.

7. The Greek & Latin fathers in their order, Especially those of the first Ages Clement, Ignatius, Polycarp &c. as also Epiphanius Gr: lat: with annot: Cyprian according to the very many excellent vncollated Copies we haue by vs. Euthymius vpon the Psalmes, not yet extant in Gr:

8. Ephrem Syrus & other eastern fathers in Syriack. especially those parts of them which are not extant in Greek.

9. Josephus Gr: l. with the Annot: of S. Petit & others.

10. Maimonides, More novochim, as written by himself in Arab:, Arab: lat:

11. The history of Tamerlain in Arab: & Persian. with the lat:

12. A history of Insects, more perfect than any yet Extant.

13. A Description of Coins & Medals, such as haue not hitherto bin describd; from the Uniuersitys, & other priuate collections.

14. The Classical authors both greek & latin; Historians, Philosophers, Orators, & Poets, with new & more vsefull annotations, then haue bin hitherto publisht.

15. The ancient Mathematicians Greek & latin in one and twenty Volumes; part not yet Extant, the rest collated with MS. perfected from the Arabick versions, where the originals are lost, with their Scholia & comments: & all illustrated with Annotations. if this proposal shall be thought too vast, we shall enter vpon such authors, & publish them in such formes as shall be desird.

16. The authors of the Middle age from our Sauiours birth, in seueral faculties, that merit publick light, but as yet are not extant.

We shall farther adde Subsidiary books in seueral parts of learning; & treatises of learned men now liuing both in Latine & English.

Fell's publishing programme drawn up early in 1672 (All Souls MS. 239, fol. 641).

The press would derive authority from the University and in return would discharge a duty for it and add to its fame in the ears of mankind. 'We conceivd', Fell wrote, 'that it was a Service to the university to put our Selves upon a certainty of great trouble and Expence, to bring the trade of Printing hither, meerly for their honour and advantage.'[1] The lease of the privilege to the partners drawn by Yate and sealed on 5 October 1671 puts very clearly the view that the lessees were acting on behalf of the Chancellor, Masters, and Scholars. It recites that the latter considered:

that Printing and the full use and exercise thereof in the said University may redound to the great honour, renowne and benefitt of the same; and that it cannot be managed with better advantage to the publique, then when it is committed to some select Persons, who not only have an interest common with the rest of the said University, that so publique a work may be promoted, but who also shall of their own accord undergoe a hazard and expence . . .[2]

Fell and Yate as publishers and printers certainly accomplished more for the University than an organization under its collective control would have done at that time, but there were essential differences between theirs and a true university press. First, the partners (in effect Fell) had liberty to choose the books to print (and many do not so much as bear the imprimatur of the Vice-Chancellor). Second, the financial risk was run wholly by the partners, and the University even withheld from them the revenues it had allocated to learned printing. Third, the partners were given no inducement to act as agents, but on the contrary had to pay for rendering a service.

Nor was it the printing-office for which Laud made his plans. Once Fell's lease took effect the *typographi universitatis*, elected by Convocation, were debarred from the Theatre, and the post of Architypographus, so long as the lease lasted, was a sinecure. Disappointed of having Thomas Bennett in the post, Fell made arrangements for the Architypographus and Law Bedel, Norton Bold, to be moved to the better-paid place of Bedel of Divinity[3] and made a second, determined, attempt to secure the election of his candidate. He armed himself with a mandamus from the King addressed to the Vice-Chancellor enjoining Convocation to 'choose the most capable person that you can find to oversee and governe your

---

[1] S.P. (Dom.), Car. II, 293, No. 95, 8 Oct. 1671.
[2] Univ. Arch. S.E.P. 7; printed in *Print and Privilege*, pp. 162–4.
[3] *Ath.* iii, 883. Cf. 757–8.

The interior of the Sheldonian Theatre, looking towards the north

Thomas Guy (1645–1724), founder of Guy's Hospital and printer of
Bibles at Oxford. By John Vanderbank, c. 1706

Robert Plot (1640–96), author and Keeper of the Ashmolean Museum

presses' and reminding it of the statutory qualifications of an architypographer.[1] Anthony Wood describes the disgraceful sequel: how a
faction among the masters, 'perceiving full well that Dr. Fell was resolved
to get his man in meerly by his authority', elected 'a meer stranger, who
lived remotely from Oxon, named Christop. Wase . . . But Dr. Fell, who
had received a character of him, would never let him execute the archityp.
place, because as he usually said, he was not fit for it, as being not a
person of sobriety, &c. So that from the death of Mr. Clarke to this time
[*c.* 1690], the superior beadleship of the civ. law and the architypographer's place hath been disjoyned.'[2]

So Fell threw overboard Laud's designs for a *typographia universitatis
publica* and set off on a new course leading to a modern business. The
transition from Fell's to a university press was a matter of substituting
control by a representative committee for his and involving the University's money in the hazard of gain or loss.

STAFFING, PREMISES, AND MATERIAL

We are ill-informed, or rather not informed at all, about the recruitment
of a work-force by the partners, excepting only their fetching the typefounder from Holland.

It may be supposed that they took over some of the men whom Scott
had gathered for the *Synodicon*. John Bagford said that four compositors
were brought from Paris, and one was named Dell.[3] John Delle, of Paris,
compositor, was still here and was matriculated in 1691, aged 45.
Another Frenchman, to judge by his name, may have been Gallot, who
set part of Wood's *Historia*.[4] Not all of Scott's men stayed: Anthony
Izard, the London Stationer, who had a position of responsibility, disappeared as soon as the *Synodicon* was done.

John Hall, son of William Hall, printer of Oxford, was matriculated
as a printer in 1667. He was a grandson of Henry Hall, *typographus
universitatis*. The Vice-Chancellor paid him £200 in 1669–71 for work on
the *Synodicon*. Fell and Yate took him on as their leading hand, listened
to his advice about buildings, and trusted him with money to buy
materials. With the title of Warehouse-Keeper he was in charge at the
press during the partnership, kept accounts, engaged and dismissed
workmen, sold books at the door, and sent out bills. The Delegates
continued his employment in that capacity until he died in 1708.

[1] P.R.O. S.P. (Dom.), Entry Books, No. 31, fol. 77.   [2] *Ath.* iii, 883.
[3] B.M. MS. Harl. 5901, fol. 85.   [4] *Wood's Life and Times*, ii, pp. 261, 264 n.

We know the names of four apprentices bound to Hall in the early days of the Sheldonian Press.[1] Two of them, Thomas Hearne of Oxford, a namesake of the antiquary, bound in 1667, and John Crooke of Oxford, bound in 1675, stayed and became compositors at the learned press.

In November 1672 Fell reported 'above twenty hands at work'.[2]

Coming new to industrial management, Fell found his employees trying. 'To make them always attend their work, is I think beyond any Skill: Printers having a peculiar obligation to be idle, as being paid for it: Holiday mony being a certain stile in their Bills.'[1] Having to pay them for the customary waygoose on Bartholomew Day (August 24) must have been fresh in his memory; for when not on holiday the men were paid piecework rates. Yate asks himself 'What rate Presse work. and composeing for 3000. what lesse for 5000 what lesse for 10000 etc.'.[3]

Some memoranda jotted down by Yate and referable to the year 1671 ask: 'Whether to build any roome under the wall of the Theater for composeing and presse. J. Halle thinks it absolutely necessary.'[4] The query is answered by an entry in the Computus of the Vice-Chancellor for 1671–2, the expenditure of £104 paid to a carpenter 'for the new Print House under the East Wall of the Theater'. Besides that, Mr. Delgardno was paid in 1668–9 for vacating a dwelling, 'Tom Pun's House', very close by, which became 'the little Print House', part of it occupied by John Hall as living quarters. It had seven hearths,[5] and so was a useful adjunct to the New Print House, which had none. Though all books from Fell's press have an imprint 'from the Sheldonian Theatre', it is doubtful whether much printing was done there.

It appears from various items of expense that at least 5 presses were bought or made locally.[6] That was a big complement: only three of the London printers in 1668 had as many. The King's Printers, with 6 presses, 8 compositors, and 10 pressmen had the most; Flesher and Streater each had 5.[7] Not all the presses would normally be in use, and the 13 frames for compositors must have allowed for future expansion of

---

[1] Univ. Arch., Chancellor's Court Papers 130. See below, pp. 195–6.

[2] S.P. (Dom.), Car. II, 317, No. 188.

[3] Univ. Arch. S.E.P. P17^b(1)^m. He was muddled: the rate for composing would not be affected by the quantity.

[4] Univ. Arch. S.E.P. P17^b(1)^m.

[5] V.-C.'s Computus 1669–70.

[6] V.-C.'s Computus 1667–8: Mr. Rainsford for materialls for 3 Presses, Mr. Clarke for Hebrew Letters and a Printing-Presse (cf. Hart, *A Century*, p. 157); Computus 1668–9: Mr. Norman of London for one new Presse with Cases and furniture.

[7] S.P. (Dom.), Car. II, 243, No. 181.

the business. By the end of Fell's lifetime the number of presses had increased to 8.[1]

Paper, mostly French or from Genoa, was bought from merchants in London.[2] Fell announced in the autumn of 1672 that the partners had bought more than a thousand reams costing about £900.[3] In the same advertisement he wrote that 'We have paper made within two miles of

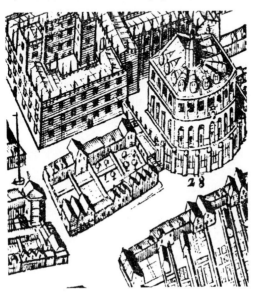

Part of Loggan's map of Oxford (1675), enlarged to show the Printhouse leaning against the wall round the Sheldonian Theatre on the east side.

the town that is usefull in printing.' That could refer only to the mill at Wolvercote, where in 1674 Robert Plot found 'a coarse paper' being made;[4] but in fact white paper of respectable quality was made there at least two years before that: the *Oxford Almanack* for 1673 in book form used 80 reams of Wolvercote paper costing 4s. 6d. a ream and 2 reams of Genoa at 6s. 6d.[5] John Bagford credited Fell with encouraging the fitting-up of a paper mill there.[6] Wolvercote Mill was bought for the University's use in 1855 and acquired outright in 1872.[7] It has since been the principal supplier of paper to the Press.

[1] Schedule to the 'Christ Church Specimen', reproduced in Morison, *Fell*, facing p. 73.
[2] R. W. Chapman, 'An Inventory of Paper, 1674', *The Library*, 4th ser. vii (1927), pp. 402–8.   [3] All Souls MS. 239, fol. 666; Madan, *Oxford Books*, iii, p. 412.
[4] Bodl. MS. Hearne's Diaries 158, p. 15.
[5] Univ. Arch. S.E.P. P17^b(1)^c. The size of the sheet is not given.
[6] B.M. MS. Harl. 5901, fol. 86.   [7] Carter, *Wolvercote Mill.*

ABANDONMENT OF THE PRIVILEGED BOOKS

The venture into school book publishing lasted six months. On 7 October 1672 Fell told Williamson: 'We are here put in some expectation of having some of the Stationers with us to treat concerning their Priviledged books'; but he adds, 'whither they bring such terms as will be decent for us to accept, I cannot yet guesse.'[1] A week later a deputation from the Stationers' Company arrived in Oxford. The price offered for the partners' forbearance to print books for which the Company had patent rights was a yearly £120, an advance (Fell wrote) of £30 on the Stationers' share of the £200 paid in previous years to the University. But, as negotiations progressed, it was agreed, in consideration of a lump sum for the school books already printed by the partners, to be taken over 'at the rate of paper and printing',[2] the annual rent payable by the Stationers would be abated to £100.[3]

It appears from one of Yate's calculations[4] that before agreeing to buy up all Fell's printed editions of school books more or less at cost price the Stationers had offered to employ the Sheldonian Press to print 22 of such books in editions of 3,000 every year, a total of 377 sheets. That would have solved the problem of providing bread-and-butter work for the printers; but the rates offered were no more than a third of the cost of producing the books at Oxford, and Yate had no difficulty in showing that acceptance would have been disastrous.

The Stationers treated only for their corporation on this occasion: in earlier years they had dealt with the University on behalf of their members who had patents of their own, therefore the rent that they paid for forbearance included contributions from the King's Printers for Bibles and Roger Norton for the *Grammar*. Fell and his partners signed a separate agreement with Norton,[5] but they were prepared to brave the King's Printers by keeping liberty to print Bibles in the sizes that were permitted to the Universities.

So the partners gave up all but the Bible of the privileged books, the books that Fell had argued would by their profitable sale sustain a learned press and make his enterprise viable. He explained to Williamson that 'the avoyding trouble is to us a valuable consideration';[6] so for securing peace and quiet he accepted the Stationers' terms, though he

[1] S.P. (Dom.), Car. II, 316, No. 65.
[2] Bodl. MS. Rawl. D. 397, fol. 356; *Print and Privilege*, pp. 69–70.
[3] So I understand S.P. (Dom.), Car. II, 316, No. 167.
[4] Univ. Arch. S.E.P. P17ᵇ(1)ᵇ.   [5] S.P. (Dom.), Car. II, 316, No. 197.
[6] Ibid., No. 142.

knew that his forbearance to print almanacs alone was worth more to them than £100 a year.

A relic of the school books printed by Fell and Yate in 1672. The title-page of Aesop reproduced from the copper plate at the Press.

Yate's accounts[1] reveal more sales to the Stationers of the partners' printed stock besides the school books. The Londoners bought up the little pocket-book *Oxford Almanack* for 1673 and one in the form of a sheet for the same year. Perhaps they destroyed them, for very few

[1] Univ. Arch. S.E.P. P17ᵇ(1)ᵖ.

copies are known,[1] though 20,500 of the booklet and 15,000 of the sheet were printed. There was no monopoly that the Stationers guarded so closely as that of almanacs. For less obvious reasons they also took the bulk of the editions of two books by Rapin on eloquence and Daniel Brevint's *Missale Romanum*.[2]

In fact, as it soon became clear, Fell's partnership was quite unequal to competing in the market for cheap school books, a kind of work for which the Stationers' English Stock employed poor printers at cut prices. A few examples[3] will show it all too clearly.

Ovid's *Tristia*, for which the partners estimated for an edition of 3,000 £13. 5s., cost them £16. 10s. 6d. or 1s. 2d. a copy, while the Stationers sold it in quarterns of 25 for 9d. The so-called Cato's *Disticha*, estimated at £12 for 3,000, cost £12. 17s. 6d., while the Stationers' price was $2\frac{1}{2}d$. a copy, as compared with Oxford's $9\frac{1}{2}d$. Aesop, estimated at £25. 5s., cost the partners £30. 18s., or 2s. 7d. a copy, while the Stationers charged 12s. for a quartern. The *Sententiae Pueriles* printed at Oxford worked out at 7d. a copy, and the Stationers charged $1\frac{3}{4}d$.; the *Pueriles Confabulatiunculae* $6\frac{1}{2}d$. as against 2d. And the buyer of a quartern got a 26th copy free.

So it was not only the jealousy of the Company of Stationers that kept Fell and his partners out of the school book business. Superior as their product may have been and doubtless was, it would have found few buyers willing to pay their prices; and in the event, of Oxford educational books it was only the 'Grammar with accidence and notes'[4] that established itself in the face of opposition from the patentees. It had the advantage of being newly edited under guidance from Fell.

Doubts about their capacity to sell books would account for compliance on the part of the managers of the new press. They had discouraging news from their country salesman. Peter Yate, a nephew of the Principal, had been visiting provincial booksellers and was obliged to report, 'I planely perceive that it must be a good Bargaine that will divert their Trade from their old acquaintance.'[5] In the nature of things, the London booksellers were unlikely to favour them, for almost all these tradesmen were Stationers and had shares in the Company's English Stock. In these

[1] Madan, *Oxford Books*, iii, Nos. 2957–8. D. Wing's *Short Title Catalogue* locates a copy of the booklet at Harvard besides the one at the Bodleian. Madan knew of no copy of the sheet; but Miss H. M. Petter has lately found a cropped copy at the Bodleian (MS. Carte 114, fol. 546).
[2] Madan, *Oxford Books*, iii, Nos. 2941, 2944, 2921.
[3] Univ. Arch. S.E.P. P17b(1)c, Yate's estimates and accounts.
[4] Below, pp. 219–21.
[5] Bodl. MS. Rawl. D. 397, fol. 380.

circumstances Fell was apt to appreciate the advantages of ready money over an uncertain prospect of profit.

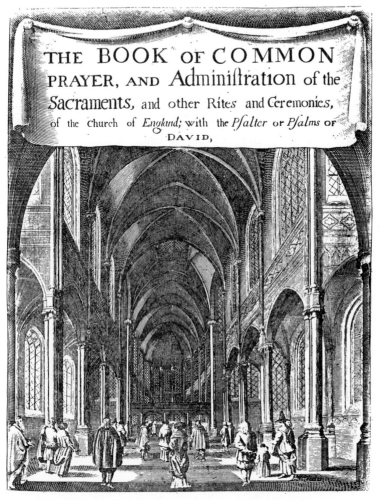

THE BOOK OF COMMON PRAYER, AND Adminiſtration of the Sacraments, and other Rites and Ceremonies, of the Church of *England*; with the *Pſalter* or *Pſalms* of DAVID,

The engraved title of the Book of Common Prayer printed at Fell's press in 1675. Reproduced from the copper plate at the Press. Reduced.

The first Oxford Bible was put to press in 1673, and the New Testament part of it is dated in that year. The complete Bible, with a title-page dated 1675, was on sale before 7 February.[1] It is a Crown 4to, one of the sizes allowed to the Universities by the Order in Council of March

[1] Prideaux, p. 35.

1636. It is said that Yate's investment in the business, £3,000 or £4,000, was used to pay the cost.[1] The quantity of the first printing was probably 5,000. It was sold in sheets for 8*s*. The Book of Common Prayer and the metrical psalms were produced in the same year in a form suitable for binding with the Bible.

To call this an Oxford Bible might convey that it had authority from the University; but that is not the case. It is very much Fell's Bible. He made minor alterations in the text of the Authorized Version as it had been improved and printed at Cambridge,[2] and, what is more, he subjected it to his idiosyncratic spelling—mainly a matter of putting i where y was usual, as eies for eyes and daies for days, but also bin for been. A good deal of latitude was taken, and perhaps not noticed, in writing English then, but in print our orthography was relatively stable. Contemporaries found Fell's reformed spelling troublesome. On seeing the Bible, a former pupil of the Dean's, Humphrey Prideaux, wrote: 'A Bible hath lately come forth from us; if you hear anything of it pray inform us. I must confesse, since Mr. Dean hath taken the liberty of inventeing a new way of spelleing and useing it therein, which I thinke will confound and alter the analogy of the English tongue, that I doe not at all approve thereof; and I could hartyly wish that he would be a looser by the experiment, that we may have noe more of it.'[3]

Severe inroads into the King's Printers' monopoly of the Bible in English were made by editions printed in Holland and sold illicitly here;[4] the Cambridge privilege was exploited in some printed for the profit of George Sawbridge, Treasurer of the Stationers' English Stock, who had secretly taken the University Printer, Hayes, into his service.[5] The patentees were determined to have no more competitors. Fell writes of their 'molesting them [the Oxford partners] in the printing and sale of such Quarto Bibles as they had undertaken'.[6] Whatever form the molestation took, it had the intended effect; Fell and his associates did not print another Bible.

The first agreement between the partners and the Stationers was for 3 years from March 1672. When it expired another was signed that was

[1] Bodl. MS. Ballard 49, fol. 237.
[2] Madan, *Oxford Books*, iii, No. 3084.
[3] Prideaux, p. 38.
[4] 'Dutch Bibles, which to the equal shame and damage of the Nation, supply half this Kingdom, all Scotland, all Ireland, and all our Plantations': Fell to Sancroft [January 1679/80], J. Gutch, *Collectanea curiosa*, i (Oxford, 1781), p. 270.
[5] D. F. McKenzie, *The Cambridge University Press 1696–1712* (Cambridge, 1966), i, pp. 4, 5.
[6] Bodl. MS. Ballard 49, fol. 190.

rather more favourable to the Oxford press.[1] The rent was still £100, but the deed reserved to the partners a right to print a sheet almanac every year, besides the 'singing psalmes' to fit their Bibles, and the works of Virgil, Terence, Cicero, and Ovid with critical notes physically inseparable from the texts, 'soe printed that they be not prejudiciall to the sale of [those authors] as commonly printed and sold by the Company of Stationers', disputes to be submitted to Obadiah Walker, Master of University College, and Robert Scott, bookseller, for arbitration. Where classics were concerned, the only advantage taken of the concession was to include in a composite volume the dialogue in Greek, *De exilio*, considered as the work of Cicero, but now relegated to his *spuria*.[2]

[1] Printed from a deed in the custody of the Stationers' Company in *Print and Privilege*, pp. 165–7 (Stationers' Company Serial No. 335, 9 Mar. 1674/5).
[2] Madan, *Oxford Books*, iii, No. 3264.

CHAPTER VII

The Books from Fell's Press 1672–1680

IN the 15 years of Fell's management the Sheldonian Press put out some 150 books, besides reprints and ephemera. Falconer Madan in 1931[1] catalogued those that were printed before 1681 with a fullness of detail and comment that modern cost of printing would not permit, an accuracy less than that of the modern scientific bibliographers, and a humanity and humour rare in that school.

For the present purpose it is enough to extract history from Madan's bibliography with reference to the contemporary sources and to give a brief account of a few of Fell's publications that are of intrinsic interest still and of others whose history is interwoven with that of the Press.

Wood's Historia et Antiquitates Universitatis Oxoniensis

This is one of the books that had been undertaken by the Delegates of the Press before Fell and his partners entered upon their lease. Wood said that the Delegates, Fell and Yate among them, 'had been informed of the worth of the book by Mr. Obad. Walker and Mr. Will. Stone of New Inn', who had perused his manuscript.[2] It must have been common knowledge at Oxford that Anthony Wood of Merton College, a notorious recluse, had been at work since 1660 on a history of Oxfordshire of which the annals of the University since 1066 was one section. He had copied inscriptions in churches and graveyards and made persistent demands on the custodians of college muniments and University Archives. The Delegates, meeting on 22 October 1669, agreed to buy the copy, written in English, for £100, 'to be printed in Latin or English, according to their discretion'.[3]

In his autobiography Wood gives more information about this meeting. He says it was a condition of the sale 'that he would suffer the book to be translated into Latine, for the honour of the university in forreigne countries, and that he would take more paines in recovering transcripts

---

[1] *Oxford Books*, iii.
[2] 'The Life of Anthony à Wood written by himself' in *Ath.* i, lxv.
[3] *First Minute Book*, p. 6.

of original charters which he cites in his book, as also *verba ipsa*, the words themselves, of old MS. authors &c. to be put in Italic character, and thereby add to the authority of the book. These proposalls, tho' they were suddain to the author, yet he granted them their desires.'[1]

Establishing the wording of the documents put him to a great deal of trouble. He made several journeys to London to copy from records in the Tower and manuscripts in Sir John Cotton's library. The Delegates further desired of him that he would add to his accounts of the colleges and halls summaries of the lives of writers bred in them. He did so, and his notes on the writers were the nucleus for that famous work, Wood's *Athenae Oxonienses, an exact History of all the Writers and Bishops who have had their Education in the most famous and ancient University of Oxford*, published later in London. Sir Leoline Jenkins put him up for a week, admitted him to the Wills Office of the Prerogative Court of Canterbury, and presented him to Archbishop Sheldon.

The translation (said not to be good) caused much resentment in Wood. The Dean committed it to a Bachelor of Arts, Richard Peers, and an usher of Magdalen College School, named Reeve;[2] 'but all the proofs that came from the press went thro' the doctor's hands, which he would correct, alter or dash out, or put in what he pleased . . . so much that many look'd upon the copie as spoyl'd by him.'[3] Fell took special care to delete Wood's praise of Thomas Hobbes for learning and benevolence,[4] and inserted in its stead opprobrious expressions about *Leviathan* and Hobbes's mathematics. At the end of the book is an anonymous diatribe by Fell in answer to Hobbes's defence of himself. There was a struggle between author and editor, too, about a passage in the preface where Wood disclaims responsibility for offence given by matter inserted in his copy by others; and in this instance he prevailed.

The history, as Wood wrote it in English and revised after its publication in Latin, was carefully edited in 1791–6 by John Gutch. Its lasting value as an authority on the earlier history of the University is almost wholly due to the use made in it of material collected by Brian Twyne, the Keeper of the Archives in the years 1634–44. 'Wood did little more than put together materials collected by Twyne', said his scrupulous editor in 1895, Andrew Clarke; and he adds, 'In the *Hist. et Antiq.* printed in his lifetime, we find an entire absence of acknowledgement of debt to

[1] *Ath*. lxv.
[2] Quarrels between Wood and the translators are narrated by Prideaux (pp. 10–12).
[3] *Ath*. i, lxviii.   [4] Ibid., p. cxxxvi.

Twyne's Collections.'[1] The omission accords with the author's morosity and vanity, but also with the practice of his day. It must be allowed that where Twyne stops Wood carries on with a respectable amount of information that he had gathered from Oxford records.

When he wrote the preface to the Latin edition Wood expected that Loggan's copper engravings of views of Oxford and the colleges would be available to any who wanted them for binding in his book; and several times he refers to the engravings as 'the cuts belonging to my book'. They were published separately in 1675 as *Oxonia illustrata*, but often presented to distinguished visitors as a companion to the *Historia*. Wood's book, also, is ornamented with handsome headpieces printed from copper and, towards the end, with fantastic woodcut initial letters.

At first it was intended that subscriptions should be invited to pay the cost of production,[2] but in the event Fell paid for translating and printing, Jenkins contributing £50. The dedication to King Charles II is from the *Procuratores rei Typographicae in Universitate Oxon.* The University paid Wood £100 for the copy and gave him another £50 for the trouble caused by the exigences of the Delegates.

How many were printed is not known. The ordinary copies are Demy folio, but some were done on Royal for presents. On publication 17 copies were bought by the University and richly bound; one was given to the King. Another 100 in sheets were set aside for regaling notable visitors in future; the Prince of Neuburg, the Grand Duke of Tuscany, and the Queen were among the first to receive them. Wood was given 14 copies. When the Delegates sold off their stock in 1712 the remaining 4 copies on large paper, priced at £2, and 10 on small, price £1, were spared.[3]

The Catalogue of Bodleian Printed Books, 1674

The Delegates of the Press had determined on the printing of this book before Fell and his partners took charge of the press. The editing was finished by July 1672, when the Delegates decided to put it in hand at the expense of the University and that the 'farmers of the Universitys Privilege for printing' should be paid for their services in producing it.

The book, *Catalogus impressorum librorum bibliothecae Bodleianae, in academia Oxoniensi*, was ready by December 1674 and on sale by the

[1] *Wood's Life and Times*, iv, pp. 223–4.
[2] D.O. 26 Oct. 1670; *First Minute Book*, p. 8.
[3] D.O. 8 June 1713; *First Minute Book*, p. 38.

following January.[1] The Delegates fixed the price at 19*s.* for the two folio volumes and decreed that 'no person have leave to propose a Dispensation to study in the Library; but shall first bring a Certificate from the Janitor that he has bought and payd for one Copie of the Catalogue'.[2]

This was the third published catalogue. Unlike its predecessors it was confined to printed books and arranged by authors in alphabetical order. It runs to 706 pages. Thomas Hyde, the *protobibliothecarius*, impliedly taking all the credit for the work, complains much in his dedication to Archbishop Sheldon and his preface of the burden he had borne for nine years compiling it, enduring weariness of mind and body and the intense cold in winter. Thomas Hearne believed that Hyde 'did not do much in the Work besides writing the Dedication and Preface'.[2] He attributed most of the labour and endurance to the Janitor (under-librarian), Emmanuel Pritchard.

Since Thomas James's second catalogue was published in 1620 the number of the printed books had grown from an estimated 15,000 to about twice that number.[3] A catalogue of the accessions for use in the Library was perfected in 1646, but by 1652 things were getting out of hand and Gerard Langbaine began work on a subject-catalogue, for which one of 15,000 entries under authors was made as a preliminary.[4] The bulk of Selden's bequest of 8,000 volumes reached the Library in 1659.

The *Catalogus* of 1674 was the biggest yet made of printed books, therefore a great service to the literate world.[5] Nearly all the learned books being then in Latin, it could still be claimed, as Thomas James had claimed for his catalogue of 1620, that 'Non solum publicis per Europam universam bibliothecis, sed etiam privatis musaeis, aliisque ad catalogum librorum conficiendum usui esse possit.' It was bought and used interleaved to catalogue other libraries: until 1760 a marked copy was the only catalogue at the Bibliothèque Mazarine in Paris,[6] and John Locke used it for an inventory of his books.[7] Yate foresaw in 1671-2 a need to

---

[1] D.O. 24 July; *First Minute Book*, p. 93; T.C. I, p. 199.

[2] Hearne, iv, p. 431.

[3] F. Madan, 'A Statistical Survey of the Bodleian Library', *Bodleian Quarterly Record*, i (1917), pp. 254-62.

[4] *Summary Catalogue of Western Manuscripts in the Bodleian Library at Oxford*, ed. R. W. Hunt, i (Oxford, 1953), pp. xxi-ii; G. W. W[heeler], 'A Projected Subject-Catalogue (1652)', *Bodleian Quarterly Record*, iii (1921), pp. 193-4; M. Purver, *The Royal Society: Concept and Creation* (1967), pp. 112, 121-6.

[5] Strickland Gibson summarized in Bibliographical Soc. *Transactions*, xiv (1919), pp. 2-4.

[6] Macray, *Annals*, pp. 140-1 n.

[7] J. Harrison and P. Laslett, *The Library of John Locke*, 2nd ed. (Oxford, 1971), plates 3, 4.

provide for additions in manuscript: 'If wee print the Catalogue to do it in a Larg Letter, Larg Paper, a Larg Margent, and on Paper will beare Inke'.[1]

Hyde was paid £160 for the editing, and Pritchard, the Janitor, was rewarded with £5 and 100 copies at a discount of 1s. to sell. The Vice-Chancellor paid Fell and his partners £725 for printing 1,000. There is no indication of the arrangements for sale, but the edition sold out more quickly than many; for no copies were left in 1696, when the Warehouse-Keeper made the earliest extant list of the Delegates' stock.

The Oxford Almanack

Members of the University, resident or in country vicarages, like every-one in the seventeenth century, would have felt lost without an almanac. Their requirements being in some respects peculiar, it was a happy idea of the prospective lessees of the press to provide for one adapted to the needs and taste of such people. Yate noted in anticipation of taking charge: 'A designe and cut for a Leafe Almanack on a Brasse plate. . . . A cut in wood for Sheet Almanack', and 'Paper. All markes for Almanackes and Bibles'.[2]

By printing a book almanac and a sheet almanac in 1673 they fell foul of the Stationers' Company, and their whole editions, 20,500 copies of the one and 15,000 of the other, were bought up by the Company.[3]

Almanacs were printed in large numbers and the profit on their sale, though moderate, amounted to a substantial sum. The Stationers' Company acquired its monopoly of publishing them and selling them whole-sale by Letters Patent of 1603.[4] In 1673 it was distributing two dozen varieties of them to its bookselling members and valuing them at £2,455, which was almost 40 per cent of the revenue of its publishing business, the English Stock. Whenever they were free to do so, in the absence of an agreement to the contrary, the Oxford printers had printed almanacs.[5] The action taken in 1673 to suppress competition from Oxford was an incident in the Stationers' constant struggle to keep this market to themselves.

The great bulk of the almanacs sponsored by the Company were in the form of printed sheets intended for binding, often with interleaves, as

---

[1] Univ. Arch. S.E.P. P17ᵇ(1)ᵐ.   [2] Ibid.   [3] Above, pp. 69–70.
[4] Blagden, p. 75; and his 'Distribution of Almanacks in the Second Half of the Seventeenth Century', *Studies in Bibliography*, xi (Charlottesville, 1958), pp. 107–16.
[5] Madan, *Oxford Books*, iii, p. 393.

pocket books. Many people wrote their accounts and diaries in the blank pages and spaces.[1] They provided prognostications based on astrology besides valuable memoranda. The exceptions were only two varieties in the form of flat sheets for sticking on walls, and the fact that they were of an unpretentious kind may have made it comparatively easy for Fell and Yate in 1675 to wrest from the Stationers' representatives the concession allowing them, without loss of compensation for forbearing to exploit the University's privilege, to print one sheet almanac every year. It must have been understood that the *Oxford Almanack* would be of high quality, unlikely to affect the sale of their popular series.

The earliest *Oxford Almanack* of the illustrated series begun by Fell and his partners and continuing until now is that for 1674. It can have been no hindrance to the Stationers' business. Its very size, 39 by 30 in., sets it aside from the common run; and the design and the quality of the drawing and engraving are calculated for an educated taste. It is made of four sheets of paper pasted together, each of them printed all over from engravings in copper. Joined together they form a composition depicting classical gods and goddesses with the calendar and tables of useful information inserted in it.

The daunting cost of the first of the partners' *Almanacks* is a possible reason for there being none for the next year, 1675. The second, for 1676, is more modest in size, a single sheet about 23½ by 20 in., but in conception and execution as fine as the first. Since then there has been no interruption of the series.[2]

Fell paid the artists and engravers.[3] Dates of movable feasts, phases of the moon, and eclipses were furnished by the Savilian Professors of Astronomy.[4]

Copies printed on stuff are known. In early days some were printed by (or for) the wife of the Warehouse-Keeper. Yate refers to them in his accounts for 1676 and 1677;[5] in 1676 he received 'Of John Halls wife for printing off at the Rolling Presse upon Cloath 290 Almanackes at 3*d.* per peice over and above 5*s.* was given her £3 7*s.* 6*d.*' (she paid 3*d.* each less a deduction of 5*s.*). In the following year he calls them 'Handkerchers'.

[1] E. F. Bosanquet, 'English Seventeenth-Century Almanacs', *The Library*, 4th ser. x (1930), pp. 361–97.
[2] The *Almanack* is dealt with fully by Miss H. M. Petter, *The Oxford Almanacks* (Oxford, 1974), and briefly later in this book (pp. 201–3).
[3] His accounts in Chancellor's Court Cause Papers for Hilary Term 1687/8 and copied by Yate in Bodl. MS. Rawl. D. 397, fol. 424.
[4] Until 1806: D.O. 16 May and 25 June 1806.
[5] Bodl. MS. Rawl. D. 397, fols. 417ᵛ, 422.

In 1677 the Almanack was sold as single copies for 6d. and wholesale for 4s. a hundred.[1]

Sequels to the Whole Duty of Man

The most commercially valuable copyrights that Fell had were in four books by the anonymous author of The Whole Duty of Man. The first of them, The Ladies Calling, came out in 1673, and it was reprinted four times in that year. It reached the 12th edition in 1712. In rapid succession came The Government of the Tongue (1674), The Art of Contentment (1675), and The Lively Oracles given to us (1678). All these are described on their title-pages as 'By the Author of the Whole Duty of Man'.

To identify the writer with certainty has defeated inquirers who have spent abundance of time and pains on it; but the reasonable demonstration by C. E. Doble in 1882, confirmed in 1951 by Paul Elmen,[2] that probability favours Richard Allestree has been so generally assented to that in most libraries the books are catalogued under his name. Allestree, Regius Professor of Divinity at Oxford, 1663–79, was a close friend of Fell, and there is little doubt that he let Fell dispose of his copies and get them printed, great care being taken to conceal his identity.

The Whole Duty of Man was printed and published in London in 1658. It was followed by The Gentlemans Calling (1660) and The Causes of the Decay of Christian Piety (1667), both printed there and proclaiming on their title-pages that they were by the author of the Whole Duty. Edition upon edition of that book came out; it was translated into several languages, and its popularity lasted into the middle of the eighteenth century.[3]

The author's design was to promote virtue and piety. He aimed the books at gentlefolk of both sexes, but their prodigious sale can only be explained by a general desire to adopt the ethic of a leisured class. The religious instruction is derived from the Bible, therefore was acceptable to Dissenters as well as Churchmen. To understand the appeal of these books would be to understand a great deal about the minds of our ancestors during four reigns. 'The literary style', Madan says, 'is justly admired.'

Five editions of the Government of the Tongue, four of the Art of Contentment, and three of the Lively Oracles were printed at the Sheldonian

[1] Bodl. MS. Rawl. D. 397, fol. 424ᵛ.
[2] 'Who wrote "The Whole Duty of Man"', Academy, xxii (1882), pp. 348–9, 364–5, 382–3; 'Richard Allestree and "The Whole Duty of Man"', The Library, 5th ser. vi (1951), pp. 19–27.   [3] See below, p. 272.

Press in Fell's time. The temptation to pirate them was too strong for some of the London publishers. In a letter to Williamson of 6 August 1674 Fell complains of pirated impressions of the *Ladies Calling* and the *Government of the Tongue*, and proposes that the King, as a special favour to the University, should forgo half the fine recoverable by the successful prosecution of an unauthorized edition of any of his publications and so make prosecution worth his while.[1] He attributed the offending counterfeit impressions to 'the combination and fraud of several Printers and Stationers'. Robert Battersby admitted printing the *Ladies Calling* without licence, evidently in collusion with the Stationers' searcher, Samuel Mearne; but Sir Roger L'Estrange, the Licenser, found out about the edition and 'put it down'.[2]

Fell's Greek Testament

In the same year as his English Bible, 1675, Fell published his variorum Greek Testament.[3] It is a modest octavo set in small type and by no means easy to read or consult, but his collection of various readings, the biggest yet made, was judged very favourably by competent scholars. Henry Aldrich thought it 'preferable to others, not excepting Dr. Mill's' (of 1707), and Thomas Hearne agreed.[4] Heinrich Wetstein praises it highly in the preface to his edition (Amsterdam, 1711). The text is that of the Elsevier edition of 1633; for Fell considered that departure from it might undermine faith. The variants, collected by Fell and his friends from published sources and manuscripts in the Bodleian and Oxford colleges, are packed into the tail margins. John Mill relates (in Latin) a conversation about the book with Edward Bernard, who 'much wondered that its experienced editor had resolved to cram the mass of variant readings into so small a book, when it was obvious that the tail margin was incapable of holding so much as the bare readings from such a multitude of sources, let alone naming the sources from which they came, which was a thing essential to the objects of the book'.[5] The defect must not be judged without taking into account the price of the book. It cost 3*s*. unbound.

[1] S.P. (Dom.), Car. II, 361, No. 188 with enclosure.
[2] Hist. MSS. Comm., 9th *Report*, App. p. 77.
[3] Madan, *Oxford Books*, iii, No. 3087 and p. 322.
[4] Hearne, xi, p. 211.
[5] John Mill in the Prolegomena to his *Novum Testamentum cum lectionibus variantibus* (Oxford, 1707), p. cliii.

The frontispiece of Fell's variorum Greek Testament of 1675.
Reproduced from the copper plate destroyed in 1918.

Loggan's Oxonia Illustrata

This volume of illustrations of Oxford and its colleges and halls, enlivened by conventional figures of the inhabitants and their animals, is incomparably the most interesting and attractive of all that bear the imprint of the Sheldonian Press. Unlike the rest it gives a delight that is unaffected by the passage of time.

What was its connection with the Press is difficult to determine. It is printed wholly from engraved plates, and the printing was done in

David Loggan's house. The royal privilege conferring the sole right of printing for 15 years is granted to Loggan. The book is not mentioned in the Orders of the Delegates of the Press.

The imprint is 'Oxoniae e Theatro Sheldoniano', therefore Fell and his partners were in some sense the publishers. If they sold copies, there is no record of their doing so. The work is included in 'A Catalogue of Books, printed at the Theater in Oxford', issued probably early in 1678; but Anthony Wood noted on his copy of it, 'this was not printed in the Theater, but in his house in Halywell.'[1] The partnership bought seven copies from Loggan in 1677 at the price of £1. 2s. 6d. each.[2] When the Vice-Chancellor in 1675 needed one to send to 'mounsier Justellus', he bought it from Loggan for £1. 5s. in quires. His successor in 1688–9 paid Loggan £50 for 50 copies.

Although the connection between this book and the accredited undertakers for printing can have been only tenuous, the University adopted it to the extent of making presents of it to distinguished visitors.

Madan gives a detailed account of the contents.[3]

Prideaux's Marmora Oxoniensia, 1676[4]

Among the works announced in Fell's draft prospectus of January 1672[5] as 'begun to be printed at the Theater' (meaning that the Delegates had decided to publish it) is 'The Arundel Marbles with their Explication in fol: together with a Discourse of Mr: Lidiats upon the Epocha, and others of like nature with cutts'. By 'epocha' the learned would understand the means of dating in Greek chronology.

Part of the collection of Greco-Roman sculpture and inscribed stones made by the second Earl of Arundel had been given to the University by Henry Howard, the Earl's grandson, in 1667, and was exposed to public view in niches in the walls enclosing the courtyard of the Sheldonian Theatre. Fell was the most active of the Heads of Houses who were anxious to mark by issuing a handsome catalogue their appreciation of the liberality of the gift. Scholars at home and abroad expected a publication of the inscriptions, and in particular of one, the Parian Marble, a

---

[1] Bodl. MS. Wood 660 B (8). It is also in *Catalogus librorum in Theatro Sheldoniano Oxon. impressorum* of 1694.

[2] Yate's accounts: Bodl. MS. Rawl. D. 397, fol. 407ᵛ.

[3] *Oxford Books*, iii, No. 3035.

[4] The subject is dealt with again in a notice of the definitive edition of the marbles by Richard Chandler, 1763; below, p. 393.

[5] Above, p. 60.

chronicle of events in the Greek world giving indications of the Olympiads in which they happened. This was one of 27 inscriptions that had been copied by Selden, Patrick Young, and Richard James when the stones were brought to England in 1627 and published by Selden in 1628; but by the time of the gift to Oxford that edition was out of print and scarce.

Part of Loggan's view of the Sheldonian Theatre from the south, showing Arundel Marbles built in the surrounding wall.

It was known that Thomas Lydiat, a noted chronologer who died in 1646, left unpublished a treatise relating this chronicle to other sources of knowledge. That and Selden's annotations were part of the book that Fell envisaged.

The Dean entrusted a favourite pupil, Humphrey Prideaux, then a young Student of Christ Church, with the edition. The Arundel Marbles at Oxford with 20 given by Selden were 150 pieces. Selden had catalogued 27. It was necessary to transcribe from the stone 123 epigraphs, annotate them, translate them into Latin, and provide illustrations of the reliefs. Michael Burghers, successor to Loggan as University Engraver, was given the 'cuts' to do in copper with the aid of his journeymen. Prideaux groaned under the weight of his assignment and protested that his attainments in scholarship were unequal to it. Fell had also burdened him with editing the chronicle of John Malalas, a project left in suspense since Convocation adopted it in 1633. However, Prideaux managed to secure another postponement of Malalas and concentrated on the Marbles.[1]

The title-page of Prideaux's *Marmora*.

The work evidently interested him, and he formed large designs for notes and appendices. He was learning Semitic languages from Edward Pococke, a teacher whom he loved. That was the branch of learning in which he afterwards made his name by his famous *Connection*. He was able to quote Hebrew, Arabic, and Syriac in his notes to the *Marmora*. Fell, in the peremptory way that he had with authors, importuned him

[1] Prideaux, pp. 14–43 *passim*; preface to the *Marmora*.

to make haste. As soon as six sheets of notes were written, Prideaux tells the world in his preface, he was ordered to commit them to the press and told for the future not to keep the compositors waiting for copy. He excuses shortcomings in his performance by these 'extremely difficult conditions'.

It is a hurried performance, begun in August 1674 and at press by the following December, 'wonderfully defective' as Hearne called it.[1] Prideaux printed Selden's transcript of the Parian Chronicle without attempting to read the original. He explains his decision on the grounds that the stone had suffered from the weather since 1627 and half of it had been used to mend a chimney in Arundel House and had disappeared. The volume is a muddle: the contributions by Selden, Lydiat, and Prideaux are not distinguishable and all follow a half-title 'Thomae Lydiati Oxoniensis annotationes'.

The Vice-Chancellor paid the partners £30. 10*s*. for an unspecified number of copies in 1676.[2]

Obadiah Walker's Paraphrase of the Epistles of St. Paul, 1675–8

The book is interesting as the vestige of a plan that Fell worked out at the outset of his management of the press. In April 1672 he wrote to Jenkins about an 'attempt at an Edition of the Bible':[3]

> The truth is, Mr. Principal and my self, have had long debates upon that head; for as it is certain that we can never carry on our Expensive businesse of printing without the help of Subscriptions; so it seems evident to us that nothing can be so usefull, as be[side?] classical Authors wherein Scholars are concernd; to propose also such an universal book as will be acceptable to all conditions not only of men, but the Women likewise, and doubtlesse what you recommended to us, the Setting out an English bible, with all the advantages of print and paper, and exterior ornaments, and the accession of practicall annotations fitted for the use of Every Christian reader, had advantages beyond any other design that we can think of.

He had, accordingly, thought of six doctors of divinity who might write notes of sufficient authority; moreover he had persuaded the Regius Professor, Richard Allestree, to revise the whole, 'which I confesse is a Point gaind so much beyond expectation; (for you know with what unwillingnesse he is brought to work)'.

---

[1] Hearne, vii, p. 6.   [2] Bodl. MS. Rawl. D. 397, fol. 421ᵛ.
[3] S.P. (Dom.), Car. II, 305, No. 117. It is printed by Madan (*Oxford Books*, iii, p. 415) very incorrectly.

Fell made a rough draft of directions to the annotators.[1] They were to aim at rendering 'the mind of the Text, so as to be understood by the unlearned reader', but also to 'enforce the meaning of such Texts, as establish the Orthodoxe truth', paying special attention to passages perverted by Papists, Socinians, and Anabaptists, and sparing to quote humane authors. They must be brief, in order that the text and notes might not exceed the limits of a folio volume.

Perhaps the impossibility of meeting this last requirement killed the project. Henry Hammond's paraphrased and annotated New Testament of 1653 ran to 1,008 folio pages. Fell had a page set as a specimen.[2] His plan was manifestly unworkable: the type had to be much too small, and the paraphrasing and noting huddled into the tail margin would not be read. It would doubtless have been a popular book if it had been feasible.

Walker was not one of the doctors selected by Fell to illuminate the Scripture. He was a close friend of the Dean, whose end is said to have been hastened by Walker's reception in 1685 into the Roman Catholic Church. When the first part of the *Paraphrase on the Epistles* came out in 1675 the intention to complete the Bible had not been given up. Prideaux wrote in December 1674: 'We are likewise printeing here a comment on the Epistles, writ by Mr. Walker, which is to be a specimen of what we designe to doe on the whole Bible, severall men haveing been formerly imployed on the worke and don a great deal in order thereto.'[3]

Walker's book is unlike the original conception of an annotated Bible in several respects. It is an octavo and the explanatory words, in Italics and enclosed by square brackets, are inserted in the text. The notes are at the foot and, like the text, are well arranged and easily legible. The preliminaries and pages 1–168 are found bound as a volume, and the remaining pages (169–349) are said by Madan to have been printed 'after a (short) interval'. In the Bodleian Catalogue this second part is dated 1678.[4] It is a rare book, perhaps put out to test the public reaction.

Though the partners were not tempted to pursue the scheme for a whole Bible, the *Epistles* had the commercial success that Walker's learning and lucidity deserved. Fell reprinted them in an improved form in 1684, two later editions were published in London and one in Oxford.

---

[1] Bodl. MS. Rawl. D. 398, fol. 127.
[2] Bodl. MS. Smith 22, fol. 81.
[3] Prideaux, p. 27.
[4] I do not know on what evidence. The accounts of the Press 1676–9 (Bodl. MS. Rawl. D. 397, fols. 403–26) have no entry for it.

Bernard's Josephus

One of the books described by Fell (in anticipation) as 'begun to be printed' early in 1672 was Josephus. An edition of the *Jewish Antiquities* and *Jewish Wars* of Flavius Josephus in the original Greek with a Latin translation had been decided on by Fell as early as 1669, when the Delegates agreed to buy the collations made for a similar purpose by 'Mounsier Peteet'.[1] Edward Bernard, fellow of St. John's College, was entrusted with the editing, and Fell arranged for the cost of printing to be borne by the University.

Bernard was elected to the chair of astronomy in 1673. He was a learned orientalist whose special interest was in the recovery of the writings of ancient Greek mathematicians, a pursuit for which his knowledge of Arabic equipped him. He made slow and intermittent progress with Josephus, on whom his annotations were copious in the extreme.

The work has a long and disappointing history.[2] Soon after it was begun it was laid aside, either as being too expensive to print or because it became known that an edition by J. A. Bose of Jena was in an advanced state of preparation. Bose died in 1678 before completing his task, and after negotiations in which Sir Leoline Jenkins took part,[3] the widow Bose sold his collections to the Oxford partners for £40, an amount which the Delegates of the Press repaid to them.[4]

Bernard set to work again and 'laboured at it a good while with the utmost vigour and resolution'. A specimen was set and issued,[5] collation of manuscripts far and wide was set in train, and Bernard wrote to scholars at home and abroad for help with his problems.[6] As he progressed and some printed sheets came from the press, critics found matter for complaint. They objected that various readings were incorrectly transcribed and that the old Latin version, by Epiphanius, was inadequate. The Delegates were horrified by the amount of copy, 'with the length of the commentaries, in which whole dissertations were inserted without

---

[1] Samuel Petit (d. 1643), orientalist, professor of Greek at Nîmes.

[2] It is told by Siwart Havercamp in the preface to his edition of Josephus (Amsterdam, 1726), basing himself on personal knowledge and the correspondence of Bernard and Robert Huntington. His account is summarized, not very clearly, in the article on Bernard in *Biographia Britannica* (1748).

[3] Bodl. MS. Smith 5, fol. 155, Job Ludolf to Bernard, 20 Mar. 1678.

[4] D.O. 17 Dec. 1678; *First Minute Book*, pp. 12–14.

[5] There is a charge in the accounts of the Press for 1678 for setting and printing two specimens of Josephus: Bodl. MS. Rawl. D. 397, fol. 409ᵛ. No copy is known.

[6] His letters in Bodl. MS. Smith 9 are almost illegible. He consulted John Pearson, Bishop of Chester, as to the lapse of time between the Flood and the birth of Abraham: MS. Smith 5, fol. 353 (1679).

any apparent necessity'. So printing was discontinued and relations between the learned editor and Fell ceased to be friendly.

The later part of the history is obscure. There was a resumption of printing before 1683, when Bernard broke off work on the book to go to Holland for the sale of Daniel Heinsius's library. Fell wrote of his 'belated exertions over Josephus' and continued, 'Lest the expectations which he has excited periodically should lead to nought, I have arranged for the Books of the *Jewish War* to go forward under new auspices, with Dr. Aldrich, a canon of our cathedral, to see them through the press.'[1] The first Book and part of the second (out of a total of seven) were printed with a title-page dated 1687.[2] It must have been to print this truncated edition that the Vice-Chancellor paid Fell a total of £244. 10*s*. in 1684-6. He also paid £189 for the paper.

Fell died in 1686, and the hope that the University would sponsor the Josephus died with him. Seven or eight years later three Oxford book-sellers persuaded Bernard to make a fresh start, and in 1694 they issued a specimen of their proposed edition, described as being in hand at the Sheldonian.[3] However, the reluctant editor could not be driven beyond the middle of the fifth of the twenty Books of the *Antiquities*, and in 1696 he died.

The fragmentary *Jewish War* printed in 1687 and what Bernard did of the *Antiquities* were combined in a volume issued with the Sheldonian imprint and dated 1700 without dedication or prefatory matter. A record in the Press Accounts for 1702 of the receipt of the University's surcharge on 25 sheets of Josephus printed for a private customer probably relates to this book and means that it was published at the expense of someone other than the University. It was a poor outcome for the work that Fell imagined.

Bernard was internationally reputed a great scholar, but he left little or nothing of value in print, unless we credit him with the catalogue of manuscripts in British libraries which goes by his name.[4] Most of his projects failed to mature.[5] The edition of Josephus by John Hudson, published by the University in 1720, makes little use of Bernard's

---

[1] Bodl. MS. d'Orville 470, p. 238, a copy of a letter to Isaac Vossius in Latin.

[2] 800 sets of the sheets were unloaded on the Company of Stationers in 1692-5: 1st Accounts, 1695.

[3] Bodl. Wood 658 (774). It is headed, 'Sciant eruditi novam Josephi editionem, secundum typum et chartam istius speciminis, jam in Seldonio adproperari, sumtibus Joh. Crosley, et Hen. Clements, et Joh. Howell bibliopolarum Oxoniensium.' Wood wrote on it that Bernard gave it him on 30 Aug. 1694.

[4] Below, p. 245.   [5] Wood, *Ath*. iv, 706-7.

apparatus; but that of Siwart Havercamp (Amsterdam, 1726) makes extensive use of it and in the preface gives him high praise.

Plot's Natural Histories of Oxfordshire and Staffordshire

'The Natural History of England was a Thing never dream'd of, till the Viscount of St. Albans (Sir Francis Bacon) began to publish his own Discoveries in Experimental Philosophy; and by his great Example and Success, set some lesser Heads a working.' This was the opinion of Bishop William Nicolson.[1] He continues:

'Twas this great Man who first observ'd to our English Philosophers, that we wanted two Parts in three of a just Natural History; which he calls *Expatiatio Naturae et Artis.* Under the former he ranks all the uncouth and uncommon Occurrences in Simple Nature; and under the other, her several Modifications (and the many useful and instructive Discoveries that are made of her) in Arts Mechanical.

One of the 'lesser Heads' was that of Robert Plot, D.C.L., Vice-Principal of Magdalen Hall, who later became Curator of the Museum presented to the University by Elias Ashmole, and a Fellow of the Royal Society.[2] He embarked on a natural history of England and Wales and achieved a volume on Oxfordshire and another on Staffordshire, both printed at Fell's press, the one in 1677, the other in 1686. He went on to collect material for Middlesex and Kent, but did not persevere with his scheme.

He proposed his idea to Fell in a letter:

The Design in general is a Journey through England and Wales, for the Promotion of Learning and Trade, which indeed are the Things chiefly aim'd at. But beside these of Profit there are others of Pleasure that fall within the Verge of this Design, intending in the same Journey to make a strict Inquiry after all Curiosities both of Art and Nature, such I mean as transcend the ordinary Performances of the one, and are out of the ordinary Road of the other . . .[3]

He quotes Bacon often and conforms to a great extent with his prescription, with a bias towards the uncouth and monstrous. His science is mixed with a great deal of folklore. He gives in *Oxfordshire* an excellent history of natural and experimental science in the University from Roger

[1] *English Historical Library*, 3rd ed. (1736), p. 7.
[2] Gunther, *Early Science in Oxford*, xii (Oxford, 1939), pp. 333–418.
[3] Ibid., p. 336 (Bodl. MS. Jones 19(12), dated by the Bodleian in 1670).

Bacon to John Wallis, Christopher Wren, and Halley; but in spite of his knowledge of the astronomy, physics, and chemistry of an élite, he shares many of the beliefs of the ordinary man. He accepts that the weather is affected by the planets, that little frogs and caterpillars fall with rain, that live toads are found embedded in stones, that fossil teeth of fishes cure cramp, and the flowing of an intermittent bourne (or 'vips') presages woe.

The two volumes are consequently the most readable of all that Fell printed. Plot travelled indefatigably and observed carefully, reporting much that is good history. He liked to rely on his own perceptions ('I had then the curiosity to go see myself, which otherwise, perhaps, I should have as hardly credited as some other persons now may do'), but he links what he saw with what he had read in the writings of philosophers from Aristotle onwards and with reports of other observers. He was well read and evidently affable. Even when the second-hand information strains his credulity, he thinks it worth reporting; as that fairy rings in turf were caused by witches dancing in a circle backwards, though he prefers to believe that lightning causes them. For him, moreover, the Old Testament is final authority: he will not have Ray's theory that all water reaches the earth as precipitation from above because it conflicts with the Book of Genesis.

The books were intended for issue to subscribers, of whom landowners were the most likely; so the books pay sufficient, though not disproportionate, attention to gentlemen's houses and are provided with maps on which they can easily be found. Plot claims that his maps of the two counties are the most detailed yet made, and made from his own surveys. The seats of liberal subscribers are depicted in folding plates of considerable charm drawn and engraved by Michael Burghers. Other plates show phenomena in the heavens, remarkable landscapes, fossils, plants, monsters, and man-made engines closely observed and rendered with great skill by Burghers with his burin.

The volumes are folio: of *Oxfordshire* 700 were printed 'upon the worst fools cap and 50 upon the best flour deluce' (Demy).[1] It was sold at the Press and by Simon Miller in London for 9s., to subscribers 8s. It was reprinted with additions by the author at Oxford in 1705 by Leonard Lichfield for the booksellers.

There is a prospectus for *Staffordshire*.[2]

---

[1] Bodl. MS. Rawl. D. 397, fol. 426.
[2] B.M. MS. Sloane 1039, fol. 136.

FELL'S NEW-YEAR BOOKS

It was a pleasant habit of the Dean's to print every year a book to be given to the young men of Christ Church and to his friends on 1 January. They were plain texts of works hard to come by that would be useful to students of theology (Pachymeres, Clement I (the Pope), Nemesius, Faustinus, Cyprian) or of the classics (Alcinous, Epictetus, Theocritus, Pliny), while not of great bulk.

In the Latin preface to his gift book for 1669, the (first) *Epistle of St. Clement to the Corinthians*, he explains his motive for adopting this anniversary habit. At the onset of each new year, he says, the young men of the House observed a solemn custom of thronging his doorstep to vie in good wishes and congratulations, and he was ashamed in return to have to extend an empty hand and be worsted in a contest of giving. Though he would always yield to any man where brains, learning, eloquence, riches, or rank were concerned, he could not bear to be beaten for feelings of good will and the offices of friendship. So, as Annus bent with age and made ready to join up with himself, he (Fell) was obliged to look out for an author to put in print, as he regularly did, and was able with his aid to requite good wishes and letters with thanks and a little book.

He was modest about the quality of the books: 'My yearly Trifles are designed either to my friends who will not see faults, or my young people who can not.'[1] Dean, Vice-Chancellor 1666–9, Bishop after 1676, Fell had not much time to give to editing; it is not surprising that the texts were taken, often unamended, from printed copy and annotation was slight— still less surprising that the printing shows signs of haste.

The series goes back to an origin in 1666 and extends to 1686, the year of Fell's death. The list of New-Year Books as tentatively constructed by Falconer Madan,[2] has blanks for 1668 and 1673 and uncertainty about three other years.[3] Of the Faustinus of 1678 only 250 were printed,[4] but the edition of Theocritus (1676) was 500,[5] perhaps leaving some for sale. Copies of Cornelius Nepos (1675) were certainly sold.[6]

---

[1] S.P. (Dom.), Car. II, 272, No. 79.   [2] *Oxford Books*, iii, p. 521.
[3] J. S. G. Simmons gives reasons for preferring, of Madan's alternatives Lactantius to Epictetus for 1680 and the same author to Theophilus for 1684: Morison, *Fell*, pp. 221, 223.
[4] Bodl. MS. Rawl. D. 397, fol. 403ᵛ.
[5] Ibid., fol. 423.   [6] Bodl. MS. Rawl. D. 398, fol. 159.

CHAPTER VIII

The Beginning of the Bible Press

THE SUB-LEASE OF THE PRIVILEGE FOR BIBLES

WHILE Fell and Yate were publishing these and other worthwhile books they were made increasingly aware of the difficulty of selling them. Prospectuses issued in 1675 and 1676 (probably)[1] proclaim to the learned world that unless more subscriptions were received, the partners' 'readiness to serve the public, and answer the desires of the friends of Learning' would be frustrated; 'it will be impossible to support the charge of such an attemt, and carry it on with vigour and success.' Therefore, on behalf of the undertakers of the Press at Oxford, the prospectuses promised that 'whatever Book shall be desired to be publisht, of whatsoever Subject or Language, upon the assurance that when tis finisht, 500 copies will be taken off, shall be printed'.

It is not surprising that no one rose to the bait. It meant in effect finding a publisher willing to employ Fell as general editor and printer while relieving him of the burden of finding subscribers and collecting their money. There were publishers enough who could get learned books printed if they foresaw a sale for them. The prospectuses are eloquent of a serious state of affairs.

The obstacle to success, as Fell saw it, was combination among booksellers against him. 'Booksellers', according to the second of these appeals, 'thinking it not their interest to prefer and forward the Sale of any Book, beside their own and fellow Traders; no Edition of the said Undertakers, of a just Volume, or large Book, will ever be sold by them.' In other words, the London booksellers were members of the Stationers' Company and had shares in its English Stock.

Fell had come to a composition with the Company in 1675 promising in return for £100 a year not to compete with it by printing school books, almanacs (excepting a sheet almanac), or metrical psalms (excepting such as were needed to go with his Bibles).[2] The agreement was

---

[1] Morison, *Fell*, App. v, Nos. 2 and 3; Madan, *Oxford Books*, Nos. 3069, 3117. The second is reproduced in *Print and Privilege*, facing pp. 84, 85.　　　　[2] See above, p. 73.

due to expire on Lady Day 1678. Bibles were left outside this bargain, to which the patentees, the King's Printers, were not party; they had ceased after 1672 to buy the University's forbearance, 'presuming the University had not Stock enough to Comprint Bibles with them'.[1] In the mean time the experience of producing one Bible in 1675 had taught the Oxford partners that this was true: they lacked resources enough to compete in that market. The King's Printers could undersell a particular Oxford Bible and recoup their loss by raising the prices of editions in other formats.[2]

When his compact with the Stationers was coming to an end Fell tried to induce them as a premium for its renewal to buy his unsold stock for £3,800.[3] That they declined to do, and Fell put the same proposition to Moses Pitt.

Pitt had gained his freedom of London from the Haberdashers' Company, but had traded since 1669 as a bookseller and publisher, as the custom of the City permitted. He dealt in Latin books imported from abroad, and by 1678 he had published works by Oxford scholars, John Wallis and Thomas Gale. There is no evidence to show how his collaboration with Fell and Yate began. He issued proposals in 1678 for publishing under royal patronage an atlas of the world in eleven volumes which would outdo in splendour the atlases of Blaeu and Jansson.[4] From the first the project had associations with Oxford: Fell, Yate, Jenkins, Wallis, and Obadiah Walker were among the original subscribers, and security for the performance of Pitt's promises had been given to Sir Joseph Williamson. The proposals were followed by an announcement that the volumes would be printed at the Theatre in Oxford, and in 1680 a leaflet invited the payment of subscriptions to Dr. Yate, Principal of Brasenose College.

Whether the plans for this giant atlas preceded negotiations for a sublease of the privilege of printing or followed them must be left uncertain. Pitt put it on record that he paid the £3,800 for the partners' printed stock,[5] and on 26 September 1678 he and three other London booksellers signed a counterpart lease from Fell, Williamson, Jenkins, and Yate of the University's right 'to print and comprint all Bookes which by any Letters Pattents have bin graunted to . . . the Stationers of the Citty of London, unto the King's Printer, or to Roger Norton'.[6] It was a sublease of the privilege to last for three years at a rent of £200 a year.

1 Parker and Guy's Case: Bodl. MS. Ballard 49, fol. 237.
2 B.M. MS. Add. 36081, fols. 186–92.   3 Blagden, p. 197.
4 Bodl. Wood 658 (791, 795).
5 Letter from Parker to Fell, 1684: Univ. Arch. S.E.P. P15, fol. 17.
6 Madan, Oxford Books, iii, pp. 418–21.

Writing in 1691 John Wallis remembered that the original intention was to grant the sublease to Pitt and one other bookseller, 'but finding these not enough to do the work, they further took in Mr. Parker and Mr. Guy.'[1] Doubtless the other bookseller was William Leake, the fourth member of this syndicate. Leake had been selling and publishing books since 1635; he was a Stationer and had a share in the English Stock. Peter Parker and Thomas Guy, founder of Guy's Hospital, were also Stationers.

In joining with Fell and his partners in a total defiance of the mono-polists of printing the four sublessees were not necessarily actuated by malice against the Company of Stationers. They readily agreed with the Company to forbear printing the books covered by its patents in return for an initial fine of £200 and a yearly payment of £100.[2] The Stationers undertook to supply the Oxford sublessees with metrical psalms to be sold with their Bibles.

This new alliance of Oxford academics with London booksellers was for war with the King's Printers. Fell, who had never resisted an accom-modation with the Stationers, said that the King's Printers 'had alwaies put us at defiance'.[3] The sublessees also may well have had a grudge against the Bible-patentees, who had prosecuted Pitt and Parker for dealing in Bibles smuggled in from Holland.[4] Guy is said to have done big business in this illicit merchandise and to have adopted the un-amiable practice of buying up quantities of Dutch Bibles which the patentees had seized and selling them to retailers, who ran the risk of a second seizure and prosecution. There is reason to think that he acted in collusion with the Stationers' court.[5]

It is likely enough that about 1678 business in smuggled Bibles was becoming unprofitable, owing to improved methods of the Customs and the King's Printers for stopping it, and the four sublessees had seen in the University's privilege their best hope of continuing a lucrative specialized trade. There was room for more than one Bible-printer.

The real importance of the sublease is that it founded the Oxford Bible Press. It was a scion that soon overshadowed the stock, leaving Fell's

---

[1] 'A Copy of the Account, which Dr. Wallis gave to Dr. Bernard' (concerning the business of printing), printed in *Philosophical Experiments of Robert Hooke* (1726), pp. 217–24. A manu-script copy is Bodl. MS. Ballard 49, fol. 243; another was listed and printed in Maggs Bros. Catalogue No. 509 (1928), No. 252. Neither is in Wallis's handwriting. It is also printed, from the Bodleian MS., in *First Minute Book*, pp. xx–xxv.
[2] Blagden, p. 197.   [3] Univ. Arch. S.E.P. P15, fol. 51.
[4] Ibid. P16(11); printed in *Print and Privilege*, pp. 78–9.   [5] Ibid.

learned imprimery far behind in the volume and commercial value of its production, and for two hundred years to come it was to be the dominant part of the University's business in publishing and printing.

For Fell the great inducement to the delegation of Bible-printing to outsiders, whose motives must have been distasteful to him, was that it relieved him of his unsold books and promised help with sales in the future. Pitt told Peter Parker 'that such a day hee bought a parcell of Bookes above £3,800 worth and contracted for the privilege which would not be granted without his buying the bookes'.[1] John Wallis recollected that Fell and Yate 'found it necessary to take in with them some London Booksellers, as well for the better vending of Books, which did already lie upon their Hands, as for the Increase of their Stock, that they might be in a Capacity to print in other volumes also' (i.e. reprint their books in cheaper formats).[2]

On 24 February 1679 Moses Pitt held an auction in London at which he offered thirty Oxford-printed books in quantity. Among them were Fell's Bible and Book of Common Prayer of 1675, Wood's *Historia*, the *Marmora*, Hyde's *Catalogus* of Bodleian printed books, and Plot's *Oxfordshire*.[3] In 1678 three new Sheldonian editions, Spelman's *Life of Alfred*, the Psalter from *Codex Alexandrinus*, and Gale's Iamblichus, were advertised in the Term Catalogue as sold by Pitt. Duty of Man's *Lively Oracles*, printed at Oxford, were advertised as sold by Pitt, Leake, Parker, and Guy. In 1679 Pitt began advertising the *Oxford Almanack*. Promotion of this kind encouraged Fell and Yate to put out a series of the classics in pocket formats, many of them Fell's New-Year books with minor emendations, in impressions of 1,000. In 1678 Parker and Guy announced ten of these as 'School-Books printed at the Theatre in Oxford' available at their shops in London.[4]

The Londoners occupied the Sheldonian Theatre, where they were bound by the terms of their lease to keep four presses at work. The

[1] Univ. Arch. S.E.P. P15, fol. 17.
[2] Letter to Bernard cited on p. 95, p. 220 of *Philosophical Experiments*, etc.
[3] Madan, *Oxford Books*, iii, No. 3202.
[4] On p. 279 of an edition of Bond's Horace (1678): Bodl. Auct. Jur. III 79. Some, I suspect, are reprints not separately noticed by Madan. The books, with relevant numbers in *Oxford Books* were:

Pliny, *Epistolae et Panegyricus*, 3156   Sallust, 3195
Homer's Iliads in Greek, 3109   Justinus, 3014
Theocritus in Greek, 3124   Cornelius Nepos, 3066
Herodian, Greek and Latin, 3177   Quintilian, 3073
Tho. Lydiat, *Canones*, 3064   Maximus of Tyre, 3146

Such, and so great, was the literacy of the schoolboys.

earliest of their editions was a Bible in quarto dated 1679 with the prayers and metrical psalms to match.[1] A New Testament in Latin was printed for them at Fell's press in the same year. The King's Printers acted promptly: they brought the matter before the King in Council on 19 December by a petition alleging that the Bible was really an octavo, or could be trimmed to the size of one, therefore it contravened the Order in Council of March 1636; further, that the University had no right to print the Testament alone. They averred moreover that 'several Booksellers of London having undertaken the Oxford Presse' had in hand 'an Impression of near 30,000 (as the Petitioners are informed) of the New Testament in 12mo. to sell apart also'. The King was willing to hear the complaint argued in the January following and directed that the Vice-Chancellor of Oxford should be represented.

At the deferred hearing counsel for the petitioners argued, among other things, that the undertakers at Oxford, who had only a short lease, 'do in this Time print such vast Numbers, as that, if the University should be found to have a Right, it would be hereby made uselesse to them, as well as to His Majesty's Printers; for so many would be printed in this Time, that there would be no Occasion of printing any more in this Age, at least not these twenty Years.' The King dismissed the suit, finding the issues too complicated to be settled at the Council board and advising the parties to refer their differences to a court of law.[2]

These proceedings were enough to bring to light a weakness in Fell's armament against the monopolists: that litigation, even defensive, even successful, is costly. Resistance to the petition, Wallis wrote, 'put us to 2 or 300l. Charges; which was born partly by the University, partly by the Bishop, and partly by our printers'.[3] There was reason to fear worse to come.

It was five years later when the King's Printers took the dispute to court, this time to the Court of Chancery. Meanwhile they did their utmost to ruin the Oxford Bible Press by underselling. 'Their next attempt', Wallis wrote, 'was, the setting of a Multitude of Presses to Work, to print vast Numbers off, and by selling them cheap, to break our Printers; so that the Contest was, whether should print most, and sell cheapest; whereby the Price of Bibles, for the Advantage of the Publick, was brought down to less than Half of what they were before sold at; and

---

[1] Madan, *Oxford Books*, iii, No. 3243.
[2] 'An Account of the Hearing at the Council Table, 16 January 1679/80': Reg. Conv. Tb, at the end of the book.
[3] Letter to Bernard, printed in Hooke's *Philosophical Experiments*, at p. 220.

many hundreds of Thousands of Bibles, printed and sold, more than otherwise would have been; and our People at home, and abroad in our Plantations, furnished from hence, which before were wont to be furnished in vast Numbers from Holland.'[1] Fell wrote a memorandum on 'The State of Bible Printing' in 1684, giving the effect of the struggle on prices: folio Bibles were reduced from £6 to £1. 10s. and others in proportion, so that the smallest could be had for 1s. 4d.; and he adds, 'very many well disposed persons have laid out considerable sums of money for great quantities of Books, to be distributed in Charity to the poor.'[2]

Of the four sublessees Leake died and Pitt withdrew his active support in 1683, leaving Parker and Guy to compete with the King's Printers and ward off their attacks. From the first they printed Bibles and Testaments and prayer books in all sizes, disregarding the Order in Council of 1636 restricting the Universities to two. 'The matter in dispute', Fell told Archbishop Sancroft in 1679, 'is the right of printing Bibles in small forms; wherein if we are justified, the advantage will extend to our Sister University; and indeed to the whole Nation.'[3] By 1682 the Oxford printers were ready to offer Bibles in five sizes with prayers and metrical psalms to bind with them.

Rehearsing their services to the University in 1685, Parker and Guy affirmed that they and Moses Pitt had taken off the hands of Fell and Yate books 'to the vallue of £5,000 and expended £3,000 in materials for Bible printing. With this Strugling and with these Expenses the University were established in a Condition to print Bibles.'[4] If the figures are exaggerated, the last sentence is true: Parker and Guy made Oxford Bibles a widely known and honoured commodity.

Their Bible Press from about 1683 onwards must have been the biggest printing-office in the kingdom. They were reticent about the number of their presses when challenged to disclose it in the Chancery proceedings before the Lord Keeper in 1684. They did not like Pitt's putting in writing his belief that 'there were sometimes 4 6 8 9 presses imployed in the Theatre which last hee knew to be false and I fear yt will lye hard upon us as any thing the number of presses before my Lord Keeper.'[5] It is unlikely that the King's Printers, who in 1668 had six

[1] Letter to Bernard, p. 221.

[2] Printed in J. Gutch, *Collectanea curiosa* (Oxford, 1781), i, pp. 269–70. Fell sent a copy to Jenkins, P.R.O. S.P. (Dom.), Car. II, 438, No. 12.

[3] Gutch, *Collectanea curiosa*, i, p. 270.

[4] Parker and Guy's case: Bodl. MS. Ballard 49, fol. 237.

[5] Parker's letter to Fell: Univ. Arch. S.E.P. P15, fol. 17.

presses,[1] were as largely equipped; but unlike the Universities, they were allowed by their patent to put their Bible work out to other master printers, so they had all the London trade at their service. In answer to the King's Printers' bill of complaint to the Lord Keeper the University confessed to there being 13 presses and 2 proof presses in Oxford;[2] but how these were apportioned between the Bible Press, Fell's learned press, and Leonard Lichfield, master printer, there is no means of telling.

THE STRUGGLE FOR SURVIVAL OF THE BIBLE PRESS

The arrangement of 1675 between the Company of Stationers and its two members at Oxford secured a truce until Henry Hills became Upper Warden of the Company in 1684, and in the usual absence in the country of the Master, Roger Norton, was the chief power in their court.[3] Hills was likewise the dominant partner in the business of King's Printer;[4] therefore he was able to drag the Stationers into battle against Oxford in the interests of his trade in Bibles.

Hills caused the Treasurer of the English Stock to put difficulties and delays in the way of deliveries of the metrical psalms to Parker and Guy,[5] who, in consequence, printed a large number themselves and put them on general sale. It was strong provocation of the Stationers to trespass on their monopoly of the 'Singing Psalms', and after Midsummer 1684 they discontinued paying the rent for forbearance.[6] Fell disapproved of the action of his sublessees: 'It looks a little foul', he wrote to Wallis, 'that when the Stationers were at an agreement with them at a rent not to comprint their books, yet to print their Psalms.'[7]

Neither side got any benefit from litigation. At a hearing of the Chancery suit on 24 November 1684, Lord Keeper North decided that the validity of the patents on which both parties relied must be tried at common law, and he refused any relief to the King's Printers in the mean time.[8] He was of opinion 'that it was never meant by the patent to the University, that They should print more than for their own Use, or at least but some small Number more, to compensate their Charge'. John

---

[1] S.P. (Dom.), Car. II, 243, No. 181.
[2] Reg. Conv. Bb, p. 30. An estimate of 15 presses is in the Stationers' records: Liber F, 23 June 1687.
[3] Blagden, p. 171.
[4] R. L. Haig, 'New Light on the King's Printing Office 1680–1730', *Studies in Bibliography*, viii (Charlottesville, 1956), pp. 157–67.
[5] Blagden, p. 197.   [6] Reg. Conv. Bb, p. 86.
[7] Univ. Arch. S.E.P. P15, fol. 25.   [8] 1 Vernon's Reports, p. 274.

Wallis thought 'the Lord Keeper North bore very hardly upon us (and was afterwards convinced that he had done so).'[1]

A month or two later, in Hilary term 1685, two actions in the Kings Bench against Parker and Guy came on for hearing, one in the name of the King's Printers, the other in that of the Company of Stationers. The brief report of the case[2] throws light on the privilege as lawyers saw it at that time. Nobody doubted that the royal prerogative, unsupported by Act of Parliament, extended to controlling printing and granting monopolies of it. Fell had noted of the Chancery suit, 'my lord keeper was glad to see that we claimed under the kings patent, and did not affront his prerogative';[3] and he described the gist of the action in the King's Bench neatly: 'The issue between the King's Printers and us seems plain and short: whither the king by granting to some Persons a power to print, abridges himself of liberty to grant the like power to others.'[4] Before the King's Bench it was argued that in the event of two exclusive grants of the same thing the earlier alone should prevail if the thing were an interest, but not if it were an office. If the king conferred an office, he might afterwards curtail or abolish it. The court was disposed to favour Parker and Guy, but because of an earlier decision in *The Company of Stationers* v. *Seymour*[5] felt obliged to hear further argument.

The case was never decided; it was adjourned many times and still pending in 1691, when events rendered it out of date.

To strengthen the defences of Parker and Guy in these court proceedings it was thought advisable to make them employees of the University. To do this effectively in time for their answer to the bill of complaint preferred against them in Chancery in April 1684 meant telling a deliberate lie. In Convocation on 11 July the University's seal was put on a deed of appointment dated 27 March of that year, reciting that Parker and Guy had been servants of the University for five years past.[6]

---

[1] Letter to Bernard, in Hooke's *Philosophical Experiments*, p. 221.
[2] (1685) Skinner's Reports, p. 233.
[3] Univ. Arch. S.E.P. P15, fol. 18.
[4] Ibid.
[5] (1677) 1 Modern Reports, p. 256. It was regarded by the judges in the action against Parker and Guy as a 'hard case'. Seymour had a patent from Charles II for the sole printing during 41 years of 'all Almanacks . . . whose Originalls the said John Seymour or his executors or assignes shall purchase or otherwise obtayne . . . during the said terme from the respective Authors'. The Company pleaded that an almanac printed for Seymour infringed their earlier patent for all almanacs. A jury found that Seymour's book did not differ from the almanac in the Book of Common Prayer. Judgement was given for the plaintiffs. The reasoning does not appear.
[6] Reg. Conv. Bb, p. 42; *Print and Privilege*, pp. 92–4.

To this double deception Fell, the Bishop, was privy, though at first he opposed it.

By consenting to this appointment Fell did not resign his interest in the University's privilege of printing: Parker and Guy were thenceforth servants and printers of the University but still lessees of Fell, Jenkins, and Williamson (Yate died on 22 April 1681). The bishop, as always, was ready for an amicable settlement with the Stationers, but he would not consent to exclusion from printing the Bible. When Hills came to Oxford in April 1685 and proposed a treaty of forbearance with the King's Printers as well as the Company of Stationers, Fell countered with a suggestion that he should retire from dealings with the Stationers, leaving them to treat directly with the University. As for agreeing not to comprint Bibles, he would not hear of it. 'And so they are gon with a bravado, of being sure to carry every thing by Law.'[1]

In spite of his professed confidence Hills did not carry the Stationers with him. Fell's suggestion was adopted, and on 30 September 1685 an agreement was sealed between the Chancellor, Masters, and Scholars and the Worshipful Company of Stationers. The University in return for a rent of £160 promised to forgo for three years the printing of books named in a schedule, being for the most part school books, but also the metrical psalms and almanacs. There was an exception for the benefit of the University of the Oxford Almanack and editions of Latin and Greek classics with annotations or variant readings not adapted for use in school. As for the Singing Psalms, the Stationers undertook to supply the University with copies at the prices they charged to the King's Printers whenever they were asked to do so by Fell or by the Vice-Chancellor for the time being.[2] By a separate agreement of even date Fell and his partners, in consideration of the privilege of printing Bibles, covenanted to make the sum due for forbearance up to the customary £200.[3]

Fell departed this life on 10 July 1686.[4] By his will he directed his executors to apply the stock of the partnership in printing for the service of the University, and to cede to it after four years all his typefounding equipment of punches, matrices, and moulds, if in the mean time they were satisfied that 'the interests of learning and printing were encouraged in the said University'.[5] A lease of the University's privilege of printing

[1] Univ. Arch. S.E.P. P15, fol. 30.
[2] Stationers' records, Serial No. 338, Univ. Arch. S.E.P. 8 (16); Reg. Conv. Bb, p. 104.
[3] Reg. Conv., as above; S.E.P. P8(17).
[4] Newdigate Papers B413.
[5] A certified copy is in the University Archives.

was granted to the executors when the last lease to Fell expired in 1688,[1] and Parker and Guy attorned tenants to them at a rent of £60 a year.[2]

Hills did not cease to harry the Oxford Bible-printers by delaying deliveries of the metrical psalms. Losing faith in his constantly deferred action at law to stem the growing output of their presses, he instigated a prosecution of the University by a writ of *Quo warranto*, a dreaded proceeding which would put the Chancellor, Masters, and Scholars at the great expense and trouble of strictly proving their grant of the right to print and comprint and its legality. Rather than face it several corporations had compromised with King James by allowing him to remove persons hostile to him from their boards and put in their places men of his choice. In his petition to the king in the name of the Stationers' Company of 29 April 1688, designed to promote the prosecution, Hills based himself on public policy: there were too many men brought up to the trade of printing to be needed for lawful work; hence the profusion of scandalous books and leaflets which so exercised the government. The Stationers' Company, he affirmed, was doing its best with much success to control the printers in London, but it had difficulty in stopping irregularities in remoter places. He mentioned York, and continued:

> That Guy and Parker, the present Farmers of the Priviledges, in this point, of the University of Oxford, have assumed to themselves a Liberty to erect and imploy many more printing Presses than are granted to them by the letters Pattents of the said University: And, for a supply to this Irregularity, they constantly breed up, or which is worse suffer their Journeymen to breed up, many more Apprentices, than by their Priviledges they are allowed to doe.
>
> That Except this deluge of Workmen be stopt, it will be very difficult, if not impossible for us to do his Majestie that service we earnestly desire.
>
> The said Master and Wardens therefore humbly pray, That your Majestie would be graciously pleased, to give them leave in Your Majesties name to take such course to Redress their Exorbitances, both in York Oxford and elsewhere, as the Law directs, and according to such Methodes as your Majesties Attorney, Or Solicitor General shall advise.[3]

Guy and Parker were positive that 'fowerteen of the Principal men of their Company attended at the Attorney-General's Chamber in the Prosecution of the Quo Warranto';[4] and Wallis, probably relying on their

---

[1] The counterpart, signed by the executors, is, strangely, in the custody of the Stationers' Company (Serial No. 343). Dated 26 Apr. 1688.
[2] Ibid.   [3] Univ. Arch. S.P.D., fasc. 3(12).
[4] Bodl. MS. Ballard 49, fol. 237ᵛ.

word, wrote that 'a Plate of 500 Guineas went one Way, and a Tun of Wine another Way; and £300 allowed to Henry Hill upon his Account, for secret Service.'[1] Mr. Attorney addressed to the king an opinion pointing out the weaknesses in the University's position, if it were taken to court.

Peter Parker and Thomas Guy who are two of their Printers, though they have taken houses in Oxford, yet are really and truly inhabitants of London and not of Oxford as they ought to be And that they now imploy eleven Presses there And about fourty eight Apprentices and workmen. I do not find that any particular mischiefe hath happened from thence save only the Company of Stationers in London are dampnified thereby And though it doth not appear to me that any seditious or scandalous pamphlets are printed there, but that the Vice Chancellor is very carefull to prevent the same: yet the breedinge of such number of persons to print is contrary to the intention and design of the Statute for Regulating Printing[2] and is no way warranted by the Grants aforesaid; but may prove a forfeiture of their Priviledge of appointing and licensing Printers in case your Majestie should impeach that Priviledge in a Quo Warranto.[3]

The summons was served on the Vice-Chancellor on 13 June. The prospect was at best of a prolonged lawsuit in which all the privileges of the University would be investigated. Many would be attacked by the corporation of the city of Oxford; that of printing in particular would face an Attorney-General who had asserted an unfavourable view of it, backed by two wealthy and powerful interests. At worst this privilege would be found unlawful or confined, as Lord Keeper North would have had it, to a private press printing small editions to supply academic needs.

The Prince of Orange put an end to the uncertainty and left the University secure in the possession of a source of revenue enough to keep its learned and educational publishing solvent. The prosecution due to open on 25 October was withdrawn by a general pardon announced on the 3rd of that month. The Prince's *Declaration* was received in London on 29 September.

The new reign brought relief but not peace to the Bible Press. Henry Hills, once an Anabaptist and Printer to His Highness the Lord Protector, King's Printer to Charles II, turned Roman Catholic and King's Printer to James II, was voted out of office in the Stationers' Company and died in

---

[1] Letter to Bernard, 1691, in Hooke's *Philosophical Experiments*, p. 222.
[2] The current re-enactment of the Licensing Act of 1662 (13 & 14 Car. II, c. 33). It was renewed periodically until 1695, with an interval in 1675-9.
[3] From a copy in Univ. Arch. S.P.D., fasc. 3 (4).

exile. The Stationers, none the less, nursed a grievance against Parker and Guy for comprinting some of their books after they had withheld the rent for forbearance during five quarters. For this they demanded reparation, and in December 1688 they filed a bill in Chancery seeking an account of their scheduled books printed at Oxford since the agreement of 1685 and a renewal of the agreement. They complained that the Oxford printers had 'for several months past printed or caused to be printed many hundred thousand Psalms in metre in several sizes' and other scheduled books and almanacs.[1]

Nevertheless talks continued, and the Stationers were disposed to be reasonable. They offered a deed of release of their claims against the University and its printers in March 1689, reserving only their right to a renewal of a covenant not to print their books, as the agreement of 1685 had promised. Articles to this effect were sealed on 6 March, and dated back to 30 September 1688.[2]

In September 1685 Fell had reserved to himself for three years the right to use the University's privilege of printing Bibles, grammars, and books not covered by the Stationers' patents.[3] A like grant was made to his executors in 1688.[4] Parker and Guy had their appointment as Printers to the University renewed in August of that year for an indefinite time (*quamdiu nobis placuerit*).[5] In return they advanced to the Vice-Chancellor the £240 owed by the Stationers as arrears of forbearance money. They had spent between them more than £450 on defending court proceedings, to which sum their co-defendants, the University, ought to have contributed.[6]

From such generosity of its tenants it is fair to conclude that the Bible Press was doing good business. In 1691 it was revealed that the Vice-Chancellor and Delegates of the Press had given permission for 40,000 small Bibles, 1,500 prayer books, 1,000 folio Bibles, and 40,000 Testaments for Ireland to be printed.[7]

It is not now easy to find the Oxford-printed books by which the Stationers were aggrieved. Oxford Bibles of the period with which the metrical psalms are bound are generally folio or quarto, and in these formats the University had an agreed right to print them. The British

[1] P.R.O., Chancery Proceedings, Mitford's Div., 351, No. 160; R. L. Steele, 'The Oxford University Press and the Stationers' Company', *The Library*, 3rd ser. iii (1912), pp. 104–12.
[2] Univ. Arch. S.E.P. P14ᵇ; Stationers' records, Serial No. 344.
[3] Reg. Conv. Bb, p. 104; S.E.P. P8(17).   [4] See above, p. 102.
[5] Reg. Conv. Bb, p. 215.
[6] Bodl. MS. Ballard 49, fols. 237ᵛ–238.   [7] Ibid., fol. 234.

Museum and the Bodleian between them can muster one 12mo edition of the Singing Psalms printed here, and one 24to. The enormous quantities of which the patentees complained must have gone among the wastes of Time. However, Parker and Guy did print two almanacs for 1689, Partridge's and Pond's, of which copies are known.

The leases and agreements affecting the University's printing were due to expire in September 1691. The question whether to leave Bible-printing in charge of Parker and Guy had been canvassed in the colleges for a year or more and aroused strong feelings.[1] What were the grounds for a division of opinion is not easily found out: for that time there are not even minutes of the Delegates of the Press. It is clear that on the one hand the Vice-Chancellor elected in 1688, Jonathan Edwards, was a determined opponent of the sitting tenants and favoured an approach from the Stationers proposing to take the King's Printers under their wing and add Bibles to the privileged books let to the Company, for which they would pay a rent of £200. Of the other party John Wallis, Savilian professor and Keeper of the Archives, was a firm and outspoken supporter. Asked by the Delegates for a state of the question in June 1691, he wrote the memorandum quoted several times above and ended it: 'I do not know that Parker and Guy (who are now your Printers) have ever failed in paying you to a Penny whatever they promised. Nor do I find that the Company do charge them to have ever failed in any Agreement tho' but Verbal.'[2]

To a great extent the two Bible-printers put down their eventual defeat to the appointment in 1691 of a new Delegacy of the Press. Of original members of the one appointed in 1662 Fell was the last survivor; and since he died the board had been attended by men added in recent years, Halton, Jane, Aldrich, and Mill, the Testament scholar. The Delegacy as reconstituted took in these, excepting Mill who retired, and four more. Of the new Delegacy Edwards was able to persuade four to his purpose;[3] so the Stationers' tender for the whole of the privilege, including Bibles, was accepted.

It was a very tempting offer, holding out a great hope of rescuing the learned press from its chronic inability to sell off its output. It was made to the Delegates by three prominent Stationers, Ambrose Isted, Master of the Company, Henry Mortlock, a Warden, and John Bellinger, a

[1] *Print and Privilege*, pp. 117 ff.
[2] As printed in *Philosophical Experiments of Robert Hooke*, p. 224.
[3] Bodl. MS. Ballard 49, fol. 238.

past-Master, personally, for fear lest the Company, as a corporation, might have unpleasant associations for Oxford. The King's Printers, *a fortiori*, were not mentioned. A contemporary note of the heads of agreement is the following:

1. They [the three Stationers] shall pay to the University the Annual Rent of £200 as formerly.

2. They shall take off the Stock of Books now by them, a Catalogue of which is made, and the Prices agreed to; and take off what Books shall be printed at the Charge of the University, not exceeding 500 of a sort, at a fifth part clear profit to the University.

3. To Collect and send to Oxford-library, what Books are, or shall be, due to them by vertue of two Acts of Parliament, without any Charge.[1]

4. To keep up the Printing of Bibles, Common Prayer &c.: in the Precincts of Oxford, Prices to be set by the Vice-Chancellor and Delegates.

5. To Indemnify the University, and the late Bishop Fell's Executors, from any Suit that is or shall be commenced against them touching Printing, either by the King's Printers, Stationers' Company, or any other person or persons; and such Suits to be maintained at the Charge of the Persons agreeing.

6. Not to transfer the Right of Printing Books here, either in part or in whole, to any Company or person, without leave first had under the Common-Seale.

7. To indemnify and save harmless, the University, and the said Bishops Executors, from a Debt of £240 claimed by Mr. P: and G. and from another Debt claim'd by them of £250: they say to have expended in Law-Suits.[2]

Counter-proposals from Parker and Guy were only a little less large. Instead of the Stationers' undertaking to buy the surplus stock of learned books and sell whole editions in future (which proved impossible of performance) Parker and Guy 'do hope in a few Months time to put our Affairs in such posture that we may dispose of Books to the Universitys Content'.[3] For the rest, they would write off claims against the University for expenses in defending lawsuits.

The decision to conclude an agreement with the three Stationers acting for their Company appears to have been taken by the Delegates at a meeting early in October 1691.[4] Whether formal notice to quit was

[1] The allusion, as the subsequent deed shows, is to s. 17 of the Licensing Act, 1662, and one of its re-enactments.

[2] Bodl. MS. Ballard 49, fol. 195ᵛ.   [3] Ibid., fol. 196.

[4] Ibid., fol. 238; *Print and Privilege*, p. 127.

given to Parker and Guy is not reported;[1] but on 12 October Jonathan Edwards, the Vice-Chancellor, with a bedel, John Hall, the printer, and a carpenter went to the Theatre and took four presses to pieces and removed them.[2] They were forcibly resisted, and, if contemporary report can be believed, not even the Vice-Chancellor's person was inviolate. Again, on 23 December Edwards and Henry Aldrich, Curators of the Theatre, went and ordered the printers to cease working there on pain

Bocardo, the old north gate of the city. The room over it was the University's prison. (From James Ingram's *Memorials of Oxford*, 1837.)

of imprisonment. Thereupon many gave up and left, but at least one, Robert Elliott, refused. He had been warned twice by the Vice-Chancellor, so on 2 January 1692 an order was made in the Chancellor's Court for Elliott's imprisonment until he gave security to stop printing in the Sheldonian. Two days later the Court ordered Parker to cease printing there and to take away all his presses by the 7th of the month on pain of being sent to prison. Elliott was set free by 12 February, when he made a public confession and apology. He owned to having slandered and scandalled the Vice-Chancellor, saying he was 'a rash, hotheaded passionate man, that he had kicked up his heeles and thrown him on his back and done the Welsh mans busines for him'. He was fined £40 and deprived of his status of a privileged person.[3]

[1] Their immediate landlords, Fell's executors, had surrendered their lease in 1690; but the University had allowed Parker and Guy to remain in possession and had accepted rent from them.
[2] Probably those that the University let to the Bible-printers in 1678.
[3] Chancellor's Court Cause Papers, Hilary 1692.

Surprisingly, the Vice-Chancellor accepted a quarter's rent from Parker and Guy on 22 December 1691.[1] Their contract as servants and printers of the University was not terminated by Convocation until 21 October 1692, on the ground of their misconduct.[2]

The Stationers bought from Parker and Guy the presses, type, and white paper left in the Theatre.[3] If there had been any ill will, business sense conquered it.

Meanwhile, the University's formal agreement to employ Isted and his two companions as its servants and agents 'for the carrying on and for the management of the Manufacture of Printing within the precincts of the said University' was approved by Convocation and dated 27 January 1691/2. It would have been approved at an earlier meeting, had not the Senior Proctor declined to be present and sat in an adjoining room objecting that the proposal ought first to be sanctioned by the Heads of Houses. Threatened with a prosecution for the reform of his morals, he gave in.[4]

There were regrets afterwards about the breach with Parker and Guy.[5] Assertions that their printing was bad are not confirmed by inspection of their Bibles, if 'bad' is to be understood as meaning below the prevailing British standard. The big Bibles are set in good Dutch type and well printed on fine paper. Only the smallest leave much to be desired, but they are no worse than those of the King's Printers or any English printing of that day in small type on soft paper.

A fair construction to put on the events of 1691–2 is that Fell's passion for Bibles had led to a state of affairs causing uneasiness in many minds. While sharing the deceased Bishop's appreciation

How necessary it is for the service of our protestant religion that bibles should not be a monopoly, it being manifest by experience, that our comprinting has put bibles into thrice as many hands as formerly had them . . . nothing besides filling the market can steddily make a commodity cheap,[6]

they recoiled before the spectacle of so much comprinting. Some were comforted by the thought that the Stationers' Company, armed with the agreement of 1692, would exploit their new privilege of printing the

[1] Bodl. MS. Ballard 49, fol. 238ᵛ.
[2] Reg. Conv. Bb, p. 376.
[3] Stationers' records, schedule to an agreement of 6 Oct. 1693 to form an Oxford Stock.
[4] Chancellor's Court Cause Papers, Hilary 1692.
[5] Bodl. MS. Ballard xxii, fol. 24.
[6] Bodl. MS. Rawl. lett. 93, fol. 99.

Bible in competition with the King's Printers.[1] They forgot that His Majesty's Printers were Stationers too.

There was a party in the ascendant at Oxford in favour of a tight control of printing. Had not the printing in Oxford itself of a scandalously heretical book, Arthur Bury's *Naked Gospel*, in 1690 opened eyes to the risks inherent in the press?[2] The Stationers' Company, it was said, gave some protection against irregularities, therefore it should be allowed to enjoy its monopolies unchallenged; moreover by guarding publishers' copies it did good service to authors. Oxford did not desire an end to censorship or the withdrawal of a statutory limit to the number of presses. At the last gasp of the Licensing Acts it tried to put new life in them.[3] To look back on the number of Bibles and psalms that 'those mercenary fellows', Parker and Guy, had been allowed to bring out in the University's name prompted a feeling that on such a scale printing was not proper work for an academy, and to abet it meant undermining an old order and opened the way to freedom of the press.

With the sealing of a deed by Fell's executors on 2 October 1690 surrendering to the Chancellor, Masters, and Scholars the rights and property let to them and releasing the equipment bought by the partners since 1672[4] we come to the beginning of the true University Press.

[1] [James Harrington] *Reasons for reviving and continuing the Act for the regulation of printing* (1693), a broadside.
[2] Reg. Conv. Bb, pp. 285–92.   [3] [Harrington] op. cit.
[4] Univ. Arch. W.P. R8ᵇ(2).

CHAPTER IX

The Books 1678–1690

DURING the last years of Fell and the tenure of the Press by his executors some notable books, besides Bibles, were printed at Oxford. It remains for a bibliographer to give an account of those published after 1680, the last year with which Madan dealt in his *Oxford Books*. The most remarkable will be noticed here briefly.

Pitt's English Atlas, 1680–3

Certainly in point of format the most ambitious, and perhaps the finest, English book of the seventeenth century is this unhappy *Atlas*. Failure to bring out more than four of the eleven volumes originally proposed is no reason for not recognizing the merit of its printing.

Credit for the *Atlas* cannot, however, be claimed for the University or for Fell's partnership, for all that the volumes bear the imprint, 'Oxford, printed at the Theater for Moses Pitt',[1] nor can the failure to complete the series be put down to the weakness of Oxford salesmanship. It is safe to say that the production of the four volumes was controlled by Moses Pitt and he sold them. The types are not those to be seen in Fell's printing, and they with the woodcut initial letters and a tailpiece reappear in the folio Bibles of Pitt, Parker, and Guy. The *Atlas* must have been printed in the cellar of the Sheldonian, not in the Printhouse where Fell's staff worked.

The conception of the book is probably traceable to a sale at Amsterdam in January 1676 by the personal representatives of Joannes Janssonius of his remaining atlases and the copper plates for the maps in them.[2] In one of his prospectuses issued in 1678 Pitt announced that he had 'the advantage of making use of divers plates already graven, but more especially of those of Jansson's Atlas'.[3] He did some renewing of the engraving and made corrections. The format is Elephant folio (23 × 14 in.),

---

[1] Some were issued with the names of Jan Jansson van Waesberge and Steven Swart at Amsterdam in substitution for Pitt's: M. M. Kleerkooper and W. P. van Stockum Jr., *De boekhandel te Amsterdam, voornamelijk in de 17de. eeuw* (The Hague, 1914–16), p. 304 n.

[2] Ibid., p. 304.

[3] Pitt's *Proposals*, Bodl. Wood 658 (791*).

and Pitt, not being able to buy sheets big enough through the trade, rented a mill in France and had them made there.[1]

The four published volumes deal with the Arctic regions, Muscovy, Poland, and Scandinavia, Germany, and the Netherlands, described in

Specimens of the two sets of woodcut initial letters bought by Moses Pitt for his *English Atlas* printed at Oxford in 1680-2. The original blocks are still at the Press.

much detail by Oxford scholars, Obadiah Walker, William Nicolson, Richard Peers, and John Cooper. Madan gives a full description of the book.[2]

The woodblocks for the fine initial letters of two sizes,[3] typical Dutch work of the time,[4] finally came to rest in the store-room of the Press,[5] and electrotypes made from them are often used still.

[1] Ibid. (791, 795), B.M. MS. Harl. 5901, fol. 86.
[2] Madan, *Oxford Books* iii, No. 3253.   [3] Morison, *Fell*, pp. 191-4.
[4] Very similar letters are in the *Specimen typorum* of Johannes Elsevier (Leyden, 1658) and the sale-catalogue of the successors to Joan Blaeu (Amsterdam, 1695), and there are some ascribed to the seventeenth century in the collection of Messrs. Joh. Enschedé en Zonen at Haarlem: C. Enschedé, *Fonderies de caractères et leur matériel dans les Pays-Bas du XVᵉ au XIXᵉ siècle* (Haarlem, 1908), facing p. 107.
[5] The block for the E of the larger set is in the Bodleian Library (Gough Collection).

Spelman's Life of King Alfred

Obadiah Walker, elected Master of University College in 1676, took a particular interest in Alfred, whom he regarded as the founder of his college. He resuscitated a manuscript life of the king written in English by Sir John Spelman, who died in 1643, a son of the better-known Sir Henry. Walker had the work put into Latin and added notes by himself assisted by others of the college.[1]

Spelman's text is a digest of information about Alfred in the *Vita Ælfredi* by Asser and other ancient chronicles with critical observations. He relied on the printed edition of Asser sponsored by Archbishop Matthew Parker of 1574, with all its interpolations and omissions. As history it deserves little respect. Spelman's criticism is mainly concerned with contesting the genuineness of a passage in William Camden's printed text of Asser[2] where it is stated that Alfred sent his mass-priest Grimbald to Oxford to compose discord among the students. Camden was guilty of inserting the passage in Asser as printed for Parker without any indication that he had done so, and an old manuscript that he afterwards cited as his authority is unlikely to have existed.[3] Spelman was right to denounce the fabrication, on which arguments for Oxford as the older of the two Universities had been based. He did so at too great a length, without humour, and went on to adduce weak evidence for the greater antiquity of Cambridge.

Many of Walker's annotations contribute usefully to the history of Alfred's time from a wide reading of the chronicles and from archaeological finds. He prints quotations from the sources in Old English; when it comes to Camden's fabrication, he deprecates contention between the Universities as to priority, but he defends the fabricated passage. What is most discreditable to both Spelman and Walker is that neither recognized, or admitted, the supreme authority of MS. Otho A. xii in the Cottonian Library as the parent of all other manuscripts of Asser,[4] though it had been pointed out by Ussher in 1639.[5] Spelman had seen it and noticed that it did not include the passage about Oxford, but evidently without appreciating its importance to him. Walker refers to

---

[1] *Ælfredi Magni Anglorum Regis invictissimi vita . . . a clarissimo Dno. Johanne Spelman . . . conscripta.* Oxonii, e Theatro Sheldoniano, 1678; Hearne, ii, p. 180.
[2] In *Anglica, Normannica, Hibernica, Cambrica, a veteribus scripta* (Frankfurt a. M., 1602–3). It is also quoted in his *Britannia* of 1600.
[3] A. G. Watson, *The Manuscripts of Sir Henry Savile of Banke* (1969), App. iii.
[4] *Asser's Life of King Alfred*, ed. W. H. Stevenson (Oxford, 1904), Introduction.
[5] In his *Britannicarum ecclesiarum antiquitates*, pp. 341–2.

it several times without admitting its primacy or correcting Spelman's text by it. The Cottonian MS., dated by Humfrey Wanley A.D. 1000 or 1001, was burnt in 1731; posterity must deplore that the Oxford publication throws so little light on it.

Hearne published Spelman's *Life* in English in 1709 from the author's manuscript in the Bodleian Library 'with considerable additions' of his own in the form of footnotes and appendices. In the notes Asser is quoted from the edition by Camden and there is no comment on Spelman's single mention of 'an ancient manuscript' which Archbishop Ussher enabled him to see.

Spelman's *Life of King Alfred*, a poor thing in itself, is memorable for its part in the Oxford–Cambridge controversy as to precedence (for even now the 'Alfred myth' has its place in every history of the University); but it is memorable also as testimony to the growth at Oxford of interest in the Old English language and our early chronicles. Oxford made its first contribution to this branch of philology in 1659 by publishing William Somner's great *Dictionarium Saxonico-Latino-Anglicum*. The notes to Spelman were the next step towards a mastery of the language and familiarity with the chronicles.[1]

Fell's edition of St. Cyprian, 1682

That Fell should have chosen St. Cyprian as material for his *magnum opus* is in no way surprising, seeing how great was the regard in which the saint was held by the Anglican Church in the seventeenth century. Cyprian had combated schism in the shape of the Novatian and Donatist heresies, over baptism he had come to an open breach with the Pope, and he had suffered martyrdom. In all three respects he was a model for high Anglicanism, insulted by enthusiasts, encroached upon by the Roman Church, and deprived of its head in the person of William Laud.

In one of his manifestos, issued probably in 1676,[2] Fell declared a willingness on the part of the 'Undertakers for the Press' to effect 'the design of Dr. James', beginning with St. Cyprian. Thomas James, D.D., Bodley's Librarian, had moved in Convocation of the clergy in 1625 'that some persons might be commissioned to peruse the manuscript fathers in all public and private English libraries, that thereby the forgeries of foreign popish editions might be detected'.[3]

Cyprian was an obvious choice for a beginning because of doubts

---

[1] For Fulman's and Gale's editions of the chronicles, see below, p. 227.
[2] Morison, *Fell*, p. 252.   [3] Wood, *Ath.* ii, 465.

about the authenticity of passages in the text of the treatise *De Ecclesiae Catholicae unitate* attributing to the see of Rome in particular the authority given to St. Peter and, on that account, asserting its 'primacy'. Some good manuscripts omit these passages, which were very inhibiting to Protestant controversy. It is believed now that Cyprian wrote the 'Primacy Text', but after disagreeing with the Pope rewrote the *De unitate* without the passages conferring primacy and stressing the equality of the Disciples and therefore of bishoprics. It is a subject, which, a modern editor regrets, 'has been the cause of such endless, futile, and as we now see, misplaced controversy'.[1]

In his edition Fell argues vehemently for the falsity of the passages favouring Rome. Naturally he wanted a Protestant apparatus: in his notes he is irritable with the Roman Catholic scholar, Jacobus Pamelius, who was responsible for an edition at Antwerp in 1568, and politely critical of that of 'doctissimus Rigaltius' (Nicolas Rigault) at Paris of 1649. However his fear of Rome may have been a reason for his bestowing his scholarly pains on Cyprian, he is equally concerned to enforce the saint's condemnation of schism. His annotation does little to soften the saint's terribly rigorous churchmanship. Where Cyprian consigns to perdition a schismatic who suffers martyrdom for Christianity, Fell notes that this is a tenet of the Eastern Church.

Fell had forgiven the British dissenters nothing they had done in his lifetime.

We remember very well [he wrote in 1681] the time when blood and rapin put on the mask of Godliness and Reformation, and we lost our King, our libertye and property, and religion by fighting for them. As it then appeared that we poor Cavalliers were protestants, though scandalld with the names of malignants and papists: so I hope we shall still continue: and be as ready to suffer and die for our religion, as others are to talk of it.[2]

Discussing the degree of guilt separating Cyprian's *sacrificati* from the *libellatici* among the lapsed, he fetches a parallel from his experience. He writes in Latin to this effect:

Assuredly in this country when the rebel forces had borne down the best of princes and the victors were irresistibly oppressing such as remained loyal, there were many who went over to the other camp and openly changed sides. Those were the apostates (*sacrificati*). There were also many,

---

[1] Maurice Bévenot, S.J., *Cyprian De lapsis and De Ecclesiae Catholicae unitate*, Oxford Early Christian Texts (Oxford, 1971), p. xv.

[2] To Sir Richard Newdigate, 11 May: Newdigate Papers, B 413.

less culpable in their own esteem, who secured the token that was given to any who swore allegiance to the rebels by buying it or misrepresenting their identity, while maintaining that they had not broken faith or bound themselves to a wicked confederacy. The token, they said, meant only that they had protected themselves by a timely lie. They were the *libellatici* [people who had falsely secured certificates that they were not Christians].[1]

Those were his memories, and his apprehensions of future events were as vivid. He is said to have been one of two or three bishops who voted to exclude James, Duke of York, from succession to the throne.[2] The thought of young English noblemen going abroad and coming under the influence of Jesuits tormented him.[3] 'The Church is now assaulted by the furious malice of Papists on the one hand and Fanaticks on the other.'[4]

Fell undoubtedly regarded the works of St. Cyprian as highly relevant to his own time. He valued the saint's support for the view that the Christian Church entire, not the Church of Rome more than another, inherited the authority given to St. Peter, and that infallibility in matters of doctrine resided in councils of bishops. However, if contention played a large part in Fell's aims as editor, conscientious and laborious scholarship reinforced it. In his preface he puts first the need to separate the *spuria* and the authentic writings; and in that he must be taken to have succeeded, for his canon is virtually the same as that of Wilhelm Hartel, the last editor (1868–71) of the complete works. His collection of various readings is testimony to his industrious research, and his notes are proof of a mastery of patristic learning and of the text of the Hebrew Bible as well as the Septuagint. Hartel writes of Fell's edition respectfully.

The volume contains besides the genuine and supposititious treatises and letters of St. Cyprian the annals of his lifetime gathered by the learned John Pearson, Bishop of Chester. When Fell wrote the preface he expected that the lengthy *Dissertationes Cyprianicae* by Henry Dodwell would be in it too, and they are sometimes bound with it. Dodwell was a historian, he enlarged on the annals, but he also supplied an interest in theology, which Fell lacked. So compacted, it is a monument to the Church of England at one stage of its development.

For a reason which is not obvious the Archbishop of Canterbury, Sancroft, was apprehensive of danger in what Fell might have written,

[1] p. 133.   [2] Hearne, iii, p. 444.
[3] To Williamson, 14 Nov. 1683: B.M. MS. Add. 28104, fol. 15; to Sir W. Trumbull, 11 Oct. 1685: Hist. MSS. Comm., *Downshire*, i, p. 48.
[4] Bodl. MS. Tanner xxxi, fol. 156 (1685).

and not being willing to read the work, asked Peter Gunning, Bishop of Ely, for a report on it. The report was reassuring.[1]

Hearne said that the book was extremely hard to come by in his day.[2] In foreign Protestant countries it was clearly thought to be saleable. There was a pirated edition from Bremen of 1690, and that was copied in one by Abraham van Someren at Amsterdam in 1691. The unscrupulous pirate, J.-L. de Lorme, went so far as to put a title-page reproducing Fell's, complete with the imprint and engraving of the Sheldonian Theatre, on some copies of his reprint at Amsterdam in 1700.[3]

Bull's Defensio Fidei Nicaenae, 1685

George Bull, a poor and humble parson in a country living, first ventured into authorship with *Harmonia apostolica*, printed in London in 1669. In it he maintains the doctrine of the Epistle of St. James as to the necessity of good works for salvation and reconciles it with the emphasis on faith as a means to that end in the Epistles of St. Paul. He was attacked by the more Calvinistical clergy for his insistence on good works, and his opponents insinuated that Bull was sympathetic with unitarianism.

To answer the charge of heterodoxy Bull wrote his famous *Defensio*. He had learned, moreover, that students of theology were reading the *Nucleus historiae ecclesiasticae* by Christopher Sandius, published at Amsterdam in 1669, 'an open and barefaced defence of the Arian blasphemy', as Bull called it.[4] Those who disbelieved in the divinity of Christ were encouraged by the view of some respectable scholars that before the Council of Nicaea the fathers of the Church were Arians, and among these scholars was Dionysius Petavius, a Jesuit, whom Bull considered as 'a great man, extremely well-read in all kinds of learning'.[5] It was this mistaken opinion that Bull set himself to combat by a thorough examination of the writings of the ante-Nicene Fathers, and as proof that it was erroneous his book has been the undisputed authority ever since.

[1] B.M. MS. Add. 29546, fol. 96.   [2] Hearne, ii, p. 208.
[3] Notes by J. S. G. Simmons in Morison, *Fell*, pp. 222, 224; Hearne, ii, pp. 208–9. De Lorme worked closely with the Abbé J.-P. Bignon in providing editions of books in French and Latin which would be forbidden in France but of which Bignon, Superintendent of the book-trade, wanted a few copies to be brought into the country: I. H. van Eeghen, *De Amsterdamse boekhandel 1680–1725*, i, *Jean Louis de Lorme en zijn copieboek* (Amsterdam, 1960). The Bibliothèque Nationale has three copies of De Lorme's reprint of the *Cyprian*.
[4] The imprint is Cosmopoli, apud Libertum Pacificum. It is said, on the authority of Rahir, to have been printed on the presses of Joan Blaeu at Amsterdam: M. M. Kleerkooper and W. P. van Stockum Jr., *De boekhandel te Amsterdam*, i, p. 1177.
[5] Denis Petau, who died in 1652.

The *Defensio*, when written, was offered to three booksellers in turn, and they all declined it, thinking, as Bull surmised, that the author was too obscure and the matter too abstruse to attract readers. After a time the manuscript came to the notice of William Jane, Regius Professor of Divinity at Oxford, and he recommended it to Fell, who undertook to print it at his own expense.

After its acceptance by Fell the book was a long time in the press, which was 'taken up with other things by other men, so that for some time this treatise made no progress at all and later did so at intervals'.[1] The author saw a proof only of the last sheet; he begs indulgence from readers for the errors of the compositor and, after him, of the drowsy corrector.

The great Bossuet warmly commended the book in his *Histoire des variations des églises Protestantes* of 1688.[2] He invoked God's blessing on 'le savant Bullus' for his zeal in proving the divinity of Jesus Christ and prayed that his eyes might be opened to the light of the Catholic Church.

A second edition was printed at the Theatre in 1688. No copies were in stock in 1696. Bull's Latin works were reprinted at Oxford in 1703, 1827, and 1846. They were translated into English in 1844, and a translation of the chief of them was added to the Library of Anglo-Catholic Theology in 1851–5.

WALKER'S PRESS AND THE ANTI-POPERY TRACTS

The Popish Plot and the accession of James II irresistibly directed publishers' resources to religious controversy in the closing years of Fell's press. At Oxford one good effect of Protestant anxiety was the reprinting at the Theatre in 1684 and 1687 of William Chillingworth's *Religion of Protestants a Safe Way of Salvation*, first printed here in 1638. With its exaltation of conscience, of revelation interpreted by reason and learning, of tolerance, it had, if constant reprinting can be trusted as a sign, a profound effect on religion in England at the end of the century and in the early part of the next. Chillingworth's belief 'that there are certain basic intellectual propositions which are necessarily true also pervaded the "enlightened" classical rationalism and empiricism of the eighteenth century'.[3]

---

[1] Preface, 3rd page.
[2] Livre xv, para. clii, at Vol. ii, pp. 439–40 of the edition of 1730.
[3] R. R. Orr, *Reason and Authority: The Thought of William Chillingworth* (Oxford, 1967), p. 183.

On a lower level of intellect, the collected *Works of the Author of the Whole Duty of Man*, with a preface written for this edition by Fell, printed partly at the Sheldonian in 1684, upheld Anglican piety in a time of stress.

Obadiah Walker, Master of University College since 1676, had been reproached before the accession of King James for tendentious writings bordering on Roman Catholicism. In 1680 the Vice-Chancellor had forbidden the sale in Oxford of his (anonymous) *Benefits of our Saviour*. At the outset of the new reign Walker avowed obedience to the Church of Rome, and a year later the King gave him the sole right for him and his assigns to print and sell during 21 years 36 named books of Roman Catholic apology or devotion.[1] The books were nearly all written by Abraham Woodhead, a former fellow of University College, who died in 1678, leaving his manuscripts to be disposed of by Walker. The first that the Master put to press was *Two Discourses on the Adoration of our Blessed Saviour in the Eucharist*. He took it to Leonard Lichfield, third Oxford printer of the name, in the High Street, who allowed Arthur Charlett to take away sheets of the book as they came off the press for the purpose of writing a Protestant answer to the argument.[2] When Walker understood that Lichfield had dealt falsely by him, he 'set up cases of letters and a press in the back part of his lodgings belonging to him as master of Univ. Coll.'[3] (in the stables, as Hearne was told).[4]

From this little press came a dozen booklets, seven of them certainly by Woodhead,[5] attacking Protestantism. The Sheldonian press, in the tenure of Fell's executors advised by Timothy Halton, Henry Aldrich, and John Mill, was kept busy with Protestant replies. These, known collectively as 'Oxford Anti-Popery Tracts', are attributed by Anthony Wood to William Wake, Charlett, Aldrich, Francis Atterbury, George Smalridge, and James Harrington. The contestants on both sides were learned and honourable, so that the controversy is erudite and, generally, urbane; if anyone were desirous of learning what divides the two Churches he could learn it from these exchanges without being offended by the language.

---

[1] J. Gutch, *Collectanea curiosa* (Oxford, 1781), i, pp. 288–9.
[2] The writer knew that 'A. C.' would answer him (p. 8 of the first Discourse). Presumably Walker added to Woodhead's copy.
[3] Wood, *Ath.* iii, 1161, also iv, 440.
[4] Hearne, i, p. 72.
[5] According to Falconer Madan in a letter to John Johnson of 30 Apr. 1931 in the Printer's copy of the Tracts.

A fortnight after the arrival in London of the Prince of Orange the press in University College was dismantled,[1] the printed stock having been lodged in a place of safety by Walker.[2] Two of the books, one unfinished, bear the date 1689 but must have been printed the year before.

ANGLO-SAXON GRAMMAR

Hickes's Institutiones Grammaticae Anglo-Saxonicae et Moeso-Gothicae, 1689

George Hickes's grammar of Old English of 1689 was the first to be printed. It was enlarged and corrected to form part of his monumental *Thesaurus* of 1703-5.[3] In the intervening years it was the tool and the inspiration of a generation of Saxonists. By propagating a study of the northern languages in succession to the younger Francis Junius, Hickes widened the scope of learning at Oxford for a lifetime.

In the preface he tells of a conversation with Fell, who deplored the want of the rudiments for learning Gothic and Anglo-Saxon. He regretted that Thomas Marshall had not written a work of the kind to be prefixed to the dictionary of five languages by Junius, which at one time Fell meant to print.[4] Hickes felt bound to supply the want.

In a long preliminary discourse, discussing the relationships of the northern languages and recommending them to English students of divinity, law, classical philology, and rhetoric, he credits John Josselin with being the father of Anglo-Saxon learning. He says that Josselin, William Somner, Junius, and Marshall edited good texts because they had mastered the grammar: Henry Spelman, Selden, even Wheelock, he puts on a lower plane as not having done so.

Part of the volume, though the pages are numbered separately, is an Icelandic grammar by Runolf Jonas, an Icelander. It has its own title-page describing it as 'Recentissima antiquissimae linguae incunabula'; but in fact the grammar had previously been printed in 1651 at Copenhagen, sponsored by the Royal Danish Academy. Hickes says he annexed it to his book because the Icelandic is pure Cymbric, uncorrupted by contact with other languages.

The volume was the first to make extensive use of the type for northern languages given to the University by Francis Junius. The

---

[1] Wood, *Ath.* iv, 440; *Wood's Life and Times*, iii, p. 282.
[2] Wood, *Ath.* iii, 1163.
[3] Below, p. 261.
[4] Below, p. 126.

Icelandic words in the grammar are set in a German Schwabacher face for which Junius gave only a fount, not matrices or punches.[1] It has no thorn (þ); Junius had supplied the capital form of the letter, but ᵺ had to be used for the lower-case form.

A third part of the volume, contributed as a mark of his friendship with Hickes, is a tract by Edward Bernard, 'Etymologicon Britannicum'. Bernard had extravagant notions of the derivation of languages one from another. He finds words akin to the English in Welsh, Czech, Russian, Armenian, Croat, Hungarian, Polish, Portuguese, Gothic, Icelandic, Persian, Basque, and Turkish, among other languages.

WELSH

One of the arguments used to support the setting up of a press at Oxford shortly before 1585[2] was its foreseeable usefulness for supplying the needs of Wales; and until printing began at Shrewsbury in 1696 this was the most convenient place to which Welshmen could bring their copy.

Miles Coverdale's English version of a book by Otto Wermüller, *The Spiritual and most Precious Pearl*, translated into Welsh by Hugh Lewis, was printed here in 1595.[3] The next piece of Oxford printing in Welsh is believed to have been *Carol o Gyngor, yn Datennig yr Cymru* (A carol of counsel, as a gift to the Welsh), by Matthew Owen, a four-page poem giving religious advice, of 1656.[4]

The Oxford master printers, Henry Hall and the Lichfields, produced four books in Welsh in the 1670s: *Y Ffydd Ddi-Fuant*, a history of Christianity by Charles Edwardes, of which there were editions in 1671 and 1677; John Jewel's *Apologia ecclesiae Anglicanae*, put into Welsh by Maurice Kyffin as *Dad Seiniad Meibion y Daran . . .; An Eccho of the Sons of Thunder*, and edited by Charles Edwardes, with an *Epistle* to the Welsh people by Bishop Richard Davies, in 1671; and *Profiad yr Ysprydion* (The trial of the spirits) by Rondl Davies in 1675.

At Fell's press in its last ten years rather more frequent attention was paid to the established Church in Wales. Marshall's *Catechism*[5] translated into Welsh by John Williams of Cambridge was issued from the Theatre in 1682, and the *Llyfr Gweddi Gyffredin* (Book of Common Prayer) in 1683. A second edition of *Ffordd y Gwr Cyffredin yn ei Addoliad* (The way

---

[1] Morison, *Fell*, p. 245.   [2] Above, pp. 19–20.
[3] Madan, *Oxford Books*, i, pp. 38–9.
[4] Ibid. iii, No. 2406. The Bodleian has the only known copy.
[5] Below, p. 221.

of the ordinary man in his worship) by the same John Williams was printed here also in 1683. A treatise of the Lord's Prayer, *Gueddi'r-Arglwydd wedi ei Hegluro* by George Griffith, Bishop of St. Asaph, was published in 1685 with an introduction by William Foulkes. A poem highly regarded by Welsh readers, *Cerdd-Lyfr* by Foulke Owens, printed at the Theatre in 1686, exists only in a sadly defective copy at the National Library of Wales. Bishop Ken's *Practice of Divine Love*, an exposition of the Catechism, translated by William Foulkes (*Esboniad ar Gatechism*) followed in 1688, and in 1689 *Y Rhybuddiwr Cristnogawl*, a translation of *The Christian Monitor* of John Rawlet.[1]

In the imprints the name 'Oxford' is rendered in Welsh as Rhydychen, but the word Theatre was then used in both languages.

[1] The books named above, excepting (I believe) the two first and the one by J. Williams, are in the National Library of Wales at Aberystwyth. The exceptions are in the Bodleian.

CHAPTER X

Technical Matters 1670–1690

THE DEVELOPMENT OF FELL'S TYPEFOUNDRY

HARMAN HARMANSZ., whom Thomas Marshall persuaded to leave his employment in a typefoundry at Amsterdam and enter the service of Fell and Yate,[1] had arrived in Oxford by 1 August 1672.[2] That he or his employers were dissatisfied with the service or thought Harmansz. by himself was not enough is an inference from a letter that Fell wrote in the August following to Henry Aldrich, then in Cologne, asking him to look out for 'some ingenious young man who would help us in the affair of letter founding . . . especially one who cutts and goes through the whole manufacture'.[3]

Harmansz. is described late in 1672 as having cast hitherto only the imperfections;[4] that is to say, he was using the matrices got from Holland to supply extra letters for the founts of type brought from there. The last sign of him in our records is a payment 'to Harman' on 1 March 1675 (N.S.) in Fell's accounts.[5] Fell's apprentice typefounder, William Hall, was working under Harmansz. in November 1674.[6]

Casting in the Dutch matrices was not all that Fell wanted from his typefounder, as his letter to Aldrich testifies. He needed a man who would make new typefaces by cutting punches and striking matrices for them. His programme drafted early in 1672[7] would not be carried out unless he got type for Coptic and Syriac, and Marshall had been able to find neither, even in Holland. Further, to make him independent of the London founders he needed matrices for big Romans and Italics.

The finding of a man capable (in whatever degree) of meeting the Dean's requirements is probably creditable to Sir Leoline Jenkins while he was in Holland as a plenipotentiary for negotiating the Peace of Nijmegen. At all events, by 25 February 1676 Peter de Walpergen arrived in Oxford and was given a workroom in the Dean's Lodging at

---

[1] Above, p. 57.
[2] S.P. (Dom.), Car. II, 313, No. 177.
[3] Ibid. 336, No. 212.
[4] Yate's accounts: All Souls MS. 239, fol. 667, printed in Madan, *Oxford Books*, iii, p. 413.
[5] In the Chancellor's Court Cause Papers 1687–8.
[6] Ibid.
[7] Above, p. 63.

Christ Church, where he cut punches and made matrices.[1] His initial salary of £36 a year was later increased to £40, and he had his 'diet' from the Dean. Payments to him occur regularly in Fell's accounts from the date of his arrival, and one is for 'diet for the Founder and boys'.

Of this typefounder's earlier life little is known. He was almost certainly the Pieter Walberger who contracted with the Dutch East India Company at Batavia in 1671 to serve them as printer and letter-founder for a period terminable at will.[2] The imprint of Pedro Walberger is on an Aesop in Portuguese published in Batavia in 1672.[3] In the records of Dutch typefounding there is no trace of him, and it seems probable that he was one of a family settled since 1586 at Frankfurt am Main, descended from a Protestant refugee from Antwerp.[4]

The earliest sign that De Walpergen was making new typefaces at Oxford is a letter from Fell to Archbishop Sancroft of September 1681, telling him that he had had a Syriac type cut and fitted.[5] In the next year a big Roman and Italic, the 'Fell Double Pica', attributable to him, was used in an edition by John Wallis of Ptolemy's *Harmonics*. In all he must be credited with 16 complete typefaces, besides many odd characters, cut for Fell or, after Fell's death, for the University. His masterpiece is a type for music, made no doubt under supervision from Henry Aldrich and modelled on his handwriting.[6]

The music-type, known to modern bibliophiles by its use in the *Yattendon Hymnal* of 1899, was shown in the University's *Specimen of the several Sorts of Letter* in 1695, and the schedule at the end of the booklet describes the punches as 'cut by Peter Walpergen'. The peculiar shape of these punches makes it possible to recognize others in the custody of the Printer to the University as made by the same man. Among them are the punches for the big Roman and Italic faces which came into use at the Press one after another in the years 1682–7. They are not to everybody's liking: they partake of the severe and economical style of German

---

[1] Depositions in the cause of De Walpergen against the Executors of John Fell: Chancellor's Court Cause Papers, Michaelmas 1687 to Easter 1688.
[2] A copy of the contract is in the Algemeen Rijksarchief at The Hague (Kol. Arch. 586, fol. 23).   [3] In the Bodleian Library.
[4] Information from the Archivdirektor of the City of Frankfurt; Alexander Dietz, *Frankfurter Handelsgeschichte* (Frankfurt a. M., 1911), ii, p. 317.
[5] Bodl. MS. Tanner 290, fol. 159.
[6] Aldrich was Dean of the Cathedral and Vice-Chancellor in 1694, when the type was finished. It was made with a view to a proposed volume of church music: Bodl. MS. Ballard, i, fol. 95; xxiii, fol. 39. Two anthems by Aldrich are set in it: Christ Church Library, Music Collection, No. 1208. Music scores in that Library believed to have been written by Aldrich are very like the type in style.

printing after the Thirty Years' War; they have none of the suavity or
French type of the sixteenth century, they lack the regularity of stress
and slope that distinguishes good lettering; but the big 'Fell' types are
crisply cut and they give a peculiar character to work set in them. In

The music-type made for the Press by Peter de Walpergen, evidently modelled on the
handwriting of Dean Aldrich. Reset as it was shown in the University's *Specimen* of 1695.

their day they were appreciated by the trade, for types cut at Fell's
expense found their way into London printing, and De Walpergen was
credibly accused of abusing his employer's trust by surreptitiously selling
punches to London typefounders.[1]

A propensity of his typefounder for 'ill company' troubled the Dean,
and by various names De Walpergen was sued four times in the
Chancellor's Court for debts to tavern-keepers and cooks.[2] Intemperance
seems not to have impaired his industry; he went on making new
typefaces for the University until his death in 1703, and added to his
duties waiting on the Dean at table when there was company to dinner.

THE GIFT OF FRANCIS JUNIUS

The younger Francis Junius had type made in Holland for Gothic,
Runic, and the peculiar characters for Anglo-Saxon. The Anglo-Saxon

---

[1] Chancellor's Court Cause Papers, as above; depositions of Henry Cruttenden.
[2] Chancellor's Court Acta.

he used for his edition of Caedmon's poetical paraphrase of the Book of Genesis at Amsterdam in 1655, and all three for *Quatuor D.N. Jesu Christi Evangelia* in Gothic and Anglo-Saxon edited by him and Thomas Marshall at Dordrecht in 1665.

In 1674 he came to spend his remaining years in England, where his former pupil, Marshall, was Rector of Lincoln College at Oxford and his nephew, Isaac Vossius, was a canon of Windsor. He arrived in Oxford in October 1676, moved to Windsor in the following August, and died there in November 1677.[1]

Junius brought with him his founts of type besides punches and matrices for the three dead northern languages, and founts of type only

The Anglo-Saxon, Gothic, and Runic letters for which punches and matrices were given to the University by Francis Junius in 1677.

for a Roman to supplement the Old English characters and two sizes of German Schwabacher, one of them supplied with extra letters for Danish, Norwegian, and Icelandic. All this equipment he gave with his manuscripts to the University of Oxford in 1676 or 1677.[2] The type was sent to Oxford by barge from Eton in April 1679 and was received at the Bodleian Library.[3] Marshall had most of the matrices when Fell asked for them some time later.[4] The punches, not needed for present use, were found, as Thomas Tanner related in 1697, in the study of the Proto-bibliothecarius at the Bodleian.

Mr Thwaites and John Hall took the courage last week to go to Dr Hyde about Junius's matrices and punchions, which he gave with his books to the University. These no body knew where they were, till Mr Wanley discovered some of them in a hole in Dr Hyde's study. But upon Mr Hall's asking, Dr Hyde knew nothing of them, but at last told them he thought

[1] Life of Junius by Georgius Graevius prefacing the edition of Junius's *De pictura veterum* at Rotterdam, 1694.
[2] It is said (*D.N.B.*) that Junius made the gift of his manuscript by deed while he was in Oxford. Inquiries have failed to locate a deed. The Register of Convocation is silent about the benefaction. Payments to F. Junius of £40 in 1676 and the like sum in 1677, by order of 'the Delegates', are recorded in the V.-C.'s Computus.
[3] Bodl. MS. Add. C. 78, fol. 30.
[4] Bodl. MS. Marshall 134, fol. 18, not dated.

he had some old Punchions about his study, but he did not know how they come there, and presently produces a small box full, and taking out one, he pores upon it and at last wisely tells them that these could not be what they look'd after, for they are Æthiopic: but Mr Thwaites desiring a sight of them found that which he look'd upon to be Gothic, and in the box were almost all Junius's Saxon, Gothic and Runic Punchions, which they took away with them and a whole Oyster barrel full of old Greek letter, which was discovered in another hole. (10 August 1697.)[1]

Fell had begun the printing of the *Glossarium quinque linguarum*, or dictionary of five languages, by Junius when he asked Marshall for the matrices, but that project was abandoned, and the Junian types were first used in quantity for Hickes's *Institutiones grammaticae Anglo-Saxonicae et Moeso-Gothicae* of 1689.

THE STOCK OF TYPE AT FELL'S DEATH

A specimen of the University's equipment of type was printed but not published about the time of Fell's death in 1686 or soon after. A single copy exists in the Library of Christ Church in the form of 12 unbound leaves without title, imprint, or date.[2] The collection of typefaces displayed is the same as that in *A Specimen of the several Sorts of Letter given to the University by Dr. John Fell*, dated 1693, omitting those that came into use at the Press after Fell's day. The types given by Junius are among the omissions.

The 'Christ Church Specimen' and the *Specimen* of 1693 illustrate the justice of an opinion of contemporaries that Fell left the Press equipped with 'type of all kinds' and 'for all languages'.[3] When he and his partners took charge in 1672 the University already had some matrices (but no means of casting in them): the Greek given by Sir Henry Savile in 1619 and the Hebrew and Arabic got from Leyden in 1637.[4] Fell added four sizes of Greek and six sizes of Roman and Italic got from Holland besides Coptic, Samaritan, and Syriac, and three big Romans and Italics with a set of bigger Roman capitals cut by De Walpergen. The gift of Junius brought in Anglo-Saxon, Gothic, and Runic. One language for which Fell lacked the distinctive type was English: he needed a Black Letter for

---

[1] Bodl. MS. Ballard iv, fol. 30. The punches and matrices are now safe at the University Press.
[2] Christ Church Library, D. 124.
[3] John Bagford, B.M. MS. Harl. 5901, fol. 35; John Mill, *Testamentum Novum* (1707), p. clxv; Thomas Smith, *Vita Edwardi Bernardi* (1704), p. 33.
[4] Above. pp. 33–4.

words in the vernacular in polyglot works. Matrices were provided for that by De Walpergen soon after the bishop's death, presumably by his order.

For these scripts the Press could get new type as it was needed from its typefounder. Only the printing-office at Rome of the Sacra Congregatio de Propaganda Fide outdid Oxford for the number of languages that it could print. Besides type from its own foundry Fell's press had founts of exotic faces cast elsewhere: the Anglo-Saxon bought in London for Somner's *Dictionarium* of 1659, and two sizes of Schwabacher appropriate for modern Germanic languages.

One of the tasks given to De Walpergen, and one that must have occupied him for a long time, was to add many to the ligatures and abbreviations in the two Greek typefaces used for John Mill's variorum *Testament* finished in 1707.[1] In the Prolegomena Mill recalled a promise by Fell that 'he would act like a good Printer (for so he called himself among friends) and have a big type cast for the text, which, if the skill of his typefounder were equal, would at least rival the letters of Stephanus for magnificence.'[2] His way of keeping the promise was to add 150 ligatured letters to the text type and 125 to the type used for notes, bringing the total of ligatured sorts in the one to 260 and in the other to 277.

Fell's fondness for ligatured Greek was old-fashioned. His friend Thomas Gale, writing in 1687, recommended a type freed from these encumbrances, and Heinrich Wetstein, prefacing his Greek Testament of 1698, blamed the *compendia* for corruptions in texts due to misreading.[3] The University Press did not discard them altogether until 1824.

Though a few ligatures, ει and ος for example, help to preserve the rhythm of truly Greek writing in print, there is nothing to be said for ugly and disturbing abbreviations such as ει̃) for εἶναι, ϗ for καὶ, and final ϑ̵. Fell, however, was of another mind.

COPPERPLATE AND WOODCUTS

Most books from the Sheldonian Press had some copperplate printing in them. At first Fell followed the Dutch fashion of beginning a book with an engraved title; later he was content to embellish a type-set title with

---

[1] Below, pp. 259–61.

[2] p. clviii (in Latin). Stephanus was Robert Estienne, who set Greek Testaments in the biggest of Garamond's beautiful *Grecs du Roi*.

[3] Reed, *Old English Letter Foundries*, p. 224.

a publisher's device engraved in copper. His private accounts for 1674–6[1] record his payments to Michael Burghers and George Edwards for engraving the *Oxford Almanack* of 1676 and to unnamed artists for the pictorial title-pages or frontispieces of the Bible and Book of Common Prayer of 1675, the *Grammar* of the same year, and the sequels to *The Whole Duty of Man*.

Of the heathenish Gods of the Laplanders.   41

One of the woodcuts by George Edwards illustrating Johann Scheffer's *History of Lapland* (1674).

Edwards, on whom Fell relied very much in the early days, worked mostly on wood. According to Bagford, he was 'a cutter of the great Letters, and Engraved many other things made use of in printing of Books, and had a Talent in Maps, altho' done with his left hand'.[2] He cut an alphabet (most likely two alphabets) of fantastic capitals for Fell,[3] did the delightful illustrations in Scheffer's *Lapland* (1674), and earned £25 from Edward Bernard by cutting 315 diagrams to illustrate a proposed edition of Euclid.[4]

---

[1] Chancellor's Court Cause Papers, Michaelmas 1687–Easter 1688.
[2] B.M. MS. Harl. 5901, fol. 86ᵛ.
[3] Morison, *Fell*, p. 191; Bodl. MS. Rawl. D. 398, fol. 120ᵛ. He may plausibly be credited with the bigger initial letters shown in Morison's book at pp. 189–90. The blocks for both are kept at the Press.
[4] Bodl. MS. Savile 101, fol. 107. For the Euclid see Madan, *Oxford Books*, iii, No. 3141.

Other copper-engravers at Oxford mentioned by Bagford are Henry Savage, son of a Master of Balliol, whom Fell invited to become Engraver to the University, Robert White, Woodfield, and Michael Burghers. Savage did some fine engravings for Morison's *Herbal*, Vol. ii (1680). White engraved the first *Almanack* (1674) and the grandiose frontispiece of Anthony Wood's *Historia*. Woodfield and Burghers were assistants to Loggan in his *Oxonia illustrata*, and after Loggan gave up work here, seemingly in 1675 or earlier, Woodfield was often commissioned by Fell in the next two or three years. He made three plates of the Theatre for use as a device and he engraved titles for the *Ladies Calling* and the *Art of Contentment*. Burghers comes into prominence with his illustrations for the *Marmora Oxoniensia* of 1676 and Plot's *History of Oxfordshire* of the next year, and thereafter carried all before him. He was using the style of Engraver to the University by 1695.

The earliest of Fell's engraved titles is that of Aratus (1672). It is signed 'D. L. sc.'. Several anonymous plates of the years 1672–4 bespeak the hand of Loggan, unaided or not, by their clean cut and gracious drawing; notably the two titles for Fell's Bible of 1675 and the Greek Testament of the same year.

The engraved devices begin with one in the second impression of the *Ladies Calling* in 1673. It is made up of the University arms and a cherub surrounded by a wreath with the arms of Fell and his three partners roughly represented in the corners. It was superseded a year later by the Theatre, occurring first in Wood's *Historia*, beautifully but anonymously engraved. The figure of Athene armed with spear, Gorgon shield, and caduceus sitting in front of the Sheldonian Theatre, used in learned quartos and folios, was engraved first by Loggan as part of the title to *Oxonia illustrata* in 1675 and may owe its design to Henry Aldrich, since the goddess has a close resemblance to one in his collection of prints.[1] It was engraved again in a rectangular frame for the *Marmora Oxoniensia* of 1676.

The Press kept many of the plates made in the seventeenth and eighteenth centuries until 1918, when most were sacrificed to the needs of war. Of those that are left the oldest would appear to be the engraved title to Aesop's *Fables*, one of the school books printed by Fell and Yate in 1672–3, and the sole relic of an edition bought up and destroyed by the Stationers.[2] Of the 15 illustrations by Burghers for Charleton's *Exercitationes de differentiis et nominibus animalium* of 1677 one plate is left—of the

[1] Information from Miss H. M. Petter.   [2] Above, p. 69.

sinister-looking *rana piscatrix*. The handsome frontispiece to the Bodleian
Catalogus impressorum librorum (1674) survives and so do dozens of engraved
initial letters, and many headbands, coats of arms, and portraits. Plates
for the *Oxford Almanack* from 1716 until it ceased to be printed from
hand-engraved surfaces are preserved too.

The male sea frog from Walter Charleton's *Exercitationes de
differentiis et nominibus animalium* (1677). Reproduced from the
copper plate destroyed in 1918. Reduced.

The prices paid for work at the rolling press were absurdly low. In 1676
the printer charged the partners 3*s*. for a thousand impressions of the
Theatre on a title-page, and for a frontispiece and a Theatre 6*d*. a
hundred.[1]

Humphrey Prideaux tells the story of Fell's surprising an attempt to
use his rolling press to print illustrations for Pietro Aretino's sonnets on
the postures adapted to sexual intercourse. Writing to his friend Henry
Ellis, the future Dean of Norwich tells the story:

[1] Yate's accounts: Bodl. MS. Rawl. D. 397, fol. 422.

(24 January 1674/5) The presse hath often furnished me with something to tell you. You little thinke it hath been imployed about printeing Aretins postures. I assure you we were like to have had an edition of them from thence were it not that last night the whole worke was mard. The gentlemen of All Souls had got them engraved, and had imployed our presse to print them of[f]. The time that was chosen for the worke was the eveneing after 4, Mr. Dean after that time never useing to come to the theator; but last night, being imployed the other part of the day, he went not thither till the work was begun. How he tooke to find his presse workeing at such an imployment I leave to you to imagin. The prints and plates he hath seased, and threatens the owners of them with expulsion; and I thinke they would deserve it were they of any other college then All Souls, but there I will allow them to be vertuous that are bawdy only in pictures.[1]

At least six printer's marks printed from woodcuts were used by Oxford master printers before Fell's time. He found it advisable to have his device of the Theatre cut on wood for use in cheaper books. A block for the University's arms printed on a notice in 1689 survives.[2]

A LONDON WAREHOUSE

There is an entry in Thomas Yate's accounts dated 9 July 1676, 'For my journey to and from London and expences there when I went to remove the Warehouse &c. £5. 12s. 0d.'[3]

There is no other mention of a warehouse in London for the sale of the secular books of the Press until 1758, when for a brief spell 'honest Tom Payne' held an appointment as 'Warehouse-Keeper or Publisher' to the University at his shop in Castle Street.[4] The lessees of Bible-printing at Oxford naturally had depots from which they sold their books as printed sheets in London; one of them, where there was a fire in 1770, was in Paternoster Row.[5]

The likeliest explanation of Yate's journey is that he went to supervise the transfer of a stock of books deposited with some other bookseller to the shop of Simon Miller 'at the Star near the west end of St. Paul's'. Miller's name occurs in the imprints of two books printed at the Theatre in 1677 announcing that he sold them,[6] and Fell's *Proposal tending to the*

[1] Prideaux, p. 30.
[2] Bodl. Wood 276 A (380). Mr. Reynolds Stone pointed out that it is a very early example of engraving with a pointed tool on the end-grain of boxwood.
[3] Bodl. MS. Rawl. D. 397, fol. 422.   [4] Below, p. 370.
[5] *Annual Register*, 1770, p. 66.
[6] Madan, *Oxford Books*, iii, Nos. 3130, 3144.

Advancement of Learning, issued probably in 1676,[1] says of the books 'ready or preparing for the Press' that they 'are to be bought at the Theater in Oxford, or at Mr. Simon Millers, . . . in London'. In 1677 Miller paid £262 to the Oxford partners. The arrangement with him seems not to have outlasted that year, and soon afterwards Moses Pitt succeeded as salesman in London.

[1] Morison, *Fell*, p. 252.

PART II

THE AUGUSTAN AGE
1690–1713

CHAPTER XI

Corporate Ownership and Committee Management

THE TRANSFER TO CORPORATE CONTROL

SATISFIED after an experience of four years that 'the interests of learning and printing are encouraged in the said University',[1] the executors of John Fell made over to the Chancellor, Masters, and Scholars by a formal release dated 2 October 1690[2] all the equipment for printing that the Bishop and his three partners had gathered together during a tenancy of eighteen years.[3]

The press named after the Sheldonian Theatre, which had been corporately owned since Sheldon gave the building in 1669 and equipped by the University with what it had in the way of furniture, type, and matrices, thus came under corporate management. Since Lady Day 1672 the lessees headed by Fell had been entrusted with all the powers, duties, and interests that the University had in the business of publishing and printing and given a discretion to publish and print what they thought best. Apart from an ill-tempered refusal by Convocation to approve

[1] That was the condition of Fell's bequest.   [2] Univ. Arch. W.P. R8ᵇ(2).
[3] How Fell was able to dispose of the partnership assets is not quite clear: Sir Joseph Williamson survived him. However, the last lease of the Press, of 1688, was to Fell's executors only; so presumably Williamson withdrew and waived his claims. On the other hand, Fell's right to the large investment made by Yate must have rested on survivorship. Blackstone got over the difficulty by calling Fell 'the academical survivor' (Philip, p. 64). Williamson had spent nothing on the Press.

Fell's nominee for the post of Architypographus,[1] the lessees had had complete freedom to manage. Their additions to the equipment had more than trebled the resources of the Press. Their printed stock and rights to 'copies' were a substantial asset.

Ever since the release by the executors all these powers and duties have been exercised and all this property has been managed by the University's appointed agents, the Delegates of the Press. The 'Learned Press' has been subject to their immediate control without interruption since then, and they had wide powers of supervision over the 'Bible Press' while it was managed by lessees in the years 1690–1780. The origin of the existing University Press was certainly not later than 1690.[2]

For a university to own premises and plant for printing and to employ directly the various tradesmen who contribute to it is still a rarity. In 1690 there was no precedent for it. The number of presses owned before the end of the seventeenth century by fictitious persons who could not die is extremely small. The earliest appears to have been one belonging to the Jesuits' College in Rome, which lasted from 1556 until 1616.[3] In 1587 Pope Sixtus V constituted by his Bull 'Eadem semper' of 27 April the Typographia Apostolica Vaticana, an institution which in one form or another has persisted up to the present.[4] The conduct of this press was originally entrusted to a Venetian master printer, Domenico Basa, a contractor rather than a servant to the Papacy. It was the imprint of Basa that appeared on the publications, the Pope raised his rent for premises occupied by the press,[5] and Basa, like his successor Guelfi, paid for type.[6] The popes, particularly Gregory XIII, subsidised the Typographia liberally, bore the cost of having type made for foreign scripts,[7] and

[1] *Print and Privilege*, p. 50. Above, pp. 51, 64.

[2] A. W. Pollard (*The Library*, 4th ser. iii (1923), pp. 66–7) took [R. W. Chapman] to task for entitling a book *Some Account of the Oxford University Press, 1468–1921*. It is not easy to fix a date for the beginning. 1690 leaves out of account the facts that the University owned matrices since 1619, a type store since 1652, and premises furnished with printing presses, compositors' frames, and type since 1669. If 'Press' can mean a publishing organization, this one goes back at least to 1633.

[3] G. Castellani, 'La tipografia del Collegio Romano', *Archivum historicum Soc. Iesu*, ii (Rome, 1933), pp. 11–16.

[4] The history of the Vatican Press is traced in outline by Luigi Huetter, 'La Typografia Vaticana', *Gutenberg-Jahrbuch 1962*, pp. 273–9, and by H. D. L. Vervliet in his introduction to *The Type Specimen of the Vatican Press 1628* (Amsterdam, 1967).

[5] Otto Baumgarten, *Neue Kunde von alten Bibeln* (Krumbach, 1922), pp. 104–6; L. von Pastor, *Geschichte der Päpste*, ix (Freiburg i. Br., 1923), note on pp. 198–9.

[6] A. Bertolotti, 'Le typografie orientali e gli orientalisti a Roma nei secoli xvi e xvii', *Rivista Europea*, ix (1878), pp. 217–68, at p. 245.

[7] The printer, Zanetti, in his foreword to the *Homilies* of St. Chrysostom (in Greek), Rome, 1581, referring to Gregory XIII.

decided what books were to be printed. The Apostolic Press was devoted to learnedly corrected editions of the Fathers and manuals in oriental languages for missions. The popes as secular monarchs had, from 'about 1530'[1] another press, the Stamperia Camerale, mainly for notices affecting their temporal domain. That also was confided to master printers, the well-known Antonio Blado and his descendants. Paul V combined these two printing-offices in 1610 so as to form the Typographia Vaticana, and from then onwards the Papacy may be said to have had a truly institutional press. At much the same time there came into being a third papal printing-office, that of the Sacra Congregatio de Propaganda Fide, devoted to the needs of foreign missions.

The Propaganda Press was far ahead of any other in its capacity for polyglot work, and its advantage to the Roman Catholic cause must have been apparent as far away as London and Oxford, given the addiction of ecclesiastics and scholars at that time to seeking, if not converts, support for their various doctrines in the eastern churches. When Fell wrote, in 1680, that one of his motives to develop printing at Oxford was 'preventing foreign Universities and Cities . . . to impose their Wares upon us, and oblige us to receive not only Books at their prizes, but opinions from their dictates'[2] he had in mind the well-equipped Romanist and Calvinist presses abroad, as Archbishop Laud had when he prompted the Vice-Chancellor at Oxford in 1636–7 to send to Holland for 'oriental' types.[3]

Soldiers of lead in religious strife were an argument for institutional presses, for few master printers could afford the range of foreign scripts needed for it. Attempts to buy founts of them, as by the Duke of Buckingham and Archbishop Ussher, from owners of a different religious persuasion failed.[4] Laud and Fell knew that they must equip a type-foundry for casting them. The University of Oxford by acquiring matrices for Greek in 1619 and for Hebrew and Arabic in 1637 had gone some way towards forming an institutional press, though it relied on accredited university printers to use the types. At Oxford, as at Rome, an intermediate stage, where the institution supplied learned types and controlled

[1] Vervliet, *The Type Specimen of the Vatican Press 1628*, p. 14.

[2] *An Account of the State of the Press in the Vniversity of Oxford as it now stands, January 9. 1679* (Morison, *Fell*, App. v, No. 4).

[3] Morison, *Fell*, pp. 22, 233–43.

[4] *Correspondance de P. P. Rubens*, ed. M. Rooses and Ch. Ruelens (Antwerp, 1909), vi, pp. 79, 149; A. Bernard, *Antoine Vitré et les caractères orientaux de la Bible Polyglotte de Paris* (Paris, 1857), pp. 17, 24; Ussher, *Works*, ed. C. R. Elrington and J. H. Todd (Dublin, 1847–64), xv, pp. 340, 342.

the choice of books to be printed came between the accredited printer as a wholly independent contractor and the corporately-owned institutional press.

Two other models must have helped to shape the plans of Laud and Fell for the 'publica Universitatis typographia' provided for in the academic statutes approved in 1636.[1] The French monarchy and the University of Leyden had fostered and subsidized printing of a learned and not necessarily profitable kind from motives partly religious. In 1539 King Francis I appointed Conrad Neobar as Royal Printer for Greek and charged him to produce correct editions of Greek manuscripts, 'the fount of all instruction'.[2] Neobar's successor in office, the famous Robert Estienne, got from the royal treasury the cost of commissioning Claude Garamond to cut the *typi regii Graeci*, the envy of all learned printers.[3] Laud did not enjoy his freedom long enough to experience the work of the French royal press; but Fell did so. L'Imprimerie royale du Louvre, set up in 1640, was designed for 'la gloire de la France et à l'honneur des lettres'.[4] Fell refers to the world's esteem for it as one of his reasons for hoping that the public would support his press.[5] Aldrich, his successor as dean and as encourager of learned printing, had the Louvre edition of the *Imitatio Christi* on his shelves;[6] his lieutenant, Arthur Charlett, refers to the 'fine Louvre editions'.[7]

Fell thought that the Hollanders had gained much credit by printing well.[8] English scholars of his generation read largely the editions of Dutch printers annotated by Dutch professors, and the example of Leyden can never have been far from his thoughts. The university there never has achieved an institutional press; but it always took a lively interest in publishing and printing and its professors acted as literary advisers and correctors at the presses in the town. As early as 1577 the senate of Leyden's university and the burgomasters induced an eminent printer, Willem Silvius, to leave Antwerp and become their first official printer.[9] His second successor in the post was the great Christophe Plantin, for

[1] Tit. xviii, sect. v; Griffiths, *Laudian Code*, p. 188.
[2] Letters patent quoted in *L'Art du livre à l'Imprimerie nationale* (Paris, Imprimerie nationale, 1951), p. 3.
[3] A. Bernard, *Histoire de l'Imprimerie royale du Louvre* (Paris, 1867), p. 8.
[4] *L'Art du livre à l'Imprimerie nationale*, p. 10.
[5] Letter to Williamson, 8 Apr. 1672, S.P. (Dom.), Car. II, 305, No. 98, quoted above, p. 62.
[6] Hearne, iii, p. 302.
[7] Hist. MSS. Comm., 2nd *Report*, p. 254b.
[8] Letter to Williamson cited above.
[9] Colin Clair, 'Willem Silvius', *The Library*, 5th ser. xiv (1959), pp. 192–205, at p. 200.

sixteen months, and he was followed by his learned son-in-law, Frans Ravelingen (Raphelengius), printer and professor.[1] A very high standard for learned printing had been set at Leyden by the time that the first of the Elseviers to own a press, Isaac, was made University Printer in 1620.[2] The senate obliged Abraham and Bonaventure Elsevier to equip themselves with exotic types,[3] and although the members of this family were contractors to, not servants of, the university, their publishing was the means of spreading its learning abroad.

The Dutch model is evident at Fell's press in the make-up of the volumes and the style of printing—and in typography. Anyone in England then would have gone to Holland for good type, as the University had done in 1637 for its orientals. Samuel Clarke, the Oxford Architypographus, was trying in 1668 to find matrices and a letter-cutter in Holland for the 'new intended Presse',[4] as Fell did with better success a few years later. Fell was set on getting 'Waesberg's Greeks', meaning those that Jan van Waesberge used at Amsterdam.[5] He could have admired the same types in books printed at Antwerp or in France or Germany if he had not read the Greek classics in Dutch editions and liked them best. It was to Isaac Vossius that Fell confided his hope of founding a press devoted to learning.[6]

Such was the meagre background of institutional printing when Fell and his partners undertook to conduct a press from Lady Day 1672 'that Printing and the full use and exercise thereof in the said University may redound to the great honour, renowne and benefitt of the same'.[7] It was still an experiment when in 1690 Fell's executors were succeeded as managers by the University's Delegates.

THE DELEGACY

The beginning of a Delegacy for Printing was in 1633, when Convocation, after listening to the royal charter authorizing the University to print and sell 'all manner of books', determined to show itself worthy of it and

---

[1] Leon Voet, 'Het Plantijnsche huis te Leiden', *Verslag van de algemeene vergadering van de leden van het Historisch Genootschap, Utrecht, 31 Oct. 1960*, pp. 10*–36*.

[2] D. W. Davies, *The World of the Elseviers, 1580–1712* (The Hague, 1954), p. 48.

[3] P. C. Molhuysen, *Bronnen tot de geschiedenis der Leidsche Universiteit, 2e. deel, 1610–47; Rijks geschiedkundige publicatiën No. 29* (The Hague, 1916), p. 128.

[4] B.M. MS. Add. 22905, fol. 84; Thomas Marshall at Dordrecht to Clarke, 9 Nov.

[5] Hart, p. 168a.

[6] Universiteitsbibliotheek, Leyden, Burm. Cod. Fo., No. 11, ii, fol. 62; 12 Mar. 1670/71, quoted above, p. 61.

[7] Univ. Arch. S.E.P. P7.

grateful for it. The Vice-Chancellor asked whether the venerable assembly would not name delegates 'who after thorough deliberation would find a way of making these most ample privileges procure the utmost benefit and credit for the University'. These delegates, he proposed, should 'settle the undertaking to be required of the printers, a press for printing in Greek, and an annual choice of a manuscript book in the Library to be published'. Thereupon the Proctors named eleven men, doctors or masters, 'as delegates for hearing, ordering, and effecting the matter proposed, that is to say the printers, the press, and what relates to printing'; the delegacy to consist of the eleven or a majority of them and the Vice-Chancellor and the Proctors.[1]

Convocation had been used, at any rate since the latter part of the sixteenth century, to depute committees for detailed business: the name 'delegates' was used in 1614 for a group entrusted with codifying the University's statutes.[2] The tasks given to these committees could be accomplished once and for all, and when that had been done the committees dissolved, *functi officio*. It is not unlikely that the Delegacy for Printing of 1633 was intended to be of this kind. It was told to arrange for an annual choice of a book, but not necessarily to make it; and 'what relates to printing' (*ad imprimendum*) might be understood, with reference to the question put to Convocation, as applying to the printing of a particular book (*res typographica* was the usual expression for printing generally). After it had decided that the *Chronographia* of Johannes Malalas of Antioch[3] was the best Greek text to publish no more is heard of this Delegacy for some time. The University's statutes drawn up a year after its appointment, in 1634, do not mention delegates in their provisions for printing.

However, the delegates nominated in 1633 were called upon to undertake more work four years later. The so-called 'Great Charter' of 1636[4] made it as clear as the King could make it that the University had the right to print Bibles, psalm-books, grammars, and other school books notwithstanding monopolies previously granted respecting them, and the London Stationers promptly offered an annual rent for forbearance to exercise the right. A proposal by the Vice-Chancellor that the money

---

[1] Reg. Conv. R, fol. 61; *Print and Privilege*, p. 12 n.

[2] Strickland Gibson, *Statuta antiqua Universitatis Oxoniensis*, p. lvii. For earlier committees, see ibid., pp. xxiii ff.

[3] Univ. Arch. S.E.P. P17ᵇ(3), fol. 1. It was published in 1691.

[4] Strickland Gibson, 'The Great Charter of Charles I to the University of Oxford (3 March 1636)', *Bodleian Quarterly Record*, vii (1932), pp. 73–94.

should be spent on printing learned books at Oxford was approved by Convocation and the delegates previously appointed were assigned to take charge of the business and to render an account of receipts and expenditure.[1] The proceedings of these persons are not recorded.

Sir Leoline Jenkins, Judge of Admiralty and an eminent civilian, doubted whether a permanent delegation of powers as wide as those exercised by the Delegates of the Press was good law.[2] Certainly the second Delegacy, nominated by the Proctors in 1653, was intended to last indefinitely, and it was entrusted with powers of a general kind: 'to supervise the University Press, and to take charge of printing generally'. The members were the holders of the offices of Vice-Chancellor, Proctor, professor, and Savilian praelector, University Orator, Principal Librarian, and Keeper of the Archives, as well as seven persons named. Unlike the previous Delegacy it was instructed to give Convocation a report of its proceedings.[3]

The expression 'University Press' (*praelum Academicum*) is remarkable, there being at that time no such thing. An obligation to set up the 'public press of the University' as soon as suitable premises could be found, in accordance with the statute approved in 1636, must have been present to the minds of some active members of Convocation. Moreover the project was—or, at any rate, almost was—considered by this delegacy.[4] There is no report of a meeting of this body, but its composition shows that great importance was attached to the business committed to it.

The Proctors wrote in 1756 with reference to this appointment: 'N.B. This Delegacy was probably look'd upon at the Restoration as appointed by illegal Authority; for an entire New Delegacy was soon after appointed, which, it is apprehended, subsists, by various substitutions, to this day'.[5]

The Delegates of 1662 were all doctors, Bailie, Yate, Barlow, Say, Pococke, Fell, Jenkins; all but the last three heads of colleges. They are not described in the Register of Convocation as 'standing' (*stati*),[1] but

[1] Reg. Conv. R, fol. 143ᵛ.

[2] Univ. Arch. W.P. γ 16(1), fols. 99, 100; *Print and Privilege*, p. 54.

[3] Reg. Conv. T, p. 191. '. . . ad Statuta Typographica condenda; lites, si quae inciderint, dirimendas; praelum Academicum supervidendum et rem Typographicam in universum procurandam'.   [4] Above, p. 45; B.M. MS. Add. 22905, fol. 9.

[5] *Observations relating to the Delegates of the Press: with an account of their succession from their original appointment* (Oxford, 1756), p. 3.

[6] This qualification was given, as a rule, only to the Delegates for Accounts: see the note (by Blackstone) in *A Reply to Dr. Huddesford's Observations* (Oxford, 1756), at pp. 14, 15; but Huddesford found instances of its being used of Delegates of the Press: ibid., p. 20, and Blackstone's *To the Reverend Dr. Randolph* (Oxford, 1757), pp. 23, 25 n. (Philip, pp. 64–5).

the scope given to them meant that they would be in permanent session. Their charge was 'To deliberate and act with regard to publishing and printing (*de re typographica*) and to report to Convocation', or, more exactly, 'to accept and expend money from the London Stationers, &c., to look for and secure a suitable place for printers and do all that is required for the purpose, and to render annually to Convocation an account of receipts and expenses at the time of the Vice-Chancellor's making up his account'.[1]

The Proctors did not appoint the Vice-Chancellor or themselves to this Delegacy: the holders for the time being of these offices were added to it by the Proctors in 1691.[2] At that time, soon after the cession to the University of the additions to the plant and stock of the Press made by Fell and Yate, they clearly purported to supersede the existing delegacy. They named Delegates 'to deliberate on and decide about printing, who shall also provide for and effect all that has to be done for it, together with the Vice-Chancellor and Proctors for the time'. However, since Convocation had not dissolved the old Delegacy, it could be argued that the nominations of 1691 operated only as a substitution of members. John Mill, Principal of St. Edmund Hall, added in 1688, was not named as one of the new body; so it is uncertain whether he was a member of it or not.

In later times the right of the Proctors to nominate new members to the Delegacy of the Press without the concurrence of the Vice-Chancellor was questioned. The matter came to a head in 1756, when the Proctors asserted it.[3] Precedents were found in favour of the contestants on either side. The revised statute for the Press adopted a year later provided that appointments of new Delegates must be made by the Vice-Chancellor and Proctors, or a majority of them, and approved by Convocation.[4]

The Delegates appointed in 1691 were Timothy Halton, Provost of Queen's, William Jane, Regius Professor of Divinity, Henry Aldrich, Dean of Christ Church, William Levett, Principal of Magdalen Hall, Jonathan Edwards, Principal of Jesus, Edward Bernard, Savilian Professor of Astronomy, and Fitzherbert Adams, Rector of Lincoln. They were all doctors of divinity. Their average age was $50\frac{1}{2}$.

---

[1] '. . . ad deliberandum et determinandum cum relatione ad Dom. Convoc. de re typographica, viz. Qui pecunias a Stationariis Londin. &c. accipiant et erogent, de loco typographis idoneo aliisque omnibus in hanc rem faciendam prospiciant et transigant, et rationem quotannis reddant de receptis et expensis quo tempore V-Can. Computum suum fecerit': Reg. Conv. Ta, p. 154.

[2] Reg. Conv .Bb, p. 309; *Print and Privilege*, p. 121.

[3] p. 327 below.

[4] *Corpus statutorum Universitatis Oxoniensis*, 1768, App., p. 68.

Whether these Delegates held meetings, and if so how often, cannot now be told. Their minute-book[1] is blank between 1678 and 1694, in which year Arthur Charlett, Master of University College, and John Hough, Bishop of Oxford, were added. Halton, Jane, Aldrich, Edwards, and Charlett were regular attendants at Delegates' meetings in the ten years following 1694.

In their provisions for delegacies the statutes of 1636 did not prescribe a period for their meetings: they only obliged them to convene when duly summoned in a place appointed by the Vice-Chancellor. The Delegates of the Press, so far as the records show, met twice in 1694, once in 1695, once in 1700, and five times in 1703. The attendance seldom exceeded half a dozen. The statute adopted for this Delegacy in 1757 fixed the number of meetings at four in every year or more if business so required. It fixed the number of Delegates at eleven, including the Vice-Chancellor and the Proctors, and at that number it remained until 1856. The first sign of a quorum is in 1760, when two meetings were adjourned because a majority of the Delegates was not present.

A board of as many members meeting at some such intervals of time could transact much of the business of publishing, but it could not conduct a printing-office. It is evident that the printing-office was largely left to its own devices; also that other people besides the Delegates devoted their energies to publishing.

THE ARCHITYPOGRAPHUS

Before discussing the persons who were active in promoting the affairs of the Press in its Augustan Age, 1690–1712, it will be as well to dispose of the University's officer established for that purpose, who did not act at all during those years and disappeared soon afterwards.

The modern statutes of the University make scant reference to a Printer to the University. Before their extensive reform in 1969 he was mentioned only among those eligible to professorial fellowships: since the reform he occurs also as an officer to be appointed by the Delegates of the Press.[2] The Laudian statutes, in force from 1636 until 1856, contemplated (Tit. XVIII) that there would be a number of master printers who would be allowed to use the title of *typographus Universitatis* and work on their own account, not as servants of the academic body,

---

[1] It has been published as far as 1756 in *First Minute Book*. The minutes of 1758–60 are printed in Philip, pp. 90–113.
[2] (1968) Tit. XXIV II; (1970) Tit. III LXXVII, s. 2.

though doubtless sometimes as contractors to it. The Architypographus was to rule over them. He was the University's officer charged with maintaining standards both of scholarship and of workmanship in books printed within its precinct. He was appointed by, and answerable only to, Convocation. One thing he lacked: a salary; so the difficulty was got over by annexing to his office that of Esquire Bedel of Civil Law. As both the man chosen for the post was entitled to a salary and fees.

The truth is that the momentous step taken by the University of engaging directly in printing and bookselling, which the University of Cambridge took six years later,[1] was taken by accident. The public academic press which Archbishop Laud had in mind when he framed the statutes in 1634 would have been one where licensed printers could work at their own risk. In the previous year Convocation had instructed delegates to find a suitable place for the printers;[2] the post for an architypographus established in 1636 was designed to make their work a credit to the University.

The master printers of Oxford did execute works for the University at its own press, when at last it was given space for printing in the Sheldonian Theatre. The Vice-Chancellor paid one of the *typographi* to produce, with the imprint 'Oxonii, e Theatro Sheldoniano' the verses for the death of the Queen Mother which Anthony Wood said was the first book to be finished there.[3] At least eight other books with the same imprint were done by contractors' labour in the years 1669–72. The first book to be put in hand at the corporately-owned press, Beveridge's *Synodicon*, was contracted out to a London bookseller, Robert Scott.[4] When Scott asked to be relieved of his bargain, the Delegates agreed to finish the book, employing the workmen brought to Oxford by the contractor and to take the whole impression as security for their costs.[5] Presumably Scott was able eventually to repay the University and redeem his books;[6] but this experience of the printing and bookselling trades was enough to persuade Convocation to entrust Fell and his three partners with the Press as from Lady Day, 1672.

Under Fell's management the press in the Sheldonian Theatre set a pattern for his successors and, in some respects, determined its organiza-

---

[1] D. F. McKenzie, *The Cambridge University Press, 1696–1712* (Cambridge, 1966), Introduction; S. C. Roberts, *The Evolution of Cambridge Publishing* (Cambridge, 1956), pp. 1–21.
[2] Above, p. 138.
[3] Madan, *Oxford Books*, iii, No. 2916.
[4] D.O. 7 Sept. 1668; *First Minute Book*, p. 3.
[5] 13 Jan. 1669; ibid., pp. 6–7.
[6] There is no record of copies being left in the Delegates' stock.

tion for many years after his day. It was not the kind of press that Laud had envisaged, though it produced books that he would have liked and rose in point of quality of workmanship above the depressed standard of English printing that he had deplored.[1] Instead of being paid for out of funds belonging to the University, this press was financed mainly by Fell and Yate. They, indeed, paid £200 a year for the privilege. The choice of books to be published lay, not with a committee, but with the providers of the funds for them. The manner and quality of the production was the concern of the 'undertakers', not of the University's officer, the Architypographus.

Nothing better illustrates the changed character that events forced on the learned press, or for lack of purposefulness were allowed to affect it, than the history of this official. Established as the supervisor of printing at Oxford, controlling the academic printing-house, its equipment, staffing, and materials, a corrector of copy and a superior proof-reader, he soon became little more than a runner of errands between the Delegates and the printers and an accountant before being suppressed in all but name. To be effective an architypographus would have needed not only the rare combination of attainments contemplated by the statutes but an uncommon force of character. If he did not control the funds for printing, he was without the means of enforcing his will or the corporate will of his employer—especially if it meant crossing the redoubtable Dr. Fell.

Lack of money prevented the only Architypographus with qualifications that measured up to his task, Samuel Clarke, from exercising them. Clarke, the first of holder of the office, elected in 1658, was a student of Hebrew and Arabic who had borne a share in the correction of the London Polyglot Bible and had plans for more polyglot publishing.[2] He was energetic and earned from Anthony Wood the character of 'a most useful and necessary person' to the University.[3] He interested himself in the mechanics of printing, catalogued the Greek types brought to Oxford in Laud's time,[4] and made inquiries in Holland for matrices and a letter-cutter.[5]

The admirable Clarke lived to see presses installed in the Sheldonian Theatre and the first book with the Sheldonian imprint come off the presses in October 1669. Two months later he died. Fell, Dean of Christ

[1] *Reports of Cases in the Courts of Star Chamber and High Commission*, Camden Soc., 2nd series 39 (1886), p. 305.
[2] Bodl. MS. Rawl. D. 397, fol. 155.
[3] *Ath.* iii, 882.
[4] Bodl. MS. Rawl. D. 317, fol. 53.
[5] B.M. MS. Add. 22905, fols. 67, 70–2, 81, 84–8, 90.

Church, accomplishing his term as Vice-Chancellor, a Delegate of the Press since 1662, had taken up the cause of University printing and did not lightly forgive interference with his plans for it. He had his candidate chosen for the post vacated by Clarke, and proposed to Convocation Thomas Bennett, M.A., whom he trusted to correct copy and proofs. The memoirs of life at Oxford at that time make it clear that many things besides fitness of the candidates swayed elections here. Fell's peremptoriness and Bennett's omission to canvass votes provoked a majority of Convocation to vote for Norton Bold, who could pretend to none of the statutory qualifications.[1] Bold occupied the post for three years without performing any of its functions, and then Fell saw an opportunity to promote him to a more lucrative bedelship and proposed Bennett once more for architypographus. The Dean went so far this time as to get a Mandamus from the King in Council declaring the election of 1669 of no effect and ordering a new one.[2] Despite the royal injunction to choose the 'most suitable person to govern your printing presses', Convocation repeated its rebuff to the Dean of Christ Church and elected Christopher Wase, a man lately incorporated from Cambridge who was not even resident.

The lease of the University's privilege of printing to Fell and his partners, signed in October 1671, took effect on Lady Day following. Wase, who had been surprised by his appointment and owned his incompetence,[3] did not attempt to act in it but was content to enjoy its emoluments until he died in 1691. He was succeeded by Gerard Langbaine the younger, who held the office for little more than a year.

Under Fell's constant and close supervision the Press afforded little scope for such a responsible officer as the Architypographus. The leading man there was John Hall, the Warehouse-Keeper. He had been matriculated as a printer in 1667,[4] the son of William Hall, and grandson of Henry Hall, Printer to the University. When Fell's partnership took over the concern John Hall was in charge of the men working on Anthony Wood's *Historia*.[5] The extent of his responsibilities was not as yet settled, but Yate suggested that he be entrusted with a fund for buying ink,[6] and before long Hall was answerable to the partners for the day-to-day management of the printing-house: some of the accounts that he rendered

[1] Wood, *Ath.* iii, 884; Reg. Conv. Bb. 29, fol. 301.
[2] P.R.O. S.P. Misc. Entry Books, 31, No. 77, 16 Sept. 1671.
[3] P.R.O. S.P. (Dom.), Car. II, 293, No. 108.
[4] Reg. Conv. Pb. 348ᵇ.
[5] Univ. Arch. S.E.P. P17ᵇ(1)ᵐ; *Print and Privilege*, pp. 57–8.   [6] Ibid., p. 58.

to them, for the years 1676–9, have found their way to the Bodleian.[1] Lest Bennett, the corrector, might try to be a sort of architypographus, the partners noted: 'Corrector not to intermeddle in any thing, but to mynd his bussinesse.'[2]

The Warehouseman–manager was taken over as part of a going concern by the Delegates in 1690, and Hall signed the annual accounts rendered to the Vice-Chancellor until he died in 1707. At this point the Archi-typographus, Giles Thistlethwaite, elected after the death of Langbaine in 1692,[3] was put in possession of some of his functions. He was not competent to undertake technical supervision, but he acted as go-between carrying messages from such Delegates as were active to the workmen. Hall's widow received payments for work done, paid the printers, and lived over the Little Print-House adjoining the Sheldonian Theatre.[4] The Architypographus drew up the annual accounts.

Thistlethwaite died on 15 January 1714/15, and four days later Thomas Hearne was elected Architypographus in his stead—by a large majority of votes.[5] He had in abundance the qualifications as a scholar that the statute framed in 1634 required; he was an experienced editor with ten publications to his credit besides the correcting and indexing of others; since 1701 he had been on the staff of the Bodleian Library and had accumulated a wonderful knowledge of books and manuscripts. His industry and method would have made him invaluable in a tightly-governed publishing business. In such a loose organization as the University's press was at that time, Hearne, a conceited, touchy, and quarrelsome man and a stickler for method, would have been a disaster: he would have spent his energies on arguing with Mrs. Hall on the one hand and the Delegates on the other in his determination to work to rule. Two days after Hearne's election the Delegates met and appointed Stephen Richardson Warehouse-Keeper in charge of the Press, clearly intending that he should act as Hall and Mrs. Hall had done while Hearne ran errands and copied out the accounts.[6] Hearne, rather dis-ingenuously, claimed that Richardson, a compositor in the University's service since 1691, had been made Architypographus.

Nobody who has read Hearne's diaries will fail to understand what the Vice-Chancellor, Bernard Gardiner, meant when he said: 'Mr. Hearne, you are certainly the fittest person that is in Oxford for this place. But

---

[1] MS. Rawl. D. 397, fols. 404–26.   [2] *Print and Privilege*, p. 57.
[3] Hearne, ii, p. 122.
[4] Ibid., pp. 121–2; see p. 66 above and p. 197 below.
[5] Hearne, v, p. 17.   [6] D.O. 17 Jan. 1715; *First Minute Book*, pp. 42–3.

your principles are not suitable.'[1] Hearne's outspoken Jacobite loyalties had offended some of his seniors and alarmed others; his rigid Non-Juring professions and his poverty were a reproach to them. Always determined to be an oppressed man, after many acrimonious passages, he resigned the office on 8 November 1715, and on 12 November William Mussendine was elected to succeed him.[2] It had been shown that the will of Convocation could not now prevail over that of the Delegates of the Press.

It does not appear that Mussendine, in his capacity of Architypographus, did more than put his name to the Press accounts; and when a successor to him, Herbert Beaver, was chosen in 1732 some were of opinion that the post had ceased to exist and Beaver was only Esquire Bedel of Civil Law.[3] He was called upon, nevertheless, by the Delegates in 1756 to make plans for printing Edmund Gibson's *Codex* and to act as its corrector.[4] Still, we have Blackstone's authority for saying that from the time of Beaver's election until 1757 the post of Architypographus was vacant.[5]

It was a ground of Blackstone's complaints of his seniors on the Delegacy that this office had been allowed to lapse: 'the laying aside of the office of architypographer and employing a mere labourer in his stead',[6] but it seems likely that the vacancy interested him only as colour for his charges of neglect. He admitted that there was little for the Architypographus to do, that his functions 'would be absurd and impracticable in works that are printed for private persons' and that the most to be expected of him was 'a general oversight' of correction, workmanship, and quality of material.[7] In his draft for a new statute defining the province of the Delegates[8] he mentions the Architypographus as an exception from their power to appoint and remove officers and servants of the Press; but the new statute adopted in consequence in 1757 omits any mention of him. He remained statutable until 1856.[9] The Superior Bedel of Civil Law in the capacity of Architypographus was consulted by the Delegates of the Press in 1770[10] and they asked him to correct proofs of Polybius in 1783.[11]

Blackstone's reforms[12] led to the appointment of a fit man, Daniel Prince, to assume the office of Warehouse-Keeper or Overseer.

[1] Hearne, v, p. 32.   [2] Hearne, vi, pp. 4–7.   [3] Hearne, xi, p. 124.
[4] *First Minute Book*, p. 58.
[5] *To the Revd. Dr. Randolph*, p. 11; Philip, p. 52.
[6] *To the Revd. Dr. Randolph*, p. 23; Philip, p. 63.
[7] *To the Revd. Dr. Randolph*, p. 10; Philip, p. 52.
[8] Philip, p. 73. For the revised statute see ibid., pp. 75–6; Griffiths, *Laudian Code*, p. 309.
[9] *Addenda ad Corpus Statut. Univ. Oxon.*, pp. 528–33.
[10] D.O. 28 Oct.   [11] Ibid. 4 July.   [12] See Chapter XXI, below.

THE ACTIVE MANAGERS

Fell, by his will, had recommended to his executors the 'Advice and Direction' of Dr. Timothy Halton, Dr. Henry Aldrich, and Dr. John Mill. These three and Dr. William Jane, Regius Professor of Divinity, were the Delegates of the Press who assumed the power of management in 1691. Dr. Jonathan Edwards, Principal of Jesus College, as Vice-Chancellor, was their chairman.

Halton, Provost of Queen's, was a Delegate of the Press from 1688 until he died in 1704; but of any effect that he may have had on its policy or productions there is no trace. Fell is said to have liked him because Halton 'would be ruled by him'.[1] He was not a literary man: his monument is rather the magnificent building of the library added to his college under his supervision.

The papers belonging to Aldrich were destroyed in accordance with his will soon after his death in 1710, so that information about his part in publishing and printing is sadly hard to find. There can be no doubt, though, that his was the main influence on the press in its first twenty-five years of committee-management. Looking back in 1757 Blackstone singled him out for continuing 'in some degree' Fell's spirit and example at the learned press.[2]

Aldrich kept up Fell's custom of producing 'New-Year Books', presents for pupils and friends.[3] These editions of Greek and Latin classics or Christian texts were put on general sale, but the Dean paid for a number of copies (apparently some 200)[4] for his own use. In this way he subsidized solid works of scholarship, two volumes of the Xenophon edited by Edward Wells and Grabe's *Spicilegium* of the early Fathers, and a series of texts useful to students which were hard to come by.

In Hearne's opinion (and he was a good judge of this) Aldrich was one of the best scholars and literary critics then living.[5] It may be true that his interests were confined, as Charlett thought, to 'polite learning';[6] but if so his predilection is not reflected in the University's publishing. Unlike other Oxford scholars of his generation he achieved distinction as

---

[1] *Wood's Life and Times*, i, p. 348.
[2] *To the Revd. Doctor Randolph*, p. 26.
[3] Wood, *Ath.* iv, 652; Madan, *Oxford Books*, iii, p. 521; Hearne, i, p. 123. Five of them are named in an undated advertisement by Jonah Bowyer, bookseller in London, for the sale, with other Oxford books, of 'a small number remaining of the late Dean of Christ Church's five last New-Years-Gifts': the *Odyssey* in Greek, 1705; Grotius, *Baptizatorum puerorum institutio*, 1706; Epictetus, *Enchiridion*, 1707; Ignatius, *Epistolae*, 1708; Palladio, *Antiquitates urbis Romanae*, 1709; B.M. Harl. 5932(9).
[4] Hearne, xi, p. 278.   [5] Hearne, viii, p. 120.   [6] Hearne, vi, p. 47.

an amateur of music, architecture, and the graphic arts.[1] His publications were two defences of the Anglican Eucharist against the Romanist Abraham Woodhead, of 1687 and 1688, the *Artis logicae compendium*, first printed in 1691, the acknowledged ancestor of a long series of manuals on its subject,[2] and an *Institutio geometrica* of 1709, which did not get beyond *Pars prima* 'impressa sed non edita; secundas enim cogitationes expectat'. He also wrote the first part of a treatise intended to cover the whole of architecture, and had a few copies of it printed with illustrations engraved from his own drawings.[3]

Hearne, who wrote of Aldrich as a 'great man' and an 'excellent Dean', paid tribute to his conscientiousness as head of the House and as supervisor of studies.[4] As such he incited younger men to edit and publish. The Euclid which came out in 1703 with the name of David Gregory as editor was promoted and planned by Aldrich and Charlett;[5] the Dean 'directed' Wells's series of the works of Xenophon;[6] and set Hugh Hutchin on the ill-fated project of a Polybius.[7]

Aldrich acted for the University in accepting Clarendon's *History* for the Press.[8] He helped the Earl of Rochester to prepare the final draft which was copied for the printers. One of Rochester's household remembered that 'Dr. Aldrich frequently came over to Cornbury House and assisted in revising it.'[9] The printed form of the first edition, it is easy to suppose, owed a great deal to the Dean; its handsome folio format, big type, and engraved ornament conform with all that is known of his taste.[10]

Other proposed publications in which the Dean was interested came to nothing: an edition of Caesar 'with noble cuts of his own contriving'[11] was one, and another was a 'set of books for the service of choirs',[12] identifiable with 'your design'd volume of church-musick' of which Samuel Pepys wrote hopefully.[13] Of this work four sheets in folio were printed and remained in the list of the Delegates' stock for several years.

---

[1] W. G. Hiscock, *A Christ Church Miscellany* (Oxford, 1946).
[2] *D.N.B.*
[3] The fragment was published in 1789 with an English translation as *Elementa Architecturae civilis*. It will be noticed in the second volume of this history.
[4] Hearne, iii, p. 89.
[5] Bodl. MS. Ballard i, fol. 109; Hearne, i, pp. 88–9.
[6] Hearne, x, p. 143.
[7] Hearne, i, p. 195; J. M. G. Blakiston in *The Library*, 5th ser. xvii (1962), at pp. 33–4.
[8] Hearne, iii, p. 179; Macray, *Annals*, p. 225.
[9] John Burton, *The Genuineness of Ld. Clarendon's History . . . Vindicated* (1744), pp. 18–19.
[10] As to Aldrich's part in the prefaces, see below, pp. 234–5.
[11] Hearne, iii, pp. 302, 329.
[12] List of books 'sub prelo' at the Sheldonian Theatre, 1696.
[13] Bodl. MS. Ballard i, 93.

Pepys had seen a specimen of the 'musick-characters' to be used in the book and found them 'very agreeable'; this was evidently the genesis of De Walpergen's pretty music-type, which met the public eye first in the *Yattendon Hymns* of 1895.[1] The University's *Specimen of . . . Letter*, 1695, the second edition, gives a small sample of it, and in Christ Church Library there is a sixteen-page setting in this type of anthems, one of which is attributed to Aldrich.[2] De Walpergen's rendering of hand-written notes in a somewhat old-fashioned decorative style is likely to have had guidance from the Dean; for he was considered to be a master of ornament, the only man for inventing borders (head and tail pieces) for a book.[3]

The justice of Hearne's opinion is confirmed by a recent discovery. Designs for initial letters, headbands, and tailpieces in an album kept at the Press have been identified by Miss H. M. Petter, basing herself on the collections at Christ Church, as drawings by Aldrich.[4] Many of them were engraved by Michael Burghers and printed in the first edition of Clarendon's *History of the Rebellion*. The designs are accomplished and beautiful drawings in brown ink with brown and grey washes. Miss Petter has found that several of the subjects correspond closely with engravings after old masters in the collection at Christ Church made by Aldrich. The plates by Burghers convey the designs accurately, but his hard, insensitive lines cannot do justice to the delicate originals. The comparison shows how much more the ornament of the *History* owes to Aldrich than to the engraver.

The death of Aldrich in 1710 was a turning-point in the history of Oxford publishing. His position as an eminent man generally liked and admired was unique, and the want of such a man in the direction of the Press is miserably apparent in the quarrels and neglect in the succeeding age.

John Mill, Principal of St. Edmund Hall, does not appear to have been an active or prominent member of the Press Delegacy, and no doubt he owed his place in it to Fell's patronage. He died in 1707 within a month

---

[1] Morison, *Fell*, pp. 205 ff. The complete *Yattendon Hymnal* followed in 1899.
[2] G. E. P. Arkwright, *Catalogue of Music in the Library of Christ Church* (Oxford, 1915–23), No. 1208. [3] Hearne, i, p. 287.
[4] The attribution is supported by Mr. H. M. Colvin and by Mr. Gordon Christian, Assistant Curator of Christ Church Gallery. The album is inscribed, 'Collected from the papers of Horace Walpole Earl of Orford left by the Honble. Anne Seymour Damer to Sir I. W. Waller Bart. G.C.H.' Falconer Madan inserted a slip on which he wrote, 'Original designs by Michael Burghers who engraved for the Oxford Press from 1676 to 1720, and in 1692 was appointed Engraver to the University'.

of publishing his great variorum Greek Testament, on which he had been working since 1681.[1] A very learned man, sharing with John Wallis the distinction of being the best disputant in theology of his day,[2] he had difficulty in making up his mind.[3]

Of those who came after the advisers recommended by Fell, Arthur Charlett bore the main burden of directing the Press, as he bore much of the burden of stimulating the literary energies of Oxford. 'A man of a strange Rambling Head, much addicted to maintain Correspondence, to hear and to tell news in Company, which he is seldom free from',[4] his hospitality, his fine library, his care for his pupils made University College, where he was Master from 1692, a focus for social and intellectual life.

Hardly an author himself, he delighted in promoting authorship. Besides helping Aldrich to plan the Euclid of 1703 and getting David Gregory and John Hudson to work at it, he put Jonas Proast on the subject of toleration,[5] set Edmund Gibson to catalogue the libraries of Tenison and Dugdale, and promoted Gibson's edition of Camden's *Britannia*.[6]

The two 'visitors' deputed by the Delegates to inspect and control the farmed-out Bible Press[7] in 1708 were Aldrich and Charlett.[8] They were well chosen for this onerous duty because one was trusted and the other active. From the time of his appointment to the Delegacy in 1694 the Master of University was busy selling the work of the Press and thinking of books to print. He knew better than anyone what books were in preparation, and from 1694 until 1716 he compiled and issued to likely buyers lists of publications to be expected from the Sheldonian presses and lately come from them.[9] His letter-writing and hospitality kept together a group of friends of the Press informed by him of its activity and capable of informing it of criticism. To work with people of such conflicting opinions and irritability as the Oxford scholars of his day needed tact, and it is no wonder if Charlett was accused of having so much of it as to amount to duplicity.[10] He was the 'great patron' of the

[1] Wood, *Fasti* ii, p. 381.   [2] Hearne, viii, p. 59.
[3] Adam Fox, *John Mill and Richard Bentley, a Study of the Textual Criticism of the New Testament 1675–1729* (Oxford, 1954).
[4] Hearne, i, p. 215.   [5] Hearne, ii, p. 5.
[6] Hearne, ii, pp. 45–6; Bodl. MS. Add. C. 217, fol. 63.
[7] See below p. 160.
[8] Bodl. MS. Rawl. letters, 38, 1811.
[9] Copies of his 'sub prelo' lists are extant for the years 1694, 1696, 1697, 1701, 1705, 1708, 1711, 1716.
[10] Bodl. MS. Ballard xiii, fol. 36.

learned Edmund Gibson,[1] disliked at Oxford for his Whiggery, and advised Browne Willis on local history,[2] while Hearne had grudgingly to admit that he was 'a great Encourager of good Letters'.[3] Like Aldrich, he bought quantities of some of the books from the Press to give as presents to his pupils and friends at the New Year.[4]

If the University can be said to have acted as publisher during the twenty years after the death of Fell it was owing to the Dean and the Master. That the publishing was unprofitable was certainly not the Master's fault: he did what he could to sell the books, but finally had to admit 'the vending of books we never could compasse'.[5] As the Delegates grew less inclined for new ventures the Press was kept going by aspiring authors and by booksellers who paid it to print.

John Hudson was conspicuous among the scholars who were disposed to print. From 1692 until he died in 1719 some work of his editing was passing through the Press, and he lent a hand with a good deal of work by others. Though never a Delegate, he must have been of considerable weight in the counsels of the Press, prompting authors and editors and suggesting improvements in what they did.[6] 'Besides the Works going under his name,' Hearne noted, 'he has likewise assisted in most of the things which have of late years come from the Theatre Press, in some of which he is gratefully mention'd, in others not.'[7] As a young tutor he had his abridgement of Bishop Beveridge's Chronology printed by Leonard Lichfield for the benefit of his pupils, and he followed it with a dialogue by Erasmus (1693).[8] These he paid for, and in later life he commissioned the Theatre Press to print for him Eutropius and Justin Martyr in 1703. His study in the Bodleian Library was described in 1711 as a warehouse for books that had been printed for him.[9] His nickname, the Bookseller, may have been earned in his dealings with Bodleian duplicates,[10] but an intimate acquaintance with the trade is implicit in his purchase in 1713, with two of his friends, of the whole stock in the Press Warehouse for £751.[11] How he disposed of it is a mystery, but he died rich,[12] so the speculation is likely to have done him no harm. As Bodley's

[1] Bodl. MS. Add. C. 217, fol. 63.
[2] Hearne, iv, p. 84.   [3] Hearne, v, p. 55.
[4] Velleius Paterculus, 1693, Plutarch, 1694: Wood, *Ath.* iv, 452, 460.
[5] Hist. MSS. Comm., 2nd *Report*, p. 254b.
[6] Hearne, i, pp. 239–40; ii, pp. 8–9.
[7] Hearne, i, p. 240.   [8] Wood, *Ath.* iv, 451–2.   [9] Hearne, iii, p. 262.
[10] Conrad von Uffenbach quoted in J. E. B. Mayor, *Cambridge under Queen Anne* (Cambridge, 1911), p. 386.
[11] D.O. 8 June 1713; *First Minute Book*, pp. 38–9.   [12] Hearne, viii, p. 92.

Librarian from 1701 he evidently gave to authors the help that Bodleian librarians can and do give, and this is a great strength of Oxford publishing.

Of the Vice-Chancellors who presided briefly over the fortunes of the Press little is known to our purpose: of Adams, who followed Aldrich in 1695, nothing; of Meare, who held the office for a year, that 'he was never noted for Learning or for anything else';[1] of Paynter and Mander, 1698–1701, nothing. That brings us to the notorious Dr. William Delaune, the President of St. John's. He was the Delegates' chairman when the first two editions of Clarendon's *History* were published, and his receipts for books sold and other income of the Press were computed at £2,773. 3s. 9d. Of that he paid into the University Chest £493.[2] He accounted satisfactorily for £200 rent from the Stationers' Company for the Bible Press in each of his four years and a payment of £493 from Thomas Bennett, bookseller, in 1702/3.

Delaune admitted the debt, 'which he hath both by Letters and by promises severall times undertaken to pay or give unexceptionable security for', according to a minute of the Delegates of 1709.[3] Hearne affirmed that Delaune was made President of the College 'upon the Account of his supposed Riches, some Relative of his having left him a vast sum of Money, which as 'tis reported he squander'd away by shaking his Elbow; whence a certain *terrae Filius* in the Publick Act of 1703 beginning with some Hesitation to speak something of the Vice-Chancellor broke out with a Resolution to do it with these words, *jacta est alea*'.[4]

Oxford opinion was not hard on his 'misfortunes'.[5] Rumours that £1,000 or £600 were in the University chest when he took office and were missing and unaccounted for at the end of his term[6] were an exaggeration: in 1709 the Chancellor, Masters, and Scholars sued him for a debt of £231. 1s. 2d., and when he admitted his inability to pay sequestered his presidency of his college.[7] It may not have been true that

[1] Hearne, ii, p. 395.   [2] D.O. 26 Mar. 1708; *First Minute Book*, pp. 23–4.
[3] D.O. 5 Apr. 1709; *First Minute Book*, p. 28.
[4] Hearne, i, p. 100; N. Amhurst, *Terrae filius* (1726), i, pp. 3, 18–20. Hearne's hearsay and the jibe of the *terrae filius* are our only authority for Delaune's being a gambler. A scurrilous lampoon on him ascribed to Thomas Wagstaffe the younger accuses him of many kinds of moral obliquity and silliness, but not of gambling (Nichols, *Lit. An.* i, pp. 36–7). He may have had some other way of getting rid of a great deal of money leaving nothing to show for it. The *terrae filius* was the clown traditionally licensed to enliven the University's solemnities.
[5] Hearne, v, p. 25.   [6] Hearne, i, pp. 315, 320.
[7] Chancellor's Court Acta, 1706–12, 16 July 1709.

he received a bequest of £20 to Stone's Almshouse in Oxford and failed to pay it over.[1] If Hearne can be believed, he had expensive tastes: 'a good Companion, and one who understood Eating and Drinking very nicely'.[2]

Delaune was so unfortunate as to be succeeded as Vice-Chancellor by 'the Northern Bear', William Lancaster, Provost of Queen's, who roundly charged him with owing the Press £2,280. 3s. 9d. and when he did not pay, got an order from the Chancellor's Court to sequester his rectory of Long Hanborough.[3] The sequestered rectory and a prebend of Winchester yielded to the University payments in the years 1711–20 amounting to £2,804 (the stipend of a curate for Long Hanborough included).[4] Means had to be found for easing Delaune's need of money: he was elected Lady Margaret Professor of Divinity in 1715. Later, in 1721, during the Vice-Chancellorship of Robert Shippen, Principal of Brasenose, he was made a Delegate of the Press and of Accounts (!). The stone under which he was buried in his college chapel lacks the customary laudatory epitaph.[5]

The case of Delaune is believed to be the only one of a Vice-Chancellor diverting revenues from the University to his own use. The documents enabling the succeeding Vice-Chancellor to prove it do not survive; but at the risk of taxing the reader's patience, it seems worth while to investigate the likelihood of these large sums being paid to the account of the Press at this time, and in particular to test the truth of the assertion that Delaune made away with the proceeds of the sale of Clarendon's *History of the Rebellion.*[6]

The money that Delaune was accused of (and admitted) receiving and not accounting for was all paid by John Baskett in the years 1703–6.[7] Delaune was Vice-Chancellor from October 1702 until October 1706. Baskett was a paper-merchant doing a big business with the University and a member of the Court of Assistants of the Stationers' Company. In August 1706 he succeeded Thomas Bennett as sole wholesaler of Clarendon's *History.*[8]

The Delegates' Orders of 28 November 1704 and 4 December 1705

[1] Hearne, ii, p. 89.   [2] Hearne, i, p. 193.
[3] D.O. 4 July 1710; *First Minute Book*, p. 31.
[4] V.-C.'s Computus 1697–1735.
[5] For more about Delaune, see W. C. Costin, *The History of St. John's College, Oxford, 1598–1860* (Oxford, 1958), pp. 165–81.
[6] Hearne, i, p. 315; J. Ayliffe, *The Antient and Present State of the University of Oxford* (1714), i, p. 216.
[7] The year as printed '1708' in the *First Minute Book* is a misreading of 1703 in the original.
[8] Below, p. 167.

record their decision to sell to Thomas Bennett, bookseller of London, wholesaler's rights in two volumes of Clarendon's *History*. These were the third volume of the first (folio) edition and the first of the edition in octavo. However, a draft agreement sanctioned at an unreported meeting of the Delegates[1] and an account kept in the Stationers' records[2] make it clear that he acted as wholesaler, with the assent of the Stationers' Company, of all the volumes of both editions, including second impressions of two volumes of the first, leaving the University only the copies on large paper to sell or give away. The price that Bennett had to pay for the eight books may be roughly estimated at £3,000. That is approximately what Lancaster accused Delaune of misappropriating, if we add the £685 that he said was due from Baskett and deduct the £485 received from Bennett which is credited to the University in the Computus.

Yet it is unlikely that Bennett had paid the whole of his debt for Clarendon when he died in August 1706,[3] and other debts of London Stationers are likely to be represented in the payments that Baskett made to Delaune.

As a result of their agreement made with the University in 1692 the Stationers held a stock of Oxford books for which they paid from time to time as the books were sold. In 1699/1700 Benjamin Tooke, Treasurer of the English Stock, sent the Warehouse-Keeper £860 in all, and Bennett paid him £229 in 1703, of which £113 was for Clarendon.

There are amounts credited to the Vice-Chancellor in the Press accounts which ought to have appeared in Delaune's Computus and did not. One of them is for sales of the *Almanack*, bringing in £472 in 1703–6, and the number printed was such that London was the only market capable of absorbing it. Baskett bought a large quantity at wholesale rates in 1711 and for many years thereafter.

It is remarkable, too, that items standing to the Vice-Chancellor's credit regularly in other years are lacking in those for 1703–6. There is usually £30 or £40 received for the University's poundage on books printed for authors and booksellers and often the money paid for printing such books; but in Delaune's time it must be inferred that these revenues did not come into the hands of the Warehouse-Keeper. They must have been substantial: reference to the Appendix to this volume will show that

---

[1] Delegates' files, Pkt. 75. See below, pp. 164–5.

[2] Printed in N. Hodgson and C. Blagden, *The Notebook of Thomas Bennet and Henry Clements* (Oxford, 1956), pp. 209–11.

[3] The V.-C.'s Computus for 1709/10 has an entry for £240 'from Basket and London Stationers for Lord Clarendon's books'.

a number of books were published in 1702–5 which are not traceable in the accounts of the Press, some of them printed for London Stationers.

The conclusion can only be that Delaune misappropriated a sum due to the Press equivalent to the proceeds of sale of the University's two editions of Clarendon's *History*. The sequestration of his living and prebends had restored £2,327 by 1719, in which year Delaune himself paid £265, presumably to meet the University's costs in recovering the money and its expenses at Long Hanborough, which in 1718 were computed at £155.[1]

There is reason to believe that of the succeeding Vice-Chancellors Lancaster (1706–9) and Bernard Gardiner (1712–15) were weighty men, but information about their part in conducting the Press is hard to get. Hearne, our most copious informant, was violently, and probably unreasonably, prejudiced against both.

In Lancaster's term an attempt was made to tighten up accounting for Delegates' books. Delaune's defalcations and difficulties in persuading the Stationers to accept their quota of the University's editions made finance a pressing problem for the Delegates. They agreed in 1707 'That a distinct Account be kept by John Hall the Printer of each Book printed by it selfe, together with what profit to the University, how many sold, where the money, what books remain and what presents'.[2] The effect of the injunction was slight and not lasting; for some ten years thereafter the Warehouse-Keeper added to the charge to the Delegates for each book a 'discharge' showing the return from it assuming that all copies were sold at the full price. Answer to the question 'where the money' there was none.

This slight reform was beneficial in cases where the bulk of an impression was disposed of quickly to the booksellers, but not if the profit depended on sales over a long time. It was far from being an adequate reform of accounting for the Press. To find out to what extent successful publications paid for the unsuccessful or the commissions from authors and booksellers to print subsidized the publishing, whether debts were recovered, whether the rent from tenants of the Bible Press, the surplus

---

[1] Figures taken from the V.-C.'s Computus. Delaune's final payment is the nearest thing I can find to a justification for the statement in the *D.N.B.* 'He paid a composition of £300 in full discharge of the debt in 1719.' I can find no justification for Ayliffe's assertion: 'There were some laudable Efforts made to recover part of this Sum in the Vice-Chancellor ship of Dr. Lancaster [1706–9], by Vertue of a Sequestration; but his honest Endeavours have been rendred vain and fruitless, by the base Spirit of one of his Successors' (*Antient and Present State of the University of Oxford* (1714), i, p. 216).

[2] D.O. 28 Feb. 1707 (N.S.); *First Minute Book*, p. 21.

of the endowments for repair of the Schools and the Theatre were applied to publishing, as they should have been, it is no good looking in the Accounts of the Warehouse-Keeper. Much of the needed information was known only to the Vice-Chancellor, and not all of it can be found in the part of his annual Computus headed the Schools Account. Items paid to or by him for the business of the Press may or may not have been entered by the Warehouse-Keeper, differently expressed. These were matters awaiting the attention of Blackstone later in the century.[1] They were ordered better at Cambridge, where an annual Press Account struck a balance of all income and expenditure.[2]

Despite a reputation as a 'conscientious, indomitable, stern, uncompromising man',[3] in the records of the Press Bernard Gardiner cuts an inglorious figure; for it was under his chairmanship that the Delegates remaindered their stock of books at a miserable price, and the incompetent and nepotistical Stephen Richardson was appointed to take charge of the printers.

[1] Philip, pp. 77–8.
[2] McKenzie, *The Cambridge University Press, 1696–1712*, ii, pp. 44 ff.
[3] *D.N.B.*

CHAPTER XII

The Lessees of Privilege

UNTIL late in the eighteenth century bookselling in England was effectively controlled by the Company of Stationers of London.[1] Great efforts were made by the Company during the last twenty years of the seventeenth century to restrict the book trade to its members by procuring the transfer from other livery companies of freemen who exercised the stationer's trade and by obtaining orders prohibiting bookselling by haberdashers and by hawkers.[2] These efforts were not wholly successful, but broadly speaking booksellers were bound by the by-laws of the Stationers' Company and amenable to its court.

The main concern of the Company was not with retail bookselling or with printing but with publishing, that is to say with bringing new books on to the market and selling them wholesale. It fought for the property of its members in their 'copies' and for the monopoly of its trading concern, the English Stock, in a large collection of 'copies'. This joint stock in which members of the Company held shares exploited royal privileges granted to the Company for printing and selling particular books and classes of books and others bought from the original patentees: the most important of its monopolies covered school books from the ABC to cheap editions of the Latin classics, almanacs and prognostications, catechisms and primers, and the metrical psalms. The right of the two Universities by virtue of their charters to 'comprint on' the English Stock was a threat which the Stationers had to combat or buy off.

The Keepers of the English Stock were trusted not to let the books on their list go out of print. They placed orders with printers for new editions, bought paper for them, paid the bills, and warehoused the books, which they sold wholesale to bookselling members of the Company.[3] In the early part of the eighteenth century shareholders were usually paid a dividend of 9 per cent.

[1] Cyprian Blagden, *The Stationers' Company, a History, 1403–1959* (1960).
[2] Stationers' records, Liber D, Liber F; Moxon, *Mech. Ex.*, pp. 481–2.
[3] Stationers' records, Warehouse Accounts, English Stock.

If it heard that a royal monopoly in a class of books or in a particular book was for sale, the Stationers' Company would try to buy it. It would also buy the right to the copy of a book likely to be in constant demand if the owner would sell.

Certain monopolies escaped the Stationers' net. Chief of them was the exclusive right to the Bible and the Book of Common Prayer, which had been vested in the King's Printer since 1577.[1] When, after the Restoration, the office of King's Printer was revived, a brief spell of Bible-printing by the Company came to an end. The Crown received large sums of money for the grant of this office in possession and in reversion. It was generally held by partners, of whom nearly all were members of the Stationers' Company; and yet the Company was not always disposed to protect the interests of these members if they conflicted with those of its English Stock. Between the Company and the King's Printer there was a fragile alliance most of the time.

The (Latin) Grammar monopoly was a valuable vestige of the office of King's Printer in Latin, Greek, and Hebrew. The Stationers made several attempts to buy it, but during most of the eighteenth century it remained in the family of Norton.[2] The patent for books of the Common Law also was in private hands.

It was the view of the Stationers that the two Universities should confine their publishing to learned books. When, in 1692, they bought Oxford's forbearance to print the 'scheduled books', meaning those reserved for the English Stock, they conceded:

> . . . that this restraint upon the University of Printing and Comprinting the Books above named shall be understood to be of the Books as they have usually been Printed by the Stationers of London, but not extend to Classical Authors when illustrated by new Annotations or Various Readings, or printed in formes or with Letters not for the use of Schools.[3]

They agreed that 'what Classick Authors shall be printed at the University Press [Cambridge] with new Notes or Lections or other Improvements shall not be interpreted as a Breach' of a similar covenant of 1704.[4] When, in 1696, Cambridge, led to it by Richard Bentley, decided to set up a new academic press the Stationers were given an assurance that it would print 'Classick Authors and such books of Learning'.[5] Books of

---

[1] A. W. Pollard, *Records of the English Bible* (1911), pp. 322 ff.
[2] Blagden, *Stationers' Company*, p. 163. I have not been able to discover when they ceased to hold it.
[3] Reg. Conv. Bb, pp. 336–43; *Print and Privilege*, p. 177.
[4] Stationers' Records, Liber G, 3 Apr. 1704.   [5] Liber F, 7 Sept. 1696.

this kind from the Universities they would not object to their members buying and retailing.

From the Company's point of view these learned publications were on a par with books published by subscription. Members of the Stationers' Company were free to print and to sell any book that was not the 'copy' of another or the subject of a royal monopoly. The *Term Catalogues* are proof that many books printed for the authors at Oxford or Cambridge were advertised for sale by London booksellers.

That the Universities had the right to print the books reserved to the English Stock was recognized by the Stationers early in the seventeenth century, and they secured covenants of forbearance to do so, in return for annual payments, from Oxford in 1637 and from Cambridge in 1639.[1] Bibles and prayer books not being 'scheduled', were the concern of the King's Printer, and until 1672 they were included in the covenants by arrangement between him and the Stationers, he contributing a share of the money. The Stationers' covenants with Oxford were renewed periodically with a gap between 1643 and 1662 until 1672. Three years later the University in the persons of Dean Fell and his partners renewed the covenant as for the 'scheduled books' but reserved the right to print Bibles and prayer books[2] (a like reservation was made by Cambridge in 1726).

The unsuccessful experiment of Fell and his partners in braving the hostility of the Stationers by printing school books, pocket almanacs, and the metrical psalms has been described in an earlier chapter,[3] and so has the surrender to the Stationers by the University of the Oxford Bible Press in 1692.[4]

The court of the Stationers heard on 1 February that:

. . . The Master and Wardens had at last agreed with the University of Oxford for their privilege of printing, which had been near twelve months depending, but that the University absolutely refused to treat with the Company, they haveing been much misrepresented to them by Mr Parker and Mr Guy,[5] by means whereof himselfe, Warden Mortlock, and Mr Bellinger were under a necessity of treating with the University in their own names, and Mr Roger Norton[6] has become bound with them. And the Master and the rest declared in Court they had entred into the said

---

[1] Blagden, p. 104.
[2] See above, pp. 68, 70.
[3] Ibid.
[4] Chapter VIII, pp. 105–8.
[5] The survivors of the four renegade Stationers who held the previous lease. See above, p. 95.
[6] Owner of 'the Grammar' as King's Printer in Latin etc.

Articles in trust for & for the only benefitt, interest and advantage of this Company.[1]

By May 1692 a declaration of trust for the Company at large had been executed by the three lessees and £1,000 voted for carrying on business at Oxford.[2] It was resolved that a 'New Stock' similar to the English Stock should be formed to finance printing at Oxford and Cambridge, to sell the books printed there at a warehouse in London, and divide the profits annually among the shareholders. Sixty-seven shares were taken up and the formalities completed by October 1693, and by then the lessees had rented a house in Oxford, altered it, and stocked it with presses, type, and paper at a cost of £735.[3] Lewis Thomas, Stationer, was appointed to manage it.

The partners, styling themselves 'the University Printers', issued the first of their Oxford Bibles in 1695. They also printed the Book of Common Prayer and the metrical psalms by Sternhold and Hopkins. Twenty editions of the Bible in English were printed at Oxford in the years 1695–1711. The only one in folio format, of 1701, is a handsome book. Copies of it are usually ruled in red by the binder and some have a set of the illustrations available wholesale at that time[4] inserted in them.

New agreements with nominees of the Stationers' Company were sealed by the University in 1698, 1703, and 1708.

So the University vicariously discharged what it conceived to be a duty to the public, to supply it with the Scriptures and the prayer book. The terms of the leases gave its Vice-Chancellor ample powers to deter-mine the quantities and formats of the editions and their prices, to approve the material, and to enter and inspect work in progress. Mean-while, to the extent of £200 a year Bibles were subsidizing learned pub-lishing. Fell had found the demand for it a disappointment, and he and his partner, Thomas Yate, had sunk much of their own capital in it. The Delegates who took over the business after him found the problem no less and were not in a position to mitigate its severity by private subventions. Charlett bemoaned the inability of the Press to sell its books,[5] and Archbishop Wake wished that the Press 'had better means of selling

---

[1] Liber F, 1 Feb. 1691/2.
[2] Ibid. 2 May, 7 Aug. 1692.
[3] Printed from a document in the Stationers' Records in *Print and Privilege*, p. 186. The house was in St. Aldates: B.M. MS. Harl. 5901, fol. 85.
[4] *T.C.* III, 299.
[5] Hist. MSS. Comm., 2nd *Report*, p. 254b.

Henry Aldrich (1647–1710), Dean of Christ Church. By Sir Godfrey Kneller

Nicholas Hawksmoor's design for the south façade of the Clarendon Building

abroad'.[1] The offer by the Stationers to take whole editions off their hands at a small profit must have seemed to the Delegates a release from their main burden.

In the correspondence of scholars during the late seventeenth and early eighteenth centuries there is much dislike of booksellers; but it is aimed at these people as publishers and concerns their treatment of writers. Samuel Pepys, lamenting the shelving of Bernard's Euclid in 1699, writes: 'but what better is to be hoped for from our Booksellers, while they continue our Maisters? An Evill; that noe Lover of Letters should sleep till it bee cur'd.'[2] George Hickes complained that the booksellers 'governed learning',[3] Edmund Gibson thought them 'a slippery sort of men',[4] Hearne thought they had rather employ hacks as editors than learned men.[5] There is no suggestion that booksellers did not want to sell books if scholars could get them published.

Even Hearne noted when Thomas Bennett, bookseller in St. Paul's Churchyard, died in 1706 that 'A great many in the University seem sorry for the Death of Mr. Bennett, as if there were no bookseller of the same Public Spirit, and who would be so serviceable as he to the University.'[6] Two of Bennett's former apprentices, Henry Clements and Jonah Bowyer, would get Oxford books for customers in London;[7] and Clements the elder in Oxford and his son of the same names at the Half-Moon in St. Paul's Churchyard had a twice-weekly delivery service one to another.[8] A look at a list of books from the University's press is enough to show that many were sponsored by booksellers in Oxford or London. There is no reason to suspect that its members were ill served by 'this useful profession', as Bishop Atterbury called it.[9]

The University had great hopes of that part of its bargain with the Stationers which obliged them to 'take off' its books.[10] It proved to have been a rash undertaking, but when the Stationers jibbed at renewing it in 1698 at the expiration of their five-year lease a strong party in Convocation resisted any mitigation.

[1] Bodl. MS. Ballard iii, fol. 139. [2] Ibid. i, fol. 109.
[3] Ibid. xii, fol. 164.
[4] Bodl. MS. Ashm. 1815, No. 177.
[5] Hearne, iii, p. 373; xi, p. 376.
[6] Ibid. i, p. 286.
[7] Ibid. ii, p. 14.
[8] Ibid. iii, pp. 107, 242, 247. For Bennett and the two Clements, see N. Hodgson and C. Blagden, *The Notebook of Thomas Bennet and Henry Clements* (Oxford, 1956), Introduction.
[9] Plomer, *Dictionary, 1668–1725*, s.v. Bennett.
[10] See above, p. 106.

In 1697/8 the Stationers alleged these facts:[1]

They have taken off Books the Five Years they have been concerned to the Value of	£1671 7s. 6½d.
They have paid	1356 18 6
They have receiv'd for them but	434 0 0
There is remaining in Books unsold	1237 7 3 [sic].

They pleaded that 'if more such Books be put upon them, they must inevitably sink under the Burden', and they proposed that if in future they were offered books that they judged would be unsaleable, they should be quit of all obligation if they paid 2s. in the £ towards the cost of producing them. Finally, they suggested that Bibles and prayer books might be left out of the prospective agreement.[2] They would leave the King's Printer to look after himself.

Against them it was argued that the article that they most objected to was of their own proposing. At Oxford it had been foreseen that 'they would be apt to say at every turn that what we printed was unsaleable', but had answered 'That we should never be troubled with such complaints, that they were men of Trade, and had put themselves into a method to vend whatever Books we printed'.[3] The Stationers' figures were misleading, it was said: they did not take account of books sold but not yet paid for; and it was known that they had sold £400-worth of Wallis's *Works* alone.[4] They let the books lie in their 'Oxford Warehouse', as they called it, and made no attempt to advertise their existence, but simply waited for booksellers to inquire for them.

This dispute brings us near the heart of the matter: was the University producing books that were not wanted, that no bookseller could sell? The consciences of the Vice-Chancellor and Delegates for Printing appear to have been touched; for at a meeting, not recorded in their Minute Book but held some time in 1697–8, they resolved 'That great care be taken by the Delegates for Printing, to recommend such Books to the Press as are Vendible, as well as Usefull'.[5]

No controller of a learned press in recent times would expect to clear his stock every five years. It is true that among the books unloaded on the Stationers in 1692–8 there were some going back to the early days of Fell's regime: the *Historia et antiquitates Universitatis Oxoniensis* of 1674, for

---

[1] Univ. Arch. W.P. R8ᶜ(6).   [2] Ibid. (5).
[3] 'Case between the University and the Farmers of their Privilege of Printing': Univ. Arch. W.P. R8ᶜ(4).
[4] The Accounts for the Stationers' English Stock Warehouse 1696–7 record the sale of 34 copies of Wallis's *Works*.   [5] Univ. Arch. W.P. R8ᶜ(9).

example. But those were not the subject of complaint: what were objected to were books published during the five-year period of the lease or, like Morison's Herbal and Wallis's *Opera mathematica*, a series completed during that time; these in particular:

800 Josephus, fol.
400 Wallis Opera Mathem: 2 vol. fol.
470 Hyde de Ludis Orientalibus, 8°
550 Gibson's Portus Iccius, 8°
500 Homeri Ilias, 8°, gr.
250 Kennet's Parochial Antiquities, 4°
500 Cotton's Catalogue.

Of these the Stationers owned to have sold in the first four years 100 of Wallis, 50 of Kennett, 130 of Cotton.[1] Morison's *Historia plantarum*, three volumes, folio, the hardest of all to move, was the matter of a separate complaint.

Surely this was a desirable 'back list' for the University, a stock that any publishing firm might be glad to carry over a long time if there were a slow sale? Oxford had yet to learn that a university press must expect to need a big warehouse. We shall see that the Delegates, like their Stationer-lessees, were alarmed to the point of remaindering their stock unwisely.

Aye, but we are accustomed to university presses that have money. The Oxford press of 1698 could not finance new books until it had got back the capital it had spent. 'If we do not insist on this Article', the objector wrote, 'we shall want stock to carry on Printing for the future with that vigour we have of late done to the Honour of the University and the benefit of the Learned world.'[2]

The agreement with the Stationers sealed in June 1698 for a second term of five years made concessions to their unwillingness to accept the learned books. Their liability for the five years was limited to £1,000, they would not be obliged to take any part of an edition of which they had not been given advance notice and a specification, they were not bound to take more than 200 copies of any book.[3]

The accounts for the Stationers' Oxford Warehouse are not available: those for their English Stock record the sale of a few Oxford books in 1698–1701: 7 copies of Wallis, 32 of the *Catalogi* of English and Irish manuscripts, 26 of the *Iliad*, 100 of the Grammar. The signatories to the

---

[1] Ibid. (11).   [2] Ibid. (1).
[3] Reg. Conv. Bc (1693–1703), fols. 170 ff.

second lease were still far too sanguine about their ability to sell these books from a repository to which retailers were used to come for almanacs and school text books.

The Stationers' Court of Assistants in June 1700 appointed a committee to advise on the disposal of Oxford books. It 'met several times, but could not dispose of them to any Advantage. Therefore the Committee were of opinion to send them beyond the Sea and that Mr Buckley, a bookseller,[1] was thought by them a fitt person to be Employed.'[2] Accordingly, these were delivered to Mr. Buckley:[3]

[The list]	Paris	Holland	[Expanded titles]
Dr Hyde	160	140	De ludis orientalibus, 1694
Gibson	155	170	Julii Caesaris Portus Iccius, 1694
Wallis Comp[lete]	100	75	Opera mathematica, 3 vols., 1693, 1695, 1699
Oxon. Cat. MSS	90	50	Catalogi librorum Mss., ed. Bernard, 1697
Lycophron	100	60	Ed. J. Potter, 1697
Cotton's Cat.	225	140	Catal. librorum MSS. Biblioth. Cottonianae, ed. T. Smith, 1696
Oxon. Antiq.	20	20	A. Wood, Historia et antiquitates Universitatis Oxon., 1674
Sco—	12	10	(?) Scotus, De divisione naturae, ed. J. Gale, 1681 or 1687
Josephus	3	3	Antiquitates Judaicae, ed. E. Bernard, [1687]
Dr Cave's 2 vol ⎱ Mr Chiswell's ⎰	200	—	Scriptorum ecclesiasticorum historia literaria, 1688, 1698, published by Richard Chiswell in London (not Oxford books)

Buckley got back from his travels in 1703, owing the Company £16 on his transactions.[4]

By the time that the Stationers learned that they had realized £16 for a stock of books for which they had paid nearly £600, the first volume of Clarendon's History had been printed at Oxford, and thereafter no complaints are recorded. Twelve copies of Volume i reached the Treasurer of the English Stock on 8 July 1702, and on 12 August 40 copies were delivered from the Stationers' warehouse to Thomas Bennett, the book-

1 Samuel Buckley. John Dunton wrote: 'He is an excellent linguist, understands the Latin, French, Dutch, and Italian tongues': Plomer, Dictionary, 1668–1725, p. 57.
2 Stationers' records, Liber G, 3 June 1700, 17 Apr. 1701.
3 Ibid. Warehouse Accounts, English Stock, 10 May 1701.
4 Liber G, 22 Apr. 1703.

seller.[1] The accounts of the Delegates' Warehouse-Keeper at Oxford show that 90 copies were sold quickly by him but are silent as to the rest of the edition of 1,100. At Michaelmas 1702 twenty-nine copies remained unsold at Oxford. It seems likely that the whole edition on 'small' paper was sold by Thomas Bennett on commission for the Company of Stationers.

It is certain that the second impression of Volume i of the *History*, of 1703, was disposed of in that way. On 2 February 1703/4 Bennett gave the Treasurer of the English Stock orders from 46 booksellers for the second edition amounting to £293. 5s. That would account for the bulk of the edition of 500 on small paper at £1 a copy, if the Stationers and Bennett shared a discount. For the second volume, published in 1704, he collected 37 orders,[2] and for the third, also of 1704, he took delivery from the press at Oxford of 2,000, the whole edition on small paper. For Volume iii the Stationers received £789. 10s. Similarly, Bennett sold the first octavo edition, of 1705–7, on behalf of the English Stock, the Delegates at Oxford ordering that he should have 'the whole impression of the Small paper and 300 of the large',[3] leaving themselves 200 on large paper to sell or give away.

Not without reason Lord Weymouth thought Clarendon in folio 'profited only the booksellers'.[4] The Stationers' court felt obliged to Lewis Thomas, their manager of the Bible Press at Oxford for the share their Stock had in this business. It was resolved to give him the three volumes in quires 'in consideration of his good services done to the Company relating to the buying of the said booke'.[5]

The History of the Rebellion was exceptional among Oxford books of its time in the breadth of its appeal; still, it showed that, given a vigorous wholesaler with contacts inside the trade, the London booksellers could vend an Oxford book, and that the University would make little attempt to do so. There was scope for an individual to supplant the Company of Stationers, and if he were enterprising and knowledgeable, to push the sales of at least some of the University's output with a profit to himself. John Baskett appears to have conceived this idea. After Bennett's death in 1706 he told the Stationers' court, of which he, as Assistant, was a member, 'that he had been at Oxford since the death of Mr. Bennett and

---

[1] Stationers' records, Warehouse Accounts, English Stock.

[2] Ibid. The names of booksellers who subscribed for the *History* are printed by Hodgson and Blagden, *The Notebook of Thomas Bennet and Henry Clements*, pp. 209–11.

[3] D.O. 4 Dec. 1705; *First Minute Book*, p. 21.

[4] Bodl. MS. Ballard x, fol. 64.   [5] Liber G, 2 Apr. 1705.

has entered into an Agreement with the University about printing of Clarendon at Oxford in the same manner as Mr. Bennett had'.[1] In 1706–7 he commissioned two editions of the *History* from the Press at Oxford, an octavo in four volumes and a folio in three. The Stationers showed their resentment of Baskett's interloping by declining to take his Clarendons into their warehouse;[2] nevertheless he must be supposed to have sold them well, for he ordered three more editions of the work before he died in 1742. It is the measure of the University's vigour as publisher then that it sponsored its second edition of the *History* in 1807, contenting itself in the mean time with a profit on the printing, a fee of £100 for the copy, and 100 or 150 copies for stock. It would be charitable to suppose that the Delegates thought their resources and energies should be devoted to more learned works.

JOHN BASKETT

As a supplier of paper, a wholesale bookseller, a publisher, and a printer of Bibles and prayer books John Baskett had a prominent part in the English book trade for fifty years. He saw the press at Oxford as potentially useful to him in all his concerns; he made use of it and was a clever manipulator of its interests when they conflicted with those of the Stationers.

The son of Roger Baskett of 'Sarum in Salisbury', gentleman, he was apprenticed in 1682 to Edward Dorrell.[3] His master, often called Captain Darrell, was a 'Paper Stationer' and a supplier to the Ordnance, the Excise, and the English Stock of the Stationers' Company.[4] Baskett was made free of the Company in 1690 and was called to the livery forthwith.

In public records he appears first in 1692 as the lender of a large sum, £1,109, to the Treasury towards paying a debt of £12,000 to the King's Printers.[5] In later years John Baskett of Paternoster Row is often named in the Treasury Books as a supplier of paper and parchment.[6] That he was a young man of a bold spirit appears by his application for a post of commissioner for collecting a duty on paper imposed in 1696.[7] He took an apprentice in 1695.[8]

The Oxford records refer to him first in 1695, when the Warehouse-

[1] Liber G, 5 Aug. 1706.   [2] Ibid. 1 Dec. 1707; 30 Mar. 1708.
[3] Stationers' records, Register of Apprentices, 4 Dec.
[4] *Calendar of Treasury Books, 1681–5*; Stationers' Liber F, 7 July 1690.
[5] A. F. Johnson, 'The King's Printers, 1660–1742', *The Library*, 5th ser. iii (1949), at p. 35.
[6] *Calendar of Treasury Books, 1695*, and succeeding volumes to 1717.
[7] *Calender of Treasury Papers*, vol. xxxi, p. 46.   [8] Liber F, 2 Dec.

Keeper's Account for Printing records a debt of £500 for paper received from him during the two previous years. After 1696 he is the only provider of paper named in the Accounts until 1709, when a small amount was bought direct from John Beckford, the paper maker at Wolvercote close by. Archives do not indicate the sources of Baskett's supplies, except that some Oxford books were stated in the Accounts to be on Dutch paper. Some of the watermarks in others suggest origins in Normandy or Brittany. Some of the paper is so badly made that it is likely to be English. Later, in 1720, Baskett was getting the paper for his Oxford Bibles and prayer books from millers at Wolvercote, Eynsham, Burford, and High Wycombe.[1]

Evidence of Baskett's turning publisher and wholesale bookseller dates from 1706. It was on 5 August in that year, according to the Stationers' records, that Baskett informed the Court of Assistants of his agreement with the University about the printing of Clarendon.[2] This refers to the folio edition of 1707, of the *History*, and in the next year he commissioned the University to print the work again in six volumes octavo. For some reason the Stationers' English Stock declined the offer to deal in both these editions, and the Court ordered that Baskett 'be desired to take them away';[3] but it is likely that he disposed of them profitably, for he was allowed to print more editions of the *History* at the press at Oxford in 1711, 1716, 1719, and 1728. The editions that Baskett sponsored do not bear his name, and only entries in the Accounts of the Press show that they are not, as they appear to be, publications of the University. From 1711 onwards he bought large quantities, sometimes as much as two-thirds of the impression, of the *Oxford Almanack*, for which he also furnished the paper. In sum, he was a substantial financier of the work of the Oxford Learned Press from 1707 until 1729.

It must be supposed that Baskett spent some time laying plans for capturing the trade in Bibles and prayer books. They came to light soon after he bought a sixth share in the reversion to the patent of King's Printer in 1710, when the term granted in 1635 to Charles and Matthew Barker was about to expire and a grant in reversion to Henry Hills and Thomas Newcombe made in 1675 to take effect.[4] By agreement with the

---

[1] Deed of transfer of mortgage, 23 May 1720, Brookes, Baskett, and others to Latane, in the custody of the Printer to the University, Oxford.

[2] Liber G, 5 Aug. 1706.   [3] Ibid. 9 Feb. and 30 Mar. 1707/8.

[4] A. F. Johnson, 'The King's Printers, 1660–1742', *The Library*, 5th ser. iii (1949), pp. 33–8; Robert L. Haig, 'New Light on the King's Printing Office, 1680–1730', *Studies in Bibliography*, viii (Charlottesville, 1956), pp. 157–67.

other shareholders, 'and for the benefitt of them', Baskett was sworn Queen's Printer 'about the month of April [1712]'.[1] He held the appointment for the rest of his life, and since his name appears alone in the imprints of the King's Printing Office from 1724 onwards there is an inference that he bought out the other shares in the patent about that time.

In 1711 Baskett bought a third share in the patent granted to Robert Freebairn of Queen's Printer in Scotland.[2] It is clear that he was on good terms with Freebairn, for soon afterwards these two tried, unsuccessfully, to oust the holder of the third share. Baskett, therefore, had secured the two exclusive privileges of printing and selling Bibles and service-books in Great Britain. It remained to protect his monopoly against the two English Universities, whose charters gave them the right to print 'all manner of books' including any that were the subject of royal monopolies.

It surprised the Stationers on 10 September 1711 when 'the Master informed the Court that he understood that the University of Oxford had granted the privilege that the Company had lett to them and which would expire at Lady Day come twelve month to some other person than the Company.' They ordered that a deputation should meet Mr. Baskett and Mr. Williams and try to get from them some security against damage to the English Stock by reason of the change. The new lease from the University to Baskett, John Williams, and Samuel Ashurst was dated 2 January 1711/12.[3] The previous lease, of September 1708, was made for five years to Phillips, Mortlock, and Andrews, trustees for the English Stock, but the new lease, for twenty-one years from 1713, was for the benefit of Baskett.

The Company, if it had been disposed to war with Baskett, might have printed Bibles at Cambridge, where the University Printer, Hayes, and his press were subject to its absolute control by virtue of a lease of 1705 for 21 years.[4] Cambridge had not produced a Bible since 1682. However, the Company chose the way of peaceful negotiation with Baskett, and no Bible was printed at Cambridge until 1743.

Agreement was reached in October 1712. Baskett finally contented himself with an annual payment of £200, the equivalent of his rent for

---

[1] Haig, op. cit., p. 166.
[2] [J. Lee] *Memorial for the Bible Societies in Scotland* (Edinburgh, 1824), p. 179; Appendix, No. xxx.
[3] Univ. Arch. S.P. A.1 (counterpart).
[4] Liber G, 20 Dec. 1705.

the University's privilege, for not printing the books reserved for the English Stock, plus the £30 a year paid by Roger Norton to the Company for not contesting his exclusive right to the *Grammar*. Baskett abandoned a claim to print enough metrical psalms to go with his Oxford Bibles and agreed to buy them from the English Stock, folio copies for 1*s.* and quarto for 6*d.*[1]

Two Bibles with Baskett's imprint at Oxford were published in 1715, and in the same year he printed a Testament and a Book of Common Prayer there. In the same year his name with those of the assigns of Newcombe and Hills first appears on a Bible from the King's Printing House in London. In Edinburgh he is said to have set up a printing office in 1725, and the first of his Edinburgh Bibles came out in the following year.[2] He continued to print the Bible, the New Testament, and the prayer book in various formats and sizes of type at London and Oxford until his death in 1742, when his sons succeeded him as King's Printers and lessees of the University.

It was a condition of Baskett's lease of the Bible Press at Oxford that he should contribute 'Two Thousand pounds . . . for and towards the building of a new Printing house within the said University', and that 'the manufacture of printing' by him and his co-lessees should be 'carried on at the new printing house which is designed to be erected'. The move to the Clarendon Printing House took place in October 1713, six months after Baskett's lease took effect.[3] Probably it was to inaugurate the press in its magnificent surroundings—the building was the third in England to be designed for printing and of unexampled architectural splendour for the purpose—that a Bible of the grandest kind was put in hand. Hearne wrote on 18 November:

> They are just now beginning to print the Bible in a large Folio Volume, on fine Paper, & with a large, noble Letter, at the new Printing House in Oxford; and they propose to follow the first Edition of King James's Translation, which came out in the year 1611 in a large Folio, with Broughton's Genealogical Tables (which commonly go under the name of John Speed) and the Maps, which bear Speed's name also. So that in this new Edition they propose to take no more Notes into the Margin than are in the said first Edition; but whether, or no, the Persons, who are to be Correctors, are really well qualify'd for the Undertaking time will discover.[4]

It is doubtful whether Baskett deserves much of the credit for the

---

[1] Ibid. 1 Sept. 1712.   [2] [Lee], *Memorial*, p. 182.   [3] Hearne, iv, p. 254.
[4] Ibid., p. 258.

superb typographical quality of the 'Vinegar' Bible or all the obloquy he has earned for its errors. His lease bound him to keep four presses working and to employ 'the workmen who have been employed in the Theatre', paying them the wages customary in the trade, on printing Bibles, Testaments, and prayer books in such formats and quantities as the Delegates should direct, within limits as to quantity. With regard to this particular Bible the University appears to have intervened to give it a special excellence, and the intervention extended to establishing the text and designing the page.

A letter from Charlett to Humfrey Wanley, dated from University College, 9 December 1713, is contemporary evidence of the academic share in this 'Basket-ful of errors':

> We are here printing a most Magnificent English Bible, some very few Copys will be in Vellum for a present to the Queen & my Ld Treasurer. You know Dr Wallis and Dr Gregory pronounced Mr Dennison absolutely the best Corrector they ever met with. If this Work have not the Advantage of his nice Ey at least in giving the first Directions, and settling the Distances of Lines & Words and the great Art in a beautifull and Uniforme Division of Syllables, with several other minute Regulations, invisible to vulgar Eys, the Work will want of its proposed Splendor. I Committed the Corrector & Him together in my Studdy and left them alone together, I understand He ownd himself, after twenty years Practise, to be much enlightned—Mr Denison says the Fount of letters, is the very best He ever saw, and you know his Ey examines all the Tayls sides & Topps of letters &c. To do justice to Mr Basket, He spares no Cost nor Pains. We shall throw out all the vast Numbers of References added by some late Reformers & Improvers of the Bible, reserving only those of the Original Translators themselves, as beleiving they who were at the Pains of the version, had good Reasons for theyr References, tho I feare by this omission We may incurre the Censure of some Rt Reverends, but we have been so often & so long under them, as to be almost insensible of theyr Weight.[1]

It may be allowed that William Dennison, fellow of University College, was a corrector in an older sense of the word, a person responsible for establishing the text rather than for the drudgery of eliminating misprints in the proofs,[2] but he seems to have been charged with a general oversight of proof-reading by an anonymous corrector.

When the Bible was published in 1717 complaints of printer's errors

---

[1] Printed from the autograph at Welbeck Abbey in Percy Simpson, *Proof-Reading in the Sixteenth, Seventeenth, and Eighteenth Centuries* (1935), p. 195.
[2] Ibid., p. 126.

were not long in coming. Charlett's friend William Bishop writes in February of that year asking whether the tetragram for Jehovah were not wrongly engraved in the frontispiece and fears 'there will be found other oversights'.[1]

Bibles at that time all had misprints in them, and only an exceptionally conscientious and leisured historian could tell how far the Vinegar Bible fell below the ordinary standard of accuracy.[2] However, this was a Bible unsuited by reason of its bulk for anything but reading from a lectern in church, and for that purpose it was not accurate enough. A letter to Charlett from William Lowth, on behalf of the clergy at Winchester Cathedral, makes the point forcefully.

Winchester. 1 July 1718. I am desired by some of my Brethren here to acquaint you, that the Great Church Bible lately Printed at the University Press in a very fair Character if extremely [?] which they lately bought for the Use of our Cathedral is very false Printed. In the 2 Lessons upon St. Peters day we found two Considerable Mistakes. Acts iii: 24. Instead of, you and all the Prophets from Samuel and these that follow, it is Printed, you and the Prophets from Sam. and all these &c. And Acts iv: 24 Instead of, And when they heard that, it is Printed And when they had that. Finding 2 such Faults in two successive Chapters, we have reason to fear the whole Edition is faulty, and severall others have bin observed by those of our Quire who read the daily Lessons. One might expect, besides the dishonor don to Religion by such Careless Editions of the Bible the Printer should have a little consulted his own Reputation, and the Interest he has in the sale of the Book, which we shall take all Occasions to let the world know how unfit it is for Publick Use. And I must further beg leave to take notice to you, that Mr Basket by reason of his Interest in the King's and the University Printing House, has got the Monopoly of Bibles, and so has of late raised the common Bibles that use to be sold for 4s. to 4s. 6d., and hereby has laid a Vast Tax upon the Common People, as well as upon those that give away Bibles in Charity. Your known Concern for the Honour of Religion and the University made us give you the Trouble of this Information.[3]

No such handsome Bible was printed at Oxford until the Lectern Bible designed by Bruce Rogers of 1935. Only Baskerville's, printed at

[1] Bodl. MS. Ballard xxxii, fol. 11, 16 Feb. 1716/17.
[2] A list of the errors is kept in a copy belonging to the British and Foreign Bible Society (Darlow and Moule, No. 942), and some of the worst are cited by Percy Simpson in *Proof-Reading in the Sixteenth, Seventeenth, and Eighteenth Centuries*, at pp. 196–7.
[3] Bodl. MS. Ballard xxxiv, fol. 67. Percy Simpson (op. cit., p. 196) mistook the year in the date.

Cambridge in 1763, is its equal among Bibles in English for beauty of type, impression, and paper, and the richness of its decoration gives the Vinegar Bible a unique distinction. Not that the copperplate headpieces and initials by Sir James Thornhill, Chéron, Louis Laguerre, and others repay much study as works of art, but they serve their purpose as enrichment, punctuation, and relief from the monotony of print. Fame has fastened on the errors: what might have been one of the glories of English printing is one of its curiosities. The sheets, sold originally for £4. 4s., were offered in 1728 for £3. 5s.[1] and would not be worth much more now. Moreover, it must be admitted that one of Charlett's correspondents hardly exaggerated in saying that the book needed a crane to lift it.

The quarto Book of Common Prayer printed by Baskett at Oxford in 1720 was said to have 'many gross omissions';[2] and others besides William Lowth complained of rising prices. Reporting to Charlett on a suit brought by Baskett against James Watson, who printed Bibles in Edinburgh, in the House of Lords, Smalridge, Bishop of Bristol and Dean of Christ Church, wrote on 15 February 1717/18:

> Council for Watson inveighed severely against Mr Baskets endeavours to get to himself an entire Monopoly of printing Bibles, &c. and enlargd very much upon his having rais'd the price of 'em to an exorbitant Degree; and on this Occasion several Lords, not in publick Debate, but in private Conference, complain'd very much of our leasing to Him the right of Printing, which ought to have been us'd as a check against his enhansing the price of Bibles &c. I have good reason to think that unless due care be taken by the University, that the Covenant we have made against his selling these Books at an higher price than by Us fixt be strictly executed, our Privilege will be endanger'd, if not from the Courts of Law, Yet from the Legislative.[3]

The bishop was alluding to a term in Baskett's lease of 1712 providing that 'the lessees shall sell all such Books as shall be by them . . . printed within the said University at such rate and price and no other as by the Vice-Chancellor of the said University . . . shall be sett', and there was a declaration of the intent of the parties that 'the price of Bibles and more particularly of little Bibles in duodecimo or other little forme [shall not be] advanced or increased'. The Courts did indeed show a growing distaste for the royal prerogative's interference with printing;[4] and

---

[1] Advertisement by Sam. Birt in the London *Evening Post*, 10 Oct.
[2] Bodl. MS. Ballard xxxii, fol. 122.   [3] Bodl. MS. Ballard vii, fol. 31.
[4] See pp. 347–8 below.

Baskett's high prices and misprints were calculated to bring the exclusion of competition from this branch of the book trade into bad odour.

Of the series of Bibles printed at Oxford in Baskett's time some twelve editions in folio, quarto, octavo and duodecimo are distinguishable, those in quarto and duodecimo being reissued from time to time with new title-pages. He gave the quantities of the editions that he was printing in 1720: octavo in Nonpareil type 10,000; duodecimo in Minion type 10,000. Besides these he printed some sixteen editions at Oxford of the Common Prayer in various formats, and he described a duodecimo New Testament in the press in 1720 as 'always printing'.[1] The quality of the impression varies with the size of the type and format: Baskett's big Oxford Bibles and Prayers are above the average standard of English printing in his day; but the little ones are so roughly printed as to be virtually unreadable.

In due time the Church or the Crown was impelled to act by general dissatisfaction with the available editions of the Scriptures. In 1724 King George I issued by way of proclamation 'Directions to Printers of Bibles and Prayer-books for remedying faulty printings and regulating the prices'.[2] He ordered that specimens for proposed editions should be deposited with the two Secretaries of State, the Archbishop of Canterbury, and the Bishop of London, and that the editions, when issued, should be as good as the specimens. As for correction, the King directed the printers 'That they shall employ such correctors of the press, and allow them such salaries, as shall be approved from time to time by the Archbishop and the Bishop of London'. Further, the patentees were instructed to print in the title-pages of their Bibles and prayer books the exact price at which they were sold to the booksellers.[3]

Of Baskett's compliance with these regulations it is known that for eight or nine years he printed prices at the feet of his title-pages. His folio Bible of 1727 from Oxford cost 36s. in sheets, folded and quired, and his 24to Bible of the same year, also unbound, 2s. He sold a duodecimo Book of Common Prayer for 20d.

His relations with the Delegates of the Press were not easy. They showed concern in their minutes of 1708 about dilatoriness in his settlement of accounts rendered for the printing of Clarendon's *History* to his order, and evidently thought that their Warehouseman had allowed Baskett to deliver more paper than was needed so that the supplier might

[1] Transfer of mortgage, Brookes, Baskett, and others to Latane, cited above on p. 167.
[2] So described in Steele, *Bibliotheca Lindesiana*, viii, p. 25, under date 1724, 24 April.
[3] John Lewis, *A Complete History of the Several Translations of the Holy Bible and New Testament into English*, 3rd ed. (1818), pp. 350–1.

have the more to set off against his debt.[1] Again in 1721 he owed the University £1,000, and one of the Delegates, Shippen, Principal of Brasenose, wrote that he dishonoured bills drawn on him and would not answer letters.[2]

There are signs by that time that Baskett had exhausted his capital on his multiple enterprises. He mortgaged his leasehold of the Oxford Bible Press in 1718 for £4,500, and for default in payment of the interest the mortgagee had sold £1,500-worth of the stock of books by 1720.[3] His co-lessees, John Williams and Samuel Ashurst, had only a fictitious interest: Williams was the manager of the King's Printing House,[4] and Ashurst finished an apprenticeship to Baskett the year the lease was signed;[5] it is not surprising that they joined in the mortgage of 1718 to declare that they had no beneficial interest in the property and were trustees of it for Baskett.

The mortgage was transferred in 1720 to another lender, and in the following year Baskett mortgaged his interest in the Bible Press again, this time to two Stationers, Gosling and Knaplock. Here it would seem that he overstepped the bounds of legality, for the transaction gave rise to a suit in Chancery between rival mortgagees.[6] In 1724 he sold to (John) Eyre for £10,000 the reversion for 30 years to the office of King's Printer, which Baskett had bought from the Crown in 1716.[7] By March 1727 he was insolvent, and John Eyre, as assignee of his mortgages, demanded of the Stationers' Court that the Company's payments for forbearance to print the 'Scheduled Books' at Oxford should be made to him.[8] Two years later Baskett had been declared a bankrupt.[9] His place in the accounts of the Press as wholesale dealer in the *Oxford Almanack* was taken by Eyre. Baskett ceased until June 1733 to sit as Assistant in the Stationers' Court; but a rule of the Company that an insolvent debtor should be removed from the list of Assistants[10] was not invoked in his case.

Baskett's rent for the Bible Press, £200 a year, was not paid regularly. He began defaulting in 1716/17, and by 1719/20 he owed the rent for four years. He paid £300 the next year, but nothing the year after, and

[1] D.O. 9 March.   [2] Bodl. MS. Ballard xxi, fol. 215ᵛ.
[3] Transfer of mortgage, Brookes, Baskett and others to Latane, cited above.
[4] Robert L. Haig, 'New Light on the King's Printing Office, 1680–1730', *Studies in Bibliography*, viii, at p. 162.
[5] Stationers' records, Register of Freemen, 7 Apr. 1712.
[6] Memorial from Eyre's attorney to the Stationers' Court, Liber H, 7 Feb. 1728/9.
[7] R. A. Austen-Leigh, *William Strahan and his Ledgers* (1922), p. 9.
[8] Liber H, 7 Mar. 1726/7.   [9] Ibid. 7 Feb. 1728/9.   [10] Liber G, 5 May 1701.

it was not until 1727/8 that he caught up with arrears. In 1740/1 the lessees were once more behind with the rent, and the debt was not paid in full until 1744/5, two years after Baskett's death, when his sons Thomas and Robert had succeeded to the lease.

A gradual mending of his affairs appears by his having paid off one mortgage by July 1731;[1] and in July 1732 the Delegates at Oxford agreed to grant a new lease of the privilege of printing to Baskett jointly with Samuel Ashurst and Robert Gosling after the expiration in 1734 of the one then in being.[2] The new lease dated 28 June 1734[3] (which, incidentally, increased the number of presses to be kept at work from four to five) describes the half of the new Printing House devoted to the Bible business as 'now in the possession of . . . Baskett, Ashurst, and Gosling'. A change of lessees since 1713 would explain a passage in a letter addressed to Charlett in 1720:

> Yesterday in the afternoon Mr Goslyn met Mr Sare and then told him, it was true, they were allowed Partners in the Lease with Baskett, as Mr Baskett own'd to Them, but it was without Their knowledge; as for himself Goslyn said He knew nothing of it, till he asked Baskett of it, and as he assured Mr Sare he then knew not the reason or meaning of it, which causes many guesses, not much to Basketts reputation.[4]

Sare died in 1724; there must have been two new leases in the mean time.

Baskett's devious and mysterious ways are apparent, also, in his dealings with Robert Freebairn, the Scottish printer. This man, appointed Queen's Printer for Scotland in 1711, took part in the Rebellion of 1715 and printed manifestos for the Pretender.[5] Baskett and the widow of Andrew Anderson secured a new patent to themselves in 1716 in which the privileges of Freebairn are solemnly revoked.[6] None the less by 1725 Baskett and Freebairn were in partnership,[7] and from 1734 until the time of Baskett's death, despite Baskett's tenure of the patent, Edinburgh Bibles had the imprint of Robert Freebairn. Baskett was content with liberty to sell his London and Oxford Bibles in Scotland.[8]

When Baskett told their Court on 3 December 1734 that he had renewed his agreement with the University of Oxford, the Stationers at

---

[1] Liber H, 6 July 1731.   [2] D.O. 31 July 1732.
[3] Univ. Arch. S.E.P. 6, A. 12(3).
[4] Bodl. MS. Ballard xxxii, fol. 124, William Bishop, 30 Aug. 1720.
[5] [Lee], Memorial, App. xxx, p. 183.   [6] Ibid., App. xxxi.
[7] I. H. van Eeghen, De Amsterdamse boekhandel, 1680–1725, iv (Amsterdam, 1967), p. 109.
[8] [Lee], Memorial, pp. 180–2.

once decided to continue their annual payments to him for forbearing to comprint on the English Stock. 'He had been at a very Great and unusual Charge', he said, in securing the new lease, and 'he hoped that as the Company were to receive a like benefitt therefrom with himself, they would also contribute the Summe of £250.' This premium, too, was paid. Three years later he invited the Stationers to commute their yearly payments to him for a lump sum; but this offer was declined.[1]

By that time Baskett had reached the age of 70. The records at Oxford and at Stationers' Hall are silent about his remaining years, which came to an end on 22 June 1742.[2] His son John predeceased him by a month; his other two sons, Thomas and Robert, succeeded him as King's Printers and lessees of the Oxford Bible Press.

No trace of Baskett's accounts or other papers remains at Oxford. Daniel Prince, the Delegates' Overseer, wrote in 1795: 'About the year 1762, all Baskett's stock, &c. was removed to London.'[3]

---

[1] Liber H, 6 Sept. 1737.

[2] *Gent. Mag.*; according to Plomer, *Dictionary*, 1668–1725, his will was proved on the 23rd. The fire which burned his house and the King's Printing House adjoining it was on 14 Jan. 1738: *Gent. Mag.* viii (1738), p. 49.

[3] Nichols, *Lit. An.* iii, p. 705.

CHAPTER XIII

The Learned Press in the Early Eighteenth Century

SALESMANSHIP

CHARLETT is the only man who makes his mark in the records of the time as salesman on behalf of the Press, and after his death in 1722 all attempt to sell direct to the public was given up. In this capacity Charlett was successor to Thomas Yate, Fell's partner, and his lot was made easier by the pioneer work that Yate had done towards organizing the sale of Oxford books through the trade as well as to subscribers.

Besides a voluminous correspondence[1] in which doings at the Press are brought to the attention of his acquaintance, Charlett busied himself with maintaining a body of regular subscribers. He circularized them with prospectuses and specimen pages, even arranged for copies of new books to be shown to them by messengers, and for their information compiled lists of forthcoming editions.

It is probable that by the time of Fell's death there was a circle of potential buyers of his books who might be considered regular sub-scribers. The Dean had put out two appeals for the formation of a body of supporters and had sent out at least three lists of books printed, in course of printing, and in contemplation.[2] Charlett, by the time he was made a Delegate of the Press in 1694, was in the habit of sending presents of Theatre books and specimens of some in preparation to likely patrons.[3] In that year was produced a *Catalogus librorum in Theatro Sheldoniano Oxon. impressorum*, an octavo of 8 pages giving the short titles of works printed by Fell's partnership or ordered by the Delegates since 1669.[4] It is not a complete list, and if it comprised the books available for sale in 1694 their number had been much reduced by 1696, when John Hall first recorded 'Books remayning in the Warehouse' in his accounts.

[1] Much of it is digested briefly in a thesis by S. G. Gillam, 'The Correspondence of Arthur Charlett (Master of University College 1692–1722) in its Antiquarian and Historical Aspect' (1948). Bodl. MS. B.Litt. d. 45.

[2] Morison, *Fell*, pp. 251–2.   [3] Bodl. MS. Ballard xxx, fol. 27.

[4] Bodl. 258 b. 272. Charlett told Hearne that it was his compilation, according to Hearne's note on that copy.

The *Catalogus* was followed in the same year by a leaflet, the first of a series, giving titles of works in course of printing at the Sheldonian, also drawn up by Charlett.[1] There are variants of these folio leaves headed *Anno Domini* [year and day] *in Theatro Sheldoniano apud Oxonienses sub prelo sunt libri sequentes*, some with a note about large paper copies in Latin, others with the corresponding 'Advertisement' in English. The Warehouseman's accounts witness to revisions being made in them at brief intervals of time. Twelve of such lists issued in the years 1694–1716 are known, that there were more seems clear from Hearne's diaries and the Press Accounts. They include books being printed for the authors or for booksellers as well as those sponsored by the Delegates. Sometimes Charlett inserted books that were only in mind and never got beyond that stage.[2]

Advertising in the newspapers was resorted to rarely. The Warehouse-Keeper charged in 1693 and 1701 for insertions in the *London Gazette* of publications by the University, four in all. Hearne advertised his Leland's *Itinerary* in the *Daily Courant* and the *Post-Boy*.[3] The University did not get its books into the *Term Catalogues*, but booksellers who stocked them did so.

Subscription was the main source of revenue for publishing. Henry Dodwell noted 'The Booksellers dare not now undertake anything but Pamphlets, but by subscription' (1707).[4] They subscribed one another's publications besides canvassing their customers. By 1698, if not before, Charlett had collected an entity to which he referred as 'the Subscribers'.[5] Referring probably to a Specimen of Thomas Smith's edition of the letters of Ignatius, he writes to Thomas Tanner in May: 'I have directed Mr Hall to send the Epistles to all the Subscribers.' The service reached as far as London, where deliveries were made by the wagoner's messenger ('a silly woman . . . very exacting and troublesome').[6]

Tanner in 1698 was doing small services for Charlett in London. He was asked to deliver a letter to Sir Hans Sloane, 'a most Humane and Obliging Gentleman and very well worth an Hours discourse with alone',[7] and he made the mistake of calling upon London subscribers to engage themselves for a book printed at the Theatre but not sponsored by the Delegates. Charlett's letter, read carefully, gives some insight into the constitution of the subscribers:

It has always been thought convenient, out of Respect, to shew the

[1] Hearne, ii, p. 180.   [2] Ibid., p. 12 (Tacitus).   [3] Hearne, iii, pp. 162, 496.
[4] Hearne, ii, p. 331.   [5] Bodl. MS. Tanner xxii, fol. 37.   [6] Ibid., fol. 20.
[7] Bodl. MS. Tanner xxii, fol. 33.

[Upper notices rotated and largely illegible]

Anno Domini MDCCV. *Jun.* die 12. in Theatro *Sheldoniano* apud *Oxonienfes* fub Prelo funt libri fequentes.

NOvum Teftamentum Græce, cum variis Lectionibus, &c. Fol.
An Expofition of *Daniel's* Prophecy of LXX Weeks,
with Chronological Tables of thofe Weeks and other
matters relating to the fame; by the Right Reverend Father in God, *William* Lord Bifhop of *Worcefter.* 4to.

Archæologia Britannica; Containing fome account, additional to what has been hitherto publifhed, of the An-
cienteft Languages, Cuftoms and Monuments of the *Britifh* Ifles: From Obfervations and Collections in Travels
through *Wales, Cornwall, Baffe Bretagne, Ireland* and
Scotland. By *Edward Lhwyd* A. M. Keeper of the *Afh-
molean Mufæum.* Vol. I of the Languages. Fol. The
Tome contains I. Some Obfervations in general, relating
to the alteration of Languages. II. The various Dialects
of the *Britifh* and ancient *Scotifh* Languages compar'd.
III. A fhort Grammar and Vocabulary of the *Cornifh.*
IV. The Roman names of Perfons and Places in *Britain,*
parallel'd with *Britifh* names yet remaining, and partly
interpreted. V. An examination how far the *Britifh*
Tongue agrees with the *Greek* and *Latin.* VI. The *Britifh, Celtic* and *Teutonic,* compar'd with Obfervations as
to the Origin of the *Britains.* VII. A Catalogue of *Britifh* MSS. VIII. A Grammar of the *Irifh;* for ancient
Scotifh) with a Catalogue of MSS. in that Language.
IX. An *Irifh-Englifh* Dictionary: and laftly the *Irifh* Language collated with the *Cantabrian, Celtic* and *Teutonic*;
with an Enquiry into the Origin of the Ancient *Scots*
and *Picts.*

Jofephus, feu *Jofephi Ben-Gorionis* Hiftoria Judaicæ Li-
bri fex integri hactenus inediti, nunc primum ex Hebræo
in Latinum tranflati, & Notis illuftrati, opera & ftudio
Joannis Gagnier A. M. 4to.
Novum Teftamentum Græce cum Var. Lect. 8vo.
Jo. Ernefti Grabe Differtationes tres de verfione LXX
Interpretum. 4to.
Athenagoræ Athenienfis, Philofophi Chriftiani, Opera.
Ex vetuftis Exemplaribus recenfuit, Adnotationibufque
Gifneri, Suffridi, Kortholti.Lang, Rechenberg, Stephani,
aliorum, fuas qualefcunque adjecit *Edv. Dechair* A. M.
Coll. *Linc.*
Sophoclis Ajax Flagellifer, & Electra Gr. Lat. cum
Scholiis antiquis & Annot. per *Th. Johnfon Etonenfem.*
Introductio ad Veram Phyficam: feu Lectiones Phy-
ficæ habitæ in Schola Naturalis Philofophiæ Academiæ
Oxonienfis. Quibus accedunt *Chriftiani Hugenii* Theore-
mata de Vi Centrifuga & Motu Circulari demonftrata.
Per *Jo. Keill* A. M. & Reg. Soc. Socium. Editio fecunda
Emendatior & Auctior. 8vo.

Nuper etiam ex eodem Typographeo prodierunt,

The Hiftory of the Rebellion and Civil Wars in
England, Begun in the Year 1641. Written by the
Right Honourable *Edward* Earl of *Clarendon,* &c. In
three Volumes. Fol.
Linguarum Veterum Septentrionalium Thefaurus
Grammatico-Criticus & Archæologicus; necnon, de
Linguarum illarum Ufu & Dignitate differtatio Epifto-
laris: Opera & ftudio *Georgii Hickefii,* S. T. P. Ac-
cedunt *Andreæ Fountaine* Equitis Aurati Numifmata
Saxonica, & *Humpbredi Wanley* Librorum Veterum
Septentrionalium, tam eorum qui in Anglia excufi funt,
quam qui in Membranis fcripti nondum eduntur, Cata-
logus, quam fieri licuit, locupletiffimus.
Dionyfii Halicarnaffenfis opera omnia Gr. & Lat. Fol.
duobus Voluminibus comprehenfa. Curâ *J. Hudfon* Bibl.
Bodl. Præfecti.
r. Multa Maimonidis Tractatus Duo: I. De Doctrina
Legis, five Educatione Puerorum. II. De natura & ratio-
one pœnitentiæ apud Hebræos. Latinè redditit, notifque
illuftravit *Robertus Clavering,* A. M. Coll. Univ. Soc. 4to.
The *Englifh Euclide,* being the Firft Six Elements of
Geometry, Tranflated out of the *Greek,* with Annotations
and ufeful Supplements; by *Edmund Scarburgh* A. M.
De Bibliorum Textu Hebraico, & Verfionibus Græca

&-Latina Vulgata Libri IV. Auctore *Humfredo Hodio*
S. T. P. & Ling Græc. Profeff. Fol.
Marci Antonini Imperatoris *τῶν εἰς ἑαυτὸν* libri XII. Gr.
& Lat. cum Annotationibus. 8vo.
M. Juniani Juftini Hiftoriarum ex Trogo Pompejo li-
bri XLIV. MSS. Codicum Collatione recogniti, Annota-
tionibufque illuftrati, per *Tho. Hearne,* A. M. ex Aul. S.
Edm. 8vo.
S.P.N. Cyrilli Hierofolymorum Archiepifcopi opera,
quorum quædam nunc primum ex Codd. MSS. edidit, re-
liqua cum Codd. MSS. contulit, emendavit, notifque illu-
ftravit *Tho. Milles* S. T. B. ex Æde Chrifti. Fol.
Ex recenfione *Davidis Gregorii* M. D. Aftronomiæ Pro-
feffora Saviliani, & R. S. S.
Novum Teftamentum, una cum Scholiis Grecis, operâ
Job. Gregory Archidiac. Glouc. Fol.
S. Irenæi, Libri quinque adverfus Hærefes, quorum La-
tinam verfionem antiquam è Codicibus MSS. emendavit,
&c. *Joan. Ernefus Grabe.* Fol.
Europii Breviarium Hiftoriæ Romanæ,cum Pæanii Me-
taphrafi Græca. Meffala Corvinus de Augufti Progenie.
Julius Obfequens de Prodigiis. Anonymi Oratio Funebris
Gr. Lat. in Imp. Conftant. Conftantini M. fil. cum variis
Lectionibus & Annotationibus, per *T. Hearne,* A M. 8vo.
Xenophontis opera omnia Grece & Latine cum variis
Lectionibus, fex Voluminibus. 8vo.
A Prefervative againft *Socinianifm:* in 4. Parts, by Dr.
Edwards Princip. of Jefus Coll. in *Oxf.* 4to.
Aftronomiæ Phyficæ & Geometricæ Elementa, Auctore
Davide Gregorio M. D. Aftronomiæ Profeffore Saviliano
Oxoniæ, & R. S. S. Fol.
A general View of Ancient and Prefent Geography,
together with a Sett of Maps, by *Edw. Wells* S. T. P.
Sir *Robert Cotton's* Catalogue of MSS.
Librorum Manufcriptorum Angliæ & Hiberniæ Cata-
logus, cum Indicibus Accuratiffimis. Fol.
Dr. *Pocock's* Commentary on Micah, Malachy, and
Joel. Fol.
Hiftoria Plantarum Oxonienfis: per *Robertum Morifo-
num* M. D. & *Jac. Bobartium.* 2 Vol. Fol.
Joannis Wallifii nuper Geometriæ Prof. Savil. Operum
Tomus III.— Fol.
Geographiæ Veteris Scriptores Græci Minores (cum In-
terpretatione Latina, Differtationibus Cl. *Dodwelli,* ac An-
notationibus) duobus Voluminibus comprehenfi, opera &
cura *Joan. Hudfon* Biblioth. Bodl. Præfecti.
C. Plinii Cæcilii Secundi Epiftolæ & Panegyricus cum
variis Lectionibus & Annotationibus. Accedit Vita Plinii
ordine Chronologico digefta, per *T. Hearne,* A.M. 8vo.
Sancti Juftini Philofophi & Martyris Apologia prima
pro Chriftianis ad Antoninum Pium; cum Latina Joannæ
Langi verfione,quamplurimis in locis correcta, &c. edita
à *Joan. Ernefto Grabe.* Ejufdem Apologia fecunda cura
Hugonis Hutchin A M. ex Æd. Chr. 8vo.
Aftronomiæ Cometicæ Synopfis, autore *Edm. Halleio*
Geometriæ Profeffore Saviliano.

Prelo parantur.

Geographorum Græcorum minorum Volumen ternum.
Auctorum nomina & feriem in fingula Voluminibus fiftit
pagina proxime excipiens *H. Dodwelli* Differtationes fe-
cundo Volumini præfixæ. 8vo.
Apollonii Pergæi libri duo *περὶ λόγου τομῆς* ex Arabico
in Latinum converfi, per *E. Halleium* Geom. Prof. Savil.
Verfio LXX Viralis juxta exemplar Alexandrinum
cum Var. Lect. Annott. & locis Parallelis, Fol. per *Jo.
Ernefum Grabe.*
Livii Opera cum Variis Lectionibus Chronologia &
Notis &c. Accurante *T. Hearne* A. M.
Sir *John Spelman's* Life of King *Alfred* the Great,
from the Original Copy, with feveral additions from
MSS. &c. by Mr. *Hearne.*
Quintiliani Inftitutiones Oratoriæ & Hermogenis
Rhetoric cum Notis & var. Lect. 2 Vol. 8vo.

*Rogandi funt viri docti & bonarum artium Fautores, qui libros, quantquot è Theatro Oxonienfi in pofterum pro-
dibunt, in charta Regia vel majori impreffos habere malint quam communes, ut nomine fuo ad* Joannem Hall *Typo-
graphei Sheldoniani cuftodem mature mittere velint.*

Two of Charlett's advance notices of books being printed at the University Press.
Reduced.

Subscribers any Books printed at the Theatre, but it was never intended, to oblige them to buy such, as *printed* and *prised* by Booksellers: And therefore, to clear this matter, I have ordered the Porter to wait upon you, and go to all the Subscribers, as by order from the Governers of the Presse, to acquaint them with this, and to *offer to returne the mony back again*. . . . As for Dr Wake, he is only a Subscriber, for Greek and Latin, and therefore at liberty for all other Languages, however I think it but a Civil Respect to shew him any others without any Intention to engage him beyond his Inclinations.[1]

'I am thinking', Charlett wrote in 1698,[2] 'of proposing Subscriptions for the two Universitys and Royal Society, not exceeding in one year from each Body a certain Summe suppose 30 shillings.'[3] That was a day-dream; but any such idea of a book-club whose members were given no exclusive privileges would hardly withstand economic reality. After 1698 nothing more is heard of the subscribers to the Delegates' series of publications. By 1705, when the whole edition of Volume iii of Clarendon's *History* was sold to the booksellers, it is hard to see how the University can have had obligations to regular customers.

The arrangement to which the Company of Stationers rashly agreed in 1692 in their anxiety to gain control of the Bible Press drew off a considerable amount of stock from the Delegates' warehouse. The Stationers agreed to take 500 copies of any volume that the University published, 500 being at that time the normal edition from the Theatre of a learned work. This arrangement, modified in 1698 by reducing the Stationers' quota to 200, is dealt with on another page.[4] A large delivery, 12,672 volumes, priced at £2,416, was made to the Stationers in 1695 and slowly paid for. The Londoners were unwilling buyers of much of the Oxford output, and it does not appear from the Press accounts that another big consignment was made to them until 1711, when they received 600 books priced at £303.

The University felt justified in planning editions on the assumption that sales to the Stationers would be enough to make them profitable—or so Edmund Gibson thought. 'Tis true,' he wrote in 1697, 'Spelman was begun and has been thus far carry'd on by the encouragement of the Delegates and at the expence of the University, in order to sell it to the Tenants.'[5]

---

[1] Bodl. MS. Tanner 22, fol. 20.   [2] Ibid., fol. 33.
[3] Alternative draft forms of agreement to this effect in Charlett's handwriting are in B.M. MS. Sloane 4019, fol. 192.
[4] See p. 163.
[5] Bodl. MS. Tanner 23, fol. 21.

Among the Oxford books there were some that the London Stationers could easily sell and must have accepted willingly. 'Dr Marshalls Catechisme at 3*d*.' (14 to the dozen) was always saleable: 12,000 were printed at the Theatre in the years 1691–1709, and in 1692 the Stationers took 2,000. 'The Grammar', i.e. *A Short Introduction of Grammar generally to be used*, deriving from the original by William Lily, in a volume also containing the *Brevis Institutio grammatices cognoscendae*, selling at 12*d*. with a 25th copy free, was printed in 1687, 1699, 1709, and 1714 in quantities of 3,000 or 2,000. The Stationers bought 2,425 in 1693–6, though it could be got from other printers too. 'Oxford verses', that is to say dutiful poetry, mostly Latin, in honour of royal persons or eminent benefactors of the University sold quite well in London. Five hundred of the Oxford *Gratulatio* for the safe return of King William from Ireland were printed in 1690, and by Michaelmas 1691 only a hundred were left; and of the *Pietas* for the King's death in 1702 all but 60 were sold or given away within six months. When George I came to the throne in 1714 the University was more cautious and printed 400 of which 163 were presents, but the rest were sold at once.

The *Oxford Almanack* was good business, the number mounting from an impression of 3,000 in 1691 (N.S.) to 4,000 in 1696, 7,000 in 1703, 8,000 in 1707, 10,000 in 1711. In most years about two-thirds went to the Stationers, priced at 32*s*. a hundred. In addition there were copies on large paper, rising in number from 150 to 500.

Dealing with distant places was troublesome. Ralph Thoresby writes from Yorkshire in 1717, 'The inconvenience of paying moneys at, and receiving books from, Oxford, hinder[s] your friends in these parts of seeing many of your curious books, which are more accurately printed than most authors';[1] and when Sir Daniel Fleming in Westmorland got his undergraduate son to send him a book in 1697 the carrier advanced the cash for it.[2] Owing to the problems about payment foreign sales hardly came in question: it was almost impossible to trade unless by barter. More than once the Press was called upon to supply books in exchange for some got from abroad for Bodley's Library. In 1691–2 the famous Amsterdam bookseller Johann Heinrich Wetstein was sent a parcel of 55 volumes from the Warehouse 'in exchange for Bookes which he sent to the publique Library'.[3]

[1] Hearne, vi, p. 55.
[2] *The Flemings in Oxford*, ed. J. R. Macgrath, iii (Oxford Historical Society, vol. lxxix, 1923), p. 357.
[3] 1st Accounts, p. 3.

REMAINDERING

Within ten years of taking over the management of the Press the Delegates must have despaired of selling their stock of books by the means they had relied on. In their anxiety to recover some of their liquid capital they resolved in 1698 to entrust John Owen with books priced at £755. 8s. to take abroad and exchange for foreign publications. The consignment was made to Owen in London, the University paying freight to Holland. The Vice-Chancellor advanced him £145 for expenses, and further sums of £120 were made available to him in London and in Holland through the medium of John Baskett, the London Stationer who supplied the Press with most of its paper. Who Owen was and how he had gained so much credit with the Delegates nobody can tell. When he was sued for debt in the Chancellor's Court in 1702 he was described as 'Typographus', printer or compositor; at Cambridge in 1701 he was styled 'Bookseller of Oxford'.[1] No doubt he was the Johannes Owenus whose name appears in the imprint of books printed at the Theatre in 1699 and 1700 and another of 1702.[2] Analogy with Owen's later dealings with the Syndics at Cambridge[3] suggests that he had paid for the printing of these books and proposed to sell the editions. The fact that he owned a printing press in 1702[4] is an indication that he had been or had ambitions to be a master printer. His name is not to be found in the records of the Stationers' Company.

The Delegates 'imployed [Owen] to exchange some bookes of considerable value for the University'.[5] Nothing more detailed is known of his commission. Judging by what he did, he was to bring back books of equivalent value from abroad and deliver them to the University, which would keep such as it wanted for the Bodleian Library and sell what were left. In the event Owen arranged a sale by auction in the School of Moral Philosophy at Oxford on 20 June 1700, by which time the Library had taken books valued at £154. The sale was conducted by John Bullord, a London bookseller and auctioneer of repute.[6]

---

[1] R. Bowes, 'Biographical Notes on the University Printers', *Cambridge Antiquarian Soc. Communications*, v (1883–4), at p. 312. He had an address in Oxford: D. F. McKenzie, *The Cambridge University Press, 1696–1712*, i, p. 64 n.

[2] Miscellaneous writings of Johannes Crenius, 1699 (a curious book without a trace in the Accounts); Grabe's *Spicilegium*, 1700; and Potter's *Lycophron*, 2nd ed., 1702.

[3] McKenzie, op. cit. i, pp. 63–7.   [4] Ibid. i, p. 44.

[5] D.O. 16 Dec. 1700; *First Minute Book*, pp. 15–16.

[6] A preliminary advertisement ([MS.] Wood C. 51) and a catalogue (Vet. A. 4. e. 772) are in the Bodleian Library. Another, issued after the sale, is catalogued there but cannot be found.

The outcome of the auction-sale was a failure. A sum of £75 in cash was realized and books valued provisionally at £497 were knocked down to trusted buyers at prices to be settled later.[1] These amounts with the value of the books acquired for the Bodleian were roughly equal to the prices set on the books that Owen had taken abroad. Expenses turned the failure into a disaster. They came to £186, and the Delegates felt obliged to allow Owen £100 for his time and £100 for his 'loss in Appraysement of the bookes'[2] (the Oxford books had been priced too high).

The London bookseller Thomas Bennett complained of the effect on the market of selling foreign books too cheap. 'Mr Owens sale by Auction at Oxon has done the Latt and Greek Bookes an Injury for they sold most of them much under the Prizes I pay for them in Holland Ready Money though the Charges of selling them cost above 50 pounds Sterling besides the Expenses of bringing them over.'[3]

So far there was no hint of opprobrium in the Delegates' statement of their account with Owen. He had done what they employed him to do, though with ill success. However, he owed them £11. 16s. 2d. on the transaction and had acquired books to the value of £140. Then there were books missing or imperfect, and when all allowances had been made he was debtor to the University for £105. 10s. 2d. When the debt had been owing for two years the University proceeded by a decree of the Chancellor's Court to arrest Owen's goods in Oxford, which were 500 copies of Potter's Lycophron appraised at £108. 6s.[4] The seizure appears to have closed the account for the Dutch adventure.[5]

Daunted from the foreign market and, as it seems, without a reliable body of subscribers at home, the University was thrown inexorably into the clutches of the English booksellers and, owing to the difficulty of trading with remote places, virtually into those of the Oxford and London booksellers, though Cambridge, Bath, and Eton are heard of rarely. Like other publishers, the Delegates were sometimes driven to disposing of the slow-selling books (or those of which they had printed too many) to auctioneers at large discounts. Christopher Bateman of London was famous for his auctions,[6] and in 1705–6 he took 160 volumes

---

[1] Bodl. MS. Ballard iv, fol. 41. [2] D.O. loc. cit.

[3] N. Hodgson and C. Blagden, *The Notebook of Thomas Bennet and Henry Clements, 1686–1719* (Oxford, 1956), pp. 58–9. [4] Chancellor's Court Cause Papers, Michaelmas 1702.

[5] In 1707 the Delegates noted that Delaune, Vice-Chancellor 1702–5, held a bond from Owen for £100: *First Minute Book*, p. 21. The debt may have been paid off meanwhile. The Cambridge Press accounts for November 1708 refer to 'the late John Owen': McKenzie, ii, p. 57.

[6] H. R. Plomer, *Dictionary of Printers and Booksellers, 1678–1725* (1922).

from the Press Warehouse at reduced prices. Homer's *Iliad*, normally 8*s.*, he had for 3*s.* 6*d.*, Xenophon, published at £1. 18*s.*, for 17*s.*, Bernard's *Catalogi MSS. Angliae et Hiberniae*, originally £1. 2*s.* 6*d.*, for 14*s.*, Ludolf's Russian grammar, reduced from 1*s.* 6*d.* to 1*s.*[1]

As the time came near for moving the equipment and stock of the Press to new quarters in the Clarendon Printing House there was added reason to re-examine the unsold books and decide on their disposal. In 1712 there were 8,500 volumes in the Warehouse, whose published price came to £4,447. Their average age was about ten years, and the older ones were selling at a rate of one or two a year. It was resolved to make a clean sweep. The University's biggest investment in print, and financially the worst, Morison's *Herbal*, standing in the Accounts at £2,056, was sold to the deceased author's personal representative for £460. The other books, excepting only Anthony Wood's *Historia*, were sold to a triumvirate headed by John Hudson, Bodley's Librarian, for £751.[2]

Hearne thought the decision was prompted by the need to pay for the new Printing House and he reprobated it vigorously.[3] It took no account of a probable slow sale for some very valuable books, Clarendon's *History*, of which 200 were in stock, Bernard's *Catalogi*, Wallis's mathematical works, for instance. However, Christopher Bateman, the experienced auctioneer and bookseller, did not respond to an offer by the Delegates to let him have the whole for £1,200.[4]

This clearance was a confession of failure and, no doubt, was regarded as such by those responsible for it. It marks the end of a period of adventurous publishing begun by Fell and carried on by Aldrich and Charlett. They had overestimated the effective demand for learned works. They had been rash in agreeing to publish Morison's *Herbal* before it was complete and unfortunate in being saddled with two parts of a work of which the third never was written,[5] but their impression of 750 was too big. They printed 750 of the *Catalogi* of English and Irish manuscripts and of the manuscripts of the Cotton Library, and of these too they were left with large surpluses. Their minimum edition for learned books was 500; but Charlett did not think Thomas Smith would sell 300 of his edition of the *Epistles* of Ignatius and Polycarp with Bishop Pearson's notes,[6] and Hearne was advised that 150 was the right quantity for Camden's *Annals of Queen Elizabeth*.[7]

[1] 1st Accounts, p. 243.　　　　　[2] D.O. 8 June 1713; *First Minute Book*, pp. 38–9.
[3] Hearne, iv, pp. 91, 94.　　　　[4] D.O. 2 Mar. 1713; *First Minute Book*, pp. 36–7.
[5] Madan, *Oxford Books*, iii, No. 2917.　　　　　　　[6] Hearne, ii, p. 124.
[7] Hearne, v, p. 233.

Aug. 2*f*. 1713.

Books to be had of Stephen Richardfon *at the* Theater-
*Prefs by any Gentlemen of this University at the fol-
lowing rates till the end of* Michaelmas *Term.*

Folio.	*l.*	*s.*	*d.*
Lord *Clarendon*'s Hift. Royal paper in 3 Vol.	2	5	0
To be had feparately { 1*ft* Vol. Royal paper	0	15	0
2*d* Vol. Royal paper	0	15	0
3*d* Vol. Small paper	0	10	0
Apollonius's Conica, by Dr. *Halley,* Gr. Lat.	0	15	0
Euclid's Works, Gr. Lat. Large paper	0	17	6
Small paper	0	12	6
The 3*d* Vol. of Dr.*Wallis*'s Works, Large paper	0	17	6
Small paper	0	12	6
Dr. *Pocock*'s Commentaries on *Joel*	0	4	6
Micah	0	2	6
Malachi	0	2	6
Dr. *Inett*'s Ch. Hiftory, 1*ft* Vol. Small paper	0	7	6
2*d* Vol. Large paper	0	10	0
Small paper	0	7	6
Catalogue of MSS. in *England* and *Ireland*	0	12	6
Verfes on the Duke of *Gloucefter*	0	0	6
on King *William*	0	0	6
Plaufus Mufarum, &c.	0	0	6

Quarto.			
Dr. *Hody*'s Tractatus, &c. cum Excerptis è Cod.			
MS. Borocciano	0	0	6

Octavo.			
Xenophontis Memorabilia & Oeconomicus Gr.Lat.	0	2	6
De re Equeftri &c.	0	1	6
Dr. *Halley*'s Apollonius de Sectione Rationis	0	2	6
Greek Geographers 2*d* Vol. Large paper	0	5	6
Small paper	0	3	6
Grotius in Decalogum, &c.	0	1	0
Levi's Hebrew Grammar ———	0	0	9
Dr. *Marfhall*'s Catechifm *per* dozen	0	4	0
Trigland's Inftitutions	0	1	0

An offer of Delegates' books at reduced prices to clear the stock in
1713 (B.M. Harl. 5932, fol. 7).

The best form for wisdom after the event to take remains a difficult
question. The gentry were, no doubt, rightly blamed for not reading and
the clergy for not buying;[1] smaller editions at higher prices might have

[1] Hearne, v, p. 81; viii, p. 11. Burnet's opinion of the social classes of the English bear him
out: *History of my own Time* ('Conclusion').

paid better; a better-organized printing-office would have produced books at lower prices and got more work from outside; perhaps the Delegates had too narrow an idea of the scope for a university press.

The market for learned, or serious, or durable, books was in a state of uncertainty about Latin. In 1711 John Woodward wrote from London that 'Our Booksellers care not to meddle with any Thing that is in Latin', and inquired about the possibility of having a book written in it on natural history printed at Oxford, where there was no such disinclination.[1] Old-fashioned scholars like Hearne deprecated translations of the classics or Latin grammars in English;[2] he was indignant at the thought of prefacing his *Collectanea* in English,[3] and in 1706 considered that Wotton's life of Boyle ought to have been in Latin,[4] the catalogue of Thoresby's museum and Camden's *Britannia* as well.[5] Scholars' vanity required that they should be known beyond seas, but in England the death-throes of Latin as an idiom widely and thoroughly mastered did not long outlast the seventeenth century. Convocation in St. Mary's was tickled by the Registrar's inability to put '1708' into Latin on the spur of the moment.[6] The disadvantages of printing in Latin began to outweigh the advantages about then. 'Tell Dr. Sloane I do not at all like Dr. Tod's proposals, of printing the Natural History of the Diocese of Carlisle, in Latin,' Charlett wrote in 1707, 'it is much more proper in English and more vendible, such books being more used by Ladys and Country Gentlemen.'[7] It was a misfortune that great works of scholarship begun in the days of a universal language, Hickes's *Thesaurus* of the northern languages, the prolegomena to Mill's *Testamentum Novum*, Inett's *Origines Anglicanae*, were finished when their language made them inaccessible to, or inconvenient for, too many potential readers. Add to the drawbacks of Latin that it made books printed in it more liable to be pirated abroad.[8]

The decline of Latin was the opportunity for publishing in English. The Delegates cannot escape blame for not exploiting their very valuable copies in vernacular books—for farming out to other publishers the works of the author of *The Whole Duty of Man* and Clarendon's *History of the Rebellion* in return for small fees. London publishers, Tonson, Lintot, Benjamin Tooke, were building up flourishing businesses on English

[1] Hearne, iii, p. 202.
[2] Hearne, ii, p. 158; xi, p. 333.
[3] Hearne, iv, pp. 325, 328.
[4] Hearne, i, p. 286.
[5] Hearne, v, p. 86; iii, p. 136.
[6] Hearne, ii, p. 105.
[7] To Cockman, 12 Feb. 1706/7: B.M. MS. Slo. 4064.
[8] Hearne, v, p. 225.

books for serious reading, a market captured largely from the Latin classics in Dutch and French editions.[1]

The Oxford press sank into a twilight for thirty years and did not recover the vigour of its Augustan Age, 1691–1713, until the middle of the nineteenth century. 'There is hardly anything that the University print', Hearne lamented in 1712,[2] and, in 1733, 'The University prints nothing of Learning, indeed nothing at all hardly but a sheet Almanack.'[3] It was virtually true.

THE JOURNEYMEN

There are many questions about the journeymen printers at Oxford which records do not answer: how many were they, how much did they earn, what hours did they work, what was the ratio of compositors to pressmen, what qualifications had they?

First, the staff of the Learned Press: the names of 12 compositors occur in matriculations, Hearne's diaries, the Act Books of the Chancellor's Court, J. E. Grabe's accounts, and the annual accounts of the Warehouse-Keeper in the years 1692–1713, but do not occur in records of the Bible Press. Six pressmen may be assigned to the Learned Press on similar grounds. Apprentices to both trades, an unknown number, must be added. When there was work for them 'smouts', casual helpers, were employed.

The rules of a friendly society formed by the staff of the Bible Press printed in 1708/9 give the names of 21 journeymen working there.[4] They do not distinguish compositors and pressmen.

These rules describe the men who worked regularly at the Press as having 'a place in the Printing-House'. Who gave them the place, whether management or fellow workmen or a combination of the two, there is no knowing. It was a closed shop inasmuch as only those who paid contributions to the friendly society were admitted. '*xi*. That every person who shall hereafter have a Place in the Printing-house . . . shall be Obliged, within Three Months after he shall have such Place, to Sub-scribe and Seal these Articles, and to Conform himself in all things thereunto.'

---

[1] W. Roberts, *The Earlier History of English Bookselling* (1889); E. T. Wood and A. Heal, 'Notes on London Booksellers and Publishers, 1700–1750', *Notes and Queries*, vols. 161 (1931) and 162 (1932).

[2] Hearne, iii, p. 288.   [3] Hearne, xi, p. 229.

[4] *Articles agreed upon by the Workmen of the University Printing-House, Oxford* (dated 1 Mar. 1711/12), a broadside of which the Printer has a copy.

All the men were on piecework, and when there was no work for them they earned nothing. 'At present they are not fully employ'd' Daniel Prince told Blackstone in 1756.[1] 'They complain of the Want of a regular Supply of Work; and allege, that as they may lie idle for half the Year, they must be paid in proportion when employed', Blackstone told the Vice-Chancellor.[2] There is an item for £19 'subsistance money' in the Warehouse-Keeper's Account for 1700, which may be taken to imply that in an extremity the University would pay to keep its printers from going elsewhere.

In one year, 1695, the Warehouse-Keeper received sums amounting to £466 'to pay Workmen', but nothing of the kind is entered in the accounts for other years. He doubtless paid for work chargeable to the Delegates.

As for the rates of pay for composing and printing, Blackstone said in 1756 that the workmen at Oxford claimed that they were fixed by 'long and immemorial custom'.[3] When Fell and Yate entered upon their lease of the Sheldonian Press in 1672 they appear to have bargained with the journeymen for prices by the sheet. 'If we agree to pay by the sheet. And give 6s. for composing (though it may not be worth more than 5s.). And give for pressworke 3s. the 1000.' So Yate wrote.[4] His rough note over-simplified the matter, for a reasonable rate depended on the size of the sheet, the density of the composition, and the language. The charges to the Delegates for composing in the accounts for 1690–1719 range from 3s. a sheet in Demy folio for the occasional verses to 24s. for the *Iliad* in Greek, Lumber 8vo. Clarendon Medium folio cost 8s. to set in 1702, but 18s. in Demy 8vo in 1706.

In presswork, also, the price was affected by the size of the sheet, the space taken up by margins, and the size of the type. The charges vary between 2s. a sheet for Pococke's *Micah* and *Malachi*, 250 copies in Fool-scap folio, and 24s. for Marshall's Catechism, 6,000 in Pott 8vo. In this department of the work, naturally, it was the length of the run that mainly affected the price for a sheet, but format and size of type made a difference. 'Press-men reckon their Work by Hours. . . . They make their prizes of different Work by the Hour', Moxon said.[5] According to a scale written in the seventeenth century,[6] an hour's work on a sheet of Pott

[1] Philip, p. 20.   [2] Ibid., p. 23.   [3] Ibid.
[4] Univ. Arch. S.E.P. P17b(1)p.
[5] *Mech. Ex.*, p. 344.
[6] Queen's Coll. MS. Vol. 504, in a seventeenth-century hand.

set in Double Pica cost 2*d*., while on a sheet of Caen Royal set in Non-pareil it cost three times as much.

These were amounts payable to the workmen; the overseer added a percentage for ink and other consumable stores, and the master (the University in this case) added his poundage for overhead expenses.

Although it is easy to believe that charges for sheets of the various sizes set in the different kinds of letter had become conventional at Oxford by 1690, when the Delegates took over management of the Press, and might be said without much exaggeration to be fixed by immemorial custom, they rested ultimately on a bargain with the journeymen. 'The Manager should set the General Price, treat with the Workmen for their Part, and reserve the proper Profit on the whole for his Superiors', Blackstone was told by Daniel Prince in 1756,[1] and Moxon in 1683 speaks of a price being made for a whole book after weighing up the quality of the copy, the good parts against the bad.[2]

This conception of the compositors and pressmen as contractors for a book at a time is foreign to a modern way of thinking. To have a place in an institution where work is brought by the customers and to undertake it on agreed terms is associated in our minds with professions, the Inns of Court, the College of Heralds, or the Stock Exchange. They are closed professions, making rules for themselves.[3] The bargaining power of journeymen printers, however it may have been on the wane in 1690, implies combination. Yet of any organization of workmen at Oxford frequenting the Printing House or of qualifications for doing so there is no trace until the nineteenth century.

Trades came under the purview of the University, the extent to which they did so being perpetually disputed between town and gown. Merchants and mechanics were incorporated and chartered by grant or licence from the University,[4] but those who exercised trades had to be freemen of the city and to abide by its by-laws. In the period 1690 to 1716 a barber, a fishmonger, several booksellers, a cook, and a wine-merchant were prosecuted in the Chancellor's Court on presentments by fellow tradesmen for plying their crafts without proper authority. In these cases

[1] Philip, p. 19.   [2] *Mech. Ex.*, p. 203.
[3] An old way of thinking was expressed by the journeymen printers of Lyons in 1571: 'Les Compagnons font société avec les Maistres, & sont les vray imprimeurs à proprement parler: Là ou la plus part des Libraires & Maistres pretenduz, sont plustôt marchans four-nissans les matières, oustilz & instrumens': *Remontrances et Mémoires pour les Compagnons Imprimeurs de Paris et de Lyon*, Paris, Bibl. Nat., Rés., Coll. Morel de Thoisy, No. 328, fols. 138–43.
[4] H. E. Salter, *Oxford Council Arts, 1626–1665* (Oxford, 1933), pp. xii–xiv.

the gravamen was that the intruder had not served, or completed, an apprenticeship.[1] Certain occupations, printing, typefounding, bookbinding, and bookselling among them, were reserved for 'privileged persons'. Here, as in university cities generally, the book trades came under close academic control and were exempt from any other.

The quality of a *persona privilegiata* was conveyed by the formality of matriculation. To a tradesman it meant exemption from the jurisdiction of the mayor and bailiffs, from an obligation to be free of the city and belong to a guild, and it conferred a right to sue in the Chancellor's Court for trespass, debt, and defamation, and to be sued or prosecuted only there unless for matters concerning freehold land and the more serious criminal offences.

Hearne records in his diary the matriculation of a bookbinder in 1721.[2] The man owed the privilege to the interest of a fellow of Jesus College. The formality took place in the Apodyterium of the Divinity School, and the fee paid was 5s. Hearne thought it should have been 2s. 2d. 'of which 2s. is to the Government for the Stamp'.

Of the printers mentioned in records of the years 1690–1713 26 are known to have been matriculated and 37 are not. A likely explanation is that those who worked at the Bible Press as employees of London Stationers were not matriculated.

Universities admitted members from anywhere, so long as they would subscribe the required religious tests and take the oaths of allegiance; so it is not surprising to find (mainly in the Matriculation Book) that the employees of the Learned Press about 1700 included a Frenchman, a Dutchman, a Scot, and men from distant parts of England. In this respect it was like the printing trade in London, for it also had a wide area of recruitment.[3]

Admission to the University's privileges precluded enjoyment of those of the city of Oxford,[4] but several of the printers, at least 5, had the freedom of London from the Company of Stationers. The power of a Stationer to make his apprentices free of the Company was valuable; but for those in Oxford there was the disadvantage of having to go to London to seal the indentures at Stationers' Hall or pay a fine for sealing them

[1] The London printers had this grievance too: E. Howe, '*The Trade*', *Passages from the Literature of the Printing Craft* (1943), p. 10.
[2] Hearne, vii, pp. 239–40.
[3] D. F. McKenzie, 'Apprenticeship in the Stationers' Company, 1555–1640', *The Library*, 5th ser. xiii (1958), at p. 298.
[4] Griffiths, *Laudian Code*, tit. II, sect. 9.

elsewhere. Henry Hall, a master printer in Oxford, was fined 30*s*. in 1663 for binding an apprentice in his own city.[1]

However, these privileges and freedoms cannot much have affected the lives of the Oxford printers. What we should like to know is how they were governed or governed themselves. Presumably they had a 'chapel' of the kind described by Moxon. We know, chiefly from Hearne's diaries, that customers formed close associations with particular compositors.[2] Grabe in 1707 was aggrieved because John Hall, the overseer, had taken the Dutch compositor, Pieter La Mouche, off setting his Septuagint. The Vice-Chancellor wrote to Hall telling him to restore La Mouche to Grabe's work pending a decision by the Delegates on the priorities.[3]

The extent to which the compositor might be directly responsible to a customer of the Press appears in an undertaking by two workmen, dated 14 September 1705:[4]

I do hereby promise & engage, to print or cause to be printed, without intermission, thirty sheets of the first volume of the Archaeologia Britannica, beginning at page 81, at the rate of three sheets per fortnight compleatly finished: & doo hereby oblige my self in default thereof of the forfeiture of five shillings each fortnight, on condition that I am allowed six-pence an hour for all the time I shall want copy, which shall be call'd for in Library hours. Witness my hand

Edmund Bush
Pieter la Mouche

Subscribe'd in the presence of
> Mary hall
> Daniel Parry
> Sillvester Andrewes

The two signatories were compositors. Mrs. Hall, in charge at the Press, was a witness, and another, Andrews, was the typefounder.

The staff of the Bible Press, tenanted at that time by John Baskett, printed the rules of their friendly society in 1709. Its members bound themselves to pay a shilling every third Saturday and an extra shilling 'at each of the Three usual reckonings in the Year; viz. Christmas, Easter, and the Wake-goose' into a chest. The first charges on the fund were 'morts' (funeral expenses) and the relief of members' widows and orphans; subject to that, a majority of members might decide to lend money at interest to a subscriber amounting to no more than half his

[1] Blagden, p. 179.   [2] See p. 256.   [3] Bodl. MS. Ballard xxi, fol. 70.
[4] Bodl. MS. Ashm. 1820ᵃ, No. 231.

subscriptions. If he left Oxford a contributor might recover four-fifths of what he had paid in. Clause *xi* is 'That every person Smouting in the said Printing-house and receiving Copy-money, shall pay out of this Copy-money Two pence a week to the said Chest . . . so long as he shall continue Smouting; but if such Smouter shall have a Place in the said Printing-house, he shall then be Obliged forthwith to subscribe and seal these Articles . . .'. No dealing with the fund was allowed without the consent of a majority of subscribers, and a majority had power to elect trustees, key-keepers of the chest, and an assistant to keep accounts, which had to be rendered to a meeting annually on 1 March. The trustees in 1712 were Baskett, the master printer, and his manager Lewis Thomas.[1]

Besides the agreed rates of pay the journeymen had perquisites. The copy-money referred to in the *Articles* is defined in some Regulations made by the Company of Stationers in 1635: 'That every Jorneyman Printer shall forever hereafter have of the Master Printer with whome he worketh, in lieu of an Auncyent Custome which they the said Jorneymen Printers have had, for to have a Copie of every Booke they worke uppon, Three Pence a weeke'.[2] Thomas Yate, Fell's partner, reckoned about 1672 that at Oxford 'Hollidayes and copie-money' would add 1½*d.* in the shilling to the cost of composing and presswork.[3] A single passage in Hearne's accounts may be taken to mean that authors who had their books printed at the Press had to meet this extra charge. He paid 8*s.* to the compositor and 8*s.* to the press-crew as copy-money in 1731.[4] At Cambridge the Syndics agreed in 1699 to pay 4*d.* a week copy-money.[5] As for holidays, Hearne is to the point:

Memorand. that formerly the Theater Printers at Oxford kept no other Holidays at Christmass but the three days immediately following Christmass day, and the Circumcision commonly called New Year's day. The other days, excepting Christmass day it self, they used to work, not so much as keeping Epiphany or 12th day Holyday, only at night they did not use Candles, a Thing I note, because the Custom hath of late been altered, so as little work is done during all the 12 days.

This he wrote in 1727.[6] Moxon witnesses that 'It is now customary that Journeymen are paid for all Church Holy days that fall not on a Sunday,

    1 *Articles agreed upon by the Workmen of the University Printing-House, Oxford.*
    2 Printed in E. Howe, '*The Trade*', p. 12. It was a report of referees appointed by the Stationers' Court to consider the complaints of journeymen and master printers, 16 Nov. 1635: W. W. Greg, *A Companion to Arber* (Oxford, 1967), pp. 94–5.
    3 Univ. Arch. S.E.P. P17b(1)c.   4 Bodl. MS. Rawl. Q.e. 18, fol. 2v.
    5 McKenzie, ii, p. 3.   6 Hearne, ix, pp. 252–3.

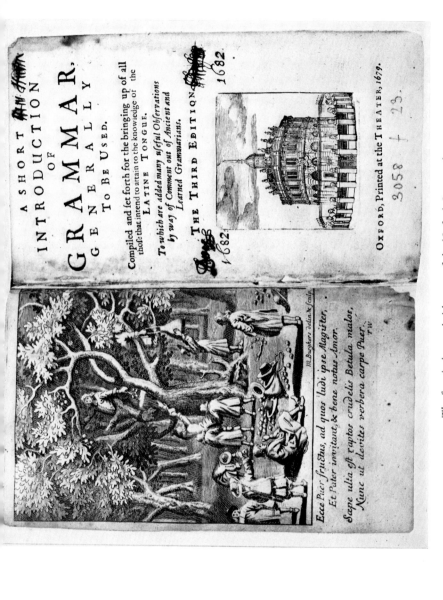

A SHORT
INTRODUCTION
OF
GRAMMAR
GENERALLY
To Be Used.

Compiled and set forth for the bringing up of all
those that intend to attain to the knowledge of the
LATINE TONGUE.

*To which are added many useful Observations
by way of Comment out of Ancient and
Learned Grammarians.*

THE THIRD EDITION.

OXFORD, Printed at the THEATER, 1679.

Ecce Puer fructus, ad quos ludi ipse Magister,
Et Pater invitant, & bene notus Amor.
Sæpe ultia est raptor crudelis Betula malos,
Nunc ut docritis verbera carpe Puer.
T.V.

M. Burghers delin. & sculp.

The frontispiece and title-page of the 'Oxford Grammar'

Aldrich's designs for the headbands and initial letters of Clarendon's *History of the Rebellion*, with copper plates engraved from them by Michael Burghers

Whether they Work or no'; and if they did not work they were paid an average day's earnings.[1]

In his accounts from 1693 onwards the Warehouse-Keeper entered yearly the sum of £2 'to the Workmen according to Custom on St. Barthol. Day'. This was the master's contribution to the Wake-goose (Waygoose, Wayzgoose) to which the *Articles* of the workmen refer. Moxon said that this treat took place 'about Bartholomew-tide'.[2] The Saint's day is 24 August, but it fell 13 days later in the season than it does in our present calendar. From that day onwards printers would work by candlelight. Sunlight on 6 September would serve for a working day of 13 hours—from 5.30 a.m. until 6.30 p.m.

A privileged compositor was paid a wage of £4 a year for 'looking after the Letter' (i.e. type).[3] Laying new founts of type in cases was paid for: a pair of Greek cases was filled for 10s., an Arabic for 5s.[4] Pressmen charged £2 in 1762 for 'working down' a new press. Compositors found it necessary to rub new type: they charged 9s. in 1744 for rubbing five founts delivered by Caslon, whom one would expect to have rubbed them adequately already.

Printers might expect a gratuity now and then. A typefounder, Joseph Leigh, sent half a crown to each compositor who set the type he had cast for the *Synodicon* in 1669 and entreated him to be careful with it.[5] In 1729 Hearne gave the two pressmen a shilling when they began to print his edition of Caius's *Vindiciae*, and 1½d. for tobacco (snuff, probably). He gave the compositor a shilling when he had set signature O of the book and did likewise for signatures Oo, Ooo, and Oooo. He gratified the compositor at other times with 10d. and 2s. 6d. to drink.[6] When visitors came and were honoured with a printed keepsake they reciprocated with money for beer.[7]

Though they were not above accepting these *douceurs* the status of journeymen printers was honourable. It has been justly remarked that Hearne regarded those at Oxford as his equals. He enjoyed discussing antiquities with Joseph Brookland, the compositor of his later years, and spent convivial evenings with Lewis Thomas, manager of the Bible Press.[8] William Ellis, compositor, was the son of a vicar of Sunningwell;[9] William

---

[1] *Mech. Ex.*, p. 327.   [2] Ibid.
[3] V.-C.'s Computus 1694–5; 1st Accounts, 1701–12, regularly.
[4] 1st Accounts, pp. 28, 250.   [5] Hart, p. 156.
[6] Bodl. MS. Rawl. Q.e. 18, fol. 2ᵛ.
[7] Alicia D'Anvers, *Academia* (1691), pp. 26–7. It was written in 1682.
[8] Hearne, iv, p. 259; viii, p. 71.   [9] Hearne, ix, p. 267.

Findall had an estate at Marston and his daughter married a don;[1] Thomas Hearne, compositor, owned land in Holywell and at Binsey.[2]

I do not know why one compositor, John Croke, had his name (excudebat Johannes Croke) added to the imprints of four books printed at the Theatre in 1696–8.

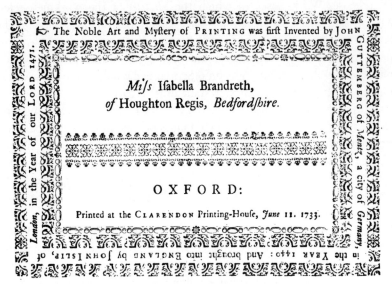

A keepsake for a visitor to the Press. The name and date were altered as the occasion required and the visitor pulled the press. (Bodl., J.J. Collection.) Reduced.

For John Hall, the Warehouse-Keeper and Overseer, nobody had a good word. Thomas Smith, the orientalist scholar, is one who accused him of peculation.[3] An anonymous writer alleged that Fell, on his deathbed, said that Hall was dishonest;[4] but the handwriting of this note is that of Henry Cruttenden, who would have liked to supplant the Overseer. Besides taking charge of the press Hall and his widow after him were entrusted with showing the Theatre to visitors.[5] Mrs. Hall, left rich by her husband, was 'nothing behind him in the arts of gaining wealth'.[6]

Charles Combes, born in Oxford, by trade a compositor, was put in charge of the Bible Press by John Baskett in succession to Lewis Thomas at some time between 1713 and 1720. He died in 1731.

[1] Hearne, v, p. 274; viii, p. 71; ix, p. 267.
[2] Hearne, vi, pp. 199–200. There were three contemporary namesakes: one a fellow of Merton College.
[3] Hearne, ii, p. 90.   [4] Bodl. MS. Ballard 49, fol. 208v.
[5] Hearne, ii, p. 121.   [6] Hearne, xi, p. 141.

A mysterious figure with a name occurring in records of the Press is Henry Cruttenden. What is known of him suggests that he occupied a position intermediate between manager and workman. A native of Lee in Kent he was free of the Stationers' Company in 1675 by servitude to Anne Maxwell,[1] and he was matriculated at Oxford in 1683. He was given charge of the press in the stables of University College, where Obadiah Walker, protected by King James II, printed Roman Catholic propaganda.[2] *The Speech of Sir George Pudsey Kt. to the King . . . Sept. 3. 1687* has the imprint 'Oxon: printed by Henry Cruttenden, One of His Majesty's Printers, and Printer to his Army'.[3] In 1688 he deposed in the Chancellor's Court to having bought punches clandestinely from Fell's typefounder on behalf of London typefounders. Hearne refers to him as 'a broken Printer and a great Acquaintance of Dr. Charlett's'.[4] He paid for Edmund Gibson's edition of Quintilian printed at the Theatre in 1693; and in that year he appears to have been working as a compositor there.[5] He wanted to reprint Fell's St. Cyprian, and 'If Mr. Hall's coming in makes any difference, I believe Mr. Cruttenden would agree to it', Gibson thought in 1694.[6] He died late in that year.[7]

Besides compositors and pressmen and a copperplate printer the Press had a gatherer.[8]

APPRENTICES

I have failed to find any mention of apprentices in contemporary descriptions of the Press in its early days. They must have been an appreciable part of its manpower: the charter from Charles I of 1633 allowed the University's three printers, each to have two presses and two apprentices.[9] Of their way of life there is nothing on record.

There have lately been found two bundles of notes, some cut to form indentures, made by a University Registrar, Richard Witt, of the binding of apprentices in the Chancellor's Court during the years 1666–85.[10] This record, without parallel for other years, is confined to trades whose

---

[1] Stationers' Company records, Register of Freemen.
[2] Wood, *Ath.* iv, 440; see above, Chapter IX, pp. 117–18.
[3] *The Religion of Martin Luther neither Catholick nor Protestant* from the same press dated 1688 has a similar imprint.
[4] Hearne, i, p. 217.   [5] Bodl. MS. Ballard iv, fol. 24.
[6] Ibid. v, fol. 10.   [7] Ibid. v, fol. 66.
[8] Hearne, ix, p. 341.
[9] Printed by Madan, *Oxford Books*, i, p. 283.
[10] I am indebted to Mr. Michael Turner for a knowledge of them. Univ. Arch., Court papers 130.

members were admitted to the academic body as *personae privilegiatae*, among them barbers, bookbinders, booksellers, cooks, printers, scriveners, and stone-carvers.

As for the printing trade the notes give some useful information. This example will convey the common form.

17 July 1675. John Crooke son of John Crooke of Cuxham within the County of Oxon' bound himselfe an Apprentice to John Hall of the University of Oxon' Printer him to serve from the 16th of this Instant till seaven yeares be fully compleate & ended &c.

The parties do not sign, all the apprentices bind themselves and parents or guardians do not occur, few mention conditions for maintenance of the servant. Only one, apprenticed in 1668 to William Hall, printer, stipulates for 'meate, drinke, washing, & lodging, shoes, and stockings'. Unlike the Cities of London and Oxford, the University did not recognize freedom of a trade by patrimony: there are several examples of sons binding themselves to serve their fathers for 7 years.

In this period six apprentices were bound to John Hall, the foreman at Fell's press, five for 7 years, one for 8. Two were bound to journeymen working there or in the Bible Press, both for 7 years. Moses Pitt, a partner in the lease of the Bible Press, took a Londoner as his apprentice for 10 years in 1681. 'The worshipfull Dr. Fell', Dean of Christ Church and a Delegate of the Press, appears in a new capacity, as master typefounder: William Hall, son of the printer of the same names, bound himself to serve the Dean for 7 years from Michaelmas 1672 to learn the art of letter-founding.

Of John Hall's six apprentices five came from Oxford or Oxfordshire and one from Pembrokeshire.

PREMISES

Not long after the Theatre had been fitted up with movable equipment for printing, in 1668-9, John Hall the foreman printer was urging on Fell and his partners the absolute necessity of adding 'a roome under the wall of the Theatre for composeing and Presse'.[1] It is not surprising that he did so, for having to clear the Theatre when it was needed for a function of the University other than printing must have been very burdensome. In February 1671/2 the Delegates minuted, 'That a Shed or building under the Wall by the little Printhouse be forthwith erected and built at

[1] Univ. Arch. S.E.P. P17^b(1)^m; *Print and Privilege*, p. 58.

the charge of the University'.[1] The Vice-Chancellor's accounts record a payment in 1670–1 of £105 to Richard Frogley and others 'for building the new Print House of the Theater under the East Wall'.[2] Frogley, as it appears by several entries in the Accounts, was a carpenter: the shed was probably wooden. It is discernible in Loggan's map of 1675,[3] a low penthouse fastened to the wall of the Theatre Yard, not very big—say 50 by 15 feet.

This workshop had proved inadequate by 1691, when a 'new Print House', costing £128, was put up by the carpenter. In that year, too, he was paid for building a 'Founding-House'.[4] Room for expansion had been made available in 1681 by the assignment to John Hall, the printer, of the lease of 'a garden adjoining the Printing House'.[5]

At its southern end Fell's Printing House adjoined a bastion of the city wall spared when the rest of the wall hereabouts was destroyed. In this former bastion a dwelling-house known as Tom Pun's House had been contrived. The University leased it in 1667[6] from the city, and it also was called at one time 'the Printing House' or the 'little Print House'.[7] It had seven hearths,[8] and was partly a dwelling for the Warehouseman in charge of printing. John Hall was living there in 1699, when it was described as 'the Tower in the Town Wall, . . . part of the Print House'.[9] Hall's widow occupied it,[10] and after her day the Delegates let it to the Architypographus, Giles Thistlethwaite. He was given notice to quit in January 1713, when the tenement was due for demolition.[11] It was probably pulled down at the same time as the wall of the Theatre Yard, in 1714.[12]

The wooden Printing House was demolished before then, in 1712, to make room for the new Clarendon Printing House, which renamed the Clarendon Building stands on the northern part of its site. Hearne lamented its passing; he thought it 'one of the best in the world', and doubted whether the new Typographeum would be as good and convenient.[13] He noted in January 1712 (N.S.), 'Yesterday the Workmen

[1] First Minute Book, p. 9. [2] V.C.H. Oxfordshire, iii, p. 52.
[3] D. Loggan, Oxonia illustrata (Oxford, 1675).
[4] V.-C.'s Computus 1690–1.
[5] H. E. Salter, Oxford City Properties (Oxford, 1926), p. 297.
[6] Print and Privilege, p. 41.
[7] Wood's Life and Times, iv, pp. 70–1. [8] Ibid., p. 69.
[9] Salter, loc. cit.; Univ. Arch. W.P. β 24(1), p. 294. The rent was 40s. and 'two fatt Capons' or 5s. for the Mayor.
[10] Bodl. MS. Rawl. letters, xxxviii, fol. 182. [11] First Minute Book, p. 36.
[12] Hearne, iv, p. 429. [13] Hearne, iii, pp. 221, 288.

began to move their Cases and Letters & other Utensils from the Printing House to the Theater, where (as formerly) they are to work 'till the New Printing-House is built.'[1]

The most recent occupation of the Theatre by printers had ended in 1692, when the Stationers' Company, in fulfilment of an agreement with the University signed by their nominees on 23 March of that year, rented a house in St. Aldates for the purpose of printing Bibles and service-books.[2] Fell's sublease of the Bible privilege to the four renegade Stationers of 1678[3] allotted to them for Bible-printing 'the use of the large Gallery or Roome in the Circuler part of the Theater aforesaid where the [Frames][4] and Cases for composing are now placed, And also the use of all the Lower Roomes under the Theater aforesaid where the Presses for printing are now placed and which are now used for the Custody and Drying of Paper together with the use of the said Frames Presses and Cases'.[5] That the Bible-printers had the accommodation in the Theatre all to themselves is an inference to be drawn from the Stationers' agreement with the University of 1691/2 to 'employ all those printers as were [in January 1692] imployed in the theatre . . . either at presse or case as they have been brought up in the trade'.[6] It seems clear, also, that these Bible-printers had no access to the Printing House; for in 1681, when the House of Commons sat in the Theatre, the printers took their cases to the School of Moral Philosophy.[7] When Celia Fiennes visited the Sheldonian Theatre, about 1694, the printers were in the cellars and the attic was used for drying printed sheets.[8]

Hearne's praise of the old Printing House was extravagant, but had some justification inasmuch as premises designed for printing were hardly to be found when he wrote.[9] In England, where printers had been obliged by an Ordinance of 1653 to work 'in their respective Dwelling Houses and not elsewhere',[10] only the two Universities had accommodation designed for this trade. Cambridge led the way by building a Printing House in 1655.[11]

The new Printing House, to which the Oxford printers moved on

---

[1] Hearne, iii, p. 293.
[2] *Print and Privilege*, pp. 178–81, 186; Hearne, iii, p. 288; B.M. MS. Harl. 5901, fol. 93.
[3] Madan, *Oxford Books*, iii, pp. 418–21.   [4] 'Formes' in the original.
[5] Madan, *Oxford Books*, iii, p. 419.   [6] *Print and Privilege*, p. 179.
[7] *Wood's Life and Times*, ii, p. 532.
[8] *Journeys of Celia Fiennes*, pp. 32–3.   [9] Moxon, *Mech. Ex.*, p. 15 n.
[10] *Acts and Ordinances of the Interregnum, 1642–1650*, ed. C. H. Firth and R. S. Rait, ii (1911), p. 698.
[11] D. F. McKenzie, *The Cambridge University Press, 1696–1712*, pp. 16–25.

28 October 1713,[1] provided room for the Learned Press under the immediate control of the Delegates and for the Bible Press then in the tenure of John Baskett. Bibles were printed in the eastern half of the building.[2]

There is no longer a need for a history of the building. The design was Nicholas Hawksmoor's and William Townesend, master mason of Oxford, was responsible for carrying it out.[3] Of its two purposes, to ornament the University city and to accommodate printers, it served the former better. Men carrying heavy loads had many stairs to climb. An occupation needing a strong light was hampered by projecting cornices and bulky columns. The windows, though they are bigger than an architect of the classical school would like, are too far apart to allow of an economical use of floor-space. The pressmen, relegated to the basement, can have been served little better by the light of day than by their tallow candles.

It must be supposed that the expectation of a large profit from Clarendon's *History* inclined the University to undertake the expenditure on such an elaborate structure and to name it after the author. They exacted £2,000 from Baskett as part of the price of his lease. Profits from the sale of the book came to much less. The profit to the University by the sale of the third volume of the first edition came to £174. 17s.,[4] and the other two volumes are unlikely to have brought in more than twice as much. The first of three volumes of the octavo edition of 1705–6 made a profit of £29. 5s. 4d.[5] The charge for printing the folio edition of 1707 for John Baskett would hardly have been more than £250. Moreover Delaune's defalcations[6] obliged the University to wait for its money. In 1715 the Vice-Chancellor rendered an account of £6,185 spent on the new printing house.[7] The extent to which a grateful University was indebted to Clarendon for this splendid addition to its buildings has often been exaggerated.

The verses in honour of Queen Anne, recited at the Act of 1713 and printed in that year, were given the imprint 'e Typographeo Clarendoniano', but the precedent was not followed; the imprint at the Sheldonian Theatre continued to be normal for many years and is found as late as

---

[1] Hearne, iv, p. 254.   [2] Hearne, ix, p. 75.
[3] See *V.C.H. Oxfordshire*, iii, pp. 54–5; *Country Life*, vol. lxiii, No. 1637 (June, 1928), pp. 800–7.
[4] D.O. 28 Nov. 1704; *First Minute Book*, pp. 19–20.
[5] Ibid., p. 20.   [6] Above, pp. 152–5.
[7] *V.C.H. Oxfordshire*, iii, pp. 54–5.

1783.[1] Tanner's sentiment 'tis pity that Typograph. Clarendonianum should swallow up the names & Memory of Abp. Sheldon & Bp. Fell, who were as great Benefactors' was evidently not confined to him.[2]

The New Printing House afforded in its western half a magnificent room for the meetings of Delegacies, for which it serves still. Jokers named it 'Golgotha' because Heads (of Houses) were to be found there and were thought to lack animation.[3] It was used for a dissection in 1715.[4] One of the rooms was appropriated to printing copper plates,[5] and another to the typefoundry.[6] There were complaints of cold and damp in the new building causing a sickness of which one compositor died.[7]

COPPERPLATE

The greatest advance in printing and publishing during the seventeenth and eighteenth centuries was an increased use of intaglio engraving for illustration and ornament. The taste for engraved title-pages, frontispieces, headbands, and tailpieces came to England at the Restoration from Holland. Designs by Rubens for the Plantinian office at Antwerp set an example of grandiose allegorical and emblematic ornament which was followed by the Dutch in their own manner and inspired the *Oxford Almanack* a century later. The magnificent Dutch atlases, the writing manuals of Clement Perret and Van de Velde, as well as engraved music, were proof of the advantages in point of delicacy and freedom of copperplate over woodcut. In England the Book of Common Prayer and the Odes of Horace were offered in editions printed entirely from copper plates.

Two rolling presses for printing intaglio are entered in the schedules appended to the University's *Specimens* of type issued in 1693, 1695, and 1706. Two were bought in 1702.[8] Hardly a book, unless, like the Catechism or the *Parecbolae*, it was aimed at the cheapest market, came from the Press without a copperplate print of some kind, at the least a view of the Sheldonian Theatre on the title-page.

Oxford was not rich in artists or engravers. A vacuum was filled when David Loggan, 'of Dantsic', was appointed *Publicus Academiae Sculptor* in

[1] F. Madan, *A brief Account of the University Press at Oxford* (Oxford, 1908), p. 11.
[2] Bodl. MS. Ballard iv, fol. 110.
[3] Hearne, vi, p. 34.
[4] Hearne, v, p. 59.   [5] Hearne, x, p. 87.
[6] Hearne, vi, p. 295.   [7] Hearne, iv, p. 295.
[8] V.-C.'s Computus 1697–1735.

1669.[1] Engravers who worked for Fell, George Edwards, Robert White, Woodfield, were either Loggan's pupils or were influenced by him. Michael Burghers, from Amsterdam, came to Oxford with Loggan; he told Hearne in 1724 that he was 76 years old and had worked for the University of Oxford for 55 years, part of the time as journeyman under Loggan.[2] He had succeeded to the title of Engraver to the University by 1694.[3] Hearne believed that Burghers was the best general engraver in England in the latter part of his life and that he had 'a vast deal of business'.[4]

No artist has been so closely associated with the University as Burghers. His engravings of the University arms and his decorative headpieces after drawings by Aldrich have been reproduced in recent years to ornament and authenticate the academic journals and ephemera. He did a great deal of work for Fell. Prideaux's *Marmora Oxoniensia* of 1676 has the earliest of his title-page devices, copies of that by Loggan in *Oxonia illustrata* of 1675, showing Athene seated in the Theatre yard.[5] A large task for him was Robert Morison's *Historia plantarum* of 1680–1700 of which the second volume has 167 of his plates. The 16 plates of fossils and curiosities in Robert Plot's *Natural History of Oxfordshire* of 1677 testify to remarkable powers of observation.

Above all, Burghers is remembered for the series of *Oxford Almanacks*[6] which he engraved, if he did not design, from 1676 until 1724.

The first of these illustrated almanacs, large broadsides printed on one side from an engraving of the calendar and other useful information surrounded or surmounted by a picture, was for the year 1674. It was an invasion of the most cherished monopoly of the Stationers' Company, bought by them in 1603 and relied on to produce a large part of the profits of their English Stock.[7] Fell at the outset of his career as a publisher had put 'Designe and Cut for a Leafe Almanack on a Brasse plate' in the list of things to be considered,[8] but an agreement of 14 October 1672 with the

---

[1] Madan, iii, p. xxxv.

[2] Hearne, viii, p. 284.

[3] He is so called in the Vice-Chancellor's Accounts for that year.

[4] Hearne, ix, p. 254.

[5] Miss H. M. Petter has found the original for the buxom goddess in a French engraving which belonged to Dean Aldrich (now Christ Church Library, Aldrich N. p. 65). It is signed Poilly and dated 1674.

[6] H. M. Petter, *The Oxford Almanacks* (Oxford, 1974). Nothing like a complete account of the subject is attempted here.

[7] Figures for 1663–4 are given by Blagden, p. 185.

[8] *Print and Privilege*, p. 58.

Stationers[1] debarred him from printing during the next three years 'any Booke or bookes or part of bookes' to which the Company had exclusive rights, in return for annual payments of £120. When that agreement reached its term a new one of March 1675 reserved to Fell and his partners 'a broad Almanacke with a large border . . . to be engraven upon a Copper plate and to be wrought of at the roleing press not exceeding Five thousand' and the payment for forbearance was in consequence reduced to £100.[2] Negotiations for the agreement of 1675 may account for there being no *Oxford Almanack* for that year.

The drawing by Burghers for the *Almanack* of 1676 has been preserved,[3] and he and George Edwards were paid for the engraving.[4] Edwards was employed for some of the engraving of the issues for 1677 and 1678, very likely the calendars, for Burghers received a fee for 'the figures about the sheet' of 1678. His signature as engraver and often as draughtsman too is on one or more plates until 1724. Sir James Thornhill did the design used in 1720[5] and Burghers cut one plate for it and Vandergucht another.

Duplication of the plates so that more than one press might work off the *Almanack* at a time is discernible by slight variations from 1703 onwards, and for 1709, 1711, and 1712 there were triplicates. The Warehouse-Keeper's Accounts for 1720–4 refer to a 'London Plate' and an 'Oxford Plate' from both of which impressions were sent to John Baskett for sale in London. The difference was probably in the places of origin, Vertue in London doing one while Burghers did the other.

The peak year for sales of the *Almanack* was 1717, when 10,112 were printed, some 500 were given away and the rest were sold, 9,025 to Baskett. Some copies were always on large paper. In later years almanacs had to contend with severe taxation in the form of stamp-duty, rising to as much as 1s. 3d. before its abolition in 1834.[6] The small amounts levied on sheet almanacs in the eighteenth century had no apparent effect on the one issued from Oxford. A statute of 1711[7] required sheet almanacs to bear a revenue stamp for one penny. The paper had to be stamped at the Stamp Office in London before it was printed. The Delegates obliged Baskett to supply paper to the Press stamped.[8] In 1757 the duty was increased to 2d. and in 1781 to 4d.[9] By 1811 the *Oxford Almanack* had to

---

[1] *Print and Privilege*, pp. 69–70.   [2] Ibid., p. 166.

[3] In Christ Church Library with that for 1689.

[4] Bodl. MS. Rawl. D. 397, fol. 322.

[5] In Worcester College Library with that for 1688.   [6] 4 & 5 Will. IV, c. 47.

[7] 9 Anne, c. 23, ss. 23, 25.   [8] D.O. 4 Dec. 1712; *First Minute Book*, p. 35.

[9] 30 Geo. II, c. 19, s. 1; 21 Geo. III, c. 56, s. 1.

bear a shilling stamp. The presence of a revenue stamp in the margin is a guarantee that a copy is one of the original impression and not a modern reprint. One plate for every year from 1716 to 1880 has been kept at the Press, and in 1886 and again about 1909 impressions from the whole series were offered for sale.[1]

The intention behind the allegorical plates is in nearly every case difficult to divine, nor is it known who chose the themes they illustrate, except that Charlett is credited with one and (probably) Aldrich with another.[2] The change to topographical subjects after 1722 may be connected with Charlett's death in that year. Hearne witnesses to a scandal caused by the *Almanack* for 1706. It was taken as reflecting on Godolphin the Lord High Treasurer, and as expressing Jacobite sympathies.[3] 'I am told by a very good Hand', he writes, 'that the Oxford Almanack is now in Consideration before the H. of Lords and that Bennett the Bookseller has sent to Mr. Hall to send up to London without fail an hundred of them.'[4] No proceedings in the matter are recorded. Rowe Mores, an untrustworthy writer, repeats a story about an *Almanack* (he does not tell which), that 'a celebrated Vice-Ch. was examined upon the surmise, and was at last very decently dismissed thus; "if you mean nothing you are fools: if you mean any thing you are knaves".'[5] The Vice-Chancellor did not claim expenses for a visit to London in 1706. The Whig newspapers of 1717–18 complain much of the *Almanack* and its 'hieroglyphics'.[6]

Early Oxford Bibles have copper-engraved frontispieces and title-pages; but the illustrations to be found in many copies of them are insertions by the bookbinder of sets that could be had from the engravers.[7]

In an age of copperplate illustration and ornament woodcuts served for such purely utilitarian purposes as diagrams in scientific works. Engravers named North and Lightbody were employed for the 'schemes' in the folio Euclid of 1703, and 230 for the same book were supplied by

---

[1] Advertisement in the Bodleian album and one inserted in C. F. Bell's article on the *Oxford Almanack*, *Art Journal*, Aug. 1904, at the Ashmolean Museum. As late as 1928 the Oxford University Press *Catalogue* offered the whole series.

[2] Hearne, iii, p. 133; ii, p. 318.

[3] Hearne, i, p. 56. [4] Hearne, i, p. 177.

[5] *A Dissertation upon English Typographical Founders and Founderies* (1778), ed. H. Carter and C. Ricks (Oxford, 1961), p. 14.

[6] W. R. Ward, *Georgian Oxford* (Oxford, 1958), pp. 75–6; *Hieroglyphica sacra Oxoniensia: being an Explanation of the Ch. Ch. Almanacks since the Commencement of this Century* (1702): B.M. Harl. 5932, fol. 93.

[7] As advertised in the *T.C.* in 1694 and 1702 (II, p. 597, III, p. 299).

Cookoe (an Oxford name) and Mr. Gardiner of London.[1] The block for Fig. 190 in Volume i of John Wallis's *Mathematical Works*, 1695, was found in 1892 by workmen enlarging a window of the basement of the Sheldonian Theatre.[2] It is cut with engraving tools on the end-grain of box-wood.

The wood-engravers of that time had few opportunities for showing their capabilities. A few examples have been kept at the Press of cuts of the University arms and of the Sheldonian Theatre device which date

from the years 1690–1710. The block for the arms on the title-page of a folio Bible of 1701 is a most skilful copy of a copper-engraved original cut with a knife on the long grain.

EQUIPMENT

The schedules appended to the University's *Specimens* of type dated 1693, 1695, and 1706 give the number of its printing presses as 7. It was a large number for those days. There is no contemporary list of London printing offices which gives the numbers of their presses: in 1668 only

---

[1] 1st Accounts, pp. 172, 196.
[2] Letter from E. W. B. Nicholson to Lyttelton Gell, 25 Jan. 1892, in the Printer's archives.

the King's Printers had as many as 6.[1] The 7 presses were the property of the University and in what came to be called 'the Learned Press'. Its tenants in the Bible Press were bound by their leases from 1678 until 1708 to keep 4 presses at work. The opinion of the Attorney-General that 11 presses were in use there in 1688 is probably not far off the mark. One informant put the number as high as 20, perhaps adding together those of the Learned and the Bible concerns.[2]

Frames to support cases of type while the compositors worked at them were made in 1668–9 by an Oxford joiner, John Rainsford.[3] Thirteen of them were in use at the University Press within living memory, but gifts or permanent loans have reduced the total to 5. The legs of these frames were lengthened at some recent time by adding blocks of wood to the feet so as to raise the level at which the compositor worked by 6 inches. They are made of oak, panelled at the back, and have decorative turned legs, features which would not have been found in the furniture of an ordinary printing-office but made these frames worthy to stand in so grand a building as the Sheldonian Theatre.

Rainsford also made cases to hold the type. None of those at the Press looks old enough to be his work, though a few are very old. If Joseph Moxon can be trusted, there has been no change in the construction or dimensions of the pair of cases used for bookwork since he wrote his *Mechanick Exercises* of 1683.[4] The partitions of the cases provide a 'box' (so called) for every letter and sign, and Moxon gives a plan for 'the most common way of Laying them' (i.e. the pair of cases), but he adds that the compositor before he lays type in the cases 'considers how the rest of the Cases in that House ly, viz. into what Boxes the several Letters are to be disposed; for they are not in every Printing-House disposed alike'. Virtual uniformity in the lay has since been reached in British printing-offices, but the University Press at Oxford is an exception. In the lower case the Oxford lay differs in important respects from the standard, and where it does so it approximates to the French. This vagary might be explained by the employment of French compositors to set the first book put in hand at the Sheldonian Press. The book was Beveridge's *Synodicon*, which the London bookseller Robert Scott undertook to print at the Theatre. John Bagford noted 'Mr. Robert Scott . . . brought over from Paris 4. of the most reputed Workmen there, one of whose names was

[1] S.P. (Dom.), Car. II, 243, No. 181.
[2] *Print and Privilege*, pp. 105, 106.
[3] V.-C.'s Computus 1668–9, 'Schools Account'.   [4] Edition of 1962, pp. 27–8.

Dell.'[1] Dell(e) was still working at the Press in 1691, when, as the son of John D. of Paris, he was matriculated in the University. Another compositor there had a French surname, Peter La Mouche; but he sometimes wrote his bills in Dutch,[2] so he was certainly a Dutchman. Another possible explanation for the peculiarity of the Oxford lay is that it is

A	B	C	D	E	F	G	A	B	C	D	E	F	G
H	I	K	L	M	N	O	H·	I	K	L	M	N	O
P	Q	R	S	T	V	W	P	Q	R	S	T	V	W
X	Y	Z	J	Œ	U	Æ	X	Y	Z	J	Œ	U	Æ
1	2	3	4	5	6	7	1	2	3	4	5	6	7
8	9	0	æ	œ		j	8	9	0				
						k						[ ]	( )

(second group of figures marked "superior figs.")

&		'	hair spaces	q		;	–	—	?	!		fi
b	c	d		e	thin and middle spaces	h	f	ġ				ffi fl / ffi ff
y	l	m	n	i	o	r	p	w	en quadrats	em quadrats
z / x	v	u	t	thick spaces	a	s	, : / . -	quadrats

The 'Oxford lay' of a pair of type cases, formerly distinctive of the Learned Side, but adopted by the Press as a whole since 1901.

better suited than the normal for setting Latin, the language which predominated at the Press in its early years.

All the cases at the Press are now laid according to the plan inherited from the former Learned Press; but this uniformity is of comparatively recent origin. Until 1901 the Bible Press had its own lay, which was a variant of the arrangement prescribed by the printers' manuals and adopted almost universally elsewhere.

It is easy to understand that there should have been this difference between the two 'Sides' of the Press, one continuing a tradition handed

[1] B.M. MS. Harl. 5901, fol. 85.
[2] Bodl. MS. Grabe 53, fol. 220; MS. Ballard xxi, fols. 70-1.

down from Fell's French compositors setting mainly Latin, the other deriving from Londoners brought here to set the Bible in English.

The Bible Press lay differed sufficiently from the British standard to be of historical interest, as well as a sign of the imperviousness of Oxford printing to outside influences. The arrangement of type-cases in western

A	B	C	D	E	F	G	A	B	C	D	E	F	G
H	I	K	L	M	N	O	H	I	K	L	M	N	O
P	Q	R	S	T	V	W	P	Q	R	S	T	V	W
X	Y	Z	Æ	Œ	J	U	X	Y	Z	Æ	Œ	J	U
ä	ë	ï	ö	ü			â	ê	î	ô	û	§	‡
1	2	3	4	5	6	7	à	è	ì	ò	ù	‖	†
8	9	0	£	ç	Hair spaces	k	á	é	í	ó	ú	¶	*

&	]	æ	œ	'	j			Thin spaces	)	?	!	;		fl
	b	c	d	e			i		s	f	ģ			ff
														fi
ffi	l	m	n	h		o	y	p	,	w	en quadrats	em quadrats		
ffl														
z	v	u	t	Spaces.	a	r	q	:		Quadrats				
x							.	-						

The usual British lay, for comparison with the diagram opposite. (Taken from William Savage's *Dictionary of the Art of Printing*, 1841.)

Europe retains features which must be as old as the art itself and bespeak a common origin at a time when Latin was the prevailing language. Of the departures of the British case from a primeval pattern we know only that before Moxon in 1683 published the first plan of the case used in this country the London printers had evolved a lay that was moderately well adapted for the English language. It has undergone no essential alteration since.[1] Compositors whose earnings depended on familiarity

[1] Philip Gaskell, 'The Lay of the Case', *Studies in Bibliography*, xxii (Charlottesville, 1969), pp. 125–42. All lays of the case had to be reformed to some extent early in the nineteenth century when the long-s and its doublets were given up, leaving eight boxes vacant.

with the lay of the case would hardly be induced to change it, and none of many attempts to rationalize it by substituting a more convenient arrangement has been seriously considered.

&	]	æ	œ	(	j	e	f	'	?	!	;	—	fl
ffl / ffi	b	c	d				i	s	g	*Thin spaces*	*Mid spaces*	ff / fi
em quadrats	l	m	n	h		o	y	p	,	w	*en quadrats*	*thin en quadrats*
z / x	v	u	t	Thick spaces	a	r	q / .	: / -	Quadrats

Lay of the lower case on the Bible Side until 1901.

The Oxford Bible Press lay may well be as old as the one published by Moxon and as good an indication of practice in London in the late seventeenth century. Only the lower-case plan is shown here, the upper case being virtually the same as that used in England generally.[1]

An old tradition with more serious consequences for the modern Press is responsible for the abnormal height of its type. It has been attributed, probably enough, to the import by Fell of founts of type of Dutch height in 1670 and 1672, and though it is unlikely that anything like standardization had been achieved at that time in either country, Dutch type was higher than English.[2] Here again there was a difference between the Learned and the Bible Presses, and both differed from the British norm. When the two Presses were merged on 31 March 1906 it was 'Learned height' that was adopted as the standard for the University Press. All its type, as well as its Monotype and Linotype moulds have to be made of this supranormal 'Oxford' height and its printing machines have to be modified to suit it.

[1] Pairs of cases are almost a thing of the past. Compositors correcting machine-set matter use, instead of a pair, one double case which has boxes for capitals, lower-case letters, and figures. The lower-case part is laid here according to the Oxford plan. For the increasing use of double cases, see Lewis A. Pryor, 'The History of the California Job Type Case', *Journal of the Printing Historical Soc.*, 7 (1972), pp. 37–50. Double cases were a nineteenth-century invention; six were bought for the Bible Press as early as 1861.

[2] Fell wrote in 1671 'If we could be furnisht presently, we would take up with the Dutch height': Hart, p. 165b. Marshall had written: 'Voskens . . . utterly refuseth to conform to the size of your letters, which are much lower (and consequently will be dearer) than those used here': ibid., p. 161a.

That the Learned Press rather than the other imposed its standards on the combined University Press was inevitable in the circumstances at the time of the merger. Of a total of some 150 compositors working here at the turn of the century no more than 30 were employed on Bible work.

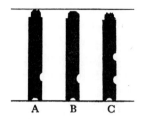

The height of Oxford Type

A. The former 'Learned Press' height, now adopted as the standard for all type at the Press (0.9396 in.).

B. The former 'Bible Press' height, disused since 1906 (0.931 in).

C. British and American standard height (0.918 in.).

The Bibles were printed from electrotype plates, whose height could easily be adjusted, while a great deal of learned work was in process of composition or standing in type awaiting reprints with alterations.

Confusion due to variation in the height of its type was worse at the Press while the founts given to it in 1677 by Francis Junius were in use. They were cast in Amsterdam, and if the relics of his Schwabacher can be relied on, they were 0·987 in. high—very much taller than 'Learned' height. Roman, Italic, and Black Letter for use with the 'Junian' types had to be specially cast to conform with them. Edward Bernard noted in 1689, 'the Junian types exceed in height the modules of the Sheldonian Press.'[1]

It is of no use to look for advances in technique or improvements in equipment of printers in the years 1600 to 1740. In this country average performance declined in quality from a decent standard reached in Queen Elizabeth's time owing much to French immigrant printers and type-founders. A few minor innovations can be noted. Hearne had his Neubrigensis 'scabbarded' (the lines spaced apart with strips of scale-board) so that 'the book will look more beautifully'.[2] That was an early

[1] Note preceding Bernard's 'Etymologicum Britannicum' in George Hickes's *Institutiones grammaticae Anglo-Saxonicae* (1689).

[2] Hearne, vi, p. 155.

example of 'leading'. Brass rules for printing lines must have been in use at the Press by 1690, when an engine for making them was ceded to the University by Fell's executors.[1] The typefounder was paid in 1711 for 91 brass rules.[2] Tin rules were bought in 1703 for Bishop William Lloyd's chronological tables.[3]

If the Press rose to a level well above average, particularly in Clarendon's *History* and Hickes's *Thesaurus*, it was largely owing to its excellent type, its abundant copperplates, and the use of superior paper. The possession of a typefoundry stocked with Fell's matrices meant that its founts were in better condition than those of the London houses and could be replaced more easily. The fashion of Fell's bigger typefaces is not to everyone's taste, but there is no denying them a rude strength which makes folio pages set in them impressive.

In the post-Fell era the Delegates made considerable additions to the stock of type. In 1692 they bought from Peter de Walpergen the matrices for his Pica Roman and Italic,[4] a face which passed for a 'Fell' type in recent years until 1930, when Stanley Morison pointed out the better claim of 'True Fell Pica' and caused its belated revival. An Ethiopic of a somewhat primitive kind was got from Holland in 1692–3.[5] De Walpergen's music-type was acquired in 1694, commissioned, no doubt, for the book of services and anthems for choirs of which only 16 pages were printed.[6] The Delegates agreed with H. W. Ludolf to pay for the making of a Cyrillic type for his Russian grammar of 1696.[7] The preface mentions a type for Armenian in progress. Founts were bought from London too: a 2-line English Roman probably cut by Dirk Voskens of Amsterdam and the companion Italic by Nicholas Kis in 1695.[8] Paragon Roman and Italic, sixteenth-century types by Robert Granjon, were added in 1706,[9] and founts of two excellent old Black Letters were got in 1701.[10]

Fell's typefounder, Peter de Walpergen, died in 1703.[11] Thomas de Walpergen, letter founder, a son of Peter,[12] was sued in the Chancellor's Court for a debt in 1704.[13] No more is heard of him. Payments to 'the

[1] Morison, *Fell*, p. 228.   [2] 2nd Accounts, p. 22.

[3] 1st Accounts, 1690–1708, p. 202.   [4] V.-C.'s Computus 1691–2.

[5] Morison, *Fell*, p. 246.

[6] Bodl. MS. Ballard i, fol. 95; xxiii, fol. 39. See above, pp. 148–9.

[7] J. S. G. Simmons, 'H. W. Ludolf and the Printing of his *Grammatica russica* at Oxford in 1696', *Oxford Slavonic Papers*, i (Oxford, 1950), pp. 104–29.

[8] Hart, p. 47.   [9] Ibid., p. 69.   [10] Ibid., pp. 70–1.

[11] Register of Burials, St. Mary the Virgin, Oxford, 7 May.

[12] Bagford's notes, B.M. MS. Harl. 5901, fol. 85.

[13] Chancellor's Court, Acta, 27 Oct.

Founder' are entered in the Press Accounts for 1706 and some to 'the Founders' in 1707. Sylvester Andrews witnessed a document relating to the Press in 1705.[1] Mr. Andrews was paid for casting type in 1708 and 1712. Sylvester Andrews, letter founder, brought a suit in the Chancellor's Court in 1716.[2] According to Rowe Mores, he was a son of Robert Andrews, typefounder in London,[3] who also supplied the Press. The last mention of a founder in the Accounts is of 1733. Sylvester Andrews sold his matrices to John James of London in that year.[4] Thereafter there was no typefounder in Oxford until the Press installed casting machines in 1853.

There are expenses in the Accounts for making typemetal. The first typefounder, Harman Harmansz., and the second, Peter de Walpergen, were paid for refining antimony, and there was one purchase of old nails, which were thought to help in freeing the antimony from dross.[5] Seven hundredweight of crude antimony was bought in 1691–1702, and it must be supposed that typemetal was made by mixing refined antimony with old type, since there are no charges for supplying lead, nor tin. The founders who succeeded De Walpergen evidently felt unequal to the task of extracting antimony from the ore, which Moxon describes as herculean. In 1705 four hundredweight of 'Mettle' was bought ready made.

A payment to the typefounder for making 'Mettle Letters' in 1694 relates to a practice of reproducing big wooden letters by using them as patterns for moulding in sand or plaster. A shallow casting of typemetal from the mould was 'dabbed' before it froze on another equally fluid casting serving as a mount.[6]

Of the Oxford typefounders only De Walpergen cut punches and made matrices and so could originate typefaces. The first that he made was a Syriac (1681), and in all he has 22 faces to his credit, half of them made after Fell's death in 1686.[7] The Accounts record rather frequent payments to him for punches and matrices for odd letters and signs to supplement existing founts. His successors did no more than cast, so the creative period of Oxford typefounding came to an end in 1703.

Fell paid his typefounders a salary and provided them with a 'workhouse' in the Dean's Lodging at Christ Church. After the bishop's death

---

[1] See p. 191.   [2] Chancellor's Court, Acta, 2 Mar. 1715/16.
[3] *Dissertation upon English Typographical Founders* (1778), p. 48.
[4] Ibid. (misprinted in the edition of 1961, to my regret).
[5] Fry's Metal Foundries Ltd., *Printing Metals* (1956), pp. 1–3.
[6] An explanation by T. B. Reed is quoted in the *O.E.D.* s.v. Dab, in sense 9.
[7] Morison, *Fell*, pp. 254–5.

De Walpergen worked casually for the University and doubtless for
other customers too. The Bible Press and Leonard Lichfield's press in
High Street were equipped with some of the typefaces made at Fell's
expense, and some reached printing houses in London.[1] While he was
salaried by the bishop De Walpergen cut punches surreptitiously for the
London typefounders Head and Andrews.[2] Sylvester Andrews was given
a room in the Clarendon Printing House. Hearne, in 1719, refers to it:
'Last Night the New Printing House . . . had like to have been burnt,
occasion'd by the Letter Founder's Fire, whose Room is above Stairs . . .
The old Room of the Letter Founder was below Stairs, as it ought to be.
The Letter Founder was at work now, not for the University, but for
himself. Indeed, he seldom works for the University, but uses the Room
for his own Affairs.'[3]

Figures in the tail-margins occur in books printed at the 'Learned
Press' in 1704–10. Bibliographers name them 'press figures' and consider
that they served to identify either a press or a press-crew of two men.[4]
William Savage in his *Dictionary of the Art of Printing*, published in 1841,
gives a clear account of the matter: 'In printing offices where there are a
number of presses employed, it is usual to distinguish them by numbers;
as 1st press, 2d press, &c.; and the pressmen put a figure into each form
they work, corresponding to the number of their press.'[5] There are no
press figures in Savage's book, but he wrote when they were common
within living memory.

Given that in 1706 the Learned Press had 7 presses, it is not surprising
to find only five represented by figures in the books printed there about
that time, for it is likely that one would be reserved for proofing and one
might be manned only when exceptional pressure of business required it.

The Bible Press conducted by London Stationers began to use press
figures in 1683 and kept up the practice until late in the next century.
In a folio Bible and a quarto Book of Common Prayer of 1683 the figures
range from 1 to 8, and an undated folio prayer book of the reign of

---

[1] Morison, *Fell*, pp. 148–9, 153.

[2] Chancellor's Court Cause Papers, Hilary 1687/8, Cruttenden's deposition in *De
Walpergen v. Crosse and others*.

[3] Hearne, vi, p. 295.

[4] William B. Todd, 'Observations on the Incidence and Interpretation of Press Figures',
Studies in Bibliography, iii (Charlottesville, 1950), pp. 171–200; Philip Gaskell, 'Eighteenth-
century Press Numbers: Their Use and Usefulness', *The Library*, 5th ser. iv (1950), pp. 249–
61; K. Povey, 'A Century of Press-Figures', *The Library*, 5th ser. xiv (1959), pp. 251–73;
D. F. McKenzie, 'Press-figures: A Case History of 1701–1703', *Transactions of the Cambridge
Bibliographical Society*, iii (Cambridge, 1959), pp. 32–46.

[5] At p. 814.

James II has figures up to 9. The allegation in the *Quo Warranto* proceedings of 1688 that the Bible Printers 'imploy eleven Printing Presses'[1] may well have been justified.

Assuming that press figures came into use at the Learned Press in 1704, they serve to distinguish books printed in or after that year but given an earlier date in their imprints, and to date parts of books that were a long time in the press. The several impressions of Volume i of the first edition of Clarendon's *History* all bear the date 1702 in their imprints; copies in which there are press figures belong to the third impression, which, as the Warehouse-Keeper's Accounts show, was printed before Michaelmas 1704. Copies of it were received at the Stationers' warehouse in London on 26 January 1704/5.[2] The presence of figures in a copy of Volume ii means that it belongs to the second impression, finished by Michaelmas 1704, which reached the Stationers' warehouse on 19 June 1705. Volume iii, of which there was only one impression, finished by Michaelmas 1704, has press figures only in the pages of the index, which Hearne compiled.[3] Mill's variorum Greek Testament, published in 1707, took many years to print. In the text there are no press figures, but the prolegomena have them regularly after page cxxvi.

It may be inferred from a letter of Edmund Gibson's of 1694[4] that London booksellers thought New-Year's Day the best for publishing.

It is safe to assume that the dates in Oxford imprints from the Restoration onwards are of years beginning on 1 January,[5] though it is otherwise with Oxford documents and letters.

John Wallis alleged that it was a common practice with bookseller-publishers to put the date of the following year on books issued late in a year,[6] and Hearne supplies an instance of this in a book dated 1714.[7]

PAPER

The Press Accounts of 1690–1713 show that the cost of paper was seldom less than half the expense on producing a book. The paper for a folio volume, unless the composition was abnormally complicated, came to more than twice the bill for printing. The relation was otherwise if the

[1] *Print and Privilege*, p. 105. See above, p. 103.
[2] Stationers' records, Warehouse Accounts, English Stock.
[3] Hearne, ii, p. 160.   [4] MS. Ballard v, fol. 69.
[5] Madan, *Oxford Books*, iii, pp. 111–12. I have found nothing that conflicts with this.
[6] In the preface to his treatise on *Algebra*, Vol. ii of his Mathematical Works (Oxford, 1693), first paragraph.
[7] Hearne, iv, p. 251.

format were small and the composition intricate or in small type. These are some examples:

	Printing	Paper
Clarendon's *History*, Vol. ii, 1st printing, folio, 1703	£174 14s.	£470 10s.
do. Vol. i, 3rd reprint, folio, 1704	128 13	189
do. Vol. iii, folio, 1704	305 18	758 12
Ignatius, 4to, 1709	30 2	32 8
Clarendon's *History*, 8vo, vol. i, 1706	127 10	267 10
Halley's Apollonius, 8vo, 1706	22 14	10 16
Marshall's Catechism, 8vo, 1705	12 2	10 8
Levi's Hebrew Grammar, 8vo, 1705	15 0	5 10

The following table will give an idea of the kinds of paper bought by the Press in the years 1692–9 and the prices paid for them, excluding the cost of carriage. Only a very rough comparison of the prices is legitimate, because quality, weight, and number of sheets in the ream are unknown.

	Per ream			
	1692	1694	1695–6	1698–9
Pott	4s.			
Foolscap	6s.	5s. 8d.	8s.	11s.
Crown			6s.	
Demy	10s.		13s.	12s.
Dutch Demy	20s.		22s.	
Genoa Demy				11s.
Lumber	13s.		15s. 6d.	16s.
Royal		38s.		35s.
Elephant	23s.		30s.	22s.
Imperial			40s.	
Atlas		45s.		57s. 6d.
Double Royal			55s.	50s.

Source: Warehouse-Keeper's Accounts.

Most of the paper was supplied to the Press by London stationers, after 1694 by one of them, John Baskett. Their trade was mainly in French paper, but got largely from Dutch merchants who owned or rented mills in France.[1] Direct import from France while it was at war with England and Holland in 1689–97 virtually ceased and never recovered

[1] Auguste Lacroix, *Historique de la papeterie d'Angoulême* (Angoulême, 1853), pp. 8, 9; D. C. Coleman, *The British Paper Industry, 1495–1860* (1958), p. 22.

its former volume. Thereafter Holland and Genoa were the sources of our fine papers. It is probable that the English product equalled the foreign in quantity by the end of the seventeenth century, but not in quality for another forty years.[1]

Oxford was well served by the Thames for transport of paper from London by barge and for driving paper mills close by. Paper from the mill at Wolvercote was used for the pocket-book *Oxford Almanack* of 1673[2] and for the greater part of Fell's edition of Faustinus in 1678,[3] and the initials TQ in the watermark of some sheets of Pococke's *Hosea* of 1685 are likely to indicate Thomas Quelch, the miller there. The very poor paper of the second volume of John Wallis's *Mathematical Works*, 1695, marked Q is attributable to him.

The watermark TM in sheets of the *Ladies Calling*, 1693, points to Thomas Meale, papermaker, tenant of the mill at Eynsham near Oxford from 1667(?) until 1706.[4] Charlett was thanked in 1695 for a sample of 'Ensum' paper.[5] A second Thomas Meale at Eynsham was a regular supplier of paper to the Bible Press at Oxford in 1720.[6]

In 1692, while war restricted imports, paper costing £304 was delivered to the Press by the Company of White Paper Makers in England. This chartered corporation, renting English mills and employing Huguenot refugees, had been given in 1686 a monopoly of making paper in this country for sale at more than 4s. a ream.[7] It had a brief career. The Company sold another consignment of 60 reams to the Press in 1694, but two years later it was regarded as defunct or moribund.[8]

John Beckford, who succeeded Quelch as miller at Wolvercote, supplied the Press in 1708 with 86 reams of Crown at 9s. the ream for use in the Grammar. The quality of the paper in the book bears out Hearne in his very favourable opinion of Beckford's work.[9] John Beckford and his son and his son's widow were suppliers to the Press until 1738, usually for the Grammar and the complimentary Latin verses prompted by state occasions. Like Meale at Eynsham, the second Beckford was making paper for the Bible Press in 1720.

---

[1] Coleman, op. cit., fig. 2 following p. 90.   [2] Univ. Arch. S.E.P. P17b(1)c.
[3] Bodl. MS. Rawl. D. 397, fol. 403v.
[4] Bodl. MS. Wills Oxon. 93, 296v, and 107, 305.   [5] Bodl. MS. Ballard xxv, fol. 15.
[6] Transfer of mortgage, Brookes and Baskett to Latane. Deed in the custody of the Printer to the University.
[7] W. R. Scott, *The Constitution and Finance of English, Scottish, and Irish Joint-Stock Companies to 1720*, vol. iii (1911), pp. 65–70.
[8] Bodl. MS. Locke c. 30, fol. 43, 'Reasons why the Paper Manufacture in England has not succeeded'.   [9] Hearne, vi, p. 231; ix, pp. 230–1.

Several of Hearne's books were done on Wolvercote paper, from his Leland of 1710–12 onwards. He bought it from William Seale, a book-binder, who, it would seem, acted as agent for the mill.[1]

The Warehouse-Keeper's accounts provide rather unsafe material for a comparison of the prices charged by the local millers with those of the London stationers. Foolscap from Wolvercote cost 5s. 8d. a ream in 1694: Baskett in London charged 8s. in 1695; but whether Baskett's was of English or foreign origin and whether there was a difference in quality and weight there is no means of telling. The White Paper Makers charged low prices as compared with those of the stationers in London: 6s. for Foolscap as against 8s., 10s. for Demy as against 13s., 13s. for Lumber as against 15s. 6d. The Company, however, did not last long.

The slight use made by the Learned Press of the paper mills close by was very likely due to prejudice, for as late as 1738 Chambers's *Encyclopaedia* could still assert that 'the English manufacture hitherto has been in no great reputation' (s.v. Paper), or to the limited capacity of these small mills which were already supplying the Bible Press, a very much bigger concern. There is evidence enough in the Press accounts that John Baskett secured a virtual monopoly of supplying paper for the Delegates' books from 1695, when his bill amounted to £1,870, until he got into financial difficulties in 1726. He began in 1707 to commission printing from the Press; his editions of Clarendon's *History* of 1707 and 1708 cost him £685, and he owed large sums for the *Oxford Almanack*, which he sold in London. A suspicion that he was sending more paper than was needed in order to reduce his debt is apparent in an Order of the Delegates in 1708, 'That from this time no paper be received at the Printhouse sent from Mr Baskett unless by Order from the Delegates at a Meeting',[2] and another of 1710, 'That no paper be received from Mr Baskett but what shall be sent for'.[3]

Customs duty on imported paper was increased and excise duty on British paper was imposed by the statute 10 Queen Anne, chapter 18.[4] Imported paper paid a duty of roughly 30 per cent of its value and the excise on the home product was about a sixth of its price before the Act

[1] Bodl. MS. Hearne's Diaries, pp. 184–189.
[2] 9 Mar. 1708; *First Minute Book*, p. 23.
[3] 8 Aug. 1710; *First Minute Book*, p. 31.
[4] 10 Anne, c. 19 in Ruffhead. There had previously been an excise on paper in the years 1643–60 (R. C. Jarvis, 'The Paper-Makers and the Excise in the Eighteenth Century', *The Library*, 5th ser. xiv (1959), p. 100) and in the two years 1696–7 and 1698–9: D. C. Coleman, *The British Paper Industry 1495–1860* (Oxford, 1958), p. 67.

was passed. The Press had to pay £164 in excise on the paper in its store in 1712.[1]

The Act of 1712 allowed the Universities of Oxford and Cambridge and those in Scotland a drawback (refund) of duty on paper that had been used for printing in the Latin, Greek, oriental, or northern languages.[2] Neither English university took advantage of this concession until Blackstone took the matter in hand in 1760.[3] He referred in 1757 to a single attempt to recover the duty. It was made, he said, by Edward Lye for the paper in his edition of the *Etymologicum Anglicanum* of Junius printed for him at the University Press in 1743. Blackstone wrote, 'When Mr. Lye some years ago printed his edition of Junius here, and made his application for the drawback, I have heard that he met with great trouble upon that account, the demand being entirely new and unprecedented.'[4]

But this, as it appears, was not quite true. The business-like John Hudson wrote in December 1712 complaining of the burden of taxation on the paper used in his edition of Josephus and others of his publications by subscription printed at the Press: 'I know that I shall, at last, have the advantage of the Drawback; but in the mean time I cannot spare my money',[5] and John Burton, fellow of Corpus Christi and later of Eton, is credited with making arrangements for the allowance of drawback to Thomas Hutchinson for his editions of Xenophon (1727, 1735, 1745) and with ensuring that 'in future editors would not be put off by delays and difficulties from claiming this relief'.[6] It is most surprising that the University should have been so behindhand in claiming it for its own publications.

Allowance to the Universities of drawback of import-duty on paper had been proposed in a Bill before Parliament in 1699 which failed to pass.[7] That the privilege should be enlarged to cover Bibles and Books of Common Prayer was a suggestion by a correspondent of Charlett in 1712;[8] but eighty years had to go by before the legislature gave effect to it.[9]

---

[1] 2nd Accounts, p. 24.   [2] Sect. 63.
[3] Philip, pp. 13–14, 114. For Cambridge, see McKenzie, i, pp. 161–2.
[4] *To the Reverend Doctor Randolph* (1757), p. 8.
[5] B.M. MS. Add. 4163, fol. 107, a transcript of a letter from Hudson to Wanley.
[6] Edward Bentham, *De vita et moribus Johannis Burtoni* (Oxford, 1771), pp. 12–13.
[7] Bodl. MS. Ballard iv, fols. 17, 28.
[8] Bodl. MS. Ballard xxx, fol. 75.
[9] 34 Geo. III, c. 20, s. 31 (1794).

CHAPTER XIV

Delegates' Books 1690–1713

THE history of a press, particularly of one that publishes, is incomplete without an account of its product. Faced by the task of reviewing the books put out by this learned press an author is bound to say as Humfrey Wanley said, 'sensi me imparem tanto negotio.'[1] Wanley's task was to index a catalogue of the manuscripts in English and Irish libraries. He goes on (in Latin), 'it presupposes a man competent in all manner of languages, arts, and sciences, and one familiar with authors and the titles given to them to distinguish them.' Nevertheless, he compiled the index.

Publishing by the Delegates can be considered under the three heads of religion, education, and learning or scholarship. These are, broadly, the scope of the University as publisher at the present time, and they are implicit in the manifesto issued by Fell in 1680: '. . . to supply the occasions of the University, in printing Books of ancient learning, and principal use in Divinity and other sciences: and in receiving and vending the modern works of learned men in their several faculties, both within and out of the University'.[2]

Books printed by order of the Delegates of the Press and charged to the University were a small part of the output of the printing business. They are distinguishable by entries in the Accounts of the Warehouse-Keeper from 1691 onwards giving for each edition the quantity printed, the charges for setting type, correcting, and printing, and the year ending at Michaelmas in which these operations were done. At intervals in the account-books there are lists of books unsold in the warehouse, which usually give the prices at which the books were offered for sale. The only trace in the early records of the Press of books printed for the authors or for booksellers is a note of receipt in the Accounts of 'poundage' for the University's overheads.

A distinction between Delegates' books and other books does not mean that the latter were not considered to deserve the honour of being

---

[1] [Edward Bernard] *Catalogi librorum manuscriptorum Angliae et Hiberniae* (Oxford, 1697), fol. 3★2ʳ.

[2] *An account of the state of the Press in the University of Oxford as it now stands, January 9, 1679.* See Morison, *Fell*, p. 252.

accepted for publication by the University. The Delegates would, no doubt, have sponsored Mill's variorum New Testament and Hickes's *Thesaurus* of the northern languages if the authors had not chosen to bear the cost of printing and make their own arrangements for selling. The justification for paying special attention to Delegates' books is only that it may bring to light a policy for publishing and indications of the quality of the members of the board as business men.

EDUCATION

In the period we are considering, texts and manuals for schools were rarely undertaken by the University. They were the jealously guarded preserve of the Stationers' Company, and it paid an annual sum to the University for forbearance to trespass in it. The lists of 'scheduled books' appended to the agreements to forbear[1] were largely of books for use in school from the horn-book to Hesiod. There was little room for another publisher of cheap classics. On the other hand annotated editions embodying original work were expressly excepted from the agreements,[2] so that the Delegates had scope in higher education.

Moreover there were two texts for elementary schooling which the University did publish and presumably thought it had a duty to publish.

The Grammar

The work generally known as 'Lily's Grammar' was regularly printed at Oxford in large editions which were taken for the most part by the London Stationers.

The composition between the University of Cambridge and the Company of Stationers and the King's Printers sanctioned by the Privy Council on 16 April 1629[3] allowed the University to print 3,000 copies of Lily's Grammar every year (in despite of the monopoly of the King's Printer in Latin). Another Order of 9 March 1635/6[4] conferred on the printers of the University of Oxford all the benefits of royal grants to those of Cambridge.

The book was in two parts, the first in English on accidence entitled *A Short Introduction of Grammar generally to be used*, the second in Latin on syntax, *Brevissima institutio grammatices cognoscendae*, each with its title-page but continuously signed. This arrangement had been adopted

---

[1] *Print and Privilege*, pp. 175–7, 204–6.   [2] See p. 73.
[3] Greg, *Companion to Arber*, p. 76.   [4] Ibid., p. 100.

by 1574 and lasted for more than two hundred years. The second title-page bore the claim 'Quam solam Regia Majestas in omnibus scholis docendam praecipit'. The edition of 1732 by a competent scholar, John Ward, is prefaced by a history of the book tracing the assertion of the exclusive royal sanction to a passage in Thomas Eliot's *Castle of Helthe* of 1541.

The authorship of the texts has lately been investigated by C. G. Allen.[1] 'Both halves of Lily's Latin Grammar', he says, 'were the work of a committee.' The *Short Introduction* owes a good deal to Colet's *Aeditio*, written in 1509, and to Lily's *Rudimenta*, written probably some nine years later. It preserves some of Lily's manual of syntax, *De constructione*, which Erasmus revised. The *Brevissima institutio*, in print by 1540, took Lily's rules in Latin verse for the genders, but was mainly a collection from earlier grammars.

The complete work was printed at Oxford first in 1636. The Stationers might have been expected to object to the University's comprinting on their member, Roger Norton, who as King's Printer for Latin, Greek, and Hebrew claimed a monopoly in the Grammar and printed it himself. In 1710 Norton entered this work in the Stationers' Register as his copy, an abnormal thing for a patentee to do. There must, however, have been a friendly understanding with him about the Oxford editions, for the University received a poundage for the one done in 1692, and the Stationers' English Stock dealt largely in it.[2] The whole edition of 2,000 printed in 1699 went to the Stationers;[3] but after the expiration of their lease of the Bible Press an edition of the same quantity done in 1709 was charged to the Delegates and half was taken by two Oxford booksellers.[4]

It may be that the Oxford editions of the Grammar would in any case have been regarded as not infringing Norton's patent because they were annotated. Fell and his partners in leasing to the four renegade Stationers the privilege of overriding monopoly in 1678 reserved to themselves 'Lillies Grammar with [blank] Notes as it hath been printed heretofore at the Theater'.[5] The Grammar, as it had been printed at Oxford, was extensively revised at Fell's bidding by Thomas Bennett in 1672–3,[6] and

---

[1] 'The Sources of "Lily's Latin Grammar": a Review of the Facts and some further Suggestions', *The Library*, 5th ser. ix (1954), pp. 85–100.

[2] Stationers' records, Warehouse Accounts, English Stock, 1692–4.

[3] 1st Accounts, p. 149.   [4] 2nd Accounts, p. 7.

[5] Madan, *Oxford Books*, iii, p. 419.

[6] John Twells, *A General Examination of the Oxford Grammar* (1683), p. 26 of the pre-liminaries.

Fell is the probable author of the preface to the first part of the book in the edition of 1673 and later years. The title-pages of the *Brevissima institutio* of 1692 and 1699 claim that it embodies new matter by Vossius, Busby, and others. Editions printed by the patentee, Roger Norton, in 1682 and 1699 were of the *Short Introduction* without the Latin sequel.

The last Oxford edition was of 1733, but the patentees, then Longman, Hurst, and Company, issued one in the traditional form in 1814.

Marshall's Catechism

This booklet without covers, selling for 2*d.* 'sticht', was printed four times at Oxford in the years 1690–1713 in editions large for those times and was evidently in steady demand. Of the 9th edition, dated 1692, 6,000 were printed and in February 1692/3 2,000 were bought by the Stationers' English Stock. The 10th edition was printed in 1698 in an unknown quantity for the London bookseller Thomas Bennett. The 11th, of 1,000, came out in 1700, and in 1704 there was a 12th edition of 3,000.

The Catechism set forth in the Book of Common Prayer briefly explained by short notes grounded upon Holy Scripture 'was drawn up and composed', Wood said, 'by our Author upon the desire and motion of Dr. John Fell, bishop of Oxon., to be used by the ministers of his diocess in the catechising of the children of their respective parishes'.[1] The author, on the same authority, was Thomas Marshall, Rector of Lincoln College. The series of editions from the University Press ended in 1835.[2]

DIVINITY

Given the divisions between English Christians at this time it is surprising that the University published so little in the way of religious controversy. It printed and published its own solemn condemnation of Arthur Bury's *Naked Gospel* in 1691, the last pronouncement by an English university of true doctrine. Bury's pamphlet, one of the most persuasive devotional books of its time, might well be accepted for publication by the Delegates now, the term 'religion' being differently understood.

In the late seventeenth century the Delegates seem to have given the authority of the University to controversial religious books that were valuable as scholarship. They sponsored Humfrey Hody's *Redargutio* (Denial) in 1691 that a schism had occurred in the Anglican Church when

---

[1] Wood, *Ath.* iv, 171.   [2] Madan, *Oxford Books*, iii, p. 373.

bishops were deprived of their office, albeit unjustly, for refusing the oath of allegiance, provided their successors were orthodox. He supported the thesis by printing an argument to the same effect by Nicephorus, an early Father, from a manuscript at the Bodleian.[1] The ensuing controversy was printed elsewhere. As printer the University had less objection to contentious matter: Jonathan Edwards against Socinianism, Jonas Proast against toleration, William Lowth for the divine inspiration of the Scriptures, George Bull on the divine nature of Christ, Benjamin Wood-roffe in defence of Luther, William Buckeridge against occasional conformity, issued from the Press at the expense of the authors or of booksellers. Much of the large output of sermons, including one by Henry Sacheverell, was aimed at liberal theologians; and the numerous tracts with which Edward Wells belaboured the Dissenters came from it too.

Pococke on the Minor Prophets

The fourth of Edward Pococke's commentaries on the Minor Prophets, on *Joel*, was published by the Delegates in 1691, a few months after the author's death. His volume on *Micah* and *Malachi* was reprinted in the same year. In his preface to *Joel* he writes, 'Many difficulties there are in this Prophet, which were incumbent on me to clear.' He elucidates obscurities in the Hebrew text by reference to other Semitic languages, and it was well said that the greatest imperfection in his work was the excessive modesty which prevented his expressing a preference for one reading over another. The resources of the Press in the way of type for Hebrew, Arabic, and Syriac were put to good use.

Five hundred copies were printed for sale at 4s. 6d. In 1712 there were 140 copies left in the Warehouse, and they were among the books sold at a knock-down price to John Hudson.[2]

When the *Theological Works of the Learned Dr. Pocock* were edited by Leonard Twells in 1740 errors in the first editions proved 'so very numerous as greatly retarded the Work'. Thomas Hunt, the orientalist, believed he had corrected more than two thousand errors in the texts.[3]

Aristeas

Pseudo-Aristeas on the 72 Interpreters was published by the Delegates in 1692. It is the spurious text on which the miraculous origin of the

[1] Bodl. MS. Barocci 142, 4.   [2] See p. 184.
[3] P. Simpson, *Proof-Reading in the Sixteenth, Seventeenth, and Eighteenth Centuries*, pp. 145–6.

Septuagint rests. Humfrey Hody had shown clearly in 1684 that the work was not authentic,[1] so the reason for giving it a new lease of life in this edition is not obvious. The anonymous editor in his preface is un-decided as to the genuineness of the work, but thinks scholars should read it. He undertook the editing, he says, at the instance of Edward Bernard and added an appendix suggested to him by a very eminent man. This last is likely to have been Henry Aldrich, who gave away copies of the book as New-Year presents. The editor of the book can hardly have been Hody, who has been credited with it,[2] for he was convinced of its worthlessness. Moreover, the unsigned preface by referring to an edition of Xenophon which the writer had been obliged to lay aside identifies him with Edward Wells, like Bernard and Aldrich a Christ Church man.

Six hundred copies were printed of which 150 were sold to Dean Aldrich at 9d. each, the price to other customers being a shilling. In 1697 there were 80 unsold, after which year the book disappears from the Accounts.

The Cathedral Service

Christ Church Library has 16 folio pages of words and music intended to be part of a choral service-book.[3] The setting and printing of 'four sheets of the Cathedral Musick' were charged to the Delegates in 1696-7, and the four sheets, valued at 25s., were in stock two years later. The first eight pages are an anthem, 'Have mercy on me', by Aldrich, the seven following are 'Behold, thou hast made my days', set by Orlando Gibbons, the last page is the beginning of another anthem by Aldrich, 'Give the King thy judgments'. The type for the music is the one by Peter de Walpergen shown in the University's type-specimen book of 1695. No doubt it was made for this proposed book, and is modelled on Aldrich's handwriting.[4] Samuel Pepys wrote to Charlett on 4 August 1694 acknowledging receipt of a specimen of a music type and hoped to see a proof of words and music 'before you enter (for good & all) upon your design'd volume of Church-Musick'.[5] As for the abandonment of the project the records are silent.

---

[1] *Contra historiam Aristeae de LXX Interpretibus dissertatio* (Oxford, 1684). Modern criticism finds some value in the text: S. Jellicoe, *The Septuagint and Modern Study* (Oxford, 1968), pp. 29-53.
[2] *D.N.B.*; Catalogue of the British Museum.   [3] Music MS. No. 1208.
[4] For comparison see the Dean's writing in Christ Church Music MS. No. 33, the first ten lines.
[5] Bodl. MS. Ballard i, fol. 95.

The beautiful music type was used for illustrations in Wallis's edition of Ptolemy's *Harmonica* in 1699;[1] but not again until Robert Bridges revived it for his Yattendon *Hymns* of 1895-9.

The Letters of St. Ignatius

Ignatius was an author in favour with Anglicans of the seventeenth century because of his insistence on the authority of bishops. Archbishop Ussher had edited him at Oxford in 1644 with learned notes, two years before Isaac Vossius published the first text based on Codex Mediceus (since regarded as the best) and rejected spurious letters.

John Pearson, the learned Bishop of Chester, who died in 1686, contemplated an edition of the letters, but left his copious notes unfinished and unrevised. A collation of Codex Mediceus was made for Pearson by John Ledgard. The notes and recension were made available to Thomas Smith, librarian to Sir Robert Cotton, for an edition sponsored by the Delegates and published in 1709. Smith arranged and completed Pearson's notes, adding some, and used Pearson's recension of the Greek text.

The book has a troubled history. Aldrich had decided on the letters as his New-Year book for 1708 and set his nephew, Charles Aldrich, to work on it. An accurate transcription of the Medicean text was made for him by Antonio Salvini, and the little book was printed 'at the Theater' at the Dean's expense and was ready by the end of 1708. Though dated 1708, it was made the Dean's present for 1709. Smith's much more elaborate work came from the Press only two months later. However, the Dean's edition was small in number, the notes were slight, and Hearne thought it did not lessen the demand for Smith's.[2]

The correction of Smith's edition was done mainly in Oxford. Hudson, Bodley's Librarian, undertook a general care of production, and Hearne read the proofs. Revised proofs were sent to Smith in London.[3] So many wrong citations were found in Pearson's notes that printing had to be stopped and two sheets had to be reset. A month before printing was finished J. E. Grabe moved to suspend publication until the book 'had been approved by proper judges'.[4] His intervention should be associated with an objection by 'a most venerable ecclesiastic' (Cumberland, Bishop

---

[1] In Wallis's collected *Works*, vol. iii.
[2] Hearne, ii, pp. 24, 158, 167, 247.
[3] Hearne, ii, p. 129; P. Simpson, *Proof-Reading in the Sixteenth, Seventeenth, and Eighteenth Centuries* (Oxford, 1935, reprinted 1970), pp. 198-200.
[4] Hearne, ii, pp. 175, 438.

of Peterborough) who thought that Pearson's notes in their unfinished state did not do him justice.[1]

Later authorities on Ignatius have found many faults in Smith's text.[2] On the other hand, Aldrich's little book has, perhaps, had less recognition than it deserves.[3]

All the same, Smith's edition sold well; so well that Peisley, the Oxford bookseller, bought the Delegates' stock soon after copies became available.

Inett's Church History

Mainly at Charlett's instigation the Delegates agreed in 1709 to print and publish a second volume of John Inett's *Origines Anglicanae* continuing his history of the English Church from the year 401.[4] His first volume, ending at the Norman Conquest, had been printed in London for Matthew Wotton in 1704. The author complained of printer's errors and made over his copy in the second volume carrying the history on to 1216 to the University.[5] The previous volume cannot have sold well, for when the second was ready the Stationers did their utmost to resist taking the 200 copies which the terms of their lease of the Bible Press obliged them to take. However, in the end they took them.[6]

Hearne judged the work unfavourably as relying on secondary sources,[7] and William Nicholson politely expected to see 'the latent sources' of Inett's information brought to light by another author.[8] The history was edited in 1855 by John Griffiths with many corrections.

Five hundred and fifty copies were printed in 1710. When the Delegates' stock was sold in 1713, 378 copies were left.

ARTS AND SCIENCES: THE CLASSICS

When the Delegates took charge of printing in 1690 very few classical texts had been printed at Oxford. Students at the University must have read Dutch editions or those published in France *in usum Delphini*.

---

[1] Smith's preface to *S. Ignatii epistolae genuinae* (Oxford, 1709), fol. a3ʳ.
[2] T. Zahn, *Ignatius von Antiochien* (Gotha, 1873), pp. 546 ff.; J. B. Lightfoot, *The Apostolic Fathers*, 2nd ed. (1889), Part II, vol. i, pp. 78 n., 81 n.; vol. iii, p. 7.
[3] Zahn, op. cit., mentions it with approval on p. 553.
[4] Hearne, ii, p. 341.
[5] Bodl. MS. Ballard xv, fol. 47; *Origines Anglicanae, or, a History of the English Church from the Conversion of the English Saxons till the Death of King John*, ed. J. Griffiths (Oxford, 1855), pp. xxi–xxiv.
[6] *First Minute Book*, p. 32.　　　　　　　　　　　　　[7] Hearne, ii, p. 269.
[8] *English Historical Library*, 3rd ed. (1736), pp. 102, 109.

Nothing of Virgil, Horace, Livy, Juvenal, Lucretius, Caesar, Catullus, or Martial had come from the Press, and of the Greeks only Homer and Theocritus. Fell had at one time proposed to print plain texts of the classics in order to keep the presses busy, but it was very likely the fear of quarrelling with the Stationers that deterred him.[1] The Stationers claimed a monopoly in school editions of the Greek and Latin authors, though it may be doubted whether they kept them in print. Fell contented himself with producing small editions with few notes of Epictetus (the *Enchiridion*), Cornelius Nepos, Theocritus, and Pliny's letters for New-Year presents.[2]

In the first ten years of their management of the Press the Delegates sponsored a three-volume edition of lesser Greek geographers by John Hudson, a complete Xenophon by Edward Wells, Potter's Lycophron, and Pindar. The texts belong to the era before Bentley, and there is no need to linger over them now, however well they may have served their generation. A 'noble edition' of Caesar projected by Aldrich with 'cuts of his own contriving' came to nothing.[3]

Xenophon in seven volumes, costing £1 the set, completed in 1705, in quantities varying from 1,000 to 500 according to the demand for each volume, sold well: only 87 sets were left in 1712. The Stationers could not sell Lycophron, and sent 160 of their allocation of 200 for sale by auction in France and Holland in 1701.

ARTS AND SCIENCES: HISTORY

Malalas

An edition of the chronicle in Greek of John Malalas published by the University in 1691 is memorable for an appendix by Richard Bentley.

The author, who lived at Antioch at some time between A.D. 600 and 1000, wrote what appears to have been a history of the world from the birth of Adam. His work was preserved for modern readers only by a manuscript in the Bodleian Library[4] and in a mutilated state. The first of two volumes is lost and the second lacks leaves at the beginning and end.

Archbishop Ussher's attention was drawn to the chronicle, and it was probably for him that Edmund Chilmeade made a transcript at some date

---

[1] Charlett to Hearne: Hearne, v, p. 122.
[2] Madan, iii, p. 521.
[3] Hearne, iii, pp. 302, 329. Aldrich had 12 copies printed of part of one of Horace's *Satires* rearranged to his liking (ibid., p. 115). The Bodleian has one (Mar. 576).
[4] Bodl. MS. Barocci 182.

before 1654.[1] Fell also had a transcript, and put this work in his list of publications in preparation in 1676.[2] In 1674 the Dean had entrusted his pupil Humphrey Prideaux with the editing. Prideaux scouted the assignment: 'We are continually pestered', he wrote, 'with letters from forrain parts to set it forth, out of a conceit that rare things ly hid therein, wereas more than halfe the book is stuffed with ridiculous and incredible lys.'[3] R. C. Jebb called it 'a dismal swamp'.[4] It was left to John Mill after Fell's death to take general charge of an edition and to Hody, the Greek professor, to supply an introduction.

In 1690, when proofs were available, Bentley was staying in Oxford, and Mill lent him the proofs and persuaded him to write his comments. Bentley's 'Epistola ad Johannem Millium', appended to the book, was the first of his writings to appear in print. At the age of 28 he astonished the learned world by his erudition and the acuteness of his criticism.

Ludwig Dindorf, a later editor, found many errors and omissions in the Oxford text.[5]

English Chronicles

The three volumes of early English chronicles completed in 1691 by the issue of *Historiae Britannicae et Anglicanae Scriptores xv* edited by Thomas Gale were prompted by Fell. In his prospectus of 1681 he put among books ready or preparing 'English ancient historians not yet printed', and the first volume of the series, *Rerum Anglicarum scriptorum veterum Tom. i*, came out in Fell's lifetime, in 1684. It was published without an editor's name and has been regarded as the work of the bishop himself; but the transcribing and editing was done by William Fulman, who, as Wood testifies, was 'totally averse from making himself known'.[6] In this volume are the spurious Annals of Croyland and, printed for the first time, the valuable Chronicle of Melrose and the Annals of Burton.

Gale edited the subsequent volumes, numbered i and ii, the latter dated 1687 and the other 1691. The earlier, *Historiae Anglicanae scriptores quinque*, anonymously edited, contains the Annals of Margam Abbey, not previously printed, and the History of Walter de Hemingburgh as far as

---

[1] *Catalogi librorum MSS. Angliae et Hiberniae* (Oxford, 1697), Vol. ii, Part ii, No. 180.
[2] Bodl. MS. Auct. T infr. 2. 5, formerly Fell No. 8713; *A Proposal tending to the Advancement of Learning* (Oxford, 1676).
[3] Prideaux, pp. 16, 22.
[4] R. C. Jebb, *Richard Bentley* (1902), pp. 9–13.
[5] *Ioannes Malalas*, Corpus Scriptorum historiae Byzantinae (Bonn, 1831), p. viii.
[6] *Ath.* iv, 239–43; D. C. Douglas, *English Scholars* (1943), pp. 213–17. (Charlett's) *Catalogus librorum in Theatro Sheldoniano impressorum* of 1694 attributes it to Fulman.

1272. In Volume i are Gildas, Nennius, and Eddi besides authors of less account and Fordun's Scotichronicon. The text of Gildas was an improvement on any printed before, and Nennius and Eddi were printed for the first time.

In the preface to Volume i, *Historiae Britannicae, Saxonicae, Anglo-Danicae scriptores xv*, Gale owns that he was set to work by repeated exhortations from Fell. He had transcribed some of the unprinted chronicles with his own hand, others were copied at his expense. He names the libraries and archives where the sources of medieval English history had been found at a cost to him of much time and eyestrain.

The chronicles are printed virtually without introductions or apparatus and are not in advance of their time in point of accuracy. Gale did not always specify the manuscripts from which his text was taken, nor did he estimate the value of one source as compared with another. Nevertheless, these closely-packed folios are monuments to the industry of the compilers and served three or four generations of historians of England.

Defects at least as serious are to be found in Edmund Gibson's edition of the *Anglo-Saxon Chronicle*, which the Delegates published in 1692; but that also was superseded only in the nineteenth century.

Hyde's De ludis orientalibus

The book, dated 1694, begins with a complaint (in Latin) about the Press: 'You see that, however belatedly, this little book appears at last. It is lamentable that, through the fault of the printers, it may truly be said to have groaned in the press for two years, while, given ordinary diligence on the workmen's part, it could have been finished in six months. Such is the slowness of our press. . . . As a result of the delay I have been obliged to cut out and dispense with a large part of the copy: otherwise this little work might not have appeared at all.'

In view of the thirty-one books begun by Hyde and left unfinished,[1] the printer given knowledge and opportunity, might have said equally damaging things about him. This man of stupendous learning, professor of Hebrew and Arabic and Bodley's Librarian, had a preference for the byways of knowledge. While he published this history of table games he declined to bear a part in the catalogue of the manuscripts in England and Ireland, being, as he said, too old and tired.[2] He died in 1703.

[1] Wood, *Ath.* iv, 525-7.
[2] R. W. Hunt, *A Summary Catalogue of Western Manuscripts in the Bodleian Library at Oxford*, i (Oxford, 1953), p. xxvi.

The greater part of the book is a history of chess and had been printed before at Oxford at the author's expense in 1689. To it Hyde added a history of backgammon and similar games played on boards. A large part is quotations in Persian and a good deal is in Hebrew and Greek. The text is in Latin and Latin translations follow the passages in other languages. Words in Russian and Georgian are rendered by woodcuts, Chinese by copper-engravings.

Five hundred copies were printed for sale at 3*s*. 6*d*. After 1695 none were left in the Delegates' warehouse. The Stationers took at least 350 at 3*s*., thirteen to the dozen, for their English Stock, but they had to send 300 to France and Holland for sale in 1701 and write them off as a loss.

Kennett's history of Ambrosden

At first sight it is surprising that White Kennett's *Parochial Antiquities attempted in the History of Ambrosden, Burcester, and other adjacent Parts in the Counties of Oxford and Bucks* (1695), source material and professedly limited in its scope to a small area, should have been published at the expense of the University. The history has really a much wider application than the title would suggest, because Kennett printed *in extenso* the documents on which he relied, many of them of much more general interest than the purpose for which he cited them. Moreover, a good many of the deeds printed in the book were in private hands and have since disappeared. Being so closely related to original authorities, it served as a pattern for local history and a corrective of national history as it was written in Kennett's time.

Hearne, who was on the worst of terms with this author, accused him of 'putting in all papers he met with'.[1] His was a perceptive criticism of the book as a history of Ambrosden and Bicester, but regarded as a repository of documents its disregard of strict relevance is all to the good. Kennett's biographer does well to call it 'a microcosm of feudal history, which, in its examination of a particular instance, threw a powerful light on the general question'.[2]

Of 312 printed all but 6 copies were sold within a year.

Spelman's Remains

Edmund Gibson undertook to prepare for the press some works by Sir Henry Spelman left unpublished at the author's death in 1640.

---

[1] Hearne, i, p. 244.   [2] G. V. Bennett, *White Kennett, 1660–1728* (1957), p. 162.

Charles Spelman had sold the 'copies' in his grandfather's writings to the University in 1672.[1]

The most notable of the pieces in this thin folio, *Reliquiae Spelmanianae* (1698), is the treatise on 'Feuds and Tenures by Knight Service in England' in which Spelman argued against the bench of Irish judges that hereditary tenure subject to military obligations was unknown in this country before the Norman Conquest. It was with reference to this treatise that Maitland said: 'Were an examiner to ask who introduced the feudal system into England, one very good answer, if properly explained, would be Henry Spelman.'[2]

Gibson prefaced the book with a life of Spelman written in his pleasant, easy style. The cost of the book was charged to the Delegates, but the title-page affirms that it was printed for the London booksellers Awnsham and John Churchill. The booksellers bought the impression after it was printed.

Clarendon's History of the Rebellion

Of the books published at Oxford in the years 1690–1713 the hardest to reconcile with the normal pattern of university publishing is the most famous. Clarendon's *History* can hardly be considered a work of learning: it has nothing of an academic character about it. The author's association with the University as its Chancellor from 1660 until 1667 must be supposed to have induced his sons, Henry, second Earl of Clarendon, and Laurence, Earl of Rochester, to give the copy in the book to the University in the person of Aldrich, the Vice-Chancellor.[3] The manuscript used by the printers[4] was returned to and kept by Rochester at Cornbury Park, but he and his brother allowed the University to claim the sole right in the printed work—a right recited in Queen Anne's exclusive privilege of printing the book for 14 years from 1703. Clarendon's original manuscript of his 'History' (Books i–vii)[5] was left in the custody of Dean Aldrich and reached the Bodleian after 1711 but before 1743.[6] The fair copy used by the printers was given to the University in 1785 or 1786 by the sister and nieces of Rochester's son, Lord Cornbury, who would

[1] D.O. 11 Nov. 1672; *First Minute Book*, p. 10.
[2] *Constitutional History*, 5th ed. (1919), p. 151.
[3] Hearne, iii, p. 179.
[4] Bodl. MS. Clar. 114–20.
[5] Bodl. MS. Clar. 112.
[6] Hearne, iii, p. 179. Macray, *Annals*, p. 225. In 1735 George Clarke had it in his room at All Souls: J. Burton, *The Genuineness of Lord Clarendon's History Vindicated*, p. 138.

have given all Clarendon's manuscripts in trust for the University if he had survived his father.[1]

The fair copy used by the printers was made in 1699 partly by William Wogan, a King's Scholar of Westminster School, and partly by an amanuensis named Low at the bidding of Thomas Sprat, Dean of Westminster and Bishop of Rochester.[2] Wogan and Low transcribed a copy made by Clarendon's secretary, William Shaw, of a draft by Clarendon himself. It was the text that Clarendon composed by fitting together his 'manuscript History' and the greater part of his 'manuscript Life',[3] and Shaw's copy had alterations and additions in the author's handwriting. Shaw's copy has disappeared; it may have been burnt in a fire at Rochester's house at Sheen.[4] It was read by a number of eminent people, Archbishop Sancroft in 1685, Turner, Bishop of Ely, Sir John Nicholas, perhaps by Queen Mary II, and it was lent to Bishop Sprat.[5]

When the author's sons decided to publish the book, as their father had given them a discretionary power to do, a revision of Shaw's manuscript was undertaken by Rochester in consultation first with Sprat, famous for the purity of his literary style, and then with Dean Aldrich.[6] No doubt it was at this stage that Clarendon's archaic and arbitrary spelling was modernized and made regular,[7] for the transcript by Wogan and Low differs only slightly in its spelling from the printed volumes. Clarendon's involved sentences were rewritten in plainer language. In a few instances expressions hurtful to the memories of the living relations of Clarendon's contemporaries were softened.[8] An example of this kind of revision, which the author had expressly authorized ('by Suppressing or Publishing . . . all my papers and writings'), occurs in the character of the Earl of Arundel,[9] whom Clarendon had portrayed with unwonted harshness. Arundel's grandson had been a benefactor to Oxford in giving some of the Arundel Marbles to the University,[10] and there were grounds for hoping that his posterity would give it more. A few such alterations were made; but Atterbury was told by Aldrich that nothing was added,[11] and Rochester's reluctance to allow any significant changes is attested in the preface to Volume i.

[1] Macray, *Annals*, p. 225.   [2] Burton, pp. 90–2.
[3] C. H. Firth, 'The History of the Rebellion', *English Historical Review*, xix (1904), pp. 26–7; Preface by W. D. Macray to his edition of the *History* (Oxford, 1888).
[4] Burton, p. 94.   [5] Ibid., pp. 86–7, 89.   [6] Ibid., pp. 91, 127.
[7] Extracts from the *History* in Clarendon's spelling are printed in D. Nichol Smith's *Characters from the Histories and Memoirs of the Seventeenth Century* (Oxford, 1918).
[8] Burton, pp. 136–7.   [9] Nichol Smith, op. cit., pp. 264–5.
[10] Above, p. 83.   [11] Burton, p. 127.

The transcript by Wogan and Low has corrections by at least two hands. When it was shown to Wogan in 1732 he 'observed here and there some literal Mistakes which I had made in Copying, rectified; but most, if not all, of them in the Earl of Rochester's Hand.—Besides these Alterations in my Copy I observed none but some Typographical Marks for directing the Composers while the Book was at the Press.'[1]

So far as the text of the *History* in Books i–iv is concerned, the marks for the guidance of the printers are brackets indicating new paragraphs. Commas are inserted and capitals are substituted for small letters, though by no means consistently. In Books v–xii the beginnings of printed pages are indicated by crosses scratched, pencilled, or in red ink.[2] The preface to Volume i is marked more fully for the printers: page-endings corresponding with those of the printed book are marked in six instances by pencilled crosses between words in the manuscript; but other crosses, some rubbed out, do not correspond with any breaks in the printing. These marks are confined to the first third, approximately, of the preface. A direction to alter a small letter to a capital is given by a stroke at the head, and the opposite is conveyed by a stroke at the foot. These strokes, done in ink, are likely to have been made by the corrector to save alterations in proof, but the crosses would have been made by a compositor.

The reason for marking the beginnings of printed pages, it must be supposed, was that the fount of type did not extend to setting all the eight pages in a quire of four leaves of folio, so that the compositor would have to rely on an estimate of the extent of at least two pages before he set the others. Whoever marked pages in the preface to Volume i cannot have known that it would be printed for gathering in single sheets, as it was, and therefore there would be type enough for the four pages of each. As soon as he understood that, he discontinued the marking.

The corrector, Thomas Terry, assured George Clarke in 1726 that the book was 'most exactly printed from the written copie'.[3] That must be understood as relating to essential things. Changes in the preface to Volume i were evidently made in proof, as the marks for the estimated ends of pages show. A paragraph reprobating the country's participation in King William's wars, in true Tory vein, a hit at Rochester's arch-enemy, Marlborough, is in the copy but not in the book. Differences

---

[1] Burton, p. 138.
[2] P. Simpson, *Proof-Reading in the Sixteenth, Seventeenth, and Eighteenth Centuries*, pp. 90–4.
[3] Burton, pp. 134–5.

between manuscript and print in spelling, capitalization, and punctuation are interesting as pointing to a good deal of latitude for the compositor and the emergence of a 'style of the house'. The following are some departures from the copy in the printed pages:

Vol. i, p. i, l. 9.   Restauration: MS. Restoration.
p. ii, l. 1.   he received: MS. He received.
l. 3.   Somerset: MS. Somersett.
suffer'd: MS. suffered.
l. 9.   Approaches: MS. Approches.
l. 16.   he adorn'd: MS. He adorned.
l. 25.   ignorant that: MS. ignorant, That.

Nouns beginning with a small letter in the manuscript are regularly given a capital in print, adjectives and pronouns are deprived of their capitals, and subordinate clauses lose a capital for the opening word. The Oxford compositors of 1702–4 were of the kind commended by Joseph Moxon twenty years before, whose 'Judgment should know where the Author has been deficient, that so his care may not suffer such Work to go out of his Hands as may bring Scandal upon himself'.[1]

The consternation caused by the state of the copy when it first reached Oxford and the pains taken to prepare it for the printers may be gauged by a letter from Aldrich to Sprat, luckily preserved by a transcript.[2]

Christ Church
August 18 1700

My Lord. I had the honour of your Lordship's of the 10th. instant: . . . We make all the hast we can possibly without spoiling my Lord Clarendon's Book: but we are not so far advanc'd as I hoped we might have been, partly because of a violent Rheum which fell upon my right Eye, and swell'd it so, that I could not for a fortnight so much as look upon a book without great pain, and manifest Danger; but chiefly by the great and till we came nearly to consider it unimaginable Incorrectness of the Copy, which we are to print by. The Capitals are seldom or never true; the points of Distinction wholly omitted, or so misplaced, as to pervert the sense, which is likewise in many places represented under such Expressions, as we know not how to reconcile either to the known truth of History, or indeed the plaine meaning of the Author. Yet we aim to be scrupulous even to superstition to represent our Copy to a title, except in some few spellings, which yet we do not alter without advising with

[1] *Mech. Ex.* ii, sect. 22, para. 5; ed. Davis and Carter, p. 219.
[2] B.M. MS. Add. 4253, fol. 114. (A copy made for Thomas Birch, before 1766.)

Dr. Wallis, the fittest person I know of in the World to direct us upon such Occasions. These and many matters relating to this Affair would furnish matter sufficient almost for a Volume, at least for a much longer Letter than it is fit to trouble your Lordship with: And 'tis probable that even such matters would not give an account so satisfactory, as to put an end to all our Doubts. The best way I can think on is to beg your Lordship to make good your promise of allowing me to meet you halfway between this and London, and three or four Hours Discourse may effectually settle what cannot be so well transacted by Letters in a twelve month. I can borrow a Day, or at most two, but hardly more, at least till we have done with our poetry: otherwise I would come to London.

I must earnestly beseech your Lordship, if you can spare Terry (for Tommy, I know, I must not ask for) to send him to me as soon as may be; for I have abundance of necessary business, which stands still, and must stand still for want of him.

It is pleasing to be told that John Wallis, that eminent and wise grammarian, had a hand in the beginnings of Oxford house-style.

The accepted opinion that Rochester wrote the preface to the first volume is open to question. The main reason for thinking that he did is the testimony of the corrector, Terry, who said he supposed that Rochester wrote it, 'for it was delivered to him written all in the Earl's hand, and printed from that Copy'.[1] That was his recollection twenty-four years after the event; but in fact the copy that is marked for the compositors is written in Low's hand, Sprat's amanuensis, and has only some corrections in Rochester's. On the other hand, some expressions in the preface referring to Rochester and his elder brother come unnaturally from one of them: 'We take them both to be men of so much Piety to their Father, and so much Spirit in themselves, that they would by no means be bribed to omitt any thing . . .';[2] 'Whoever are acquainted with the Sons of the Noble Author, must do them this justice to own, they have often declared . . .'.[3] Rather than Rochester's own words these seem likely to be survivals from a draft by another writer that he had worked over.

Since authorities of the standing of C. H. Firth and W. D. Macray studied the Clarendon manuscripts the Bodleian bought (in 1913) a draft for the preface to Volume i which is clearly an earlier state of it than the copy given to the printers.[4] It is a good deal longer and differs strikingly from it in having many more quotations from the Latin classics. The

[1] Burton, pp. 127, 135.   [2] Preface, p. xv.   [3] Ibid., pp. xxii–xxiii.
[4] Bodl. MS. Clar. 112.

handwriting is of an older fashion than Low's. The writer was a man with an academic frame of mind, such as Aldrich's or Sprat's, and his draft had to be largely remodelled to suit Rochester.

The dedications to Volumes ii and iii lack the prevailing magnanimity of the preface to Volume i and may be ascribed to Rochester unaided.

The first edition of the *History* is made up of several printings not easy to distinguish. Only of the third volume are all copies alike: all those dated 1704 were printed before Michaelmas in that year. Of Volume ii there were three printings from different typesettings, of 1704, 1704–5, and 1707, all dated 1704. Volume i, first printed in 1702, was printed again in 1703, 1704, and 1707. A new edition of all three volumes in folio format was printed at the Theatre in 1707 for John Baskett, the London Stationer, who paid for it and sold it. Since it is indistinguishable, except by its date, from the University's edition of 1702–4, sets of three volumes are sometimes a mixture of the two.

Books warehoused after printing in those days were all folded sheets and might remain such for a long time before being bound. Sheets printed at different times might be put together to make volumes: it is not an infallible guide to the date of Volume i of Clarendon that it includes the Queen's privilege for the work granted a year after it was first printed, or that the engraving of the frontispiece or title-page device has a late date. These things can at most indicate the earliest date for the binding.

The presence of press figures in the tail margins of Volumes i and ii is a sign that the sheets belong to a late printing. Figures of the kind occur first in Oxford books of 1704 (apart from Bibles and prayer books),[1] therefore sheets of Clarendon that have them almost certainly belong to the third or fourth printing of Volume i or the second or third of Volume ii. Volume iii, printed late in 1704,[2] has full points, asterisks, and brackets in the tail margins, no doubt serving the same purpose as press figures, and figures only in the index.

Although the Accounts do not specify the number of copies printed on large paper of Volume i, it is probable that the several printings of the first edition amounted to 2,000 of each volume on small paper and 350 on large.

The Delegates distrusted their capacity to warehouse and dispose of such a quantity of books and chose to farm out the edition. Assuming that a draft agreement in their files[3] was executed, they agreed on 17 June 1702 to sell to Thomas Bennett, the London bookseller, the greater

[1] See p. 212.   [2] Charlett to Wanley, 13 Oct. 1704: Welbeck Papers.
[3] Pkt. 75. The Delegates' meeting therein recited is not reported in the Minute Book.

part of the impression of 1,100 copies of the first printing of Volume i. Bennett agreed to take 750 on small paper and 50 on large. A subsequent clause binds him to buy the whole impression of the forthcoming other two volumes, provided he were consulted as to the number to be printed. For small paper copies, priced at 15*s.*, he was to pay 14*s.*, and for the large, priced at 24*s.*, 20*s.* Mindful of its obligations to its lessees of privilege, the Stationers, who to their cost had taken from it large consignments of unremunerative books, the University stipulated that Bennett should let the Company, if it wished, take half the quantity allotted to him at the price that he paid.

It is evident that some such arrangement took effect. At any rate of Volume ii the Delegates sold all the copies on small paper (2,000) to Bennett,[1] and the accounts of the Warehouse of the Stationers' English Stock record the orders that Bennett collected from booksellers for all three volumes of the *History*.[2]

Similarly, of the first octavo edition, published in 1705–6, all the 2,000 copies on small paper and 300 on large were sold to Bennett, reserving to the University only 200 large-paper copies.[3]

Leland De Scriptoribus Britannicis

Encouraged by Edward Thwaites, Anthony Hall, fellow of Queen's College, made a transcript of a Bodleian manuscript of this work by Leland. The Delegates published it in 1709. The edition is of little value and is remembered chiefly for the distress that it caused in Thomas Tanner, who had been engaged, he said, for fifteen years, on enlarging and continuing Leland's book.[4] Tanner did not finish his work, but it appeared after his death, in 1748, edited by David Wilkins.

ARTS AND SCIENCES: PHYSICAL SCIENCES AND MATHEMATICS

Morison's Herbal

A specimen of Robert Morison's *Plantarum historia universalis Oxoniensis*, one section of his Part ii on herbaceous plants, was the second book put in hand at the Sheldonian Theatre. It came out in 1672, a folio with 12 copper-engraved plates given by admirers of the author at Oxford.

---

[1] D.O. 28 Nov. 1704; *First Minute Book*, p. 20. [2] See p. 165.
[3] D.O. 4 Dec. 1705; *First Minute Book*, pp. 20–1.
[4] Bodl. MS. Ballard iv, fols. 89, 107.

Morison, a protégé of Charles II, came to Oxford as Professor of Botany in 1669 with the title of Royal Botanist and Curator of the King's Gardens. Great things were expected of his *Historia*, which was planned on a grand scale and was clearly meant to show a new interest on the part of the University in the natural sciences.

The specimen set out the classification that Morison would adopt in his treatment of trees and plants, a much more systematic arrangement than any devised by earlier English botanists.[1]

The author intended to issue the work to subscribers, but the sums raised from them were not enough to meet his expenses, and the University lent him £200 in 1677 and a further £200 three years later on the security of the forthcoming books. Thenceforward the 'Herbal' becomes a Delegates' book subject to an equity of redemption in the Morison family.

Volume ii, on herbaceous plants, was published from Fell's press in 1680.[2] The Vice-Chancellor advanced £200 towards the cost of paper and printing.[3] In the event, Volume i, on trees, was never written. Of the 16 classes in which he divided herbs Morison dealt with 5 in Volume ii. Before he died in 1683 he had written another 4. Jacob Bobart the younger, a pupil, though a critical one, of the professor, commissioned by the Delegates to complete the third volume, did so.

In 1696–9 the Press printed 750 copies of Volume iii, 100 of them on large paper, probably matching the edition of the previous volume, of which the number is not known. Small-paper copies of Volume ii were priced at £2. 10s. and of Volume iii at £3.

To the eye of a layman the illustrations, particularly of Volume iii, are truly beautiful. They must be among the earliest of botanical subjects to be rendered by copper-engraving. In the third volume, mainly by Bobart, there are 167 plates showing more than three thousand subjects. Many of the best draughtsmen and engravers of that day are represented by signed plates, including Loggan and the English illustrator Francis Barlow. The printing of the illustrations and the engraving of some of them in this last volume were charged to the University, and it paid Bobart his author's fee of £400.

'The Herbal' was a crushing burden on the Press in its early days. The University's expenditure on it with interest on the loan was reckoned

---

[1] My authority on the value of the book to a botanist is Hermia N. Clokie, *An Account of the Herbaria in the Department of Botany in the University of Oxford* (1964), pp. 10–15.

[2] Madan, *Oxford Books*, iii, No. 3271.

[3] Univ. Arch. S.E.P. z. 27.

in 1693 at £2,153.[1] In 1705, 417 copies of Volume ii and 515 of Volume iii were unsold. The Stationers, having formally agreed in 1692 to take 430 of Volume ii,[2] found reasons for going back on the bargain. When the final volume was ready the University and Morison's widow agreed to divide the proceeds of sale until the advances and charges for printing

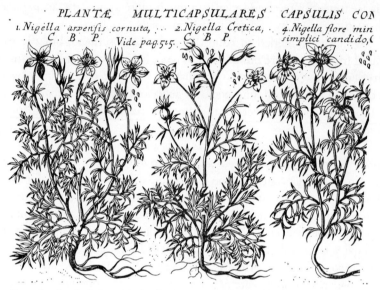

Part of a plate in Robert Morison's *Plantarum historia universalis Oxoniensis*, Part iii (1699). Engraving by F. H. Vanhove, reduced by one-third.

were recovered.[3] But the book did not sell: in 1713 the stock of Volume ii was 184 perfect copies, 364 without the frontispiece, and 184 lacking some plates; while of Volume iii there were 560, 36 of them imperfect.[4] The Delegates decided to part with their claims for £460.[5] 'Heads of Houses and other Gentlemen of the University' were given a chance of buying the set of volumes for 40s.

Volumes ii and iii came on the market again in 1715 with added preliminary matter and a new title-page announcing them as sold in London by Isaac Vaillant.[6]

---

[1] Univ. Arch. S.E.P. z. 27.
[2] By a term of their lease of the Bible Press: *Print and Privilege*, p. 178.
[3] Ibid., pp. 139–40 note.   [4] 2nd Accounts, p. 27.
[5] D.O. 8 June 1713; *First Minute Book*, p. 38.   [6] Bodl. Sherard 732, 733.

It was a thoroughly unsatisfactory publication. To supply the want of a first volume the specimen issued in 1672, though superseded by a section of Volume ii, is often bound up as part of the set and numbered i. As a scientific work it is of little account. Linnaeus said that what was good in it was copied from Caesalpinus, and it was Ray's classification that soon made Morison's out of date.[1]

Wallis's Mathematical Works

The impact of John Wallis's mathematical genius had been felt long before his collected mathematical and miscellaneous *Works* were published at the Delegates' expense in 1693–9. The series of books by him began in 1652 and extended to his *Algebra*, in English, of 1683. Collected in three volumes the texts were all in Latin, revised, and with additions. Wallis ascribed the idea of such an edition to the Delegates.[2]

Volume ii came out in 1693. It contained the Algebra, given priority because Wallis was afraid he might die before he had put it into Latin; whereas his other treatises were nearly all in Latin originally, and could without much disadvantage be reissued posthumously. The Algebra in Latin and enlarged was of importance to the learned world: it summarized recent methods of Newton and Leibniz not previously published.

Volume i came two years later, devoted to arithmetic, conic sections, and mechanics. The third volume, of 1699, reprints Wallis's edition of Ptolemy's *Harmonica* and brings into print other ancient Greek writers on music extant in manuscript in the Bodleian. Wallis justified his ample treatment of harmonics by the curiosity of scholars about these manuscripts and by the terms of Sir Henry Savile's endowment of the Professorship of Geometry which he held. The preface to Ptolemy goes into detail about the accentuation of Greek, quoting the Cambridge professor Ralph Winterton as authority. Harmonics are followed by a treatise on speech (*De loquela*) and a grammar of the English language. At the end of the volume are letters from Leibniz, Newton, and other members of the Royal Society. Wallis describes them as relating to recent discoveries and methods, among them the arithmetic of infinite series, interpolation, and the fluxional or differential calculus.

Wallis, Savilian Professor of Geometry and Keeper of the University Archives, was a successful transplant from Cambridge by Cromwell in 1649. He was not disturbed at the Restoration. He has been called 'the

---

[1] Clokie, op. cit., pp. 11, 12.   [2] In the Preface to vol. i.

greatest of Newton's English precursors'.[1] His interests were diverse. He was rated as one of the best disputants in theology of his day,[2] and he wrote tracts on religious matters and published sermons. His languages included Hebrew. He was expert in deciphering. In defence of the University's privilege of printing he stood beside Fell and was always ready with an opinion, a history, or a draft. He bore the brunt of the Stationers' assaults in 1679–88.[3] His death in 1703 left the Press without a stout champion until Blackstone was made a Delegate in 1755.

Wallis's treatise on speech and his grammar of English are valued as evidence of the pronunciation and usage of his time. No scientific treatment of articulate vocal sounds had been attempted until he gave his mind to teaching 'dumb' children and published his method in the *Loquela*. His grammar, first published in 1652, reached its fifth edition in 1676. A modern author considers it 'undoubtedly one of the most distinguished works of English linguistic scholarship'.[4]

Gregory's Euclid

Thomas Smith, in his life of Edward Bernard, refers to a design inchoate at Oxford soon after the Restoration to publish the ancient mathematicians.[5] Fell, in his list of works that 'We purpose to Print, if we may be encouraged' (1672), put 'The ancient Mathematicians Greek & latin in one and twenty Volumes; part not yet Extant, the rest collated with MS. perfected from the Arabick versions'.[6] Bernard drafted a synopsis of the Greek, Latin, and Arabic texts to be comprehended in the scheme.[7] In 1668 the Delegates of the Press authorized the Vice-Chancellor to advance £30 or £40 to Bernard towards his expenses in copying the Arabic version of the conic sections of Apollonius from a manuscript at Leyden.[8]

Proposals for an edition of the fifteen books of Euclid with copious annotations by Bernard were issued about 1690,[9] but the response from subscribers was not considered to warrant proceeding with it.

The volume of Euclid's extant works, which came from the Press in

---

[1] A. M. Clerke in the *D.N.B.* See generally Joseph F. Scott, *The Mathematical Work of John Wallis* (1938).

[2] Hearne, viii, p. 59. [3] *Print and Privilege*, pp. 98–113.

[4] E. J. Dobson, *English Pronunciation 1500–1700*, 2nd ed. (Oxford, 1968), pp. 218–46, at p. 246.

[5] *Vita Edwardi Bernardi* (1704), p. 23. [6] Above, p. 63.

[7] Printed in Smith's life of Bernard as an appendix.

[8] D.O. 12 Dec. 1668; *First Minute Book*, p. 5.

[9] Madan, *Oxford Books*, iii, p. 347, No. 3141.

The *Opera mathematica* of John Wallis (1616–1703) printed at the Press in 1693–5. The woodblock at the foot printed the diagram on p. 866 of Volume I

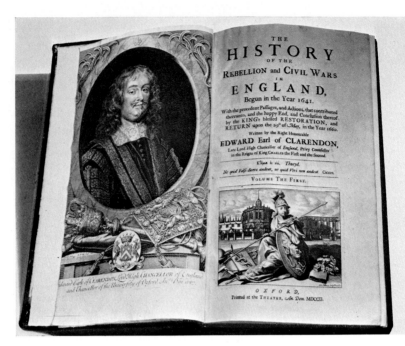

Clarendon's *History of the Rebellion*. Volume i

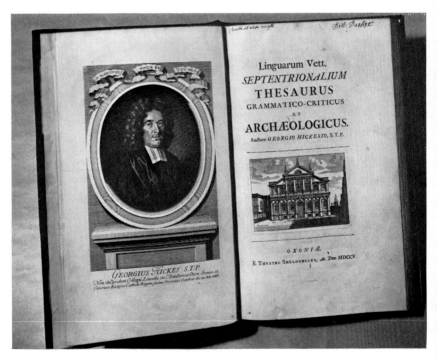

Hickes's *Thesaurus*. The first volume

1703 with David Gregory's name as editor was prompted by Henry Aldrich and Arthur Charlett.[1] Gregory was entrusted with the mathematics and John Hudson with the Greek text. John Mill and John Wallis kept an eye on the progress of the book and composed differences between the editors. In the end Hudson generously withdrew his name from the title-page and dedication. Bernard's recension of the text and some of his notes and translations were used. Gregory supplied a preface reviewing the manuscripts and printed editions.

The book, a thick folio, was an edition of 750, of which 250 were on large paper, priced at 15s. the small, and 20s. the large. In 1712 there were 245 unsold, and these were included in the sale of the stock to Hudson in the following year.

Apollonius De sectione rationis

As soon as he was appointed Savilian Professor of Geometry in succession to Wallis in 1703 Edmund Halley was enlisted by Dean Aldrich in the revival of ancient Greek analytical geometry. He chose to devote himself to Apollonius of Perga, famous for his eight books on conic sections composed in the second century B.C.[2]

He began with a lesser work of Apollonius surviving only in an Arabic translation and unpublished. Edward Bernard had been made aware of this manuscript at the Bodleian, entitled the equivalent of 'The Book of Apollonius on sections of lines in given ratios',[3] and had begun to translate it into Latin, but laid it aside when about a tenth was done. After Bernard's death David Gregory revised the translation. Halley accomplished the extraordinary feat of deciphering (as he put it) the remaining nine-tenths of the text without knowing Arabic, using Bernard's partial translation as a key.[4] He had guidance from introductory matter and lemmata by Pappus; and relying on them Halley was able to reconstruct another work of Apollonius, *De sectione spatii* (Cutting off a space), and add it to the volume.

The book, a modest octavo published in 1706, is a Latin text with diagrams. Some 550 copies were printed for sale at 2s. 6d., and of these 122 were remaindered to John Hudson in 1713.

---

[1] Hearne, i, pp. 88–9; Bodl. MS. Ballard i, fol. 109, xx, fol. 3.
[2] Halley's preface to *Apollonii Pergaei conica* (Oxford, 1710).
[3] Bodl. MS. Arch. Seld. A 72(3), No. 32. The English term is 'cutting off a ratio': *Encyclopaedia Britannica*, art. Apollonius.
[4] So he says in his preface to *De sectione rationis*; but Hearne, characteristically, knew of a rumour that a man named Jones translated it for him: Hearne, ii, p. 167.

Apollonius on Conics

Books v–vii of this work were lost to the western world until a German scholar, Christian Ravius, bought a manuscript in Arabic of the whole work, except Book viii, at Istanbul in 1641.[1] It is believed to have been translated from the Greek in the ninth century by Thabit ibn-Korra of Harran.[2] Ravius allowed the eminent orientalist Jacob Golius to have the part not extant in Greek transcribed by an Arab at Leyden in 1643; but he took his manuscript back before the proofs and diagrams were copied.[3] Ravius published Books v–vii in Arabic with a Latin translation at Kiel in 1669.[4] In 1668 Edward Bernard went to Leyden and transcribed Golius's transcript.[5] In the following year Thomas Marshall was expecting the arrival in London from Dordrecht of the 'Mathematical Figures of Apollonius Pergeus' for which Bernard was waiting.[6] Bernard made a Latin translation of Books v–vii.[7] Books i–iv in Greek, without proofs or figures, were in manuscript in the Savilian Library at Oxford.[8]

In 1703 or soon after, the two Savilian Professors, Gregory and Halley, set about an edition of the complete work in Greek for the first four books with an old Latin version by Commandini[9] and in Latin for the remainder in Bernard's translation with the lemmata of Pappus in Greek, all with considerable revisions by the two editors and John Hudson. The treatise on conic sections of Serenus in Greek, copied for Aldrich in Paris, was added. In 1708 Gregory died, and the volume published at the expense of the Delegates in 1710 is substantially the work of Halley. It includes the lost eighth Book of Apollonius reconstructed by Halley from notes and lemmata by later Greek geometers.

Narcissus Marsh bought the transcript made for Golius at the sale of the Dutch scholar's library in 1696 and lent it to Halley for the purposes of his edition.[10] It came to the Bodleian by bequest from Marsh and is now

---

[1] M. Th. Houtsma, 'Uit de oostersche correspondentie van Th. Erpenius, Jac. Golius, en Lev. Warner', *Verhandelingen der Koninklijke Akademie der Wetenschappen, Afdeeling Letterkunde*, vol. xvii (Amsterdam, 1887), p. 85. Miss W. M. C. Juynboll, in her *Seventiende-eeuwsche beoefenaars van het Arabisch in Nederland* (Utrecht thesis, 1931), p. 138, says that Golius bought one such manuscript in Istanbul and Ravius bought another. Houtsma prints contemporary letters about the copying of the Ravius manuscript for Golius, making it seem unlikely that Golius possessed the work.

[2] Juynboll, as above.   [3] Houtsma, pp. 85, 87.
[4] Copy in Bodl. Savile Y. 35.   [5] T. Smith, *Vita . . . Bernardi*, p. 11.
[6] B.M. MS. Add. 22905, fol. 81. According to Juynboll, Golius had boxwood blocks cut for the figures in Istanbul (op. cit., p. 139).

[7] Bodl. MS. Lat. class. e. 2.
[8] Bodl. MS. Savile 7. It has diagrams added by Gregory.
[9] Published at Bologna in 1556.
[10] Preface to *Apollonii Pergaei conica* (Oxford, 1710).

in MS. Marsh 720. The codex bought by Ravius also found its way there. It was bought at Amsterdam by Thomas Marshall,[1] and is now MS. Thurst. 3.

Halley's is the first, and the only complete, edition of this work of Apollonius. Sir T. L. Heath in 1896 called it 'a monumental work, beyond praise alike in respect of its design and execution'.[2]

Four hundred copies were printed, priced at 22s. 6d. In 1712, when the Delegates decided to sell off their stock, 95 copies were left in the warehouse.

ARTS AND SCIENCES: LANGUAGES

Ludolf's Grammatica Russica

Edward Bernard, appointed to the Delegacy of the Press in 1691, was one of the seventeenth-century philologists who sought to undo the confusion of tongues due to the Tower of Babel. He published in 1689 a table to illustrate his theory that the scripts of the literate world all derived from the alphabet of the Samaritans.[3] Similarly, he aimed at grouping spoken languages according to degrees of their descent from a common origin. In a Japhetic group he put the Slavonic and Russian. In order to gain some knowledge of these languages he engaged correspondents abroad in a search for books in them, and through Nicholas Witsen, burgomaster of Amsterdam, he was put in touch with Heinrich Wilhelm Ludolf.[4] After spending a year and a half in Russia Ludolf was preparing for the press 'a short Russish grammar, with a Vocabulary, and the most common idiotisms; as soon as I am sure to have it printed at an other man's charge'.[5]

This was in November 1694, by which time Bernard had persuaded the Delegacy to sanction the making of type for Cyrillic. Whether at that or a later time the Delegates consented to print and publish Ludolf's book. Punches for the type were cut at Amsterdam and typefounding was finished in time for a specimen of the 'Sclavonian' to appear in a supplement to the University's *Specimen of the several Sorts of Letter* of 1695.

[1] Macray, *Annals*, p. 129, prints Marshall's inscription to this effect in the codex. An account of its history is in the *Bodleian Quarterly Record*, No. 31 (1921), p. 152.

[2] *Apollonius of Perga: Treatise on Conic Sections* (Cambridge, 1896), p. 9.

[3] *Orbis eruditi literatura a charactere Samaritico deducta*, 1689, reprinted in 1700.

[4] J. S. G. Simmons has written an admirable account of the genesis of the book and the type: 'H. W. Ludolf and the Printing of his *Grammatica Russica* at Oxford in 1696', *Oxford Slavonic Papers*, i (1950), pp. 104–29.

[5] Ibid., p. 111.

The Grammar was printed at Oxford under Ludolf's supervision in the early part of 1696, an edition of 300. By 1699 all but 14 copies had been sold at a price of 1s. in quires.

(43)

PHRASES
ET
MODI LOQUENDI
Communiores.

Гла́ва а̃.	C A P. I.
Ѿ Соѵине́нїи	De Conſtructione
предло́га.	Præpoſitionum.
Гдѣ ты́ был̃. (1)	Ubi fuiſti ?
У бра́та мое́во, У	Apud meum fra-
сестрѣ̀ твое́и.	trem , apud ſororem
	tuam.
Ѿ кУди приде́ш̃. (2)	Unde venis ?
Ѿ батУшки, Ѿ	à patre, à matre.
матУшки.	
ИЗ̃ агле́нскои (3)	Ex Anglia adve-
ЗЕмли привоЗа́т̃	hunt pannum.
сУкно.	
давно́ли ты́ сз мо-	Diune è Moſcovia
сквы̀.	diſceſſiſti ?

Cap. 1.
Von der Conſtruction der Praepoſition.

(1) wo ſeyd ihr geweſen ? bey meinen bruder, bey deiner ſchweſter.
(2) wo kombt ihr her ? vom vatter: von der mutter.   (3) Aus
England bringen ſie tuch. Wie lange iſt es dafs ihr aus der Moſcau
kommen.

G   BYE-

Russian phrases with Latin equivalents in the *Grammatica Russica*
of H. W. Ludolf (1696).

This is the oldest grammar of the Russian language. The type reproduces the Church-Slavonic script in which Russian was written and
printed until Peter the Great devised a new character for the Russian
alphabet early in the eighteenth century. Ludolf's Grammar has been
reprinted in a critical edition by the late Professor B. O. Unbegaun,[1] who

[1] *Henrici Wilhelmi Ludolfi Grammatica Russica, Oxonii A.D. MDCXCVI* (Oxford, 1959).

considered that 'one could hardly expect to find a better seventeenth-century description of the Russian language', and that 'its value for the history of spoken Russian can hardly be overestimated'.

Levi's Hebrew Grammar

The Delegates financed this little compendium published in 1705. Philip Levi, a converted Jew, was teaching Hebrew at Oxford at the time.[1] According to Zachary Pearce, Bishop of Rochester, the real author was Robert Clavering, later Professor of Hebrew at Oxford and finally Bishop of Peterborough.[2] There appears to be little novelty or profundity about the book.

Five hundred were printed, priced at 1s. Two hundred were left to be remaindered in 1713.

BIBLIOGRAPHY

The Catalogues of Manuscripts

Two great catalogues of manuscripts were printed and published at the University's expense in 1696 and 1698. They had a common origin in a project abandoned in Fell's time but revived about 1692 by persons of eminence at Oxford to sponsor a catalogue of manuscript books in the libraries of the two English universities and famous public and private collections in this country and Ireland with an alphabetical index.[3] Edward Bernard, the former Savilian Professor of Astronomy, took general charge, and in 1694 proposals and invitations to submit lists of private collections were issued in his name.[4] The *Term Catalogue* for Hilary 1695 announces the forthcoming publication and 'desires such of the Nobility, Clergy, and Gentry as have any MSS. in their possession, and are willing to Oblige the World with Catalogues of them; that they would be pleased to send them in, with all speed, to the Theater, for the

---

[1] Chancellor's Court Acta, Michaelmas 1706.

[2] The Superintendent of the Reading Room of the B.M. kindly supplied this information from his records: 'A copy in Westminster Abbey Library has a manuscript note "The gift of the author Dr. Clavering, Ld. Bishop of Peterborough, to me Z. Pearce" and a further note by another hand "The Bishop told Dr. Pearce that he gave leave to Levi to publish this Grammar in his own name".'

[3] Thomas Smith, *Vita Edwardi Bernardi*, p. 47. A full account of Bernard's *Catalogi* of 1698 and its origins is given by R. W. Hunt in *A Summary Catalogue of Western Manuscripts in the Bodleian Library at Oxford* i, (Oxford, 1953), pp. xxv–xxxv.

[4] B.M. Harl. 5932, No. 92; *Philosophical Transactions*, xviii (1693/4), p. 160; Bodl. Wood 658 (815b).

Editor, Dr. Edward Bernard, in Oxford'.[1] Another such announcement appeared in Trinity term.

As time went on it became clear that the world must be satisfied with less than had been planned. By the middle of 1695 the University of Cambridge and all but four of the colleges there had dropped out, a belief that William Cave would supply a section on Lambeth Palace library[2] was disappointed, and the owner of the most important private collection, Sir John Cotton, decided to have his catalogue published separately.[3]

The *Catalogus librorum manuscriptorum Bibliothecae Cottonianae* was printed at Oxford and published in 1696. The compiler and editor was Thomas Smith, Cotton's librarian and one-time fellow of Magdalen College, a learned orientalist. His catalogue is a most respectable performance, and has gained an adventitious importance from the fire which consumed many of the manuscripts in 1731.

An edition of 750 of the Cotton *Catalogus* was sold out by 1714, according to Hearne.[4] So it was, so far as the University was concerned; but the unfortunate Stationers had taken the bulk of it and had to send 365 copies abroad for sale in 1701 and get virtually nothing for them.[5]

The *Catalogi librorum manuscriptorum Angliae et Hiberniae* followed two years later. It is made up of four parts separately signed and paginated, the last two of them headed Tomus II. Tomus I, Part iii, has no heading and carries on the series of signatures begun in Part ii, but it has its own index. There is only one title-page. Whether the book is two volumes or one, it is usually bound as one. The last five sheets were printed in 1698, and publication was announced for November of that year in the Term Catalogue.[6] There is no obvious explanation of the year 1697 being put on the title-page.

Bernard, the general editor, did not live to see the printed work. It goes by the name of 'Bernard's Catalogue', but his part in it was not large, revisions for the most part of existing lists.[7] In the later stages of the work Arthur Charlett was the organizer, and so it is fitting that the preliminary *Epistola*, anonymous but by Edmund Gibson,[8] was addressed to him. Humfrey Wanley wrote an anonymous introduction, dealing chiefly with the difficulty of indexing, and Gibson contributed a life of Bodley.

[1] *T.C.* II, pp. 545, 563.   [2] Bodl. MS. Ballard xxxiv, fol. 31.
[3] The 'Epistola' prefacing Bernard's *Catalogi* (1698).
[4] Hearne, iv, p. 419.   [5] See p. 164.   [6] *T.C.* III, p. 95.
[7] Hunt, *Summary Catalogue of Western MSS.*, i, p. xxxi.   [8] Ibid.

The Catalogue is the work of many scholars. Attributions to them in the list of contents are not wholly reliable. For a large part of the Bodleian collections old lists by Emanuel Pritchard and Gerard Langbaine were used in amended form. White Kennett, Thomas Tanner, Edmund Gibson, Edward Lhuyd, Michael Maittaire, and Wanley were among the compilers. Four colleges at Cambridge furnished lists by Joshua Barnes, editor of Homer, and Henry Laughton. For the other colleges there lists were made from Thomas James's *Ecloga Oxonio-Cantabrigiensis* of 1600 for want of better. Cambridge, therefore, was poorly represented, but the cathedral libraries, many private libraries, and libraries in Ireland were dealt with thoroughly. The five indexes by Wanley, who was strictly enjoined to brevity, have been praised,[1] no doubt justly.

Of 750 copies printed, priced at £1. 2s. 6d., 96 were in stock in 1712. The Stationers despaired of selling the quota they were obliged to accept and sent 140 abroad for sale at a great loss in 1701.[2]

Here was a case of the University acting for the benefit of literate mankind. James's *Ecloga* of 1600 was the only British precedent for a published catalogue of manuscripts, and the *Bibliotheca Belgica* of Sanderus, of 1640, the only foreign one. The *Catalogi* has not been wholly superseded; since it was issued in 1698 a copy has been kept close to the entrance to Duke Humphrey's Library in the Bodleian and constantly used.

The Verses

The Delegates, taking charge after Fell's day, did not put an end to a series going back to 1587 of books of verses in which members of the University rejoiced or lamented over events of public significance. These exercises by dons and undergraduates supported the University's pretensions to be a keeper of the nation's conscience and showed that its peaceful precinct was not out of touch with a larger world outside.

In the years 1690–1713 eleven of such volumes of collected poetry were published at the University's expense. *Academiae Oxoniensis gratulatio* of 1690 was to celebrate the safe return of William III victorious from Ireland. There followed (titles abridged):

Theatri Oxoniensis encaenia, 1693. Verses recited at the Encaenia.
Pietas Oxoniensis in obitum Reginae Mariae, 1695. The queen died on 28 December 1694.

[1] Macray, *Annals*, pp. 164–6.
[2] Stationers' records, Accounts of the Warehouse of the English Stock, 10 May 1701.

Exequiae Gulielmo Glocestriae Duci, 1700. Queen Anne's only child who lived for more than a few weeks died on 30 July.

Pietas universitatis Oxoniensis in obitum Gulielmi III, 1702. The king died on 8 March 1701/2.

Comitia philologica in honorem Annae Reginae, 1702.

Epinicion Oxoniense ob res feliciter gestas, 1702. That summer Marlborough relieved Holland from encircling French armies and took Liège.

Plausus musarum Oxoniensium, 1704. After the Battle of Blenheim.

Academiae Francofurtanae ad Viadrum encaenia secularia, 1706. For the centenary of the University of Frankfurt an der Oder.

Exequiae Georgio Principi Daniae, 1708. For the death of Queen Anne's consort.

Academiae Oxoniensis comitia philologica in honorem Reginae Annae, 1713. Rejoicing for the Peace of Utrecht. A song by Dr. Pepusch was printed to go with it.

The series went on until 1762. It is hard to find a good word for it from subsequent writers. How many of the Latin poems were deserving of print few can tell now (many fewer those who can judge of the Hebrew, Greek, Arabic, Armenian, Anglo-Saxon, Runic, Phoenician, or Etruscan); but the poet who confessed

<blockquote>Too weak the Voice to speak the hasty zeal</blockquote>

was not unfair to the compositions in English. There is evidence that the contributors were hurried; and the bill for printing *Plausus musarum* of 1704 included '10s. to the Workmen for expedition'. Rowe Mores, 'seconded by Mr Vicechancellor', appealed without effect to Edward Lye in 1761 for 'some congratulations and complts in the Septentrional languages upon the present occasion; I mean his majesties marriage with the Princess of Meckl', and asked for 'a speedy gratification'.[1]

Large numbers were given away. Of 300 books printed in 1708 for the death of Prince George 100 on large paper and 100 on small were delivered to the Vice-Chancellor and Delegates, leaving 100 small for sale at 3s., and these were taken promptly by Peisley, the Oxford bookseller. Four hundred were printed of the verses at the *Comitia* of 1713: 150 were presents and Peisley took the rest at 3s. 4d. The demand was evidently not negligible. On the other hand, if the sale were not quick quantities of such topical matter were left in the warehouse. Of the 500 done in 1700 for the little Duke of Gloucester 100 had to be written off after 1705, and

[1] B.M. MS. Add. 32325, fol. 176.

so did 125 of the *Plausus* for the victory at Blenheim, of which 700 were printed.

As gifts they were acceptable by bibliophiles, printed, since Fell's day, in folio format with big new type, some of them ornamented with copper-engravings by Burghers from drawings by Aldrich, the large paper copies on 'best Dutch Demy'.

Samuel Johnson must be reckoned among defenders of these collections, since in conversation he contradicted somebody who derided them. He argued that a university should take the opportunity of a state occasion to show that it had two hundred scholars, if not as many poets, and tell the world 'Here is a school where every thing may be learnt.'[1] In his Life of Dryden he was at least as effective to the contrary:

In an occasional performance no height of excellence can be expected from any mind . . . In the fate of princes the publick has an interest; and what happens to them of good or evil, the poets have always considered as business for the Muse. But after so many inauguratory gratulations, nuptial hymns, and funeral dirges, he must be highly favoured by nature, or by fortune, who says any thing not said before. Even war and conquest, however splendid, suggest no new images; the triumphal chariot of a victorious monarch can be decked only with those ornaments that have graced his predecessors.[2]

[1] Boswell, ii, p. 371.
[2] *Lives of the Poets*, ed. Birkbeck Hill (1905), i, pp. 424–5.

CHAPTER XV

Authors' Books 1690–1713

MOST of the books printed at the Theatre and the Clarendon Printing House were commissioned, not by the University acting through its Delegates, but by authors or by booksellers in their capacity of publishers.[1] In the Press these were traditionally styled 'authors' books'.

The contract for undertaking work of this kind was made with the Warehouse-Keeper in charge at the Press or with a senior compositor on his behalf. He or a compositor would cast off the copy and tell the potential customer how many sheets of the desired format the work would make and quote him a price for a sheet.[2]

It is difficult to be sure whether the Delegates of the Press exercised an effective control over the acceptance of work by their Warehouse-Keeper, even after, in 1708, they had expressed a determination to do so. It is true that some time in 1697 they met and resolved 'That, for the future, No Books of what Kind soever be committed to the Press, but such as are first approved off by the Vice-Chancellor for the time being, and the Major Part of the Delegates under Their Hands, at a publick meeting';[3] nevertheless, and notwithstanding such conclusive language, the context shows that they had in mind Delegates', not authors' books. That the University had a collective conscience about the books published in its precinct is evident from the survival of the 'imprimatur'. It must have been revived by the scandal of the printing in Oxford of Arthur Bury's *Naked Gospel* in 1690 and its public cremation in the Schools Quadrangle. 'This book the Rector [Bury], being then Pro-Vice-Chancellor of Oxford, carried to the Press; and, by the authority of his Character prevail'd with the Printer [Lichfield] to print it without any other license.'[4] Hearne used to go and ask the Vice-Chancellor for his imprimatur, and a compositor once did so on his behalf.[5]

---

[1] Using the word in its modern sense. At that time it was applied rather to an author or editor: e.g. Hearne, iii, pp. 301–2 (1712).

[2] Hearne, vii, p. 34.

[3] Univ. Arch. S.E.P. R8ᶜ, fol. 9. It is not recorded in the Minute Book.

[4] [James Harrington] *An Account of the Proceedings of the . . . Lord Bishop of Exeter* (Oxford, 1690), p. 23. Leonard Lichfield printed the two Oxford editions of the book: ibid., p. 55.

[5] Hearne, iv, pp. 116, 126.

Hearne considered that the imprimatur conveyed leave to use the University's press,[1] and it is difficult to resist a conclusion that in his time (1705–35) it was generally so understood. Yet, strictly, the imprimatur meant another thing, and its proper significance appears by the fact that it was put in books ordered by the Delegates as well as in those ordered by authors and booksellers. It must have been thought necessary for all books published in Oxford, since it is found in many of the books printed there by Leonard Lichfield, who was in business on his own. It applied to texts, not editions, for succeeding editions were given the imprimatur of the first. It was a vestige of the Chancellor's power and duty of approving books printed in the University's precinct. This liberty within the general censorial arrangements for the realm was expressly conferred on the Chancellors and Vice-Chancellors of the two Universities by the Licensing Act of 1662;[2] but it probably was considered, rightly or wrongly, to exist at an earlier time, for the charter of 1632 required that all books, before they might be printed in Oxford, must be approved by the Vice-Chancellor and three doctors, one of them a doctor of divinity.[3]

Queen Elizabeth I in her Injunctions of 1559 for the book trade had included the Chancellors of both Universities among the people qualified to sit on panels for perusing and licensing books,[4] and had continued: 'the names of such as shal allowe the same, to be added in thende of every such worke, for a testimony of the allowaunce therof'. Perhaps with a vague memory of these Injunctions in mind and obeying them in the spirit Oxford Vice-Chancellors had their imprimaturs put at the beginnings of some books from 1656 onwards[5] and did so more or less regularly from 1691 until about 1770. To account for the numerous exceptions from this more or less regular practice does not seem possible. Naturally, the University did not censor its own pronouncements: complimentary verses and addresses, statutes, and the like have no imprimaturs; some Vice-Chancellors were said to license books without allowing their authorization to appear in them.[6] The imprimaturs were dated. They were granted at no particular stage in the progress of a book, but sometimes before printing began and sometimes when it was finished[7] (as the New-Year books, among others, show). A book with an earlier imprimatur was not necessarily the earlier published.

[1] Hearne, vi, p. 371.   [2] 13 and 14 Charles II, c. 33, s. 4.
[3] Madan, Oxford Books, i, p. 282; Reg. Conv. Sb. 25, p. 57.
[4] Arber, Transcript, i, p. xxxviii.   [5] Madan, Oxford Books, iii, No. 2318.
[6] Hearne, iv, pp. 126, 173.   [7] Bodl. MS. Tanner 23, fol. 54.

Leave to print at the University's press was, at any rate in theory, another matter. The Delegates considering whether to grant it might be expected to take into account other things besides harmlessness of the content. In 1708 they adopted an order, prompted, as it would seem, by a private pique of Charlett's because Hearne had been given leave to print a life of King Alfred, founder of his college, without his privity, 'that no book or paper for the future be printed in the University press without the consent of the Delegates at a meeting'.[1] This was proper in theory but, given the rarity of the meetings, hardly practicable. The Delegates' minutes from 1690 until 1713 record permission given to two London booksellers, who presumably had written for it, to print at the Press: they do not mention any applications from authors, who must usually have applied informally.

There can be no doubt that force of circumstances made the Vice-Chancellor's imprimatur a leave to use the Press. Its earlier significance was forgotten. An instance is reported of the Vice-Chancellor in 1697 being asked by the author of a scientific book to approve its content and being nonplussed by such an unusual request.[2] Lancaster, Vice-Chancellor, was afraid in 1707 that his imprimatur in Mill's variorum Greek Testament might be taken to mean that he had approved disrespectful references to Charles II in the dedication.[3] The Delegates' order of 1708 was sometimes remembered; as in 1718, when 'there was like to be a great Difference and Falling out' between the Vice-Chancellor and Gardiner, Warden of All Souls, one of the Delegates. It concerned Hearne's Neubrigensis. ' "You gave him leave", says Gardiner, "but he hath not my leave." "Ay, I say my Leave", replys the V. Chancellour. "Why, your leave", says Gardiner, "is not sufficient. He ought to have Leave of the Delegates. No book can be printed at the Theatre-Press without the Delegates' Leave." '[4]

A charge for the University's overheads, known as 'poundage' was made for books not ordered by the Delegates, and it was credited to the Vice-Chancellor. It must not be confused with a charge for 'necessaries' added to all bills for printing. The latter was a payment to the Warehouse-Keeper for ink, lye, oil, and other consumable materials which that officer had to provide.[5] 'Poundage' was for use and wear and tear of

---

[1] D.O. 19 Oct. The trouble about Alfred is related by Hearne, ii, p. 180.
[2] *Print and Privilege*, pp. 9–10; Nichols, *Illus.*, iii, p. 261.
[3] Bodl. MS. Ballard xxi, fol. 45.   [4] Hearne, vi, pp. 411–12.
[5] A list of things covered by the term is in the second volume of the Warehouse-Keeper's Accounts, extending from 1709 to 1746 and is printed on p. 282 of this book.

plant and type, rent of premises, profit, and interest on capital. It was charged at the rate of 4s. for every £1 of the bill, or 2s. 6d. if the number of copies was small.[1] It may not have been enough to make the enterprise profitable; but Robert Plot's argument that it was not enough because it would not be an adequate remuneration for an editor of a work sponsored by the Delegates was wide of the mark.[2] It was not (after 1693) charged on accounts for Delegates' work or added to the selling prices of their books, and in the cases of their paying for editing they paid sums not related to cost of production. Poundage was levied on users of the Press who had to provide the editing and sell the books.

Author-publishers nearly always sold to subscribers. A good many of the 'proposals' or prospectuses which they sent to likely buyers survive.[3] Group-subscription was often encouraged by giving a seventh copy to a subscriber for six.[4] Commonly payment was made by two instalments, one at the time of subscription, the other on receipt of the book. Booksellers usually subscribed a large part of the edition, and the frequency of advertisements by booksellers of publications that had been canvassed by their authors for subscription suggests that one or two men in the trade often acted as agents for selling them and held the stock, as Robert Gosling evidently did for Browne Willis.[5] Other booksellers might be willing to take copies on 'sale or return'.[6]

Small and inexpensive books were printed at the University Press for booksellers, who took the whole edition, no doubt exchanging copies for other books with their fellows. Sermons were a common case. A Vice-Chancellor instructed Henry Clements of Oxford to pay the preacher copy money. ' "Copy-Money", says Mr. Clements, "Sure, Mr V. Chanc., you are not in earnest . . . I will be so far from giving him any thing that I hope you will take care that I be indemnifyed, being very much afraid that I shall lose by it." '[7]

The many imprints of Oxford books associating booksellers with the editions by such expressions as 'impensis', 'sold by', or 'prostat apud', probably cover a variety of relationships between Press and retail trade. There is no reason to doubt that 'impensis' and 'printed for' mean what they say and that the whole of the edition so described was delivered to

[1] Hearne, viii, p. 241. An assertion that poundage was not charged to 'private booksellers' (Bodl. MS. Tanner 23, fol. 20) needs confirmation.
[2] Bodl. MS. Ballard xiv, fol. 43.
[3] Some are included in the Appendix. John Hudson had a sensible recipe for framing proposals: Hearne, ii, p. 127.
[4] Hearne, v, p. 84.
[5] Hearne, v, pp. 54–5, 73.
[6] Bodl. MS. Tanner 25, fol. 138.
[7] Hearne, vi, p. 32.

the man or men who paid for it. When a court order was made against the unlucky John Owen in 1702, 500 copies of Potter's Lycophron (presumably the second edition done at Owen's expense in that year) were found on his premises and taken in execution.[1] 'Sold by' merely indicates an agency.

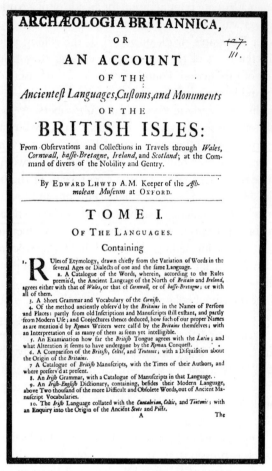

ARCHÆOLOGIA BRITANNICA,

O R

AN ACCOUNT

OF THE
Ancientest Languages, Customs, and Monuments
OF THE

BRITISH ISLES:

From Obfervations and Collections in Travels through *Wales, Cornwall, baffe-Bretagne, Ireland,* and *Scotland*; at the Command of divers of the Nobility and Gentry.

By EDWARD LHWYD A.M. Keeper of the *Aſh-molean Muſeum* at OXFORD.

TOME I.

OF THE LANGUAGES.

Containing

1. Rules of Etymology, drawn chiefly from the Variation of Words in the feveral Ages or Dialects of one and the fame Language.
2. A Catalogue of the Words, wherein, according to the Rules premis'd, the Ancient Language of the North of *Britain* and *Ireland,* agrees either with that of *Wales,* or that of *Cornwall,* or of *baffe-Bretagne*; or with all of them.
3. A Short Grammar and Vocabulary of the *Cornifh.*
4. Of the method anciently obferv'd by the *Britains* in the Names of Perfons and Places: partly from old Infcriptions and Manufcripts ftill exftant, and partly from Modern Ufe; and Conjectures thence deduced, how fuch of our proper Names as are mention'd by *Roman* Writers were call'd by the *Britains* themfelves; with an Interpretation of as many of them as feem yet intelligible.
5. An Examination how far the *Britifh* Tongue agrees with the *Latin*; and what Alteration it feems to have undergone by the *Roman* Conqueft.
6. A Comparifon of the *Britifh, Celtic,* and *Teutonic*; with a Difquifition about the Origin of the *Britains.*
7. A Catalogue of *Britifh* Manufcripts, with the Times of their Authors, and where preferv'd at prefent.
8. An *Irifh* Grammar, with a Catalogue of Manufcripts in that Language.
9. An *Irifh-Englifh* Dictionary, containing, befides their Modern Language, above Two thoufand of the more Difficult and Obfolete Words, out of Ancient Manufcript Vocabularies.
10. The *Irifh* Language collated with the *Cantabrian, Celtic,* and *Teutonic*; with an Enquiry into the Origin of the Ancient *Scots* and *Picts.*

A   The

A prospectus by Edward Lhuyd. Only Volume I was published
(in 1707).

It appears rarely in Delegates' books (Quintilian, 1692) and very often in those printed for authors. Spelman's *Reliquiae* changed its character in course of printing. It was begun as a Delegates' book, but was sold, at the request of the editor, Edmund Gibson, to the London booksellers

---

[1] Chancellor's Court Cause Papers, Michaelmas 1702.

whose names appear on the title-page as publishers.[1] Editions shared by the Delegates and booksellers are uncommon (Herodian, 1699). The absence of a bookseller's name from the imprint cannot be relied upon as showing that the Delegates paid for the book: the opposite is true of the editions of Clarendon's *History* for which Baskett paid and of many books printed for authors.

According to the notions prevailing at that time (before the case of *Donaldson* v. *Becket*, 1774), publishers, whether booksellers or printers, would respect a claim by one of their number to a perpetual right to the copy in a work that he had entered in the Stationers' Register and first printed or one that he had acquired by purchase.[2] Several Oxford titles are among the copies that had belonged to Henry Clements sold in March 1719/20 after his death.[3]

Keil, Introductio ad veram physicam.	Sold for £37	
—— Introductio ad veram astronomiam.	35	
Musae Anglicanae, 2 vol.	21	
Grabe, Specilegium patrum. $\frac{1}{3}$-share	}	5 5s.
—— part of the Septuagint. $\frac{1}{4}$-share		
Boyle against Bentley.	—	
Homer, Iliad, Oxon. $\frac{1}{4}$-share.	2 3s.	
Hudson, Thucydides	}	
—— Dionysius Halicarnassius		
Justin Martyr, 2nd Apology	}	5 5s.
Alsop's Aesop		
Wells's Cyropaedia		

'The dearness of the University Press', Blackstone wrote in 1756, 'has been long, and very justly, a Matter of Complaint both to Authors and Booksellers.'[4] He gave examples of prices charged there then which tally very closely with those in the Warehouse-Keeper's Accounts from 1690 onwards. They remained stationary until the reform by Blackstone which took effect in 1758. The evidence that he collected is, broadly speaking, that a sheet that would have cost 15s. 6d. to set and print in London cost 17s. 6d. in Oxford.

Thomas Smith told Hearne that in Fell's time the prices charged at the Press were very moderate, 'but afterwards the excessive rates you referre

---

[1] Bodl. MS. Tanner 23, fols. 21, 49.
[2] W. W. Greg, *Some Aspects and Problems of London Publishing between 1550 and 1650* (Oxford, 1956), chap. iv.
[3] Catalogue in the J.J. Collection, Bodleian Library.
[4] Philip, p. 23.

to, were brought in by the cunning & artifice of John Hall [the Ware-house Keeper], who knew how to influence his new Masters, and at the same time to make a good hand of it to his own profit and advantage.'[1] Authors were not attracted to the University Press for the sake of economy. Nor had it a good reputation for speed. There were complaints of delay in producing Clarendon's *History*;[2] Edward Twells's life of Pococke, the second edition, was done in London because the Press at Oxford was so dilatory;[3] Edmund Gibson said it was too slow to get work from London booksellers,[4] and advised a correspondent in 1693 to get his book printed in London: 'Our press Sir, is soe slow, that you could not reasonably hope to see it finish'd under 4 or 5 years. Our workmen are few, our stock of Letter small, besides a hundred accidental obstructions to which the London-presses are not subject.'[5]

Presses are generally accused of being expensive and slow: what lends colour to the criticisms of the Press in the first half of the eighteenth century is the downward trend of business here while in London the book trade was rapidly gaining volume.[6] Hearne thought, in 1718, that the Delegates took no interest in the books printed at their press at the authors' expense;[7] and his account of his dealings with the institution, which were by direct contact with the compositors, is enough to convict it of a lack of organization. He writes of 'his' compositor and 'his' press-men; he did his best to keep 'his' workmen continuously employed.[8] Likewise, Lancaster was worried because 'Dr. Hudson's workmen' were kept waiting for their pay.[9] In the absence of any effective chain of command it was hard on Hearne to say that 'his private way of printing perverts the Use of the Press.'[10]

To set against this, the Press was 'very well furnished with types'.[11] Fell had left it equipped with its own matrices for casting Roman, Italic, Greek, Syriac, and Coptic letters, and these with the Hebrews and Arabic bought by the University in 1637 and the Armenian and Cyrillic acquired by the Delegates since Fell's death were enough to tempt learned authors into putting up with disadvantages of printing at the Theatre. A commission from a London publisher to print the Lord's Prayer in exotic

---

[1] Hearne, ii, p. 90.
[2] Bodl. MS. Ballard v, fol. 52.
[3] Ibid. xxviii, fols. 30, 33.
[4] Ibid. v, fol. 23.
[5] Bodl. MS. Aubrey xii, 138ᶜ.
[6] F. Madan, *A Chart of Oxford Printing '1468'–1900* (Oxford, 1904).
[7] Hearne, vi, p. 237 n.
[8] Ibid. vii, p. 1; vi, pp. 67, 103.
[9] Bodl. MS. Ballard xxi, fol. 42.
[10] Archbishop Wake in 1716: MS. Ballard iii, fol. 118.
[11] Hearne, ii, p. 177.

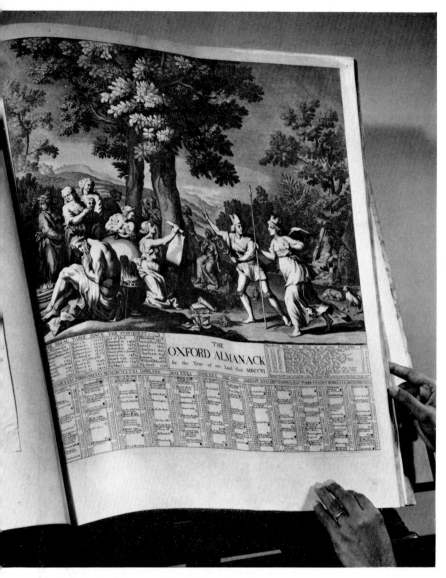

An *Oxford Almanack* in the collection at the Press

Edmund Halley (1656–1742), Savilian Professor of Geometry
1703–42

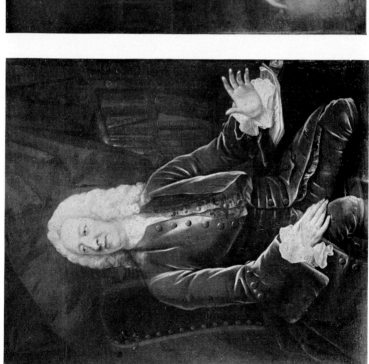

William King (1685–1763), Tory and Jacobite, Principal of St.
Mary Hall

scripts in 1700 is proof of its unique resources of the kind, so far as England was concerned. By then it had deserved the tribute paid to it by Daniel Prince thirty-six years later: 'all Greek, the Hebrew, and other Oriental and Foreign Letters are better than in any other Printing House.'[1]

Corrector there was none in the house. In Blackstone's day the relatively high rate of pay to the compositors was justified partly by their undertaking to work 'so cleanly as not to need any other Corrector than the Author himself'.[2] That being so, it is unlikely that the Press had a proofreader on its staff at an earlier time.[3] The Delegates employed graduates casually to correct their books unless the author or editor were available to do it, and the names of several such are to be found in the accounts. They were normally paid 2s. 6d. a sheet for octavos and 2s. or 1s. 6d. for bigger formats. The Architypographus, whose functions nominally included supervising the correction of the press (or, rather, presses) in the University's precinct, evidently did not concern himself with it. In the case of a private work, if the author were not in Oxford, a friend would sometimes read the proofs for him, as Hearne did for Thomas Smith,[4] and Thomas Tanner for Edmund Gibson;[5] but sometimes proofs were sent to London, as were those of Smith's edition of the letters of Ignatius of 1709.[6]

It must be allowed that the books from the Learned Press of the late seventeenth and eighteenth centuries were, on the whole, free from printers' errors. Even that Zoilus Hearne, when he brings to light faults in Oxford editions, blames authors not printers. Gibson, warning Lluyd to expect 'a trial of patience now and then, upon the Compositor's getting drunk, or bringing a sheet three or four days later than he promis'd, or making two faults by mending one',[7] was being irresponsibly facetious. In point of quality Oxford printing was unsurpassed in England at that time. In composite volumes of sermons and tracts the ones printed at the Theatre (or at Cambridge) stand out from the rest by the superiority of their paper and print.

[1] Philip, p. 19.   [2] Ibid., p. 33.

[3] I would assume that Moses Carterius, 'imployed for above ten years [before 1686] as Corrector in the Presse at the Theater' (Reg. Conv. Bb. 29; *Wood's Life and Times*, iii, p. 189), was really an orientalist called in by Fell when he was needed and paid by Fell. He does not figure in the Accounts.

[4] Bodl. MS. Rawl. letters, xxviii, fols. 24, 32.

[5] Bodl. MS. Tanner 25, fol. 231.

[6] Hearne, ii, p. 127. Correction at the University Press is dealt with by Percy Simpson in *Proof-Reading in the Sixteenth, Seventeenth, and Eighteenth Centuries* (Oxford, 1935), pp. 161–3, 193–4, 204.

[7] Bodl. MS. Ashmole 1815, No. 85; Simpson, op. cit., p. 204.

The Delegates left the profitable field of religious controversy to private authors; unless the University's fulmen against the *Naked Gospel*, in 1690, may be considered as an exception. The best sellers printed at the Theatre were Anglican polemics directed at Dissenters. Jonathan Edwards's *Preservative against Socinianism*, begun in 1693, had its first part reprinted within a year and again five years later. That and Edward Wells's *Letter from a Minister of the Church of England to a Dissenting Parishioner* (1706), of which there were five editions in its first year, exceeded in popularity any other works that the Press was willing to print. These best-sellers were all 'authors' books'.

Bodleian MSS. Grabe have preserved useful information about the proceedings of an author getting his works printed and published at Oxford in the years 1698–1711. For his edition of Irenaeus printed at the Theatre in 1702 Grabe contracted with the London bookseller Thomas Bennett.[1] The bookseller undertook the charge for printing, £114, plus a poundage of £22. 18s. to the University for overheads.[2] He promised Grabe for editing £80 to be paid on publication and an additional £20 if he could engage 250 subscribers besides 'what shall be subscribed by booksellers' or 500 'as well from Gentlemen as Booksellers'. Grabe had previously issued proposals for the edition.[3]

In other cases Grabe found all the subscribers and paid for the printing. Bills presented to him for his *Apologia* of Justin Martyr (1700) by compositors and pressmen are extant.[4] He paid them directly and got signed receipts from the workmen. There are more of such bills for his Septuagint of 1707.[5] They include charges for carriage and postage for which the compositors had paid. Brookland, one of the compositors, had paid the corrector, Moses Williams, undergraduate of University College, a fee of 16s. 6d. and recovered it from Grabe.[6] Another compositor, Pieter La Mouche, had paid £4 to two press-crews working on the book.[7] The cost and profit of the edition of Volume i of the Septuagint were shared by Grabe and a London bookseller, Richard Smith, who took a quarter-share.[8]

It is clear that besides paying the workmen Grabe had to square accounts with the Warehouse-Keeper, John Hall, and after his day with Mrs. Mary Hall, the widow. He would owe the Warehouse-Keeper for 'necessaries' (ink, lye, etc.), charged at 8s. a sheet, and for the University's

---

[1] Bodl. MS. Grabe 53, fol. 316. [2] 1st Accounts, p. 171.
[3] Bodl. J.J. Coll., f. 25. [4] MS. Grabe 53, fols. 6, 7. [5] Ibid., fols. 44, 131.
[6] Ibid., fol. 44. [7] Ibid., fol. 79. [8] Ibid., fol. 85.

poundage at 6s. a sheet;[1] but it looks as though Hall were responsible for seeing all the workmens' bills paid. He gave Grabe a quittance for all the charges for Justin's *Apologia*, composing, presswork, necessaries and poundage, though Grabe had already paid the compositors and press-crews, at any rate in part.[2] Mrs. Hall refused to release the printed sheets of the Septuagint (Vol. i) until she had 'security as to the payment of the Remainder of the Money', saying she would not trust the bookseller, Smith, and relied on Grabe for the whole.[3]

Henry Clements, the London bookseller, advanced part of the cost of the Septuagint in payments to Thistlethwaite, the Architypographus, and La Mouche, the compositor.[4] John Hudson lent Grabe £100 towards the expenses of preparing the edition.[5] The Architypographus would advance money to pay the pressmen if Grabe would authorize him.[6]

The printing of Grabe's *Spicilegium* of the early Fathers was partly financed by contributions from the Dean of Christ Church, John Rance a compositor, the Principal of Jesus, and the Provost of Queen's.[7] There is no trace of this book in the Warehouse-Keeper's Accounts, so presumably the University forwent the usual poundage as its contribution.

Thomas Hearne in 1710 arranged with Rance, the senior compositor, to pay an inclusive price for the sheets of Leland's *Itinerary*, with part of which Rance would pay the pressmen and the copperplate printer.

I agreed to give Mr Rance 25s. per sheet for Leland's Itin. so as that I should have no other Trouble with any other Printer about printing it, he the said Mr Rance being to satisfy both himself and others out of that sum, which should have been less had he not promised for it together, and dry them, and bring them home without insisting upon any future gratuity . . .[8]

The image and credit of this University Press in the eyes of the world depend to a great extent on books which it printed but did not publish. The imprint 'Oxford, at the Theater' conveys to all but the most inquiring mind the character and authority of an academic publication. Famous books have borne this mark of their origin with no sign that it relates only to printing. One of them is John Mill's *Novum Testamentum cum lectionibus variantibus* of 1707. It was originally intended to be a

---

[1] Ibid., fols. 93, 155. [2] Ibid., fol. 8. [3] Ibid., fol. 78.
[4] Ibid., fol. 132. [5] Hearne, i, p. 171. [6] MS. Grabe 53, fol. 140.
[7] Ibid., fol. 213.
[8] Bodl. MS. Hearne's Diaries 184, under 1710.

Delegates' book: in his Prolegomena[1] Mill relates (in Latin) how the change came about:

My mind was not made up to undertake a new edition until the most experienced of our authors, the famous Bishop of Oxford, John Fell, looked at my papers, and seeing the pile of variant readings that I had got together and my untidy notes on them vehemently insisted on my putting them in order and setting about an edition as soon as might be. . . . And when we had got no farther than the 24th Chapter of Matthew we lost our revered 'taskmaster' and our plans were brought to confusion. For he was taken away whose money, types, and patronage had availed me so far.

From that point onwards Mill paid for the production and sold the edition to subscribers. He went so far as to refund to the University the amount that Fell had spent on the first fifteen sheets.[2]

The book, begun in 1681,[3] was a very long time in the press; it was rumoured that Queen Anne had sent Mill an order to hasten with it.[4] He died a fortnight after publication.

F. H. A. Scrivener has made eloquent acknowledgement of the debt owed by later New Testament scholars to Mill's great work.[5] Oxford opinion was shocked by the dedication to Queen Anne, which Mill altered at the last moment on advice from William Lloyd, the puritanical Bishop of Worcester.[6] Some found it too fulsome: others were horrified by its strictures on Charles II for allowing his government to be corrupted by French gold and the influence of the Papacy. These were charges not previously seen in print. The Vice-Chancellor, William Lancaster, whose imprimatur is on the book, found it incumbent on him to censure them in his speech at the end of his first year of office,[7] but Thomas Smith thought his condemnation of Mill's offence was much too mild.[8] In private Lancaster was of another mind: 'And what of Dr. Mill's Testament?', he wrote to Charlett, 'I fear it will be thought I licenced that Admirable Dedication.'[9]

Canon Adam Fox has noticed that copies of the book vary in the first 88 pages of the text and in some other pages as far as 144.[10] Presumably subscriptions exceeded the expected demand, so that the early sheets had to be reprinted and some others fell short and had to be made up to an

[1] pp. clviii–clxiv.   [2] Wood, Fasti, ii, 381.
[3] Ibid.   [4] Hearne, i, p. 29.
[5] In his Introduction to the Criticism of the New Testament (1861), quoted by Adam Fox, John Mill and Richard Bentley (Oxford, 1954), p. v.
[6] Hearne ii, pp. 20, 25, 29, 30.   [7] Hearne ii, p. 61 n.
[8] Ibid., p. 62.   [9] Bodl. MS. Ballard xxi, fol. 45.   [10] Op. cit., p. 63.

average number before the book left the press. The Warehouse-Keeper's Accounts do not help here: they are silent as to this book. The University did not charge poundage.

An author's book which must be rated as one of the great feats of English scholarship is Hickes's *Thesaurus* of the northern languages, two bulky folios issued in 1703–5.[1] J. M. Kemble in 1837 called it 'a miracle of mistaken energy and learning'. 'Though modern attention', he continues, 'has detected so many errors as to render his Grammars rather dangerous than useful, we owe to him hearty thanks for his labours. . . . A host of Saxon students rose around him.'[2] It was the culmination of the studies of Oxford Saxonists, 'that Revolution' as Tanner called it,[3] beginning with William Somner's *Dictionarium Saxonico-Latino-Anglicum* of 1659.

Though time has dealt hardly with Volume i of the work, the appended 'Dissertatio epistolica' dealing with Anglo-Saxon charters retains its authority,[3] and Volume ii, Humfrey Wanley's list of manuscripts containing Old English 'is a book which scholars will continue to use or neglect at their peril'.[4]

The *Thesaurus* was paid for by subscribers with subventions from the author's friends. The University did not charge the usual poundage for its overhead expenses, so there is no mention of it in the Accounts. The book is excellently printed, and no other press in the world could have printed it then.

Phalaris

The small book which started the controversy between a group of classical scholars of Christ Church and Richard Bentley[5] was one of those that Dean Aldrich ordered to give away as New-Year presents. It was his gift for New Year's Day 1695.

The accounts are proof that the Delegates did not sponsor it. They received an amount of £4. 10*s.* for overheads on the printing, which means that it was an edition of some 500.[6] How many were sold is not known.

The dedication to the Dean acknowledges that the impulse to edit these suppositious letters of a Sicilian Greek tyrant came from him and that he had borne the cost. Charles Boyle, a grand-nephew of the famous chemist,

---

[1] An excellent history of the book by Professor J. A. W. Bennett is in *English Studies 1948* (Essays and Studies collected for the English Association by F. P. Wilson), pp. 28–45. Professor D. C. Douglas gives an enthusiastic account of it and the author in *English Scholars*, ch. 4. [2] Quoted by Douglas, op. cit. 1951 ed., p. 90.
[3] Bodl. MS. Tanner 25, fol. 172.
[4] N. R. Ker, *Catalogue of Manuscripts containing Anglo-Saxon* (Oxford, 1957), p. xiii.
[5] R. C. Jebb, *Richard Bentley*, pp. 40–85. [6] 1st Accounts, p. 53.

had been allotted the task (and no doubt his tutor, Francis Atterbury, helped with it).

A preface to the reader makes it clear that this is a slight work done at short notice. The writer recommends enjoying the letters rather than disputing their authorship. It may be thought that this is much to ask when the text ostensibly is of historical value and written in the 52nd Olympiad. If the editor were content to abdicate his function as critic so far, it might have been better to say that the letters had been brought into prominence by extravagant praise of them in the second of Sir William Temple's *Miscellanea*, published in 1692, and should be available to the curious.

The writer of the preface goes on to review, very briefly, the state of opinion as to the genuineness of the text. He anticipates the main points of Bentley's subsequent attack, that the dialect is Attic and that one of the cities referred to did not exist in the lifetime of Phalaris. Admitting some corruption, he leaves the question open and will listen to the verdict of more learned men.

All might have been well, the book might have passed as an inconspicuous exercise by an immature scholar, if Boyle had not seen fit to put in his preface a complaint that Bentley, 'with his usual politeness', had not allowed him the use of a manuscript in his care as Royal Librarian long enough for a transcript to be finished.

Bentley believed that the quarrel was begun by his being overheard to say, while the edition was in the press, that the *Epistles* were spurious and should not be printed.[1] As for the loan of the manuscript, his account of the matter was that he had been obliged to see it put back in its place before he went away for a time and that Boyle had not asked for it again.[2] With that the controversy becomes part of the larger dispute about the comparative merits of ancient and modern literature.[3] The spirited but ineffectual defence of Boyle's friends to Bentley's demolition of Phalaris[4] was not printed at the Press, or, indeed, at Oxford.

---

[1] R. Bentley, *A Dissertation upon the Epistles of Phalaris, with an Answer to the Objections of the Honourable Charles Boyle, Esquire* (1699), p. v.

[2] Ibid., pp. iii–v.

[3] The relevant books are noticed in the edition of Swift's *Tale of a Tub* by A. C. Guthkelch and D. Nichol Smith (1920), in their notes to 'The Battle of the Books'.

[4] *Dr. Bentley's Dissertation on the Epistles of Phalaris and the Fables of Aesop examin'd by the Honourable Charles Boyle, Esquire* (1698). It is attributed to Atterbury. Of another Oxford champion Johnson wrote that he 'tried what Wit could perform in opposition to Learning, on a question which Learning only could decide': *Lives of the English Poets*, ed. Birkbeck Hill ii, p. 27.

Would it be surprising if Oxford clung to a belief in this author? An unaltered reprint of Boyle's edition was issued by the Clarendon Press at the expense of Stephen Fletcher, a local bookseller, in 1718.

Thomas Hearne's Publications

The books that Hearne edited and sold to subscribers in the years 1703–35 form an appendix to the work of the University Press. Everybody knew that they did not carry the authority or even the approval of the academic body and that Archbishop Wake's feeling that Hearne's 'private way of Publishing perverts the Press'[1] was commonly shared. All but two of these editions were printed there, and if the Delegates disliked them they must have been aware that they kept the printers occupied. After 1716, when he was ousted from his post at the Bodleian, Hearne made his living by publishing.

The fact that he left £1,000 at his death means that he was, in his small way, a successful publisher, unlike the University in his lifetime. He gauged the demand for learned books more nearly and limited the size of his editions to suit it, charging prices high enough to yield him a modest profit. The Delegates seldom printed fewer than 500: Hearne was content with 150 for several of his books,[2] and a usual number was 200 or 240, with 60 or 70 on large paper.[3] His subscribers, many of whom were people of eminence, stood by him firmly, and he appears generally to have sold out his stock. He tells us that large paper copies of Leland's *Itinerary*, published in 1710–12 at 45s., were being sold for 12 guineas in 1714, and 15 guineas were offered in 1719.[4] The unscrupulous Edmund Curll had pirated part of Dodwell's *De parma equestri* in 1713, and John Woodward blamed Hearne for not entering the book at Stationers' Hall and for printing too few.[5]

He did not believe in issuing printed proposals, finding it enough to announce the forthcoming book at the end of the preceding one,[6] and he got a friend in London to put an advertisement in the *Courant* or the *Postboy*.[7]

By the end of 1713 nine of Hearne's thirty-seven editions had appeared. His anonymously-edited *Reliquiae Bodleianae* of 1703 (printed by Lichfield at Oxford) and his Volume ii of *Ductor historicus* (printed in London) are

---

[1] Bodl. MS. Ballard iii, fols. 116, 118 (1716).   [2] Hearne, ix, p. 374.
[3] Hearne, v, p. 336; vi, p. 404; vii, pp. 36–7, 75, 115, 156, 195, 350.
[4] Hearne, iv, p. 335; vii, p. 33.   [5] Hearne, iv, p. 176.
[6] Hearne, vii, pp. 135, 149.   [7] Hearne, iii, pp. 162, 496; vi, p. 410.

Thomas Hearne, the antiquary.

the only ones that were not printed at the University Press. For the rest, the straitness of his means and the need to supervise the press prevented him from placing his work elsewhere.

The value of the texts that Hearne made available was assessed fairly as early as 1748 by David Wilkins,[1] and it must be granted that modern English history owes a great deal to him.[2] The economic spur that forced him to set about a new work as soon as he finished the last, his enforced reliance on transcripts, the obligation to gratify the vanity of his friends and subscribers by printing the documents that they lent him, have to be allowed for. He worked from hand to mouth, accepting additions and alterations to texts that were in the press.[3] He professed to do no more than reproduce the manuscripts that came to his hands with little or no criticism.[4]

In the history of the University Press he is of immense help as a witness. Nobody else of his day cared as he did for printing and printers or kept such a sharp and discriminating eye on editions. He is also of great use as an indicator of the limits set by the University to the expression of opinion over its imprint.

Hearne's passionate championship of the Pretender was notorious, and he did not conceal it from strangers in his capacity of under-librarian.[5] It was enough to make the rulers of the University eye him narrowly as an author; and, added to the offence he had given Charlett by editing the life of King Alfred without the Master's privity, it brought the wrath of the Heads of Houses down upon him in 1713. Their order banning the sale of Hearne's edition of Dodwell's *De parma equestri*[6] was based on expressions in the preliminary apparatus. Hearne had written (in Latin) of Dodwell, 'Being one of those honest men who thought it wrong to break an oath to a king, he was upon that account treated with contumely by many and subjected to repeated insults, and, sad to say, was driven from the Camden lectureship.' He had described Thomas Milles, then Bishop of Waterford, as a person of 'mediocre learning' and asserted that he attacked Dodwell 'as an aid to preferment'.

The Heads allowed the book to be sold if the offending preliminaries were removed;[7] but Hearne, uncharacteristically, 'got the Preface transmitted to those who had receiv'd copies without it'.[8] To the Vice-Chancellor he objected that the offending passages were true. 'Truth is

---

[1] In the preface to Thomas Tanner's *Bibliotheca Britannico-Hibernica*, pp. xliii–iv.
[2] D. C. Douglas, *English Scholars*, ch. ix. [3] Hearne, vii, p. 370.
[4] Hearne, iii, p. 109; vii, p. 131. [5] Hearne, iv, pp. 111–14.
[6] Ibid., pp. 124, 137. [7] Ibid., pp. 125, 141. [8] Ibid., p. 126.

not to be spoke at all times', the Vice-Chancellor (Bernard Gardiner) said, adding that ' 'Twas not fit that the book should be said to come *e Theatro Sheldoniano.*' The President of Corpus joined in to say 'We shall be looked upon all as Jacobites . . . and very severe Censures will fall upon us, if we permit Books of this kind to pass from the Theater Press unregarded.'[1]

Hearne was mildly rebuked by the Vice-Chancellor for criticizing, in his Leland's *Collectanea*, the removal of the Arundel Marbles from the Theatre Yard and for his reflections on the Archbishop of Dublin for treason to James II and Bishop Milles for deserting the Non-Jurors. 'He said he wished I had left these Reflexions out.'[2]

Hearne was unrepentant. A note in his *Life of Henry V* by Livius Foro-Juliensis referring to 'smutty' letters from Henry VIII to Anne Boleyn 'gave offence';[3] and in Roper's *Life of More* strictures on the same monarch 'displeased'.[4] The Vice-Chancellor forbade the appearance of Oxford or the Theatre in the imprints of Hearne's books for the future.[5] Subject to that, he was given leave to print Camden's *Annals of the Reign of Queen Elizabeth.*

The *Annals*, published in 1717, brought matters to a head. Hearne's provocations to received opinions could no longer be borne, and the world must be assured that the University disowned him. He was cited to answer in the Chancellor's Court the office of Vice-Chancellor suing for reformation of his morals.[6] He had defamed the University, and the penalties were public recantation, imprisonment, or expulsion, at the Vice-Chancellor's discretion. In the preface to Camden he had written (in Latin) of Henry VIII, benefactor of the University and founder of Christ Church, 'it is well known that he may be called crueller than Nero, more barbarous than Caligula, more immoral, almost, than Heliogabalus, sacrilegious, if ever a man was'; of Queen Elizabeth I, benefactor, founder

---

[1] Hearne, iv, pp. 117, 139.

[2] Hearne, v, pp. 74–5. 'It is very rash for any one, especially for Scholars, to attempt the Alteration of ancient Monuments, that they may be the more conveniently placed. . . . My Lord Arundel was very cautious in this Affair. . . . It is, therefore, very much to be lamented that . . . they have been permitted to be cut and mangled' etc.: Leland, *Collectanea* (1715), vi, p. 276.

[3] Hearne, v, p. 329. He printed the letters in the volume of Avesbury's *History* (1720). He had exaggerated their carnality.

[4] Hearne, v, p. 328. (In Latin:) 'More is the pity that he should have been slaughtered by a ruler too much given, if our historians can be believed, to the venereal and all other pleasures': Preface to Roper's *Life* (1716), p. xviii.

[5] Hearne, v, pp. 328–9. There is no imprint on three of his books published in 1716–17. The Theatre imprint was resumed in 1719 with Neubrigensis.

[6] Hearne, vi, pp. 350 ff.

The title-page of Roper's *Life of More* edited by Hearne while he was
forbidden to use the Oxford imprint, substituting *vadum boum vetus*
(the old ford of oxen) for it.

of Jesus College, that her execution of the Queen of Scots was a heartless
crime. He had calumniated the Chancellor, Masters, and Scholars by
writing that 'the dignity and splendour of a university lie, not in the size
of its buildings nor in the number of people living in comfort and

indolence, but in a multitude of learned and studious men.' He had complained that Archbishop Marsh's magnificent bequest of manuscripts was relegated to a dark corner of the Bodleian; he had reminded heads of colleges that Queen Elizabeth wished them not to live in enviable luxury with wives and children within the walls.

Hearne was willing to express sorrow for offending, but he stood by his words. By a series of agitated letters to his more influential patrons he sought to bring persuasion to bear on the Earl of Arran, Chancellor of the University, to stop the prosecution. It dragged on for seven months and was allowed to drop with the end of the Vice-Chancellor's term of office. Hearne had been frightened by the threat of expulsion and his morbid belief that he was a hunted man was made worse; but his love of putting 'crude and extraneous matter' (as Gibbon called it)[1] in his prefaces was ineradicably part of him.

Work on his edition of Neubrigensis, stopped by order of the Vice-Chancellor and Delegates during the prosecution, was allowed to go on again after three months. He was using the imprint of the Theatre once more by 1719.

Parallel instances of intervention by authority for fear that Oxford books might offend are reported by George Smalridge in a letter of 1698:[2]

Our Vice-Chancellor has shown a good deal of caution in doing any thing that might offend the Government or any one that is in the favour of it. He suppressed for some time the Aesop published by Mr. Alsop, because in the preface of it there was a gentle touch upon Dr. Bentley.[3] He has at last given leave to the vent of it on condition that his *Imprimatur* be not printed with it. He put a stop to a Discourse of Mr. John Keill's, a Scotchman, of Baliol,[4] because notice was taken in it of an astronomical mistake of Dr. Bentley's; but after expostulating with him, he has at last granted that it come out, even with his *Imprimatur*, on its being approved by our Mathematical Professors. An 'Anglo-Saxonicum Pentateuchum', i.e. the Five Books of Moses, and Joshua, and Judges, in Saxon,[5] is suppressed by

[1] *Miscellaneous Works of Edward Gibbon, Esquire*, ed. John, Lord Sheffield, ii (1796), p. 711.
[2] Nichols, *Illus.* iii (1818), p. 261.
[3] He made light of a stain on the honour of the Press. Of the contention that the fables were not written by the fabled philosopher he wrote, 'quod nuperrime fecisse audio Richardum quendam Bentleium, virum in volvendis lexicis satis diligentem'.
[4] *An Examination of Dr. Burnet's Theory of the Earth* (Oxford, 1698). The reference to Bentley is on p. 70.
[5] *Heptateuchus, Liber Job, et Evangelium Nicodemi Anglo-Saxonice* edited by Edward Thwaites (Oxford, 1698).

him, because dedicated to Dr. Hickes, a Nonjuror, though there is no other compliment paid him, but that he is skilled in Saxon, and has promoted the study of it.

Ælfric's Heptateuch

This ineffectual 'suppression', amounting to no more than the withdrawal of the Vice-Chancellor's imprimatur and some delay to the appearance of the volume, is a miserable episode. Thwaites's edition of the abbot's Old English version of the Pentateuch, Joshua, and Judges is rated by a modern editor of the work as 'a scholarly performance'.[1] It is an edition of a Bodleian manuscript (Laud Misc. 509), and Thwaites filled up its lacunae from one in the Cambridge University Library and another in Sir Robert Cotton's, providing a text for a long time without a rival.

In his dedicatory 'Epistle' to George Hickes the editor eulogizes his friend and master in the accustomed way. The Delegates of the Press agreed to publication of the book,[2] and the Vice-Chancellor (Meare) gave his imprimatur on 27 December 1697. One of three copies in the Bodleian has the imprimatur.

Hickes lay until 1699 under threat of prosecution and was in hiding under assumed names, at this time as the guest of William Brome near Hereford. Thwaites made no allusion in his dedication to his friend's Non-Juring or defiance of the order depriving him of his deanery; nevertheless the Vice-Chancellor was persuaded by Arthur Charlett to forbid the sale of the book. 'Now the Vice Chancellour has confessed, he was put upon this by Dr. Charlett', Thwaites wrote to Brome on 6 January 1697/8. 'He said he found noe fault in the dedication, all that was improper was the Patron. for Dr. Charlett had told him, 'twas the greatest affront to the Court that could be invented; and that the whole design was driven on for this particular end, viz. a dedication, and that if he lett it pass, all the interest of this place was ruined.'[3]

The Master denied it; but he wriggled ignominiously. Wanley put Charlett's case to 'Mr. Potter' c/o Brome in a letter of 18 February: he denied having spoken to the Vice-Chancellor before the ban was imposed,

---

[1] S. J. Crawford, *The Old English Version of the Heptateuch*, Early English Text Soc., o.s. 160 (1922), Preface.

[2] The expression in Thwaites's dedication, 'ubi de edendis hisce monumentis convenerit inter rei typographicae curatores' might mean that they originally agreed to publish it themselves.

[3] Bodl. MS. Rawl. letters 108, fol. 245.

but 'He thought the bringing of you out of a Retirement, which you had voluntarily chosen, into the World again, was quite contrary to your Inclination',[1] and much else.

The outcome was that a new title leaf was printed without an imprimatur on the verso and sooner or later the embargo must have been lifted. The dedication was not affected: Thwaites had told Meare he was 'resolved not to change one word'.[2]

Why the year in the imprint is set as 'MDCXCVIII', with the last letter bigger than the others, is a minor mystery—possibly a whim to indicate that the dating is New Style. It is so in the copy given the imprimatur, which Thwaites had seen by 6 January 1697/8; therefore it cannot stand for 1699.

The Accounts for the Press have no entry for this book; so the Delegates neither published it nor charged, as was usual, for their overheads on the printing.

[1] Bodl. MS. Eng. hist. c. 6, fol. 19.   [2] His letter cited above.

PART III

THE BAD TIME
1713–1755

CHAPTER XVI

The Neglected Press

THE Press partook fully of the lethargy into which the University sank in Hanoverian times,[1] and if the Press shook it off earlier than other academic organs it was thanks only to the genius of Blackstone. The want of good books was a fundamental defect, perhaps a cause as much as an effect of the low condition of society in this place. Newspapers, sermons, essays, and pamphlets on politics offered an easy substitute for more serious reading. Energy that might have gone into editing texts or compiling dictionaries found an easier vent in controversy, much of which was stifled by the more prudent seniors fearful of losing patronage by offending the court. It was not only their own chance of preferment in the Church that was at stake: association of Oxford with Non-Juring and Jacobitism was reason to fear restriction of the autonomy and privileges of the University by the Whig ascendancy in Parliament. The failure of the University to sell its publications in the previous twenty years and the ability of the Press to make ends meet by working for other publishers were inducements to let printing look after itself and publish nothing.

Delegates not chosen for their interest in scholarship, literature, or

---

[1] C. E. Mallet, *History of the University of Oxford*, vol. iii (1927), and in *Johnson's England* (1952), ii, pp. 209–42; W. R. Ward, *Georgian Oxford* (Oxford, 1958); A. D. Godley, *Oxford in the Eighteenth Century* (1908). Dame Lucy Sutherland's Bryce Memorial Lecture, *The University of Oxford in the Eighteenth Century: a Reconsideration* (Oxford, 1973) corrects some of the excessive severity of earlier judgements.

business had no other qualification than being Heads of Houses, the small group which, as Hearne said, ordered things as it pleased.[1]

And yet books and printing of all kinds were wanted then as never before. Multiplication of booksellers in London and in the provinces, a new frequency of book-sales, shorter periods between issues of news-papers and periodicals go far to proving it; and the record of William Bowyer the elder, 1686–1737, and the son, 1737–71, as printers of serious and learned works shames both Universities.[2]

Besides new books, old favourites were in demand; but the University showed little interest in exploiting its rights in them. One such, whose popularity indicates the character of eighteenth-century England, was *The Whole Duty of Man*, a mixture of piety, courtesy, and worldly wisdom, first published in London in 1658. Everyone knew it: the Duchess of Marlborough quoted it to Queen Anne in pleading for a renewal of their friendship;[3] an edition printed at Oxford (1730) is so arranged that families might read through it three times a year on Lord's Days; innumerable editions appeared in the eighteenth and early nineteenth centuries. Four sequels by the same anonymous author, beloved almost as much as the original, were considered as being the University's copy-right, but it farmed out its rights to booksellers, reserving to itself only the printing.

It did the same thing with Clarendon's *History*, with Maundrell's *Journey from Aleppo to Jerusalem . . .*, and even with its Greek text of the *Odyssey*. The Oxford Grammar was last printed in 1733, and the only one of its copyrights that the University kept in print, unaltered until the end of this period, was Thomas Marshall's Catechism.

Funds were available for subsidizing learned editions, but they were untouched if not forgotten. After a struggle lasting three years Blackstone was able to revive a separate Delegacy for the Press, to put its accounts on a proper footing, to install a competent overseer, and remedy the misapplication of funds destined for it; what he failed to do was to find worthy objects to spend the funds on. It might well be asked what was the use of subsidizing a press that had nothing to print. Daniel Prince, an Oxford bookseller, consulted in 1756, suggested *The Whole Duty of Man* and Clarendon's *History of the Rebellion*. The proposal to reprint Clarendon at the University's expense was adopted by the Delegates in 1759,[4] but not pursued. Blackstone's adumbration of a series of plain editions of the

[1] Hearne, xi, p. 137.
[3] D.N.B. art. Anne, p. 461.
[2] Nichols, *Lit. An.*, vols. 1–3.
[4] Philip, pp. 107–8.

classics, beginning with a 5-volume Cicero, 4to, at 4s. 6d. a volume, and a
completion of Hearne's annotated but unfinished Cicero were unanimously
approved but dropped as editors proved unwilling to persevere with
them.[1]

Mount Tabor.   Pag. 114.
1 Naim. 2. Endor. 3 Mount Hermon. 4 The mounta:
ins of Gilboa. 5 The mountains of Samaria. 6 The
river Kishon. 7 The Plain of Esdraelon 8. valley of Iezrael.

An illustration from Henry Maundrell's *Journey from
Aleppo to Jerusalem at Easter* A.D. *1697*. First published
in 1703, it was printed at the Press seven times by
1749. Reduced.

The general belief that the law protected perpetual copyright kept the
University out of the market for school books until it was dispelled by
the judgement in *Donaldson's* case in 1774.[2] Until then the Stationers'
Company maintained a monopoly of the commonly-used educational

[1] Ibid., pp. 110–12, 115.
[2] *Donaldson* v. *Becket* (1774) in the House of Lords, 4 Burrow's Reports, 2408; 7 Brown's
Parliamentary Reports, 88.

books.[1] After the Grammar in 1733 the Delegates published nothing of the kind for more than a hundred years.

Among Delegates' books of the first half of the eighteenth century none was more praiseworthy than the *Catalogue of Printed Books in the Bodleian Library* of 1738, and the failure to sell it is a reflection not only on the literate world of that time but also on the means that the Press had for selling its books. Sales at the door seldom amounted to as much as £20 in a year, and sales to booksellers declined almost to none. Of the Bodleian Catalogue 24 copies were sold at the door of the Press in the first five years and none in the five years following. Seventy-five were consigned on publication to a bookseller in London and 17 to the Vice-Chancellor at Cambridge. Thirty-four more which had disappeared by 1742 were probably given away. The discount offered to booksellers on the two volumes priced at 3 guineas for large paper and 2 guineas for small was 5*s*. A fly-sheet advertising the book was issued in 1738 and the lists of the University's publications printed from time to time would doubtless include it. Perhaps the Catalogue was advertised once or twice in London newspapers; but on the whole the Press had to rely on selling to customers on the spot.

SUBMERGENCE OF THE PRESS DELEGACY

In the years 1690–1712 the Delegates published 23 titles: in the succeeding period, 1713–55, they published 14 new ones besides reprinting 5 that were old.

The flagging of their activity may be put down partly to memories of the failure to sell the University's publications in the past, partly to ignorance that Convocation had voted funds to subsidize learned publishing, and partly to the appropriation by the Heads of Houses of the Press Delegacy. The last of these causes is likely to have been the most efficient, because Delegates chosen for their interest in scholarship and literature might well have overcome the other two difficulties.

From 1710 until 1745 appointment to the Delegacy of Accounts carried with it that of Delegate of the Press. The Proctors, who nominated Delegates, generally with the consent, if not at the bidding, of the Vice-Chancellor, almost invariably conferred both offices at once, or one followed after a short interval by the other.[2]

---

[1] See the list of the Company's English Stock books in 1766 on p. 243 of Blagden.

[2] Invariably according to the table on p. 32 of *A Reply to Dr. Huddesford's Observations* (1756). Blackstone thought that Dobson (1719) was not a Delegate of Accounts: manu-

The pair of appointments was given since 1691 only to Heads of Houses, and followed approximately the order of their seniority, the number of Delegates being about one-third that of Heads. The Vice-Chancellor in 1755 told the Proctors 'that the Delegacies were one and the same, and always went together ... that it had been usual to nominate only Heads of Houses to this Trust; that the Delegacy of the Press was always considered as a proper Compliment to the Vice-Chancellor for the time being'.[1]

This was said to a recalcitrant Proctor, who thought 'the many abuses, which had crept into the University-Press' and had long been a matter of public complaint, were due to 'the numerous avocations of those to whose charge it was committed'. He was, he said, determined 'to intro-duce a Gentleman to this trust, who it was presumed might be induced to attend it'.[2]

Records of Delegates' meetings after 1716 until 1755 are very infre-quent, generally one for each year and none between 1732 and 1742. Of the 27 members of the board during that time 17 are reported as having been at one meeting or more.

Humphrey Prideaux may have been too censorious when he wrote in 1695 that most of the rulers of Oxford colleges were 'such as I could scarce committ a dog to their charge';[3] but there is little doubt that their average attainments were mediocre or worse. The extent to which merit entered into the choice of a delegate may be judged by the appointment in 1721 to be Delegate of Accounts and the Press of William Delaune, President of St. John's, who as Vice-Chancellor in 1702–6 had failed to account for £2,500 belonging to the Press and the University. Two Deans of Christ Church, Smalridge (1713–19) and Conybeare (1748–55), stand out for respectability, though not for any obvious effect that it had on the Press. John Purnell, Warden of New College, while he was Vice-Chancellor in 1747–9 deserved credit for being the first to get rid of stocks of unsaleable books.

Had the choice not been restricted to the Heads, it would still have been difficult to think of members of the University who would have graced and animated the Press Delegacy. Thomas Hunt, professor of

script note in his proposed revised edition of *To the Reverend Doctor Randolph*, Bodl. MS. Top. Oxon. d. 387, at p. 31. Joseph Morley, whose name appears among those approving the accounts for 1726–7, is not in the table.

[1] *A Reply*, etc., pp. 4, 6.
[2] Ibid., p. 3.
[3] Hist. MSS. Comm., 5th *Report*, p. 374 *b*.

Arabic, 1738–74, and Hebrew, 1747–74, comes to mind. His letters[1] display an interest in literary criticism and publishing not confined to his own field of study.

THE FINANCES OF THE LEARNED PRESS

The following table summarizes the balance of accounts between the Vice-Chancellor and the Warehouse-Keeper during the years 1690 and 1755 as it is shown in the Account for Printing rendered annually by the latter.

THE BALANCE OF ACCOUNTS FOR THE PRESS, 1690–1755

as shown in the accounts of the Warehouse-Keeper

Year	Excess of Expenses or Receipts	Amount £ s. d.	Payments to the V.-C. £ s. d.
1690–1	E	10 7 2	—
1691–2	E	78 5 0	—
1692–3	E	109 13 5	—
1693–4	E	108 8 1	—
1694–5	E	140 6 2	—
1695–6	E	180 10 11	—
1696–7	E	185 19 8	—
1697–8	E	131 10 8	—
1698–9	E	192 14 9	—
1699–1700	E	36 7 3	—
1700–2	E	15 11 0	—
1702–3	E	113 13 1	—
1703–5	R	12 14 4	—
1705–6	E	150 7 0	—
1706–8	E	80 5 2	—
1708–9	R	12 6 2	—
1709–10	R	54 4 3	—
1710–12	R	228 6 6	238 8 6
1712–15	R	100 10 0	—
1715–16	E	32 18 3	—
1716–18	R	13 1 2	—
1718–23	R	219 2 1	200

[1] In Bodl. MS. Rawl. letters 96.

		£ s. d.	£ s. d.
1723–4	R	139 16 1	100
1724–5	R	178 0 10	115
1725–6	R	212 16 0	100
1726–7	R	236 11 3	100
1727–8	R	100 8 6	—
1728–9	R	114 0 5	100
1729–30	R	120 7 11	—
1730–1	R	148 17 9	50
1731–2	R	142 17 0	50
1732–3	R	125 11 3	150
1733–4	R	88 18 10	50
1734–5	R	94 7 9	50
1735–6	R	96 14 0	—
1736–7	R	75 18 4	50
1737–8	R	74 9 1	70
1738–9	R	99 10 7	80
1739–40	R	86 16 1	50
1740–1	R	119 13 11	50
1741–2	R	116 14 6	100
1742–3	R	82 12 10	100
1743–4	R	36 5 6	150
1744–5	R	31 3 6	60
1745–6	R	21 16 6	50
1746–7	R	2 9 2	40
1747–8	E	9 9 7	50
1748–9	R	12 12 2	50
1749–50	R	12 10 8	90
1750–1	R	10 15 9	100
1751–2	R	15 0	50
1752–3	R	14 14 7	—
1753–4	R	13 8 3	50
1754–5	R	24 15 8	—

NOTE. These figures are taken from the account books of the Press. On the whole they accord with those in the Computus of the Vice-Chancellors. In many years the Computus enters the profits from the Press a year late: the £238. 8s. 6d. credited to the Vice-Chancellor in the Warehouse-Keeper's account for 1710/12 occurs in the Computus for 1712/13.

There are some serious discrepancies. According to the Computus, the Press paid £150 in 1713/14, and in 1714/15 as much as £4,677 (a year in which there was a loss on printing). This large amount was the product of a premium of £2,000 charged on Baskett for his lease of 1711, with debts collected from him and other booksellers, and the money from the sale of all the Delegates' stock of books. In 1736/7 the Vice-Chancellor did not enter receipt of £50 from the Press, nor did he in 1748/9. Otherwise the two accounts, allowing for a delay of a year sometimes, are conformable.

When payments were made by the Warehouse-Keeper to the Vice-Chancellor, as they were in most years from 1709 onwards, the amounts are included in the expenditure of the Press.

These figures are not a precise indication of the profits of printing and publishing. The Vice-Chancellor paid for paper used in the University's publications, for the design and engraving of the annual *Almanack*, sometimes for the typefounder's and smith's bills, and occasionally an honorarium for an editor or corrector. Since the University did very little publishing, the Vice-Chancellor's expenditure under this head in the early eighteenth century was very moderate. The amounts shown in the Computus as spent on printing in various periods of time averaged yearly:

Years	£
1703–10	307
1711–20	114
1721–30	217
1731–40	109
1741–50	136
1751–5	117

No allowance was made for depreciation of plant or stock. Peculations of the Warehouse-Keeper and workmen amounted to some £3 a year at least.

The balances are warrant enough for saying that the Press from the time of Charlett's death in 1722 was treated as a source of revenue to the University. That was the opposite of what Laud and Fell had intended. At their instance Convocation voted three sources of income for the support of a learned press, that is to say, the rent received from the Stationers for the Bible Press and forbearance to print 'scheduled books' (1662), the surplus of Sheldon's endowment for the repair of the Theatre (1669), and the Schools money (1660).[1] These revenues, amounting to £400 or more in a year, ceased after Fell's time to be paid to the Press. If income is balanced against expenditure, from the Delegates' assumption of management in 1690 until Blackstone's reform was given effect in 1758 the cost of the Press to the University never came to as much as £200 in a year.

The Press was not only starved but milked. Only the Heads of Houses, who were also the Delegates of Accounts, knew that this was so or what became of the money drawn off from the Press or that should have been

[1] *Print and Privilege*, pp. 16–17.

spent on it. Nobody else had access to the Vice-Chancellor's Computus or to the Warehouse-Keeper's Account for Printing.[1] No doubt these worthies had rather 'drive a little peddling trade, with a small but certain gain', as Blackstone said,[2] than risk such losses as the Press had made under more daring leadership by publishing works that were useful but not vendible. Besides that, amounts received by the Vice-Chancellor from booksellers for licence to print the University's copies[3] were not allocated to publishing.

In case it were contended that the Press ought to pay contributions towards amortizing a debt on the new Printing House to which it moved in 1713, it should be made clear that in the financial year 1714–15 printing paid £4,617 of the amount of £6,185 that the building had cost up to that date. A fine of £2,000 extracted from Baskett for his lease of the Bible Press and £974 that he paid 'on another account' (probably for the printing of his editions of Clarendon's *History* and for the *Almanack*), Hudson's purchase of the stock, and other profits of printing made up the Press's share. Some £1,200 paid to Townesend, the mason, and Minn, the joiner, during the next ten years may have been for work on the Printing House. At all events, that building was as much an ornament to the University's precinct as a workshop. The leaden figures on the parapets[4] and the statue of Clarendon for which Mr. Bird was paid £55 in 1721 were rightly debited to the University's general account.[5]

The Account for Printing

The Warehouse-Keeper's Account for Printing rendered to the Vice-Chancellor at Michaelmas for the previous twelve months was essentially a balance struck between those two officers. Neither was concerned to throw light on the solvency of the Learned Press either by showing how much it spent or declaring the value of its assets. The Warehouse-Keeper confined himself to defining the Vice-Chancellor's debt to him or his to the Vice-Chancellor.

The series of these Press accounts, written in folio-sized volumes, is kept in the Delegates' archives. The three books extend from 1690 to 1780. The year's accounts were written by a scrivener, once in these folio

---

[1] Blackstone, *To the Reverend Doctor Randolph*, p. 21.   [2] Ibid.

[3] See below, p. 306.

[4] Hearne, vi, p. 106.

[5] The figures in this paragraph are taken from the Computus of the Vice-Chancellor, 1697–1735 (Univ. Arch. W.P. β 21b).

books and again in quarto leaflets which were given to the Vice-Chancellor. The Vice-Chancellor's quartos, being his personal property, have generally not been kept: one, for the year 1735–6, has found its way to the Printer's archives.

The Delegates of the Press were bound by statute to approve the year's account and pass it to the Vice-Chancellor in time for him to use it in preparing his annual Computus for submission to the Delegates of Accounts at the end of his term of office in November.[1] In the eighteenth century all he did with it was enter in the Computus sums that he paid to the Warehouse-Keeper or received from him.

In the Computus there are many items relating to printing that the Vice-Chancellor had paid for and that do not appear in the Warehouse-Keeper's accounts: purchase of paper, artist's and engraver's work on the *Almanack*, new founts of type, structural work at the Printing House. There are also receipts from sales of books and hire of rights in copy. A conscientious inquirer into the affairs of the Press must look at both books.

Blackstone in 1755–8 was an extremely conscientious inquirer, and he was not content with the Warehouse-Keeper's book, which was all that as Delegate of the Press he was allowed to see. Believing that the Computus was in the University Archives, as it ought to have been, he applied to the Keeper of the Archives, Francis Wise, and got the following reply.

[n.d., but in July 1758.] Thursday. Sir, I will be ready to meet you at the Archives between six and seven on Saturday morning. But I am afraid you will not meet with the satisfaction you expect. The Vicechancellor's accounts were formerly wrote on Parchment Rolls and laid up in the Archives, but that practice has been discontinued many years. The accounts are now kept in books, and the Press accounts, I believe, separate. These have of late years been kept a mystery, only to be seen by the Delegates, and I believe are lodged in the Vicechancellor's Black Trunk, which is a sort of private Archives.[2]

The other Delegates, given their dual capacity, had less to complain of on this score; nevertheless from an early time their Orders complain a good deal at the insufficient information given them by the Warehouse-Keeper. Stephen Richardson, chosen for the post in 1712, had no head for book-keeping. Thistlethwaite, the last effective Architypographus,

[1] See p. 140 above.   [2] Bodl. MS. Top. Oxon. d. 387, fol. 40.

kept the books until he died in 1715; then Richardson did so for three years, but in 1718 he broke down. A peremptory order from the board in April 1721 to present his accounts within a month failed to move him, and it was only a threat of dismissal in November two years later that extracted from him an account for the years 1718–23.

Richardson needed reminders. He was told in 1717 to declare what paper he had received and what he did with it; also to declare his receipts from books for which he was paid the University's poundage when he printed for authors and booksellers. In 1724 he promised not to forget this, but when he died in 1756 it became apparent by one means or another that he had not entered in the accounts the poundage received for small books, sermons mostly. The amount due for a sermon was 3s. or 5s., and the Press had been printing about six a year; in an average year the number of small books not accounted for would be about ten. Daniel Prince, the overseer appointed in 1758 to succeed Richardson, used to enter all such small receipts and an annual expense of £4 or more on 'Workmen's and Overseer's allowance for books printed and paper bought for the University'. It is a fair inference that this allowance was a composition extinguishing the employees' claim to perquisites and gratuities. Richardson's son-in-law, Wood, left in temporary charge of the Press, was ordered by the Delegates to produce 'an Account of such Books as have been printed at the University Press for three years past and not brought to account'.[1] When, after a long delay, the list was submitted it named 34 sermons printed in 1755–7 that had not appeared in the accounts for those years. The poundage on them came to £12. 1s. 10½d.

By 1730 the Warehouse-Keeper's accounts had settled into a routine, the items differing little from one year to the next: 1. receipt of poundage, 2. outlay on repairs, rent, jobbing work, and petty cash, 3. balance of expenditure and receipts for the annual *Almanack*, 4. charges for printing Delegates' books, if any were done during the year, 5. sales of Delegates' books, 6. a list of books in stock, 7. paper left in the warehouse, 8. balance of receipts and expenditure.

Salaries are absent from the accounts, for there were none. Compositors, pressmen, and, sometimes, correctors got their pay from the charge for printing, always reckoned 'per sheet' (the single exception was a payment of £4 a year to a favoured compositor for 'looking after the Letter', i.e. type). The Warehouse-Keeper drew his legitimate emoluments from the

[1] D.O. 9 Feb. 1758; Philip, p. 92.

charge on every sheet for 'necessaries'. They are defined at the end of the Accounts, 1709–47, thus:

Ordinary Necessaries Incidental to Printing.

Fire, Candle, and Ink	Lye-Brushes
Wool	Lye
Balls	Past
Ball-stockes	Postage of Letters and Parcells
Nails	Gathering, Collating, and Drying of Books
Parchment	Packing, Cordage, Packing paper, and spunge.
Blankettes	

Charges for maintenance of unspecified nature are found in both accounts, the Vice-Chancellor's and the Warehouse-Keeper's. The joiner's bills were large enough to cover repairs and small additions to plant such as cases, frames, and wooden furniture, but never enough for a new press. The blacksmith and the turner were constantly called in to mend the rolling presses for printing copperplate.

Typefounders' bills, also, were carried on both accounts. The Vice-Chancellor's Computus for 1732–3 is the last to record a payment to (Sylvester) Andrews, the man who had carried on his trade in the Clarendon Printing House. He sold his equipment in 1733,[1] and thereafter the Press was dependent on the founders in London or remoter places for more than a hundred years. An entry for the cost of 'Carriage of a Box of Letter from Mr. Caslon' in 1736–7 is the earliest sign of dealings with the eminent artist, William Caslon, whose types gradually superseded those of Fell's bequest in Oxford books during the next twenty years.[2] The commission given him in 1736–7 was presumably to cast in matrices belonging to the University, for type of Caslon's own design is not found here until later; in fact it was the resolve of the Delegates in 1742 to print a 'beautiful' edition of Shakespeare that involved them in buying a fount of Caslon's Roman and Italic. They bought more, including several sizes of his Hebrew in 1743–4; and the Advertisement of 1744 for Forster's Hebrew Bible, published in 1750, announced that it would be set 'in a new letter provided by the University'. Arabic type 'by the famous Mr. Caslon' was lent by the Society for Promoting Christian Knowledge for Thomas Hunt's Abdollatiphus, which, however, got no further than a prospectus issued in 1746.

[1] E. Rowe Mores, *Dissertation upon English Typographical Founders*, p. 49, regrettably misprinted '1723' in the edition by Carter and Ricks (Oxford, 1961), p. 48.
[2] The dates of acquisition of various founts are given by J. S. G. Simmons, 'The Undated Oxford Broadsheet Specimen', *The Library*, 5th ser. xi (1956), at p. 16.

CHAPTER XVII

The Printing of Oxford Opinion

> Sermons are mere drugs. The trade is so vastly stocked with
> them, that really, unless they come out with the name of
> Whitefield, or Wesley, or some other such great man as a
> bishop, or those sort of people, I don't care to touch; unless
> now it was a sermon preached on the 30th of January; or we
> could say in the title-page, published at the earnest request of
> the congregation, or the inhabitants; but truly, for a dry piece
> of sermons, I had rather be excused; especially as my hands are
> so full at present. (*Joseph Andrews*, Book i, ch. xvii [1742].)

SERMONS AND RELIGIOUS CONTROVERSY

SAMUEL JOHNSON reminds us (and perhaps we need to be reminded
now) that 'Sermons make a considerable branch of English literature; so
that a library must be very imperfect if it have not a numerous collection
of them.'[1] The Delegates at Oxford did nothing to furnish libraries in this
respect beyond allowing the use of their presses to clergymen who were
anxious, or booksellers who were willing, to publish work of this kind.
In the period 1690–1800 sermons were a large part of the output of the
Press: an unprofitable part, but it must at times have saved the workmen
from having nothing to do.

It was known that Leonard Lichfield, the printer in the High Street,
could produce sermons rather more cheaply than the University. In 1725
he charged 26s. a sheet for about 4,000 in 8vo 'with abundance of notes'.[2]
Lichfield printed a great many, but still it is evident that a significant
number of the clergy valued the Sheldonian imprint and paid the higher
price. A printed sermon might be a qualification for a doctorate in
divinity and a step towards a chaplaincy or a benefice. The University's
imprint would recommend it.

Lichfield's press was less intimately connected with the University
than the other, and it may have taken some time to live down the odium
of printing the scandalous *Naked Gospel* in 1690; in any case there is
reason to think that sermons of dubious orthodoxy or tending to make
trouble would go to him. He printed seven sermons by Sacheverell to the
University's one, and William Tilly's assize sermon of 1705, which

---

[1] Boswell, iv, p. 105.   [2] Hearne, ix, p. 37.

displeased the judges by reflecting on the government,[1] came from Lichfield too.

It should be borne in mind in estimating the importance of printed sermons in the eighteenth century that they were almost the only cheap literature—the serious man's alternative to ballads and chap-books. Single ones were priced at 4*d*. or 6*d*. As an influence on opinion the pulpit had the advantage over the periodical press of not attracting stamp duty. It was probably the prospect of much more severe taxes on paper that caused sermons to change from 4to to 8vo format about 1710. Nearly all ran to more than 16 pages, or one sheet, therefore they escaped the duty on pamphlets.

The resident members of Oxford University in the earlier part of the eighteenth century spent a great deal of time composing, delivering, repeating, and (like the generality of men) hearing, reading, and discussing sermons. Anyone who had patience enough to read these compositions now, with an adequate knowledge of the circumstances, would become an authority worth reading on the character of the place at that time. The dons were exasperated by the Hanoverian succession to the throne, but might not say so in the pulpit; they were exasperated by the adaptation of the Church to the succession, and said so. In a word they were obsessed by the Bangorian Controversy. So much is easy to find out from a cursory inspection of this branch of Oxford printing.

The University kept a check on printed theology. Thus, the Vice-Chancellor and Heads of Houses issued a notice in 1695 disapproving a sermon preached at St. Peter's in the East;[2] in 1710 Charlett would not allow a sermon by William Tilly to be sold with the imprint of the University because it was critical of the government's choice of clergy for preferment, and it had to be issued with a new title-page falsely asserting that it had been printed in London.[3] A sermon by Peter Maurice of 1719 was judged to have offended the Article about the 'unworthiness of the minister', and he was required to recant and submit. He had his discourse printed in London.[4] George Stubbs after preaching to the University in 1722 in favour of a search after truth in religion did not (he was of Exeter College) receive the customary request from the Vice-Chancellor to publish. His sermon appeared with a London imprint, prefaced by a sarcastic letter to the Vice-Chancellor.[5]

[1] Hearne, i, p. 12.   [2] B.M. 714. i. 8(65).   [3] B.M. 225. h. 12(17).
[4] *The true causes of the contempt of Christian ministers*. . . . *With a preface in vindication*; Hearne, vi, pp. 262, 263, 294.
[5] Bodl. 100 aa. 12(6). The preface gives the facts.

The relevance of these eighteenth-century Oxford sermons to the history of the Press is in their witness to an unproductive frame of mind. A hidebound theology has much to do with the decline of the University, in publishing as in other things. But for that, the sermons were best forgotten. If publishing almost ceased and the Vice-Chancellor and Heads of Houses were *ex officio* Delegates of the Press in the years 1710–48, and the Delegates kept no minutes in 1732–42, it was largely because Oxford had nothing new to say and did not like anything new to be said.

The contrast is remarkable between the easy-going neglect of secular duties by the Oxford dons of this time and their fervid campaigning against innovation in religion or the Church. On the text from Jeremiah, 'Ask for the old paths, where is the good way, and walk therein', William Tilly in 1710 spoke for them all, and his sermon ran into four editions in twelve months. Lecky did not fail to observe that 'Every great step which has been made by the English intellect, in connexion with theology, has been made in spite of the earnest and persistent opposition of the University of Oxford.'[1]

Preaching was directed against the use of reason in approaching sacred mysteries, whether by infidels and scorners or avowed Christians. Locke's notion of human personality and his doubts about the resurrection of the earthly body were confuted to the satisfaction of the preachers.[2] Whiston's attempt at reconciling the Book of Genesis with Newton's laws was attacked.[3] The more adventurous brethren from Cambridge, Thomas Burnett, Whiston, Hoadly, Thomas Bennet, Samuel Clarke were anathematized—and inevitably Woolston, the denier of miracles. Philip Stubbs in 1729 denounced Woolston from the pulpit as a favourite of Satan and much else.[4] Thomas Newlin's sermon to the judges of assize of that year was partly a covert plea for the renewal of Woolston's prosecution for blasphemy. These discourses are not edifying, not aimed as Johnson thought they should be, at making the hearers 'drink the cup of salvation to the bottom'.[5]

Clergy at Oxford preached to the clergy. Their tendency was didactic, not persuasive, 'more like essays', Hearne thought.[6] The preachers seem intent on keeping intruders out of their City of God rather than enticing anyone into it. If clerics of a more generous mind—Smalridge was one of

[1] *Rise and Influence of Rationalism in Europe*, ed. of 1910, p. 158.
[2] Holdsworth, 1720; Felton, 1725. (See in the Appendix.)
[3] Dodwell, 1743; Hind, 1717; Parker, 1713.   [4] *Further advice to the Clergy*.
[5] *A Johnsonian Miscellany*, ed. Birkbeck Hill (1897), ii, p. 429.
[6] Hearne, xi, p. 455.

a few, and those who praised music as conducive to religion—brought their sermons to the Press, they were rarely sermons delivered here. Whatever one may think of Mark Pattison's view that this was 'an age destitute of depth or earnestness, an age whose poetry was without romance, whose philosophy was without insight',[1] the work of the Press affirms the justice of his remark that 'Every one who had anything to say on sacred subjects drilled it into an array of argument against a supposed objector.'[2]

Preaching at Oxford was heard gratefully if it exalted the priestly calling or confined it to the Anglican ordained. One preacher cites the example of Uzza, who was not a Levite but dared to put his hand on the Ark to save it from falling. Uzza was preternaturally struck down.[3] Exclusion of Presbyterian ministers from the benefit of genuine ordination was the theme of numerous pamphlets and several sermons.[4] The University was to a great extent a society for protecting the rights of the beneficed clergy.

A claim, going beyond this, that a degree from a university was necessary for ecclesiastical preferment was rebuffed in 1719, when the Archbishop of Canterbury conferred a B.D. on Samuel Peploe to qualify him for the wardenship of Manchester Collegiate Church and the Court of King's Bench held that it was a sufficient qualification. *The Bishop of Chester's Case* for refusing to appoint Peploe was published by the Delegates in an edition of 3,100, ornamented with copper-engravings and selling for 6d. That was to overestimate popular interest in the matter: after seven years the London booksellers returned 1,500 to the Press, where they remained until, in 1748, the Vice-Chancellor ordered them to be wasted.

For much of the reign of Queen Anne and all that of George I Oxford, the focus of Non-Juring and Jacobitism, was in opposition to the government. The feeling that it was exiled from favour and denied its fair share of patronage declared itself in exasperated sermons. *Honesty and plain dealing an usual bar to honour and preferment* was printed three times in 1710. Charlett's attempt to suppress William Tilly's sermon in that year and his refusal of the Oxford imprint to Thwaites's *Heptateuch* in 1699 were prompted by a fear that reflections in them might impair such interest as Oxford had at court. It was a sad day for the University when its solemn decree of 1683 that non-resistance to the sovereign was a Christian

---

[1] *Pattison's Essays*, ed. Nettleship (1889), ii, p. 42.　　　　[2] Ibid., p. 48.
[3] Joseph Betty, *The divine institution of the ministry* (Oxford, Lichfield, 1729).
[4] Sermons by Newlin, 1718, Coker, 1720.

obligation was burnt by the common hangman at the bidding of the House of Lords in 1710.[1]

The currents of politics run through the sermons. When a Whig ministry was formed in 1706 fear that concessions would be made to the Dissenters caused a spate of pamphlets directed against these people's pretentions; and when the first Earl Stanhope, who was known to favour repeal of the Test and Corporation Acts, became First Lord of the Treasury in 1717 there was a fresh outburst of preaching and writing against the 'false prophets'. It was a mood of sullenness and jealousy that to a great extent cut Oxford off from the spirit of inquiry and the increasing tolerance of that time. Newman explained the decline of the University by his observation that the old Oxford Toryism 'had in it no principle or power of developement'.[2]

POLITICS IN PRINT

To find Oxford at its most animated in this early eighteenth century it is necessary to turn to party politics.

There was a nice irony about Charlett's programmas of 1715 warning Jacobite rioters of the serious displeasure of the University authorities. One issued on 4 June begins, 'Whereas on Saturday and Sunday last, late at night, a multitude of persons, to us unknown, did in a tumultuous and riotous manner, of which we had never seen an example in this place, assemble together in the publick streets . . .'; and on 25 July he writes, 'Whereas Monday the first of August next, is appointed for a day of public thanksgiving for His Majesty's happy accession to the Throne; least so just an occasion of rejoycing should be turn'd into excess and tumult . . . [he warned] all persons whatsoever to avoid all odious and contumelious words of reproach and distinction which may tend to create discords and animositys'.

Unequivocally Jacobite expressions are hard to find in Oxford printing, it being the constant preoccupation of the Heads of Houses to keep them out. The attitude of the Heads of Houses towards the new king was unexceptionable. At a meeting on 16 March 1716/17 they ordered:

That thanks be given to Mr. Dod for his Assize Sermon preached before the Judges on Thursday the 14th of this instant March where in he

---

[1] H. of L. Journals, 19, p. 122. The decree had been reprinted in *An entire confutation of Mr. Hoadly's book of the Original of Government* (London, 1710), which the Lords also consigned to the flames.

[2] *Apologia pro vita sua* (1865 ed., p. 291).

expressed so just a zeal and indignation against the groundless and uncharitable imputation of Schism charged against the whole body of the Church of England by those, who have unwarrantably separated from our Communion, and have by their principles and practises plainly discovered a seditious disposition to subvert our present happy Establishment in Church and State, and to alienate the affections of the people from his most sacred Majesty King George and the Protestant succession in the Royal Family.

And that Mr Dod be desired to print the same.[1]

George Coningsby's sermon of 1727, in which he praised King Charles the Martyr as 'a Prince that was not alien by Birth, and that he preferred to Dignities in the Church men of true worth and Learning',[2] was not printed, and Coningsby was censured by the Heads and forbidden to preach in the precincts for two years. The accession of George II was greeted by verses of the usual warmth and loyalty, and Philip Stubbs, a high churchman, disgusted Hearne by preaching a year later on the happiness of the event.[3]

Nor did the Rebellion of 1745 leave much trace in our publishing. Sermons delivered here while the Pretender's army was not far away, by Francis Potter and John Free, could not have been more severe on the rebels and the Church of Rome; but they were printed in London. Edward Bentham, a prominent Whig, urged his countrymen in Latin to come to the rescue of the state and reprinted Cicero's praises of some who had done so.[4] John Burton, fellow of Eton, formerly of Corpus Christi, the chief apologist of Whiggery at Oxford, was chosen to preach to the University on the day of public thanksgiving for the defeat of the insurgents.

Latent Jacobitism was brought to the surface in 1748 by the riotous behaviour of some students after a private dinner-party shouting defiance of the house of Hanover in the streets and insulting a don, Richard Blacow, who tried to disperse them. Blacow failed to persuade the Vice-Chancellor to act and brought the matter to the attention of the Ministry. Three of the culprits were brought to justice and given severe sentences.[5] An order by the Vice-Chancellor enforcing a rule that undergraduates

---

[1] At the tail end of the first Minute Book of the Delegates of the Press.

[2] Hearne, ix, p. 266; Hist. MSS. Comm., *Portland*, vii, p. 455.

[3] Hearne, x, p. 101.

[4] *Associatio Ciceroniana, sive cohortatio ad rempub. tuendam* (Oxford, 1745); *M. T. Ciceronis sententiae duae de iis honore augendis, qui periculum vitae adierunt reipub. causa* (Oxford, 1746).

[5] Bodl. MS. Top. Oxon. e. 145(7–8).

must dine in college halls and a sermon by John Tottie condemning intemperance referred to this unhappy episode.

In this year, 1748, exasperated feelings in the two parties found vent in pamphlets. The Tory champion, William King, Principal of St. Mary Hall, was accused of instilling sedition in youthful minds by Edward Bentham in *A letter to a young gentleman by a tutor*, printed at the Press. King replied with *A proposal to publish a poetical translation both in Latin and English of Mr. Tutor Bentham's letter* and *A poetical abridgement* of the letter in 1749, both printed in London. When Burton came to the aid of his former pupil by addressing King in two open letters, *altera peregrinantis, altera rusticantis*, King answered him in *Carmen rhythmicum, monachicum, Momo dicatum, a rusticante Oxon.* (London, 1749).

Only King's close friendship with the University's Chancellor, Lord Arran, could explain his being trusted to deliver one of the two orations at the opening of the Radcliffe Library in 1749. He made the most of the opportunity for mischief. In elegant Latin and by skilful innuendo he longed for the return of the house of Stuart and affronted the reigning monarch, the Ministry, and the arch-informer, Richard Blacow. His peroration was a series of pleas beginning with *redeat* for a return of the impersonation of goodness and truth, and culminated in words to this effect:

May he come back, the great genius of Britain [*Redeat magnus ille genius Britanniae*], whether he be the messenger or the very spirit of God, the firmest guard of liberty and religion; and let him banish into exile, into perpetual exile, from among our countrymen all barbarous wars, slaughters, rapines, years of pestilence, haughty usurpations, infamous informers, and every evil! May he come back and prosper, that the common weal may revive, faith be recalled, peace be established, laws ordained—just, honest, useful, salutary laws, to deter the abandoned, restrain armies, favour the learned, spare the imprudent, delight all!

The Ministry wisely disregarded the speech. Burton had his *Remarks on Dr. K's speech* printed in London, and King extracted the opprobrious epithets from them and had them printed in an ornamental frame as *An answer to dr. King's speech: by the Rev. Mr. John Burton*, a broadside twice printed at Oxford in 1750 (but not at the University Press). King treated the imprints of his squibs with as much levity as the subject-matter, so that it is hard to tell the place of printing of *Elogium famae inserviens Jacci Etonensis* (Oxford, 1750) or *The old lady in her tantarums* (Eton, 1750). By

1755 he was allowed the use of the University Press, and it produced his *Doctor King's apology, or vindication of himself from the several matters charged on him by the Society of Informers.*[1]

[1] For the biography of the 'Old Trumpeter' and a list of his writings see David Greenwood, *William King, Tory and Jacobite* (Oxford, 1959).

CHAPTER XVIII

The Books 1713–1755

Menelaus on Spherics

THE Delegates were charged in 1713–14 with the cost of setting and printing Menelaus and 'cutting schemes' (making woodcuts for the diagrams).[1]

This was a step towards accomplishing a programme for publishing the ancient Greek mathematicians announced by Fell in 1672 and pursued by Edward Bernard.[2] Euclid had been done by Gregory and Hudson in 1703, Theodosius on spherics by Costard in 1707, Apollonius and Serenus on conics by Halley in 1710. Halley undertook to edit Menelaus for the Delegates in 1714.[3]

Menelaus of Alexandria, who flourished about A.D. 100, wrote on spherical trigonometry. The Greek original is lost and extant manuscripts derive from an Arabic translation made in the ninth century. The Arabic was soon translated into Hebrew. The Bodleian has two manuscripts in Arabic, two in Hebrew, and one in Greek.

Halley made a Latin translation of Menelaus, and it was printed in 1713–14 as pages 7–70 of a book. He provided no preliminary matter, and the printed sheets containing only the text were kept for many years in the Delegates' stock. From 1750 onwards some sets of the sheets were sold: the British Museum and the Bodleian have copies of the book in its imperfect and unpublished state.

At length, in 1758, the Delegates 'agreed that the copies of Menelaus now lying in the University Warehouse be forthwith published, and that Mr. Costard be desir'd to prepare it for Publication'.[4]

George Costard could only provide a title-page and preface enough to precede the printed page 7; and for that the Delegates paid him a guinea. He was an Arabist and a mathematician, and in the preface he is informative about the transmission of the texts. As for the sources from which

---

[1] 2nd Accounts, p. 40. [2] See above, pp. 63, 240.
[3] D.O. 20 Apr. 1711; *First Minute Book*, p. 33.
[4] D.O. 1 Mar. 1758; Philip, p. 94.

Halley worked he knew nothing; he could only point to some footnotes in the printed text where Halley refers to manuscripts in Hebrew and Arabic. Costard guessed that one of Robert Huntington's Hebrew manuscripts in the Bodleian was the original that Halley translated.[1] How the great astronomer, who knew neither Hebrew nor Arabic, extracted a text from the manuscripts (perhaps aided by earlier printed editions) is more than Costard could tell, and he alludes cryptically to difficulties which prevented Halley from rounding off his task with a preface. Halley was made Secretary to the Royal Society in 1713.

The preliminary pages were printed and the book was published in 1758. The quantity was probably 250; for in that year 16 were sold, at 1s. 2d., leaving a stock of 220. In 1799 the number of unsold copies was 188.

The Coptic Gospels, 1716

A proposal to print the Gospels in Coptic was part of Fell's programme drawn up in 1672.[2] They were to be edited and translated into Latin by Thomas Marshall, the Rector of Lincoln College, basing himself on 'a copy of venerable antiquity in his hands'.[3] The project got as far as a specimen page[4] set in a Coptic type made to Fell's order, doubtless for this book.[5]

Marshall died in 1685 leaving the work unfinished, and he left three manuscripts containing the Coptic New Testament, or parts of it, to the Bodleian Library. Another two, which had been the property of Robert Huntington, were acquired by the Library in 1693.[6]

The Coptic version of the Gospels had not been printed. Publishing in that language was confined to a vocabulary and a list of manuscripts compiled by the Jesuit, Athanasius Kircher, issued at Rome in 1636, and a psalter edited by Theodore Petraeus, printed in Greek letters at Leyden in 1663.[7]

Having the manuscripts and the type, Oxford wanted only an editor. Fell engaged Thomas Edwards, a Cambridge orientalist, to carry on

---

[1] Bodl. MS. Huntington Or. 96; see A. A. Björnbo, 'Studien über Menelaus' Sphärik Beiträge zur Geschichte der Sphärik und Trigonometrie der Griechen', *Abhandlung zur Geschichte der Mathematischen Wissenschaften*, xiv (Leipzig, 1902), pp. 1–154, at pp. 17–18.

[2] Above p. 63.

[3] He bought one at Amsterdam in 1668: B.M. MS. Add. 22905, fol. 85.

[4] B.M. Harl. 5929, No. 108.   [5] Morison, *Fell*, pp. 158–61.

[6] Bodl. *Catalogue of Oriental MSS.* (Uri), i, Cod. Copt. xiii; Macray, *Annals*, pp. 154, 161

[7] A. Rahlfs in *Nachrichten von der Kön. Ges. der Wissenschaften zu Göttingen, Philol.-Hist. Klasse*, Jrg. 1917 (Berlin, 1918) at p. 294; Nichols, *Lit. An.* ix, pp. 11–12.

Marshall's work,[1] but he failed to do so. Meanwhile, the type was used for a poem of four lines by Edward Bernard in the University's *Pietas* of 1695 for the death of Queen Mary II and, for a London publisher, in a polyglot Lord's Prayer of 1700.

The Delegates agreed in August 1715 to publish an edition of the Gospels edited by David Wilkins, and 500 copies were put in hand at the University's expense.[2] Wilkins, born at Memel of German parents in 1685, had travelled about Europe acquiring at various universities some knowledge of Arabic and the dead languages of the Middle East. Archbishop Wake made him librarian at Lambeth Palace in 1715.[3]

At Amsterdam in November 1714 Wilkins was negotiating with a Dutch firm for the publication of the Gospels in Coptic,[4] and the Bodleian has a prospectus for the edition dated there in the following year with a specimen set in Coptic type.[5] Perhaps he changed his plans when he learned that Oxford had Coptic type too, as well as the best manuscript.

This manuscript, one of Huntington's, was the basis for Wilkins's edition published by the Delegates in 1716, and he collated it with the four others at the Bodleian, two at the Vatican, and two in Paris.[6] Given the state of knowledge of the language, which even Egyptian Christians could not understand, and the almost total want of apparatus for learning it, it is easy to believe that Wilkins's performance was defective both in the transcription and in the translation into Latin.[7] Nevertheless, it was useful as a starting-point for later scholars.[8]

The book was hard to sell. The first hundred had gone by 1760, and the Delegates never gave up hope of disposing of the rest. The last remaining copy was sold in 1907.[9]

In a letter dated 26 March 1686 Nicholas Witsen, burgomaster of Amsterdam, reminds Edward Bernard of a Coptic dictionary which Witsen had given him for publication and asks what had become of it. He also offers to send to Oxford about a hundred punches for a Coptic type (Bodl. MS. Smith 8, fol. 37). Only one set of punches for Coptic is

---

[1] *D.N.B.* art. Edwards, Thomas, 1652–1721.

[2] D.O. 17 Aug.; *First Minute Book*, p. 44.   [3] *D.N.B.*

[4] M. V. Lacroze, *Thesaurus epistolicus* (Leipzig, 1742–6), i, p. 372.

[5] I do not know what led to the making of this type. It is shown in a specimen by the Widow and Son of Dirk Voskens, typefounders of Amsterdam, which must have been printed not long before or after 1700 (in Leyden Univ. Library).

[6] According to Wilkins's Prolegomena; see the Introduction to G. W. Horner's *Coptic Version of the New Testament in the Northern Dialect* (Oxford, 1898–1905).

[7] Lacroze, *Thesaurus*, i, p. 173; iii, pp. 154–5, 159, 161.

[8] E. Quatremère, *Recherches sur la langue et la littérature de l'Égypte* (Paris, 1808), pp. 80–2.

[9] *The Periodical* (of the Oxford Univ. Press), May, 1907, p. 128.

recorded in the schedules of equipment at the Press and only one remains there. That was evidently cut by Peter de Walpergen, Fell's typefounder, and it is the face used for Wilkins's edition of the Gospels. Since that type was almost certainly in existence before 1686, it is likely that Bernard declined Witsen's offer and his biographer's statement that Witsen gave Oxford University the punches for Coptic is incorrect.[1]

Plato's Parmenides, 1728

At their meeting of 14 March 1726 the Delegates agreed 'to print some part of Plato called [blank] . . . the Gentleman Mr. [blank] that undertakes to bring the book to the Press desiring nothing for his pains'.[2]

Thus authorized, *Parmenides* edited by John William Thomson issued from the Press in 1728. The author, a member of St. Edmund Hall, aged 25, was, however improbably, born at Königsberg, *gente Borussus*. He came to Oxford in 1722 and left without taking a degree here. John Burton, highly appreciating Thomson's command of Greek (not common then at Oxford),[3] urged him to edit the dialogue.[4]

The editor did no work on the text, and the Latin version is of Marcello Ficino in the sixteenth century. Thomson contributed footnotes and a substantial preface showing that his interest in the dialogue was theological.

The price was 1s. 4d. Five hundred were printed, of which 401 were in stock in 1755 and 245 in 1804.

The Bodleian Catalogue of Printed Books, 1738

The Delegates of the Press, meeting on 29 February 1716, agreed that '1000 Catalogues of the Library with references according to the Specimen produced be printed at the University charge'.[5] Noting this, Hearne[6] tells us that a great deal of the work in the collected material was done by him. This was to be the fourth of the printed catalogues of the books in the Bodleian, the third having been issued in 1674, when Thomas Hyde was Librarian.

---

[1] Thomas Smith, *Vita . . . Edwardi Bernardi* (1704), p. 33.
[2] *First Minute Book*, p. 51.
[3] A. D. Godley, of the early eighteenth-century verses: 'Oxford of that day was fluent and fairly correct in Latin, but expressed itself seldom and for the most part abominably in Greek. This improved later: John Burton of Corpus Christi writes good Greek in the middle of the century': *Oxford in the Eighteenth Century* (1908), p. 232.
[4] *Epistola critica ad J. Gul. Thompson Graece conscripta* (Oxford, 1750).
[5] *First Minute Book*, p. 45.   [6] Hearne, vi, pp. 8–9.

Soon after his appointment as Janitor of the library in 1702, when 'a vast number of books were placed and never so much as catalogued', Hearne began correcting Hyde's edition. He went round comparing every book with the printed entry, correcting many mistakes and adding books that were not entered. That done, he 'consulted many books in order to recover anonymous authors', and 'retrieved' a good number. All these corrections and additions he wrote in an interleaved copy of the old catalogue.

Dr. Roger Mander, Vice-Chancellor in 1700-2 and made a Delegate of the Press in 1704, wanted an appendix to Hyde's catalogue to be printed, so Hearne copied his work in two folio volumes, and the Librarian, John Hudson, favoured reprinting the old volumes with Hearne's corrections and additions as an appendix. Hearne's work remained in manuscript and was kept for use in the library.[1]

Hudson died in 1719, and Joseph Bowles succeeded him. Bowles digested Hearne's supplement into the body of the work, and printing began in 1727.[2] The Accounts of the Press for 1727-8 charge the Delegates for composing and printing 84 sheets (256 pages). The quantity ordered at first was 300 on large paper and 2,000 on small; but when 19 sheets had been printed the number for the small copies was altered to 500. According to Hearne late in 1728, the Delegates ordered two compositors to be set to work on the book.[3]

In 1729 fifty sheets were printed, in 1730 twelve, in 1731 eighteen, in 1732 twenty, in 1733 twenty-four, in 1734 twenty-six, in 1735 twenty-four, in 1736 thirty, in 1737 forty, in 1738 seven.

The result was two folio volumes, the first of 611 pages, the second of 714. Of these pages Bowles completed the first 244 of Volume i and 292 of Volume ii. Robert Fysher, following Bowles as Librarian in 1729, finished the catalogue with the help of his friend Emmanuel Langford.

The slow progress of the book can hardly be blamed on the Press. Granting that there was type enough for only one sheet, fluctuation of the output indicates slowness of editing in most years.

It looks as though 40 sheets (160 pages of folio format) were a typical year's work while editing and correcting kept pace with printing. Twenty-seven pages were ornamented with copper-engravings, so had to be printed twice. The time taken in the press meant that the catalogue, when published, was ten years out of date.

Copies on large paper sold at 3 guineas and on small at £2. 5s. Fifty

---

[1] Ibid.   [2] Macray, *Annals*, pp. 212-13.   [3] Hearne, x, p. 75.

were presents, 75 were consigned to the London trade through Richard Gosling as wholesaler, four were sold by the Warehouse-Keeper in the first year. In 1746 633 were in stock. It is said that of 100 sent abroad 8 were sold there;[1] but the Press Accounts do not show a drop of this magnitude in the stock until 1762, rather late to think of foreign sales. The retail price was reduced in 1748 to 2 guineas and 30s., booksellers being charged 5s. less.

Finally, 442 copies, all but 20 of the stock, were disposed of as waste paper in 1785.

Of the merits of the work there can be few competent to judge. One of them, W. D. Macray, praised it highly for its 'remarkable accuracy and the abundance and minuteness of its cross-references'.[2] He attributed these praiseworthy qualities mainly to Hearne, who is given no credit in Fysher's preface.

Surely it was a pardonable mistake, if it was a mistake, of the Delegates to publish this book: an example of a public service ill-rewarded such as university presses have to risk.

Other Delegates' Books

A polemic by Jean Gagnier in defence of Conrad Kircher's concordance to the Septuagint was published by the Delegates in 1718 (*Vindiciae Kircherianae*). It was an attack on the criticisms of Abraham Trommius, then a very old man, and lacked moderation and good manners. Gagnier's severity should have been suspect, because Trommius had forestalled him in bringing out a revised edition of the concordance, a design which Gagnier had announced in proposals of 1715.[3] Of Gagnier's polemic 200 were printed, 77 were sold, 44 given to the author, and the remainder wasted in 1785.

Gassendi's *Logica*, of which 750 priced at 1s. 2d. were issued in pocketable format in 1718, was a commercial failure. There were more popular works on the subject. Of these the Delegates had printed Fell's *Grammatica rationis* the year before; but for some reason they did not put it on sale, and in 1721 they disposed of their impression of 1,000 to Peisley, the local bookseller. Aldrich's much-favoured *Artis logicae compendium* was printed at the Press for Peisley in 1723. It is strange that the University's copy in these two manuals was not exploited. The 519 copies of Gassendi's book left in 1785 went as waste paper.

---

[1] Macray, *Annals*, pp. 214–15 n.   [2] Macray, *Annals*, pp. 212–13.
[3] Hearne, vi, p. 253.

It is curious, considering how few books the Delegates published at this time, that they undertook *Census habitus nascente Christo* by John Reinolds in 1738. It is a learned, but too lengthy, investigation of the difficulty of reconciling St. Luke's statement at the beginning of Chapter ii with the facts ascertainable from other sources. Five hundred were printed and offered at 2*s.* 6*d.*; but in 1785 all but 20 of the stock of 413 were sold as waste.

Also pulped in 1785 were 467 copies of Dr. Courayer's speech in the Sheldonian Theatre. The 800 printed in 1733 were offered at 6*d.* or 32*s.* a hundred. Pierre-François Le Courayer was a canon of St. Geneviève at Paris. His defence of the validity of Anglican orders brought persecution on him. Oxford gave him an honorary D.D. in 1727, and in the following year he took refuge in this country, where he was received with acclaim by prelates and clergy. His speech of 1733 was an acknowledgement of the University's favour and a declaration of his respect for the Church of England, for all that he was a Roman Catholic.

This melancholy tale must reflect to some extent on the Delegates' flair for publishing, but much more it exposes their failure to win the help of booksellers. They did not offer enough discount or do anything else to encourage the London trade to interest itself in Oxford books.

The Gothic Gospels, 1750

The translation by Ulphilas of the Bible into the language of the Goths as it was in Moesia in the fourth century is preserved in a fragmentary state by the Codex Argenteus at Uppsala. It was first edited by Francis Junius the younger with the help of Thomas Marshall and printed for them at Dordrecht in 1665 in the Gothic type that Junius caused to be made and afterwards gave to the University of Oxford.

Being fragmentary and representing a Greek original too late to be of much textual interest, the Ulphilas Bible has a mainly linguistic value. Not more than half the Greek text of the Gospels is rendered by the existing Gothic version. Junius made great use of it in tracing the etymologies of English words, and when Edward Lye came to edit the unpublished work of Junius on that subject he found that the edition from Dordrecht contained obvious errors and learned that a better transcription and Latin translation were being made in Sweden. In his *Etymologicum Anglicanum* of 1743 Lye acknowledged help with the Gothic words from the Archbishop of Uppsala.

Eric Benzelius the younger, Archbishop for a year before he died in
1743, had been engaged for many years on an edition of the Codex with a
new Latin translation and notes.[1] On completing his studies at Uppsala in

[1]

❖❖❖❖❖❖❖❖❖❖❖❖❖❖❖❖❖❖❖❖❖❖❖❖❖❖❖❖❖❖❖❖❖❖❖❖

EVANGELIUM
SECUNDUM
MATTHÆUM.

· • • • • Superiora defunt. ΛΚ ΛΝΛ ΛΠΚΛΚΝΛ·STΛψΛN.   15.
ϬΛh ΛΙΠΓΕΙψ ΛΛΛΛΙΜ ψΛΙΜ ΪΝ ψΛΜΜΛ ΚΛΖΝΛ: SψΛ   16.
ΛΙΠhΤϬΛΙ ΛΙΠhΛψ ΪΖψΛΚ ΪΝ ΛΝΔψΛΙΚψϬΛ ΜΛΝΝϬ. ΕΙ
ΓΛSΛΙΟΛΙΝΛ ΪΖψΛΚΛ ΓϪΔΛ ψΛΝΚSΤψΛ. ϬΛh hΛΝh-
ϬΛΙΝΛ ΛΤΤΛΝ ΪΖψΛΚΛΝΛ ψΛΝΛ ΪΝ hΙΜΙΝΛΜ: ΝΙ hΠΓ-   17. ΛΓ·
ϬΛΙψ ΕΙ ΝΙ ΠΕΜϬΛΝ ΓΛΤΛΙΚΛΝ ψΙΤϪψ ΛΙψψΛΝ ΠΚΛΝ-

Sed fuper candelabrum (a) & lucet omnibus, qui in illa do-   Cap.5.v.15.
mo. Sic luceat lux veftra in confpectu hominum, ut videant ve-   16.
ftra bona opera & glorificent patrem veftrum, illum in cœlis.
Ne putate quod venerim (b) diffolvere legem aut prophetas, non   17.XXXIII.

(a) Sed fuper candelabrum ΛΚ ΛΝΛ ΛΠΚΛΚΝΛSTΛψΛΝ. Sic MS.
utrumque tamen recte fe habet; nam ΛΝΛ, & tertium & quartum cafum re-
git, ficut ixi eadem fignificatione apud Græcos.

(b) Diffolvere legem ΓΛΤΛΙΚΛΝ ψΙΤϪψ. Proprie foret difrumpere, di-
fcindere, deftruere legem, nam de templi deftructione utitur quoque Gothus nofter
hoc vocabulo Marci 14. 58. 15, 29. Prudentius, refolvere, fed metro id requi-
rente καθμιϛ. IX. 103. Poft, ut occafum refolvit. i. e. mortem deftruxit. Lati-
nius diceres abrogare legem, vel antiquare, vel etiam obrogare legi, i. e. legis in-
firmandæ cauffâ aliam ferre. Τῃ̈ ϰατιλύϛη opponitur hoc loco πληϱῶϛη i. e. βιϭαιῶ-
ϛη. Philo de LL. Spec. p. 805. c. ὑπομίϛϛη γὰρ διϛ' ἑτέϱϛη ὕπεϱ μηδεμίαϛ ἔχοϛϛη κοινωίαϛ,
ὰλλὰ τῖϛ ἤδλϛη ἀπϛϱτμϛϛϛη, κατωλύϛϛη ἡμαϛ ἰϛη, ἢ βιϭωϛϛϛη, nam id agere, ut qui pu-
niuntur, luant pœnas à delicto diverfas, atque nullatenus convenientes, non eft fta-
bilientis leges fed diffolventis.

A   (a) Ve-

A page of the Gospels in Gothic edited by Edward Lye and Eric Benzelius
in 1750. Reduced.

1702 he was made librarian of the university, and soon afterwards set
himself to producing a better edition of its most famous manuscript. He
wrote in later years that Junius had made little attempt to read the more

[1] The following is mainly extracted from an account of the history of the book which
Dr. Sten G. Lindberg, of the Royal Library, Stockholm, very kindly wrote for me, based on
the Swedish authorities and particularly on the Benzelius Correspondence in the Stifts-
bibliotek, Linköping (Corr.).

difficult passages and that his grasp of the grammar of the language was defective.[1]

In 1706 Benzelius distributed to his friends a woodcut facsimile of a page of the manuscript with a note of his proposed publication; but he knew that a complete facsimile by the means then available was not feasible,[2] and he must have meant to get type made in Sweden for the Gothic characters when he made an approach to King Charles XII in 1717 for patronage. The approach, made through a colleague, Olaus Rudbeck the younger, was favourably received, but the king was killed in the following year, and Benzelius gave up hope of publishing in Sweden.

He told J. A. Fabricius in 1720 of his intention to go to England to make arrangements for the edition.[3] He knew that the Gothic type made for Junius was at Oxford,[4] and he made inquiries to see whether similar type could be had in Holland or Germany. In the event the visit to England never took place; the appointment of Benzelius as bishop, first of Gothenburg in 1726 and then of Linköping in 1731, delayed the book. However, in 1732 the Swedish scholar Jacob Serenius, then in London, was corresponding with him about proposals to be issued there for an edition of the Ulphilas later in the year.[5]

It occurred to Benzelius that an English patron might be found to recommend the work, and he suggested to Serenius the Bishop of London, Edmund Gibson, or Sir Hans Sloane. Sloane was approached and proved willing; he told Benzelius that he had discussed the project with several members of the University of Oxford and all were well disposed. Oxford would do the printing, but a publisher must be found to bear the cost and collect subscriptions.

Benzelius sent his son on a foreign tour including England in 1738 and entrusted him with the material for a specimen to be given to Sloane and the offer of the complete copy as soon as a bookseller would consider publishing it.[6] Sloane suggested Edward Lye as the best person to supervise the impression at Oxford. Lye, he said, was engaged in editing the *Etymologicum* of Junius, but he was believed to be willing to act as husband to the Ulphilas.[7] After an interview with the young emissary Lye began writing to the Bishop in Sweden about the textual problems.[8]

---

[1] E. Benzelius, *Monumenta vetera ecclesiae Sveogothicae* (Upsala, 1709), p. xv; *Brefwäxling imellan ärke-biskop E. Benzelius och dess broder*, ed. J. H. Lidén (Linköping, 1791), p. 275; B.M. MS. Slo. 4055, fol. 322.   [2] *Brefwäxling*, p. 275.

[3] H. S. Reimar, *De vita et scriptis J. A. Fabricii* (Hamburg, 1737), pp. 222 ff.

[4] *Brefwäxling*, p. 7.   [5] Corr., xiii, Nos. 15 and 37.

[6] B.M. MS. Slo. 4055, fol. 322.   [7] Ibid.

[8] Corr. xvi and xvii, *passim*; answers from Benzelius in B.M. MS. Add. 32325.

At this point Wasenberg, the Swedish minister in London, intervened strongly advising Lord Carteret rather than Sloane as patron. Carteret while ambassador in Sweden had made the acquaintance of Benzelius; Sloane was sick and might die at any time.[1] Carteret succeeded through the good offices of the Archbishop of Canterbury, Potter, and the Bishop of Oxford, Secker, in persuading the Delegates at Oxford to undertake the book at the University's charge. Wasenberg wrote in April 1741 that the Delegates would not pay Benzelius a fee but would give him 20 or 30 copies of the book and were ready to start setting at once.[2]

The Delegates registered their formal consent to undertaking the expenses of production at a meeting in August 1743.[3]

During the summer of 1741 the complete work of Benzelius had reached Wasenberg, and by October was in the hands of Edward Lye, who writes to the Bishop, 'I was very sensibly pleas'd to find, that most of the Irregularities, which are to be met with in the Junius Edition, will be remov'd in that complete one of Bishop Benzelius.'[4] Benzelius replies in Latin vehemently insisting that Lye should favour him with his criticisms. Their friendly correspondence was ended by the death of Benzelius on 23 September 1743. The following letter from Lye dated 30 August cannot have reached the Archbishop:

I shou'd have long ere now acknowledg'd the favour of Your most obliging letter of the 31st of March, had I not waited for some certain account to give you in regard to the Gothic Gospels. I now tell you, that the University have agreed to print three hundred Copies upon a very fine Dutch paper. They do not propose to themselves any advantage by the impression: all they desire is, that they may be no losers. They are in hopes, that the North will take off a number of their Copies. The paper is provided, and I have deliver'd the 1st sheet to be compos'd, so that you may expect shortly that together with the Etymologicum, which is finish'd, I'll transmit to you the sheets, as they are work'd off for your revisal. As I live at a good distance from Oxford, there will of consequence be more time requir'd for finishing the work. However I will do my utmost to forward it by visiting the University sometimes, which, tho expensive, I shall do with pleasure, as knowing it will be agreeable to the Archbishop of Upsal. Tho I fall so very short of You in learning, I will presume to equal you in my wishes.[5]

---

[1] Corr. xvi, 104.
[2] Ibid. 121 and 125. Holmes, President of St. John's, undertook to bring the matter to the attention of the Delegacy: B.M. MS. Add. 32 325, fol. 64.
[3] *First Minute Book*, p. 54.
[4] Corr. xvi, 164.   [5] Corr. xvii, 165.

For reasons now impossible to divine the book was a further seven years in the press. Lye added notes of his own and a grammar of the Gothic language; the preface by Benzelius was found by his son and sent to Lye in 1744.[1] Three hundred copies, all on large paper, were issued in 1750 at the price of 15*s*. Lye was given 92. In 1800 there were 152 unsold, and by 1882 the stock was reduced to 3.[2]

Hanmer's Shakespear

By publishing Shakespeare's plays in 1744 the University made its first bow to English literature. The publication was a departure from the tradition of the Press and out of accord with the policy of the Delegates before or since, for it was an edition fit neither for scholars nor for school-boys. It was a luxurious edition fit only for bibliophiles.

The idea of a grandiose edition, outdoing Pope's in splendour with a text freed from the corruptions that Rowe, Pope, and Theobald had allowed to pass, improving on Shakespeare in the regularity of the metre, was Sir Thomas Hanmer's. He had made a considerable figure in politics as a Hanoverian Tory during the last years of Queen Anne, and had been Speaker for a short spell in 1714–15. After quitting public life in 1727 he 'made it the amusement of his leisure hours', as he says in his preface, 'for many years past to look over [Shakespeare's] writings with a careful eye'. His emendations and notes written in a copy of Pope's edition[3] served as copy for the Oxford printers.

In the work of establishing a text Hanmer had help from Warburton, the irascible Bishop of Gloucester, given in an exchange of letters and by word of mouth at Hanmer's country house. The letters[4] give the impression that neither faced soon enough the problem as to whose property the improved text would be and both were disingenuous in not admitting one to the other an intention to publish an edition of his own. By May 1739 Hanmer had asked two London booksellers, Gyles and Tonson, to estimate on the book and had their assurance that no bookseller would

---

[1] Letter from Carl Jesper Benzelius to Lord Carteret, 19 Oct. 1745: B.M. MS. Add. 43417, fol. 429; to Lye Add. 32325, fol. 66.

[2] *The Gospel of St. Mark in Gothic*, ed. W. W. Skeat (Oxford, 1882), p. xiii. In 'On writing and printing Gothic' (*Speculum* xv, Cambridge, Mass., 1940, pp. 313–30) Sidney Fairbanks and F. P. Magoun Jr. criticize the letters made for Junius. These authors were misinformed as to the existence of the Junius type: the punches, two sets of matrices, and a small fount are at the Press. By 1734 William Caslon was also offering Gothic. The two faces would be hard to tell apart.

[3] Bodl. Malone G. ii. 1–6.

[4] B.M. MS. Eg. 1957; Nichols, *Lit. An.* v, pp. 589–90.

undertake it in the form that Hanmer wanted. Gyles told Warburton of the inquiry, and so recrimination began. Warburton published his edition in 1747.

Hanmer's approach to the University of Oxford was by way of Joseph Smith, the Provost of Queen's. Before his election by the College in 1730 Smith had been a prominent London clergyman, and as Lecturer of St. George's, Hanover Square, is likely to have had Hanmer, who spent his winters in Grosvenor Street, in his congregation. Smith was not a Delegate, so he passed on the proposal to Robert Shippen, Principal of Brasenose, who sat on the board.

A letter from Hanmer to Smith of 18 March 1742[1] implies a call from the Delegates for fuller information. It was given as follows:

I have received the favour of your letter, by which you desire me to open a little the plan I would propose for a new impression of Shakespeare . . .

My aim in general is to promote a correct and a beautiful edition of his dramatic works, more worthy of the author than any of those which have hitherto been bestowed upon him. It must be in six volumes in quarto, in as large a letter at least as that published by Mr. Pope, but upon much better paper . . . I propose to have a good cut prefixed to every play, done by the very best designer and engraver; which copper plates are now under hand, and in pretty great forwardness: and these I design shall be at my expence. I will give them freely to the publick, that the book my be brought within the compass of a reasonable price, which I would not have exceed four pounds at the most: if it can be afforded cheaper, I shall be glad, nor do I desire more copies for myself than ten or twelve to give to my particular friends.

The principal point of all is to employ some gentleman of great care and exactness to be corrector of the press . . .

Hanmer expected that printing could begin the next winter.

Six months later there was indecision on the part of the Delegates to be overcome, and Hanmer writes again to Smith.

There seem to arise some difficulties with respect to the design of printing a new edition of Shakespeare, and I beg it may be laid aside, if you are not fully satisfied that some advantage may arise from it to the University . . .[2]

A fear of Warburton's malice may have influenced some of the Delegates; but the feeling that it was time the University did honour to

---

[1] *Biographia Britannica*, vi, p. 3743 (the 'cancelled leaf').
[2] Ibid.; Nichols, *Lit. An.* v, p. 588, wrongly addressed.

Shakespeare, whose surpassing merit had been guaranteed by no less a person that Pope, prevailed. The decision to publish was taken a month or two later and is recorded in the Minutes of the Delegates without an exact date.[1] By then it had been agreed that publication would be by subscription among friends and no copies would go to booksellers.[2] Some of the leading booksellers were afraid of Warburton.[3]

The Account for Printing shows that Hanmer and the Heads of 9 colleges shared out the edition of 600 unequally and each sold his quota. An advertisement with specimen pages was printed in 1743 or the year following.

Hanmer subsidized the book to the extent of supplying the whole-page plates, printed and ready for insertion. The University paid for the engraving and printing of the device on the title-page and 27 tail-pieces.[4]

The Vice-Chancellor's expenditure and receipts were these:[5]

	£	s.	d.
Paper, 560 reams of Royal	800	0	0
The printers' bill	305	0	0
Copperplate printing	24	7	6
Engraving, to Gravelot	14	14	0
A corrector's journey to London	2	2	0
For the pressmen to drink Sir Tho. Hanmer's health	2	2	0
Correctors	84	0	0
Caslon, letter-founder	39	2	0
Wood, pressman, for delivering copies	6	6	0
Binding and delivering Sir Tho. Hanmer's copy	6	1	0
	1,283	14	6
Receipts from sales			
1744–5, 575 sets	1,811	5	0
1745–6, 6 sets	18	18	0
1746–7, 3 sets, being the last	9	9	0
	1,839	12	0

Sixteen sets were given as presents.

[1] *First Minute Book*, pp. 53–4.
[2] Hanmer's letter to Zachary Grey, 30 Dec. 1742: Nichols, *Lit. An.* v, p. 589.
[3] [Philip Nichols]. *The Castrated Letter of Sir Thomas Hanmer in the Sixth Volume of Biographia Britannica* (1763).
[4] The Account for Printing, 1709–49, fol. 202. Porters were paid 1s. 6d. for 'letting down into the Ware House a large box with all the Cutts for Shakespear's Works'.
[5] Univ. Arch. W.P. β 21, V.-C.'s Computus 1735–68.

These figures take no account of the University's overheads or the expenses of the dons who sold the edition, so the profit was quite modest. The selling out of an edition in so short a time as three years is without precedent in the history of the Delegates' publishing. Nor was an edition ever before done at the University's expense and sold by subscription.

Hanmer's Shakespear was much to the taste of the age. The price of a second-hand copy had risen by 1763 to £10, while Pope's edition was sold off in 1767 for 16s.[1] Warburton's, published at £2. 8s., was being sold off within a year at 18s.[2] Appreciation must have been due to its being, as Dibdin said,[3] the first Shakespeare 'which appeared in any splendid typographical form', and therefore a necessary accession to any rich man's library. Nevertheless the text must have passed for a time as the best: a group of London booksellers pirated it a year after it was published, and it was reprinted four times in London and Dublin before the University issued a second edition in 1770–1.

The poet William Collins hailed the book in stanzas addressed to Hanmer, for example:

> Those Sibyl-Leaves, the Sport of ev'ry Wind,
> [For Poets ever were a careless Kind]
> By thee dispos'd, no farther Toil demand,
> But, just to Nature, own thy forming Hand.

Some of Hanmer's emendations are adopted by modern editors, others are so absurd that even the eighteenth century would not countenance them.[4] Aldis Wright's dismissal of him as 'a country gentleman [who] amused his leisure hours by scribbling down his own and his friends' guesses in Pope's Shakespeare' is a little severe inasmuch as Hanmer scribbled in Theobald's edition too[5] and shows in his letters an occasional awareness of the readings of the 'old editions'. The defects of his text could hardly be summed up better than they were by Samuel Johnson soon after it was first printed:

From the little that I have seen, [I] think it not dangerous to declare that, in my Opinion, its Pomp recommends it more than its Accuracy. There is no Distinction made between the antient Readings, and the Innovations

[1] Nichols, *Lit. An.* v, p. 597; *Biographia Britannica* vi, p. 3743 n.
[2] T. F. Dibdin, *The Library Companion* (1824), p. 794.   [3] Ibid.
[4] Horace Walpole, *Letters*, ed. W. S. Lewis, 18 (1955), pp. 566–7, on Hanmer's changing 'damn'd in a fair wife' to 'damned in a fair phyz' in *Othello* I. i. 20–1, because it appeared elsewhere that the character concerned had no wife.
[5] H. B. Wheatley, 'Shakespeare's Editors, 1623 to the Twentieth Century', *Transactions of the Bibliographical Society*, xiv (1919), at p. 159.

of the Editor; there is no Reason given for the Alterations which are made; the Emendations of former Criticks are adopted without any Acknowledgement, and few of the Difficulties are removed, which have hitherto embarrassed the Readers of Shakespeare.[1]

The conception of the book was wholly Hanmer's, and it took shape just as he had conceived it. If the Delegates had troubled to read the copy or the proofs they would have seen that the editing fell far short of an academic standard. The title 'Works' is a misnomer, for the narrative poems and sonnets are left out; but nobody noticed that Hanmer, in using Pope's edition for his copy, had forgotten to alter the title. Sadly enough, it was generally known as the 'Oxford Shakespeare', there being no editor's name in it.

For this exercise in fine printing the Press was supplied with Roman and Italic type by William Caslon. It was used increasingly as time went on and little by little it displaced the types of Fell's bequest. The new fount of Caslon's Great Primer looks magnificent in the Shakespeare, excelling even the fine Dutch type of Pope's edition. It is remarkable that a press which Blackstone described so convincingly a few years later as inefficient and lacking direction could set and print so well. For all that, the effect of grandeur and elegance is a veil between the reader and the Elizabethan playhouse.

The incongruity is very marked where the illustrations are concerned. Considerable artist as he was, Hayman had a faint vision of the plays, 'below criticism', Dibdin thought. His designs, rendered by a French engraver, are a series of *fêtes champêtres* after the manner of Watteau, peopled predominantly by sham shepherds and shepherdesses. The tail-pieces, for which Gravelot alone is responsible are decorative and done with a firm hand, but being only three, they suffer by repetition.

The engraving on the title-page is a curiosity because it shows the Radcliffe Camera finished, when it was only half-built.

The London booksellers who pirated Hanmer's work in 1745 had the good sense to mark his emendations and give an older reading as a footnote. When the Delegates printed their second edition in 1770–1 they added a table of variant readings, Theobald's and Capell's, at the ends of the volumes and had the glossary revised and enlarged.[2]

---

[1] *Miscellaneous Observations on the Tragedy of Macbeth: with Remarks on Sir T. H's. Edition of Shakespeare* (1745), p. 64.

[2] The foreword notes that the plates for the tailpieces were worn and had been engraved again by 'a very eminent artist'. That explains the existence at the Press of duplicate plates, one of each signed by Gravelot, the other unsigned.

AUTHORS' BOOKS

Eighteenth-Century editions of Clarendon's History

Until the nineteenth century the Delegates did not bear the cost of an edition of Clarendon later than the first in octavo of 1705-6, which they published but did not sell.[1] In the period 1712-55 there were five editions printed at the Press for booksellers to whom the University farmed out its right to the copy. Each of them bears the University's imprint and none has any sign that it was sponsored and financed by another publisher.

In 1711 the Delegates accepted John Baskett's 'proposall of £100 advance for printing the Lord Clarendon in Octavo beside the 4s. in the pound for the use of the University Letters'.[2] All the 1,500 copies were taken by Baskett, and none could be bought from the Press.[3] This edition is dated 1712.

Baskett agreed in 1716 to pay £100 for licence to print 1,650 for himself and 150 for the University.[4] This edition of six volumes octavo is dated 1717. Baskett paid a poundage of £40 in addition to the cost of printing.

He published another, similar, edition of 2,000 in 1720-1 on the same terms.[5]

The Vice-Chancellor entered in his Computus for 1732-3 the receipt of £200 from the London booksellers Mount and Page for licence to print the *History*. This must relate to the edition from the Press of 1731-2, of which 150 extra copies were done for the University. These copies, on large paper, presumably are what Philip Bliss called 'the master's edition; as it was printed for masters of art only'.[6]

The work was printed again in 1732 as a folio in two columns with engravings of portraits four to a page. Hearne recorded that Charles Combes, Baskett's manager at the Bible Press, 'had the managing of it'[7] (he died in December 1731), so no doubt Baskett financed it. The style of setting suggests strongly that it was done at the Bible Press—the only secular book, so far as I know, of which that can be said. The whole *History* is in one volume, though the title-page announces only Volume the First. An edition in this format had been under consideration since 1719.[8]

---

[1] See above, pp. 235-6.
[2] D.O. 20 Apr. 1711, 26 July 1711; *First Minute Book*, pp. 33-4.
[3] Hearne, iv, p. 68.   [4] D.O. 29 Mar. 1716; *First Minute Book*, p. 46.
[5] D.O. 29 May 1719: *First Minute Book*, p. 48. Volume i of the set in the Bodleian has a title-page printed for one of Baskett's customers in the retail trade.
[6] Wood, *Ath.* ed. Bliss, iii, 1024.   [7] Hearne, xi, p. 26.
[8] D.O. 29 May 1719; *First Minute Book*, p. 48.

Kennicott's Dissertation on the Text of the Old Testament

Benjamin Kennicott's *Dissertation*, printed at the Press in 1753, is to some extent a manifesto preliminary to his famous collection of variant readings of the Old Testament. In the earlier work he was concerned to show that there were inconsistencies and unintelligible passages in the Masoretic text due to scribal errors, not that it had been corrupted in later manuscripts and printed editions. The *Dissertation* was a fearless investigation of textual problems, and, as might be expected, it was fiercely attacked by Hebraists of a conservative cast of mind, in particular by Fowler Comings in Oxford and Julius Bate in London. Comings was prepared to defend every word in Van der Hoogt's edition of 1705 as sacrosanct, and accused Kennicott of undermining faith and robbing mankind of its most precious possession. Kennicott was scientific and learned, while his opponents were bound by prejudice. It is to the credit of Oxford and the English hierarchy that he was able to carry on his work. Meanwhile the Tory gadfly, William King, tormented him about his low birth and his specially-expedited academic degree.[1]

Wells's Helps to the Bible

Edward Wells's series of *An Help to the more easy and clear understanding of Holy Scripture* was, in point of bulk, a considerable part of the work of the Press in the years 1709–29. His volumes on the several Books were issued to subscribers, and those for the Old Testament were reissued in collected form in 1734. His title, *Helps*, has acquired connotations in recent years which do not fit Wells's aim, which was at a learned readership.

He had made a name as a geographer and an editor of Greek classics and as author of pamphlets combating dissent. Withdrawn in middle age from Oxford to a country vicarage, he applied himself to textual criticism and exegesis of the Bible, and virtually finished his *Helps* before he died in 1727. This was a large task for one man, and it says much for Wells's powers of application that he so nearly completed it.

Many modern readers would, I think, credit Wells with little more than that: or rather, would be impatient with him because of his want of the historical approach, of scientific method, and of candour; for he wrote for a public as little prepared as he was for a departure from tradition established in less enlightened days.

---

[1] By innuendo in *Doctor King's Apology* (Oxford, 1755) and explicitly in *The Last Blow: or an unanswerable Vindication of the Society of Exeter College* (London, 1755).

Being a Hellenist, Wells was largely concerned to emend the Greek texts by choosing among variant readings those that made the best sense or grammar. To suit his alterations he made corresponding changes in the Authorized Version. It is claimed for him that he was the first to offer an improved complete New Testament by departing from the *textus receptus* in favour of the better manuscripts.[1] He had, of course, fewer manuscripts to choose from than the modern scholars, so that inevitably the balance of authority was not where it is, and his text is of only historical interest.

As a Hebraist he is of no account. For the Old Testament he does not print the Hebrew or Aramaic, for fear, he said, of making the book unduly bulky and expensive. Only for Daniel he prints the Septuagint; for Genesis the Authorized Version as amended by him besides his paraphrase. For the rest the work dwindles to paraphrase only. Having no Mill to lean on in this part of the work, he takes his variant readings from the London Polyglot of 1657.

A paraphrase in English is more than half of the work. It is extremely copious, and not seldom it puts a strained interpretation on passages that might be given a sense unacceptable to the Anglican Church of that day. In Matthew 15:24, he paraphrases 'I am not sent, but unto the lost sheep of the house of Israel' by 'I am not yet sent', etc. He gives St. Mark's Gospel the longer ending and does not mention the want of it in some manuscripts. He contrives to discuss the prophecies of Daniel at great length without noticing a view, mooted by Hobbes and others before his time, that they were written by someone who had seen them fulfilled.

Hearne's opinion that Wells wrote 'to get a penny' is hard to reconcile with the laborious character of the *Helps*; but they were not reprinted and had nothing like the enduring appeal of Matthew Henry's almost contemporary commentary.

Petra Scandali

The text in Isaiah 8: 14 and in Romans 9: 33, 'a stone of stumbling and a rock of offence', gave its title to a small book in Arabic printed at the Press about 1725. The title-page in Latin of a copy at Christ Church describes it as an account of the separation of the eastern and western

---

[1] Adam Fox, *John Mill and Richard Bentley, a Study of the Textual Criticism of the New Testament 1675–1729* (Oxford, 1954), pp. 95–7; F. L. Cross, *Oxford Dict. of the Christian Church* (1958), art. Wells.

churches due to the undue pretensions of the Pope. This is the first of three tracts in the volume, all translated into Arabic from Greek.

A note in Jean Gagnier's hand quoted in the Catalogue of Oriental MSS. in the Bodleian Library (1787)[1] is to this effect:

> This book was translated from Greek into Arabic by order of Athanasius, Patriarch of Antioch, in 1721 for use by the Christian Arabs of his diocese against missionaries of the Roman pontiff and printed at Oxford in 1725 at the Patriarch's expense. All the copies, with very few exceptions, were sent to Aleppo in Syria.

An entry in the Press accounts for 1725–6, of the receipt of the University's poundage on 'Dr. Mayow's Arabic tract' can refer only to this book. Richard Mayo, a fellow of Pembroke College, proceeded D.D. in 1724 and was appointed Chaplain to the King in 1725.

What part Gagnier had in the work is hard to tell. He did not claim to have made the translation, but the claim is made for him in the Catalogue and a former owner of the copy at Christ Church. That an Eastern patriarch, surrounded as he must have been by people bilingual in Greek and Arabic, would have trusted an Englishman for the purpose seems unlikely. The manuscript at the Bodleian[2] is in Gagnier's hand—a simplified Arabic script approximating to the printed letter-forms. He may have copied from a script in cursive handwriting which would have been troublesome to an Oxford compositor.

Bibliotheca Biblica

This was the first book to issue from the Press in monthly parts. Like the earliest English example of publications of the kind, the *Mechanick Exercises* of Moxon, it failed to come out regularly. A proposal of 1717 was followed by five volumes of the collected parts in 1720–35. By the latter year the Pentateuch was complete, and no more was published.

The editor was Samuel Parker, the Non-Juring son of a bishop of Oxford, and notes on the Book of Genesis were contributed by Francis Lee, reputed for his rabbinical learning. Parker's death in 1730, from overwork, brought the series to an end. The commentary was designed to digest the interpretations of the Scriptures by the Fathers and by heretics up to the year 451 and to include the New Testament.

---

[1] *Bibliothecae Bodleianae Codicum Manuscriptorum Orientalium . . . Catalogus* (Oxford, 1787–1835), ii, p. 40.
[2] Bodl. MS. Or. 287(2).

The Hebrew Bible of 1750

The first Oxford Hebrew Bible, the second printed in England (the first was in the London Polyglot), was edited by Nathaniel Forster, a Prussian, chaplain to the Archbishop of Canterbury. It omits vowels and accents, therefore was not acceptable to orthodox Jews. There is nothing original about it: the text was taken from Athias's Bible, printed at Amsterdam in 1661, as revised by Jan Leusden in 1667, and the variants and notes of Van der Hoogt's edition of 1705 were added.

The words 'typis et sumtibus academicis' in the title are misleading; for proposals were sent out in 1744 for publication by subscription, and the Delegates did not bear the cost of printing or paper. They did, however, buy a fount of Caslon's Hebrew type used first in this book.

Cave's History of Ecclesiastical Writers

William Cave's *Scriptorum ecclesiasticorum historia literaria* was originally printed in London, the first volume in 1688, the second in 1698. As material for the history of Christianity in its first fourteen centuries it soon became famous, and a Swiss printer pirated it in 1705. The theft of his work so upset Cave that he would not authorize a second edition, and it remained for his friends, headed by the distinguished theologian, Daniel Waterland, to bring out the enlarged work posthumously. Cave's additions and corrections and some by other hands increased the bulk of the book by a third. It was printed at Oxford for subscribers in 1740-3.

Etymologicum Anglicanum

Francis Junius the younger, who died in 1677, bequeathed to the University of Oxford among other manuscripts the two volumes of his *Etymologicon linguae Anglicanae.*[1] It is a dictionary of English words giving related forms in Old English and kindred languages. Hearne in 1711 thought that 'Some years agoe there was a Discourse that the Etymologicon should be printed, & 'twas mightily desir'd by Graevius of Holland, as I find by some of his Letters written to Dr. Edward Bernard and now in my Possession.[2] But I believe the work was stopp'd by the Delegates of the Press, who did not care to hazard their Money upon so large a Book wch. they thought would not go off.'[3]

I think it likely that Hearne was confusing the *Etymologicon* with another manuscript attributed to Junius, known as *Dictionarium linguarum*

---

[1] Bodl. MS. Junius 4, 5.   [2] Bodl. MS. Smith 5, fol. 54.   [3] Hearne, iii, p. 274.

septentrionalium or Dictionary of the Five Northern Languages, Gothic, Cymric, Frankish, Saxon, and Icelandic. This was a composition by Fell, copying various manuscript glossaries made by Junius into eleven folio volumes.[1] Some two years before he died Fell put 'Mr. Junius his Lexicon' to press.[2] If any part was printed, it has vanished.

Later on, in 1728, Hearne was urged by Richard Meade to publish both these dictionaries; but, as he explained, the task was far beyond his means; on the other hand, he considered that 'the University ought by all means to do it.'[3]

The University published neither compilation, but after a long time Edward Lye undertook to edit the *Etymologicon* and published it in 1743. At his country vicarage Lye taught himself Old English and Gothic; he spent seven years on the book, making substantial additions and prefixing a life of Junius and a grammar of Anglo-Saxon. Emendations to Junius's readings of the Gothic Bible were supplied to him by Eric Benzelius, Archbishop of Uppsala.[4] Lye modestly entitled the book *Francisci Junii Francisci filii Etymologicum Anglicanum*. The Delegates forwent their normal charge for the University's poundage on the printers' bills; and who, knowing that Junius had given his work and the exotic types wherewith to print it, would have expected less of them?

Swinton's Works

John Swinton was the type of eccentric scholar opening up byways of knowledge—eccentric in unhygienic personal habits as in the vagaries of his learning.

It is owing to him that the Press was equipped in 1746 with type for Etruscan. He had served for two or three years as chaplain to the English merchants at Leghorn soon after the antiquities of Etruria had attracted the attention of scholars. His conclusions about the affinities of the language of the monuments and the proper decipherment of the script were far more definite than those of modern experts.[5] At Oxford in 1738 Swinton published his dissertation *De linguae Etruriae regalis vernacula* propounding a belief in the Asian origin of the people and the language. In *De priscis Romanorum literis dissertatio* (1746) he argues that an alphabet of Canaanite origin had been passed on to the Romans by their Etruscan neighbours.

---

[1] Bodl. MS. Fell 8–18.   [2] Bodl. MS. Marshall 134, fol. 18.
[3] Hearne, x, p. 58.   [4] See above, p. 297.
[5] M. Pallottino, *Etruscologia* (Milan, 1963); M. Hammarström, *Beiträge zur Geschichte der etrus., latein., und griech. Alphabeten* (Helsingfors, 1920).

By this time Swinton felt confident enough of his mastery of the language and the script to need type for it. The Etruscan was cut by William Caslon, no doubt interpreting drawings by Swinton,[1] and a box of the cast letter reached the Press during 1745–6.[2] Caslon included some lines in it in his *Specimen* of 1748 and in those of later years.[3] There is no sign that the University paid him for cutting it, and he may well have grudged his investment in the typeface, for it was used hardly at all. Some half-dozen letters of it appear in Swinton's unfinished essay *De primigenis Etruscorum literis*, of which the first eight pages were printed in 1746, and four lines of it in a poem by Swinton in the University's *Epicedia* for the death of the Prince of Wales of 1751. Another such *carmen Etruscum* by the same author is in *Pietas* for the king's death in 1760 and the inauguration of a new reign.

About this time Swinton turned to early Semitic inscriptions, especially those on coins. On these he wrote a number of articles for the *Philosophical Transactions* of the Royal Society. His command of Hebrew was enough for deciphering Phoenician and Aramaic legends, but he evidently gave up an attempt to learn Arabic.[4] Poems by him in Phoenician, Syriac, late-Phoenician, and Syriac in Palmyrene script were contributed to the academic occasional verses of 1751, 1761, and 1762, all but plain Syriac printed copperplate. There seems no reason to dispute his reading of a Semitic inscription from the ruins of Citium in Cyprus, printed at the Press as *Inscriptiones Citieae* in 1750; on the other hand, his contention in *Metilia* of the same year that a Roman coin bearing the letters CROT was struck in honour of T. Metilius Croto, mentioned once by Livy, is rejected by a modern authority as an explanation less likely than an origin in the city of Croton.[5] Swinton's fearless pioneering recommends him more than his sense of probability.

In 1752 he put to press a second dissertation on inscriptions from Citium with a new excursus on two Phoenician coins, which ends incomplete at p. 70 and has no title or preliminary pages. Of him in his last years John Nichols reports:[6]

The late Mr. Swinton of Oxford intended to have added to this work

---

[1] There are many in Bodl. MS. Auct. V 2 inf. 2 22*.   [2] 2nd Accounts, p. 211.
[3] W. T. Berry and A. F. Johnson, *Catalogue of Specimens of Printing Types by English and Scottish Printers and Founders 1665–1830* (1935), pp. 16–17. The Oxford Broadside specimen dated 1710 in that book is now known to have been printed in 1757–8 (see below, p. 380).
[4] Bodl. MS. Auct. V 2 inf. 2 22*, fol. 1.
[5] H. A. Grueber, *Coins of the Roman Republic in the British Museum* (1910), ii, p. 201.
[6] *Lit. An.* ix, p. 13.

[Scholtz's Coptic grammar revised by Woide] a dissertation De nummis Copto-Phoeniciis, part of which is actually printed off; but the remainder cannot be found among his papers.

CLASSICS

During the period 1713–55 the Press printed for the editors fine editions of Xenophon's *Cyropaedia* (1727) and *Anabasis* (1735) edited by Thomas Hutchinson and Hesiod edited by Thomas Robinson. Their quarto pages set in Granjon's biggest Greek type, which delighted Fell when he bought it in 1672, would be a pleasure to read but for the unfamiliar contractions.

The Hesiod is a curiosity inasmuch as the printing was shared by the Press with William Bowyer, the foremost London printer at the time. Bowyer set and printed the preliminary pages and the introductory dissertation (sheets a–f).[1] The accounts for the Press for 1739–40 record the receipt of poundage on the bill for 62 sheets, that is to say the text. The reason for the division of labour is not known. The title finally printed is much shorter than that written out by Robinson for the information of Richard Rawlinson.[2]

A pocket edition of Sallust dated 1730 has the imprint 'Oxonii, impensis Societatis Stationariorum', and it bears all the signs of printing at the University Press. If it was indeed done there, it was the only book printed by the University for that customer.

MATHEMATICS, NATURAL SCIENCES, AND MEDICINE

The Delegates published Menelaus on spherics;[3] private editions were printed at the Press of the great catalogue of mosses by Johannes Jacobus Dillenius and the influential book of Dr. Russell on cures by sea water.

Dillenius (Johann Dill) of Darmstadt was the first Sherardian Professor of Botany at Oxford, appointed in 1734. His *Historia muscorum* of 1741 describes and illustrates with copper-engravings about 600 species.

Richard Russell's prescription of sea bathing and drinking of sea water for diseases of the skin was largely responsible for the custom of going to the seaside for summer holidays and the rise of British watering places. Brighton, where the Doctor practised during the summer months, was the first of such places to feel the effects of Russell's teaching.[4] His book

---

[1] Nichols, *Lit. An.* ii, p. 104.   [2] Bodl. MS. Rawl. J fol. 4 (302a).
[3] See above, p. 291.
[4] O. Sitwell and M. Barton, *Brighton* (1935), pp. 47 ff.

appeared from the Press in Latin, *De tabe glandulari*, in 1750 and, translated, in 1753 as *A Dissertation on the Use of Sea Water in Diseases of the Glands.*

A DISSERTATION

CONCERNING THE USE

OF SEA WATER

In DISEASES of the GLANDS, &c.

TO WHICH IS ADDED

An EPISTOLARY DISSERTATION

To R. Frewin, M.D.

By Richard Russell, M.D. & F.R.S.

Θάλασσα κλύζει πάντα τ' ανθρώπων κακά.
Eurip. Iphigen. in Taur.

OXFORD,

Printed at the Theatre: and Sold by James Fletcher in the *Turl*, and J. and J. Rivington in St. *Paul's* Church-Yard, *London*, MDCCLIII.

Dr. Richard Russell's *Dissertation* on the curative properties of sea water, 1758. Reduced.

An early manual on electricity was printed at the Press in 1752, written by Francis Penrose, a surgeon at Bicester. His book on magnetism followed it a year later.

HISTORY AND ANTIQUITIES

Hearne's death in 1735 left no editor in Oxford of English chronicles, nor did any of the universal histories favoured by London publishers issue from here. Three of Hearne's limited editions were reprinted at the Press before 1755. Sprott's Chronicle, published by Hearne in 1719, was reprinted in 1739. There being no trace of an edition of that date, there must be a suspicion that the copies printed at that time were passed off as belonging to the original issue. James Fletcher, the Oxford bookseller, and Joseph Pote at Eton published a second edition of the nine-volume *Itinerary* of John Leland and appended to it John Ross's (or Rous's) *Historia*.

The one product of genuine historical research was *Anglia Judaica: or the History and Antiquities of the Jews in England* by the oddly-named D'Blossiers Tovey, Principal of St. Edmund Hall, printed for him by the Press in 1738. It was the earliest book on the subject, and the foremost modern authority describes it as a comprehensive work still deserving of study.[1]

Ancient monuments were discussed in two Oxford books, the White Horse near Uffington by Francis Wise in 1738 and Stonehenge by John Wood, the architect of Bath, in 1747. Wise considered the horse as Saxon, made to commemorate a victory over the Danes. Wood's Stonehenge has the usual associations with druids and Diana-worship, but his accurate measurements and plans are valuable.

[1] C. Roth, *A History of the Jews in England*, 3rd ed. (Oxford, 1964), Preface.

CHAPTER XIX

Technicalities of Publishing and Printing

PUBLISHING

THE University has a tenuous right to be considered a publisher during this period, a period beginning with the giving up of hope that the Stationers' Company would absorb its production and ending with a revival due mainly to the adoption of agent booksellers in London. The achievement of Oxford publishing in 1714–55 may be likened to that of the Abbé Sieyès under the Terror: to have lived.

Consequently it is not to be expected that the policy or methods of the Delegates at this time would repay close study. In their choice of books to promote, a matter of 20 in 40 years, it is impossible to discern any conscious aim or critical sense of scholarship or business. It must be suspected that an introduction from an influential friend was the most effective recommendation of a manuscript.

The Delegates badly needed the lecture that Samuel Johnson was to read them on discounts.[1] From its earliest days the Press offered reductions on quantities. The accounts disclose instances such as 3,000 of Marshall's Catechism priced at $3\frac{1}{2}d$. being sold for 2d. each in 1694, and the Latin Grammar costing 1s. for single copies being sold to the Stationers' Company for 10d. in 1695. Since the Stationers took 3,000, it was a small reduction. By 1724 the Catechism was selling at 4s. a dozen of 14. The Coptic Gospels, issued in 1716 at 10s., were offered to booksellers and anyone who would take twelve at 9s. The verses for the death of the Prince of Wales in 1751 sold for 6s. or £3 for a dozen of 14.

These concessions would have affected mostly the booksellers; but special prices for them come to light only halfway through the century. Meanwhile there are many instances of their paying the full price for one copy or a small number. The price of the Bodleian *Catalogue of Printed Books* of 1738 was reduced in 1748 from £3. 3s. large paper and £2. 2s. small to £2. 2s. and £1. 17s. with an allowance of 5s. to booksellers. It was going very badly. No wonder that booksellers preferred to deal with the Press by commissioning it to print editions for them.

---

[1] Boswell, ii, 424–6.

Imprints still often do not disclose the extent of the University's part in the editions. The impressions of Clarendon's *History* previously mentioned as financed and sold by booksellers[1] bear no indication that anyone besides the Delegates sponsored them. Only the accounts of the Press show that they did not do so; and this is true of other books, among them Xenophon's *Cyropaedia*, 1727 and *Anabasis*, 1735, Hesiod, 1737, Dillenius on mosses, 1741, the *Etymologicum* of Junius, 1743, that the Delegates might have been expected to publish.

The usual imprint on Delegates' and authors' books, *e Theatro Sheldoniano* or 'at the Theatre', sustains until the end of this period (and beyond it) the fiction accepted since the time of Fell; for the Learned Press had ceased to print there since 1678. 'E Typographeo Clarendoniano' as an alternative becomes increasingly common in Latin books, and 'at the Clarendon Printing-House' occurs once. There may be grounds for thinking that from about 1745 onwards this expression was used for the more learned books, but not consistently and no more often for Delegates' books than for others. The formula 'at the University Printing House' in editions by Francis Wise of 1738 and 1742 found no imitators.

There are some examples of clandestine French books with fictitious imprints at Oxford.[2] There is also a lying imprint by Edmund Curll or his son. One or other of them issued a second edition in 1728 of the Latin *Abelard and Héloïse* with the imprint of the Theatre, but the types are evidence that the book was not printed there.

The charge, described in the accounts as 'poundage', made to authors and booksellers for the University's overheads on the printers' bills had ceased by 1717 to be calculated as a percentage of the total.[3] From then onwards the amount was expressed as a rate 'per sheet', generally of 4s. but sometimes as little as 1s. What determined the rate is not discernible in the accounts; size of the edition and closeness of the author to the University, such as that of a graduate or a local bookseller, were very likely taken into account by whoever fixed it.

Publicity for Oxford editions was meagre and primitive. While Charlett lived lists of books in the press, lately published and in preparation, were issued from time to time. These folio fly-sheets announced authors' editions besides those for which the University paid. The last of which a copy survives (I believe) is that of 1716, but the accounts for 1719 charged

---

[1] Above, p. 306.
[2] Pseudo-Virgil, 1726, Meusnier de Querlon, 1746, De Pas, 1760, Voltaire, 1771.
[3] Above, p. 252.

the Delegates with the cost of 'a Catalogue of Books in the Press' and in 1720 they paid to reissue it with additions.

'A small Catalogue with Prices' for which there was a charge in 1711 would have been limited to publications of the University;[1] and a list of them dated 25 August 1713 'to be had of Stephen Richardson at the Theatre-Press' is preserved.[2] They were offered to 'Gentlemen of this University' at a reduction to clear the stock. There are entries in the accounts for printing 'Catalogues of Books sold at the Ware-House' in 1739, 1744, and 1748.

The old-established practice of printing loose title-pages and sticking them up in public places continued.[3] Instances of it concerning Delegates' books occur in the accounts for 1728 and 1748. The sticking up fell to the lot of the printers, and they charged for it. They printed and stuck up 'an Advertisement for publishing the Verses' in 1751, meaning those deploring the death of the Prince of Wales.

PRINTING

Casting a backward look at the Press as it had been during the first half of the eighteenth century, Blackstone did not spare management or workmen. What he wrote is virtually the only information we have about them. How many printers there were, how much they earned, and what hours they worked are questions that cannot be answered.

Blackstone put down 'the present deplorable condition' of the printing business largely to the want of 'an industrious, honest and skilful overseer'.[4] Some of Stephen Richardson's shortcomings have been brought to light in an examination of his accounting.[5] Blackstone directed his command of incisive language to him.

The University Warehousekeeper, or Overseer of the Press, is now quite superannuated, and entirely unfit for the Place. In a long Course of Years he has however peopled the House with a numerous Train of Descendants, Sons, Grandsons, Sons-in-Law, &c; who are employed as Workmen there; and to give them their due praise, are very good Workmen in their Kinds. To one of these, a Pressman, his Son-in-law, he has consigned the whole Care of the House; and by this Deputy are all agreements made with Authors and Booksellers for the total Price; the Wages distributed to the

---

[1] Very likely some offered by Jonah Bowyer in London: B.M. Harl. 5932, fol. 9.
[2] Ibid., fol. 7.
[3] There is a note on it in Moxon, *Mech. Ex.*, p. 13.
[4] *To the Reverend Doctor Randolph*, p. 8; Philip, p. 50.   [5] Above, p. 281.

respective Workmen; and a Residuum, small enough in reason, reserved to the University for their Profits. In this Situation, and under these Connexions, acting without Check or Controll, for the Benefit of himself and his Kinsmen, it is not to be wondered at if he suffers the Prices to remain at an excessive Rate . . .[1]

When they appointed Richardson in 1715, as a man they had rather deal with than Thomas Hearne, the Architypographus, the Delegates were too easily satisfied of his fitness for the post. They may have acted out of kindness, as their successors were on the point of doing when Richardson died in 1756, and his son-in-law, the effective overseer of the Press in the depths of its 'lazy obscurity', was a candidate to take his place. Blackstone is witness that 'A strong inclination (if not a resolution) had prevailed among many of the delegates, to commit to his hands the entire management of the house; because (I was startled at the expression) "they had most of them a kindness for Wood." '[2]

Blackstone, it is worth noting, thought that the Press had 'very good Workmen in their Kinds', but he also complains of 'the incivility, the delays, the negligence, the incorrectness of the workmen'.[3] In so far as the two views are contradictory a cursory acquaintance with the work of the Press inclines one to the former. The standard of care and correctness appears to be high, and correction, we have seen,[4] was done without a whole-time corrector.

In matters of style the Press kept abreast of an improvement which took place towards the end of the half-century. In particular, the rather crabbed title-pages, an inheritance from the previous century, boxed and intersected by a superfluity of rules, gave way about 1738[5] to a more open treatment, and the use of leads to space lines of text apart gives the pages a new seductiveness to the eye. Presswork came to rely less on force, and was presumably slower. Woodcut vignettes and headbands supply the want of copper-engraved ornament in the humbler books. These are slight improvements, and we do not know who made them.

The Warehouseman began buying 'mill'd lead to use in place of riglett' in 1733 and the Press was soon amply stocked with it. Reglet or riglet is thin strips of wood: the substitution of metal for spacing made for straighter lines and a tidier page. The use of leads was unknown to the author of the *Printer's Grammar* of 1755.

[1] 'Some thoughts on the Oxford Press 1756' MS. in the Delegates' archives; Philip, pp. 24, 25.   [2] *To the Reverend Doctor Randolph*, p. 12; Philip, p. 53.
[3] Ibid.; Philip, p. 54.   [4] Above, p. 257.
[5] Thomas Shaw, *Travels*; J. Reinolds, *Census habitus nascente Christo*.

In his 'Account' to Blackstone of the University Printing House Daniel Prince praised its Greek, Hebrew, and other oriental and foreign letters as 'better than in any other printing house'.[1] This was certainly true of the houses in Great Britain. The collection of exotics might have been increased by the punches and matrices for a Persian Avesta type made for Thomas Hyde, but the offer of it by Hyde's executors was declined by the Delegates. Finally Queen Anne bought them and they are now in the British Museum.[2]

Where Roman and Italic are concerned Caslon's types supplanting Fell's gave the pages of Oxford books an unaffected grace that they had not had since the sixteenth century, but robbed them of a distinct character. Caslon's founts on two bodies, Great Primer and Long Primer, were bought in 1743–4 for use in Hanmer's Shakespeare, and one on English, used in sermons, followed in 1746. The broadside *Specimen* of 1757/8 shows a miscellaneous collection, the big display types remaining much as they were in 1706.

Several books were printed partly at the Press and partly elsewhere. The preliminary pages of Volume i of Trapp's poetry lectures, 1711, are set in types foreign to the Press. The preliminaries of Edward Wells's *Helps* for Daniel, 1716, and the last sheets of his Samuel and Kings, 1726, are by some other printer, probably Leonard Lichfield. Sheets A–M of the letters of Abelard and Héloïse, 1718, were printed here for Edmund Curll and W. Taylor, and the book was completed elsewhere. The preliminaries and appendices of Aretaeus Cappadox, 1723, are distinguishable from Oxford work by the types. William Bowyer in London printed the preliminaries and prolegomena for Robinson's Hesiod, 1737,[3] and Charles Ackers did twelve sheets of the latter part of Volume ii of Cave's *Historia literaria*, 1743.[4] Why the work was thus shared is not known; very likely slowness on the part of the Press would explain it.

The second part of the collected *Duty of Man's Works*, 1726, was done here, doubtless because the University owned the copy, while John Baskett, who published the volume, printed the first part. Baskett appears to have printed some cancel title-pages for Clarendon's *History* of 1721 with the imprints of retailers.

[1] Philip, p. 19.
[2] Morison, *Fell*, p. 247 n.
[3] Nichols, *Lit. An.* ii, p. 104.
[4] *A Ledger of Charles Ackers*, ed. D. F. McKenzie and J. C. Ross (Oxford, 1968), p. 169.

Frontispiece to *Winter's Tale* by Francis Hayman in Hanmer's *Works of Shakespear* (1744–6)

Sir William Blackstone (1723–80). By Tilly Kettle

CHAPTER XX

The Bible Press and Other Presses in Oxford

THE BIBLE PRESS, 1713–55

THE lease granted by the University in 1712 to John Baskett and his nominees expired on Lady Day 1734, and a new one to Baskett, Samuel Ashurst, and Robert Gosling for 21 years took effect.[1] The two latter were merely trustees, and when Baskett died in 1742 his surviving sons, Thomas and Robert, as administrators of his will succeeded to his sole beneficial interest in the lease.

Oxford Bibles were published in 1743–5 with the imprint of T. and R. Baskett, and thereafter with that of Thomas Baskett alone. There is every reason to suppose that Bible-printing was carried on here as an independent and purely commercial concern. There is no sign that the ample powers reserved by the lease to the Vice-Chancellor and Delegates to regulate the number, size, quality, and price of Bibles and to enter and inspect the press were exercised. Its standard of quality was well below that of the Learned Press and reflects no credit on the University.

Blackstone in 1756 wrote that 'the Pay in Mr. Baskett's Side of the House is much inferior to what is given by the University in the other.'[2]

Litigation of much consequence to the two Universities was begun in 1743. The Syndics at Cambridge had allowed their Printer to undertake at the behest of a London bookseller in 1742 an abridgement of the statutes relating to excise on intoxicating liquors. Thomas and Robert Baskett as King's Printers claimed under their patent the sole right to print Acts of Parliament entire or abridged. They prayed in Chancery for a prohibition restraining the University from infringing the patent and for delivery up of copies of the book. At the hearing on 24 January 1743/4 the Lord Chancellor ordered that a case be stated for the opinion

---

[1] Univ. Arch. S.P. A. 12. See above p. 175. A new lease was granted to Thomas Baskett on 28 Sept. 1744. See below, p. 352.

[2] 'Some Thoughts on the Oxford Press, 1756'; Philip, p. 24.

Y

of the Court of King's Bench. Since the case could only be decided on grounds that would apply as much to Bibles and prayer books as to statutes, the liberty of the Universities to share in this market with the King's Printer was at stake.[1] Judgement was given in 1758.

OTHER PRINTERS IN OXFORD

In 1744 departed this life Leonard Lichfield, third printer in Oxford of those names, the only master of the craft in this city besides the University. If he were not overshadowed by the other, Lichfield might be distinguished among eighteenth-century printers by his substantial production.

Of him hardly anything is known, and of his plant or his employees nothing. He apprenticed himself to his father of the same names in 1681 for seven years;[2] but his father died in February 1686,[3] and the younger must have succeeded to his business, for the imprint of Leonard Lichfield continues without interruption. His grandfather, his grandmother, and his father were appointed Printers to the University, or *academiae typographi*, by vote of Convocation,[4] but it does not appear that the third Leonard held this appointment or claimed the title, though he sometimes put the arms of the University on his title-pages. His exercise of the trade before printing was set free by the expiry of the last Licensing Act in 1695 implies protection by the University, and the Vice-Chancellor's *imprimatur* in many of Lichfield's books is a sign that his press had some sort of academic status.

In the first year of his freedom Lichfield was entrusted by Obadiah Walker with a book of Roman Catholic apology, one of those that King James II gave Walker permission to publish. His betrayal of Walker's confidence has been noted on an earlier page.[5]

Lichfield did some jobbing for the University, the 'programmas' (notices) for Lenten Exercises year by year and several editions of *A Description of the Painting in the Theatre*, and printed a great many sermons for its members, being in a position to charge less for this service than the Learned Press did.[6] Poems, essays, small manuals of instruction, besides theological controversy in pamphlet form, were the staple of his business, and among them were some familiar titles: Howell's *Common*

[1] Delegates' files, Pkt. 66.
[2] Univ. Arch. Chancellor's Court Papers 130.   [3] Wood, *Life*, iii, p. 180.
[4] Reg. Conv. T 26, p. 126; Reg. Conv. T 26, p. 330, 17 Sept. 1658.
[5] Above, p. 118.   [6] Above, p. 284.

Prayer Book the Best Companion, John Wallis's *Institutio logicae*, Oughtred's *Clavis mathematicae*. He was equal to a big book now and again, Plot's *Natural History of Oxfordshire*, the 2nd edition, 1705, Wells's *Lesser Prophets*, 3rd edition, 1729, and Pointer's 2-volume *History of England*, 1714; but the most impressive for its size, Charles Leigh's *Natural History of Lancashire, Cheshire, and the Peak* (1700), a folio of 380 pages, is a dreadful muddle. He printed at least one book in Welsh.[1]

Early in his career Lichfield discarded his father's poor equipment of type and invested in a range of founts cast in Fell's matrices. These must have been supplied to him by Peter de Walpergen, the University's typefounder, with or without the consent of the Delegates. His unsigned work cannot, therefore, be distinguished from that of the University Press on purely typographical grounds.

In early years his address was 'by University College', but in 1730 he had moved to 'King Street, near the East Gate', where he renewed his lease just before he died.[2] He died insolvent, and the Delegates of Accounts cancelled his bond to the University for £100.[3]

For more than fifty years Leonard Lichfield printed charts showing the determining bachelors of every year and the trials that they had to undergo.[4] Surviving examples for 1747 and 1754 bear the imprint of Leonard Lichfield in Holywell, a fourth homonymous printer. The fourth Leonard put his imprint on a book in 1748,[5] but there is some reason for surmising that he went out of business soon after printing the Lenten Exercises of 1754, because there was a sharp rise in the number of sermons issuing from the University Press after that year.

The New Printing Office

This office, owned by Richard Walker and William Jackson, opened up and issued the first *Oxford Flying Weekly Journal and Cirencester Gazette* on 6 September 1741.[6] Originally in St. Clement's, it moved after three weeks to High Street near the Market Cross.

Jackson, a bookseller, stationer, and printer, one of the founders of the Old Bank, lived to become in 1780 a partner of the University in the

---

[1] A translation dated 1733 of Edward Synge, *De religionis Christianae fundamentalibus*, in the Library of the University of Wales.
[2] H. E. Salter, *Oxford City Properties* (Oxford, 1926), pp. 302, 305.
[3] V.-C.'s Computus 1743–4 in Univ. Arch. W.P. β 21.
[4] In Bodl. G.A. Oxon. b. 19.
[5] *Southampton: a poem by a gentleman of Oriel College*, not seen but known to Madan.
[6] Bodl. MS. Top. Oxon. e. 145, fol. 5.

Bible Press. During 1782–93 he rented Wolvercote Paper Mill from the Duke of Marlborough.[1]

In 1753 the title of the newspaper was changed to *Jackson's Oxford Journal,* and as such it was published weekly until, in 1928, it was absorbed in the *Oxford Times.*

It is indicative of the new freedom to print since the expiry of the last Licensing Act in 1695 that the University exercised no control over this business. The Vice-Chancellor's *imprimatur* is not found in any publication of the New Printing Office; neither partner in it was matriculated.

There are early indications that the new press attracted work of the kind that had been done by the Lichfields—not sermons, not jobbing for the University, but the slighter pieces, poems, and humorous or vituperative tracts thrown off by dons and undergraduates in leisure moments. When the imprint is simply 'Oxford, printed in the year —', it is not certain that a publication came from Walker and Jackson's office, but it is very likely. The partners put their names on *An authentick narrative of the Inquisition* in 1750, and Jackson put his on *Love without a mask* in 1751, on George Ballard's *Memoir of several ladies* in 1752, and on a *Poem on the Countess of Pomfret's Benefaction* in 1756.

Among academical controversial pieces that came Jackson's way was Blackstone's momentous open letter *To the Reverend Doctor Randolph* of 1757 in which he drew public attention to his campaign for the reform of the Press Delegacy and the Press.

The New Printing Office was the normal channel for publications generated by the city and county, accordingly the election of knights of the shire in 1754 brought it a spate of work, poll-lists and scrutinies, advice to voters, irrepressible abuse from either side, and comical squibs.[2]

Jackson's printing is often anonymous and is difficult to distinguish by typographical criteria from the occasionally anonymous work of the Press.[3] Both used mainly Caslon's types from about 1746 onwards, the New Printing Office being the better-equipped with the big sizes; but that office had some Fell type too.[4]

---

[1] Carter, *Wolvercote Mill,* p. 24.

[2] Bodl. Gough Oxf. 39, 91, 101; Gough Oxf. fol. A. 248.

[3] A useful indication is a different manner of signing the sheets. Jackson begins with signature A, the title-leaf being [A1]: the Press gives A to the first leaf of text and [a], b, c to the preliminaries.

[4] *A Letter to the Printer, with a Letter to the Freeholders of Oxfordshire* (1753) is obviously Jackson's publication and is set in Fell Great Primer.

PART IV

THE ERA OF BLACKSTONE
1755–1780

CHAPTER XXI

Blackstone's Reform of the Press

THE DELEGACY

WILLIAM BLACKSTONE was made a Delegate of the Press on 2 July 1755 in the room of Euseby Isham deceased. He was 32, a fellow and bursar of All Souls, doctor of civil law, barrister, recorder of Wallingford, and assessor of the Chancellor's Court at Oxford. He had failed to secure election to the professorship of (civil) law in 1752, and had begun giving at Oxford the lectures on English law of which his famous *Commentaries* are a record.

He owed his nomination as a Delegate to the Senior Proctor of the year, the Hon. John Tracy, also of All Souls. It was made in the heat of controversy, because the Vice-Chancellor wanted the vacant place for himself, said he was entitled to it by established custom, and was personally affronted by the refusal; also because the two Proctors were asserting a disputed right to make an appointment without the Vice-Chancellor's consent.[1]

Tracy alleged that there was much dissatisfaction in the University with the neglect of the Press, which, he said, was largely due to 'the numerous avocations' of the Delegates (in other words, to their being also Heads of Houses and Delegates of Accounts); therefore he was

---

[1] G. Huddesford, 'To the Reverend and Worshipful the Heads of Colleges and Halls in the University of Oxford' (10 Dec. 1756) in *Observations relating to the Delegates of the Press* (Oxford, 1756).

determined to appoint someone who was neither and could pay more attention to publishing and printing.[1]

That was not really a good reason for choosing Blackstone, who had as many avocations as any man else in Oxford and attended to them more conscientiously than any. There must be a suspicion at least that the appointment was an incident in a revolt against an old order and one in which Blackstone played the leading part. Whether there was animosity between him and the Vice-Chancellor, George Huddesford, President of Trinity College, before this incident, and if so how to account for it, history does not make clear, but they were at daggers drawn after it. Huddesford did all he could to make Blackstone's place at the board uncomfortable and to suppress his voice at it. Blackstone wrote to him demanding an explanation of an insulting reference to him that the Vice-Chancellor had made in Congregation.[2]

It may be that Blackstone had other enemies among the Delegates besides Huddesford, who was only temporarily on the board *ex officio*. One of them could have been Thomas Jenner, President of Magdalen, elected Regius Professor of (Civil) Law in 1752, when Blackstone lost the Crown's nomination because he would not promise to serve the interests of the Duke of Newcastle.[3]

Six months after joining the board Blackstone circulated to his fellow Delegates 'Some Thoughts on the Oxford Press', a memorandum on the excessive prices charged for printing and the lack of organization of the house, offering suggestions for fixing piecework rates on a rational basis generally accepted in the trade.[4] He had made some study of printing practice and had advice from Samuel Richardson in London among others.[5] This document, according to Blackstone, was received by some of the Delegates 'with seeming satisfaction' and by others 'in gloomy and contemptuous silence' and was never considered at a meeting.[6]

At the same time, that is in March 1756, the Proctors of the former year, John Tracy and Charles Mortimer, sent to the Vice-Chancellor their account of events bearing on their appointments of Delegates and their refusal to appoint him (at the end of their term they had nominated

---

[1] [J. Tracy and C. Mortimer] *A Reply to Dr. Huddesford's Observations* (Oxford, 1756), p. 3. This is evidently from the New Printing Office.

[2] To Huddesford, 22 May 1756: Bodl. MS. Top. Oxon. d. 387, fol. 14.

[3] James Clitherow's preface to W. Blackstone's law Reports (1781).

[4] Printed in Philip, pp. 23–38, from the original in the Delegates' records.

[5] Printed in Philip, pp. 39–42. Original in the Delegates' records.

[6] W. Blackstone, *To the Reverend Doctor Randolph*, 21 May 1757 (Oxford, n.d.).

Humphrey Owen, the Librarian, to a vacancy in the Press Delegacy, an appointment which Huddesford professed to have annulled by with-holding his consent). The Proctors justified their actions by the terms of the University's statutes and precedents in the records of Convocation.[1]

They followed it up a month later with a memorandum on the same subject circulated in the common rooms of the colleges.[2]

After six months Huddesford replied by printing the Proctors' two memoranda with his observations.[3] He complained much of the ir-regularity of the Proctors' proceedings and of the discourtesy to him. He makes fun of the legalistic subtleties of the 'Paper-Writer', divining no doubt rightly that though the hand was Tracy's the brain behind it was Blackstone's.[4]

Issue was joined on the right claimed by the Proctors to appoint to this Delegacy without first securing the assent of the Vice-Chancellor. The statutes admitted of argument and the precedents were conflicting. The question was settled soon afterwards by a new statute: to simplify it a little, Huddesford was right if the Delegacy was a 'stated' (i.e. standing) one; the Proctors and Blackstone were right if the Delegacy was 'occasional' (i.e. ad hoc). Since common sense is on the side of regarding the Press Delegacy as permanent, the Vice-Chancellor had the better case, so far as this narrow issue is concerned, and his view has prevailed. The justification for his opponents' contention, at any rate in the eyes of posterity, is that it enabled them to get Blackstone on to the board. So doing they breached the citadel of power, thitherto occupied by the Heads of Houses, and thrust into it an indomitable fighter against abuses and neglect.

The Proctors replied promptly to Huddesford's pamphlet contesting his argument point by point.[5] The part of their reply that retains its interest is a demonstration that the practice of naming only Heads of Houses and Delegates of Accounts to the Press Delegacy is contemporaneous

[1] 'A Copy of a Paper deliver'd to the Vice-Chancellor by the Proctors of the last year a short time before they laid down their office', in Huddesford's *Observations relating to the Delegates of the Press.*
[2] 'A Copy of a Paper sent about to the Common Rooms soon after the present Proctors were admitted', in Huddesford's *Observations*, pp. 5–16. It is dated 1 May 1756.
[3] 'To the Reverend and Worshipful the Heads of Colleges and Halls', ibid.
[4] Theophilus Leigh, Master of Balliol, wrote to Sir William Dolben on 21 May 1756 with reference to the dispute, 'I was particularly sorry that Mr. Tracey of A. Souls, son of Lord Tracey, was made a Cats-foot, while in Office last year, by the Genius above mention'd.' He ends his letter: 'If that Genius be not suppress'd, there's an End of Government here!' (Northamptonshire Record Office, Dolben Papers, D (F) 88).
[5] *A Reply to Dr. Huddesford's Observations*, 28 Apr. 1756.

with the lowest condition of the Press. To illustrate the point they printed a list of Delegates of the Press from 1633 to 1756, the best list that there is.[1]

Huddesford's term as Vice-Chancellor ended in March 1757. Until then all Blackstone's suggestions for reform were treated, he said, 'with supercilious neglect, or at best with a languid indifference'.[2] He knew of a secret meeting of the Delegacy, 'assembled in a private conclave, to elude the claim of a delegate, whom his brethren had resolved to reject'.[3] The Vice-Chancellor, he said, had left out of summons to meetings whomsoever he thought fit. He himself had been told that he might attend if he came as 'a stated delegate' (which he argued he was not).[4] He had not been allowed to see the Warehouse-Keeper's accounts, and like other members of the University he was without access to the annual Computus of the Vice-Chancellor.[5]

Professedly hoping better things of Huddesford's successor, Blackstone published his famous open letter *To the Reverend Doctor Randolph*, dated 21 May 1757, in which he exposed to the world the decayed state of the Press, the misapplication of revenues that should have been spent on publishing, and the measures that he advocated for remedying these things. If he had really expected to accomplish much by agreement with Thomas Randolph he would hardly have done so; and indeed the omens were not favourable. As a deprecator of party zeal Randolph may have been prejudiced against such a fervent devotee of the Old Interest as Blackstone; on taking office he had refused to compromise on the disputed right of Vice-Chancellors to negative appointments to the Press Delegacy or to exclude from it the Delegates of Accounts.[6]

Ill-feeling between Blackstone and Randolph reached such a pitch that in January 1758 Blackstone wrote to the Vice-Chancellor complaining that for two years past every proposal of his with regard to the Press had been treated with hauteur and neglect and threatening 'if Endeavours to serve the Publick are to be received with a silent supercilious Contempt, to bring our Proceedings with relation to the Press . . . before another less indulgent Tribunal'.[7]

---

[1] *A reply to Dr. Huddesford's Observations*, at the end.
[2] *To the Reverend Doctor Randolph*, p. 4; Philip, p. 46.
[3] Ibid., p. 6. Referring, no doubt, to Humphrey Owen.
[4] Ibid., p. 7.   [5] Ibid., p. 21; Philip, p. 61.
[6] 'Mr. Fowell's Narrative' beginning 'An accommodation of the Matters in Dispute', printed without a title, presumably at the New Printing Office. It was issued on 30 Mar. 1757.
[7] Draft in Bodl. MS. Top. Oxon. d. 387, fol. 24.ᵛ

The threat was not empty. Blackstone's reputation and influence were growing in the legal profession as well as in Oxford. His law-reporting, begun in 1746, brought him in touch with prominent men on the bench and at the bar; Lord Mansfield, Chief Justice, was his friend; one of the judges, Sir Michael Foster, wrote Blackstone a letter in 1758 explaining the motives for the judgement in *Baskett* v. *the University of Cambridge*.[1] His book, *An Analysis of the Laws of England*, published in 1756 and reaching a fourth edition within three years, was a step in his rise to celebrity, and later in 1758 he was to become the first Vinerian Professor of English Law. The diary of Sir Roger Newdigate, member of Parliament for the University, records breakfasts with Blackstone at this time.

The first sign of the old guard relenting was the passing in Convocation of a revised statute regulating appointments of Delegates of the Press in December 1757.[2] It declared that they were a 'stated' delegacy, and that the nomination of new members to fill vacancies should be the joint act of the Vice-Chancellor and Proctors or of two of these three. This was a compromise putting an end to the Vice-Chancellor's claim to a veto. Another compromise, but an important concession to Blackstone and his friends, was a provision that not more than three Delegates of Accounts should at any time be Delegates of the Press. Blackstone's recommendations were followed to some extent in requirements that the Delegates should meet at least four times a year in the Clarendon Printing House, and that the University Registrar should record their decisions in a special book. Humphrey Owen, Bodley's Librarian, whose appointment as a Delegate in 1756 Huddesford purported to have negatived, is given statutory recognition as one of the board.

Within the Delegacy there was no corresponding will to reach an accommodation. On 21 January Blackstone sent the Vice-Chancellor a draft of proposals which he intended to move at the meeting summoned for the following week. It amounted to a comprehensive scheme for remedying the misapplication of funds, failure to keep a unified and accessible account, oblivion of the relevant charters and statutes, and sufferance of an incompetent overseer—all the griefs that Blackstone had expressed clearly and at length in his open letter to Randolph of the previous year.[3] Of this communication Randolph took no notice, either by acknowledging receipt of it or by mentioning it at the meeting.[4]

---

[1] Printed in i, W. Blackstone's Reports, at p. 122.
[2] Reg. Conv. Bh. 35, pp. 5, 6; Philip, pp. 75–6.
[3] Blackstone's draft in Bodl. MS. Top. Oxon. d. 387, fol. 9.   [4] Ibid., fol. 24.

330 BLACKSTONE'S REFORM OF THE PRESS

This was the instance of 'hauteur and neglect' that caused Blackstone to write his letter to the Vice-Chancellor threatening exposure of the wrongs of the Press to the world at large.

In fact opposition to him had begun to crumble. Though he said that his proposals sent on 21 January were ignored, one of them, the transcription of the charters and statutes of the realm and of the University applicable to the Press into a book available to the Delegates was adopted at the meeting four days later. The book is in the Delegates' archives, but the transcribing never was completed. Moreover, on 1 February the Delegates resolved that the Registrar should keep a book with the minutes of their meetings starting from one end and accounts of receipts and expenditure for their publications starting from the other.

The tale told by this book, labelled at one end 'Orders of the Delegates of the Press Mdcclviii', is of a sudden and complete collapse of opposition to Blackstone's programme. The proposals he submitted to the unwilling Vice-Chancellor in January were adopted entire on 9 February; on 16 February Daniel Prince, Blackstone's candidate, was unanimously chosen to succeed the incompetent and corrupt Richardson and his peccant son-in-law Wood as Warehouse-Keeper and Overseer. On 18 March Blackstone's meticulous scheme for fixing the rates of pay of the workmen in accordance with the number of letters they set or copies they printed was put into force and his method of calculating the prices to be charged to outside customers was approved. On the 16th the Vice-Chancellor, Dr. Randolph himself, moved that the thanks of the board be given to Dr. Blackstone for his care and trouble in working out these rates and prices.

So it was peace at last; and for Blackstone to see his vision of reformation fully realized it remained only to find a procedure for claiming the drawback of duty on paper used for learned printing by the two Universities by the Statute 10 Anne c. 18 but heretofore not claimed by them.[1] That he did in 1760. It was peace after three years of exceptionally bitter antagonism, in which the forms of eighteenth-century politeness and deference do little to conceal ill-will of great intensity. Faced by a privileged class whose abuse of authority had gone unchallenged for a generation Blackstone asserted his right without a hint of a consciousness of inferiority, with as much dignity as tenacity.

It would be hard to find in English history another such victory of reform with no significant compromise. It may have saved the Press from

[1] See above, p. 217.

extinction, it almost certainly saved learned publishing by corporately-owned university presses; it also shook Oxford profoundly, for what could be done in the Press could be done in other departments of the University.

Of course, like other English reforms, it was seen by its advocates as a return to the past.

Does there even exist at this hour [Blackstone demanded of the Reverend Doctor Randolph in 1757] such a thing as a *learned* press, according to the idea that was formerly conceived by LAUD, and latterly exemplified by FELL? Has not the CLARENDON printinghouse (that monument of our former successes) been made the property of a favourite family, and a nest of imposing mechanics; while the interests of learning have so far been forgotten or neglected, that the office of architypographer has (contrary to statute) been laid aside for six and twenty years? Would this have been the case, had the care of this department been entrusted to separate hands, accountable (as directed by convocation) to those who have broke in upon their province, and who only account to themselves?[1]

Blackstone would have been incapable of suggesting anything new. English law taught him respect for the intentions of donors and the sanctity of trusts; but to him history was very real. He would look in dusty old instruments for seeds that might grow, and he would have distrusted a growth that had no roots far back in the past. A muddle like that of the eighteenth-century Press he would disentangle by tracing its history, and that he could do because of his quick grasp of principles combined with a willingness to plod. The Press keeps the rough notes that he made of a great number of documents in the University Archives.

Agitation by Blackstone and his friends was effectual in widening the qualifications of a Delegate of the Press. After 1694 until his appointment in 1755 every Delegate had been Head of a college or hall at the time of his appointment. Between 1755 and 1800 of twenty-four accessions to the Delegacy eight were of men who were already Heads of Houses. Like Blackstone himself, who became Principal of New Inn Hall in 1761, three were elected to headships soon after joining the board.

REVIVAL OF PUBLISHING

During the winding-up of the tangled affairs of Stephen Richardson in 1756, 1757, and two months of 1758, when Wood the pressman was left

---

[1] *To the Reverend Doctor Randolph*, pp. 26–7; Philip, p. 67.

in charge at the Press and Richardson's son and executor, Zaccheus, rendered the accounts, nothing was printed for the Delegates but some notices and the abridgement of the University's statutes for under-graduates in 1756.

A capital book, the second edition of Edmund Gibson's *Codex juris ecclesiastici Anglicani*, was, however, under consideration by the Delegates at this time. Gibson dying in 1748 was known to have intended to give to the University his right to dispose of the printing of this work, originally published in London in 1713, including his manuscript additions and amendments. He did not make the gift in his lifetime and omitted to do so by his will, but his residuary legatees felt in honour bound to relinquish their rights in the book to the University and did so by a deed of 26 March 1751.[1]

The Delegates had to make up their minds whether to publish. The book is the undisputed authority on its subject, and the new material added greatly to its value; but it was a large undertaking, and there were obstacles to be got over.

Henry Lintot, a London bookseller, disputed the University's right to print the *Codex*. It recited and digested Acts of Parliament, and Lintot claimed the sole right to print it as holder of the patent for 'all manner of law books which any way relate to the common or statute law'.[2] He demanded a hundred copies as the price of his permission. This number the Delegates thought was excessive, and they proposed thirty instead.[3] An agreement between Gibson's son and executor, Lintot, and the University on these terms was engrossed in triplicate for execution in September 1755, when Blackstone intervened pointing out to his fellow Delegates that the University's charters gave it a right to override patents for printing.[4] This, he said, was an instance of the disadvantage of their not having easy access to the charters.

A new agreement was drawn up substituting Thomas Baskett for Lintot. As King's Printer Baskett also had the sole right to the statutes,[5] and he was paying the University an annual rent partly for its forbearance to comprint on him. He was content with one copy of the book. This

---

[1] Copied in the Delegates' Orders; *First Minute Book*, pp. 55–6.

[2] W. M. Sale, Jr., *Samuel Richardson: Master Printer* (Ithaca, 1950), p. 135. He gives a valuable account of the devolution of the Law Patent at pp. 134–44.

[3] D.O. 26 July 1754; *First Minute Book*, p. 57.

[4] *To the Reverend Doctor Randolph*, p. 7; Philip, p. 49.

[5] The conflict of the two patents as to statutes was never resolved: Sale, *Samuel Richardson*, p. 137.

deed, passing to the Chancellor, Masters, and Scholars all Bishop Gibson's property in the work was executed on 31 December 1755.[1]

Blackstone was critical of the Delegates' indecision and delay over the *Codex*.[2] He said that they did not finally commit themselves to print it until February 1756 and took until October to conclude arrangements for doing so. In October they entered into partnership for the venture with four booksellers, three in Oxford, one in London, reserving to themselves 12 of the total of 16 shares.[3] James Fletcher of Oxford acted as treasurer and advanced the money against repayment.

The book was printed at the Press in 1756–61 and published in the latter year. The partnership was charged with the cost of paper and printing, including the usual poundage to cover the University's over-heads. The four booksellers owning between them four shares must have stocked and sold the edition, for the University did not. When an account for the venture was drawn up in 1770 of 500 printed 350 copies were unsold. What became of them our accounts do not show.

To turn to the minutes of the Delegates' meetings in the years im-mediately after the reform is refreshing as compared with the arid period before it. There is every sign of fresh energy and determination. Especially praiseworthy is a resolution of 16 February 1758 that

. . . the Royal professor of Hebrew and that the Savilian Professors, be requested to attend the next meeting of this Delegacy; in order to re-commend such Books in their several Professions, the Publication of which will be (in their opinion) the most acceptable to the Public, and most for the Honour of the University.[4]

The professors did attend a fortnight later. It may be assumed that from Thomas Hunt, Professor of Hebrew and Arabic, came suggestions that bore fruit, a new edition of Hyde's *History of Persian Religion* and a collation by Kennicott of manuscripts of the Hebrew Bible. The Savilian professors, Bradley of astronomy and Bliss of geometry, were less pro-ductive; but to them is attributable the completion in 1758 of Halley's edition of Menelaus on spherics of which the sheets printed in 1714 had since lain in the warehouse without title or preface.[5]

Some twenty years after the adoption of his proposals Blackstone

---

[1] At any rate, it bears that date. The deed and the earlier engrossments are in the archive of the Printer to the University (Box A5).

[2] *To the Reverend Doctor Randolph*, p. 5; Philip, p. 47.

[3] D.O. 26 Oct. 1756; *First Minute Book*, p. 58.

[4] D.O. 1 Mar. 1711; Philip, p. 94.   [5] See above, p. 291.

looked back with complacency on the books that the Delegacy had been enabled to publish.[1] He mentions Lord Clarendon's *Life* (1759), Hyde's *Historia religionis veterum Persarum* (2nd edition, 1760), Gibson's *Codex* (1761), Heath's notes on the Greek tragedians (1762), Chandler's new edition of the *Marmora Oxoniensia* (1763), the Greek Testament in the new type by Baskerville (1763), and Warton's Theocritus (1770). He takes special pride in the subvention (£40 a year) which the Delegates voted in 1760 towards Kennicott's collations.

These books, excepting the last, were the outcome of projects that fell into the Delegates' lap; and even Kennicott's great work is said to have been suggested to him by Bishop Secker.[2] Clarendon's *Life* was extracted from the collection of his manuscripts given to the University by his descendants;[3] the Theocritus was based on notes by James St. Amand bequeathed by him to the Bodleian in 1754.[4] The others were offered by their editors or were new editions of old titles. To get these books into print was an achievement, but the board had still to show that it could initiate works and find apt writers for them.

The acquisition of Clarendon's manuscripts and the known intention of the Delegates to print his *Life* as written by himself and his *State Papers* made it an opportune time for a new edition of the *History of the Rebellion*, of which there had been none since 1732. Preparations for such an edition were made in 1759,[5] but they came to nothing. On 19 July the Delegates agreed to print '1,000 copies of Lord Clarendon's History with the continuation of his Life' in five quarto volumes. Nine days later they decided to postpone the printing until an edition of the *Life* was done.[6] In March 1760 they resolved that 'the second edition of Lord Clarendon's History in Octavo be sold in sheets at fourteen shillings per set'.[7]

But for the last of these entries in the Orders there would be no reason to think that there was an edition of the *History* at this time.[8] No copy of it can be traced, and the accounts of the Press do not show a charge for the printing or any receipts from the sale of it. The conclusion must be

---

[1] Blackstone's copy of his letter *To the Reverend Doctor Randolph* with MS. additions for a new edition in Bodl. MS. Top. Oxon. d. 387, at p. 22 of the book.

[2] Below, p. 410.

[3] See below, p. 362.

[4] Macray, *Annals*, pp. 252–3; D.O. 17 Apr. 1758.

[5] The accounts for Delegates' books record a payment to the Overseer of £200 'for Ld. Clarendon's History' and his repayment of that sum in 1760.

[6] D.O.; Philip, pp. 107, 108.

[7] Philip, p. 111.

[8] Madan included it in his manuscript list of Oxford Books (Bodl. MS. Dep. e. 12, 13) on the faith of Philip Bliss, but with a query.

that the order made in 1760 used the word 'History' by mistake for 'Life'. The octavo *Life* on small paper issued in 1759 was sold for 14*s.*, and the second edition, printed in 1760, was selling for 13*s.* in 1764.[1]

Slowly but with increasing assurance the Delegacy in the years 1758–80 arrived at a respectable mastery of learned publishing. It ceased to depend on offers of manuscripts, and in its attempts at finding themes and writers for them it becomes possible to see the emergence of a policy and a business with a recognizable character. As publishers generally do, it dealt largely in books fortuitously offered to it, but it declined them increasingly.

Improved texts of the Greek and Latin classics predominate. The Delegates sought for, and engaged, editors for Polybius, Cicero, Xenophon (the *Hellenica* and *Memorabilia*), Plutarch's *Moralia*, Hephaestion the grammarian, Apollonius Rhodius, Strabo, Caesar. They accepted proffers of Euripides, Aristotle's *Poetics*, and Longinus.

They found editors for a corrected English Bible and Book of Common Prayer, they accepted a New Testament in Syriac, and a lexicon and grammar of Coptic. In medicine they undertook the text in Arabic of Albucasis on surgery; in mathematics and astronomy they tried to publish Pappus and published Archimedes and Bradley's *Observations*. The natural sciences are represented by the second edition of Martin Lister on shells, English literature by a second edition of the Shakespeare by Hanmer. They set Uri to work at cataloguing the oriental manuscripts in the Bodleian and Radcliffe libraries; they were willing to accept a catalogue of the Bodleian's Greek manuscripts and another of those in Slavonic languages, Coptic, German, and Tartar.

The crowning achievement of those years, Kennicott's variorum Hebrew Bible, was printed for the author, not for the Delegates; but they paid him an annual stipend while he was working at it and resolved to publish it if he could not.[2]

The board decided, 'for several reasons' (probably mainly of cost), not to adopt Thomas Hunt's suggestion that it should produce the Arabic lexicon of Golius, 'now very scarce'; and it put on record the reason for not accepting the gift of a new translation of the New Testament:

It is resolved by the Delegates not to print at the expence of the University the Works of any private Person containing either a Translation or an Exposition of any part of the Sacred Scriptures, lest they should seem by so

---

[1] 'Accounts of Lord Clarendon's Life and State Papers', manuscript in the Printer's archive. [2] D.O. 14 June 1771.

doing to give the Sanction of their Approbation, and thro' them that of the University, to Works which comprise Matter of Controversy or dubious Interpretation.[1]

Too many of the projects fell by the wayside. Polybius and Pappus were abandoned by a succession of editors; after a false start Caesar came out in ten volumes in 1783; Plutarch in 1795–1830, Xenophon in 1783, Hephaestion in 1810, Strabo in 1807. Uri's was the only eighteenth-century catalogue of Bodleian manuscripts.

The works published by the University in 1758–80 were in number 23. Toup's Longinus, Heath's notes on the Greek tragedians, Lister on shells, and Euripides sold well; the rest had, at best, indifferent commercial success.

Books strongly bound and given to the library of the College at New York in 1772 must be taken to be those in greatest estimation of the Delegates' stock:

> Marmora Oxoniensia (ed. Chandler, 1763)
> Gibson's Codex juris ecclesiastici Anglicani (2nd ed., 1761)
> Clarendon's Life (1759)
> Clarendon State Papers, vol. i (1767)
> Lister's Synopsis conchyliorum (1770)
> Hyde's Historia religionis veterum Persarum (2nd ed., 1760)
> Hyde's Syntagma dissertationum orientalium (1767)
> Potter's Works (1754)
> Evangelia Gothica, ed. Lye (1750)
> Novum Testamentum Graecum (1763)
> Hanmer's Shakespear (2nd ed., 1771)
> Burton's Sermons (1764)
> Catalogue of Printed Books in the Bodleian Library (1738)
> Novum Testamentum Gothicum (1715)
> Maundrel's Travels (7th ed., 1749)
> Plato's Parmenides (ed. Thomson, 1728)
> Menelaus on Spherics (ed. Halley, 1758)
> Heath's Notes on Aeschylus, Sophocles, and Euripides (1762)
> Census habitus nascente Christo (1738)
> Corpus statutorum Univ. Oxon. (1768)
> Warton's Theocritus (1770).

Bound copies were sent to the King of the *Marmora*, the Theocritus, the *Synopsis conchyliorum*, Toup's Longinus (1773), Scholtz's Coptic *Lexicon*

[1] D.O. 10 May 1768.

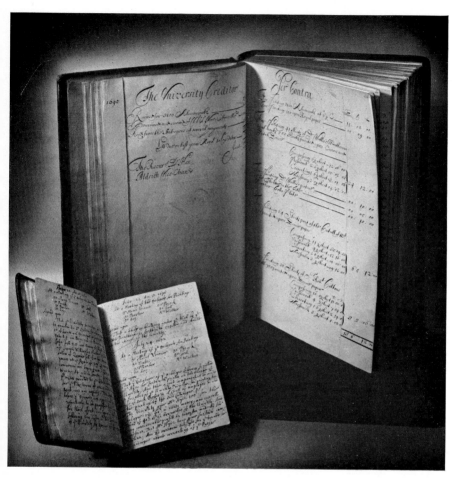

The first Minute Book of the Delegates of the Press (1668–1756) and the first book of the Warehouse-Keeper's 'Account for Printing' (1691–1708)

Frederick, Viscount North, later Earl of Guilford (1732–92), Chancellor of the University of Oxford from 1772. From an engraving after the portrait by Sir Nathaniel Dance Holland

(1774), Musgrave's Euripides (1777), and Woide's Syriac Gospels (1778). The binder of the royal copy of Theocritus was named Thompson, and he was employed by the Press to bind a good many presents about this time.

CHAPTER XXII

Press Accounting and Finances

THE Delegates, as advised by Blackstone, began keeping accounts in 1758. Previously there had been no single account of income and out-goings for their business as a whole, the Vice-Chancellor had inserted the relevant figures in his annual Computus under various heads. Blackstone drew up a model account for 1758;[1] by conforming with that the Delegates could be sure that the true state of their finances was made plain.

Under receipts were separately entered the rent from the Bible Press which included forbearance to print the books reserved to the lessee, the profit from the *Almanack*, the surplus for the year in the Schools Account and the Theatre Account, revenues of the University which Convocation had devoted to printing, and the profit, if there were any, from the Press. Under expenditure were put payments by the Vice-Chancellor for paper, for fees of editors, correctors, and artists, for taxes, maintenance of the premises, and subsidies paid to the Warehouse-Keeper to make good losses incurred in the year's work at the Press.

No account was taken of the value of premises, plant, materials, or stock: that would have been needless for a business as unlikely as this to be sold as a whole or in shares. It was in 1766 that the Delegates first demanded of the Warehouse-Keeper annual inventories of goods and type.[2]

The Warehouse-Keeper continued to render yearly accounts to the board of Delegates. His receipts were from the sale of Delegates' books and poundage on printing for others. He charged the Delegacy for printing its books and for jobbing done for the University. Under the head of expenses there was no clear line of demarcation between him and the Vice-Chancellor on the Delegates' behalf: both paid for paper and type, for maintenance, and for taxes. In theory at any rate, amounts paid to or by the Warehouse-Keeper all made an appearance in the Delegates' accounts as part of a lump sum of gain or loss.

---

[1] Bodl. MS. Top. Oxon. d. 387, fol. 26 (draft). He gave further guidance to the accountant, probably Foster, the Registrar, in a letter now in America: *The Letters of Sir William Blackstone in the Hampton L. Carson Collection of the Free Library of Philadelphia*, ed. Howell J. Heaney (Philadelphia, 1958), p. 6.　　　　　　　　　　[2] D.O. 12 July 1766.

Whoever drew up the accounts for the Delegates was strangely fallible; nor were the members of the board who certified his accuracy by signing them careful enough. In 1759 a deficit of £435 on the previous year's trading was placed to credit. When the mistake was noticed this amount was subtracted from the credit balance for 1762, but it took the accountant another year to grasp that it must be deducted once more. From 1772 to 1778 the balance is seriously wrong, by as much as £2,000 by the end of that time, because the accumulated surplus in the Theatre account, instead of its year's increase, was credited to the Press year after year. After the correction of these mistakes the balance of accounts was roughly that shown in the accompanying table (pp. 341–2).

By 1771 the Delegates were confident enough of their solvency to lend the Professor of Astronomy money to equip his observatory with a telescope and two quadrants.[1] As the University's occasional delegates for the business they signed an agreement with the instrument-maker, Mr. Bird. The amount debited to the Press in 1771–4 was £1,130, plus £17. 5s. for carriage from London. Professor Hornsby's reports to the board on the progress of the work are of technical interest.[2]

In January 1775, at which time the Delegates' credit was overstated in their accounts by more than £1,000, they made their first investment in interest-bearing securities: the Vice-Chancellor was empowered to put the yearly balance of the Press accounts into the public funds. In 1776 New South Sea Annuities were bought for £1,200 and yielded £36 a year interest.

For the years 1760, 1761, and 1767–72 there is a separate statement of a 'Lending Account'. It consisted of Lord Rolle's benefaction of £100 and one from Dr. Hodges of £200.

Rolle's benefaction is described in a memorandum written in 1758 by John Burton. Blackstone lent it to be copied in the Delegates' register-book.[3] It was not copied, but the original is preserved.

Henry Rolle Esq. at the instance of Mr Burton of CCC gave £100 to the University for a lending fund, for the use of Editors. He gave no regulations himself for the manner of disposition: but left this to Dr Holmes the Vice Canc. and Mr Burton. They accordingly did in the first instance of the Application of the Monies, make the following regulation viz. that the work propos'd by any Editor, shou'd be approv'd by the Vice Can: & Curators of the Press, as saleable & usefull—that the Editor shou'd procure

---

[1] D.O. 5 Feb. 1771. [2] D.O. *passim* from Dec. 1771 to Nov. 1773.
[3] His list of items to be copied inserted loose in the book.

a sufficient Bondsman for the repayment to the University the monies expended in carrying on the Edition (viz. for purchase of the Paper & paying the Compositor, Pressmen, Warehouse keeper & pro usu typorum to the Univ.) that the University shou'd keep in their Warehouse the work as it was printed off, as further security for the repayment, that this repayment being made, the Editor was at Liberty to make the best Advantage of his Edition.

This is what was propos'd & done in the first Instance, & approv'd by Mr Rolle.—whether any further regulation was made by Dr Holmes I know not. John Burton July 5. 1758.

The gift must have been made in the years 1732–4, while William Holmes was Vice-Chancellor. Henry Rolle became Baron Rolle of Stevenstone in 1748.[1] His £100 was lent by the Delegates in 1744 to Nathaniel Forster for his Hebrew Bible published in 1750, and his executors paid it back without interest in 1760.

Walter Hodges, D.D., Provost of Oriel and a Delegate since 1729 of the Press, died in January 1757. In April 1758 the Delegates allowed his executor until Michaelmas to pay in Hodges's 'Legacy of Two Hundred Pounds for the Use of the University Press'. Blackstone noted that 'the Clause in Dr. Hodges' will concerning his benefaction' should be copied in the register-book, but that was not done. £70 of it was on loan in 1772 to Mr. Pemberton of Oriel College towards the publication of Plutarch's *Apophthegms*.

After 1772 these benefactions disappear from the accounts; but they have since been reinstated.

A procedure for claiming the drawback of excise and import duty on paper allowed to the Universities of England and Scotland by the Act of 1712[2] was settled in an exchange of courteous letters between Blackstone and Charles Lowndes, Chief Clerk of the Treasury in 1760,[3] and the first payment in consequence was made to the Press the year after. The Act allowed the universities to recover their expenditure on these imposts if the paper had been used for printing books in the Latin, Greek, oriental, or northern languages and prescribed the manner in which claims had to be made. The chief manager of a university press had to declare in writing to his vice-chancellor the amounts, kinds, and qualities of paper used for these books and the duty paid; the vice-chancellor, thus in-

---

[1] Collins's *Peerage*, ed. Brydges, iii, p. 528.
[2] See above, p. 217. The amending Acts preserved this privilege.
[3] Lowndes's letter of 9 Oct. 1760 copied on the back of the form inserted in the Delegates' minutes. Printed in Philip, p. 114.

formed, had to forward the manager's account to the Treasury with a certificate of its accuracy and to nominate a person to receive the money.[1] Blackstone drafted a form for each of these officers to complete and sign,[2] and submitted the draft to Lowndes, who thought it 'so well considered that no alteration can be made in it, but for the worse'. The forms were printed some years later and were used regularly until duties on paper were abolished in 1861.

The sums refunded to this University in the early years were not large:

$$
\begin{array}{llll}
1761 & \pounds 18 & os. & 9d. \\
1762 & 5 & 9 & 1 \\
1763 & 41 & 3 & 9 \\
1764 & 64 & 7 & 1\frac{1}{2} \\
1765 & 16 & 0 & 6 \\
\end{array}
$$

but before 1794, when Bibles, Testaments, and prayer books were also admitted for drawback,[3] they sometimes came to as much as £100, the larger amounts reflecting the steep increases of the duties in the late eighteenth century rather than a bigger output of books in the learned languages.

BALANCE OF THE PRESS ACCOUNTS 1756–80
(Neglecting shillings and pence)

Year	Delegates' Accounts — Balance of credit or debit after correcting major errors £	Subventions from University funds included in the Delegates' Accounts as corrected — Schools Money £	Theatre Money £	Warehouse-Keeper's Accounts — Profit or loss on printing and bookselling £
1756				P 7
1757				L 17
1758	D 435	—	—	P 10
1759	C 350	102	529	L 281
1760	C 512	5	—	L 171
1761	C 197	210	—	L 152
1762	D 74	—	—	L 162
1763	D 339	358	—	L 149
1764	D 739	—	—	L 13
1765	D 651	241	—	P 45

continued overleaf

[1] 10 Anne, c. 18 (19 in Ruffhead), s. 63.
[2] Blackstone's draft and one for a memorial from the Vice-Chancellor to the Commissioners of the Treasury seeking approval of the proposed procedure are at the Press.
[3] D. C. Coleman, *The British Paper Industry 1495–1860*, ch. v; R. C. Jarvis, 'The Paper-Makers and the Excise in the Eighteenth Century', *The Library*, 5th ser. xiv (1959), pp. 100–16.

Balance of the Press Accounts 1756–80 (*cont.*):

		£	£	£		£
1766	C	590	114	—	P	43
1767	C	795	131	—	P	18
1768	C	1,470	379	—	L	63
1769	C	2,117	222	—	L	288
1770	C	2,061	319	—	L	218
1771	C	2,507	157	—	P	165
1772	C	3,231	289	132	L	204
1773	C	3,132	175	91	L	63
1774	C	2,971	61	22	L	215
1775	C	3,293	24	47	L	173
1776	C	3,100	—	27	P	47
1777	C	2,821	—	83	L	155
1778	C	2,415	150	—	L	125
1779	C	1,438	190	78	L	173
1780	C	110	142	300	L	97

RELATION OF THE PRESS ACCOUNTS TO THE VICE-CHANCELLOR'S COMPUTUS

The sums paid by the Vice-Chancellor from University funds to make up losses on the year's trading by the printing Press appear fairly regularly in his annual Computus. There are discrepancies in some years between these sums as they appear in the Computus and in the accounts rendered for printing by the Warehouse-Keeper.

The subventions to the Press (publisher and printer) from the Schools Money and the Theatre Money as they are entered in the Accounts of the Delegates are wholly different from the surplus in these two funds as it is recorded year by year in the Computus for the years 1768–1803.[1] The funds in hand from the Schools and the Theatre are in all years but one (1779–80) far greater than the amounts paid over to the Press.

The Vice-Chancellor's payments to the Warehouse-Keeper as they are recorded in their respective accounts for the years 1768/9 to 1779/80 are these:

	V.-C.'s Computus (*November to November*) £	*The Account for Printing* (*Michaelmas to Michaelmas*) £
1768/69	225	288
1769/70	261	218
1770/71	Received 165	Profit 165
1771/72	Nil	204
1772/73	504	63

[1] Univ. Arch. W.P. β 22(2).

1773/74	63	215
1774/75	215	173
1775/76	173	Profit 47
1776/77	Nil	155
1777/78	Nil	125
1778/79	125	173
1779/80	173	97

The Vice-Chancellor's payments are calculated more often than not to recoup the printer for a loss in the previous year, the Warehouse-Keeper's account, it must be supposed, having reached him too late for inclusion in his Computus. It is impossible to repress a fearful surmise that the large amount, £504. 2s. 2d., standing in the Computus for 1772/3 was due to a misreading of the £204. 2s. 2d. claimed by the Warehouse-Keeper the year before. The Vice-Chancellor and others signed both sets of accounts and should have noticed the mistake. Other discrepancies have no obvious explanation.

Where payments to the Press Delegacy of Schools and Theatre Money are concerned correspondence between the Computus and the Press accounts is totally lacking. The figures for receipts and expenditure under these two heads are conveniently set out in the Computus from 1769/70 onwards. The following is the record from that year until 1779/80 of money paid into these two accounts after deduction of expenses:

	Schools £	Theatre £
1769/70	367	252
1770/71	386	285
1771/72	521	305
1772/73	68	248
1773/74	339	269
1774/75	327	316
1775/76	399	342
1776/77	330	425
1777/78	572	422
1778/79	525	500
1779/80	472	272*

* After paying £300 to the Press.

Comparison with the table on pp. 341–2 shows that the Curators of the Schools and Theatre funds were paying only a small part of their surplus revenues to the Press. That was contrary to the University's statutes: Tit. XX. IV of the Laudian code provided that any surplus of the Schools money, after paying for upkeep of the buildings should be spent on erecting and maintaining a printing-office for the University. In accepting Sheldon's gift of the Theatre Convocation bound itself to respect the donor's desire that 'what shall every year be remaining of the Rents' with which he endowed the building 'over and above the Charge of Repayres' should be spent on the Learned Press.[1]

That was the letter of the University's constitution; but to disregard it was reasonable enough. The Curators of both funds needed a balance in hand for foreseeable and unforeseeable works, and the Press, as it was conducted in the eighteenth century, was in no state to employ large amounts of money. Laud had envisaged the printing of 'the greatest possible number of manuscript volumes, Greek and Latin, now buried in the Public Library, not fit to be perpetually at war with moths and maggots'.[2] Even under the influence of Blackstone the Press fell far short of needing the sustenance that the Archbishop would have allowed it.

There is evidence at a later date of an understanding between the Delegates of the Press and the Curators of the Schools to share the Schools money so as best to suit their respective wants. It is a memorandum, unsigned and not dated, assignable to an early year of the nineteenth century.[3]

That an account be kept of the School Money under Statute de Scholis Publicis, that is, of the Articles received and expended in the gross shall be annually transmitted to the Delegates of the Press, and the balance viz. surplus of School Money struck accordingly.

That a reserve by mutual agreement be made for the purposes of extra-ordinary repairs in the Schools, as well as for extraordinary expenses of the Press, to be replinished when diminished by such demands in such degree and proportion as may seem expedient to both Delegacies.

The disparity of the Vice-Chancellor's Computus and the Accounts of the Delegates of the Press where the Schools money is concerned points to some such liberal interpretation of the University's financial obligation to the Press in the latter part of the eighteenth century.

---

[1] Univ. Arch. Reg. Conv. Ta, p. 266.   [2] Griffiths, p. 196.
[3] A loose leaf in the 3rd A/cs. It is written on paper watermarked 1804.

CHAPTER XXIII

The Bible Press 1755–1780

THE PRIVILEGE

THE King's Printer's assault on the right of the University of Cambridge to print statutes of the realm, made in 1743,[1] came before the judges of King's Bench in 1758. Blackstone's report of the case speaks of it as having been dormant for a long time.[2] At the hearing before him in 1743 the Chancellor had ordered that a case be stated for trial at common law. This was done: a copy of the document with marginal annotations in Blackstone's hand is in the archive of the Delegates of the Press.[3] It recites the letters patent granted to King's Printers, beginning with Richard Grafton in 1547, of an exclusive right to print statutes and other publications of the King and his successors on the throne. Queen Elizabeth's grant to Christopher Barker in 1577, the first to include the Bible, is recited, but earlier patents for Bible-printing are ignored as irrelevant to the matter in hand. The subsequent history of the patent of King's Printer is traced to its vesting in Thomas and Robert Baskett as administrators with the will annexed of the goods of their father, who died in 1742.

The claim of the University is supported first by a recital of letters patent of Henry VIII dated 20 July 1534 giving it a right to have three stationers and printers or vendors of books each of whom might print within the University all manner of books approved by the Chancellor or Vice-Chancellor and three doctors. Second, the case recites the Act of Parliament of 1571 (13 Eliz. c. 29) incorporating the two Universities and confirming earlier royal grants to them. Third, it recites letters patent of Charles I dated 6 February 1629 declaring in unambiguous terms that it should be lawful for any printer appointed by the University to print within the University of Cambridge any of the books expressed in any letters patent granted to other persons by Queen Elizabeth I, King James I, or by himself.

The questions put to the judges were whether the King's Printers were

---

[1] See above, p. 321.   [2] 1 W. Blackstone's Reports, p. 105.   [3] Pkt. 66.

entitled to the sole right of printing Acts of Parliament and abridgements of them and whether the University of Cambridge had the right or privilege of printing these things.

The certificate to the Chancellor signed by Lord Mansfield, Chief Justice, and three other judges on 24 November 1758 was this:

Having heard Counsel on both sides and Considered of this Case, we are of Opinion that During the Term granted by the Letters Patent Dated the 13th. of October in the 12th. Year of the Reign of Queen Ann the Plaintiffs are Intitled to the right of Printing Acts of Parliament and Abridgments of Acts of Parliament Exclusive of all other Persons not Authorized to Print the same by Prior Grants from the Crown.

But We think that by Virtue of the Letters Patent bearing date the 20th. day of July in the 26th. Year of the Reign of King Henry the 8th. And the Letters Patent bearing date the 6th. of February in the 3d. Year of the Reign of King Charles the 1st. the Chancellor Masters and Scholars of the University of Cambridge are intrusted with a Concurrent Authority to Print Acts of Parliament and Abridgments of Acts of Parliament within the said University upon the terms in the said Letters Patent.[1]

That judgement in the cause *Baskett* v. *the University of Cambridge* is the modern foundation for the privilege of printing the Authorized Version of the Bible which the two Universities enjoy together with the Queen's Printer. It was the opinion of Sir William Holdsworth in 1935 that the case showed that the privileges granted to the Universities by royal charters, in so far as they related to books in which the king had a copyright, were not invalid.[2] It may be remarked that if the exclusive right to print the Bible is a valuable thing the University of Oxford is to some extent beholden to its sister for it, its own muniments to the purpose being less ancient and less likely to have impressed the judges in 1758.

The case of the University of Cambridge was strong and had gone unchallenged for a long time.[3] Thomas Baskett, the King's Printer, would hardly have attacked it unless he hoped that the dislike of the royal prerogative characteristic of eighteenth-century lawyers would tell in his

[1] Copied from the copy sent by Sir Michael Foster, one of the judges, to Blackstone, now in the archive of the Delegates of the Press (Pkt. 66). It is printed in Blackstone's report.

[2] Strickland Gibson, *The Great Charter of Charles I to the University of Oxford (3 March, 1636)* (Oxford, 1935), p. 9. Reprinted with additions from the *Bodleian Quarterly Record*, vii (1932).

[3] Two judges of the King's Bench advised the Privy Council in 1629 that the charters of the University of Cambridge warranted it in printing the Bible in spite of opposition from the Company of Stationers: *Acts of the Privy Council of England 1628 July–1629 April* (H.M.S.O., 1958), p. 407.

favour. His own claim, it is true, was founded on a royal patent, but it was one for which his father had given value and it imposed onerous duties on him. He may have thought that the ideas implicit in the Revolution of 1688 had made obsolete such a general, indefinite, and gratuitous royal licence to disregard private property as the privilege of printing claimed by the Universities.

The letter from Sir Michael Foster, one of the judges who tried the case, to Blackstone, dated 11 December 1758, conveys a hint that the privilege of printing claimed by the Universities needed some better justification than the royal favour of a bygone age. He underlined the words in the opinion '*are* INTRUSTED *with a Concurrent Authority*',[1] and told Blackstone:

I thought it would be agreeable to You to know the Issue of the Cause between the King's Printer and the University of Cambridge as far as concerns the Proceeding in our Court, and have therefore enclosed our Opinion. What hath been done in the Court of Chancery upon our Certificate I have not heard. The Words underlined were thrown in by way of an Intimation to the University that we consider the Powers given by the Letters Patent as a Trust reposed in that learned Body for public Benefit, for the Advancement of Literature, and not to be transferred upon lucrative Views to other Hands. I hope both the Universities will always consider the Royal Grants in that light.[2]

Strictly speaking, the decision was that Cambridge University might print Acts of Parliament. It had little interest in doing so; and in its case for the Court it disavowed ever having printed any before the abridged excise statutes of 1741, excepting only the Act of Uniformity in the prayer book. The case was of concern to that, and to the other, University because of its bearing on Bible-printing. Oxford had been given the same powers as Cambridge in its 'Great Charter' of 1636.

In *Baskett's* case Charles Yorke, Solicitor-General, argued that though the King had no power over printing he had a copyright in certain classes of publications: (1) all acts of state, (2) since the royal Supremacy was established, all books of the rites and services of the Church, (3) the translation of the Great English Bible printed by or for Grafton: this last, he said 'was performed at the King's expense, which gave him another kind of right'.[3]

---

[1] He doubly underlined 'intrusted'.

[2] Copy by Blackstone in the Delegates' archive (Pkt. 66). It is printed in 1 W. Blackstone's Reports at p. 122.   [3] 1 W. Blackstone's Reports, at p. 113.

Not being willing to grant that the sovereign might restrain the trade of printing nor to lay hands upon the established monopolies, which were valuable properties, several judges in the eighteenth century approved Yorke's line of reasoning, and the notion of a prerogative copyright became accepted. The first to propound it appears to have been William Salkeld, counsel in the case of *The Stationers' Company* v. *Partridge*, about almanacs, in 1713.[1] 'Mr. Salkeld, after positively and expressly denying any prerogative in the Crown over the press, or any power to grant an exclusive privilege, says "I take the rule in all these cases to be, that when the Crown has a property or right of copy, the king may grant it. The Crown may grant the sole printing of Bibles in the English translation, because it was made at the king's charge." '[2] Lord Mansfield, referring to *Baskett* v. *the University of Cambridge* said 'We rested upon property from the king's right of original publication.'[3]

Lord Mansfield was thinking about copyright in an old sense of the word, publisher's copyright, the sense in which Milton's poems were taken to be the property of Jacob Tonson and his assigns for ever.[4] 'Perpetual copyright', says Augustine Birrell, Q.C., 'was the law of England for five years only, viz. from 1769 to 1774',[5] at which date a majority of the judges and of the Lords decided that it was not the law.[6]

Since 1774 private copyright in a published work, though not necessarily copyright of the Crown, has existed in law only as limited to the terms of years specified in the Act of 8 Anne c. 19 and the legislation amending it, and it is normally the property of an author, not of a publisher. Lord Mansfield's justification for the King's right to bestow exclusive privileges of printing was no longer acceptable. What of Serjeant Salkeld's? If it be assumed that the Authorized Version of 1611 was made, as he said, at the king's charge, then, according to the modern law of copyright, being made 'under the direction or control of Her Majesty or of a government department',[7] it would be Crown copyright and the

---

[1] 10 Modern Reports, p. 105.

[2] As quoted by Lord Mansfield, C.J., in *Millar* v. *Taylor* (1763–9), 4 Burrow's Reports, p. 2303, at pp. 2403–4, from Salkeld's manuscript report.

[3] Ibid., at p. 2404.

[4] W. W. Greg, *Some Aspects and Problems of London Publishing between 1550 and 1650* (Oxford, 1956), ch. iv. 'A domestic affair of the Stationers' Company' (p. 66). Thus Daniel Prince, overseer of the Press, writes to John Hutchins on 21 Aug. 1766 about a proposed history of Dorset, 'I say the Copy of the Book, that is the Right of printing it hereafter for ever . . . is worth £200': Bodl. MS. Top. Gen. d. 2, fol. 362.

[5] *The Law and History of Copyright in Books* (1899), p. 141.

[6] *Donaldson* v. *Becket* (1774), 4 Burrow's Reports, p. 2408; 7 Brown's Parliamentary Reports, p. 88.   [7] Copyright Act, 1956 (4 & 5 Eliz. II, c. 74), s. 39.

THE BIBLE PRESS 1755–1780

Crown might dispose of the printing as it thought fit. But statutory Crown copyright in a published work lasts only for fifty years.

As the seventeenth century receded horror of the royal prerogative subsided and it began to seem preferable to perpetual copyright as a ground for preserving restriction of printing. Reasons of public policy were found, supplanting a prior right based on authorship or publication. Chief Baron Skinner said in 1781, in a case relating to a form of Church service:

. . . it is a monopoly supported by long usage, and standing upon very special grounds of necessity and public utility; for it is of manifest public utility to place in proper hands the right of such publication, as well upon account of the special care and superintendence which a trust of such importance necessarily requires, as because the exclusive right of doing or authorizing any acts in which the public is interested, implies an obligation to exercise that right in such manner as to answer the purposes for which it was given; and consequently, the right now in question imposes upon the crown an obligation to publish and disperse as many books of divine service as the interests of religion and the demands of the public require.[1]

The Chief Baron was echoing the underlined words in the judgement in *Baskett* v. *the University of Cambridge*, 'intrusted with a concurrent authority'; and Lord Chancellor Eldon in 1802 felt able on such grounds to grant to the Universities a prohibition forbidding a bookseller to sell Scotch Bibles in this country.[2] This view of the prerogative where the Bible is concerned was expressed a good deal later by Lord Lyndhurst, Chancellor, in his speech to the Lords in *Manners* v. *Blair* (1828),[3] upholding the right of the King's Printer for Scotland to prevent the sale of English Bibles north of the border.

But although the power of the King and his prerogative in England has never been questioned, it has been rested by judges on different principles. Some judges have been of opinion that it is to be founded on the circumstance of the translation of the Bible having been actually paid for by King James, and its having become the property of the Crown, and therefore it has been referred to a species of copyright. Other judges have referred it to the circumstance of the King of England being the supreme head of the Church of England, and that he is vested with the prerogative with

[1] *Eyre and Strahan* v. *Carnan* (1781), 6 Bacon's Abridgement, 7th ed. (1832), p. 509, at p. 512.
[2] *Cambridge and Oxford* (*Universities of*) v. *Richardson* (1802), 6 Ves. Jun., 2nd ed., p. 689.
[3] 3 Bligh's Reports, New Series, p. 391.

reference to that character. Other judges have been of opinion, and I confess, for my own part, I am disposed to accede to that opinion, that it is to be referred to another consideration, namely, to the character of the duty imposed upon the chief executive officer of the Government, to superintend the publication, of the Acts of the Legislature, and Acts of State of that description, and also of those works, upon which the established doctrines of our religion are founded—that it is a duty imposed upon the first executive magistrate, carrying with it a corresponding prerogative.[1]

Lord Lyndhurst boldly denied that, as a matter of history, King James paid for the making of the Authorized Version.[2]

That is the law.[3] In spite of the protestations of Lord Chancellor Lyndhurst and Chief Baron Skinner, any layman may be pardoned for thinking that the King has by prerogative a perpetual copyright[4] in certain books and papers, including the English Bible of 1611, entitling him to dispose of the right to print them. He has also had since 1911[5] a statutory copyright of limited duration in the same class of literature. It provides a neat example of a peculiarity of our constitution to which Maitland drew attention:

Often enough this difficulty must occur to anyone who is studying our constitutional law. He will be told that a prerogative power exists; then he will find a modern statute taking no notice of that prerogative, but enabling the king, or some one of the high officers, to exercise a more limited power. Then the question will occur to him—how far does this modern statutory power take away the old prerogative power?[6]

As though to resolve the difficulty in the matter of printing the Bible, the Copyright Act of 1956 declares (s. 46(2)) that 'Nothing in this Act shall affect any right or privilege of the Crown subsisting otherwise than by virtue of an enactment.'

That freedom to print the Bible should be restricted to three presses[7] has seemed to many minds an objectionable anomaly of our constitutional

---

[1] At p. 402.   [2] At p. 405.
[3] At any rate in New South Wales: *Attorney-General for N.S.W.* v. *Butterworth & Co. (Australia) Ltd.* (1938), S.R. [N.S.W.], p. 195. In England the constitutional position was discussed and the old cases were reviewed in *The Universities of Oxford and Cambridge* v. *Eyre & Spottiswoode Ltd.* [1964] Ch. p. 736; but the decision was only that the royal prerogative does not extend to authorizing a breach of private copyright.
[4] Prerogative affecting the Bible is considered under this head in legal text-books: *Copinger on Copyright*, 10th ed. by Skone James (1965), para. 872; *Halsbury's Laws of England*, 3rd ed. (1954), viii, p. 420.   [5] 1 & 2 Geo. V, c. 46, s. 18.
[6] F. W. Maitland, *The Constitutional History of England* (Cambridge, 1908), p. 420.
[7] The King's Printer may assign his right and has often had his Bibles printed by others.

law. There have been times when the performance of the privileged printers has fallen short of the high standards prescribed by the judges who defended the restriction on grounds of public benefit. It has cost the patentees a good deal in the way of public odium when they have enforced their right. It made the University Presses for a long time little more than factories for cheap Bibles and Testaments. All this in spite of the whittling down in course of time of the patentees' claim from the 'omnium et singulorum . . . bibliorum et novorum testamentorum quorumcunque in lingua anglicana alicujus translacionis cum notis aut sine notis antehac impressorum aut imposterum per mandatum nostrum imprimendorum',[1] reserved by Queen Elizabeth I to Barker in 1577 and by her successors to their Printers since, to merely the Authorized Version entire and without notes. Attempts at stopping Scotch Bibles from crossing the border have long since been given up.

Moreover, experienced printers of Bibles have doubted whether many of the trade would, from commercial motives, care to equip themselves for the task. Most people would agree that the law adopted in Scotland since 1839 that anyone may print the Scriptures but that his edition must be approved by a Bible Board and licensed by the Lord Advocate before publication[2] is in principle better than the dispensation prevailing here. A committee of the House of Commons, after hearing evidence, recommended that the office of King's Printer be abolished.[3] If that had been done an exclusive privilege of the Universities would almost certainly have vanished too.

Three printers of the Bible are better than one. So long as the King's Printer keeps his exclusive patent nobody but he would want to end the Universities' privilege. Cambridge, especially, has deserved well of the public by its careful editing of the Authorized Version and both the privileged presses by the more modern translations. The question is whether there need be interference with a natural selection of Bible-printers.

The Bible-privilege played a dominant part in the development of the University Press in the century following 1758, and this history will have to return to it.

---

[1] In the modern patents, 'All and singular Bibles and New Testaments whatsoever, in the English tongue or in any other tongue whatsoever, and any translation with or without notes'.
[2] House of Commons Papers, 1839 (443), xxx, pp. 605-10. For evidence as to its effect, *The Report from the Select Committee on the Queen's Printer's Patent*, Parliamentary Papers, England, 1860, xxii, 577, pp. 36 ff.   [3] Ibid., pp. i ff.

THE VALUE OF THE LEASE

Thomas Baskett, King's Printer and lessee of the Oxford Bible Press, died on 30 March 1761.[1] He and his brother Robert had succeeded to a remainder of the lease granted in 1734 to their father.[2] Robert sold his share to the booksellers, William Mount and Thomas Page, in 1744, and soon afterwards the interested parties surrendered the lease[3] and a new one was granted to Thomas Baskett for 21 years at a rent of £250 a year, which expired on Lady Day 1765, when Mark Baskett was in occupation.

There followed a series of events which does little credit to the University. They are narrated in detail by an anonymous witness identifiable by his handwriting with Samuel Forster, the University Registrar, in a booklet preserved by the Delegates of the Press.[4] Mark Baskett came to Oxford in November 1764 to solicit a renewal. The Delegates, Blackstone among them, had prepared new terms for a lease, leaving open the name of the lessee and the amount of the rent,[5] and a week later they considered proposals from Mr. Baskett and Mr. Eyre. It would be not surprising if Charles Eyre, who had bought the last thirty years, due to begin in 1770, of the term as King's Printer then current, had let it be known in Oxford that the Bible Press would be worth more to him than Baskett was paying. Nevertheless, the Delegates, after reading the two tenders, decided to grant a 21-years' lease to Mark Baskett at a rent of £550. Articles of agreement were signed by the Vice-Chancellor on behalf of the Delegates pending the drawing of a deed to be sealed in Convocation.

During their deliberations some members of the board had doubted whether it was within its competence to act for the University in such a matter: the correct proceeding, they said, was to get Convocation to appoint an occasional delegacy for the business. There was, however, a precedent for dispensing with that formality when letting the Bible Press, and the hesitant were outvoted.

Within a month Eyre circulated to the common rooms a memorandum representing himself as hardly treated, not having had a chance to make a higher bid, and on 24 December another paper offering £600 a year.

[1] Univ. Arch. S.E.P. 9 (13), draft deed.
[2] C. H. Timperley, *A Dictionary of Printers and Printing* (1839), p. 706.
[3] Univ. Arch. S.P., A. 12.
[4] An Account of the Leasing out the Clarendon Press and Priviledge of Printing by the University of Oxford to Messrs. Wright & Gill in the Year 1766. Bodl. MS. Top. Oxon. e. 19 appears to be a duplicate lacking the printed leaflets inserted in the Delegates' booklet. The younger Huddesford gave, but did not write, it. B.M. MS. Add. 6880 is the same thing written in another hand.   [5] D.O. 30 Oct. 1764.

'The merit of each competitor', Forster says, 'began now to be argued with great Skill & Warmth by their Friends.' The narrator perpetuated some gossip which is only too credible in reporting the partisans of Eyre:

Mr. Basket did not deserve any Praeference as he had even forfeited his Former Lease by his great Neglect and shameful Manner of Printing. (There was great Truth in this last Argument. Mr. Basket lived upon a genteel Private Fortune and neither understood nor gave any Attention to the Business of Printing. He left it therefore to the Care of his Servants who employed the Presses in printing a Great Number of small Prayer-books in 12mo. for Foreign Sale: so that what Mr. Eyre alledged in his Memorial, was an indisputable Fact—'That most of the Chapells in Oxford were supply'd with Folio & Quarto Prayer Books from Cambridge'. The Under Servants & Pressmen were a set of Idle Drunken Men, and the House appeared more like an Ale House than a Printing Room).

(Be it noted that since 1759 the Vice-Chancellors and chosen Delegates who exercised the University's right to inspect the Bible side of the building by an annual visit had left no word of their findings, whether praise or blame.)

It was known that in disregard of some who urged that the honour of the University would suffer if it went back on the Vice-Chancellor's pledged word, Convocation would be overwhelmingly opposed to ful-filling the agreement. It would refuse to be bound by a document that did not bear the University's common seal.

The affair dragged on for a year; counsel's opinion was taken and proved unintelligible, the Heads of Houses discussed it, a new Vice-Chancellor and new Proctors, succeeding the old, gave their minds to the problem, until on 21 October 1765 Convocation agreed to the nomination of an occasional delegacy to negotiate the letting over again. It submitted the old agreement to the House, which rejected it, and retired considering that it had done all it could. Another occasional delegacy was appointed the next week; it requested the Vice-Chancellor 'to acquaint Mr. Basket, that the Delegates, thinking themselves at Liberty to receive new Proposals, desired to know if he chose to make an offer on this Occasion'. Baskett signified that he would defer to Convocation as to the force of the signed agreement, though he was advised that it was actionable, and offered £600. Other proposals were invited for consideration on 4 December. Eyre repeated his offer of £600 and said it was final.[1] Wright & Gill, a firm of London stationers, made a bid of £750.

[1] Univ. Arch. S.E.P. 9(14).

Baskett, being informed, increased his offer to £550 and a bond for £300 a year,[1] thus surpassing Wright & Gill, whereupon these latter supplemented their tender by an extra £100 and an indemnity against the outcome of proceedings by Baskett for breach of contract. Convocation had the report of the delegacy before it on 10 December, and by a great majority awarded the lease to Wright & Gill.[2]

None of the contestants was a printer. When Charles Eyre entered upon his term as King's Printer in 1770 he took William Strahan into partnership to manage the printing. Wright & Gill, of Abchurch Lane, London, were stationers in the modern sense of the word, that is to say paper-merchants.[3]

Mark Baskett could afford to be gentlemanly: he did not go to law or equity, and after the lease to his competitors had been sealed on 28 January 1766 he gave up possession peaceably.

The lease to Wright & Gill was for 14 years from Lady Day 1765.[4] By the time it expired things were looking very different. On 21 December 1778 a delegacy for reletting the Bible Press had to report to Convocation that Mr. Wright declined to renew his firm's tenancy unless for one year at a rent of £210, and the Delegates thought it advisable to close with that offer, since they had had no other worth considering.

Wright had represented to the occasional delegates that the value of the Bible Press was greatly diminished by the decision of the Court of Common Pleas in *The Stationers' Company* v. *Carnan*[5] finally delivered in 1775. The Stationers, deprived thereby of a monopoly of printing and publishing almanacs, had since refused to pay the lessees of the Oxford privilege, as they had promised,[6] £550 a year for forbearing to print books in which the Company of Stationers claimed exclusive rights.

He also reminded the Delegates that the Boston Tea Party and the outbreak of war with the American colonists in 1775 had made the prospects much less bright for the export trade in Bibles, prayer books, and psalms (perhaps he added that the colonists had started to print

[1] Univ. Arch. S.E.P. 9(14).
[2] Reg. Conv. 1757–66 (Bh. 35), fols. 568–9.
[3] *The Earliest Directory of the Book Trade by John Pendred*, ed. Graham Pollard (1955), p. 21: 'Wright, Gill and Dalton, Wholesale Stationers'. They were very rich: Nichols, *Lit. An.* iii, 604.
[4] Blackstone's note: Bodl. MS. Top. Oxon. d. 387, fol. 18. The lease by the University to Wright & Gill cannot be found, but it is partly recited in Articles of Agreement between the Stationers' Company and Wright & Gill of 21 June 1766 in the Stationers' records.
[5] (1774) 2 W. Blackstone's Reports, 1004; C. Blagden, 'Thomas Carnan and the Almanack Monopoly', *Studies in Bibliography*, xiv (Charlottesville, 1961), pp. 23–39.
[6] In the Articles referred to in note 4.

their own Testaments).[1] Thirdly, he said that Lily's Latin grammar was so much infringed upon that the patentees had discontinued paying him £30 a year for not printing it.[2]

The judgement in *Carnan's* case was a heavy blow to the Stationers' Company as owner of nearly all the old printing monopolies, though its effects took some time to make themselves felt. For a short time it was hardly less severe on the Universities by lessening the value of their privilege; but in the long term it benefited them very much. So far as Oxford is concerned, it put an end to the expedient forced on a reluctant Fell in 1678 to exploit the right and perform the duty to print the Bible by farming them. In 1780 the University made up its mind to take a more active part in conducting the Bible Press and soon found itself in control of a big industrial concern.

The last hope of perpetuating monopoly in almanacs and so bolstering up the Stationers' Company as a publisher on a large scale vanished when Lord North's Bill for restoring the exclusive right to the three patentees was thrown out by the Commons in 1779.[3] The University's Chancellor had the backing of Convocation: the Vice-Chancellor informed the senior burgess:

At a full meeting this day, it was determined to make one vigorous push to Lord North for an act to vest the right of printing almanacks in the 2 Universities & the Stationers Company, as before.[4]

The House of Commons, swayed by Erskine's advocacy, opted for freedom, and Oxford admitted that a cause was lost.

Was our defeat owing to the eloquence of Messrs. Davenport & Erskine? The Bill is of course lost for this year. But I suppose it is lost for ever and will hardly be able to shew its head any more. It must probably pass the remainder of its days in the company of Old Almanacks.[5]

Although monopoly could not be restored, compensation for its loss might be practicable. North took a hint that had been addressed to Sir Roger Newdigate, M.P. for the University:

Lord North may put each University in possession of £500 per an. without difficulty; and without such relief, our press, I fear, will become

---

[1] H. Lehmann-Haupt and others, *The Book in America*, 2nd ed. (New York, 1952), p. 36–7.
[2] Univ. Arch. Reg. Conv. Bh. 37, fols. 64–5.
[3] *Journals of the House of Commons, 1778–80*, p. 388.
[4] Newdigate Papers, B1758, George Horne to Sir Roger Newdigate, 12 Mar. 1779.
[5] Ibid. B1751, Horne to Newdigate, 14 May.

bankrupt, having many capital works in it, which we shall never be able to get out, particularly Dr. Bradley's Observations presented to us by Lord North himself.[1]

Accordingly, the Prime Minister proposed to the Commons in 1781 that the difficulty of supplying the King's needs should be eased by doubling the stamp-duty on almanacs; and to the Bill introduced for the purpose he added a clause granting to each of the two Universities an annual payment of £500 from the Stamp Office out of the proceeds of the duty. The measure passed the Commons without a division and became law in the same year.[2] To the Universities it was ample amends for the loss of a lucrative privilege, and the higher rate of duty benefited the Stationers. 'This additional discouragement to almanac publishing', says the historian of the Company, 'put most of the small men out of the running and left the field almost entirely to Carnan and the Stationers.'[3]

The first of a long series of yearly receipts in consequence of this Act is entered in the accounts of the Delegates of the Press for 1782. Duty on almanacs was abolished in 1834,[4] and the Act of 1781 was totally repealed in 1861.[5] The annual payments to the Universities continue: fortunately successive revenue departments have taken the view that an Act of 1804[6] obliges them to maintain them.

THE STANDARD OF CORRECTNESS OF THE AUTHORIZED VERSION

The draft lease of the Bible Press approved by the Delegates on 30 October 1764 departed from precedent. One novelty was clause 4 of the draft requiring the lessee

to provide within one Year from the Commencement of the said Term one or more Copies of the Bible accurately collated with the Original or most Authentic Edition of the present Translation, and also one or more Copies of the Common Prayer Book accurately collated with the sealed Books referred to in the Act of Uniformity, which shall be produced to the Delegates of the Press at some publick Meeting, and these and no other shall hereafter be used in correcting the Books to be printed by virtue of this Lease, making due Allowance for modern Variations in mere Orthography.

[1] Newdigate Papers, B1758, Horne to Newdigate, 12 Mar. 1779.
[2] 21 Geo. III, c. 56, s. 10: 'Out of the monies which shall arise by the Duty hereinbefore granted, the Sums of Money following, to the two Universities . . .'.
[3] Blagden, p. 241.　　　　　　　　　　　　　　[4] 4 & 5 Will. IV, c. 57.
[5] Statute Law Revision Act, 1861 (24 & 25 Vict., c. 101).　　　[6] 44 Geo. III, c. 98.

Why this difficult matter came to a head at this time is not easy to tell. An obvious reason is that Cambridge had done its best to provide a model for correctness and completeness in a Bible of 1762 revised by Dr. F. S. Paris and H. Therold; and yet the subsequent discussions of this matter by the Oxford Delegates take no account of that Bible at all.[1]

Apart altogether from printers' errors, intentional changes in spelling, punctuation, italicizing, and use of initial capitals had been made in reprinting the Authorized Version from 1616 onwards, and large additions had been made to the marginal references and annotations. These changes are noticed fully and critically by F. H. A. Scrivener, the eminent textual scholar, in his book *The Authorized Edition of the English Bible (1611).*[2] There is little record of the responsibility for them: in the early days printers acted on their own initiative in bringing the spelling more into accord with the notions of their time, and Cambridge scholars revised the spelling, italicizing, and punctuation of the text carefully in the editions printed there in 1629 and 1638, correcting some errors in the original of 1611. Of intervention by civil or ecclesiastical authority there is no sign.

Oxford (from 1675) and the King's Printer had only a small part in modernizing the Bible. The first Oxford edition, of 1675, had Fell's peculiar spelling, as eies, flie, plesure, bin (for been), which set it apart from others; his sublessees, the renegade London Stationers in charge of the Bible Press, reverted to the spelling normal at that time and intro-duced marginal dates in their edition of 1679.[3] They were dates from the Creation, according to Archbishop Ussher's chronology. William Lloyd, Bishop of Worcester, worked out a new chronology, dating backwards and forwards from the birth of Christ, and his was adopted in an edition by the King's Printer of 1701. References and notes were added to those of 1611, drawn largely from an edition printed at Amsterdam in 1647 with marginal matter by John Canne, the Brownist.[4]

Apart from a variety, perplexing to the faithful, as between one edition and another in their intentional departures from the Bible of 1611, there was the fear that printers had carelessly corrupted the text. It may be claimed for Oxford that great pains were taken, though

[1] Blackstone made a note, dated 28 Feb. 1761, of the partnership of the Syndics and Benjamin Dodd, a London bookseller, in a Bible to be produced in folio and quarto, doubtless that of Dr. Paris (MS. in the archive of the Printer to the University).

[2] Cambridge, 1884.

[3] Madan, *Oxford Books*, iii, No. 3243; Darlow and Moule, 744–6.

[4] Darlow and Moule, No. 987, note.

fruitlessly, to make Baskett's 'Vinegar' Bible of 1717 splendid and correct;[1] and since then there had been no public scandal about the printing of Oxford Bibles. Scrivener even commends those produced in the middle of the eighteenth century for their typography and their accuracy[2]—surprisingly to anyone who has studied the background for them.

The desire of the Delegates in 1764 was to have a standard for text and marginal matter. They asked the Vice-Chancellor to write to the Archbishop of Canterbury 'begging his Grace to inform him, what Copy of an English Bible his Grace would recommend as a proper Standard for the University Printer'.[3] It was a difficult question, and the Archbishop, Thomas Secker, was strangely unfamiliar with the subject. In his reply he wrote that he took the first edition of the Authorized Version to be one of 1612 by Robert Barker in Roman letter. He describes the seven editions then in the library at Lambeth and continues: 'I have also heard that Dr. Paris, formerly Master of Sidney College in Cambridge, took great Pains in the same good work. And Dr. Moss hath promised me, that he will try to get Intelligence from Cambridge about the Fruits of his Labours.' Dr. Secker added that he had heard that one of his predecessors had employed Mr. Broughton, Secretary to the Society for Promoting Christian Knowledge, 'to revise a Copy, in order to a more accurate Edition than the Common ones'; but Broughton was out of town.[4]

There was nothing in this on which the Oxford Delegates could act; and after hearing the letter read they ordered that the Cambridge editions of 1743 and 1760 be collated with the first printed in 1611 and Bishop Lloyd's of 1701 and that a proper person be inquired for to undertake the task. A fortnight later Benjamin Blayney, D.D., of Hertford College, volunteered and received the commission.

Blayney's Bible, printed by Wright & Gill at Oxford in 1769, was for many years the standard by which Oxford Bibles were corrected; that is to say Blayney's as corrected in manuscript by many hands in course of time. The folio volume kept for reference has hardly a page, except in the Apocrypha, without a corrector's mark carefully written in ink. All but a few of these amendments are of slight significance: a capital instead of a small letter in a reference, a comma added, an English spelling modernized. Blayney's edition has some serious faults, reputedly 116

[1] Above, p. 169.   [2] Op. cit., p. 28.   [3] D.O. 12 June 1766.
[4] Ibid. 24 June.

misprints,[1] of which the worst is the leaving out seventeen words in Revelation 18: 2. It also fails in many places to distinguish (by small capitals) the word 'Lord' where it is a substitute for the Holy Name. Nevertheless, by any reasonable standard it was a remarkably correct edition; for, as Scrivener reminded the critics, 'All accuracy is only comparative, as every true scholar knows';[2] and few printers would disagree with the expert witness who declared before a select committee of the House of Commons in 1831, 'I should think it utterly impossible to print the Bible without an error.'[3]

Blayney erred most culpably in altering too much. If there was a verb ending in -th, he made adjacent verbs conform with it, as standeth instead of stands, loveth for loves; he changed 'seventy and one year' to 'seventy and first'; sometimes he overdid logic, as in altering 'a great multitude' to 'a great number'. Being a Hebrew scholar, he made improvements of the transliteration of names which later editors gave up as an unwise nibbling at a big problem. Some of his spellings, houshold, waggon, vallies, grashopper, travel (for travail) have not endured.

He made a report for the Delegates on the principles and method of his editing: it is copied in their minutes,[4] and was printed in the *Gentleman's Magazine* soon afterwards.[5] Unfortunately it is true that he minimized his debt to Paris, a debt of which he is convicted by his copying numerous errors which Paris first made,[6] and he claimed for his edition an unexampled purity which it did not quite achieve. He claims to have made with reference to the Hebrew extensive improvements in italicizing; to have corrected, besides adding, a great many references from Bishop Lloyd's Bible; and to have made, with guidance from learned colleagues, 'considerable changes' in the summaries at the heads of chapters. Advised by Archbishop Secker, he examined references only to be found in Scotch Bibles and selected from them (they were the references that Canne, the Brownist, was the first to print in his Amsterdam Bible of 1647). With some alterations he preserved the marginal chronology of Lloyd.

Of Paris's and Blayney's work Scrivener wrote: 'It cannot be doubted that these two editions are the great modernizers of the diction of the

---

[1] *Report of the Select Committee on King's Printer's Patents*, 1830-1, p. 163, para. 2267; evidence of John Lee, D.D. The assertion by W. J. Loftie (*A Century of Bibles* (1872), p. 21), that it 'abounds in omissions and misprints' is not justified.

[2] *The Authorized Edition of the English Bible*, p. 33.

[3] *Report of the Select Committee, 1830-1*, evidence of George Offor at p. 74.

[4] D.O. 27 Dec. 1769.   [5] Vol. 39 (1769), p. 517.   [6] Scrivener, op. cit., p. 32.

version, from what it was left in the seventeenth century.' He reprobates their 'tasteless and inconsistent meddling with archaic words and grammatical forms', in which respect he considered that the greater sinner was at Oxford.[1]

Both these editions were much depleted soon after publication by fires at the London warehouses of booksellers who acted as wholesale stockists: Dodd for Cambridge,[2] Payne for Oxford. In both fires it was the folio copies that suffered most. Of Payne's fire in January 1770 it is said that 'One thousand pounds' worth of bibles and prayer books, belonging to the proprietors [i.e. Wright & Gill] of the Oxford press, was destroyed.'[3]

In point of typography Blayney's is an excellent Bible, very restful to the eye, apart from a superfluity of apparatus cluttering up the margins.

It is, perhaps, worth remarking that the Authorized Version has been a pioneer in the sparing use of initial capital letters, and that it may have saved us from the German practice of using them for nouns. From 1611 onwards, probably for the sake of getting as many words as might be in narrow columns, our Bible has led the way to the modern style. In the seventeenth and eighteenth centuries it diverged widely from the capitalization customary in writing and in printing generally. For example, verse 3 of Hosea 10 in the Oxford Bible of 1701:

For now they shall say, We have no king, because we feared not the LORD; what then should a king do to us?

is printed in the heading to Book xv of Clarendon's *History of the Rebellion* in 1704 thus:

For now they shall say, We have no King, because We feared not the Lord; what then shall a King do to Us?

The Delegates requested Wright & Gill to make up their octavo Bibles so that certain Books began on right-hand pages and undertook to bear the cost of doing so. The Books were Joshua, Job, Isaiah, the Apocrypha, the Gospels, Acts, Romans, and Revelation.[4]

Blackstone referred to a 'beautiful and correct common-prayerbook in folio, 1768' as printed by Wright & Gill in discharge of their obligation by the terms of the lease.[5] The care of it was entrusted by the Delegates to Thomas Wintle of Pembroke College.[6]

[1] Scrivener, op. cit., p. 30.   [2] Ibid., p. 29.
[3] Timperley, p. 721.   [4] D.O. 26 Apr., 14 June 1771.
[5] Bodl. MS. Top. Oxon. d. 387, Blackstone's MS. addition to a copy of *To the Reverend Doctor Randolph*, at p. 18.   [6] D.O. 26 Oct. 1766.

The lessees employed William Jackson as agent to manage their business in Oxford.[1] He has made an appearance in these pages as owner of the New Printing Office near Carfax and of *Jackson's Oxford Journal*.[2] By this time he was an experienced and good printer and, no doubt, an able man of business. The Delegates, however, were not satisfied with the quality of his paper.[3]

[1] Ibid. 15 Dec. 1769.   [2] Above, p. 323.   [3] D.O. 15 Dec. 1769.

CHAPTER XXIV

The Clarendon Trust

EXPECTING to outlive his father, the fourth Earl of Clarendon, and succeed to his possessions, Viscount Cornbury (otherwise Baron Hyde) made a codicil to his will in 1751 bequeathing the papers of the first Earl to trustees with a discretion to publish them and apply the profit for the benefit of Oxford University in erecting a riding-school or otherwise.[1] In the event the Earl was the survivor, both dying in 1753, so that Cornbury's intended bequest was inoperative. The Clarendon manuscripts passed to the Earl's residuary legatees, his daughter, Catherine, Duchess of Queensberry, and two of his grand-daughters, Charlotte, Lady Hyde, and Mary, wife of Admiral Sir John Forbes.

These ladies made it known that they would give effect to Cornbury's intention; some time in 1758 Convocation at Oxford was apprised of the scheme and acknowledged the ultimate benefit to the University with expressions of gratitude.[2]

The papers comprised the autobiography of Edward Hyde, first Earl of Clarendon, a mass of correspondence and documents chiefly about affairs of state collected by him, and some reflections of his on religion, morals, and politics.[3] The autobiography was written by Clarendon for his descendants, not for the public at large, and when he had plundered it to make up his *History of the Rebellion* it was left a disjointed story, 'a mere fragment'.[4] The letters and documents are of the kind familiar, published in more recent times with the support of public funds, in the volumes of the Historical Manuscripts Commission.

[1] Copied in Bodl. MS. Clarendon 124, fol. 2, a book containing 'Papers received by Mr Boodle as Secretary to the Clarendon Trustees from the Revd. Tho. Randolph on the 20th of October 1823'.

[2] So it appears from the Duchess's letter of 11 July 1758 to Randolph (V.-C. 1757–9) promising 'to enable my nieces to partake their share of the Polite acknowledgement of the University & of the Satisfaction I feel, to perceive our joint offer so cordially accepted' (MS. Clarendon 124, fol. 4). I have failed to find a relevant entry in the Registers of Convocation. Randolph's draft for a motion to approve the scheme survives (ibid., fol. 28).

[3] Described by Bulkeley Bandinel in the preface to his edition of the *History of the Rebellion* (Oxford, 1826), and in *A Summary Catalogue of the Western Manuscripts in the Bodleian Library*, iii, ed. F. Madan (Oxford, 1893), pp. 557–60.

[4] C. H. Firth, *Essays Historical and Literary* (Oxford, 1938), p. 121.

The Delegates of the Press agreed on 31 October 1758 to print Clarendon's *Life as Written by Himself* 'according to the Desire of our noble Benefactresses, exactly after the Copy by them sent'. An edited transcript had been made under the supervision of the Duchess of Queensberry, and she insisted that it must be printed just as it left her.[1] Blackstone, without the authority of the board, wrote to the Duke of Queensberry objecting that the original manuscript ought to be made available as copy for the Press and was haughtily rebuked for his presumption.[2] The *Life* was published late in 1759 in a folio edition of 2,000, priced at £1. 5s., and an octavo of the same number, costing 14s. In 1760 a second octavo edition of 750 was issued, and in 1762 a third of 1,000 in octavo. The book sold slowly: in 1814 there remained of the folio 710 and of the third octavo 398; 598 of the folio edition were sold as waste in 1818, and the remainder of both editions was pulped in 1862.[3] The original manuscript of the *Life* was deposited by the trustees in the Bodleian Library for safe keeping on 18 October 1759.[4]

Of the constitution of the trust not much is known. On 10 February 1761 the Duchess wrote to Randolph, the former Vice-Chancellor, telling him that she would have a trust deed drawn up and would appoint Dr. William Markham, headmaster of Westminster School, Lord Mansfield, Chief Justice, and the Bishop of St. Asaph, Dr. Robert Hay Drummond, as trustees.[5] The terms of the deed are not available, but the subsequent activities of the trustees are enough to show that they must have reproduced those of Cornbury's codicil. By 1764 Dr. John Douglas, a friend of Samuel Johnson, was maintaining liaison between the trustees, the editors, and the Delegates of the Press.[6]

The first volume of *State Papers collected by Edward, Earl of Clarendon* came out in 1767, 650 copies in folio format and 750 in octavo. It was a selection edited and transcribed under the eye of the Duchess, and she asked that it should be put to press unaltered. The response of the public was disappointing: the Duchess promised that the next volume

---

[1] Bodl. MS. Clarendon 124, fol. 12.

[2] Bodl. MS. Top. Oxon. d. 387, fols. 49 ff.

[3] Manuscript 'Account of Lord Clarendon's Life & State Papers' at the Press.

[4] Owen's receipt, MS. Clarendon 124, fol. 21.

[5] Ibid., fol. 36. A deed of 20 March 1761 signed by the heiresses is mentioned: B.M. MS. Egerton 2183, fol. 84ᵛ.

[6] His capacity is difficult to determine. He was entrusted by Richard Powney with a collection that he contributed to the Clarendon State Papers: MS. Egerton 2183, fols. 16, 72. He does not appear to have been employed by the Clarendon trustees; but Samuel Johnson knew that he kept the accounts of their income: *Letters of Samuel Johnson*, ed. R. W. Chapman (Oxford, 1952), Nos. 459, 461 (of 1776).

would be more interesting.[1] In 1814 there were 315 left of the folios: the octavos were all wasted in 1790, and in 1818 all but 31 of the remaining 302 folios were disposed of in the same way.

The Press had borne the cost of these two productions, and Thomas Randolph, Vice-Chancellor, had put his hand in his own pocket to the extent of £1,000; while the second volume of State Papers was in the press the Delegates became worried about the adequacy of their resources for such a big undertaking, estimated to amount eventually to at least three thick volumes and to cost not less than £2,100 to produce. They had applied to the trustees in 1765 for a subvention, apparently without success. On 19 May 1767 the Delegates ordered that work on Volume ii be discontinued. They went so far as to observe in their minute that 'the University have no immediate connexion with or property in the volume.'

Editing and printing were suspended for five years, but were taken up again in 1771 when the Delegates read a letter from Dr. Douglas on behalf of the trustees. Noting that £450 was owing to the University, he proposed that £175 should be paid forthwith and in future the University should receive the yearly interest of £30 on the trustees' investment in Consolidated Bank Annuities. He hoped that these sums, added to the proceeds of selling the volumes published for the trust would induce the Delegates to resume publication. They agreed to do so.

Editing of the second and third volumes of State Papers was done at the expense of the Delegates by men of their choice, at first by Dr. Thomas Nowell and after him by Dr. Richard Scrope and Dr. Thomas Monkhouse, with occasional reference to Douglas.[2] In his letter read to the Delegates in 1771 Douglas stressed the trustees 'desire that the Editors may be allowed the utmost Latitude of Judgment in making a Selection'; but the original documents must have been made available at Oxford piecemeal, for Douglas wrote in 1772:

It had long been my wish that all the manuscripts might be put into the hands of the Delegates, to be, by them, at their Discretion, entrusted to their Editor; who, I thought, would be better enabled to execute his task, if he had the whole Collection before him.[3]

The decision to print the second volume of the State Papers was

[1] Bodl. MS. Clarendon 124, fol. 36.
[2] Bodl. MS. Clarendon 124; B.M. MS. Egerton 2183. Papers belonging to owners other than the Clarendon trustees were included: Macray, *Annals*, p. 226.
[3] Bodl. MS. Clarendon 124, fol. 41.

taken by the Delegates in June 1772, and it came out a year later, 650 copies in folio at 25s. Unlike the previous volume, it was not also issued in octavo. In 1814 there were 496 copies left, but in 1818 all but 19 were wasted.

The third and last volume was published in 1786, 650 copies in folio at £2. 2s. Of these 337 remained in 1814, and 240 were pulped four years later, leaving 19.

The final publication of the trust was Clarendon's *Religion and Policy, with a Survey of the Power and Jurisdiction of the Pope in the Dominions of other Princes*. The wish of the trustees that this book should be printed at the Press was communicated to a meeting of the Delegates in March 1810, and they assented to it with pleasure. It was published a year later as two octavo volumes matching those of the University's edition of the *History of the Rebellion* of 1807. The number printed was 1016 and the price 26s. (reduced in 1825 to £1). In 1826 there were 510 unsold, and an inquiry from the trustees whether any bookseller would make an offer for the stock met with a negative response. The 459 remaining in 1862 went for waste paper.

In estimating the commercial success of the publications of the trust it must be borne in mind that a great many copies were given to dignitaries in this country and abroad.

In 1868 the Clarendon Trust came to an end. Convocation having rejected the gift of a riding-school, the trustees, the Duke of Newcastle, the Marquis of Lothian, Sir William Heathcote, Bart., and the Rt. Hon. W. E. Gladstone, offered the accumulated trust fund for the purpose of building a laboratory for the Professor of Experimental Philosophy. This offer was accepted.[1] The trustees' investment of some £12,000 in Consols went towards the cost of the Clarendon Laboratory, now occupied by the Department of Geology and Mineralogy.[2]

It can hardly be maintained that the trust served a useful purpose. It would have been better if the papers had been given outright to the University for the Delegates to publish as best they could (they also minded the needs of natural philosophy).[3] The trustees were distinguished by nobility or otherwise eminent station rather than by an acquaintance with publishing, and they did little more in a hundred years than require of their secretary annually a statement of the proceeds of sale of their

[1] Reg. Conv. 1854–71, p. 434, and the notice by the Vice-Chancellor inserted there.
[2] H. M. and K. D. Vernon, *History of the Oxford Museum* (Oxford, 1909), p. 91; *V.C.H. Oxfordshire*, iii (1954), p. 58.
[3] Witness their loan for equipping the Observatory, above, p. 339.

books, negligible in latter days, and a letter instructing the Press to pay these proceeds to their banker. The sensible and helpful John Douglas became a bishop in 1787 and was succeeded, immediately or not, by Edward Boodle and then by his son.

The Oxford editors must be given their due: they are said on good authority to have made a judicious selection of the *State Papers* and to have printed them accurately.[1] A calendar with an entry for every item, extracts from the more interesting, and a copious index would have been preferred by scholars; and as soon as the Clarendon trust came to its end the Delegates set about producing one. Volumes were published in 1869, 1872, and 1876, but their sale was so limited that the series was not continued until 1932 or concluded until 1970.

---

[1] Macray, *Annals*, p. 227. He edited two volumes of the *Calendar*.

CHAPTER XXV

Universities' Perpetual Copyright

As soon as the House of Lords decided in 1774 that no subject had a perpetual copyright in a published work[1] and had thrown out a Bill (which the Commons had passed) aimed at reversing its decision[2] the Universities took steps to secure exceptional treatment. Oxford's dutiful Chancellor, Lord North, piloted through Parliament a measure granting to the two Universities of England and their colleges, besides the Universities of Scotland, perpetual copyright in their publications under certain conditions.[3] At committee stage the colleges or schools of Eton, Westminster, and Winchester were added.

To satisfy the conditions the right to print and sell the book must have been given outright to the favoured corporation for all time by the author or his assign with an intention that the profit should be applied as a fund for the advancement of learning or the purposes of education, the university or college must be the first publisher, must print the book wholly on its own presses, and must register the claim to copyright at Stationers' Hall.

As a result of this Act, and its re-enactments, there is a little enclave in the law as to copyright after publication where the earlier conception of the property, as founded on prior publication, not on authorship, is kept alive.

The abortive measure was promoted by booksellers, for many of them had invested large sums in copies in the belief that the law would protect their exclusive right to print them without limit of time. The Universities were hit much less hard by the judicial decision of 1774; for although it meant that many of the books in their warehouses might be reprinted by others, few of their publications were of a kind to tempt others to do so. Oxford has been alone in availing itself of the Act and with an eye to only a few precious possessions.

On 6 March 1774, while the Bill to restore perpetual copyright was in

---

[1] In *Donaldson* v. *Becket* (1774), 4 Burrow's Reports, p. 2408; Augustine Birrell, *The Law and History of Copyright in Books* (1899), pp. 122–38.
[2] [W. Cobbett,] *Parliamentary History*, xvii (1813), pp. 1077, 1400–1.
[3] 15 Geo. III, c. 53.

contemplation, the Vice-Chancellor, Thomas Fothergill, wrote to Sir Roger Newdigate, M.P. for the University, enclosing a catalogue of its stock of publications:

Should a Bill be brought into the House in consequence of the Booksellers' Petition, we shall upon seeing that, be better able to judge how far it will be likely to affect the University. In the mean While give me leave to inform You, that we have no purchased, only gift, Copies of Authors. And those, You will observe, on viewing the enclosed Catalogue, are not of a Sort that will tempt any Bookseller to invade our formerly supposed Rights in them: Lord Clarendon's History of the Rebellion only excepted. Indeed for the printing of this, and this only, the University had a Patent. But that, having been granted in the Year 1703, is long since expired.[1]

The Delegates of the Press made haste to register in a form answering to the requirements of the Act the two copies by which they set most store, the *History of the Rebellion* and Clarendon's *Life* as published in 1759. For good measure they added Bishop Robert Lowth's professorial lectures on Hebrew poetry of 1753. With these they were content until 1870, when Ruskin's *Lectures on Art* were registered. By 1904 the number of registrations had grown to ten.

In addition, and it is an important addition, Balliol College has secured to itself the sole right of printing Benjamin Jowett's translations of Plato and Thucydides and his *Politics* of Aristotle, the fact that the college has no press notwithstanding.

The Act of 1775 makes it clear that the exceptional privilege of perpetual copyright in a work shall be forfeit if it, or (probably) a part of it, is allowed to be printed elsewhere than on the grantee's own press. Until lately the Delegates at Oxford were careful to guard the University's right by a strict regard to the letter of the Act. They have had from time to time to endure embittered protests from critics who thought it high time that this anomalous restriction on the free circulation of literary classics were done away with. At times the terms of the Act have made it difficult to secure foreign copyright.[2]

When this privilege came under review by the Copyright Commission in 1874 the Delegates of the Press at Oxford had a tender conscience about it. They set about separating the profit from it as a fund for subsidizing works that were desirable but not likely to pay their way.[3]

---

[1] Newgate Papers B1682, 1683.
[2] S. Nowell-Smith, *Copyright Law and the Publisher in the Reign of Queen Victoria* (Oxford, 1968), pp. 20–1.   [3] Delegates' File FF 13.

The Act of 1775 was repealed by the Copyright Act of 1911, but that and the subsequent Act of 1956 saved the Universities' perpetual copyright as it existed before the repeal. It is unlikely to last much longer: in 1968 the Publishers' Association, among its recommendations for amendment of the law, proposed that this exceptional right should be extinguished, and both Universities have let it be known that they do not wish it to be preserved.

Favours received by the Press in the latter part of the eighteenth century, when the University was reconciled with the sources of patronage, and particularly while North's influence was dominant, make it appear somewhat covetous. The preamble to the clause of the Act of 1781 recompensing it for the loss of an interest in the monopoly of almanacs greatly exaggerates the University's deprivation by Carnan's gain;[1] that and perpetual copyright added to the Bible privilege not unnaturally antagonized liberal opinion. The favours can be defended to some extent by the prudence and restraint of their exercise, and more by the position of the University at the time of their grant as one of the two upholders of learned and literary pursuits, research, and publishing, maintainers of public libraries and correspondence with scholars abroad.

[1] It put the figure at £1,000 a year for each University. Oxford had been getting about £500 and Cambridge £200.

CHAPTER XXVI

Salesmanship

THE minutes of a Delegates' meeting on 9 July 1758 record the appointment of 'Mr. Payne of Castle Street, London,' as 'Warehouse-Keeper or Publisher' in London during the pleasure of the Delegacy. The man so dignified was 'honest Tom Payne', a prominent London bookseller.[1] There is no reason to think that he did more than stock the Delegates' books on credit terms, rendering a yearly account of his sales less his expenses. In the first year his sales amounted to £13. 4s. 3d., while sales at Oxford came to £7. 5s. 3d. For the three years following Payne remitted £83. 2s. 10d., and in 1763 £55. 1s.; by 1764 London sales had risen to £121. 17s. and those at Oxford to £129. 7s. 1d. For the remaining nine years of Payne's agency the figures dwindle, but roughly equal those from the Oxford warehouse.

That a large number of Blayney's Bibles were burnt in Payne's warehouse in 1770 is proof that he acted also as wholesaler for Wright & Gill, the lessees of the Bible Press at Oxford.[2]

Nothing was more needful at that time for both Learned and Bible Presses than a skilful and energetic salesman in London; and this was a want not provided in Blackstone's programme of reform. Payne's shop, 'the Literary Coffee-House', on part of the site of the National Gallery, was a resort of scholars, and he issued catalogues;[3] given good relations between him and the Delegates, there might have been very good business. Unfortunately, it must be supposed that Payne was dissatisfied with the terms allowed him, for what might have been a most profitable collaboration flagged and was ended by his withdrawal in 1773.[4]

As London wholesaler Payne was succeeded by Thomas Cadell and Peter Elmsley, the latter for 'learned books'.[5] Cadell's dissatisfaction is

---

[1] H. R. Plomer, G. H. Bushnell, and E. R. McC. Dix, *Dictionary of Printers and Booksellers, 1726 to 1775* (1932), p. 195.

[2] Above, p. 360.

[3] The B.M. has a large collection of them, and the Bodl. has a good many (2593 c. 4–6). Two, formerly belonging to the late Albert E. Ehrman, are described in G. Pollard and E. Ehrman, *The Distribution of Books by Catalogue . . . to A.D. 1800* (Cambridge, 1965), p. 312.

[4] D.O. 10 Dec. 1773.

[5] Ibid. 28 Jan. 1774.

reported by Canon John Douglas in a letter of 1775 with reference to the first two volumes of the Clarendon *State Papers*:

I find from Cadell that he has sold a considerable Number of the 2d. Volume, & several Sets of both Volumes. He promised to write me a Letter which I was to have sent to you to be communicated to the Delegates. He has, some time ago, writ it directly to Prince. He states the great Disadvantage that the Publications made by our University labor under from the very absurd Plan of not making the usual allowances to the Booksellers. The fact is certain; and it has but a very odd Appearance that tho our Delegates have a noble fund, & no Temptation to grasp at greater Profits than other Proprietors of Copys, yet they make so very pitifull an Allowance to their Publisher, that it is not worth the while of the Booksellers to share with him the inconsiderable Profit; by which means the Oxford Books are not distributed to the Trade, so that, at this present Moment, I dare take it upon me to say, there is not a Copy either of the Oxford Shakespear, or of the Clarendon Papers, in any one Bookseller's in London except Cadell's. I have more than once pressed the Bp. of Oxford, to use all his Interest with the Delegates to alter their narrow Mode of proceeding, which his Lordship sees the fatal Consequence of in the same Light as I do. He has, he says, often talked to Dr. Wheeler about this, but seems to expect no Change. I am sorry for it. Cadell told me that he lately disposed of, amongst the Trade, upwards of Six thousand Pounds worth of Books in which he has a Property, but he could not sell at that Sale, One Copy of any [of] the Oxford Books; there not being such an Allowance made by the Delegates as could encourage any of the Booksellers to become Purchasers.[1]

Johnsonians may remember that a complaint by 'a respectable dignitary of the Church, Dr. ✱✱✱✱✱✱', was the occasion for the Doctor's letter to Wetherell, the Vice-Chancellor, of 12 March 1776, which Boswell printed.[2] Johnson tells us the normal rate of discount:

The deduction, I am afraid, will appear very great: but let it be considered before it is refused. We must allow, for profit, between thirty and thirty-five *per cent*. between six and seven shillings in the pound; that is, for every book which costs the last buyer twenty shillings, we must charge Mr. Cadell with something less than fourteen. We must set the copies at fourteen shillings each, and superadd what is called the quarterly-book, or for every hundred books so charged we must deliver an hundred and four.

He advised allocating to the London stockist, Cadell, a shilling in the

---

[1] Bodl. MS. Clarendon 151, fols. 27–8; to Richard Scrope, 23 April.
[2] Boswell, ii, pp. 424–6.

pound, the London wholesaler, Dilly, ten per cent, the country retailer three shillings and sixpence.

Boswell notes that these rates are more than the booksellers usually demand; but in this matter Johnson is to be trusted.

Ever since Fell had it in mind to set up a press in the University 'not so much to make profits for booksellers as to further the interests and convenience of scholars'[1] the Press had resisted conforming with the trade: during a century it learned slowly to accept booksellers as a necessary evil. Undoubtedly the Delegates highly regarded an obligation to keep prices within the reach of scholars, therefore were reluctant to raise them so as to cover discounts. It was a policy that suited scholars who could call at the warehouse door in Oxford.

In 1758 the Delegates determined to allow booksellers a shilling on prices from 12s. to 19s. 6d. and 5 per cent on any higher than that, and twice as much to the warehouse-keeper in London. When the question of discounts was being discussed in 1759 Blackstone opposed an increase. He wrote a note of his argument which is among his papers at the Press.[2] His objection was, in general, that bigger discounts 'will in the end fall heaviest upon the Scholar or Consumer, as the University must set a proportionably larger Price upon their Books, to indemnify themselves against the additional Burthen'. Wholesalers intermediate between Payne, the 'publisher', and the retail booksellers were pressing for an increase in Payne's discount from 10 to 15 per cent, so that he could afford them a better allowance. Blackstone could see no need for the intermediary class (Johnson's hypothetical Dilly) and denied that the University should concern itself with it. He was opposed to letting London booksellers send their orders direct to Oxford and claim the 10 per cent allowed to Payne; if they did so, he thought they should be given only 7½ per cent off the price. His view was adopted by the Delegates on 23 May 1759.

But the Dillys could not be so easily wished out of existence: in 1770 the Delegates raised the rate for all booksellers to 15 per cent on prices above 10s. Having lost the services of Tom Payne, they agreed in 1774 to allow Elmsley 20 per cent on books in the learned languages sold to customers abroad.

Upon hearing Douglas's letter read (perhaps Johnson's as well) the Delegates acted. On 21 March 1776:

    [1] Leyden, Univ. Library, MS. Burm. Cod. Fo. No. 11, ii, fol. 62. (In Latin.)
    [2] 'Draught of Reasons for not altering the Allowance to Booksellers 1759', loose in the 'Delegates' Book'.

Information having been given to the Board by a private Letter from Dr. Douglas that Mr. Cadell, notwithstanding his Consent (near two Years ago) to sell the modern Books printed at our Press for an Allowance of 15 pr. Cent, complains that he cannot put such Books in his Sale for want of a greater Advance, Resolved, that Mr. Prince be commissioned to treat with Mr. Cadell upon this Subject in order to know upon what Terms Mr. Cadell will bona fide consent to put the University Publications in his Sale and bring them to a fair Market.

The outcome of Prince's mission is not known, but perhaps as a result of it an allowance of 25 per cent to booksellers on Clarendon's *Life* and his *State Papers* was sanctioned a month later and five booksellers were 'commissioned to sell': Cadell, Robson, White, Robinson, Payne. In 1779 the Delegates decided to allow Elmsley and Prince 20 per cent on all books.

Among the services to the Press done by the London Warehouse-Keeper was the insertion of advertisements in the newspapers. In 1762 Payne charged £10. 16s. for advertising three books in journals which he did not name. Next year he claimed for advertisements of the verses on the birth of the Prince of Wales as follows:

18 Dec. 1762		£	s	d
3 times in Gazetteer		0	9	0
3 do.	Public Advertiser	0	9	0
3 do.	Daily Advertiser	0	9	0
2 do.	Whitehall Evening [Post]	0	7	0
2 do.	St. James's Evening [Post]	0	7	0
2 do.	General Evening [Post]	0	7	0

Hyde's *Historia religionis veterum Persarum* was advertised three times in each of the *Posts* in 1768 at a cost of 10s. 6d. for the three insertions. In 1769 the *London Evening Post, Lloyd's Evening,* and the *London Chronicle* appear in Payne's bill, and the *St. James's Chronicle* in 1770. Daniel Prince placed advertisements in *Jackson's Oxford Journal* at 4s. a time.

Elmsley, when he began stocking the Delegates' books on credit in 1774, did well. His sales in the first year brought in £101, and in 1776, after deducting his expenses, £104. Cadell, who did a much smaller trade in Oxford books, drops out after 1776. In 1778 Elmsley paid in £449 net (the sales at Oxford came to £82), and after that year he figures largely in the Press accounts.

The information that we have about collaboration with London wholesalers is fragmentary but enough to show that, by the standards of that time, it greatly increased the Delegates' business. It was a big step in the progress of the Press; but further steps were needed before the Delegates fully accepted that books are sold, if anywhere, in bookshops, and publishing is best done in the capital city.

Newspaper advertisements in those days were not eye-catchers (pills and horses had still to lead the way to more effective display); there was reason to support them by other kinds of publicity. Sticking up title-pages in the streets of Oxford continued at least until 1760. A quarto fly-sheet, undated but attributable to 1758, was issued of books printed at the University Press and sold by Daniel Prince in Oxford and Thomas Payne in London.[1] A large advertisement to 'publish' Hyde's *Religio Persarum* (the second edition), the *Catalogue of Graduates*, and the Verses on the King's death was printed and pasted up in 1760. An advertisement in Latin and French was done in 1772 for Lister's *Synopsis conchyliorum*. The University would benefit indirectly from a catalogue of Daniel Prince's stock of 1767. Payne's catalogues relieved the Press of a need to print its own, until 1774, when Elmsley succeeded Payne as London warehouseman and a catalogue of 'the University Books with French directions' was printed for him. Another was done for him in 1779. Without seeing the book it is impossible to tell what 'direction' meant; but Elmsley dealt largely with foreign countries.

[1] Bodl. MS. Top. Oxon. d. 387, fol. 13. The Press accounts have a charge for a 'New Catalogue of the University Books' in that year.

CHAPTER XXVII

The Printing House 1755–1780

DANIEL PRINCE, Blackstone's candidate for the post, was appointed Warehouse-Keeper and Overseer of the Learned Press on 16 February 1758. He was a bookseller at the north corner of Catte Street and New College Lane, where he had succeeded his uncle, Richard Clements, who died in 1756.[1] He was matriculated in the University as a bookseller in 1750, probably on coming out of an apprenticeship to Clements.

It was to Prince that Blackstone turned in 1755–6 for an expert opinion on the condition of the Press and suggestions for improving it. The memorandum that Prince wrote showed that he was competent in technical matters and intimate with the printers. There is no reason to think that he had first-hand experience of the craft, but he would have learnt a good deal at second hand from the books printed across the street at the Printing House for Clements and some printed there for him during the interval between his uncle's death and his own appointment to the Press.[2] In his private capacity of bookseller he continued after the appointment to get books printed at the University Press and to publish them.

In the twenty-six years of his charge of the printing and warehousing Prince left little account of himself—perhaps because he earned no censure. His accounts are a great improvement on those that went before in fullness and ease of reading. In his time the volume of work increased very much, but there is no sign of a failure to cope with it. A few of his letters that have been kept, to an intending author,[3] are clearly expressed and helpful. A letter to another printer and bookseller, John Nichols, is delightfully candid. Prince had bought from an old bookseller some copies of Elizabeth Elstob's unfinished Anglo-Saxon *Homilies* of Ælfric, printed at Oxford about 1715. He writes: 'It is extremely well printed, as most things were here formerly. I am afraid I print worse and worse; at

---

[1] Harry Paintin, 'Some famous Oxford Booksellers', *Oxford Chronicle*, 30 Jan. 1914.

[2] In his 'Account of the University Printing House' written in 1756 for Blackstone (MS. in the archive of the Delegates) Prince claimed that he had 'expended a considerable sum in printing here these ten years past'. Philip, p. 21.

[3] Bodl. MS. Top. Gen. d. 2, fols. 361–2.

least I do not mend.'[1] When he retired from the service of the Press in 1784 the Delegates minuted:

> Mr. Prince having requested the Board to permit him to resign his Offices of Warehouse Man and Overseer of the Press, Mr. Joshua Cooke his Partner was appointed Warehouse Man . . .

Perhaps he would have expected no more by way of valediction.

In his report on the Press made for Blackstone in 1756[2] Prince concentrated attention on excessive prices. He inferred that a price for every book was set by the workmen and argued that they ought to be controlled by a skilful overseer, who would 'set the General Price, treat with the workmen for their part, and reserve the proper Profit on the whole for his Superiors'. He refers to an 'established Way' of fixing compositors' pay according to the number of ens that they set[3] and alleged that they generally earned 4d. for a thousand. At that rate a sheet of an Oxford book would cost 2s. less than it did. He admits that his suggested scale of pay would be fair to the workmen only if they were fully employed, which they were not; therefore 'stock-work' must always be available to them. When it came to naming the books to provide this permanent reserve of work, Prince, like others before him, faltered: he could think only of Clarendon's *History of the Rebellion* and *The Whole Duty of Man*, of which he believed (wrongly in the case of the latter) that the University owned the copy. He thought there might be some school books to be printed, and that candidates for holy orders needed Lactantius and Minucius Felix.

Prince pointed out that an author who went to a London printer not only paid less but had included in the price the services of a corrector, whereas at Oxford there was none. He made no secret of his opinion that Richardson, the Warehouse-Keeper, was unfit to be in charge.

---

[1] Nichols, *Lit. An.* viii, p. 476.

[2] 'Some Account of the University Printing-House; the Condition of the Letters; of what is at present wanted; and some Hints towards restoring it to an advantagious State', manuscript in the archive of the Delegates. Printed in Philip, pp. 18-22.

[3] An en is a printer's name for the letter n used as a unit of measurement. (1) In reckoning the number of letters and spaces in manuscripts or printed matter n, as being a letter of average width, is the unit. For example, a line containing 57 letters and spaces is said to contain 57 ens. It was in this sense that Prince used the word. (2) Used for measuring the width of a piece of type, an en is half as wide as an em, which is a square ■. The fact that a Roman n is not as wide as an en, or an m as wide as an em is proof enough that these printers' terms go back to a time when Black Letter was the normal and the opposite was true.

In a paper circulated to his fellow Delegates[1] Blackstone adopted in principle the suggestion that compositors should be paid by the thousand ens, but he preferred to convert it so that the module was a square inch containing a number of ens. He worked out the en-content of sheets of various sizes set in several sizes of type, and set out the result in a series of tables basing the price for a sheet on a payment to the compositor of $6\frac{1}{2}d$. a thousand ens and allowing the pressmen, the overseer, and the University to divide the difference between the compositor's part and what Blackstone reckoned would be charged for the sheet by a reputable printer in London. The justification for paying the compositors more than they would have earned for the same task in London was that they undertook corrector's work, which in London had to be paid for separately.

By taking charging out of the hands of the workmen and settling it on a regular plan Blackstone hoped to make Oxford prices equal those of the better houses in London. Of course, he had to allow for exceptions: Greek and exotic scripts, complicated works, abundance of notes, and so on, and for these he would let the overseer quote an appropriate rate. It is remarkable, though, that all work in Roman letter was charged the same, whether the language were English, Latin, or another.[2] Did the compositors really know Latin still?

Close application is needed to follow Blackstone's calculations and his explanations of them. Before submitting them to the other Delegates he sent them to two London printers, James Bettenham and Samuel Richardson, for their comments. No reply from Bettenham is to be found; Richardson could not understand the 'Calculations and Tables, having generally fixed my Prices by Practice', but he gave good advice and useful information (to which we will return).[3] The manner of the reception of his paper by the Delegacy was the subject of complaint in Blackstone's open letter *To the Reverend Doctor Randolph*:

This proposal (which cost some pains in the compiling) had undergone the strictures of many persons of learning in this place, and had been examined, corrected, and approved by some printers of the first character in London. Many also of the Delegates received it with seeming satisfaction, and professions of zeal for it's success. Others indeed treated it with

[1] 'Some Thoughts on the Oxford Press 1756. Mar. 25.', MS. in the Delegates' archive. Printed in Philip, pp. 23-38.
[2] An extra penny a thousand ens was granted to London compositors in 1785 for 'Works printed in any foreign Language, though in common Type': Howe, '*The Trade*', p. 44.
[3] Richardson's letter is printed in Philip, pp. 39-42, from a transcript at the Press. The original is at present mislaid.

a gloomy and contemptuous silence; imagining perhaps that any steps towards reformation would be an acknowledgement of former negligence. Objections of some sort or other they certainly had, and probably extremely strong ones; else it will be hard to account why, in the course of fifteen months, these proposals have never been once considered in any meeting; nor have had any other effect, than barely to alarm the favourite family in the printinghouse; who, I hear, have begun among themselves a slight and imperfect reduction, which may possibly continue till the present enquiries are over.[1]

As part of Blackstone's triumph over inertia and conservatism in the Delegacy a scheme of his for regulating the prices of printing was agreed to in 1758.[2] The rules and tables that he proposed were set up in type and distributed to the workmen and to likely customers: a copy is inserted in the Delegates' Order Book.[3] The scheme reproduces his earlier draft as to the prices, save that in the higher ranges he allows the Overseer rather more at the expense of the University. The abnormally high rate for the compositor is stated to be 'in consideration of his Care in not needing any Corrector of gross Errors, and to make Amends for any accidental Delays or Defect of Work: except in such Books as by the antient Usage of the House have been always composed at a cheaper Rate; as Marshall's Catechism, the Manual of Statutes, Occasional Verses, &c.'.

Unfortunately, the accounts are so framed as to make it impossible to tell whether this directive led to a lowering of prices. In principle it seems to be misconceived: such a minute and rigid control of prices cannot be reconciled with the variety of printer's work in point of difficulty and risk. It was indeed an example of Blackstone's 'almost oppressive spirit of orderliness'.[4] To let compositors and pressmen put a price on a manuscript was imprudent in the circumstances at Oxford in 1756; but to take the matter entirely out of their hands was equally so. Prince's recommendation that a skilful overseer should 'treat with the workmen for their part' had in it the germs of sound estimating.

Richardson, in his comments on the 'Thoughts' that Blackstone wrote for the Delegacy, makes interesting comparisons of practices at Oxford and in the London trade. He thought, while admitting that authors liked

---

[1] p. 14; Philip, p. 55.
[2] 'Orders established by the Delegates, at a Meeting, March 8, 1758, for regulating the Prices of Printing at the University Press'; printed in Philip, pp. 84–9.
[3] Thirty-two copies were printed for the workmen and 500 for 'the Publick'.
[4] G. P. Macdonel in the *D.N.B.*

to correct proofs, that the Press should conform with the London houses in employing a corrector 'in order to sweep-out, if I may so express myself, the grosser Errors of the Compositor', and so make the author's revising more pleasant to him. He was insistent on the advantages of having a salaried overseer rather than letting the man in control of printing get his living from charges for warehouse work and a commission on every printed sheet to pay him for supplying supervision and ink and other consumable stores. His status would then be intermediate between those of masters and workmen, and besides not having interests shared with his subordinates he would have more authority for deciding matters that 'cannot be decided by Rule'. Such a man would be qualified for dealing with authors and, incidentally, could undertake correction in addition to his other duties.

Richardson remarked that Blackstone had over-simplified London prices. Those that he quoted as typical were such as 'we in Town reckon to Booksellers. The Masters generally expect something more Profit from Gentlemen of Ability . . . If you treat Booksellers and Men of Fortune alike, the former will think they have Reason to be dissatisfied.'

He thought that the Overseer should be allowed to take one or two apprentices, but that the workmen should have none.

Richardson's criticisms make it evident that in depriving the journeyman printer of an original dignity Oxford lagged behind London. In Hearne's day the Oxford compositor might no longer claim his right to wear a sword, but he dealt directly with an author, quoted him a price, and presented him with a bill; he might advance the cost of materials out of his own pocket. How long the journeymen at Oxford continued to take apprentices is not clear, but in 1756 they still were responsible for making the proof conform with the copy. Despite the advice from London they went on being so for another indefinite spell of years, just as the Overseer went on gaining a living by piecework. In our Printing-House he was *primus inter pares*, not, as in London, admitted to an industrial middle class.

As soon as Prince entered upon the service of the Press he was ordered to take an inventory of the books, types, and other furniture. He did so and charged 25*s.* in 1758 for 'taking a Catalogue of all Types, Matrices, and Puncheons and other Materials'. His list of *Books printed at the University Press in Oxford* was printed,[1] but the inventory has not been preserved. So far as typefaces are concerned, the equipment at much the

---

[1] Bodl. MS. Top. Oxon. d. 387, fol. 13, a folio sheet. Its cost is entered in the accounts for 1758-9.

same time is known by a specimen bearing no date but assignable by an entry in the accounts to the period between Michaelmas 1757 and Prince's taking control in the February following.[1] It was the first specimen of the typefaces of the Press to be issued since 1706, and the only one to be issued in the form of a sheet, a Demy broadside ($22\frac{1}{2}$ by $18\frac{3}{4}$ in.). The sheet and the type displayed on it have been described fully and accurately by J. S. G. Simmons, who was the first to establish its date.[2] Although evidence to support it is lacking, his conjecture that Blackstone instigated the production of this type-specimen is plausible. Twenty-four copies were printed, of which two are known to exist.[3]

The Broadside Specimen shows the typographical equipment of the Press at an early stage of conversion from Fell to Caslon. There being no longer a typefounder in Oxford, old founts as they wore out were replaced by purchases from London, seldom, though Greek was an exception, cast in matrices from the stock at the Press. The equipment in 1757/8 was, therefore, less distinct in its character than it had been in 1693-1706, when many, though by no means all, the typefaces in the specimens issued from the Press were not available elsewhere in Great Britain. Of the 45 faces displayed in the Broadside Specimen 12 had been added since 1706: two sizes of Roman and Italic, three of Hebrew, and the Etruscan from Caslon, and four sets of full-faced capitals for titles from unidentified suppliers.

Probably put in to even up the depth of its four columns, therefore not indicative of the total wealth of the Press in such things, are 12 type-ornaments. Two others, besides two cut by Fell's typefounder,[4] had been shown in the *Specimen* of 1695. These with 6 in Fell's Bible of 1675 and another 8 discernible in keepsakes of the early eighteenth century go some way towards accounting for the 53 matrices for 'flower work' got by Fell from Holland in 1672.[5] They can almost all be found in the specimens of Dutch typefounders issued before 1710, and among them are some very fine sixteenth-century arabesques.[6] Additions shown in the *Specimen* of 1768 are of a later fashion and probably bought from London.[7]

It was in 1758 that the Delegates commissioned Baskerville to make

---

[1] The date is sometimes given as *c.* 1710 following *A Catalogue of Specimens of Printing Types by English and Scottish Printers and Founders, 1665–1830*, by W. T. Berry and A. F. Johnson (1935), p. 8, partly corrected in their 'Supplement' in *Signature*, N.S. xvi (1952).

[2] 'The Undated Oxford Broadsheet Specimen', *The Library*, 5th ser. xi (1956), pp. 11–17, with a collotype reproduction.

[3] One at the Bodleian (C. 1. 24. Art, fol. 7), one at the Press in the Printer's Museum.

[4] Hart, p. 51, Nos. 10, 11.   [5] Ibid., p. 159.   [6] Morison, *Fell*, pp. 177–87.

[7] D.O. 8 Mar. 1758: '. . . that a sufficient number of Flowers be bought of Mr. Caslon'.

a Greek type for the Press. If the words of their minute of 6 June put the matter in the right light Baskerville had approached the University with an offer to do it. At the next meeting the Delegacy deputed Blackstone to agree with him for the supply of 'a new set of Greek Puncheons, matrices and moulds in Great Primer'.

Baskerville had made a name for himself in the polite world by his beautiful Virgil, the first book in his types, published in 1757; and in a letter of 29 March 1755 Robert Dodsley had told Shenstone, with reference to one of the specimens issued from the Birmingham type-foundry, 'Mr. Baskerville's Specimen is much approv'd, and he has met with great encouragement at both the Universities.'[1] Earlier in 1758 Baskerville had come to an arrangement allowing him to print the Bible and the Book of Common Prayer at Cambridge: it may be that he fore-saw spare capacity in his punchcutter while those large works were under way. The old Great Primer Greek at the Press was the University's earliest acquisition of printing utensils, a gift of type and matrices by Sir Henry Savile in 1619.[2] It was one of the less polished sixteenth-century imitations of Garamond's *Grecs du roi* and by this time in poor repair. The other Greek types of the Press were better.

Baskerville knew nothing about Greek, and experimental work to afford him guidance was put in hand at Oxford. 'A Specimen of Double Pica Greek, all the Letters', 'A Broad Sheet of Letters &c. which will be wanted for the Greek for Mr. Baskerville', and 'A Specimen of Greek with Italick Capitals' were set and printed in 1758.

Satisfactory accounts of Baskerville's dealings with the Delegates have been published by his biographers and by Reed in his *History of the Old English Letter Foundries*.[3] Two hundredweight of the type reached Oxford in 1761 and were proofed; Baskerville was paid the stipulated sum of £210. The punches and matrices now at the Press were presumably delivered at the same time. Prospectuses of the New Testament 'on Mr. Baskerville's new Letter' were printed, 500 in quarto and 2,000 from the same type overrun to fit octavo. Someone appears to have doubted the success of the design, for in the same year there was another 'Specimen of Greek New Testament part Baskerville's and part the Large Greek'. Nevertheless in 1762 the quarto and octavo editions in the new type were put to press, and they were issued the year after.

[1] R. Straus and R. K. Dent, *John Baskerville: a Memoir* (Cambridge, 1907), p. 45.
[2] Morison, *Fell*, pp. 102-3.
[3] Straus and Dent, op. cit., pp. 51-4; T. B. Reed, 273-4 (1887).

There is no defending Baskerville's Greek against the judgements, all of them harsh, that reliable critics have passed on it. One of the most recent and most competent, the late Dr. Victor Scholderer, called it 'a mean-looking, spineless fount'.[1] Another weighty authority, Robert Proctor, saw in it the origin of the 'Porson' class of Greeks, with 'their dull monotony, ungraceful forms, and general lack of firmness and

KATA ΛΟΥΚΑΝ.   229

σαι δὲ καὶ γυναῖκες, αἵτινες ἦσαν συνεληλυθυῖαι αὐτῷ
ἐκ τῆς Γαλιλαίας, ἐθεάσαν7ο τὸ μνημεῖον, καὶ ὡς
56 ἐτέθη τὸ σῶμα αὐτῦ. Ὑποςρέψασαι δὲ ἡτοίμασαν
ἀρώματα καὶ μύρα· καὶ τὸ μὲν σάββατον. ἡσύχασαν
κατὰ τὴν ἐντολήν.

Baskerville's Greek type in the octavo Testament of 1763.

dignity'.[2] Not everyone will see so close a link between Baskerville and Porson: they may as well be regarded as two innovators, one ignorant, the other instructed, who broke in their different ways from the tradition in printing handed down from Aldus. Porson's capitals were upright and he did away with all ligatures:[3] Scholderer notes 'the only two interesting features' of Baskerville's essay, the inclination of the capitals, and, as compared with the founts then in use, 'that ligatures and contractions are still fewer and less conspicuous, the type being complete in less than 160 matrices'.

The number of matrices in 1794 was 167[4] and is now 152, but it includes two sets of Arabic numerals, a triplicate for 8, duplicates for α ε η ο s υ ω α η ω,[5] the customary alternative forms of βγθπρτ, and only 8 ligatures, for και, καὶ, ου, σθ, σπ, σσ, στ, σχ. Baskerville's was not a long step in the disuse of ligatures and contractions, a process that had been going on since the late seventeenth century;[6] the Greeks by

---

[1] [V. Scholderer] *Greek Printing Types, 1465–1927* (British Museum, 1927).
[2] *The Printing of Greek in the Fifteenth Century,* Bibliographical Society Illustrated Monograph No. viii (1900), p. 16.
[3] J. M. Mosley, 'The Porson Greek Types', *Penrose Annual,* 54 (1960), pp. 36–40.
[4] Hart, p. 131.
[5] I guess that Baskerville thought that separate matrices would be needed for casting the vowels kerned for loose accents and mistook final sigma for a vowel. The total includes a matrix for small kappa, which is missing.
[6] Reed, *Old English Letter Foundries,* p. 224.

Alexander Wilson, in use by the brothers Foulis since 1743, had no more, if as many.

The new Greek was evidently not liked by the Oxford scholars: it was rarely used again;[1] and Samuel Musgrave, who was given leave to print his Euripides in it as soon as it arrived,[2] was dissuaded from insisting on his choice, and the book was done in another type. The New Testaments sold very slowly: in 1780 there were 347 left of the 500 quartos and 1,563 of the 2,000 octavos.

At this time an equally useless accession to the typographical equipment of the Press was being withheld from it by the unconscionable Edward Rowe Mores. He had been entrusted by the younger William Bowyer with the punches and matrices for an Anglo-Saxon type as a present to the University of Oxford. The irresponsible antiquary kept them for eleven years and had type cast in the matrices for his own use, disregarding inquiries from the would-be donor or answering tardily with specious excuses.[3]

The type had been made for Elizabeth Elstob's *Rudiments of Grammar for the English-Saxon Tongue*, printed by the elder Bowyer in 1715, as a gift to the printer from the Lord Chief Justice. In sending the material to Mores on 4 December 1753 the younger Bowyer explains the circumstances:

Sir, I make bold to transmit to Oxford through your Hands the Saxon Punches and Matrices, which you was pleased to intimate would not be unacceptable to that learned Body. It would be a great Satisfaction to me, if I could by this means perpetuate my Obligations to that Personage to whose Munificence I am originally indebted for them, the late Lord Chief Justice Parker, afterwards Earl of Macclesfield: Who, among the numerous Benefactors which my Father met with after his House was burnt in 1712-3, generously procured these Types to be cut to enable him to print Mrs. Elstob's Saxon Grammar. England had not then the Advantage of such an Artist in Letter-cutting as has since arisen; and it is to be lamented that the Execution of these is not equal to the Intention of the Noble Donor, and, I now add, to the Place in which they are to be reposited. However, I esteem it a peculiar Happiness, that, as my Father received them from a great Patron of Learning, his Son consigns them to the greatest Seminary of it; and that he is, Sir, Your most obliged Friend, and Humble Servant, W. Bowyer.[4]

[1] Quotations in William Cleaver's *Decretum Lacedaemoniorum contra Timotheum* (1777) are set in it.   [2] D.O. 31 Jan. 1759.
[3] E. Rowe Mores, *A Dissertation upon English Typographical Founders and Founderies* (1778), ed. H. Carter and C. Ricks (Oxford, 1961), pp. xxxv–xliii.
[4] Bodl. MS. Eng. misc. c. 75, fol. 30.

The type had been made from drawings by Humfrey Wanley representing the characters in the English insular hand, and it is the only one ever made that attempts to reproduce that extremely beautiful writing. The cutting of the punches, however, was a miserable performance by an unnamed man who, as Wanley put it, 'was but a blunderer'.[1] There is a specimen at the Press, printed, no doubt, by Mores himself at a press in his house, of a fount of this letter that he caused to be cast.[2] He tinkered with it for years trying to get it, as he thought, improved by two punchcutters, for he was an ardent Saxon scholar and an advocate of type for the insular hand.

Mores finally parted with the punches and matrices and some type in 1764 to Joseph Browne, the Vice-Chancellor, with a letter telling him of Bowyer's gift and excusing his detention of it.[3] No acknowledgement was sent to Bowyer. Mores tried to exonerate the Vice-Chancellor, 'a most worthy gentleman, and not to be blamed upon this occasion, because I believe that he did not fully comprehend the matter'.[4] The first acknowledgement of receipt at the Press is in a letter from Daniel Prince to John Nichols, formerly Bowyer's partner, written on 8 August 1778, the year after Bowyer died:

I find that Mr. Mores, about Dec. 4, 1753, received from Mr. Bowyer a small box of Saxon punches and matrices, the same in which the letters were cast for Mrs. Elstob's Saxon Grammar; and it also appears that Mr. Mores did not send the box of matrices and punches (nor any types) till Oct. 6, 1764; when Dr. Browne was quite inattentive to business; for he died in that last year of his office.—The box of punches and matrices are now in my possession, as printer to the University.[5]

Safely stored in the Printing House, the Elstob Saxon lay unused for a century and more. It is not shown in the specimens of its types issued from the Press later in the eighteenth century,[6] but Horace Hart reproduced one of Mores's specimens of it in his *Notes on a Century of Typography at the University Press, Oxford*, in 1900.[7] Hart's book brought the

[1] Nichols, *Lit. An.* i, p. 117.
[2] There is another copy in the Bodleian (MS. Eng. misc. c. 75, fol. 32), and a variant in the St. Bride Printing Library.   [3] Bodl. MS. Eng. misc. c. 75, fol. 38.
[4] Nichols, *Lit. An.* ii, pp. 362–3, to Bowyer, 10 Jan. 1773.   [5] Ibid., p. 363.
[6] The punches and matrices are entered in the *Catalogue of Materials belonging to the University of Oxford in the Clarendon Printing House*, 1794; Hart, *A Century*, p. 132.
[7] p. 82. From the original in the St. Bride Printing Library. It can hardly have been printed, as Hart supposed, at the Press, where type for it was not available until 25 years after its date. Mores had 36 lb. of it at the time of his death in 1778: *A Dissertation upon English Typographical Founders*, ed. of 1961, p. 128.

Characteres Anglo-Saxonici per eruditam fæminam *Eliz. Elftob* ad fidem codd. mff. delineati. quorum tam inftrumentis cuforiis quam matricibus donata eft Univ. **1753.**

Oratio Dominica.

Fæðeɲ uɲe þu þe eaɲc on heoɲe-num. ɲι þιn.nama. ȝehalȝoð ꞏ co-becume þιn ɲιce ꞏ ȝepuɲðe þιn ɲιlla on eoɲþan ɲpa ɲpa on heoɲenum ꞏ uɲne ðæȝhpam-lιcan hlaɲ ɲyle uɲ co ðæȝ ꞏ ꞇ ɲoɲȝyɲ uɲ uɲe ȝylcaɲ ɲpa ɲpa þe ɲoɲȝιɲað uɲum ȝylcenðum ꞏ ꞇ ne ȝelæðde þu uɲ on coɲc-nunȝe ac alyɲ uɲ oɲ yɲele ꞏ ɲoðlιce ꞇ

Elementa Anglo-Saxonica.

A A B Ϲ C D E Ꝑ F Ϝ ᵹG H ƕ I K L ꟽ M ꞁ N O P Q R S Ꞅ Ꞇ T U V Ᵽ p p X ẏ Z Z Ꞁ æ Ꝺ þ ð þ
a b c ð e é ɲ ȝ h ι k l m n o p q ꞃ ꞃ ɲ ꞇ u p p x ẏ Ꞅ Ꞅ ẏ z æ þ ð ꞇ & þ ꞏ ꞏ ꞇ ꝥ

Cuforia majufcula 42.
Matrices majufculæ 44.
Cuforia minufcula 37.
Matrices minufculæ 39.

The 'Elstob Saxon' for which the younger William Bowyer gave the punches and matrices to the Press. A specimen printed by Edward Rowe Mores while he detained the gift for eleven years.

typeface to the notice of Robert Bridges, who experimented with it in 1908-9 as the nucleus of an extended alphabet for the English language and used some of it in one of his *Tracts* published in 1910.[1]

[1] The experimental proofs are in the Printer's archive. The tract was 'On the Present State of English Pronunciation' in the English Association's *Essays and Studies*, i (Oxford, 1910), reprinted in 1913 as *Society for Pure English Tract No. 1.*

The re-equipping of the composing room with types by Caslon had gone further by 1770, when a *Specimen of the Printing-Types belonging to the University of Oxford*, dated 1768, was issued in an edition of 150 with a supplement bringing it up to the date of publication.[1] Fell's Double Pica, Great Primer, and Pica Romans and Italics had dropped out, replaced by Caslon's, and his smaller sizes are retained only as alternatives to founts got from London. Baskerville's Greek is shown, but a fount of Caslon's old-fashioned Greek, with an abundance of ligatures, is in the supplement. Type cast on a body bigger than need be, so that it produced the same effect as putting leads between lines is shown for the first time in this specimen. It was a fount of English-bodied Roman and Italic cast on 2-line Brevier bought in 1760 for a projected edition of Cicero but used for Blackstone's *Commentaries*. Another supplement to the specimen, displaying three additional founts from Caslon was issued in 1775.[2]

For the press room a German stove with a pipe was bought in 1767, and in the same year a new press from Mr. Yalloly,[3] costing £17. 3s. 9d. The pressmen were paid the traditional fee of £2. 10s. for 'working it down'. Bedding a new stone in a press, generally done on bran or sawdust, was charged at 10d. A thousand quoins in 1768 cost 21s. A new item in the accounts for 1769 was 4d. for a black lead pencil for the Delegates.

About paper our records give all too little information that serves to measure the progress of the industry in this country. Until 1758 the Vice-Chancellor's annual computus gives the total expenditure on paper for each year, and for twenty years after that purchases of paper are entered in the Warehouse-Keeper's accounts, but only exceptionally is the supplier named in either. However, the prices paid are proof enough that the paper bought after 1758 for the Delegates' books was made in this country, the one exception being a Dutch Royal for the quarto Greek Testament of 1763 in Baskerville's type. That cost £3. 3s. a ream, while English Royal for the octavo edition cost £1. 1s. Papers often used at this time (1758–78) were Royal at £1. 8s. and Demy at 15s. The import duty at that time on a ream of foreign Demy was about 10s. for fine and 7s. 9d. for second quality; so the Demy was certainly British.

The most famous of our paper-makers comes into the Delegates' Orders once, in 1774, when Prince was directed to find out 'from Mr. Whatman

---

[1] Copies are in All Souls College Library and the St. Bride Printing Library in London. Hart, *A Century*, pp. 85–105, 187.

[2] Ibid., pp. 104–5.

[3] He was a 'printer's press carpenter' who also supplied John Wilkes: Guildhall Library (London), MS. 214/4 (Information from Mr. J. M. Mosley).

the Paper Maker what will be the price of the Paper per Rheam to be used in the new Edition of Tully'. The paper eventually bought in 1776 for Cicero's works came from Bowles, a London stationer, and cost the Press £1. 6s. a ream less 2½ per cent. It may, nevertheless, have been made by Whatman. The younger James Whatman visited Oxford in 1766.[1]

In 1778 the Delegates decided to keep a stock of paper instead of buying, as they had always done previously, enough for each edition as the need arose. They resolved:

That Mr. Prince be commissioned without delay to apply to six principal Stationers to send Specimens of three kinds of good and substantial papers for the purpose of printing Books at the University Press. That their Specimens be respectively marked with their proper and lowest Prices for ready Money.

That it is the Opinion of the Board that there be kept up a Stock of Paper from time to time agreeable to the Specimens above intended, in order that the same Paper be uniformly made use of in the same Work, and that inequality be avoided which has of late in some degree tarnished the beauty of our most elegant Editions.

That when the University has once adopted the Method of keeping up a Stock as above-mentioned, it be recommended to all who publish at the University Press to make use of the University Paper, provided they have it at prime cost, and it shall be made appear, (as it is hoped it will) that they cannot provide Paper on better Terms from any other Quarter.

At its next meeting the Board chose a 28-lb. Medium from Staples for use in all common work; the subsequent meeting selected a Demy from Chapman instead of it and directed that a thin Royal from Wright & Gill and a thick Royal from Bloxam be stocked as well. Six months later it was resolved to order from Durham (William Durham, paper-maker at Postlip, Gloucestershire) papers corresponding with the samples submitted by Wright & Gill and Bloxam for a 28-lb. best Royal at 18s. a ream and a 26-lb. Demy at 14s.

The Royal paper for Cicero bought in 1778–80 from Bowles and Bloxam amounted to 440 reams, and Durham supplied in the same period 133 reams of Demy and 84 of Royal for stock. Our records do not extend to paper bought for books printed here for authors or booksellers, nor to the Bible Press. The much larger quantity consumed in printing Oxford

---

[1] T. Balston, *James Whatman Father and Son* (1957), p. 24.

Bibles and prayer books was, to judge (rather uncertainly) by its appearance and watermarks, equally British. It may be said that the evidence from Oxford supports the accepted opinion that protective tariffs had nursed the infant white paper industry successfully in the earlier half of the century and made it dominate the home market by the end of that time.[1] Daniel Prince told an author in 1766, 'You need not fear [not] having good Paper. The Genoa sort was never very good, & is now quite out of Use.'[2] We may believe him as to the fact without sharing his opinion: he cannot have known much about Genoa paper.

It must be admitted that the supplanting of foreign paper meant a decline in quality. The ordinary English book paper of the latter part of the century is soft and of a muddy hue. This can be explained by our millers suffering more than the continental from an insufficiency of white linen rags to meet the expanding demand and being driven to use more cotton, much of it coloured. The Hollander engines replacing stampers for beating were less efficient bleachers because of their quicker action and use of less water[3] (the mill at Wolvercote was behind the times in having stampers as late as 1779).[4] Chlorine bleach was not introduced until the very end of the century.

The tariff on foreign paper was formidable in its complexity: by 1784 an importer 'would have paid duties calculated under thirteen different heads'.[5] Blackstone was not content until he had fully mastered the subject. In a draft kept at the Press he presented the result of his calculations of the excise and import duties on some fifty varieties of paper that might be used for printing. The duties in force up to 1758 he extracted from James Postlethwayt's *History of the Public Revenue*[6] and he added the 5 per cent increase imposed in 1759 (the Act of 32 Geo. II, c. 10). A glance at Postlethwayt's book will convince anyone that to extract the information from it was a feat of prodigious application and endurance and, assuming that Blackstone's results are right, of as much perspicacity. The table is as large a conspectus of the kinds of paper obtainable or within recent memory about 1760 as could be desired.[7]

---

[1] Coleman, *The British Paper Industry*, pp. 91–3.
[2] Bodl. MS. Top. Gen. d. 2, fol. 361.
[3] Coleman, op. cit., p. 110.
[4] Carter, *Wolvercote Mill*, p. 23.
[5] Coleman, op. cit., p. 129.
[6] *The History of the Public Revenue, from the Revolution in 1688 to Christmas 1753; with an appendix completing the same to Christmas 1758* (1759).
[7] In the Delegates' archive (Pkt. 62). He marked it with directions to the compositor, but I do not know that it was printed.

Reckoning the excise on a home-produced paper costing the Press £2. 19s. a ream at 8s. 6d. (which allowed the merchant 6d. interest on his payment of the tax) Blackstone calculated that the merchant was charging 3s. 3d. for advancing the money for the tax.[1]

[1] Ibid. I am not sure that I follow him. He assumes that 47s. 3d., the value of the untaxed ream, includes a profit to the manufacturer; but this may not have been so: excise was paid at the mill, and the manufacturer may have lumped it with his costs before adding a profit. And if the seller were a middleman, there would be two profits to be covered.

CHAPTER XXVIII

The Books 1755–80

DELEGATES' BOOKS

Hyde's Historia Religionis Veterum Persarum, 2nd edition, 1760

THOMAS HUNT, Professor of Hebrew and Arabic, suggested this new edition to the Delegates in 1758. The book was first published for subscribers at the author's expense in 1700. Its worth was not appreciated: it is reported[1] that Hyde 'boiled his tea-kettle with almost the whole impression left on his hands'. George Costard was put in charge of the new edition and allowed a fee of half a guinea a sheet. The number was fixed at 500. The Vice-Chancellor was asked to apply to the Trustees of the British Museum for the loan of the Persic matrices in the royal collection. By leave of His Majesty the matrices were lent and sent to Caslon, who cast a hundredweight of type in them.

These types were for the old Persian script used for the Zend and Pazend. Hyde had them made for the book, where they occur rather often besides the University's Arabic with additional characters for modern Persian. His matrices for old Persian had been offered to the University but declined, and Queen Anne bought them.[2] They passed with the deposit of the royal library by George II to the British Museum, where they still are with the types cast for the Press in 1758. Besides the types for Persian and Arabic the book called for nearly all the exotic founts owned by the Press: Hebrew, Syriac, Samaritan, Church-Slavonic, and Black Letter.

Printing began in 1758/9 and was finished late in 1760. In the January following the Delegates fixed the price in sheets at 10s. 6d. The sale was very good: Payne in London sold 94 in the first year, and by 1776 the edition was exhausted.

The new edition reproduces the first without additions: the only novelties being the words 'Editio secunda' and a brief preface by Costard.

Modern authorities on the Zoroastrian religion treat Hyde's book with the utmost respect, valuing it particularly for its exposition of the

---

[1] Nichols, *Lit. An.* ii, p. 457.   [2] Above, p. 320.

early Persian classics, which have been little studied in the West since
Anquetil Duperron in 1771 published the scriptures of Indian Parsees.[1]
It must be confessed that *Hydius, stupor mundi,* is rather too prodigal of his

An illustration from Thomas Hyde's *Historia religionis veterum
Persarum* (1700 and 1760). Reproduced from an impression of the
copper plate. Reduced.

prodigious knowledge, especially in quoting in the original language
and then translating into Latin. He was a man of the seventeenth century.
He does not fail to stress the privilege allowed to the Persians of being
the second people to be told of the birth of Christ and the messianic
prophecies in their sacred books.

---

[1] J. H. Moulton, *Early Zoroastrianism* (1913), p. 36; N. M. Dhalla, *History of Zoroastrianism*
(New York, 1938), p. 474.

Heath's Notes on the Greek Tragedians, 1762

Benjamin Heath, the studious Recorder of the City of Exeter, offered his notes on the plays of Aeschylus, Euripides, and Sophocles to the Delegates in 1758, and was told gratefully that they would be accepted for publication as soon as the presses were at liberty. William Holwell was deputed to prepare the copy and correct proofs. An edition of 500, of which 200 for sale abroad were to be on inferior paper, was put to press in 1759/60.

Holwell's commission can have been no sinecure, for he was supplied with Johnson's Sophocles and Pauw's Aeschylus at the expense of the University, and when Heath's book was published he was given a fee of £50 for 'his extraordinary trouble in revising the Work and preparing it for the Press'. Later he became an editor of some note of classical texts. Heath was rewarded with 12 copies.

The book, priced at 14s. on best paper and 9s. on the other, sold rather slowly. The more expensive sold out in 1805, when 40 were left of the others.

Acknowledgements to Heath for better readings are not infrequent in the modern editions. He was above all a metrist, and in this respect he surpassed the earlier editors. He worked entirely on printed texts.

The book conforms with the fashion adopted at Oxford in 1756 for Musgrave's *Hippolytus* of printing Greek without accents (but with rough breathings and subscript *iota*).[1]

Chandler's Edition of Marmora Oxoniensia, 1763

The Greek and Roman statues and inscribed stones, part of the collection made by Thomas, Earl of Arundel (1586–1646), brought to Oxford in 1667, were of great interest to scholars and dilettanti. Nowhere else in Great Britain were so many examples of ancient sculpture exposed to public view, until they were surpassed late in the eighteenth century by those in the British Museum.

Scholars were particularly concerned with the Parian Chronicle carved in one of Lord Arundel's stones got from Asia Minor, because it recorded notable events, fabulous or verifiable, in the Greek world up to 294 B.C., giving indications which chronologers of ancient history could not afford to neglect. Only a part of this stone came to Oxford, and it had never since it reached this country been wholly decipherable. Fortunately, the complete stone, as soon as it was brought to Arundel House

[1] Nichols, *Lit. An.* iv, p. 285.

The title-page of Swinton's dissertation on the alphabet of the ancient Etruscans.

John Swinton

Abstract of the several Duties payable upon Paper, commonly used for Printing.

Inland, at the Excise Office.

Sorts of Paper.	10 Ann. c. 19.	12 Chas. st 2. c. 9.	Total.
	s. d.	s. d.	s. d.
Demy fine per Ream	1 – 6	0 – 9	2 – 3
Demy second	1 – 0	0 – 6	1 – 6
Crown fine	1 – 0	0 – 6	1 – 6
Crown second	0 – 9	0 – 4½	1 – 1½
Fools Cap fine	1 – 0	0 – 6	1 – 6
Fools Cap second	0 – 9	0 – 4½	1 – 1½
Fine Pots	1 – 0	0 – 6	1 – 6
Second Pots	0 – 6	0 – 3	0 – 9
All other Paper, ad valorem at the next Market Town, exclusive of the Duty.	12 per cent.	6 per cent.	18 per cent.

Blackstone's tabulation of the excise payable on home-produced printing papers in 1759.
From his autograph in the Delegates' archive.

Foreign, at the Custom house.

Sorts of Paper.	Duties inclusive of the Subsidy 1747, according to Postlethwayt's Tables.	Subsidy 1759.	Total exclusive of Fractions, lower than ¼.
	s · d · 1/100	s – d 1/100	s – d
Atlas fine, ℘ Ream ..	29-8-70	1 – 0	30 – 8 ½
Atlas ordinary. - - - -	15-4·21½	0 – 8·40	16 – 0 ½
Elephant fine - - - - -	17-8·70	1 – 0	18 – 8 ½
~~Imperial fine~~	~~29-8-70~~	~~1 – 0~~	
~~Elephant ordinary~~	~~6 – 8·1 3/8~~	~~0 – 4·50~~	~~7 – 0 ½~~
Imperial fine - - - - -	29-8·70	1 – 0	30 8 ½
Second Writing Imperial ..	22·2-70	1 – 0	23 · 2 ½
Royal fine - - - -	17-8·70	1 – 0	18 · 8 ½
Super Royal fine - -	23-8·70	1 – 0	24 · 8 ½
Second Writing Royal ..	13·11·70	1 – 0	14 · 11 ½
Second Writing Super Royal	17-8·70	1 – 0	18 – 8 ½
Genoa Royal fine - -	8 – 2·71½	0 – 8·40	8 – 11
Genoa Royal second.	7 – 3·22½	0 – 6	7 – 9
Holland Royal fine ..	8 – 2·71½	0 – 8·40	8 – 11
Holland Royal second fine	5·4·72½	0 6	5 – 10 ½
Ordinary Royal - -	2 – 8·36¼	0 · 3	2 · 11 ¼
Chancery double - - -	4 – 2·36¼	0 – 3	4 – 5 ¼
Demy fine - - - - -	9 – 8 – 59½	0 – 7·20	10 – 3 ¾
Demy second ——	7 – 5 – 59½	0 – 7·20	8 – 0 ¾
Medium fine - - -	12-4·21½	0 – 8·40	13 – 0 ½
Second Writing Medium -	9 – 4·21½	0 – 8·40	10 0 ½
Genoa Medium fine -	7·1-21½	0 – 8·40	7 – 9 ½
Genoa Medium second	6 – 1·72½	0 – 6	6 7 ½
Bastard or Double Copy -	4 0·92 5/8	0·2·70	4·3 ½
Crown Genoa fine - - -	3·3·92 5/8	0 – 2·70	3 : 6 ½
Crown Genoa second -	2·6·92 5/8	0 · 2·70	2 · 9 ½
	A	B	

Blackstone's tabulation of import-duty payable on foreign printing papers in 1759, based on information in James Postlethwayt's *History of the Public Revenue, 1688–1758*. (First part.)

Sorts of Paper	Duties, inclusive of the Subsidy 1747, according to Postlethwayt's Tables.	Subsidy 1759.	Total, exclusive of Fractions, lower than 1/4.
	£ . d $\frac{100}{}$	£ . d $\frac{100}{}$	£ . d
German Crown	2 - 6 . 92 $\frac{5}{8}$	0 - 2 - 70	2 . 9 $\frac{1}{2}$
Printing Crown fine	2 - 6 . 92 $\frac{5}{8}$	0 - 2 - 70	2 - 9 $\frac{1}{2}$
Printing Crown second ordinary	2 - 2 . 42 $\frac{5}{8}$	0 - 2 - 70	2 . 5
Demy Genoa fine	4 - 0 . 92 $\frac{5}{8}$	0 - 2 - 70	4 - 3 $\frac{1}{2}$
German Demy	3 - 3 . 92 $\frac{5}{8}$	0 - 2 - 70	3 - 6 $\frac{1}{2}$
Printing Demy	3 - 6 . 92 $\frac{5}{8}$	0 - 2 - 70	3 - 9 $\frac{1}{2}$
Fools Cap fine	4 - 9 . 92 $\frac{5}{8}$	0 - 2 - 70	5 - 0 $\frac{1}{2}$
Fools Cap second	4 - 0 . 92 $\frac{5}{8}$	0 - 2 - 70	4 - 3 $\frac{1}{2}$
Genoa Fools Cap fine	3 - 3 . 92 $\frac{5}{8}$	0 - 2 - 70	3 - 6 $\frac{1}{2}$
Genoa Fools Cap second	2 - 6 . 92 $\frac{5}{8}$	0 - 2 - 70	2 - 9 $\frac{1}{2}$
German Fools Cap	2 - 6 . 92 $\frac{5}{8}$	0 - 2 - 70	2 - 9 $\frac{1}{2}$
Fools Cap printing fine	2 - 6 . 92 $\frac{5}{8}$	0 - 2 - 70	2 - 9 $\frac{1}{2}$
Fools Cap printing second ordinary	2 - 2 . 42 $\frac{5}{8}$	0 - 2 - 70	2 . 5
German Lombard	2 - 6 . 92 $\frac{5}{8}$	0 - 2 - 70	2 - 9 $\frac{1}{2}$
Genoa Pot fine	2 - 2 . 42 $\frac{5}{8}$	0 - 2 - 70	2 - 5
Genoa Pot second	2 - 2 . 42 $\frac{5}{8}$	0 - 2 - 70	2 - 5
Genoa Pot ordinary	2 - 2 . 42 $\frac{5}{8}$	0 - 2 - 70	2 - 5
Genoa Pot superfine	4 - 0 . 92 $\frac{5}{8}$	0 - 2 - 70	4 - 3 $\frac{1}{2}$
Genoa Pot second fine	3 - 3 . 92 $\frac{5}{8}$	0 - 2 - 70	3 - 6 $\frac{1}{2}$
Small Post	3 - 3 . 92 $\frac{5}{8}$	0 - 2 - 70	3 . 6 $\frac{1}{2}$
Fine Large Post, 15 lb. p Ream	6 - 1 . 72 $\frac{1}{2}$	0 - 6 -	6 - 7 $\frac{1}{2}$
Fine Large Post, under 15 lb.	5 - 6 . 54 $\frac{3}{8}$	0 . 4 - 50	5 . 11
Rochelle	6 - 1 . 10 $\frac{1}{4}$	0 - 5 . 40	6 - 6 $\frac{1}{2}$

C   D

Second part of Blackstone's table of import-duty on paper.

in London, was read by John Selden and Patrick Young and their transcription, partial as it was, was printed in 1628.[1]

The University was conscious of a duty to celebrate the gift of the stones by Arundel's grandson and to catalogue it for the information of the learned world. John Fell, Vice-Chancellor in 1666–9, laid on his favourite pupil, Humphrey Prideaux, the task of compiling the book. Prideaux, well knowing that he had less than the needed qualifications and hurried by Fell,[2] produced the catalogue, *Marmora Oxoniensia*, and it was printed at Fell's press in 1676, a folio with copper-engraved illustrations.[3] Prideaux relied, as far as he could, on previous writers, especially Selden and the learned chronologer Thomas Lydiat, for a description and annotation of the marbles.

It was felt that Prideaux's performance could be bettered, as he was the first to admit, and several scholars in succession engaged in preparing editions to supersede his, but they did not finish them until Michael Maittaire brought out an edition in London in 1732–3 with some additional matter. This also failed to satisfy the critics, many of whom knew that Maittaire, while preparing the book, had not once been to Oxford to look at the stones.[4]

When Prideaux dealt with it the collection at Oxford was of 150 statues and inscribed stones, all but 20 formerly Arundel's. After the Earl's death in 1646, the country being then in the thick of civil war, many of the objects lay neglected in the garden of Arundel House. Half the Parian Marble, the half on which the earlier events were inscribed, was used in rebuilding a chimney, and other stones were lost.[5] In 1667 Arundel's grandson, Henry Howard, decided to pull the house down and, prompted by John Evelyn, gave part of the collection to the University. At Oxford, where the Sheldonian Theatre was half-built, the stones were set in a wall enclosing the yard round the new building or stood in niches in the wall. Nearly the whole of this wall was demolished in 1712–14 to make room for the new Printing House, and the marbles were taken to a room in the Schools. From there they were moved in 1845 to the newly-erected University Galleries or New Ashmolean Museum, their present resting-place.

It is not hard to tell why the Delegates in 1760 were anxious to sponsor

[1] Madan, *Oxford Books*, ii, No. 600; Nichols, *Lit. An.* ii, p. 5.
[2] The preface to the *Marmora*, 1676. Chandler in 1763 was generous in his praise.
[3] Madan, *Oxford Books*, iii, No. 3092. Above, pp. 83–6.
[4] Nichols, *Lit. An.* ii, 1–9, 27.
[5] A. Michaelis, *Ancient Marbles in Great Britain* (1882), pp. 34–5.

a new book on the marbles, and entrusted Richard Chandler of Magdalen and Mr. Stubbs (probably John Stubb of Queen's) with the editing. A large accession to the collection had been given by the dowager Countess of Pomfret in 1755. This lady had bought from her husband's heir a part of Lord Arundel's collection that Lord Leominster acquired in 1691 and put in the grounds that he laid out at Easton Neston.[1] He had the statues repaired very badly.

The Pomfret Galleries in the Schools. A wood-engraving by Orlando Jewitt in James Ingram's *Memorials of Oxford* (Oxford, 1837).

Chandler put his proposals to the Delegates in 1762 (his fellow editor, once named, is not heard of again) for a book to be written anew. It was planned on the grandest scale, an Imperial folio with 76 whole-page copper-engraved illustrations commissioned from John Miller, a draughtsman and engraver of German birth working in London. A printer, William Howard, was specially employed to work off the plates. Of the text 750 copies were printed, and of the plates 200 sets. Chandler was paid a fee of £250.

Though the volume is dated in 1763, it cannot have been put on sale until February in the following year, when the Delegates fixed the price

---

[1] Michaelis, op. cit., pp. 36, 39-40.

at £4 and agreed to present copies to the Kings of Great Britain, France, Spain, and Naples, the two archbishops, the Dukes of Norfolk and Queensberry, the Lord Chancellor, the Earl of Pomfret, Lord Mansfield, the University of Cambridge, and the Prince of Mecklenburg-Strelitz, besides the donors of marbles then living. The Delegates had 39 free copies.

The price was high for those days, and the book was not easy to sell: 540 sets of the sheets of text were left in 1804 and 29 sets of the plates.

Unlike the previous editors, Chandler attempted nothing in the way of commentary beyond brief notes on provenance. He indexed fully. The book is a catalogue of 412 statues and smaller pieces of sculpture with illustrations that are painstaking and informative but dull. The statues, with a few exceptions, are late, hellenistic or Roman copies of the Greek, twice restored very badly. The part that retains its interest is the transcription of 245 lettered stones and an excellent double-page plate of the lettering of the Parian Chronicle. Of the existing part of this marble Chandler was able to give a virtually complete reading, a thing that Prideaux despaired of. Since the discovery in 1897 of another part of the stone Chandler's has been an incomplete exposition of by far the most important part of his subject.

The size and weight of the volume disqualify it for reference, and its scope and arrangement are insufficiently explained to the reader. A digest, more compendious and cheaper, was published in 1792. The very good paper is watermarked 'J Whatman'.

Hyde's Syntagma Dissertationum, 1767

Gregory Sharpe, Master of the Temple, an orientalist and book-collector, gave the University his collection of the works of Thomas Hyde, printed and manuscript. The gift was made with a view to a comprehensive edition of which the profits would go to a charitable object.[1]

A dozen works by the great scholar, not including his history of Persian religion, were published in 1767 in two quarto volumes. Sharpe bore the cost of the edition and gave it to the University. The *Itinera mundi*, the Hebrew part of the *Shahiludium*, and 20 copper plates were printed in London. The book makes only a small contribution to Hyde's printed works: three pieces of no great interest were previously un-published and engraved plates of several oriental scripts were added.

[1] D.O. 3 July 1767.

These also were a present from Sharpe. The biographical account of Hyde is little better than that in Wood's *Athenae Oxonienses*.

Of the text 500 were printed, but only 200 sets were worked off the plates. In 1805 326 copies were left in stock.

Lister's Synopsis Conchyliorum, 1770

Martin Lister, M.D., F.R.S., published this work on molluscs at London in 1685 at his own expense. It made a thick folio volume printed wholly from copper plates engraved from watercolour drawings by Lister's daughters, Susan and Ann. It had no text. Some 1,100 subjects are delicately drawn; and it may be said that the enlarged anatomical details of snails, slugs, and other small creatures are captivating to the eye.

The book was highly regarded by zoologists, though the system of arrangement had not fully stood the test of time, and the copper plates for it were in the Ashmolean Museum, presented, with his collection of shells, by Lister.[1] In 1768 the Delegates agreed that an impression of 250 should be worked off and published in the care of the Museum's Curator, William Huddesford. He added a brief preface and an index.

The book was put on sale two years later, the illustrations at $3\frac{1}{2}$ guineas and the index separately at 3*s*. 6*d*. Complimentary copies were sent to the King, the Kings of France, Spain, and Denmark, the Duchess of Portland, the Duke of Beaufort, the University's Chancellor, Dr. John Fothergill, and Dr. Linnaeus.

By 1804 all but 46 copies were sold.

This was one of the books that Prince, the Warehouse-Keeper, was proudest of producing:[2] certainly the rolling-press men performed a big task well. Apart from that, the University's rightful share in the credit for the book is small.

Warton's Theocritus, 1770

The book was conceived while the Delegacy was feeling the effect of Blackstone's zeal. On 17 April 1758 the board invited proposals for an edition of the poet at the expense of the University making use of the notes that James St. Amand had bequeathed to it in 1754. A fortnight later Blackstone told Sir Roger Newdigate, '[We] are meditating a very handsome edition of Theocritus in quarto.'[3]

---

[1] Gunther, *Early Science in Oxford*, iii, p. 223.   [2] Nichols, *Lit. An.* iii, p. 426.
[3] Newdigate Papers, B1495.

St. Amand had spent a large part of his life preparing for such a work and had travelled widely in search of the learning on the poet and the manuscripts.[1] By May 1758 proposals were received from the newly-appointed Professor of Poetry, Thomas Warton the younger, and the undertaking was entrusted to him. The Delegates decided that the format should be Royal quarto on thick Dutch paper and the quantity 500.

The text, making 18 sheets, was set and printed in 1758–9: the massive apparatus, 64 sheets, went to press in 1767. Warton remarks in the preface that the poet's part in the book is *minima*. He added his own lecture on the Greek bucolics, a life of Theocritus, notes by Jonathan Toup, his own notes, and indexes, but—illustrating a tendency of the time—no Latin translation. The editor regrets in his preface the Delegates' decision to print the Greek without accents, and he complains of the printers, *lubricum genus hominum atque intractabile*, for their delays. It seems likely that a higher priority given at the Press to Heath's *Notes on the Greek Tragedians*, rather than the slipperiness of the staff, had kept Warton waiting.

Toup greeted this as 'the best production that ever came from the Clarendon Press': a modern authority dismisses it as without critical value.[2] It held the field in this country until Theocritus appeared in Gaisford's *Poetae Graeci Minores* in 1814–15. It fulfilled Blackstone's hopes so far as a handsome appearance is concerned, and it was a relatively successful publication: priced at 25s. for the two volumes in sheets, it sold out in 1792. The King was given a copy. Warton was paid £180.

A cancelled leaf is found in Volume ii, where on p. 398 one of Toup's notes, relating to pederasty, gave offence and was removed by the Vice-Chancellor's wish. Toup was angry about it, and in some *Curae posteriores* on the edition, not printed here, he expresses his feelings in immoderate language.[3]

Robert Robinson's Indexes to Longinus, 1772

A proposal to publish this was adopted in 1768, on condition of its being accommodated to Toup's text of Longinus then in the press. The book was published in December 1772, priced at 2s. 6d. and the compiler was rewarded with six copies. Very few of the 500 printed were sold. The indexes are of Greek words in Longinus *On the Sublime* and in fragments

---

[1] Macray, *Annals*, pp. 252–4.
[2] M. L. Clarke, *Greek Studies in England 1700–1830* (Cambridge, 1945), pp. 63–4.
[3] Nichols, *Lit. An.* ii, p. 340.

of his, besides those in Eunapius on the *Lives of the Philosophers and Sophists* and the commentary by Hierocles on the *Aurea carmina* of Pythagoras.

Musgrave's Euripides, 1778

The Delegates resolved in February 1771 to publish five of Euripides' tragedies, and invited Robert Holmes, a B.A. of New College, to edit them. He was willing and proposed the Iphigenia in Aulis, Rhesus, Troades, Hecuba, and Andromache.

Samuel Musgrave, then a medical practitioner at Plymouth, had edited the *Hippolytus* printed here in 1765. His was the greatest authority in the kingdom on this poet, and the Delegates had been told that in his opinion a new edition of the tragedies would be justified only if it included readings from the text printed by Aldus in 1503. Benjamin Heath had pointed out that the manuscripts used by Aldus had largely escaped damage from medieval emendators.[1]

Musgrave was asked to lend his manuscript notes on the five tragedies suggested by Holmes unless it were his intention to publish them. He replied that he did, indeed, mean to proceed with an edition of the complete works of Euripides and had it almost ready. He wrote in September 1771 from Plymouth expressing his satisfaction on learning that 'the Delegates are by no means attached to that confined plan of publishing five Plays only' and his appreciation of the condescension of Mr. Holmes in being willing to bear a subordinate part in an edition or retire from it altogether. He offered to submit for the inspection of the board his notes on one of the four tragedies that he had ready.

As for a translation into Latin, Musgrave was not sure what to do.

It would appear, perhaps, paradoxical to say that the Sale of Greek Books is but little affected by the want of Translations. Yet there are some instances which countenance the Supposition. Stephen's [*sic*] Sophocles, though a much harder Author than Euripides, sells, I apprehend, without a Translation better than those Editions which have it. And it should seem as if the Dutch Booksellers did not find *literal* Translations any great help to the sale, when both the Phoenissae and Hippolytus of Monsr. Valckenaer are printed without them. The Glasgow Printers too have, I believe, taken the same Method . . .

It was decided that the University would bear the cost of publishing Euripides entire, and Musgrave was asked to proceed. He was invited

[1] See p. 392.

to give the Delegates 'such hints as may enable them to determine a proper and handsome Gratuity for his trouble'. They undertook to pay Holmes for correcting the press.

While Musgrave thought the size of the fee might be settled after publication and depend on the success of the venture, the board decided on £250 and that the volumes should be produced in the same style as the *Hippolytus* of 1756. Musgrave was delighted by the fee but thought the Greek type would be too big: Baskerville's Great Primer would have been more to his liking.

Nobody else liked Baskerville's Greek. The text was set in Fell Greek and without accents. Jeremiah Markland, for one, feared that the want of accents and of a Latin version would tell against the success of an edition;[1] and in the end the Delegates resolved to add a translation, but in a separate volume and in small type. Musgrave agreed to revise 'the old Translation' for another £80.

Annotations by the lately-deceased Archdeacon John Jortin in the margins of Commelin's Euripides came to light in 1773, and Holmes was charged with copying any that he thought original and sending them to Musgrave. Four years later the Delegates had an offer from Toup of his notes on the tragedies, and it was accepted gratefully.

Musgrave's edition was printed by March 1778, and gift copies were sent to the King, the Kings of France and Spain, the Bibliothèque Royale, the University's Chancellor, the Bodleian, and the contributors of notes. The four volumes, one hundred on large paper and the rest on Royal, selling in sheets for £3. 15s., went fairly well. Eighty-one copies on ordinary paper were left in 1804. Holmes was paid in all £149.

In January 1779 Musgrave demanded a further £200 for his pains, and declared that he would accept nothing less. He had moved to London in 1775 and was unsuccessful in his practice. He was informed that 'the Delegates think the sums already paid a sufficient Compensation.' The editor wrote again to justify his claim on 'so opulent a Body as the University of Oxford'. He died the year after.

The Euripides is one of the great achievements of English classical scholarship in the eighteenth century.[2] Musgrave's notes were reprinted in a number of editions as late as 1821, and acknowledgements of his emendations and explanations are not rare in the present Oxford Classical Text.

[1] Nichols, *Lit. An.* iv, p. 285.
[2] M. L. Clarke, *Greek Studies in England*, pp. 61–2.

Lacroze's Coptic Lexicon abridged (1775) and Scholtz's Coptic Grammar (1778)

C. G. Woide, a Polish Protestant and orientalist, who had been studying at Leyden, wrote in 1767 on behalf of the German scholar Christian Scholtz offering the University a Coptic grammar, if it would undertake to print and publish it. Woide said that the only available grammar of this language was full of gross errors. The Delegates accepted the offer immediately.

A year later their minutes refer to a Coptic lexicon compiled by Scholtz by abridging the unpublished work of Maturinus Lacroze. It was apparently intended that this and the grammar should appear as one volume; but if so the plan was altered and the two works were published separately, both edited by Woide.

Printing of the lexicon began in 1772, and it was published in 1775. Two hundred and fifty copies were printed, and the price was 15s. Copies were presented to the King of France, the Abbey of Saint-Germain-des-Prés, the Escurial, and the University of Leyden. Scholtz was rewarded with 50 copies delivered in Germany. After deduction of these, about 70 copies had been sold by 1804, but none were left in 1916.

The grammar was printed in 1774-8. It sold for 7s. 6d. and the quantity was 250. Lord North, the Chancellor, received one, and 50 were sent to Scholtz's executors; 20 to Woide. In 1804 there were 141 unsold.

John Swinton[1] was trusted to supervise the printing of these two books and correct proofs in return for a fee of £20. He was given leave by the Delegates to prefix to the lexicon a dissertation of his own, of about 8 pages, on a Coptic coin. It does not appear in the printed work; perhaps Swinton intended it for the grammar. John Nichols recorded that 'The late Mr. Swinton of Oxford intended to have added to this work [the grammar] a dissertation De nummis Copto-Phoeniciis, part of which is actually printed off; but the remainder cannot be found among his papers.'[2] Swinton died while the book was being printed, in 1777.

Toup's Longinus, 1778

Jonathan Toup offered his text and notes for Longinus *On the Sublime* to the Oxford bookseller, James Fletcher, about the year 1750. Fletcher would not venture the edition, Toup not being known then among scholars.[3] He made his name with *Emendationes in Suidam* (1760-6), and by

---

[1] See above, p. 312.   [2] *Lit. An.* ix, pp. 13-14.   [3] Nichols, *Lit. An.* ii, p. 343.

1775, when he proposed his Longinus to the Delegates, they accepted it gratefully.

They agreed on an impression of 500 copies in quarto, 100 on large paper. It was published in January 1778 at the price of 14s. for the large and 9s. for the small. The King, the Prince of Wales, Lord North, and the Bodleian received bound copies.

When this edition was one-third printed the Delegates ordered another, in octavo, of 1,500 on ordinary paper and 500 on large. The octavo was issued in June 1778, costing 5s., for the large and 3s. 6d. for the other.

No doubt it was a valuable addition to the Oxford list of the classics: some of Toup's emendations are acknowledged by modern editors. The demand for it was quite good. The quarto was exhausted by 1802, and only 180 of the octavo were left in 1804.

The preliminary dissertation ascribed to P. J. Schardam is really by David Ruhnken.[1]

Albucasis on Surgery, 1778

Thomas Hunt, Laudian Professor of Arabic and Regius Professor of Hebrew, recommended to the Delegates in 1774 a proposal by John Channing to edit Albucasis on surgery in Arabic and Latin. They agreed to publish the work, the editor bearing the cost of illustrations, and decided on two volumes in quarto, and that 350 copies would be printed, 100 to be given to the editor.

The author, Khalaf ibn 'Abbas al-Zahrawi, known as Abu al-Qasim, was traditionally a tenth-century physician at Córdoba. He compiled from Greek sources, many of which have since disappeared, a large treatise on the medical sciences. Parts of it were translated into Latin and were of high authority until surprisingly recent times. The part on surgery had been printed in Latin at Venice in 1497 and at Basle in 1541.[2]

About John Channing there is remarkably little on record. According to Nichols, he was an apothecary in Essex Street, London;[3] a man of the same name who took his degree at Oxford in 1767 and was elected a student of Christ Church,[4] was presumably his son. No explanation of

---

[1] M. L. Clarke, *Greek Studies in England*, p. 57.

[2] Nicolas L. Leclerc, *Histoire de la médecine arabe* (Paris, 1876); S. K. Hamarneh and G. Sommerbecker, *A Pharmaceutical View of Abulcasis al-Zahrawi in Moorish Spain* (Leyden, 1963).

[3] *Lit. An.* iii, p. 631; C. F. Schnurrer, *Bibliotheca Arabica* (Halle, 1811), pp. 454–5.

[4] Foster, *Alumni Oxonienses*; information from Dr. J. F. A. Mason, Librarian of Christ Church.

Channing's proficiency in Arabic has been found. In 1766 he published in London an Arabic text and Latin translation of Rhazes on smallpox, having borrowed a manuscript from the University Library of Leyden.[1]

On 31 January 1775, when some 20 sheets of the book had been printed, the Delegates were informed of Channing's death. John Uri, the Hungarian linguist employed on cataloguing the University's oriental manuscripts,[2] was asked to supervise the completion of the book. Printing was finished in June 1778, and the volumes were put on sale at £1. 16s. for large paper and £1. 5s. for small. In 1804 the copies in stock were more than the number originally ordered.

Channing's text is taken from two manuscripts in the Bodleian (Nos. 561 and 634 in Uri's Catalogue).[3]

A critical edition of the Arabic text with a complete apparatus is due has lately been published.[4]

The Philoxenian Syriac Gospels, 1778

This was the first printed edition of the Gospels used by the Jacobite sect in eastern Syria. The Syriac New Testament was previously known to Western scholars only in the older state of the Peshitta version as it was printed by Count von Widmannstadt at Vienna in 1555 and as edited by Gabriel Sionita for the Paris Polyglot Bible of 1645, from which the text in the London Polyglot of 1657 was taken.

In 1730 four manuscripts were sent from Mesopotamia to Glocester Ridley, fellow of New College, of the New Testament revised for the Jacobites by Philoxenus in A.D. 508 and again in 616 by Thomas of Harkel. The revisions were aimed at bringing the text into accord with those of the late, or Byzantine, Greek type, but Harkel noted some readings of older Greek manuscripts in the margins.[5]

The Delegates agreed in November 1772 to commit an edition to the care of Joseph White, Laudian Professor of Arabic. He was asked to finish Ridley's transcript for the press and to supply a Latin translation, making all due acknowledgements to Ridley.

Prince, the Warehouse-Keeper, was instructed to write to Caslon for

[1] *Rhazis De variolis et morbillis*, cura J. Channing (1766), preface.
[2] *D.N.B.* He will be dealt with in the next volume of this history.
[3] Schnurrer, *Bibliotheca Arabica*, p. 455.
[4] M. S. Spink and G. L. Lewis, *Albucasis on Surgery and Instruments: a Definitive Edition of the Arabic Text with English Translation and Commentary*. Publications of the Wellcome Institute of the History of Medicine, N.S. Vol. xii (1973).
[5] Sir F. Kenyon, *Our Bible and the Ancient Manuscripts* (1941), pp. 164–5; B. H. Streeter, *The Four Gospels* (1936), p. 76.

a set of small Syriac types on the model of those made for Widmannstadt, and, if Caslon could not supply it, to apply to Mr. Wilson of Glasgow. Caslon had bought the matrices in which the Syriac for the London Polyglot was cast, and though it was not a small type, it was used for text and footnotes in White's edition.[1] An impression of 250 in two volumes, quarto, was sanctioned in 1774, the year of Ridley's death.

The two volumes were ready for publication in November 1778, priced at £1. 18s. and only waited for bound copies to be sent to the King, Lord North, and the Bodleian Library.

The Delegates reckoned that at best they would lose £70 by this publication, because the quantity was so small, and they told White that they had a claim to recoup their loss from some future work of his. In the event they lost a great deal more; for in 1804 there were 176 copies left in stock, 'above half of them rotten'.

Apollonius Rhodius, 1777-9

Inquiry was made in 1771 for an editor of the *Argonautica*, and John Shaw, fellow of Magdalen, being recommended, submitted his proposals for an edition using the text and Latin translation of Hoelzlin, printed in 1641 by the Elseviers. Shaw's tender was accepted, and the Delegates authorized an impression of 250 in two quarto volumes to sell for £1. 7s. 6d.

The quartos published in 1777 were fine books and sold very well, and in the same year the Delegates desired Shaw to prepare a second edition, a single octavo volume in smaller type, adding some notes from Johannes Pierson's *Verisimilia* (1752, *apud Batavos*) and Ruhnken's letters. Toup also contributed a few notes. This was an edition of 1,500, of which 500 on large paper sold for 10s. 6d., and the rest for 6s. It appeared in 1779. Shaw was paid £140 for the quarto and £40 for the octavo. Copies were presented to the three 'great Schools', Westminster, Winchester, and Eton.

Shaw's preface makes no extravagant claims. He considered that Henri Estienne in 1574 had left succeeding editors with little to do and his main effort had gone to improving Hoelzlin's Latin version. Brunck's

[1] It is difficult to distinguish it from the copy made for Fell, of which the University had matrices. Perhaps as a result of this inquiry from the Delegates, a Long Primer Syriac by Caslon appears in the University's *Specimen* (Supplement) of 1775 (Hart, p. 104) and in Caslon's specimen book of 1786. It was used in the later volumes of the Philoxenian New Testament published here in 1799 and 1803, but when first received it was defective (D.O. 19 Nov. 1778).

edition of 1780 at Strasburg was better in all respects except the printing; perhaps that is why 1,130 copies of Shaw's remained in stock in 1804.

Aristotle's Poetics, 1780

Despite two editions having been printed at the Press in 1760 for a private customer, the Delegates resolved in February 1778 to proceed with another in the care of Thomas Winstanley. He reported that the work was much wanted in the University and proposed the text of Aldus with collations from four manuscripts in the Medicean Library and the various lections and notes of earlier editors and Goulston's Latin translation.

He was desired to add readings from a manuscript in the Escurial and two in the French king's library. Finally an edition of 1,000 on Demy paper and 500 on Royal was sanctioned, and it came out in 1780. It sold reasonably well, costing 4s. 6d. for ordinary paper and 6s. for large. In 1804 there were 356 of the small and 378 of the large left in stock.

Caesar's Commentaries, 1780

Phineas Pett, B.A., of Christ Church, was commissioned to bring out a straightforward edition of the works of Caesar using Oudendorp's text printed at Leyden in 1737 without notes or variant readings. Pett furnished the book with copperplate maps and a geographical index. The Delegates decided to set it in a new Pica type and sell it for 3s. 6d. (large paper 5s.). Fifteen hundred on small paper and 500 on large were printed. There was little demand for them: in 1804 there were left unsold 1,242 of the small and 439 of the large.

AUTHORS' BOOKS

Edward Lhuyd on Fossils, 1760

William Huddesford, Keeper of the Ashmolean Museum, produced a second edition in 1760 of Lhuyd's *Lithophylacii Britannici ichnographia*, and 300 copies were printed at Huddesford's expense.

The book, which 'laid the foundation for a new science',[1] was first printed in London in 1699. Lhuyd had expected that it would be printed at Oxford at the expense of the University, since, he said, 'it contains the Grounds of a new Science in Natural History; and is the Result of many years Searches and Observations';[2] but the Delegates declined it. Great

---

[1] Gunther, *Early Science in Oxford*, xiv, p. 263.
[2] Ibid., p. 22, quoting Bodl. MS. Ashm. 1816, fol. 62.

demands were being made on the resources of the Press at the time by Robert Morison's *Herbal*.

Sir Hans Sloane and Samuel Pepys found another eight subscribers willing to take ten copies and give one to Lhuyd, so an edition of 120 was done in London. Among the subscribers were Lord Chancellor Somers, Martin Lister, Tancred Robinson, and 'Mr. Newton of Cambridge'.[1]

The book was illustrated with 21 copper-engravings, and the plates were afterwards lodged in the Museum, where Lhuyd's collection of fossil stones gathered from Wales and England was also kept. Complaints from a growing number of geologists that the book was unprocurable made Huddesford resolve to republish it with corrections and the addition of more plates and a tract of Lhuyd's *De stellis marinis*.

Lhuyd was particularly concerned to assert that the presence of fossilized marine creatures on land was due to spawn being carried about in vapours rising from the sea and washed into the earth by rain, controverting John Woodward's thesis that they were dislodged from their original positions by the Flood. Lhuyd's letters to eminent scientists on this subject are an appendix to the book.

Jones on Natural Philosophy, 1762

William Jones's *Essay on the First Principles of Natural Philosophy*, printed here in 1762, is of some interest as an example of the 'Hutchinsonian' approach to the natural sciences.

The author, distinguished as 'Jones of Nayland', was primarily a theologian, known for his *Catholic Doctrine of the Trinity*. Like John Hutchinson, by whom he was much influenced, he was afraid of the effect that Newton's physics might have on cosmology as taught in the Bible.

Having studied the works of 'able philosophers' of the modern school, Jones 'would not dare to interpose in such a subject, unless I suspected natural philosophy to be a much easier thing than they have made of it'. For him it was enough to believe that what we see are the effects of secondary causes that God set in motion. He describes experiments proving the impossibility of the existence of a vacuum and combats Newton's theory of gravitation.

The Greek Anthology, 1766

This was the first edition at Oxford of any part of the *Anthology*. Selections

---

[1] Ibid., pp. 405–7.

by Thomas Farnaby, first published in 1629, and by Thomas Johnson, of 1699, were often reprinted in London.

The Oxford edition with a foreword by the poetry professor, Thomas Warton, is a reprint of that of J. J. Reiske, printed at Leipzig in 1754. It takes in half of the collection made by Constantine Cephalas, leaving out the sections Paedica, Variorum Metrorum, and Erotica. The editor, Thomas Warton, claims to have made improvements in Reiske's Latin versions.

It is a convenient and pretty volume, but it did not escape censure from the learned.[1] The editing and foreword are anonymous, but Warton identifies himself by disclosing that he is about to edit Theocritus.[2] He does not tell who financed the edition.

Blackstone's Commentaries, 1765-9

The Delegates did not publish Blackstone's books. He paid for them to be printed initially at the University Press, and after a time sold the copyrights to booksellers. His receipts from authorship and lecturing are said to have been £14,000.[3]

These books were a substantial part of the work of the Press from 1759 until 1777, printed in what were then considered big editions. Daniel Prince, the Warehouse-Keeper, wrote in 1783; 'In one instance (the late Judge Blackstone) I was very fully employed for ten years; and afterwards, with Messrs. Strahan and Cadell, purchased his celebrated Work.'[4] Prince's share in the copyright in the *Commentaries* was bought by him personally in his capacity of bookseller, not as agent for the University.

The syllabus for Blackstone's lectures at Oxford, called *An Analysis of the Laws of England*, was published first in 1756 and reached the fifth edition in 1762, each edition being of 1,000 copies. In 1771 Daniel Prince paid for a further 1,000, so he had presumably bought the copyright.

---

[1] Nichols, *Lit. An.* ii, p. 344.

[2] He owns it in a letter to Toup (B.M. MS. Add. 42560, fol. 156) to which Mr. David Fairer drew my attention.

[3] James Prior, *Life of Thomas Malone* (1860), p. 431. Augustine Birrell, in his *Copyright in Books* (1894), p. 131 n., wrote that Blackstone entered each of the four Books of the *Commentaries* in the Stationers' Register: 'The copyright in the whole book he afterwards sold to Cadell and two other booksellers for (I think) £4,000. On the expiration of fourteen years from the date of publication, being still alive, he assigned to the same booksellers his interest in the second statutory term of fourteen years.' I do not know the source of this information.

[4] Nichols, *Lit. An.* iii, p. 696.

Blackstone collected several of his minor works, *The Great Charter*, the *Law of Descents*, the *Essay on Collateral Consanguinity*, the *Considerations on Copyholders*, in two volumes of *Law Tracts* issued first in 1762. Two editions of 1,000 were printed at his expense by the Press.

COMMENTARIES

ON THE

L A W S

OF

E N G L A N D.

BOOK THE FIRST.

BY

WILLIAM BLACKSTONE, Esq.
VINERIAN PROFESSOR OF LAW,
AND
SOLICITOR GENERAL TO HER MAJESTY.

OXFORD,
PRINTED AT THE CLARENDON PRESS.
M. DCC. LXV.

The *Commentaries on the Laws of England* were first printed here in four volumes dated 1765, 1766, 1768, and 1769. Of the first two 1,500 were printed originally, and of the other two 3,500. Volumes i and ii were reprinted in 1767, the former an impression of 1,500, and the other of 1,000. The complete work was reprinted here in editions of 3,000 in 1773, 1775, and 1778.[1]

[1] It would be a work of some difficulty to establish the sequence of editions and number them correctly. What is described on the title-pages of Books i and ii issued in 1768 as the

It was the merit of Blackstone's lectures at Oxford, begun in 1753, and developed as the *Commentaries*, that induced Charles Viner to put the teaching of English law on a permanent footing in the University by his endowment of a professorship and scholarships.

The years that Blackstone spent mainly at Oxford, 1753-66, were the most productive of his life. He gauged his vocation truly when he wrote in 1753, that he had 'Taken up a Resolution no longer to attend the Courts at Westminster, but to pursue my Profession in a way more agreeable to me in all Respects, by residing at Oxford'.[1]

Thomas Hawkins's Origin of the English Drama, 1774

A collection of early English plays made by Thomas Hawkins, chaplain of Magdalen College, was printed at the Press in 1774 for Samuel Leacroft, a London bookseller. The three pleasing little duodecimo volumes reprint fourteen pieces, mysteries, moralities, tragedies, and comedies, of the period 1515-1606. The selection outdoes Dodsley's *Old Plays* of 1744 in point of antiquity and overlaps it only in three instances, one of them, *Gorboduc* (*Ferrex and Porrex*) being taken from a widely divergent copy. Hawkins preserves, though inaccurately, the spelling of his originals and identifies them. Many were borrowed from David Garrick's collection. He supplies an introductory note for each of the plays and a history of the English stage by way of preface, scholarly but not oppressively learned. He had benefited from reading Percy's *Reliques*.

The editor, who died prematurely while the book was printing, had supervised the second edition of Hanmer's Shakespear of 1771 and added to it the table of emendations and the glossary. So doing, he says in his preface to the old plays, he was 'naturally thrown into a course of reading the productions of our first dramatic writers, in order to explain and illustrate the obsolete phrases and allusions to ancient customs, which occur in the works of our great poet'. Hawkins thought that a re-edition of such old plays as paid a strict regard to virtue and morality would not be unacceptable to an English reader.

third edition must, I think, be one printed at the Press the year before and called in the Accounts the second edition. There is nothing in the Accounts corresponding with a second edition of Vol. i, of which the British Museum has a copy dated 1766. There is no trace in the Accounts of an edition dated 1770 described on the title-pages as the fourth edition. All these books have the imprint of the Clarendon Press, and it is hard to tell why charges for them all are not entered in the Accounts.

In calling the complete work issued in 1773 the fifth edition Blackstone (for he must be answerable) was including the partial reprint.

[1] To Sir Roger Newdigate, 3 July 1753: Newdigate Papers, B1488.

Woodcuts of the characters in *Hickscorner* made for Thomas Hawkins's
Origin of the English Drama, 1774. Printed from the original blocks.

To illustrate *Everyman* and *Hickscorner* Hawkins had copies made 'by a masterly hand' of woodcuts of the characters in the latter play in the edition printed by Wynkyn de Worde about 1515. They were copies of some in Antoine Vérard's *Therence en francois*, copied from a Strasburg Terence of 1499.[1] Two of Hawkins's three woodcuts are still at the Press.

Kennicott's Variorum Hebrew Bible, 1776–80

Benjamin Kennicott came to Oxford as an undergraduate in 1744. He learned Hebrew from the Regius Professor, Thomas Hunt,[2] and was elected to a fellowship at Exeter College in 1747. The Whig sympathies which he shared with many members of that society undoubtedly prejudiced many scholars against him. In 1753 he published a dissertation on the printed text of the Hebrew Bible attributing obscurities and conflicting passages to scribal errors and the ambiguities inherent in the script.[3] In spite of attacks by Hebraists ready to maintain that the printed text was literally inspired, he issued in 1759 his second dissertation, on *The State of the Printed Text of the Old Testament*, in which he set a high value on the Samaritan manuscripts of the Pentateuch and depreciated the Targums as indications of an early state of the text. He appended to this essay a survey of existing manuscripts of the Hebrew Bible attributable to the age before printing and a catalogue of those in Oxford libraries.

His interest in textual criticism had been aroused by Robert Lowth, the Professor of Poetry, and in 1757 Thomas Secker, a former Bishop of Oxford, urged him to embark on collating biblical manuscripts. Learned men in the past, Buxtorf, Grabe, Hottinger, Jablonsky, had pointed to the need to search for variant readings that might antedate the Masoretic recension, but without minimizing the labour and difficulty of doing it.[4]

When Thomas Hunt was asked by the Delegates of the Press in 1758 to suggest books that should be undertaken he proposed the collation of Old Testament manuscripts in Oxford. In 1760 they agreed to support Kennicott's enlarged project of a comparison of the Hebrew manuscripts prior to the invention of printing with no limit of place by a subvention of £40 a year for three years, to be reconsidered at the end of that term. To that was added a like amount from Secker, then Archbishop of

---

[1] Hart, p. 151; *Catalogue of Books printed in the XVth Century now in the British Museum*, pt. viii, p. 95.

[2] The information about his progress is given by Kennicott in the 'Dissertatio generalis' at the end of the second volume of his *Vetus Testamentum Hebraicum; cum variis lectionibus*, pp. 57 ff.

[3] Above, p. 307.   [4] *Vetus Testamentum*, i, p. vi.

Canterbury, and in 1761 the King was among many who promised subscriptions.

The Delegates attached conditions to their grant: that the editor should get annually a certificate from the Hebrew professor that satisfactory progress had been made, that copies of all the collations should be deposited with Bodley's Librarian, who would keep them under seal, and that these copies should remain the property of the University. It was agreed that the book would be printed at the University Press and sold by Kennicott, but if he died before publication the University would bear the cost of printing and sale.

From 1760 onwards he devoted himself wholly to this work. He issued a prospectus in 1763 arguing the need for the book and inviting subscriptions to the cost of editing and information as to the location of manuscripts. According to him, between 400 and 500 of these were known, of which 110 were at Oxford or Cambridge or in the British Museum. The prospectus met with a good response. The Cardinal Librarian at the Vatican was the first to allow the use of manuscripts in his care, and he sent a letter recommending the enterprise. The Académie des Inscriptions et Belles Lettres at Paris sent a testimonial, and others came from the universities of Göttingen and Mannheim and from the pastors and professors at Geneva. The King of Denmark offered to have collations made from manuscripts which he had lately got from the Levant and Africa. The Portuguese and German synagogues in London supplied a letter for Kennicott's agent to show to Jewish communities abroad. Subscriptions from all parts of Europe mounted until in the later years they came to £1,000 a year.

Kennicott employed Paul Jacob Bruns, a native of Lübeck, to work in the foreign libraries. Bruns made a tour of Belgium, France, Italy, Austria, Switzerland, Germany, and Holland, visiting 52 places.

At home in Oxford things went less well: relations between the editor and the board of Delegates became very strained. He was nettled by a reminder from them in February 1771 that he was behindhand with delivery of copies of his collations to the Bodleian. He was unwise enough to write to them that he owed far greater obligations to the public than to the University, since his income from subscriptions was far greater than his allowance from the Board, and that he would be needlessly delaying publication by doing what was demanded of him. He was evidently reluctant to put the University in a position to produce an edition of his work from which he or his posterity would not benefit.

However, the Delegates insisted on their bargain, but they promised Kennicott that in the event of their publishing the book after his death they would pay all the profit to his estate. In June 1771 they consented to release all the material in the Bodleian for the purpose of immediate publication, on Kennicott's giving his bond in £2,000 for its eventual return by him or his executors. The Vice-Chancellor was asked to make sure that the bond was duly executed.

An application by Kennicott to borrow manuscripts from the Bodleian was twice considered in Convocation and rejected.[1] The University of Cambridge and the British Museum were more accommodating.

He printed annual reports on his progress in 1760–9 and gathered them in one volume in 1770. The long gestation of the book was a test of the subscribers' patience and generosity and risked a diminution of their number. Publication of a part was decided on. Volume i, Genesis to 2 Kings, was issued in 1776 at Kennicott's expense. The number of subscribers to some division of Kennicott's labours, collating, editing, and printing was nearly 700, but since some contributors did not want to buy the book, 650 copies were printed. Kennicott personally presented one to George III. It is a weighty book, a Demy folio, not bulky, because the beautiful paper is thin. The setting is in two columns, the text, taken from Van der Hoogt's edition (which is virtually that printed by Joseph Athias in 1661), in numbered lines on the right and the various readings in the left-hand column. The 649 manuscripts consulted are identified by numbers, and omissions and erasures are indicated by signs. Readings of the Samaritan Pentateuch are set in the same type (Caslon's Long Primer Hebrew) as the rest, not, it seems, because of the essential identity of the scripts, but to make comparison easier. Vowels and accents are omitted altogether, because to notice variations in them would have added too much to the editor's labour.

Kennicott added five to the chapters set as poetry in Van der Hoogt's Bible and did not doubt that many other passages ought to be set in the same way.

The second, thicker, volume followed in 1780. It has at the end Kennicott's 'Dissertatio generalis' on what he had done. He goes into detail about his method of working and refuses to come out of it to state bold conclusions. He goes so far as to say that none of the variants is a

[1] Notices of two meetings to consider the request were printed by the Press in 1769: 3rd A/cs. pp. 279, 280. A fly-sheet giving an opinion of Bishop Thomas Barlow (d. 1691) against lending from the Bodleian was circulated in the same year.

threat to essential doctrine or increases historical knowledge. That he had forecast in his two preliminary dissertations; but it was left for Samuel Johnson to tell us 'that though the text should not be much mended thereby, yet it was no small advantage to know, that we had as good a text as the most consummate industry and diligence could procure',[1] and to modern scholars to conclude that the labours of Kennicott and of De Rossi and others after him are proof that all existing manuscripts reproduce, more or less faithfully, the Masoretic text. What was a comfort to Johnson and to his fellow Christians is a disappointment to a more inquisitive generation.

It is hard to imagine the state of mind of a man devoting twenty years of unrelenting toil to achieve a result which he must have known at an early stage would be negative. Whether it was a result agreeable to his hopes he does not say. He lived a lonely life facing much hostility from his own university and the other, childless but helped by a wife, at a task which his religion demanded of him. He was chosen F.R.S. in 1764 and made a canon of Christ Church in 1770. A copy of his book[2] has this inscription by his widow:

This book, the duplicate of one delivered to His Majesty King George the Third by Dr. Kennicott, was by his widow gratefully presented to the Honourable and Right Reverend Shute Lord Bishop of Durham, as the kindest and most highly valued friend of the editor, and of herself. For this friendship she is devoutly thankful, it having formed one of the chief blessings of her life.

[1] Boswell, ii, p. 128.
[2] Belonging to the Printer to the University.

APPENDIX

Titles of Books printed at the University Press, Oxford from 1690 until 1780

BIBLES, Testaments, and Books of Common Prayer in English are not included. The items, excepting those in parentheses, are those of which copies have been found.

The arrangement is by the years given in the imprints, and, within years, alphabetical of the names of authors, editors, or sponsoring authorities, whichever seemed most indicative of the nature of the book.

Books charged to the Delegates of the Press or entered in lists of their stocks are distinguished by *.

The locations are those of copies from which particulars have been taken. For preference the shelfmark of a copy in the Bodleian Library, Oxford (Bodl.), is given, or, if there is no copy there, the pressmark of a copy at the British Library (B.M.). 'Printer to the University' indicates that the copy relied on is in the collection of Oxford books in the Printer's room at the University Press, Oxford.

I have excluded Oxford books lacking an indication of their printer, if I could find no record of them at the Press and I judged on typographical grounds that they were not printed there.

Titles in Greek, set nearly all in capitals, have few accents, and I have not added any.

1690

1. BENSON, THOMAS. Thesaurus linguae Anglo-Saxonicae dictionario Gulielmi Somneri auctior. [Specimen pages.]
    4to. Bodl. MS. Rawl. D. 377, fols. 80, 81.   Wing S 4667
    Title-leaf and one leaf of text. The book was published in 1701.

2. EUCLID. [One leaf of a proposed edition in Greek and Latin among manuscript notes on Euclid by Edward Bernard.] Undated: *c.* 1690?
Fol. Bodl. MS. Bodl. 886, fols. 9, 64.
Madan, *Oxford Books*, iii, p. 347, No. 3141; Wood, *Ath.* iv, 706.

3*. GUISE, WILLIAM. Misnae pars: ordinis primi Zeraim tituli septem. Latine vertit & commentario illustravit Gulielmus Guisius. Accedit Mosis Maimonidis Praefatio in Misnam, Edv. Pocockio interprete. Oxoniae, e Th. Sh., A.D. CIƆIƆCXC.
4to. Bodl. Mar. 104. Wing M 2250
1st A/cs. p. 62A, price 1*s.* *T.C.* II, 411. Wood, *Ath.* iv, 114.

4. [HARRINGTON, JAMES the younger.] An account of the proceedings of the Right Reverend Father in God Jonathan [Trelawney] Lord Bishop of Exeter in his late visitation of Exeter College in Oxford. Oxford, printed at the Theatre. 1690.
4to. Bodl. Wood 631(5). Wing H 826
T.C. II, 338, 384.

5. [HARRINGTON, JAMES the younger.] An account of the proceedings [etc., as above]. The second edition, to which is added the Censure of the University of Oxford upon the Naked Gospell. Oxford, printed at the Theatre. 1690. Sold by Thomas Bennet.
4to. Bodl. C 9 4(12) Linc. Wing H 827
T.C. II, 338, 384.

6. [HARRINGTON, JAMES the younger.] The case of the University of Oxford; shewing, that the City is not concern'd to oppose the confirmation of their charters by Parliament. Presented to the Honourable House of Commons on Friday Jan. 24. 1689/90. Oxford, printed at the Theater, 1690.
4to. Bodl. Gough Oxf. 105(2). Wing C 1174
T.C. II, 323. Wood, *Ath.* iv, 393.

7. HYDE, THOMAS. Proponitur Maimonidis More Nevochim typis mandandum lingua Arabica [etc.]. Dicti operis sequitur hujusmodi specimen.
Fol. s. sh. Bodl. 4° M 13(2) Th. Wing H 3879
MS. notes in the Bodleian copy: Dec. 10. 1690. Hoc specimen tentandi causa emittitur ad monstrandum quid in hac parte fieri posset si operi tam desiderabili fautores non desint. Et hoc modo sui Laboris fructum legentibus offert autor. Per Thomam Hyde [etc.]. This was offered to our Delegates, who refused to be at the charge of printing this work.
One of Hyde's unrealized designs. See Wood, *Ath.* iv, 526.

8. HYDE, THOMAS. Tractatus Alberti Bobovii Turcarum Imp. Mohammedis IV^ti olim interpretis primarii, De Turcarum liturgia, peregrinatione Meccana, circumcisione, aegrotorum visitatione, etc. Nonnullas annotatiunculas, pro ut occasio se obtulit, passim adjecit Thomas Hyde [etc.]. Subjungitur Castigatio in Angelum a Sancto Joseph, Carmelitarum Discalceatorum in Perside praefectum olim generalem. Oxonii, e Th. Sh. 1690.
4to. Bodl. 4° M 13(1) Th. Wing B 2816

(Maimonides. In Seder Zeraim praefatio, ed. E. Pococke.
Madan notes it as 1690:22, probably because the part of No. 3 above, so headed is separately catalogued by the B.M.)

9. [MARTIN, THOMAS.] Historica descriptio complectens vitam ac res gestas beatissimi viri Gulielmi Wicami quondam Vintoniensis episcopi, & Angliae Cancellarii, & fundatoris duorum collegiorum Oxoniae et Vintoniae. Oxoniae, e Th. Sh. An. Dom. MDCXC.

    4to. Bodl. Wood 528.   Wing M 852

10*. OXFORD, UNIVERSITY. Judicium et decretum Universitatis Oxoniensis latum in Convocatione habita August. 19. Anno Dom. 1690. contra propositiones quasdam impias, & haereticas, exscriptas & citatas ex libello quodam infami haud ita pridem intra dictam Academiam perfide typis mandato ac divulgato, cui titulus est, The Naked Gospel. Quae praecipua fidei nostrae mysteria in Ecclesia Catholica, ac speciatim Anglicana, semper retenta & conservata impugnant, ac labefactant. Oxonii, e Th. Sh. Anno 1690. Sold by Thomas Bennet bookseller at the Half-Moon in S. Pauls Church-yard London. [With a copper-engraved device.]

    Fol. Imp. not dated. B.M. 1471. cc. 15(3).

10a*. — As No. 10, but with a woodcut device. B.M. 4225.1.13.

    1st A/cs. p. 62A, price 1d. T.C. II, 338.   Wing O 894

11*. OXFORD, UNIVERSITY. A defence of the rights and priviledges of the University of Oxford: containing 1. An answer to the Petition of the City of Oxford. 1649. 2. The Case of the University of Oxford presented to the Honourable House of Commons. Jan. 24. 1689/90. Oxford, printed at the Theater, 1690.

    Fol. Bodl. Wood 423(66).   Wing L 366

12*. — Another edition. 4to. Bodl. Gough Oxf. 80.105.

    1st A/cs. p. 28, '200 University cases sent to Mr Harington'. [By James Harrington.] T.C. II, 323.

13*. OXFORD, UNIVERSITY. Academiae Oxoniensis gratulatio pro exoptato Serenissimi Regis Gulielmi ex Hibernia reditu. Oxoniae, e Th. Sh. Anno Dom. 1690.

    Fol. Bodl. Pamph. 20(1).   Wing O 858
    1st A/cs. pp. 1, 2, 500, 2s.

13a*. — Another issue differing in the last sheet, which contains an additional poem. B.M. 105.f.41.   Wing O 886

14*. OXFORD, UNIVERSITY. At a meeting of the Heads of Houses, April 28. 1690. [Instructions for academic dress.]

    Broadside. Bodl. G.A. Oxon. b. 19(17).

15. [PROAST, JONAS.] The argument of the Letter concerning Toleration briefly consider'd and answer'd. Oxford, printed at the Theatre, for George West, and Henry Clements, booksellers in Oxford. A.D. 1690.

    4to. Imp. 9 Apr. 1690. Bodl. 4° M 13(3) Th.   Wing P 3538
    T.C. II, 323.

16*. SUETONIUS. C. Suetonii Tranquilli Opera omnia notis illustrata. Oxonii, e Th. Sh., MDCXC.

    8vo. Bodl. Radc. e. 80.   Wing S 6146
    See Madan, *Oxford Books*, iii, No. 3123.

17*. XENOPHON. [Title in Greek. Contains Memorabilia.] Εκ Θεατρου ἐν Οξονια. Ετει Θεογονίας αχ٩.

    8vo in fours. Bodl. Bliss B 122–126.   Wing X 3
    The first volume to appear of the works ed. by Edward Wells, completed in 1703.

1691

1. [ALDRICH, HENRY.] Artis Logicae compendium. Oxonii, e Th. Sh., An. Dom. MDCXCI.
8vo in fours. Bodl. Bliss B 127(2). Wing A 896

2. DRUMMOND, WILLIAM (?). Polemo-Middinia, carmen macaronicum. autore Gulielmo Drummondo, Scoto-Britanno. Accedit Jacobi id nominis Quinti, Regis Scotorum, cantilena rustica vulgo inscripta Christs Kirk on the Green, recensuit, notisque illustravit E. G. Oxonii, e Th. Sh. Anno Dom. 1691.
4to. Bodl. C 2. 17(7) Linc. Wing D 2204
T.C. II, 361.
[Ed. by Edmund Gibson: D.N.B.]

3*. GALE, THOMAS. Historiae Britannicae, Saxonicae, Anglo-Danicae, scriptores xv. ex vetustis codd. MSS. editi opera Thomae Gale [etc.]. Praefatio ostendit ordinem. Accessit rerum et verborum index locupletissimus. Oxoniae, e Th. Sh. MDCXCI.
Fol. Bodl. C 1. 16 Art. Imp. 3 Feb. 1690. Wing G 154
The half-title reads: Historiae Britannicae et Anglicanae scriptores xx. duobus voluminibus comprehensi.
T.C. II, 360. The previous volume was published in 1687.

4. GIBSON, EDMUND. [Specimen for an edition of Quintilian.]
4to eight pages. Bodl. MS. Rawl. D. 377, fol. 15.
MS. note in the Bodleian copy: Edmundus Gibson Art. Bac. e Coll. Reg. Taberdarius editurus Quintilianum constituit in primis notulas textui subjicere; et tres plus minus schedae hac forma impressae fuerunt. notas in 1um. librum habuit a D.D. Mill. Eum incoepti poenituit; ediditque Quintilianum nudis lectionibus ornatum.
The date of this specimen is conjectural: the book was published in 1693. See Hearne ii, p. 29.

5. HODY, HUMFREY. Anglicani novi schismatis redargutio, seu Tractatus ex historiis ecclesiasticis, quo ostenditur episcopos injuste licet depositos, orthodoxi successoris communionem nunquam refugisse. Graece et Latine ex cod. MSo. editore Humfredo Hody [etc.]. Oxon. e Th. Sh. 1691.
4to. Imp. 25 July 1691. Bodl. Pamph. 202(13). Wing H 2337, 3184
1st A/cs. p. 2: 'Mr. Hoddy's tract'. T.C. II, 382, and see II, 367.

6. HYDE, THOMAS. [Hebrew title.] id est Itinera mundi, sic dicta nempe Cosmographia, autore Abrahamo Peritsol. Latina versione donavit & notas passim adjecit Thomas Hyde [etc.]. Calce exponitur Turcarum liturgia, peregrinatio Meccana, aegrotorum visitatio, circumcisio, etc. Accedit Castigatio in Angelum a Sto. Joseph, al. dictum De la Brosse, Carmelitam Discalceatum, sui ordinis in Ispahan Persedis olim Praefectum. Oxonii, e Th. Sh., MDCXCI. impensis Henrici Bonwick bibliopolae Londinensis, apud quem prostant sub signo Rubri Leonis in Coemiterio Paulino.
4to. Bodl. 4° M 13(1) Th. Wing F 438
T.C. II, 337.

7. JANE, WILLIAM. A sermon preached before the Honourable House of Commons, at St. Margaret Westminster, on Thursday, the 26th of November, 1691. being a

day of Publick Thanksgiving. By William Jane [etc.]. Oxford, printed at the Theater, for Thomas Bennet, at the Half-Moom [sic] in St. Paul's Church-Yard, London, 1691.
    4to. Bodl. 4° W 39 Th.   Wing J 457
    1st A/cs. p. 11, dues.

8*. MALALAS. [Greek title.] Joannis Antiocheni cognomento Malalae historia chronica. Oxonii, e Th. Sh. CIƆIƆCXCI.
    8vo. Imp. 16 June 1691. Bodl. 8° M 205 Art.   Wing J 745
    T.C. II, 425. [Ed. by Edmund Chilmead.]

9*. OXFORD, UNIVERSITY. Parecbolae sive excerpta e corpore statutorum Universitatis Oxoniensis. Accedunt Articuli religionis xxxix in Ecclesia Anglicana recepti: nec non Juramenta Fidelitatis & Suprematus. In usum juventutis academicae. Oxoniae, e Th. Sh., Anno Dom. CIƆIƆCXCI.
    8vo. Bodl. Vet. A 3 f. 972.   Wing O 932
    1st A/cs. p. 10, 2,000.

10*. POCOCKE, EDWARD. A Commentary on the prophecy of Joel. By Edward Pococke [etc.]. Oxford, printed at the Theater, MDCXCI.
    Fol. Imp. 19 Aug. 1691. Bodl. A 3 6(1) Th.   Wing P 2661
    1st A/cs. p. 2, 500, 5s.; p. 243, 3s. 6d. in quantity. T.C. II, 376.

11. SPARK, THOMAS. A sermon preached at Guilford in Surrey June the 22d, 1691. at the Lord Bishop of Winchester's Visitation. By T. Spark [etc.]. Oxford, printed at the Theatre for John Crosly An. Dom. MDCXCI.
    4to. Imp. 12 July 1691. B.M. 1112.e.29.   Wing S 4820
    1st A/cs. p. 1, dues.

12*. XENOPHON. [Title in Greek. Contains Agesilaus, Spartan Polity, Symposium, Hiero, Poroi.] Ἐκ Θεατρου ἐν Ὀξονια. Ετει Θεογονίας ᾳχ⁴ά.
    8vo in fours. Bodl. Bliss B 122–126.   Wing X 3
    The second volume to appear of Xenophon's works ed. by Edward Wells.

1692

1. ABENDANA, ISAAC. The Oxford Almanack for the year . . . 1692 . . . The Jewish Kalendar, 5452–5453 [etc.]. Oxford, at the Theater.
    12mo in eights. Bodl. 8° Rawl. 698.
    T.C. II, 403.

2. ALDRICH, HENRY. Artis logicae compendium. Oxonii, e Th. Sh. An. Dom. MDCXCII.
    8vo in fours. Bodl. Bliss B 127(1).   Wing A 897
    1st A/cs. p. 23, dues. See also editions of 1691, 1696, 1704.

3*. ARISTEAS. Aristeae Historia LXXII Interpretum. Accessere veterum testimonia de eorum versione. Oxonii, e Th. Sh., An. Dom. MDCXCII.
    8vo in fours. Imp. 1 Jan. 1692. Bodl. Radcl. e. 81.   Wing A 3683
    1st A/cs. p. 12, 600, 1s. T.C. II, 394. The Printer's copy has a manuscript note: 'Ex dono Rever. Dris. Aldridge Aedis Xrti. Decani, Cal. Jan. 1691/2.' Edited by Aldrich, Hody, and Bernard.

4. CHISHULL, EDMUND. Gulielmo Tertio, terra marique principi invictissimo, in Gallos pugna navali nuperrime devictos carmen heroicum. Authore Edmund Chishull [etc.]. Oxonii, e Th. Sh. Prostant apud Joh. Crosley MDCXCII.

4to. Bodl. Vet. A 3 e. 1098. Wing C 3900
T.C. II, 426.

5. [DODWELL, HENRY.] Praelectiones academicae in Schola Historices Camdeniana. Oxonii, e Th. Sh. Vaeneunt in officina Benj. Tooke, bibliopolae Londinensis An. Dom. MDCXCII.

8vo. Imp. 29 July 1692. Bodl. 8º W 31 Art. BS. Wing D 1815, O 938
1st A/cs. p. 11, dues. T.C. II, 425, 440.

6. GIBSON, EDMUND. Chronicon Saxonicum ex MSS codicibus nunc primum integrum edidit, ac Latinum fecit Edmundus Gibson [etc.]. Oxonii, e Th. Sh. A.D. MDCXCII.

4to. Imp. 15 Aug. 1692. Bodl. 4º C 114 Art. Wing A 3185
1st A/cs. p. 37, dues. See MS. Ballard v, fol. 6.

[2nd title-page:] Chronicon Saxonicum, seu Annales rerum in Anglia praecipue gestarum, a Christo nato ad annum usque MCLIV. deducti, ac jam demum Latinitate donati. Cum indice rerum chronologico. Accedunt regulae ad investigandas nominum, locorum origines. et nominum locorum ac virorum in Chronico memoratorum explicatio. Opera & studio Edmundi Gibson [etc.]. Oxonii, e Th. Sh., A.D. MDCXCII.

7. [GIBSON, EDMUND.] Librorum MSSorum in duabus insignibus bibliothecis; altera Tenisoniana, Londini; altera Dugdaliana, Oxonii; catalogus. Edidit E. G. Oxonii, e Th. Sh. Veneunt in officina T. Bennett bibliopolae Londinensis, A.D. MDCXCII.

4to. Bodl. 4º Z 21(7) Art. Wing O 896
See MS. Ballard v, fol. 6. T.C. II, 394.

8. IRONSIDE, GILBERT. Articles to be enquired of within the Diocess of Hereford, in the first Visitation of the Right Reverend Father in God Gilbert Lord Bishop of Hereford in the year of our Lord God 1692, and in the first year of his translation. Oxford, printed in the year MDCXCII.

4to. Bodl. Vet. A 3 e. 337. Wing C 4049

9. JANE, WILLIAM. A sermon preached before the King & Queen at White-Hall in November 1692. by William Jane [etc.] Published by their Majesties command. Oxford, printed at the Theater, for Thomas Bennet at the Half-Moon, in St. Paul's Church-Yard, London 1692.

4to. Bodl. C 5. 12(7) Linc. Wing J 458
T.C. II, 437-8.

10*. [LILY, WILLIAM.] A short introduction of grammar generally to be used. Compiled and set forth for the bringing up of all those that intend to attain to the knowledge of the Latine tongue. Oxford, at the Theater. 1692. [Followed by] Brevissima institutio seu ratio grammatices cognoscendae, ad omnium puerorum utilitatem praescripta [etc.].

12mo in sixes. Bodl. 3058 e. 83. Wing L 2260
1st A/cs. pp. 2, 7, 8, 3,500, 10d., 3,000 sold to the Stationers. T.C. II, 430.

11. LOWTH, WILLIAM. A vindication of the divine authority and inspiration of the writings of the Old and New Testament. In answer to a treatise lately translated

out of French, entituled, Five letters concerning the inspiration of the Holy Scriptures. By William Lowth [etc.]. Oxford, printed at the Theater. And are to be sold by John Wilmot bookseller. An. Dom. 1692.

8vo. Imp. 13 June 1692. Bodl. 8º C 14 Linc.   Wing L 3330
1st A/cs. p. 11, dues. *T.C.* II, 421.

12*. [MARSHALL, THOMAS.] The Catechism set forth in the Book of Common-Prayer briefly explained by short notes, grounded upon Holy Scripture. To which is now added, an Essay of Questions and Answers, framed out of the same notes, for the exercise of youth. The ninth edition. Printed at the Theater in Oxford, Anno Domini 1692.

8vo. Imp. 20 Mar. 1678. Bodl. 8º N 161(2) Th.   Wing M 805
1st A/cs. p. 8, 6,000. *T.C.* II, 430, 467. Wood, *Ath.* iv, 171–2.

13. [MUSAE ANGLICANAE]. Musarum anglicanarum analecta: sive poemata quaedam melioris notae, seu hactenus inedita, seu sparsim edita, in unum volumen congesta. Oxon. e Th. Sh., impensis Joh. Crosley, & Sam. Smith, bibliopol. Lond. M.DC.XCII.

8vo. Imp. 26 Aug. 1692. Bodl. 8º St. Am. 405.   Wing M 3135
1st A/cs. pp. 1, 11, dues. *T.C.* II, 382.

14*. POCOCKE, EDWARD. A commentary on the prophecy of Micah by Edward Pococke [etc.]. The second impression. Oxford, printed at the Theater, MDCXCII.

Fol. Imp. 19 July 1676. Bodl. A 3. 6(2) Th.   Wing P 2663A
1st A/cs. p. 10, 250, 5s.

15*. POCOCKE, EDWARD. A commentary on the prophecy of Malachi by Edward Pocock [etc.]. The second impression. Oxford, printed at the Theater, MDCXCII.

Fol. Bodl. A 3. 6(3) Th.   Wing P 2662
1st A/cs. p. 10, 250, 5s.

16*. QUINTILIAN. M. Fab. Quintiliani Declamationum liber cum ejusdem (ut nonnullis visum) dialogo de causis corruptae eloquentiae. Quae omnia notis illustrantur. Oxonii, e Th. Sh. Veneunt in officina Hen. Clements, bibliopolae Oxoniensis M.DC.XCII.

8vo. Bodl. 3803 e. 7.   Wing Q 223
1st A/cs. p. 10, 1,000.

17. WHITING, CHARLES. A sermon preached July 19, 1692. at the consecration of a chapel built by the Right Honourable the Lord Weymouth at Minsterly in Shropshire. By Charles Whiting [etc.]. Oxford, printed at the Theater for Jo. Crosly 1692.

4to. Imp. 20 Sept. 1692. Bodl. 4º W 46 Th.   Wing W 2017
T.C. II, 420. Copies with a slightly different title were known to Madan (1692:24A).

1693

1. ABENDANA, ISAAC. An almanack for the year of Christ, 1693 [etc.]. To which is added the ancient Roman kalendar [with the Jewish Kalendar by Isaac Abendana]. Oxford, printed at the Theater.

12mo in sixes. Bodl. Opp. adds. 12º 23ᵃ.   Wing A 1233

2. Author of the Whole DUTY OF MAN. The ladies calling. In two parts. By the author of the Whole Duty of Man, etc. The sixth impression. At the Theater in Oxford. M.DC.XCIII.

8vo in fours. Bodl. Vet. A 3 e. 532. Wing A 1147
1st A/cs. p. 23, dues.

3. Author of the Whole DUTY OF MAN. The Government of the tongue. By the author of the Whole Duty of Man etc. The fifth impression. At the Theater in Oxford. M.DC.XCIII.

8vo in fours. Bodl. Vet. A 4 e. 1822. Wing A 1139
1st A/cs. p. 23, dues. This was really the 6th edition: Madan, *Oxford Books*, iii, No. 3001.

4. EDWARDS, JONATHAN. A preservative against Socinianism, shewing the direct and plain opposition between it, and the religion revealed by God in the Holy Scriptures. The first part. Oxon. printed at the Theater for Henry Clements. MDCXCIII.

4to. Imp. 10 July 1693. Bodl. 1243 e. 123. Wing E 216
1st A/cs. p. 55, dues for twice printing. *T.C.* II, 473.

5. — The second edition was printed in the same year.
Magdalen Coll., Oxford, a.7.21(2). Wing E 217

6*. OXFORD, UNIVERSITY. [Programma announcing the Act for 9 July.]
Broadside. Bodl. Wood 276ᵃ(393). Wing O 984
1st A/cs. p. 28.

7*. OXFORD, UNIVERSITY. [Programme for the Encaenia, 7 July.]
Broadside. Bodl. Wood 276ᵃ(404).
1st A/cs. p. 28.

8*. OXFORD, UNIVERSITY. Theatri Oxoniensis encaenia, sive comitia philologica. Julii 7. Anno 1693. celebrata. Oxonii, e Th. Sh., An. Dom. MDCXCIII.

Fol. Bodl. Pamph. 213(3). Wing O 984
1st A/cs. p. 28, 3,000.

9*. OXFORD, UNIVERSITY. Quaestiones in S. Theologia discutiendae [at the Act]. Oxoniae, E Th. Sh., An. Dom. 1693.
Broadside. Bodl. Wood 276ᵃ(437). Wing O 960

10*. OXFORD, UNIVERSITY. Parecbolae sive excerpta e corpore statutorum [etc., as in 1691]. Oxoniae, e Th. Sh. MDCXCIII.
8vo. B.M. 731.b.34. Wing O 933

11*. OXFORD, UNIVERSITY. A specimen of the several sorts of letter given to the University by Dr. John Fell late Lord Bishop of Oxford. To which is added the letter given by Mr. F. Junius. Oxford, printed at the Theater A.D. 1693.

8vo in fours. Bodl. Don. e. 563(1). Wing F 622
1st A/cs. p. 28, 'For Mr. Crooks setting the Specimen of all sorts of letter in the house . . . For stitching 52 Specimens of letter'.

12. QUINTILIAN. M. Fabii Quintiliani de Institutione oratoria libri duodecim cum duplici indice; rerum et locutionum altero, altero auctorum. Ex tribus codicibus MSS. & octo impressis emendavit, atque lectiones variantes adjecit Edmundus

Gibson [etc.]. Accedunt emendationum specimen, et Tribunus Marianus, Declamatio, nunc primum ex codice MS. edita. Oxoniae, e Th. Sh. impensis Henrici Cruttenden, typographi. MDCXCIII.

    4to. Imp. 16 June 1693. Bodl. 4º M 76 Art.   Wing Q 221
    1st A/cs. p. 16 (paper). See the preliminary specimen, 1691.

13. SOMNER, WILLIAM. A treatise of the Roman ports and forts in Kent. By William Somner. Publish't by James Brome [etc.]. To which is prefixt the life of Mr. Somner. Oxford, printed at the Theater, and are to be sold by George West, John Crosley, and Henry Clements booksellers in Oxford, 1693.

    8vo. Bodl. 8º C 155 Linc.   Wing S 4669
    1st A/cs. p. 23, dues. *T.C.* II, 476.

14. VELLEIUS PATERCULUS. M. Velleii Paterculi quae supersunt. cum variis lectionibus optimarum editionum; doctorum virorum conjecturis & castigationibus; et indice locupletissimo. Praemittuntur Annales Velleiani. Oxoniae. e Th. Sh. Prostant venales apud Joh. Crosley, Geor. West, Hen. Clements, & Joh. Howel. Anno Dom. 1693.

    8vo. Imp. 1 Jan. 1692/3. Bodl. 8º H 34 Linc.   Wing V 181
    1st A/cs. p. 23, dues. Ed. John Hudson, A New-Year Book: Wood, *Ath.* iv, 452.

15*. WALLIS, JOHN. Johannis Wallis S.T.D., Geometriae Professoris Saviliani, in celeberrima Academia Oxoniensi, de Algebra tractatus; historicus & Practicus [etc.]. Operum mathematicorum volumen alterum. Anno 1685 Anglice editus; nunc auctus Latine. Cum variis indicibus; partim prius editis Anglice, partim nunc primum editis. Oxoniae, e Th. Sh. MDCXCIII.

    Fol. Imp. 28 Aug. 1693. Bodl. B 1. 12 Art.   Wing W 566
    1st A/cs. p. 12, 500; p. 22, 450 + 50 LP; p. 28, woodcuts. The first to appear of three volumes completed in 1703.

16*. XENOPHON. [Title in Greek. Contains De re equestri, Hipparchicus, Cynegeticus.] Ἐκ Θεατρου ἐν Ὀξονια. Ἐτει Θεογονίας αχ4γ΄.

    8vo in fours. Bodl. Bliss B 128.   Wing X 14
    1st A/cs. p. 24, 500 + 12 LP. The third volume to appear of Xenophon's works ed. by Edward Wells. Others appeared in 1690, 1691, 1694, 1696, 1700, and 1703.

1694

1. BERNARD, EDWARD. Librorum manuscriptorum Academiarum Oxoniensis et Cantabrigiensis & celebrium per Angliam Hiberniamque bibliothecarum catalogus cum indice alphabetico, cura Edwardi Bernardi. Tomis duabus in folio ... [at foot:] Oxoniae Kal. Decemb. A.D. 1694. Edv. Bernardus.

    Fol. s. sh. B.M. Harl. 5932, fol. 92.
    An invitation to contribute lists of MSS. for inclusion. The *Catalogi* were published in 1698, dated 1697.

2. BULL, GEORGE. Judicium Ecclesiae Catholicae trium primorum seculorum de necessitate credendi quod Dominus noster Jesus Christus sit verus Deus, assertum

contra M. Simonem Episcopium aliosque. Authore Georgio Bullo [etc.]. Oxonii, e Th. Sh. impensis Georg. West, MDCXCIV.

8vo. Imp. 4 June 1694. Bodl. Vet. A 3 e. 437. Wing B 5418
Wood, *Ath.* iv, 493.

3. CAMPION, ABRAHAM. A sermon concerning national Providence preach'd at the Assizes held at Ailesbury in Buckinghamshire March 13. 1693/4. By Ab. Campion [etc.]. Printed for Anthony Piesly bookseller in Oxford An. Dom. 1694.

4to. Bodl. 4° G 26(3) Th. Wing C 406
Uncertainly assignable to the Sheldonian Press on typographical grounds.

4. Author of the Whole DUTY OF MAN. The art of contentment. By the author of the Whole Duty of Man. At the Theater in Oxford. M.DC.XCIV.

8vo. Imp. 24 Feb. 1675. Bodl. Vet. A 3 e. 533. Wing A 1093
1st A/cs. p. 23, dues. Probably the 7th ed.: Madan, *Oxford Books*, iii, No. 3043.

5. EDWARDS, JONATHAN. A preservative against Socinianism. shewing the direct and plain opposition between it and the Christian religion, particularly in those two great fundamental articles of our faith, concerning original sin, and the redemption of the world by the death and sufferings of our Blessed Saviour. The second part. By Jonathan Edwards [etc.]. Oxon. Printed at the Theater for H. Clements. MDCXCIV.

4to. Imp. 3 July 1693. Bodl. 1243 e. 123. Wing E 219
The first part was published in 1693.

6. EUCLID. [Specimen leaf.] Εὐκλείδου τα σωζομενα. Euclidis geometrae Opera [etc.]. Edwardus Bernardus recensuit. Oxoniae, e Th. Sh. A.D. . . . [Year trimmed off, *c.* 1694?]

8vo. Bodl. MS. Bodl. 887.
Madan, *Oxford Books*, iii, p. 347, No. 3141. Wood, *Ath.* iv, 706.

7*. GIBSON, EDMUND. Julii Caesaris Portus Iccius illustratus; sive 1. Gul. Somneri ad Chiffletii librum de Portu Iccio responsio; nunc primum ex MS. edita 2. Caroli Du Fresne dissertatio. Tractatum utrumque Latine vertit, & nova dissertatione auxit Edmundus Gibson [etc.]. Oxonii, e Th. Sh., Anno Dom. MDCXCIV.

8vo. Imp. 29 Dec. 1693. Bodl. 8° O 10 Linc. Wing S 4666, C 202A
1st A/cs. p. 38, 550. *T.C.* II, 559.

8*. (A 4-page specimen of 'Dr. Hyde's History of Egypt' was set in 1693–4: 1st A/cs. p. 44. It was probably part of the work entitled Abdollatiphi Historiae Aegypti Compendium of which a fragment, 96 pages of an 8vo in fours, is in the Bodleian Library (8° K 33(12) Th.). The fragment is undated and has a manuscript note: Hic liber inter rarissimos numerandus est—a Thoma Hyde edi coeptus est, sed morte erepto, nunquam perfectus—desinit pagina 96. Versio per Ed. Pocock fil. 'Historiae Aegypti Compendium, Arab. Lat. per Tho. Hyde' is among the books in preparation in the Catalogus Librorum Impressorum issued from the Sheldonian Press in 1694, and, according to Anthony Wood (*Ath.* iv, 525), 'Historiae Aegypti naturalis curiosae' were ready for printing in 1694.)

9*. HYDE, THOMAS. De ludis orientalibus libri duo, quorum prior est duabus partibus, viz. 1, Historia Shahiludii Latine: inde 2. Historia Shahiludii Heb. Lat. per tres Judaeos. Liber posterior continet historiam reliquorum ludorum orientis.

[Part-title to the first part:] Mandragorias seu historia Shahiludii [etc.] horis succisivis olim congessit Thomas Hyde [etc.]. Oxonii, e Th. Sh. MDCXCIV.

[Part-title to the second part:] Historia Nerdiludii [etc.]. Oxonii, e Th. Sh. MDCXCIV.
8vo in fours. Imp. 20 Sept. 1693. Bodl. 8° B 175 Art.   Wing H 3875-7
1st A/cs. pp. 12, 26, 500. *T.C. II*, 559.

10. JOSEPHUS. [Specimen leaf of Flavius Josephus, Antiquities of the Jews, in Greek and Latin, edited by Edward Bernard], headed: Sciant eruditi novam Josephi editionem, secundum typum & chartam istius speciminis, jam in Seldonio adpropriari, sumtibus Joh. Crosley & Hen. Clements & Joh. Howell bibliopolarum Oxoniensium.
Fol. s. sh. Bodl. Wood 658(774).   Wing J 1082
Manuscript note: Donavit mihi Edw. Bernard 30 Aug. 1694. Two sheets of Josephus were printed in 1690-1: 1st A/cs. p. 2.

11*. OXFORD, UNIVERSITY. Anno Domini MDCXCIV in Theatro Sheldoniano jam imprimuntur, praeter libros Anglicos [etc.].
8vo. Bodl. Don. e. 563(3).

12*. OXFORD, UNIVERSITY. Catalogus librorum in Theatro Sheldoniano impressorum.
8vo. Bodl. Don. e. 563(2).
1st A/cs. p. 42. One copy in the Bodleian has a manuscript note by Thomas Hearne: 'This was ordered to be printed by Dr. Arthur Charlett, as he told me himself. It must therefore be reckon'd among his works.' (Bodl. 258 b. 272). It is undated but datable by the contents.

13. PLUTARCH. Πλουταρχου Χαιρωνεως βιβλιον Πῶς δεῖ τὸν νέον ποιημάτων ἀκούειν, καὶ Βασιλειου Μεγαλου Ομιλια προς νεους 'Οπως ἂν ἐξ 'Ελληνικῶν ὠφελοῖντο λόγων, cum interpretatione Hugonis Grotii. Variantes lectiones & notas adjecit Johannes Potter A.B. Εκ Θεατρου ἐν Οξονια Ετει θεογονίας ᾳχͷδ'.
8vo. Imp. 1 Jan. 1693/4. Bodl. Wood 117.   Wing P 2632
1st A/cs. p. 39, dues. A New-Year book. According to the Accounts, 'Dr. Charlett's Plutarch'. Wood, *Ath.* iv, 460.

14. SYKES, THOMAS. A sermon preached at the consecration of Trinity-College Chappel in Oxford April 12 1694. By Thomas Sykes [etc.]. Oxford, printed at the Theater A.D. 1694.
4to. Bodl. Wood D. 23(6).   Wing S 6324
1st A/cs. p. 39, dues.

15. THUCYDIDES. Proposals for subscription to Thucydides Gr. Lat. Folio, now printing at the Theater in Oxford.
Fol. Bodl. Wood 658(779). Not dated, presumably 1694-5.   Wing T 1135
T.C. II, 544.

16. WHITEHALL, ROBERT. A sermon concerning edification in faith and discipline, preached before the University of Oxford. Sept. 1. 1689. By Robert Whitehall [etc.]. Oxford, printed at the Theater, for Ant. Piesley bookseller. MDCXCIV.
4to. Bodl. G. Pamph. 2322(15).   Wing W 1874

17*. XENOPHON. [Memorabilia and Apology of Socrates. A reprint of the first volume of the collective edition by Edward Wells issued in 1690.] Εκ Θεατρου ἐν Οξονια. Ετει θεογονίας ᾳχͷδ'.
8vo in fours. Bodl. Clar. Press 50 e. 5.   Wing X 15

1695

1. ABENDANA, ISAAC. An almanack for the year of Christ 1695 [etc., as for previous years]. Oxford, printed at the Theater in the year 1695.
12mo in sixes. Bodl. Opp. adds. 12° 23ᵇ.   Wing A 1234

2. BOOK OF COMMON PRAYER. O livro da oração commum e administração dos sacramentos e outros ritos, & ceremonias da Igreja de Inglaterra: juntamente com o salterio ou Salmos de David. Oxford, na Estampa do Teatro. Anno de Christo, 1695.
Fol. Bodl. C.P. Port. c. 1.   Wing L 2617
1st A/cs. p. 42, cutting punches; p. 55, dues.

3. CICERO. M. Tullius Cicero De Officiis ad Marcum F. ex MSS. recensuit Tho. Cockman [etc.]. Oxoniae, e Th. Sh. MDCXCV.
8vo in fours. Imp. 2 Mar. 1694/5. B.M. 8410.d.34.   Wing C 4297
1st A/cs. p. 53, dues. T.C. II, 559.

4. CONNOR, BERNARD. Dissertationes medico-physicae. De antris lethiferis. De Monte Vesuvii incendio. De stupendo ossium coalitu. De immani hypogastrii sarcomate. A D. Bernardo Connor M.D. Serenissimi Poloniae Regis Medico, e Regia Camerae Parisiensis Societate. Oxoniae, e Th. Sh., sumptibus Henrici Clements bibliopolae An. Dom. 1695.
8vo in fours. Imp. 5 June 1695. Bodl. Vet. A 3 e. 16.   Wing C 5885
1st A/cs. p. 53, dues.

5. Author of the Whole DUTY OF MAN. The works of the learned and pious Author of the Whole Duty of Man. The third impression. Printed at the Theater in Oxford, and in London, by Roger Norton, for Edward Pawlett, at the sign of the Bible in Chancery Lane. Anno Domini MDCLXXXXV.
[Part-title:] The second part of the works of [etc.]. Printed at the Theater in Oxford and are to be sold by Edward Paulet bookseller in London. 1695.
Fol. Bodl. Vet. A 3 b. 9.   Wing A 1084
1st A/cs. p. 53, dues. To judge by the type, the general title-page, the leaf following it, and Part 2 were printed at the Theatre.

6. [EDWARDS, JONATHAN.] Remarks upon a book lately published by Dr. Will. Sherlock Dean of St. Pauls, &c. entituled A Modest Examination of the Oxford Decree, &c. Oxford, printed at the Theater, MDCXCV. and are to be sold by H. Clements.
4to. Bodl. 4° E 26(2) Th.   Wing E 221
1st A/cs. p. 67, 'Received of Dr. Edwards for printing his remarks'.

7. GREGORY, DAVID. Catoptricae et dioptricae sphericae elementa. Auctore Davide Gregorio [etc.]. Oxonii, e Th. Sh., An. Do. MDCXCV.
8vo in fours. Imp. 18 Apr. 1695. Bodl. Savile Z 5.   Wing G 1883
1st A/cs. p. 53, dues.

8*. HOMER. Ομηρου Ιλιας και εις αυτην σχολια ψευδεπιγραφα Διδυμου. Εκ Θεατρου ἐν Οξονια ἐν τῳ ετει αχϟέ.
8vo in fours. Bod. Vet. A 3 e. 123.   Wing H 2546
1st A/cs. pp. 24, 40, 62C, 1,000, 5s.

9. JOYNER, alias LYDE, EDWARD. In obitum Mariae Mag. Brit. &c. Reginae.
Fol. s. sh. No date or imprint. Bodl. Wood 276ª(540).
Wood added a manuscript note: 'Edw. Joyner alias Lyde Author—printed at the Theatre in the later end of Feb. 1694'. *Notes and Queries*, N.S., vol. 18 (1971), pp. 299–303.

10*. KENNETT, WHITE. Parochial antiquities attempted in the history of Ambrosden, Burcester, and other adjacent parts in the counties of Oxford and Bucks. By White Kennett, vicar of Ambrosden. Oxford, printed at the Theatre. M.DC.XCV.
4to. Imp. 23 Oct. 1695. Bodl. Douce K 114.   Wing K 302
1st A/cs. pp. 40, 54, 300 + 12 LP; p. 62C, 10s.

11. LHUYD, EDWARD. A design of a British dictionary, historical and geographical; with an essay entituled Archaeologia Britannica: and a natural history of Wales. By Edward Lhwyd, Keeper of the Ashmolean Repository, Oxon. [Dated 20 Oct. 1695.]
Fol. s. sh. Bodl. J.J. Coll. Prospectuses b. 27.   Wing L 2650

12. LUCRETIUS. Titi Lucretii Cari De rerum natura libri sex: quibus interpretationem et notas addidit Thomas Creech [etc.]. Oxonii, e Th. Sh. impensis Ab. Swall, & Tim. Child, bibliopol. Lond. ad insigne Monocerotis in Caemeterio Paulino. Anno 1695.
8vo. Imp. 3 Sept. 1694. Bodl. 8° F 127 Linc.   Wing L 3445
1st A/cs. p. 39, dues.

13. OXFORD, COUNTY. Orders and constitutions made by His Majesty's Justices of the Peace for the County of Oxon, in their General Quarter Sessions held at Oxon, on Tuesday the Twenty Second day of May 1695 . . . in pursuance of an Act of Parliament . . . entituled An Act to prevent exactions of the occupiers of locks and weers upon the River of Thames westward.
Fol. 4 pp. n.d. Bodl. G.A. Oxon. 4° 6 (12).

14*. OXFORD, UNIVERSITY. Pietas Oxoniensis in obitum augustissimae & desideratissimae Reginae Mariae. Oxonii, e Th. Sh., An. Dom. MDCXCV.
Fol. Bodl. Pamph. 217.   Wing O 937
1st A/cs. p. 54, 500, some LP.

15*. OXFORD, UNIVERSITY. Advertisements from the Delegates of Convocation for his Majesties reception, for the Heads of Houses to deliver with great charge unto their companies. [At foot:] Oxford, printed at the Theater, MDCXCV.
Broadside. Bodl. G.A. Oxon. b. 19(19).

16*. OXFORD, UNIVERSITY. [Condemnation of a sermon by Joseph Bingham.] In conventu D. Vice-Cancellarii & praefectorum collegiorum & aularum Universitatis Oxon. die vicesimo quinto Novembris A.D. 1695. Cum in concione nuper habita coram Universitate Oxon. in templo S. Petri in Oriente, ad festum S.S. Simonis et Judae proxime elapsum haec verba, inter alia, publice prolata & asserta fuerunt, viz. [There are three distinct minds and substances in the Trinity . . .]
Fol. s. sh. B.M. 714.i.8 (65).

17*. OXFORD, UNIVERSITY. A specimen of the several sorts of letter given to the University by Dr. John Fell sometime Lord Bishop of Oxford. To which is added the letter given by Mr. F. Junius. Oxford, printed at the Theater A.D. 1695.
8vo in fours. Bodl. Ashm. D 27.   Wing F 623

17a. — As above, but with the addition of four pages of new matter and with the 'Account of the Matrices [etc.]' at the end revised and reset.
  Bodl. 8° F 127 Linc.
  1st A/cs. p. 56: 'For composing two pages Specimen of the Musick'; p. 96, 50 copies left in 1697, 6d.

18. PHALARIS. [Title in Greek.] Phalaridis Agrigentinorum tyranni Epistolae. Ex MSS. recensuit, versione, annotationibus, & vita insuper authoris donavit Car. Boyle [etc.]. Excudebat Johannes Crooke.
  8vo in fours. Bodl. Auct. S 6. 20.   Wing P 1960
  1st A/cs. p. 53, dues. Wood, *Ath.* iv, 669.

19. TANNER, THOMAS. Notitia monastica or a short history of the religious houses in England and Wales. By Thomas Tanner B.A. Oxford, printed at the Theater, and are to be sold by A. and J. Churchill at the sign of the Black Swan in Pater-Noster-Row, London, 1695.
  8vo. Imp. 13 Mar. 1694/5. Bodl. 8° A 26 Jur.   Wing T 144
  1st A/cs. p. 53, dues. See Hearne, i, p. 200.

20*. WALLIS, JOHN. Johannis Wallis S.T.D., Geometriae Professoris Saviliani, in celeberrima Academia Oxoniensi; opera mathematica. Volumen primum. Oxoniae, e Th. Sh. MDCXCV.
  Fol. Imp. 26 Mar. 1695. Bodl. Savile B 11.   Wing W 596
  1st A/cs. pp. 22, 42, cutting punches; p. 52, 500, some LP. The second volume had appeared first, in 1693. *T.C.* II, 559.

1696

1. ABENDANA, ISAAC. An almanack for the year of Christ 1696 [etc.]. Oxford, printed at the Theater in the year 1696.
  12mo in sixes. Bodl. Rawl. Alm. 100.   Wing A 1235

2. AESCHINES AND DEMOSTHENES. Αισχινου ο κατα Κτησιφωντος και Δημοσθενους ο περι στεφανου λογος. Interpretationem Latinam et vocum difficiliorum explicationem adjecerunt P. Foulkes, J. Freind [etc.]. Εκ Θεατρου ἐν Οξονια ετει αχ϶έ. Excudebat Johan. Crooke.
  8vo in fours. Imp. 24 Dec. 1695. Bodl. Radcl. e. 87.   Wing A 682
  1st A/cs. p. 53, dues.

2a. (— Another issue, omitting Crooke's name.   Wing A 683)

3. [ALDRICH, HENRY.] Artis logicae compendium. Oxoniae, e Th. Sh., An. Dom. MDCXCVI. Excudebat Johan. Crooke.
  12mo in sixes. Imp. 20 Apr. 1696. Bodl. 8° C 41 Linc.   Wing A 898

4*. [ALDRICH, HENRY.] Cathedral service.
  Fol. Christ Church Library, 1208. (fragments)
  1st A/cs. p. 74, paper; pp. 92, 96, four printed sheets in stock. See the letter from Samuel Pepys to Charlett: Bodl. MS. Ballard i, 95. The list of books 'sub prelo' in the Sheldonian, 1696 (No. 11 below), includes a 'Compleat set of Books for the Service of Choirs'.

5. CICERO. M. Tullius Cicero De oratore ad Q. Fratrem. Ex MSS. recensuit Tho. Cockman [etc.]. Oxoniae, e Th. Sh. 1696.

8vo in fours. Imp. 21 Apr. 1696. Bodl. Mason O 51.   Wing C 4298

6. Author of the Whole DUTY OF MAN. The lively oracles given to us, or the Christians birth-right and duty in the custody and use of the Holy Scripture. By the Author of the Whole Duty of Man, etc. At the Theater in Oxford, 1696.

8vo in fours. Imp. 10 June 1678. Bodl. Vet. A 3 e. 516.   Wing A 1155
The fifth edition: Madan, *Oxford Books*, iii, No. 3169.

7*. HOMER. [A reissue of the *Iliad*, 1695, with a new title-page and ? frontispiece.]
1st A/cs. p. 66: 'Printing the plate and first Sheet of Homer over again'. Madan 1696:13.

8*. LUDOLF, HEINRICH WILHELM. Henrici Wilhelmi Ludolfi Grammatica Russica quae continet non tantum praecipua fundamenta Russicae linguae, verum etiam manuductionem quandam ad grammaticam Slavonicam. Additi sunt in forma dialogorum modi loquendi communiores, Germanice aeque ac Latine explicati, in gratiam eorum qui linguam Latinam ignorant. Una cum brevi vocabulario rerum naturalium. Oxonii, e Th. Sh., A.D. MDCXCVI.

8vo in fours. Bodl. B 14. 13 Linc.   Wing L 3463
1st A/cs. p. 68, 300; p. 67, 1s. See J. S. G. Simmons in *Oxford Slavonic Papers*, i (1950).

(Two sheets of a New Testament in Greek, 8vo, were printed in 1696–7. 1st A/cs. p. 92; p. 96, 2 sheets in stock, valued at £4.)

9. OVID. P. Ovidii Nasonis Metamorphoseon libri xv. interpretatione et notis illustravit Daniel Crispinus, Helvetius, ad usum serenissimi Delphini. Recensuit Joh. Freind [etc.] Oxonii, e Th. Sh. impensis Ab. Swall & Tim. Child, ad insigne Monocerotis in Coemeterio D. Pauli. An. Dom. 1696.

8vo in fours. Bodl. 8° I 40 Linc.   Wing O 682
1st Ac/s. p. 87, dues.

10*. OXFORD, UNIVERSITY. [Programme for the Comitia philologica to be held on 16 April.]
Broadside. Bodl. Wood 276ᵃ(404ᵇ).   Wing O 868

11*. OXFORD, UNIVERSITY. Anno Domini MDCXCVI. Maii die 4. in Theatro Sheldoniano apud Oxonienses sub prelo sunt libri sequentes . . .
Fol. s. sh. Bodl., two slightly differing copies, Ashm. 1820ᵈ, fols. 237, 238. One has the note at the foot, about LP copies, in Latin, the other in English.
1st A/cs. p. 70.

12*. OXFORD, UNIVERSITY. Comitia habita in Universitate Oxoniensi Apr. 16. Anno Dom. 1696 in die gratulationis publicae pro salute Regis Gulielmi.
Fol. Bodl. J.J. Coll.   Wing O 868
1st Ac/s. p. 70, 2,000 given away.

13*. SMITH, THOMAS. Catalogus librorum manuscriptorum Bibliothecae Cottonianae, cui praemittitur illustris viri, D. Roberti Cottoni, equitis aurati & baronetti, vita: et Bibliothecae Cottonianae historia & synopsis. Scriptore Thoma Smitho [etc.]. Oxonii, e Th. Sh. MDCXCVI.
Fol. Bodl. H 3. 16 Art.   Wing S 4233, C 6483
1st Ac/s. pp. 52, 68, 750; p. 62B, engraving the portraits; p. 62C, 5s.; p. 70, errata. *T.C.* II, 602.

14. THUCYDIDES. [Title in Greek.] Thucydides De bello Peloponnesiaco libri octo. Quid in hac editione praestitum sit, praefatio ad lectorem indicabit. Oxoniae, e Th. Sh. impensis T. Bennet ad insigne Lunae falcatae in Coemeterio D. Pauli. Anno Dom. MDCXCVI.

Fol. Imp. 26 Dec. 1695. Bodl. C 6. 3 Art.   Wing T 1133
1st A/cs. p. 85, dues. Proposals were issued in 1694 or 1695. See T.C. II, 544.

15*. XENOPHON. Ξενοφωντος Κυρου Αναβασεως ιστοριων βιβλια ζ'. Εκ Θεατρου ἐν Οξονια. Ετει θεογονίας αχ4ς'.

8vo in fours. Bodl. in Bliss B 122–126.   Wing X 11
1st A/cs. p. 54. Included in the collected Works published in 1703.

1697

1. ABENDANA, ISAAC. An almanack for the year of Christ 1697 [etc., as for previous years]. Oxford, printed at the Theater.

12mo in sixes. Printer to the University.

2*. [BERNARD, EDWARD.] Catalogi librorum manuscriptorum Angliae et Hiberniae in unum collecti cum indice alphabetico. Oxoniae, e Th. Sh. An. Dom. MDCXCVII.

Fol. Imp. 13 Apr. 1697. Bodl. Vet. A 3 b. 27.   Wing C 1253
1st A/cs. p. 40, 750; p. 62C,£1. 2s.; p. 93, Mr. Dale correcting; p. 150, reprinting 12 spoiled sheets. T.C. II, 544–5, 563; III, 95. Hearne, i, p. 71.

3. DIONYSIUS PERIEGETES. [Title in Greek.] Dionysii Orbis descriptio, cum veterum scholiis et Eustathii commentariis. Accedit Periegesis Prisciani, cum notis Andreae Papii. Oxoniae, e Th. Sh. An. MDCXCVII. Prostant apud S. Smith & B. Walford bibliopolas Londinenses.

8vo in fours. Bodl. 8º V 26 Jur.   Wing D 1523
1st A/cs. p. 67, dues. T.C. III, 14–15.

4. EDWARDS, JONATHAN. A preservative against Socinianism: shewing the necessity of faith, and that Socinus and his followers on the contrary, by making the perswasion of the mind concerning divine truths, a useless or at best an indifferent matter, plainly undermine all revealed, and more especially the Christian religion. The third part. By Jonathan Edwards D.D. Oxon. Printed at the Theater for H. Clements. MDCXDVII [sic].

4to. Bodl. 1243 e. 123.   Wing E 220
1st A/cs. p. 85, dues. T.C. II, 473.

5. [FELL, JOHN.] Grammatica rationis, sive institutiones logicae. Oxonii, e Th. Sh. Anno Dom. MDCXCVII.

16mo. Bodl. Radcl. f. 125.   Wing F 611
1st A/cs. p. 115, dues. The 4th edition. Wood, Ath. iv, 201.

6. GREGORY, DAVID. Davidis Gregorii M.D. Astronomiae Professoris Saviliani & S.R.S. de curva catenaria demonstrationes geometricae, ad Reverendum virum D. Henricum Aldrich S.T.P. Decanum Aedis Christi Oxoniae. Oxoniae, e Th. Sh. A.D. MDCXCVII.

4to. Bodl. E 2. 26(4) Linc.

(Lloyd's tables. See 1700.)

7*. LYCOPHRON. Lycophronis Chalcidensis Alexandra, cum Graecis Isaaci Tzetzis commentariis. Accedunt versiones, variantes lectiones, emendationes, annotationes, & indices necessarii. Cura & opera Johannis Potter [etc.]. Oxonii, e Th. Sh. An. Dom. MDCXCVII.

Fol. Imp. 26 Feb. 1696/7. Bodl. L 42 Art.   Wing L 3523
1st A/cs. p. 66, 500 + 50 LP; p. 87, 10s. *T.C.* III, 79. Hearne, i, p. 227. Includes Cassandra.

8. NEPOS, CORNELIUS. Corn. Nepotis excellentium imperatorum vitae. Editio novissima. Accessit Aristomenis Messenii vita ex Pausania. Oxoniae, e Th. Sh., An. Dom. MDCXCVII. Excudebat Johan. Crooke.

8vo in fours. Bodl. Tanner 909.   Wing N 434, 4268
1st A/cs. p. 53, dues. According to the Bodleian Catalogue, edited by William Adams.

9*. OXFORD, UNIVERSITY. Comitia habita in Universitate Oxoniensi Dec. 2. [etc.] pro Gulielmi Regis auspiciis Europae reddita.

Broadside. Bodl. Wood 276ᵃ(404ᶜ).   Wing O 869

10*. OXFORD, UNIVERSITY. Anno Domini MDCXCVII. Julii die 14. in Theatro Sheldoniano apud Oxonienses sub prelo sunt libri sequentes . . .

Fol. s. sh. Bodl. Ashm. 1820ᵈ, fol. 236.
1st A/cs. p. 94, 'For Printing the Catal. of books several times'.

11*. PINDAR. [Title in Greek.] Pindari Olympia, Nemea, Pythia, Isthmia, una cum Latina omnium versione carmine lyrico per Nicolaeum Sudorium. Oxonii, e Th. Sh., MDCXCVII.

Fol. Imp. 6 Aug. 1697. Bodl. A 2. 16 Art.   Wing P 2245
1st A/cs. p. 66, 700 + 50 LP. *T.C.* III, 41. Hearne, i, p. 153.

12. POTTER, JOHN. Archaeologiae Graecae: or the Antiquities of Greece. By John Potter [etc.]. Oxford, printed at the Theater for Abell Swall, at the Unicorn, in St. Pauls Church-yard, London. MDCXCVII.

8vo in fours. Imp. 15 May 1697. Bodl. Lister F 66.   Wing P 3030
1st A/cs. p. 85, dues. *T.C.* III, 18, 108. This is Vol. i of a work completed in 1699.

1698

1. ABENDANA, ISAAC. An almanack for the year of Christ 1698 [etc., as for previous years]. Oxford, printed at the Theater in the year 1698.

12mo in sixes. Printer to the University.   Wing A 1236

2. AESOP. Fabularum Aesopicarum delectus. Oxoniae, e Th. Sh., An. Dom. MDCXCVIII. Excudebat Johan. Croke.

8vo. Bodl. Radcl. e. 99.   Wing A 729
1st A/cs. p. 173, dues. *T.C.* III, 80. Preface signed by Anthony Alsop.

3. BOETHIUS. An. Manl. Sever. Boethii Consolationis philosophiae libri v. Anglo-Saxonice redditi ab Alfredo inclyto Anglo-Saxonum rege. Ad apographum Junianum

expressos edidit Christophorus Rawlinson [etc.]. Oxoniae, e Th. Sh. MDCXCVIII. sumtibus editoris, typis Junianis.

8vo in fours. Imp. 2 Apr. 1698. Bodl. 8° M 206 Art.   Wing B 3429
1st A/cs. p. 115, dues.

4. COWPER, WILLIAM. The anatomy of humane bodies, with figures drawn after the life by some of the best masters of Europe, and curiously engraven in one hundred and fourteen copper plates, illustrated with large explications, containing many new anatomical discoveries, and chirurgical observations: to which is added an introduction explaining the animal oeconomy, with a copious index. By William Cowper. Oxford, printed at the Theater for Sam. Smith and Benj. Walford, Printers to the Royal Society at the Princes Arms in St. Paul's Church Yard, London, MDCXCVIII.

Broadsides guarded. Bodl. Vet. A 3 a. 1.   Wing C 6698
T.C. III, 47, 60.

5. DODWELL, HENRY. Annales Velleiani, Quintilianei, Statiani, seu vitae P. Velleii Paterculi, M. Fabii Quintiliani, P. Papinii Statii, (obiterque Juvenalis,) pro temporum ordine, dispositae. Ab Henrico Dodwello [etc.]. Oxonii, e Th. Sh. A.D. MDCXCVIII.

8vo in fours. Bodl. 8° I 18 Linc.   Wing D 1802A
1st A/cs. p. 85, dues. T.C. III, 60, 65, 79.

6. EDWARDS, JONATHAN. A preservative against Socinianism [etc., as in 1694]. The second part. Oxon. Printed at the Theater for H. Clements. 1698. By Jonathan Edwards D.D. The second edition.

4to. Imp. 3 July 1693. Bodl. F I 21 Linc.   Wing E 219
1st A/cs. p. 85, dues.

7. EDWARDS, JONATHAN. A preservative against Socinianism [etc., as in 1693]. The first part. By Jonathan Edwards D.D. The third edition. Oxon. Printed at the Theater for Henry Clements. A.D. MDCXCVIII.

4to. Imp. 10 July 1693. Bodl. F I 21 Linc.   Wing E 218
1st A/cs. p. 85, dues.

8. GRABE, JOHANN ERNST. Spicilegium SS. Patrum ut et haereticorum, seculorum post Christum natum I. II. & III. quorum vel integra monumenta, vel fragmenta, partim ex aliorum Patrum libris jam impressis collegit, & cum codicibus manuscriptis contulit, partim ex MSS. nunc primum edidit, ac singula tam praefatione quam notis subjunctis illustravit Joannes Ernestus Grabius. Tomus I sive Seculum I. Oxoniae e Th. Sh. MDCXCVIII.

8vo in fours. Imp. 23 Dec. 1698. Bodl. D 1. 8 Linc.   Wing G 1464, P 727
T.C. III, 158.

9*. [HUDSON, JOHN.] Geographiae veteris scriptores Graeci minores. cum interpretatione Latina, dissertationibus, ac annotationibus. Vol. I. Oxoniae, e Th. Sh. MDCXCVIII.

8vo in fours. Bodl. 8° L 101 Art.   Wing H 3260
1st A/cs., p. 90, 500; p. 89, 5s. T.C. III, 110. Vol. ii was published in 1700.

10. KEILL, JOHN. An examination of Dr. Burnet's Theory of the Earth; together with some remarks on Mr. Whiston's New Theory of the Earth. By Jo. Keill [etc.]. Oxford, printed at the Theater, 1698.

8vo. Bodl. 8° B 47(2) Jur.   Wing K 132
1st A/cs. p. 85, dues. T.C. III, 60, 66.

11. MARSHALL, THOMAS. The Catechism set forth in the Book of Common Prayer briefly explained [etc., as in 1692]. The tenth edition. Oxford, at the Theater for T. Bennet, London.

8vo in fours. Imp. 20 Mar. 1678. Bodl. Antiq. f. E 1698. 3.   Wing M 806
1st A/cs. p. 113, dues.

12*. OXFORD, UNIVERSITY. [Order by the Vice-Chancellor against opening taverns and coffee-houses on Sundays. Dated 22 Aug. 1698.]
4to single leaf. B.M. Harl. 5929, No. 106.

13. PINDAR. [As in 1697.]
B.M. 653.g.17.   Wing P 2246

14*. SPELMAN, SIR HENRY. Reliquiae Spelmannianae. The posthumous works of Sir Henry Spelman Kt. relating to the laws and antiquities of England. Publish'd from the original manuscripts. With the life of the author. Oxford, printed at the Theater for Awnsham and John Churchill at the Black-Swan in Pater-Noster-Row, London, 1698.

Fol. Imp. 17 Jan. 1698/9. Bodl. A 6. 5 Jur.   Wing S 4930
1st A/cs. pp. 68, 88, 112, 500 + 50 LP; p. 111, dues from Churchill. Apparently a publication shared by the Delegates and Churchill T.C. III, 56, 110.

15. THWAITES, EDWARD. Heptateuchus, Liber Job, et Evangelium Nicodemi; Anglo-Saxonice. Historiae Judith fragmentum; Dano-Saxonice. Edidit nunc primum ex MSS. codicibus Edwardus Thwaites [etc.]. Oxoniae, e Th. Sh., An. Dom. MDCXCVIII. Typis Junianis.

8vo in fours. Imp. 27 Dec. 1697. Bodl. O.T. Anglo-Sax. d. 1/1.
Reissued without the imprimatur: Bodl. 8° R 126 Th.

16. [WELLS, EDWARD.] Elementa arithmeticae numerosae et speciosae. In usum juventutis academicae. Oxoniae, e Th. Sh. An. Dom. MDCXCVIII. Excudebat Johan. Croke.

8vo in fours. Imp. 31 March 1698. Bodl. Savile H 1.   Wing W 1286
1st A/cs. p. 173, dues.

1699

1. ABENDANA, ISAAC. An almanack for the year of Christ 1699 [etc., as in previous years]. Oxford, printed at the Theater.
12mo in sixes. Bodl. MS. Top. Oxon. f. 43.   Wing A 1237

2. ALFRED THE GREAT. (Proposals) Hormesta Pauli Orosii quam olim patrio sermone donavit Ælfredus Magnus, Anglo-Saxonum rex doctissimus. Ad exemplar Junianum edidit Wilhelmus Elstob [etc.]. Oxoniae, e Th. Sh. An. Dom. MDCIC.
4to. 4 pp. B.M. MS. Lansd. 373, fols. 86–7.

3. CRUSIUS, alias CRENIUS, THOMAS. Thomae Crenii Animadversiones philologicae et historicae, novas librorum editiones, praefationes, indices, nonnullasque summorum aliquot virorum labeculas notatas excutientes. Cum quibusdam Josephi Scaligeri, Theodori Bezae, Hadriani Junii, Hugonis Grotii, Claudii Salmasii, Andreae Riveti, Jo. Henr. Heideggeri, & non neminis De morbo morteque Renati Des Carte

epistolis, antea nunquam editis, lectu dignissimis. Editio tertia prioribus emendatior
& auctior. Oxonii, e Th. Sh., A.D. 1699. Excudebat Johannes Owenus.
8vo. Bodl. 8° A 39 Jur.   Wing C 6882

4. GRABE, JOHANN ERNST. Spicilegium SS. Patrum [etc. as for the first volume,
1698]. Seculi II tomus I. Oxoniae, e Th. Sh. M.DC.XCIX.
8vo in fours. Imp. 26 Dec. 1699. Bodl. D 1. 9 Linc.   Wing G 1464

5*. HERODIAN. [Title in Greek.] Herodiani historiarum libri 8. recogniti & notis
illustrati. Oxoniae, e Th. Sh., An. Dom. MDCXCIX.
8vo in fours. Bodl. 90 b. 13.   Wing H 1580
1st A/cs. p. 132, 750 + 40 LP.

5a. — Another issue with the imprint: Oxoniae, e Th. Sh., impensis Georg. West,
& Anth. Peisley. An. Dom. MDCXCIX.
1st A/cs. pp. 133, 149, dues. Bodl. Vet. A 3 e. 1374.
T.C. III, 125.

6. HYDE, THOMAS. [Advertisement for his Historia religionis veterum Persarum,
published in 1700.]
Fol. s. sh. B.M. Harl. 5929, fol. 38ᵛ.

7. KEILL, JOHN. An examination of the Reflections on the Theory of the Earth,
together with a defence of the Remarks on Mr. Whiston's New Theory. By
J. Keill [etc.]. Oxford, printed at the Theater for Henry Clemens [sic] bookseller.
1699.
8vo. Imp. 30 June 1699. Bodl. Vet. A 3 e. 90.   Wing K 133
1st A/cs. p. 85.

8*. LILY, WILLIAM. A short introduction of grammar generally to be used [etc.,
as in 1692; followed by Brevissima institutio grammatices]. Oxford, at the Theater.
1699.
12mo. Bodl. 3058 e. 17.   Wing L 2302–3
1st A/cs. p. 132, 2,000, 1s.

9*. MORISON, ROBERT. Plantarum historiae universalis Oxoniensis pars tertia seu
herbarum distributio nova, per tabulas cognitionis & affinitatis ex libro naturae
observata & detecta. Auctore Roberto Morison [etc.]. Partem hanc tertiam, post
auctoris mortem, hortatu Academiae explevit & absolvit Jacobus Bobartius Horti
Praefectus. Oxonii, e Th. Sh. Anno Domini M.DC.XCIX.
Fol. Bodl. Z 4. 19 Jur.   Wing M 2772
1st A/cs. pp. 114, 136, 650 + 100 LP; p. 169, £3; p. 93, Mr. Dale correcting. For
the previously-published parts, see Madan, Oxford Books, iii, Nos. 2917, 3271.
D.O. 24 July 1677, 16 June 1694.

10. MUSAE ANGLICANAE. Musarum Anglicanarum analecta: sive poemata quaedam
melioris notae, seu hactenus inedita, seu sparsim edita, in duo volumina congesta.
Vol. II. Oxon. e Th. Sh., impensis Joh. Crosley An. Dom. M.DC.XCIX.
8vo. Bodl. 8° St. Am. 407.   Wing M 3137
T.C. III, 110.

11. MUSAE ANGLICANAE. Musarum Anglicanarum analecta [etc., as above].
Editio secunda priore multo emendatior. Vol. I. [Imprint as above.]
8vo. Bodl. 8° St. Am. 406.   Wing M 3136

12. POTTER, JOHN. Archaeologiae Graecae [etc., as in 1697]. Vol. 2. Oxford, printed at the Theater, for Timothy Child at the White Hart, and John Jones at the Dolphin and Crown, in St. Paul's Church-yard, London, A.D. MDCXCIX.

    8vo in fours. Bodl. Radcl. e. 97.   Wing P 3032
    1st A/cs. p. 85, dues. *T.C.* III, 108.

13. THEOCRITUS. [Title in Greek.] Theocriti quae extant cum Graecis scholiis. Oxoniae e Th. Sh., impensis Sam. Smith, & Benj. Walford ad insignia Principis in Coemeterio D. Pauli. An. Dom. 1699.

    8vo in fours. Bodl. Bliss B 135.   Wing T 851
    1st A/cs. pp. 89, 133, dues. *T.C.* III, 142.

14*. WALLIS, JOHN. Johannis Wallis, S.T.D., Geometriae Professoris Saviliani, in celeberrima Academia Oxoniensi, operum mathematicorum volumen tertium. Oxoniae, e Th. Sh. MDCXCIX.

    Fol. Imp. 13 Mar. 1698/9. Bodl. Savile G g. 3   Wing W 597
    1st A/cs. p. 130, 500; p. 131, £1, best paper—25*s.*; p. 138, copy bound for the King. *T.C.* III, 141.

    — The first and second parts of Wallis's works were reprinted in 1698–9, presumably to make up 3-volume sets.

    1st A/cs, p. 130.

1700

1. ABU BAKR IBN AL-TUFAIL. Philosophus autodidactus sive epistola Abi Jaafar, ebn Tophail de Hai ebn Yokdan. In qua ostenditur, quomodo ex inferiorum contemplatione ad superiorum notitiam ratio humana ascendere possit. Ex Arabica in linguam Latinam versa ab Edwardo Pocockio. Editio secunda priore emendatior. Oxonii, e Th. Sh. A.D. 1700. Excudebat Johannes Owenus.

    4to. Bodl. 4° B 53 Th. BS.   Wing A 153
    A reissue of sheets printed in 1671 with a new title-page: Madan, *Oxford Books*, iii, No. 2877.

2. BERNARD, EDWARD. Orbis eruditi literaturam a charactere Samaritico hunc in modum favente Deo deduxit Eduardus Bernardus A.D. 1689. Recognitum ab auctore A.D. 1696. Oxoniae, e Th. Sh. edidit Johannes Owenus. Anno MDCC. pret. 1*s.* M. Burghers sculp.

    Broadside. Bodl. Gough Maps 46, fol. 173.

3. Author of the Whole DUTY OF MAN. The art of contentment by the Author of the Whole Duty of Man, &c. At the Theater in Oxford, MDCC.

    8vo in fours. Bodl. Vet. A 3 e. 162.   Wing A 1094
    The 8th ed.: Madan, *Oxford Books*, iii, No. 3043.

4. Author of the Whole DUTY OF MAN. The ladies calling in two parts by the Author of the Whole Duty of Man, &c. The seventh impression. At the Theater in Oxford MDCC.

    8vo in fours. Bodl. Vet. A 3 e. 161.   Wing A 1148
    A list of editions is in Madan, *Oxford Books*, iii, p. 277.

5. GRABE, JOHANN ERNST. Spicilegium SS. Patrum [etc., as in 1698]. Seculi II tomus I. Oxoniae e Th. Sh., MDCC. impensis Joannis Oweni.

8vo in fours. Imp. 24 Dec. 1698. Bodl. Vet. A 3 e. 2464.   Wing G 1465

6. [GRABE, JOHANN ERNST.] Proposals for subscription to a new edition of Irenaeus now printing at the Theater in Oxford. [n.d.]

Fol. Bodl. J.J. Coll., Proposals, F 25 (wants the specimen page).   Wing I 1028
T.C. III, 192 (Easter, 1700). The book was published in 1702.

7. GREGORY I, POPE. [Specimen for an edition of Liber curae pastoralis in Latin and Old English.]

4to. 4 pages, 2 of which are printed. Bodl. MS. Rawl. D. 377, fol. 86.
MS. note: This is a Specimen of an Edition of Gregory which Mr Thwaites design'd.

8. GROTIUS, HUGO. Grotius De veritate religionis Christianae. Editio novissima, in qua ejusdem annotationes ipsius textus verbis subjectae sunt. Oxoniae, e Th. Sh., impensis Ant. Peisley bibliop. A.D. MDCC.

8vo. B.M. 4016.a.37.   Wing G 2105
1st A/cs. p. 171, dues.

9*. HUDSON, JOHN. Geographiae veteris scriptores Graeci minores [etc., as in 1698]. Vol. II. Oxoniae, e Th. Sh. MDCC.

8vo in fours. Bodl. 8º C 454 Linc.
1st A/cs. p. 152, 50 LP; p. 156, 5s. T.C. III, 125.

10. HYDE, THOMAS. Historia religionis veterum Persarum, eorumque Magorum. Ubi etiam nova Abrahami, & Mithrae, & Vestae, & Manetis, &c. historia, atque angelorum officia & praefectura ex veterum Persarum sententia . . . Zoroastris vita, ejusque et aliorum vaticinia de Messiah e Persarum aliorumque monumentis eruuntur . . . dantur veterum Persarum scripturae & linguae . . . specimina . . . Autor est Thomas Hyde [etc.]. Oxonii, e Th. Sh., MDCC.

4to. Imp. 12 July 1700. Bodl. 4º B 14 Art. BS.   Wing H 3876

11. JOSEPHUS. Flavii Josephi Antiquitatum Judaicarum libri quatuor priores et pars magna quinti, Gr. Lat. cum exemplaribus MSS. collati, & illustrati notis amplissimis D. Edwardi Bernardi S.T.P. Item Historiarum de Bello Judaico liber primus, et pars secundi Gr. Lat. ad codices MSS. itidem recogniti & emendati. Oxoniae, e Th. Sh. MDCC.

Fol. Bodl. E 3. 1 Th.   Wing J 1081
1st A/cs. p. 171, dues.

12. JUSTIN MARTYR. Του αγιου Ιουστινου Απολογια πρωτη υπερ Χριστιανων προς Αντονινον τον Ευσεβη. Εκ Θεατρου εν Οξονια, ετει θεογονιας αψ′. [Latin title-page:] Sancti Justini philosophi et martyris Apologia prima pro Christianis ad Antoninum Pium, cum Latina Johannis Langi versione, quamplurimis in locis correcta; subjunctis emendationibus & notis Roberti ac Henrici Stephanorum, Perionii, Billii, Sylburgii, Scaligeri, Halloixii, Casauboni, Montacutii, Grotii, Salmasii, Vallesii, Cotelerii, plurimisque novis additis; annexis insuper ad calcem annotationibus Langi & Kortholti, praemissa vero Langi praefatione, qua summam hujus Apologiae enarravit. Edita a Joanne Ernesto Grabe. Oxoniae, e Th. Sh. Anno Domini MDCC.

8vo in fours. Imp. 28 Dec. 1700. Bodl. Vet. A 3 e. 1215.   Wing J 1267

13. LLOYD, WILLIAM. Series chronologica Olympiadum, Pythiadum, Isthmiadum, Nemeadum quibus veteres Graeci tempora sua metiebantur [etc.]. Per Gulielmum Lloyd [etc.]. Oxoniae, e Th. Sh., A.D. MDCC.
    Fol. Bodl. S 11. 16 Th.   Wing S 2247, L 2698
    1st A/cs. p. 202, tin rules. T.C. III, 173. Hearne, i, p. 153. Often found bound with Pindar of 1697.

14*. MARSHALL, THOMAS. The Catechism set forth in the Book of Common Prayer, briefly explained [etc.]. The eleventh edition. Oxford, printed at the Theater in the year 1700.
    8vo in fours. Imp. 20 Mar. 1678. Bodl. 8° Q 32 Th.   Wing M 807
    1st A/cs. p. 134, 1,000.

15. MAURICE, DAVID. The bruised reed, or a sermon preach'd at the Cathedral Church of St. Asaph, for the support of weak Christians, by D. Maurice [etc.]. Oxford, printed at the Theater, 1700.
    4to. Bodl. Sermons 13 (11).

16. ORATIO DOMINICA. Oratio Dominica πολύγλωττος, πολύμορφος. nimirum, plus centum linguis, versionibus, aut characteribus reddita & expressa. Editio novissima, speciminibus variis quam priores comitatior. Londini: prostant apud Dan. Brown, ad insigne Bibliorum, & W. Keblewhite, sub Cygno in Area Boreali D. Pauli. CIↃIↃCC.
    4to. Bodl. Douce O 160.
    Two sheets, B and C, were printed at the Sheldonian Press.

17. OWEN, JOHN. Libri impensis Joannis Oweni editi vel mox edendi [announcing Lycophron's *Cassandra*, ed. Potter; Tatian's Speech to the Greeks with the *Derisio* of Hermias, ed. William Worth: Grabe's *Spicilegium* in two volumes; the Suidas Lexicon ed. Ludolfus Neocorus; and the works of Cicero ed. Thomas Cockman].
    4to. s. sh. n.d. B.M. Harl. 5932, fol. 132.
    Uncertainly attributable to the Theatre press. The first three books were printed at the Theatre in 1700–2 at Owen's expense.

18*. OXFORD, UNIVERSITY. Exequiae desideratissimo principi Glocestriae Duci ab Oxoniensi Academia solutae. Oxonii, e Th. Sh., An. Dom. MDCC.
    Fol. Bodl. AA 64 Art.   Wing O 885
    1st A/cs. p. 152, 500, Mr. Mapp correcting; p. 165, 3s.

19*. OXFORD, UNIVERSITY. Parecbolae sive excerpta e corpore statutorum Universitatis Oxoniensis. Accedunt Articuli religionis xxxix in Ecclesia Anglicana recepti. Nec non Juramenta Fidelitatis & Suprematiae. In usum juventutis academicae. Oxoniae, e Th. Sh. MDCC.
    8vo. B.M. 1471.e.9.   Wing O 934
    1st A/cs. p. 134, 1,000.

20*. OXFORD, UNIVERSITY. Anno Domini MDCC Februarii die 7, in Theatro Sheldoniano apud Oxonienses sub prelo sunt libri sequentes.
    Fol. s. sh. B.M. Harl. 5932, fol. 93.

21. [OXFORD, UNIVERSITY.] Catalogus librorum quos nuper ab Hollandia huc attulit Joannes Owenus, quorum emendorum copia quotidie in Theatro Sheldoniano

detur. [Woodblock of the Sheldonian Theatre] Oxonii. Ubi etiam catalogus gratis desideranti offeretur.
4to. n.d. Bodl. [MS.] Wood C 51.
Attributable to the Theatre press on typographical grounds.

22. [OXFORD, UNIVERSITY?] Catalogus libris exquisitissimis, rarissimisque, omnium authorum tam antiquorum, quam recentium, in re theologica, juridica, mathematica, philologica, historica omnibusque facultatibus insignium, instructissimus. [etc.] Quorum auctionem in Schola Naturalis Philosophiae Oxon. die Junii 20. faciet Joannes Bullord. Permissu Rev. D. Dris. G. Paynter, Vice-Can. Catalogues sold at six pence each, in Oxford at the Theatre by J. Owens, and by Mr. J. Bagford at Tom's Coffee-House adjoyning to Ludgate in London.
8vo. n.d. Bodl. Vet. A 4 e. 772.
Uncertainly attributable to the Theatre press on typographical grounds.

23. RIPA, CESARE. [Prospectus.] Iconologia, written by Caesar Ripa of Perugia Knight of the Order of St. Maurice and Lazarus: wherein are express'd various images [etc.]. Oxford, printed at the Theater, An. Dom. MDCC.
4to. [Title-page only]. B.M. Harl. 5929, No. 337.

24. SCALIGER, CASAUBON. Epistolae selectiores hactenus ineditae Josephi Scaligeri, Isaaci Casauboni [etc.].
4to. B.M. Harl. 5929, fol. 162. Title-page only.

25. TATIAN. Τατιανου Προς Ελληνας. Ερμιου Διασυρμος των εξω φιλοσοφων. Εκ Θεατρου ἐν Οξονια. Ετει θεογονιας αψ'.
8vo in fours. Imp. 9 July 1700. Bodl. 4° St. Am. 34. Wing T 236
Edited by William Worth: Madan 1700:6.

26. WELLS, EDWARD. A new sett of maps both of antient and present geography. By Edward Wells [etc.]. Oxford, printed at the Theater, An. Dom. MDCC.
Fol. Imp. 28 Sept. 1700. Bodl. 2027 b. 33.
It appears by the list of Contents that it was originally issued with only 14 of the 41 maps. It was reissued in 1701.

27. WOODROFFE, BENJAMIN. Examinis & Examinantis examen, sive Reformationis & reformatorum defensio adversus calumnias Francisci Foris Otrokocsi, in libro quem inscribit Examen Reformationis Lutheri & sociorum ejus [etc.]. Authore B. Woodroffe [etc.]. Oxoniae, e Th. Sh., An. Dom. MDCC.
4to. Bodl. 4° W 76 Th. Wing W 3466
1st A/cs. p. 151, dues.

28. WOODROFFE, BENJAMIN. A sermon preached at Feckenham . . . before the Trustees appointed by Sir T. Cookes, Bart. to manage his charity given to that place.
4to. B.M. 266.g.2(14). Wing W 3470
1st A/cs. p. 151, dues.

29*. XENOPHON. [Title in Greek. Contains Hellenica and Chronologia Xenophontea by Henry Dodwell.] Εκ Θεατρου ἐν Οξονια. Ετει θεογονίας αψ'.
8vo in fours. Bodl. Bliss B 124. Wing X 16
1st A/cs. p. 150. Part of the complete works published in 1703.

1701

1. [ARBUTHNOT, JOHN.] An essay on the usefulness of mathematical learning, in a letter from a gentleman in the city to his friend in Oxford. Printed at the Theater in Oxford for Anth. Peisley bookseller, 1701.

    8vo. Bodl. G. Pamph. 2831(8).

    1st A/cs. p. 171, 'Essay', dues. The *D.N.B.* attributes it to Arbuthnot.

2. BENSON, THOMAS. Vocabularium Anglo-Saxonicum, lexico Gul. Somneri magna parte auctius. Opera Thomae Benson [etc.]. Oxoniae, e Th. Sh., An. Dom. M.DCC.I. impensis Sam. Smith, & Benj. Walford ad insigne Principis, in Coemeterio D. Pauli.

    8vo in fours. Imp. 15 July 1701. Bodl. 8° K 27 Art.

    A specimen was issued in 1690. *T.C.* III, 259.

3. BOOK AUCTION CATALOGUE. Bibliotheca viri doctissimi Gul. Hopkins S.T.P. Ecclesiae Vigornensis nuper praebendarii. Libris in omni facultate, praesertim theologica, praestantissime instructa; quorum plerique omnes praelis Stephanorum, Elzeviriorum, &c. accuratissime prodeunt. Horum auctio Oxoniae in gratiam illius Universitatis habenda est decima die Februarii in Ludo Saltatorio juxta Portam Borealem. Catalogues may be had [etc.]. 1700/1.

    4to. Bodl. J.J. Coll. W.C. 3(10).

4. DODWELL, HENRY. De veteribus Graecorum Romanorumque cyclis, obiterque de cyclo Judaeorum aetate Christi, dissertationes decem, cum tabulis necessariis. Inseruntur tabulis fragmenta veterum inedita, ad rem spectantia chronologicam. Opus historiae veteri, tam Graecae, quam Romanae, quam & sacrae quoque, necessarium. Ab Henrico Dodwello [etc.]. Oxonii, e Th. Sh., prostant apud Benj. Tooke ad Medii Templi Portam in vico Fleetstreet dicto MDCCI.

    4to. Bodl. BB 41 Th. *T.C.* III, 258.

5. EUCLID. Euclidis Elementorum libri priores sex, item undecimus & duodecimus. ex versione Latina Federici Commandini. In usum juventutis academicae. Oxoniae, e Th. Sh. impensis Henr. Clements bibliopolae Oxoniensis. MDCCI.

    8vo. Imp. 1 Nov. 1700. Bodl. Bliss B 138.

    1st A/cs. p. 171, dues. The copy above cited was Gerard Langbaine's and has his manuscript note: The Editor John Keil.

6. KEITH, GEORGE. An answer to 17 queries sent to G. Keith by the quarterly meeting of the people called Quakers at Oxford; [etc.]. To which is prefixed a Letter to the Quakers, with 13 queries given in at their quarterly meeting at Oxford Octob. 1. 1700. to which their answer is again desired. By George Keith M.A. Oxford, printed at the Theater for Anthony Peisley. 1701.

    4to. Imp. 15 Aug. 1701. Bodl. 4° C 1 (23) Th.

7. MILLES, THOMAS. The happiness of those that suffer for righteousness sake: in a sermon preached at St. Maries in Oxford, on the xxxth of January 1700/01. By Thomas Milles [etc.]. Printed at the request of Mr. Vice-Chancellor, and others, who heard it preach'd. Oxford, printed at the Theater, for H. Clements bookseller. 1701.

    4to. Bodl. 4° G 26(2) Th.

    1st A/cs. p. 171, dues, 'Mr. Mills sermons'.

8*. OXFORD, UNIVERSITY. Anno Domini MDCCI Julii die 16. in Theatro Sheldoniano apud Oxonienses sub prelo sunt libri sequentes.
  Fol. s. sh. Bodl. Antiq. c. E. 9(98).

9*. OXFORD, UNIVERSITY. At a general meeting of the Vice-Chancellor, Heads of
Houses and Proctors of the University of Oxford, April the 7th. 1701 [about
academic dress].
  Broadside. Bodl. G.A. Oxon. b. 13(1).
  1st A/cs. p. 164, 'Programma about Habitts'.

10*. OXFORD, UNIVERSITY. At a general meeting of the Vice-Chancellor, Heads
of Houses and Proctors of the University of Oxford, June the 23d. 1701 [about
dealings with undergraduates and minors exceeding 5s. in value].
  Fol. s. sh. Bodl. G.A. Oxon. b. 13(2).
  1st A/cs. p. 164, 'Programma about Scholars debts'.

11*. OXFORD, UNIVERSITY. Whereas by several Letters Patents under the Great
Seal [etc. Fixing prices of wine and ale]. 7 July 1701.
  Broadside. Bodl. G.A. Oxon. b. 13(3).
  1st A/cs. p. 164, printing twice.

12. SALLUST. C. Crispi Sallustii quae supersunt, cum indicibus et variis lectionibus.
Oxoniae, e Th. Sh. A.D. MDCCI. impensis Ant. Peisly bibliop.
  12mo. Imp. 17 Feb. 1700/01. Bodl. 8° Z 216 Jur.
  1st A/cs. p. 171, dues. Dedication signed by W. Ayerst. Hearne, i, p. 239.

13. VIDA, MARCUS HIERONYMUS. Marci Hieronymi Vidae Cremonensis, Albae
episcopi, Poeticorum libri tres. Accedunt, Bombycum libri duo et Scacchia ludus,
eodem autore. Oxoniae, e Theatro Sh., impensis J. Crosley, An. Dom. 1701.
  8vo. Bodl. 8° L 103 Art.

14. WELLS, EDWARD. A treatise of antient and present geography together with a
sett of maps, design'd for the use of young students in the universities. By Edward
Wells [etc.]. Oxford, printed at the Theater. Anno Dom. MDCCI.
  8vo in fours. Imp. 28 Sept. 1700. Bodl. 4° Z 10 Art.
  1st A/cs. p. 171, dues. The Sett of maps published in 1700 was reissued as a
companion to this volume: Bodl. 2027 a. 34.

1702

1*. CLARENDON, EDWARD HYDE, EARL OF. The history of the Rebellion and
Civil Wars in England, begun in the year 1641, with the precedent passages, and
actions, that contributed thereunto, and the happy end, and conclusion thereof by
the King's blessed Restoration, and return upon the 29th of May in the year 1660.
Written by the Right Honourable Edward Earl of Clarendon, [etc.]. Volume the
first. Oxford, printed at the Theater, An. Dom. MDCCII.
  Fol. Imp. 29 Apr. 1702. Bodl. I 3. 9 Jur.
  1st A/cs. p. 168, 1100 copies. T.C. III, 303, 307.

2*. — A first reprint was done in 1702-3: 1st A/cs. pp. 192, 214; probably in 1703,
because copies of Vol. i often include the royal privilege dated 24 June 1703. No
copy with an imprint of 1703 is reported.

3. DODWELL, HENRY. Annales Thucydidei et Xenophontei. praemittitur apparatus, cum vitae Thucydidis synopsi chronologica. Ab Henrico Dodwello [etc.]. Oxonii, e Th. Sh. Prostant apud Benj. Took ad Medii Templi Portam in vico Fleetstreet dicto. MDCCII.

4to. Imp. 14 Feb. 1701/2. Bodl. 4° N 29 Art.

4. Author of the Whole DUTY OF MAN. The government of the tongue. By the Author of the Whole Duty of Man, &c. The sixth impression. At the Theater in Oxford MDCCII.

8vo in fours. Imp. 24 Jan. 1675. Bodl. Vet. A 4 e. 1822.
The preceding edition was of 1693.

5. EPICTETUS, CEBES. Epicteti Enchiridion, Cebetis Thebani Tabula, Theophrasti Characteres ethici, M. T. Ciceronis De exilio dialogus, et Prodici Hercules, cum versione Latina. Denuo recognita & notis illustrata. Oxoniae, e Th. Sh., Anno Dom. MDCCII, Impensis Georgii West bibliop.

12mo in sixes. Bodl. Bliss B 139.
A reprint of Fell's New-Year book for 1670: Madan, *Oxford Books*, iii, No. 2853.

6. GREGORY, DAVID. Astronomiae physicae & geometricae elementa. Auctore Davide Gregorio M.D., Astronomiae Professore Saviliano Oxoniae & Regalis Societatis Sodali. Oxoniae, e Th. Sh., An. Dom. MDCCII.

Fol. Imp. 3 June 1702. Bodl. D 6. 12 Art.

7. IRENAEUS. [Title in Greek.] S. Irenaei episcopi Lugdunensis contra omnes haereses libri quinque. Textus Graeci partem haud exiguam restituit; Latinam versionem antiquissimam e quatuor MSS. codicibus emendavit; fragmenta aliorum tractatuum deperditorum subjunxit; omnia notis variorum & suis illustravit Joannes Ernestus Grabe. Oxoniae, e Th. Sh., impensis Thomae Bennet, ad insigne Lunae Falcatae in Coemeterio S. Pauli Londini Anno Domini MDCCII.

Fol. Imp. 7 Feb. 1701. Bodl. B 6. 6 Th.
1st A/cs. p. 171, dues. *T.C.* III, 148, 192.

8. KEILL, JOHN. Introductio ad veram physicam. seu lectiones physicae. habitae in Schola Naturalis Philosophiae Academiae Oxoniensis, quibus accedunt Christiani Hugenii theoremata de vi centrifuga & motu circulari demonstrata, per Jo. Keill [etc.]. Oxoniae, e Th. Sh. impensis Thomae Bennett ad insigne Lunae Falcatae in Coemeterio S. Pauli Londini An. Dom. MDCCII.

8vo. Imp. 14 Feb. 1701/2. Bodl. Don. e. 414.
1st A/cs. p. 171, dues.

9. LYCOPHRON. [Title-page in Greek, as in 1697, but with the year αψβ′, and a title-page in Latin following:] Lycophronis Chalcidensis Alexandra, obscurum poema. cum Graeco Isaacii, seu potius Joannis, Tzetzae commentario. Versiones, variantes lectiones, emendationes, adnotationes, et indices necessarios adjecit Joannes Potterus [etc.]. Editio secunda, priori auctior. Oxonii, e Th. Sh. An. Dom. MDCCII impensis Joannis Oweni.

Fol. Bodl. L 6. 5 Art.

10. MILNES, JAMES. Sectionum conicarum elementa novo methodo demonstrata. Authore Jacobo Milnes [etc.]. Oxoniae, e Th. Sh. MDCCII. impensis Anth. Peisley bibliop.

8vo in fours. Imp. 19 May 1702. Bodl. 8° G 171 Art.
1st A/cs. p. 171, dues.

11*. OXFORD, UNIVERSITY. Pietas Universitatis Oxoniensis in obitum augustissimi Regis Gulielmi III. et gratulatio in exoptatissimam serenissimae Annae Reginae inaugurationem. Oxonii, e Th. Sh., An. Dom. MDCCII.
Fol. Bodl. AA 64(2) Art.
1st A/cs. p. 166, 500; p. 165, 3s.

12*. OXFORD, UNIVERSITY. Epinicion Oxoniense, sive solennis gratulatio ob res feliciter terra marique gestas a copiis serenissimae Reginae Annae contra Gallos pariter ac Hispanos A.D. 1702. Oxonii, e Th. Sh., 1702. Venales prostant apud Johan Wilmot bibliop.
Fol. Bodl. AA 64(5) Art.
1st A/cs. p. 190, 500.

13*. OXFORD, UNIVERSITY. Advertisements from the Delegates of Convocation for Her Majesties reception, to be delivered with great charge to their respective colleges and halls. 26 Aug. 1702.
Broadside. Bodl. G.A. Oxon. b. 19(20).

14*. OXFORD, UNIVERSITY. Comitia philologica in honorem optimae principis Annae D.G. Angliae, Scotiae, Franciae, & Hiberniae Reginae, habita in Universitate Oxoniensi, Julii 16. A.D. 1702. Venales prostant apud Hen. Clements bibliop.
Fol. Bodl. AA 64(4) Art.

15*. OXFORD, UNIVERSITY. Comitia philologica in Theatro Sheldoniano 3. Decemb. Anno Dom. 1702 die Gratulationis Publicae ob res sub auspiciis serenissimae Reginae Annae feliciter terra marique gestas. [At foot:] E Theatro Sheldoniano, A.D. 1702.
Fol. s. sh. Bodl. G.A. Oxon. b. 19(21).
1st A/cs. p. 176(?).

16*. OXFORD, UNIVERSITY. Anno Domini MDCCII in Theatro Sheldoniano apud Oxonienses sub prelo sunt libri sequentes.
Fol. s. sh. B.M. Cup. 645.e.5(6).

17. (According to the 1st A/cs., p. 164, two catalogues of the Proceeders at the Act were printed in 1701–2, but no copy has been traced.)

18. SACHEVERELL, HENRY. A sermon preach'd before the University of Oxford on the Tenth day of June 1702. being the fast appointed for the imploring a blessing on Her Majesty and allies engag'd in the present war against France and Spain. By Henry Sacheverell [etc.]. Printed for Geo. West, and Henry Clements, at the Theatre in Oxford. Anno 1702.
4to. Imp. 25 June 1702. Bodl. 4° G 26(5) Th.
1st A/cs. p. 171, dues.

1703

1. CYRIL, ST. [Title in Greek.] S. Patris nostri Cyrilli Hierosolymorum archiepiscopi Opera, quae supersunt omnia; quorum quaedam nunc primum ex codd. MSS. edidit, reliqua cum codd. MSS. contulit, plurimis in locis emendavit, notisque illustravit Tho. Milles [etc.]. Oxoniae, e Th. Sh., impensis Richardi Sare bibliopol. London MDCCIII.

Fol. Imp. 20 July 1703. Bodl. fol. BS 46.

The Bodleian copy was Hearne's, and he added to the title in MS. 'Accedunt 3 Indices per T. Hearne A.M.'

2. EDWARDS, JONATHAN. A preservative against Socinianism: shewing the falshood and impiety of that pernicious opinion advanced by Socinus and his followers, viz. that reason is to be the great rule of our faith, and the supreme judge of revealed religion. The fourth and last part. By Jonathan Edwards [etc.]. Oxon. Printed at the Theater for H. Clements. 1703.

4to. Bodl. F 1. 21 Linc.

3*. EUCLID. Euclidis quae supersunt omnia. ex recensione Davidis Gregorii [etc.]. Oxoniae, e Th. Sh., An. Dom. MDCCIII.

Fol. Imp. 3 June 1703. Bodl. Savile E 3.

1st A/cs. pp. 172, 195, 750 small at 15s.; 100 large at £1; p. 196, 750 + 250 LP, woodcuts; p. 214, correcting. D.O. 26 June 1703. Hearne, i, pp. 88–9.

4. EUTROPIUS. Eutropii Breviarium historiae Romanae, cum Paeanii metaphrasi Graeca. Messala Corvinus De Augusti progenie. Julius Obsequens De prodigiis. Anonymi Oratio funebris Gr. Lat. in Imp. Constant. Constantini M. Fil. Cum variis lectionibus & annotationibus. Oxonii, e Th. Sh., MDCCIII.

8vo in fours. Imp. 1 Nov. 1703. Bodl. MS. Rawl. Q e. 16.

Edited by Thomas Hearne.

5. FREIND, JOHN. Emmenologia: in qua fluxus muliebris menstrui phaenomena, periodi, vitia cum medendi methodo, ad rationes mechanicas exiguntur. Authore Joh. Freind [etc.]. Oxoniae, e Th. Sh., impensis Thomae Bennet ad insigne Lunae Falcatae in Coemeterio S. Pauli Londini. A.D. 1703.

8vo in fours. Imp. 1 Nov. 1703. Bodl. 8° L 21 Linc.

T.C. III, 389.

6*. [HUDSON, JOHN.] Geographiae veteris scriptores Graeci minores. cum interpretatione Latina, dissertationibus ac annotationibus. Vol. II. Oxoniae, e Th. Sh. MDCCIII.

8vo. Imp. 24 June 1703. Bodl. 8° C 454 Linc.

1st A/cs. p. 197, small 5s., large 8s. D.O. 26 June 1703. The first volume was published in 1698.

7. JUSTIN MARTYR. Του αγιου Ιουστινου Απολογια δευτερα υπερ Χριστιανων, Λογος παραινετικος προς Ελληνας, Περι μοναρχιας. Εκ Θεατρου ἐν Οξονια, ετει θεογονίας αψγ'. Impensis Tho. Bennet, ad insigne Lunae Falcatae in Coemeterio D. Pauli, Londini.

12mo in fours. Imp. 5 Jan. 1703. Bodl. 8° I 30 Linc.

1st A/cs. p. 225, dues. Edited by Hugh Hutchin: Hearne, i, p. 195. T.C. III, 440.

8. LHUYD, EDWARD. [Prospectus for Archaeologia Britannica.]

Fol. s. sh. Dated 10 July 1703. Bodl. J.J. Coll., Proposals b. 26. Part was published in 1707.

9*. MAUNDRELL, HENRY. A journey from Aleppo to Jerusalem at Easter A.D. 1697. By Henry Maundrell [etc.]. Oxford, printed at the Theater, An. Dom. MDCCIII.

8vo in fours. Imp. 8 Apr. 1703. Bodl. Vet. A 4 e. 448.

1st A/cs. p. 170, 500 + 50 LP; p. 191, edition sold to Thomas Bennett.

10. NEW TESTAMENT. Novum Testamentum una cum scholiis Graecis, e Graecis scriptoribus, tam ecclesiasticis quam exteris, maxime ex parte desumptis. Opera et studio Joannis Gregorii [etc.]. Oxonii, e Th. Sh. MDCCIII.

Fol. Imp. 5 Mar. 1702/3. Bodl. L 7. 14 Th.

1st A/cs. p. 191, dues.

11. PLINY. C. Plinii Caecilii Epistolae et Panegyricus cum variis lectionibus & annotationibus. Accedit vita Plinii ordine chronologico digesta. Oxonii, e Th. Sh. MDCCIII. Venales prostant apud G. West.

8vo in fours. Imp. 5 Apr. 1703. Bodl. MS. Rawl. Q. e. 12.

T.C. III, 348. Edited by Thomas Hearne.

12*. XENOPHON. [5th part. Title in Greek. Contains De administratione domestica, Fragmenta Oeconomicorum Ciceronis.] Ἐκ Θεατρου ἐν Ὀξονια. Ἐτει θεογονίας αψγ'.

8vo in fours. Bodl. Bliss B 126.

13*. XENOPHON. [6th part. Title in Greek. Contains Cyropaedia.] Ἐκ Θεατρου ἐν Ὀξονια. Ἐτει θεογονίας αψγ'.

8vo in fours. Bodl. Clar. Press 50 c. 5.

14*. XENOPHON. [Title in Greek.] Xenophontis Opera quae extant omnia; una cum Chronologia Xenophontea Cl. Dodwelli, et quatuor tabulis geographicis. Oxonii, e Th. Sh., MDCCIII.

8vo in fours. Imp. 5 Apr. 1703. Bodl. Bliss B 122–126.

1st A/cs. p. 90, 500; p. 195, £1 the set, parts 5s.; p. 214, Mr. Wells for preparing copy, Mr. Dodwell, for the chronology. A collection of the parts issued in 1690, 1691, 1693, 1696, 1700, and 1703. Edited by Edward Wells.

1704

1. [ALDRICH, HENRY.] Artis logicae compendium. Oxonii, e Th. Sh., An. Dom. MDCCIV. Venales prostant apud A. Peisley, bibliop.

8vo in fours. Bodl. 8° C 208 Art.

Previously published in 1691, 1692, and 1696.

2. MARCUS ANTONINUS. [Title in Greek.] Marci Antonini Imperatoris Eorum quae ad seipsum libri xii. recogniti et notis illustrati. Oxoniae, e Th. Sh. Anno MDCCIV. impensis Ant. Peisley, & Geor. West bibliop.

8vo in fours. Imp. 22 Dec. 1704. Bodl. F 1. 27 Linc.

1st A/cs. p. 225, dues. Edited by R. Ibbetson: Hearne, i, p. 309.

3. BUCKERIDGE, WILLIAM. A letter to a friend in which the occasional conformists are proved to be guilty of schism and hypocrisy. In answer to some arguments produc'd to the contrary in a late pamphlet, intituled The Rights of Protestant Dissenters, &c. Oxford, printed at the Theatre for Anthony Peisley 1704. Price 6d.

4to. Imp. 21 Aug. 1704. Bodl. F 1. 30(20) Linc.

4*. CLARENDON, EDWARD HYDE, EARL OF. The history of the Rebellion [etc., as in 1702]. Volume the first. Oxford, printed at the Theater, An. Dom. MDCCIV.

Fol. B.M. 596.l.14.

1st A/cs. p. 218, a second reprint was done in 1703–4 of about 750. D.O. 9 Dec. 1703: 'Agreed to print 700 of the First and Second volume in small paper and to make up the defect of the large paper'.

5*. CLARENDON, EDWARD HYDE, EARL OF. The history of The Rebellion [etc., as for Vol. i]. Volume the second. Oxford, printed at the Theater, An. Dom. MDCCIV.
    Fol. Imp. 15 Sept. 1703. Bodl. I 3. 9 Jur.
    1st A/cs. p. 200, 1300 small, 250 large.

6*. — A reprint of Vol. ii was done in 1703–5 (1st A/cs. p. 222, 700 small, 100 large), probably in 1703–4, because D.O. 3 Dec. 1703 presumably refers to it.

7*. CLARENDON, EDWARD HYDE, EARL OF. The history of the Rebellion [etc., as for Vols. i and ii]. Volume the third. Oxford, printed at the Theater. An. Dom. MDCCIV.
    Fol. Imp. 16 Oct. 1704. Bodl. I 3. 9 Jur.
    1st A/cs. p. 220, 2,000 small, 350 large; p. 272, Mr. Hearne for making the index. T.C. III, 437. D.O. 28 Nov. 1704: 2,000 sold to Bennett for 16s. each, 268 LP, to be sold by the University for 25s.

8. DIONYSIUS OF HALICARNASSUS. [Half-title:] Dionysii Halicarnassensis Opera omnia Graece et Latine in duos tomos distributa. [Title-page: Title in Greek.] Dionysii Halicarnassensis Antiquitatum Romanarum libri quotquot supersunt. Oxoniae, e Th. Sh., impensis Thomae Bennet, ad insigne Lunae Falcatae in Coemeterio S. Pauli Londini Anno Dom. MDCCIV.
    Fol. Imp. 3 July 1704. Bodl. Lister 68,9.
    T.C. III, 265, 281, 293, 302, 314–15, 420. Edited by John Hudson.

9. DIONYSIUS PERIEGETES. [Title in Greek,] sive Dionysii Geographia emendata & locupletata, additione scil. geographiae hodiernae Graeco carmine pariter donatae: cum 16 tabulis geographicis. Ab Edv. Wells [etc.]. Oxonii, e Th. Sh. A.D. MDCCIV.
    8vo in fours. Imp. 30 Nov. 1703. Bodl. 8° G 172 Art.
    T.C. III, 413.

10. Author of the Whole DUTY OF MAN. The works of the learned and pious author of the Whole Duty of Man, Printed at the Theater in Oxford, and in London by Roger Norton, for Edward Paulet at the sign of the Bible in Chancery Lane. Anno Domini MDCCIV.
    [Part-title:] The second part of the works [etc.]. Printed at the Theater in Oxford and are to be sold by Edward Paulet bookseller in London. 1704.
    Fol. Bodl. Vet. A 4 b. 27.
    1st A/cs. p. 215, payment from Paulet. D.O. 9 Dec. 1703, leave to Paulet to print the second part at the Theatre for £40. The edition of 1695 was similarly divided between London and Oxford printers.

11. HERODIAN. Herodiani Historiarum libri 8. recogniti & notis illustrati. Oxoniae, e Th. Sh., An. Dom. MDCCIV. impensis G. West & Ant. Peisley, bibliopol. Oxon.
    8vo in fours. Bodl. 23647 e. 9.
    A reprint of the edition of 1699.

12. KENNETT, BASIL. Romae antiquae notitia: or the antiquities of Rome. To which are prefix'd two essays: concerning the Roman learning and the Roman education. By Basil Kennett [etc.]. The third edition revised, corrected and augmented with

new sculptures. Oxford, printed at the Theater: for Timothy Child at the White-Hart and Robert Knaplock at the Angel and Crown in St. Paul's Church-Yard. London. MDCCIV.

8vo in fours. Imp. 18 Dec. 1703. Bodl. 8° Z 14 Art. Seld.

Previous editions were printed in London.

13*. MARSHALL, THOMAS. The Catechism set forth in the Book of Common Prayer briefly explained [etc., as in 1692]. The twelfth edition, Oxford, printed at the Theater in the year 1704.

8vo in fours. Imp. 20 Mar. 1678. B.M. 3505.c.42.

1st A/cs. pp. 216, 217, 2,000 sold.

14*. OXFORD, UNIVERSITY. Plausus musarum Oxoniensium; sive gratulatio Academiae ob res prospere terra marique gestas. in comitiis philologicis habitis in Theatro Sheldoniano calendis Januarii 1704. Oxonii, e Th. Sh., An. Dom. MDCCIV.

Fol. Bodl. L 3 3 Th.

1st A/cs. pp. 223, 224, 700, 1s., apparently with a song, which has not been found in existing copies.

15*. OXFORD, UNIVERSITY. At a general meeting of the Vice-Chancellor, Heads of Houses, and Proctors of the University of Oxford, Nov. 7. 1704. [Academic discipline.]

Broadside. Bodl. G.A. Oxon. b. 19(22).

1705

1*. BOOK OF COMMON PRAYER. Litania et ordo administrandi Coenae Domini. Oxoniae, e Th. Sh. MDCCV.

8vo. in fours. Bodl. Bliss B 140.

1st A/cs. p. 238, 'Prayers for the use of the University'.

2*. CLARENDON, EDWARD HYDE, EARL OF. The history of the Rebellion [etc., as in 1702]. Volume I (Part i, Part ii). Oxford printed at the Theater, An. Dom. MDCCV.

8vo. Imp. 29 Apr. 1702. Bodl. 8° M 40–41 Jur.

1st A/cs. p. 244, 2,000 + 500 LP; p. 243, small paper 4s. 1d., large 6s. D.O. 4 Dec. 1705, the booksellers to have the whole impression on small paper and 300 of the large. T.C. III, 503. Two books, separately paginated. The first octavo edition.

3. Author of the Whole DUTY OF MAN. The art of contentment. by the Author of the Whole Duty of Man, &c. At the Theater in Oxford, MDCCV.

8vo in fours. Imp. 24 Feb. 1675. Bodl. 26520 e. 17.

Probably the ninth edition: Madan, *Oxford Books*, iii, No. 3043.

4. Author of the Whole DUTY OF MAN. The ladies calling in two parts. By the Author of the Whole Duty of Man, &c. The eighth impression. Oxford, printed at the Theater. MDCCV.

8vo in fours. Bodl. 1419 e. 2455(2).

5. EUCLID. The English Euclide, being the first six Elements of geometry, translated out of the Greek, with annotations and useful supplements, by Edmund Scarburgh [etc.]. Oxford, printed at the Theater. 1705.

Fol. Imp. 2 Mar. 1704/5. Bodl. C 3 19 Art.

6. GRABE, JOHANN ERNST. Joannis Ernesti Grabii Epistola ad clarissimum virum Dn. Joannem Millium [etc.], qua ostenditur Libri Judicum genuinam LXX Interpretum versionem eam esse, quam MS. Codex Alexandrinus exhibet [etc.]. Oxoniae, e Th. Sh. Anno Dom. MDCCV impensis T. Bennet ad insigne Lunae Falcatae in Coemeterio D. Pauli.

4to. Imp. 31 July 1704. Bodl. Pamph. 260.

T.C. III, 483, where Mill's name is misprinted as Williams.

7. HALLEY, EDMUND. Astronomiae cometicae synopsis. Autore Edmundo Halleio apud Oxonienses Geometriae Professore Saviliano. [With the Sheldonian Theatre device dated 8 June 1705.]

Broadside, 3 sheets hinged with paste. Imp. not dated. Bodl. Savile B 13.

8. HICKES, GEORGE, AND OTHERS. [Second title-page:] Antiquae literaturae septentrionalis libri duo. quorum primus Georgii Hickesii, S.T.P. Linguarum vett. septentrionalium Thesaurum grammatico-criticum & archaeologicum, ejusdem de antiquae literaturae septentrionalis utilitate Dissertationem epistolarem, et Andreae Fountaine equitis aurati Numismata Saxonica & Dano-Saxonica complectitur. alter continet Humfredi Wanleii librorum vett. septentrionalium, qui in Angliae biblioth. extant, Catalogum historico-criticum; nec non multorum vett. codd. septentrionalium alibi extantium notitiam, cum totius operis sex indicibus. Oxoniae, e Th. Sh., An. Dom. MDCCV.

[First title page:] Linguarum vett. septentrionalium Thesaurus grammatico-criticus & archaeologicus. Authore Georgio Hickesio, S.T.P. Oxoniae. e Th. Sh., An. Dom. MDCCV.

Fol. Bodl. Douce H subt. 40–41.

Part-titles to Parts i and ii are dated 1703. The two general title-pages are numbered at the foot 1 and 2, the second being the more general.

9. HODY, HUMFREY. Humfredi Hodii, Linguae Graecae Professoris Regii et archidiaconi Oxon. De Bibliorum textibus originalibus, versionibus Graecis & Latina Vulgata [etc.]. Praemittitur Aristeae Historia Graece et Latine. Oxonii, e Th. Sh. An. Dom. MDCCV.

Fol. Imp. 2 Mar. 1702/3. Bodl. A 21. 8 Th.

10*. HOMER. Ομηρου Οδυσσεια. Εκ Θεατρου εν Οξονια εν τω ετει αψέ.

8vo in fours. Imp. 4 Dec. 1705. Bodl. 8° Z 20 Art. Seld.

11. JUSTINUS. M. Juniani Justini Historiarum ex Trogo Pompeio libri XLIV. MSS. codicum collatione recogniti, annotationibusque illustrati. Oxonii, e Th. Sh. MDCCV.

8vo in fours. Imp. 3 Jan. 1704/5. Bodl. 8° Rawl. 280.

1st A/cs. p. 225, dues. Edited by Thomas Hearne.

12. KEILL, JOHN. Introductio ad veram physicam [etc., as in 1702]. Editio secunda emendatior et auctior. Oxoniae, e Th. Sh. MDCCV. impensis T. Bennet ad insigne Lunae Falcatae in Coemeterio D. Pauli Londini.

8vo. Bodl. 8° I 47 Linc.

T.C. III, 506.

13*. LEVI, PHILIP. [Title in Hebrew.] A compendium of Hebrew grammar, compos'd for the use of beginners, by Philip Levi a converted Jew. Oxford, printed at the Theater 1705.

8vo in fours. Imp. 30 Oct. 1705. Bodl. 8° C 725 Linc.

1st A/cs. p. 240, 500. Really by Robert Clavering. See p. 245.

14. MAIMONIDES. [Title in Hebrew.] R. Mosis Maimonidis tractatus duo: 1 De doctrina Legis, sive educatione puerorum. 2 De natura & ratione poenitentiae apud Hebraeos. Latine reddidit, notisque illustravit Robertus Clavering [etc.]. Praemittitur dissertatio de Maimonide ejusque operibus. Oxoniae, e Th. Sh., impensis Hen. Mortlock bibliopola Londinensi [sic] ad insigne Phoenicis in Coemeterio D. Pauli Anno 1705.

4to. Imp. 13 Apr. 1705. Bodl. F 1. 28 Linc.

15. MATHER, JOHN. A sermon preached before the University of Oxford, at St. Mary's on Tuesday May 29. 1705. being the anniversary of King Charles II. Restoration. By John Mather [etc.]. Oxford, printed at the Theater for John Stephens 1705.

4to. Imp. 30 May 1705. Bodl. 4° L 76(5) Th.

T.C. III, 462.

16*. OXFORD, UNIVERSITY. A catalogue of all graduates in divinity, law, and physick and of all Masters of Arts and Doctors of Musick who have regularly proceeded, or been created, in the University of Oxford between . . . October 1659, and . . . July 1688 [etc.]. To which are prefix'd three continuations of proceeders to . . . March 1705.

8vo. Bodl. Vet. A 4 f. 1385.

Originally compiled by Richard Peers and published in 1689.

17*. OXFORD, UNIVERSITY. Parecbolae sive excerpta e corpore statutorum Universitatis Oxoniensis [etc., as in 1691]. Oxoniae, e Th. Sh. MDCCV.

8vo in fours. B.M. 731.a.20.

1st A/cs. p. 216, 2,000.

18*. OXFORD, UNIVERSITY. Anno Domini MDCCV. Jun. die 12. in Theatro Sheldoniano apud Oxonienses sub prelo sunt libri sequentes.

Fol. s. sh. Bodl. Ashm. 1818, fols. 78, 79.

1st A/cs. p. 226, 'For Printing several times the catal. of Books'.

18a*. The Printer to the University has another issue with five additional items and 'Imprimatur, Art. Charlett' printed at the foot.

19. RENNELL, THOMAS. The nature, causes, and consequences of divisions for the sake of greater edification. A sermon preached before the University of Oxford May 6 1705. By Thomas Rennell [etc.]. Oxford, Printed at the Theater, for George West. MDCCV.

4to. Bodl. 4° L 76(4) Th.

20. SOPHOCLES. Sophoclis tragoediae, Ajax & Electra, nova versione donatae, scholiisque veteribus, tam antehac quam nunc primum editis, illustratae. Accedunt notae perpetuae, & variae lectiones, Opera Thomae Johnson A.M. Oxoniae, e Th. Sh. 1705. impensis Sam. Smith. Benj. Walford. Tho. Newborough. Galf. Wale. Londinens. & Joan. Slatter Aetonens. bibliopol.

8vo in fours. Imp. 28 Nov. 1705. Bodl. 8° Godw. 363.

T.C. III, 494, 504. Hearne, i, p. 127.

21. TRAPP, JOSEPH. The mischiefs of changes in government; and the influence of religious princes to prevent them. A sermon preach'd before the Mayor, and Corporation of Oxford, on Friday March 8, 1705/6 being the anniversary of Her Majesty's Inauguration. By Joseph Trapp [etc.]. Publish't at the request of the Common Council. Oxford, printed at the Theater, for John Stephens 1705. and sold by J. Knapton at the Crown in St. Paul's Church Yard, London.

4to. Bodl. 4° C 116(5) Th.

T.C. III, 502 (wrongly dated).

22*. XENOPHON. [Title in Greek. Contains Memorabilia and Socratica defensio.] Ἐκ Θεάτρου ἐν Ὀξονια. Ἔτει θεογονίας ᾳψέ. [A reprint of the first volume of the collected works edited by Edward Wells, published originally in 1690.]

8vo in fours. Bodl. 2968 e. 2.

1st A/cs. p. 224.

1706

1*. APOLLONIUS PERGAEUS. Apollonii Pergaei De sectione rationis libri duo ex Arabico MS^to. Latine versi. Accedunt ejusdem De sectione spatii libri duo restituti. Opus analyseos geometricae studiosis apprime utile. Praemittitur Pappi Alexandrini Praefatio ad VII^mum. collectionis mathematicae, nunc primum Graece edita: cum lemmatibus ejusdem Pappi ad hos Apollonii libros. Opera & studio Edmundi Halley apud Oxonienses Geometriae Professoris Saviliani. Oxonii, e Th. Sh. Anno. MDCCVI.

8vo in fours. Bodl. 8° Z 32 Art Seld..

1st A/cs. pp. 242, 261, 1s. 6d. T.C. III, 545. Hearne, i, p. 18, ii, p. 312.

2. ATHENAGORAS, ST. Τοῦ ἁγίου Ἀθηναγόρου Ἀθηναίου φιλοσόφου Πρεσβεία περὶ Χριστιανων. Τοῦ αὐτοῦ Περὶ ἀναστάσεως νεκρων. Ἐκ Θεάτρου ἐν Ὀξονια, ἔτει θεογονίας ᾳψs'. [Latin title-page:] Sancti Athenagorae Atheniensis philosophi Legatio pro Christianis [etc.]. ejusdem De resurrectione mortuorum. Accedunt Latina versio, emendationes, variantes lectiones, annotationes, atque indices necessarii. Cura & studio Edwardi Dechair, A.M. Oxoniae, e Th. Sh. impensis S. & J. Sprint, A. & J. Churchill, T. Childe & R. Knaplock, bibliopol. Londin. An. Dom. 1706.

8vo in fours. Imp. 8 Jan. 1705/6. Bodl. 8° B 34 Th. BS.

T.C. III, 493–4.

3. CICERO. M. Tullius Cicero De oratore ad Q. fratrem. Ex MSS. recensuit Tho. Cockman [etc.]. Editio secunda. Oxoniae, e Th. Sh., impensis Jo. Stephens; & prostant venales apud Jo. Knapton ad insigne Coronae in Coemeterio D. Pauli Lond. 1706.

8vo in fours. Imp. 21 Apr. 1696. Bodl. 8° K 17 Jur.

4*. CLARENDON, EDWARD HYDE, EARL OF. The history of the Rebellion [etc., as in 1702]. Volume II, Part 1, Part 2. Oxford, printed at the Theater, An. Dom. MDCCVI.

8vo. Imp. 15 Sept. 1703. Bodl. 8° M 42, 43 Jur.

1st A/cs. p. 264. Two books separately paginated. A continuation of the octavo edition begun in 1705.

5*. CLARENDON [as above]. Volume III, Part 1, Part 2.
8vo. Imp. 16 Oct. 1704. Bodl. 8° M 44, 45 Jur.
1st A/cs. p. 264, 2,000 small, 1,000 LP.

6. [FREWIN, RICHARD.] Cursus chymicus Oxonii in Schola Chymiae habendus. in quo medicamenta pleraque in praxi medica usitatiora fideliter parantur: operationes chymiae primariae, ipsiusque in re medica usus, decem praelectionibus explicantur, variis experimentis illustrantur, & ad rationes mechanicas exiguntur.
Fol. Imp. 27 Feb. 1705/6. Bodl. Oxon. c. 25(3).
1st A/cs. p. 250, dues, 'For Printing Dr. Frewins course of Chym.'

7. GEREE, JOHN. A sermon preach'd in the cathedral church of Winchester, at the Assizes held there, on Thursday, July 4. 1706. By John Geree [etc.]. Publish'd at the request of the High-Sheriff and Grand-Jury. Oxford printed at the Theater for A. Peisley bookseller, and are to be sold by James Knapton at the Crown in St. Paul's Church-Yard, London. MDCCVI.
4to. Imp. 9 Aug. 1706. Bodl. 4° S 71 Th.
1st A/cs. p. 263.

8*. GROTIUS. Hugonis Grotii baptizatorum puerorum institutio: et Eucharistia: una cum ejusdem adnotationibus ad Decalogum, et ad Sermonem Christi in Monte habitum. Oxonii, e Th. Sh. An. Dom. MDCCVI.
8vo in fours. Imp. 14 Dec. 1706. Bodl. 8° Rawl. 486.
1st A/cs. p. 276, 1s. 6d.; p. 260, 1,000, 'Mr. Aldrich's Grotius . . . 210 Books to the Dean Printed on his own Paper'. Edited by Charles Aldrich, nephew of Dean Henry Aldrich.

9. JOSEPHUS BEN-GORION. יוסיפון Josippon, sive Josephi ben-Gorionis Historiae Judaicae libri sex. ex Hebraeo Latine vertit, praefatione & notis illustravit Johannes Gagnier A.M. Oxoniae, e Th. Sh. Anno Domini MDCCVI.
4to. Imp. 14 Nov. 1705. Bodl. 4° W 47 Th.
Hearne, i, p. 127.

10*. OXFORD, UNIVERSITY. Academiae Francofurtanae ad Viadrum encaenia secularia Oxonii in Theatro Sheldoniano Apr. 26. Anno Fundat. 201. Annoque Dom. 1706. celebrata. Oxonii, e Th. Sh., An. Dom. MDCCVI.
Fol. Bodl. Bliss B 412(1).
1st A/cs. p. 240, 500.
10a. — An anonymous Latin Ode in Sapphics (Bodl. 4 Δ 260(7)), printed on a single folio leaf, may be associated with this.

11*. OXFORD, UNIVERSITY. Anno Domini MDCCVI in Theatro Sheldoniano apud Oxonienses sub prelo sunt libri sequentes.
Fol. s. sh. Bodl. Fol. Θ 662(12).
1st A/cs. p. 270, 'Altering the Catal. of Books in the Press . . . Working the same at Press 9 several times'.

12*. OXFORD, UNIVERSITY. A specimen of the several sorts of letter given to the University by Dr. John Fell sometime Lord Bishop of Oxford. To which is added the letter given by Mr. F. Junius. Oxford, printed at the Theater A.D. 1706.
8vo in fours. Bodl. Gough Oxf. 142.
1st A/cs. p. 276, 114 copies in stock.

APPENDIX

13. [WELLS, EDWARD.] A letter from a minister of the Church of England, to a Dissenting parishioner of the Presbyterian perswasion. Oxford, printed at the Theater for Jo. Stephens, and are to be sold by James Knapton at the Crown in St. Paul's Church-Yard, London. 1706.

8vo. Imp. 4 Dec. 1705. Bodl. Pamph. 265(11).
T.C. III, 491.

14. — The second edition. Bodl. Vet A 3 f. 174(10).

15. — The third edition. Dr. Williams's Lib. 12.4.18(4).

16. — The fourth edition. Bodl. 1212 f. 5(9).

17. — The fifth edition. Bodl. 1305 f. 5(2).

18. [WELLS, EDWARD.] A letter from a minister of the Church of England to Mr. Peter Dowley, a Dissenting preacher of the Presbyterian or else Independent perswasion. Oxford, printed at the Theater for Jo. Stephens, and are to be sold by James Knapton at the Crown in St. Paul's Church-Yard, London. 1706.

8vo. Imp. 19 Jan. 1705/6. Bodl. Pamph. 265(1).
T.C. III, 491.

19. — The third edition. Bodl. 1305 f. 2.
The second edition was printed in London.

20. — The fourth edition. Bodl. 1212 f. 5(10).

21. WELLS, EDWARD. A true copy of a letter lately written by Mr. Dowley to Dr. Wells, and now published by Dr. Wells, together with the Doctor's answer. Oxford, printed at the Theater for Jo. Stephens, and are to be sold by James Knapton at the Crown in St. Paul's Church-Yard, London. 1706.

8vo. Imp. 10 Apr. 1706. Bodl. Vet. A 3 f. 174(6).
T.C. III, 502.

22. — The second edition. Bodl. Pamph. 265(5).

23. — The third edition. Bodl. 1212 f. 5(1).

24. [WELLS, EDWARD.] Some testimonies of the most eminent English Dissenters, as also of foreign Reformed Churches and divines, concerning the lawfulness of the rites and ceremonies of the Church of England, and the unlawfulness of separating from it. Oxford, printed at the Theater for Jo. Stephens, and are to be sold by James Knapton at the Crown in St. Paul's Church-Yard, London. 1706.

8vo. Imp. 15 June 1706. Bodl. 8° Q 32(2) Th.

25. — The second edition. Bodl. Vet. A 3 f. 174(7).

26. WOODROFFE, BENJAMIN. A sermon preached at Woodstock June 27. 1706. being the day of Thanksgiving for the glorious victory in Brabant obtain'd over the French army [etc.]. By Benj. Woodroffe [etc.]. Oxford, printed at the Theatre. 1706.

4to. Bodl. 4° S 71 Th.

1707

1*. (Clarendon, Edward Hyde, Earl of. The history of the Rebellion [etc. There was a reimpression of 71 copies of Vol. i (1702) and Vol. ii (1704), involving resetting 15 sheets].

1st A/cs. p. 262.)

2*. CLARENDON, EDWARD HYDE, EARL OF. The history of the Rebellion [etc., as in 1702]. Volume the first . . . second . . . third. Oxford, printed at the Theater, An. Dom. MDCCVII.

Fol. Imprimaturs as in the original edition. Bodl. Auct. S 10. 28–30.

1st A/cs. p. 266, 'Ld. Clarendon's Folio for Mr. Baskett'. Vol. i, 700 + 250 LP; Vol. ii, 700 + 217 LP; Vol. iii, 700 + 203 LP. Five sheets of Vol. ii had to be reset and printed again.

3*. CLARENDON, EDWARD HYDE, EARL OF. The history of the Rebellion [etc., as in 1702. 3 vols., each in 2 parts separately paginated]. Oxford, printed at the Theater, An. Dom. MDCCVII.

8vo. Imprimaturs as in the original edition. Bodl. Clar. Press 31 b. 14–19.

1st A/cs. pp. 262, 264, '2nd impr. for Mr. Baskett'; 2,000 + 1,000 LP.

4. EPICTETUS. [Title in Greek.] Epicteti Enchiridion. Theophrasti characteres ethici. Edidit C. Aldrich [etc.]. Oxonii, e Th. Sh., 1707.

4to. Imp. 1 Dec. 1707. Bodl. MS. Rawl. Q e. 15.

Hearne, xi, p. 124.

5. HUYGENS, CHRISTIAN. [Prospectus] Christ. Hugenii Zulichemii, Const. F. Horologium, oscillatorium, sive De motu pendulorum ad horologia aptato demon-strationes geometricae. Accedunt ejusdem De circuli magnitudine inventa, et Systema Saturnium. Oxoniae, e Th. Sh., An. Dom. MDCCVII.

[On p. 4:] Proposals for printing the Horologium &c. in one volume folio. To be corrected by Edw. Strong.

Fol. B.M. Harl. 5929, No. 342.

T.C. III, 513.

6. LHUYD, EDWARD. Archaeologia Britannica, giving some account additional to what has been hitherto publish'd, of the languages, histories and customs of the original inhabitants of Great Britain: from collections and observations and travels through Wales, Cornwall, Bas-Bretagne, Ireland and Scotland. By Edward Lhuyd [etc.]. Vol. I. Glossography. Oxford, printed at the Theater for the Author, MDCCVII. and sold by Mr. Bateman in Pater-Noster-Row, London, and Jeremiah Pepyat bookseller at Dublin.

Fol. Imp. 9 Apr. 1707. Bodl. T 11. 2 Jur.

A prospectus was issued in 1703. This volume was the only part published of the projected work.

7. MAUNDRELL, HENRY. A journey from Aleppo to Jerusalem at Easter, A.D. 1697. The second edition, in which the corrections and additions, which were sent by the Author after the book was printed off, are inserted in the body of the book in their proper places. By Hen. Maundrell [etc.]. Oxford, printed at the Theater, An. Dom. MDCCVII and sold by Jonah Bowyer at the Rose in Ludgate-street near St. Paul's Church.

8vo in fours. Imp. 8 Apr. 1703. Bodl. 8° H 44 Linc.

1st A/cs. p. 261, dues; p. 272, woodcuts. *T.C.* III, 579.

8. MILL'S NEW TESTAMENT. Novum Testamentum. cum lectionibus variantibus MSS exemplarium, versionum, editionum, SS Patrum & scriptorum ecclesiasticorum; & in easdem notis [etc.]. Studio et labore Joannis Millii S.T.P. Oxonii, e Th. Sh., MDCCVII.

Fol. Imp. 25 May 1707. Bodl. L 7. 13 Th.

9. MILLES, THOMAS. The natural immortality of the soul asserted, and proved from the Scriptures and first Fathers: in answer to Mr. Dodwell's Epistolatory discourse, in which he endeavours to prove the soul to be a principle naturally mortal. By Thomas Milles, B.D. Oxford. Printed at the Theater for Ant. Peisley, MDCCVII.

8vo. Imp. 3 Jan. 1706/7. Bodl. 4° Q 33 Th.

T.C. III, 533.

10. MILLES, THOMAS. De officio eorum qui de fide certant, concio habita coram Academia Oxoniensi, Aprilis 22° MDCCVII, ineunte termino, a Tho. Milles [etc.]. Oxonii, e Th. Sh. sumptibus Antonii Peisley bibliopolae, MDCCVII.

4to. Bodl. 4° W 41(25) Th.

11*. OXFORD, UNIVERSITY. Literae a celeberrimis pastoribus & professoribus ecclesiae & academiae Genevensis ad Universitatem Oxoniensem transmissae; una cum responso ejusdem Universitatis Oxon. ad easdem literas, in frequenti Convocatione omnium doct. magist. regentium & non regentium lecto & approbato, Feb. 5. 1706. Oxonii, e Th. Sh., An. Dom. MDCCVII.

Fol. Imp. 26 Mar. 1707. Bodl. V 1. 1 Jur.

1st A/cs. p. 270, 900. Hearne, ii, pp. 5, 402–5.

12*. OXFORD, UNIVERSITY. A letter from the most renowned pastors and professors of the Church and University of Geneva to the University of Oxford; together with the answer of the University of Oxford to the same letter. Read and approved in a full Convocation, Febr. 5th. 1706/7. Translated into English from the Latine originals. [At the end:] Printed at the Theatre in Oxford, Anno Dom. 1707.

Fol. Imp. 16 May 1707. Bodl. 4° Δ 260(6).

1st A/cs. p. 270, 450.

13. SEPTUAGINT. [Half-title, Greek:] Vetus Testamentum juxta Septuaginta Interpretes.
[Title-page:] Septuaginta Interpretum tomus 1. continens Octoteuchum; quem ex antiquissimo MS. Codice Alexandrino accurate descriptum, et ope aliorum exemplarium, ac priscorum scriptorum, praesertim vero Hexaplaris editionis Origenianae, emendatum atque suppletum, additis saepe asteriscorum et obelorum signis, summa cura edidit Joannes Ernestus Grabe, S.T.P. Oxonii, e Th. Sh. Prostant venales apud Richardum Smith, bibliopolam, in Cambio Exoniensi. Anno Christi MDCCVII.

Fol. Imp. 31 Aug. 1706. Bodl. P 3. 12 Th.

Includes Praefatio paraenetica in LXX by J[ohn] P[earson]. The work is in four volumes, of which the last was published in 1709, the second in 1719, and the third in 1720.

14. SEPTUAGINT. [Title and imprint as above.]
8vo. Imp. as above. Bodl. 8° Godw. 703–4.

15. THEODOSIUS OF TRIPOLI. [Title in Greek.] Theodosii Sphaericorum libri tres. Oxoniae, e Th. Sh., impensis H. Clements bibliopolae Oxon. MDCCVII.

8vo in fours. Imp. 28 Mar. 1707. B.M. 51.1.5.

Edited by Thomas Hunt.

16. WARDAPIET, THOMAS. Reverendissimi in Christo patris Thomae archiepiscopi Sanctae Crucis in Gocthan Perso-Armeniae, Peregrinationis suae in Europam,

pietatis & literarum promovendarum causa susceptae, brevis narratio. una cum dicti archiepiscopi ad serenissimam Magnae Britanniae Reginam oratiuncula, ejusque responso. Accedunt de eodem archiepiscopo testimonia ampla et praeclara. Oxonii, e Th. Sh., MDCCVII.

Fol. Imp. 27 May 1707. Bodl. 4° Δ 260(26).

17. WELLS, EDWARD. The invalidity of Presbyterian Orders proved from the Presbyterians' own doctrine of the Twofold Order [etc.]. Oxford, printed at the Theater for Jo. Stephens, and are to be sold by James Knapton at the Crown in St. Paul's Church-Yard, London. 1707.

8vo. Bodl. 1212 f. 4.

1708

1. BISSE, THOMAS. A defence of episcopacy. A sermon preach'd before the University of Oxford, at St. Mary's on Trinity-Sunday 1708. By Thomas Bisse [etc.]. Oxford, printed at the Theater for Jo. Stephens, and are to be sold by James Knapton at the Crown in St. Paul's Church-Yard, London. 1708.

4to. Imp. 23 June 1708. Bodl. G. Pamph. 38(1).
T.C. III, 608.

2. DOWNES, HENRY. The necessity and usefulness of laws and the excellency of our own. A sermon preach'd at Northampton before Mr. Justice Powell and Mr. Baron Lovel at the assizes held there July the 13th 1708. By Henry Downes [etc.]. Oxford, printed at the Theater for Anth. Peisley, and are to be sold by Dan. Midwinter at the Three Crowns in St. Paul's Churchyard, London, 1708.

4to. Imp. 30 July 1708. Bodl. 4° W 55(5) Th.
1st A/cs. p. 263, dues, 'A sermon for Mr. Piesly'. *T.C.* III, 609.

3. IGNATIUS AND POLYCARP. Sancti Martyris Ignatii Antiochensis episcopi epistolae septem genuinae, quas nimirum collegit S. Polycarpus suaeque ad Philippenses epistolae subjecit. Oxonii, e Th. Sh., An. Dom. MDCCVIII.

8vo in fours. Imp. 16 Dec. 1708. Bodl. 8° L 135 Jur.
1st A/cs. p. 278, dues. Hearne, ii, pp. 24, 247. A copy belonging to the Printer to the University has an owner's name, Henr. Turner, and in the same hand a note: 'A Newyears Gift of Dn. Aldrich c/sᵈ[?] published by his Nephew Charles Aldrich, a Student in my time & the Executor of his uncle'.

4. LIVY. T. Livii Patavini Historiarum ab Urbe condita libri qui supersunt. MSS. codicum collatione recogniti, annotationibusque illustrati. Oxonii, e Th. Sh., MDCCVIII.

8vo. Bodl. Mus. Bibl. II 7–12.
Edited by Thomas Hearne. Hearne, i, pp. 199–200.

5. LUPTON, WILLIAM. The eternity of future punishment proved and vindicated. in a sermon preach'd before the University of Oxford, at St. Mary's, Novemb. 24th. 1706. By Will. Lupton [etc.]. Oxford, printed at the Theatre for John Wilmot, and are to be sold by James Knapton at the Crown in St. Paul's Church-Yard, London. 1708.

4to. Imp. 13 July 1708. Bodl. 4° B 105 Th.
1st A/cs. p. 277, dues.

6. — [The same in 8vo, but without imprimatur.]
   Bodl. G. Pamph. 998(18).

7. NEPOS, CORNELIUS. Corn. Nepotis excellentium imperatorum vitae. Editio
novissima; nunc denuo recognita. Accessit Aristomenis Messenii vita, ex Pausania.
Oxoniae, e Th. Sh., An. Dom. MDCCVIII. impensis Ant. Peisley bibliopol. Oxon.
   8vo in fours. Imp. 26 Dec. 1696. B.M. 609.f.2.
   The previous edition was of 1697.

8*. OXFORD, CITY. An order by the Vice-Chancellor in Quarter Sessions of the
Justices to constables to enforce the laws against begging and vagrancy. Dated
22 Jan. 1707/8.
   Broadside. Bodl. G.A. Oxon. b. 19(24).
   1st A/cs. p. 270.

9*. OXFORD, UNIVERSITY. Anno Domini MDCCVIII. Augusti die 6. in Theatro
Sheldoniano apud Oxonienses sub prelo sunt libri sequentes.
   Fol. s. sh. Bodl. Ashm. 1818, fol. 77.
   1st A/cs. p. 268 (1706–8), 'For altering the Catal. of Books . . . Working the same
at Press 5 several times . . .'; p. 270 (1706–8) 'Altering the Catal. of Books in the
Press . . . Working the same at Press 9 several times . . .'

10*. (Oxford, University. An edition of extracts from the University's statutes
for the use of undergraduates was printed this year. No copy has been found.
   1st A/cs. p. 270, 'Compos'd the Statutes (somewhat added)', 500.)

11*. OXFORD, UNIVERSITY. Exequiae celsissimo principi, Georgio Principi Daniae
ab Oxoniensi Academia solutae. Oxonii, e Th. Sh. An. Dom. MDCCVIII.
   Fol. Bodl. Pamph. 277(14).
   2nd A/cs. fol. 4, 200 + 100 LP.

12. SOPHOCLES. Sophoclis tragoediae, Antigone & Trachiniae, nova versione
donatae scholiisque veteribus illustratae. Accedunt notae perpetuae, & variae
lectiones. Opera Thomae Johnson A.M. Oxoniae, e Th. Sh., 1708.
   8vo in fours. Imp. 14 Apr. 1708. Bodl. 8° B 45 Jur.

13. STEPHENS, HENRY. A sermon preach'd before the University of Oxford at
St. Mary's on Thursday the 19th of August, 1708. being the day of Thanksgiving,
for our deliverance from the late invasion, and for the victory obtain'd near
Audenard. By Henry Stephens [etc.]. Oxford, printed at the Theater, for Jo.
Stephens bookseller, and are to be sold by James Knapton bookseller, at the Crown
in St. Paul's Church-Yard, London. MDCCVIII.
   4to. Imp. 30 Aug. 1708. Bodl. 4° W 55(12) Th.
   1st A/cs. p. 277, dues. T.C. III, 609.

14. [THWAITES, EDWARD.] Notae in Anglo-Saxonum nummos. Oxoniae, anno
Domini, MDCCVIII.
   Part of Linguarum vett. septentrionalium thesauri grammatico-critici, &
archaeologici, auctore Georgio Hickesio, conspectus brevis per Gul. Wottonum,
S.T.B. [etc.]. Londini, typis Gul. Bowyer [etc.]. MDCCVIII.
   8vo. Bodl. 8° Rawl. 180.
   T.C. III, 594. The 'Notae' were printed at the Theatre: Hearne, ii, p. 78.

15. WELLS, EDWARD. Dr. Wells's Theses against the validity of Presbyterian ordination proved to hold good [etc.]. Numb. II. Third edition. Printed at the Theater for Jo. Stephens, and are to be sold by James Knapton at the Crown in St. Paul's Church-Yard, London. 1708.

8vo. Imp. 10 Apr. 1708. Bodl. 1212 f. 5(3).
Previous editions were printed by Leonard Lichfield at Oxford.

16. [WELLS, EDWARD.] Epistola ad authorem anonymum libelli non ita pridem editi: cui titulus, Stricturae breves in Epistolas D.D. Genevensium & Oxoniensium. Oxonii, e Th. Sh. Prostat apud Joan. Stephens bibliop. Oxoniensem, & Jac. Knapton bibliop. Londinensem ad insigne Coronae in Coemeterio D. Pauli. Anno Christi MDCVIII [*sic*].

4to. Imp. 19 May 1708. Bodl. EE 8(4) Th.
T.C. III, 594.

17. WHALEY, NATHANIEL. A preparatory discourse of death; in two parts. I. Of good mens willingness to die, with the reasons and motives conducing to it. II. Of the happiness of an early preparation for death: and of the means of over-coming the slavish and anxious fears of it. With an appendix. By Nathaniel Whaley [etc.]. Oxford, printed at the Theater for Jo. Stephens, and are to be sold by James Knapton at the Crown in St. Paul's Church Yard, London. 1708.

8vo. Imp. 22 Apr. 1708. Bodl. 8° K 42 Th.
T.C. III, 590.

1709

1. [ALDRICH, HENRY.] Institutionis geometricae pars prima. Impressa sed non edita A.D. 1709. Secundas enim cogitationes expectat. [No imprint.]

8vo in fours. Bodl. Vet. A 4 e. 1601. Hearne, iii, p. 363.

2. DIONYSIUS PERIEGETES. Τῆς πάλαι καὶ τῆς νῦν οικουμενης περιηγησις sive Dionysii Geographia emendata & locupletata, additione scil. geographiae hodiernae Graeco carmine pariter donatae: cum 16 tabulis geographicis. Ab Edv. Wells [etc.]. Editio secunda. Oxonii, e Th. Sh., A.D. MDCCIX. impensis A. & J. Churchill, ad insigne nigri Cygni, in Pater-Noster Roe, Lond.

8vo Imp. 30 Nov. 1703. Bodl. Vet. A 4 e. 724.
2nd A/cs. fol. 7ᵛ, dues. The first edition is of 1704.

3. EPHREM SYRUS. Τα του οσιου πατρος Εφραιμ του Συρου προς την Ελλαδα μεταβληθεντα. S. Ephraim Syrus, Graece, e codicibus manuscriptis Bodleianis. Ἐτυπώθη ἐν ᾿Οξονιᾳ, ἐν τῷ ἔτει αψθ'.

Fol. Imp. 14 Sept. 1709. Bodl. V 4 13 Th.
2nd A/cs. fol. 23ᵛ, dues.
Edited by Edward Thwaites. Reissued with a preface dated 1714.

4. GRABE, JOHANN ERNST. Septuaginta Interpretum tomus ultimus, continens Psalmorum, Jobi, ac tres Salomonis libros, cum apocrypha ejusdem, nec non Siracidae Sapientia; quos ex antiquissimo MS. Codice Alexandrino accurate de-scriptos, et ope aliorum exemplarium ac priscorum scriptorum, praesertim vero Hexaplaris editionis Origenianae, emendatos atque suppletos, additis saepissime

asteriscorum & obelorum signis, summa cum cura edidit Joannes Ernestus Grabe S.T.P. E Th. Sh.; sumptibus Henrici Clementis, bibliopolae ad insigne Lunae Falcatae in Coemeterio S. Pauli, Londini, Anno Christi MDCCIX.

Fol. B.M. 466.i.4. Bodl. MS. Grabe 53, fol. 79, presswork (12 Feb. 1708/9) folio and 8vo.

4a. Brasenose Coll. has the 8vo edition (Yarb. B 93/7).

5*. IGNATIUS. S. Ignatii epistolae genuinae juxta exemplar Mediceum denuo recensitae, una cum veteri Latina versione: annotationibus D. Joannis Pearsoni nuper episcopi Cestrensis, et Thomae Smithi S.T.P. illustratae. Accedunt Acta genuina martyrii S. Ignatii, epistola S. Polycarpi ad Philippenses, et Smyrnensis ecclesiae epistola de S. Polycarpi martyrio; cum veteribus Latinis versionibus, & annotationibus Thomae Smithi. Oxonii, e Th. Sh., Anno MDCCIX.

4to. Imp. 10 Dec. 1708. Bodl. D 5. 8 Linc.

2nd A/cs. fol. 5ᵛ, 100 LP, 650 small, prices 3s. 6d. and 2s. 3d. Hearne, ii, pp. 431–2.

6*. LELAND, JOHN. Commentarii de scriptoribus Britannicis, auctore Joanne Lelando Londinate. Ex autographo Lelandino nunc primus edidit Antonius Hall [etc.]. Tomus primus. Oxonii, e Th. Sh., MDCCIX.

8vo. Imp. 11 Dec. 1708. Vol. ii is dated in the same year. Bodl. 8° Y 23 Jur.

2nd A/cs. fol. 6, 56 LP, 500 small, prices 5s. 9d. and 3s. 9d.

7*. LILY, WILLIAM. A short introduction of grammar generally to be used; compiled and set forth for the bringing up of all those that intend to attain to the knowledge of the Latin tongue. To which are added usefull observations by way of comment out of anciant and late grammarians. Oxford, at the Theater. 1709. (The volume also contains Brevissima institutio grammatices.)

8vo. Bodl. 3058 e. 31.

2nd A/cs. fol. 7, 2,000, 12d.

8*. MARSHALL, THOMAS. The Catechism set forth in the Book of Common Prayer briefly explained [etc., as in 1692].

8vo. Lincoln Coll. Gall. 22.14(4).

2nd A/cs. fol. 7, 3,000, price 12d.

9*. OXFORD, UNIVERSITY. Encyclopaedia, seu orbis literarum prout in florentissima jam et omnium plane celeberrima Academia Oxoniensi, singulis terminis, publice in Scholis Auditoribus proponuntur . . .

Broadside. Imp. 28 May 1709. Bodl. Gough Maps 57.

10*. (Oxford, University. List of books 'sub prelo' in the Sheldonian Theatre. Madan 1709:13. No copy traced.

2nd A/cs. fol. 9, 'Printing and altering the Catall: 3 times'.)

11. PALLADIO, ANDREA. Antichita di Roma di M. Andrea Palladio racolta brevemente da gli authori antichi & moderni. Aggiuntovi un discorso sopra li fuochi de gli antichi. In Ossonio, nello Teatro Seldoniano, A.D. MDCCIX.

Antiquitates urbis Romae ab Andrea Palladio ex veterum et recentiorum authorum scriptis breviter collectae. Quibus adjicitur tractatus de veterum focis. Oxonii, e Th. Sh., A.D. MDCCIX.

8vo in fours. Imp. 17 Dec. 1709. Bodl. 8° H 45 Linc.

This copy is inscribed 'D.D. Vir clarissimus optimusque D. Henricus Aldrich Aedis Christi Decanus'.

12. (Parsons, Robert. Visitation articles, Archdeaconry of Gloucester.
Madan 1709:15. No copy traced.)

13. SPELMAN, JOHN. The life of Ælfred the Great, by Sir John Spelman Kt. from the original manuscript in the Bodlejan Library: with considerable additions, and several historical remarks, by the publisher Thomas Hearne, M.A. Oxford, printed at the Theater for Maurice Atkins at the Golden-Ball in St Paul's Church-Yard, Lond. MDCCIX.
8vo. Imp. 5 Mar. 1709. Bodl. Mus. Bibl. II 14.
2nd A/cs. fol. 7ᵛ, dues.

14. [WELLS, EDWARD.] A specimen of an help for the more easy and clear understanding of the Holy Scriptures: being St. Paul's two Epistles to the Thessalonians, and his Epistle to the Galatians, explain'd after the following manner, viz. 1. The original or Greek text . . . 2. The common English translation render'd more Agreeable to the original. 3. A paraphrase . . . 4. Short annotations. Oxford, printed at the Theater, for J. Stephens, and are to be sold by James Knapton at the Crown in St. Paul's Church-Yard.
4to. Imp. 15 Sept. 1508. Bodl. FF 25ᵇ(2) Th.
2nd A/cs. fol. 7ᵛ, 40 copies as dues.

1710

1*. APOLLONIUS OF PERGA. Apollonii Pergaei Conicorum libri octo et Sereni Antissensis De sectione cylindri & coni libri duo. Oxoniae, e Th. Sh., An. Dom. MDCCX.
[2nd title-page, after Greek title] Apollonii Pergaei Conicorum libri iv priores cum Pappi Alexandrini lemmatis et Eutocii Ascalonitae commentariis. Ex codd. MSS. Graecis edidit Edmundus Halleius [etc.].
Fol. Imp. 9 Feb. 1709[10]. Bodl. R 4. 11 Jur.
2nd A/cs. fol. 8, 400, price £1.

2. BEVERIDGE, WILLIAM. An exposition of the xxxix Articles of the Church of England. Article the first. By the Right Reverend Father in God Will. Beveridge D.D. late Lord Bishop of St. Asaph. Printed from his original manuscripts. Advertisement. Since it hath by some been questioned, whether the Right Reverend author of this exposition did design it should be published or not, and whether the publication of it would be for his honour and for the common good, therefore this exposition of the first Article is here printed singly and by way of specimen, that the learned may from hence be able to form a judgment of the whole work; and that the remaining part may be either speedily publish'd or totally suppress'd, according as the publication or suppression of it shall be thought most for the honour of the author, and for the benefit of the publick. Oxford, printed at the Theater, and are to be sold by R. Smith at his ware-house in Exeter Change in the Strand: London 1710.
Fol. Imp. 14 Oct. 1709. Bodl. 1365 c. 2.
Subsequent parts of the work were printed elsewhere. Hearne, ii, pp. 241, 248.

3. CONEY, THOMAS. Honesty and plain-dealing an usual bar to honour and preferment. A sermon preach'd at St Mary's before the University of Oxford, upon Act-Sunday July ix. 1710. By Thomas Coney [etc.]. Publish'd at the request of

Mr. Vice-Chancellor. Oxford, printed at the Theater, for Anth. Peisley; and are to be sold by Jam. Knapton, Hen. Clements, and J. Morphew, booksellers in London. 1710.

8vo in fours. Imp. 10 July 1710. B.M. 693.d.1(9).

4. — 3rd edition (Oxford, at the Theater, 1710). Bodl. Bliss B 145(1).

5. DIONYSIUS PERIEGETES. Dionysii Orbis descriptio; cum commentariis Eustathii, archiepiscopi Thessalonicensis. Oxonii, e Th. Sh. MDCCX.

8vo in fours. Bodl. Bliss B 146.

2nd A/cs. fol. 24ᵛ, dues paid by John Hudson.

6. (Gagnier, John. A sheet of Hebrew paradigms.

Madan 1710:31. No copy traced.)

7. GRABE, JOHANN ERNST. Dissertatio de variis vitiis LXX Interpretum versioni ante B. Origenis aevum illatis, et remediis ab ipso in Hexaplari ejusdem versionis editione adhibitis, deque hujus editionis reliquiis tam manu scriptis quam praelo excusis, auctore Joanne Ernesto Grabe [etc.]. Oxonii, e Th. Sh. sumptibus Henrici Clementis, bibliopolae ad insigne Lunae Falcatae in Coemeterio S. Pauli, Anno Christi MDCCX.

4to Bodl. Mar. 593.

Some accounts are in Bodl. MS. Grabe 53, Nos. 102, 103, 128.

8*. INETT, JOHN. Origines Anglicanae; or, a History of the English Church. Volume the second. Containing an account of the affairs of the Church from the Norman Revolution till the death of King John, and more especially of the rise and steps of the Papal usurpation, with the effects and consequences thereof, as well to the monarchy and nation as to the Church. By John Inett [etc.]. Oxford, printed at the Theater, in the year MDCCX.

Fol. Imp. 22 June 1710. Bodl. L 3. 8 Th.

D.O. 9 Aug. 1710. Hearne, ii, p. 269. MS. Ballard xv, 47. 2nd A/cs. fol. 14, 50 LP, 500 small, prices 12s. and 9s.

9. LELAND, JOHN. The Itinerary of John Leland the Antiquary. Vol. the first. Publish'd from the original MS. in the Bodleian Library by Thomas Hearne M.A. To which is prefix'd Mr. Leland's New Year's Gift: and at the end is subjoyn'd a Discourse concerning some antiquities latterly found in York-shire. Oxford, printed at the Theater for the Publisher. MDCCX.

8vo in fours. Bodl. Mus. Bibl. II 15.

2nd A/cs. fol. 30ᵛ, dues for two parts of Leland's Collectanea.

10. LEWIS, HUGH. The methods, unreasonableness, and danger of sinners enticing others to sin. A sermon preach'd before the University of Oxford at St Mary's on Sunday morning july ix. 1710. being Act-Sunday. By H. Lewis [etc.]. Publish'd at the request of Mr Vice-Chancellor. Oxford, printed at the Theater, for Edw. Whistler; and are to be sold by Rich. Wilkin at the King's Head in St Paul's Church-Yard, and Rob. Gosling at the Mitre near the Inner Temple Gate in Fleetstreet, booksellers in London.

8vo in fours. Imp. 10 July 1710. Bodl. G. Pamph. 1036(4).

11. — 2nd edition (Oxford, at the Theater, 1710) Bodl. 8° I 99 Th.

12. LONGINUS. Διονυσιου Λογγινου περι υψους βιβλιον. Dionysii Longini De sublimitate libellus, cum praefatione de vita & scriptis Longini, notis, indicibus, & variis lectionibus. Oxoniae, e Th. Sh., anno MDCCX. Prostat apud Joan. Wilmot

bibliopolam Oxon. qui distrahit etiam exemplaria Dionysii Periegetae cum Eustathii commentariis.

8vo in fours. Bodl. 8° W 34 Art.

2nd A/cs. fol. 24ᵛ, dues paid by John Hudson.

13*. OXFORD, UNIVERSITY. Parecbolae sive excerpta e corpore statutorum Universitatis [etc., as in 1693].

8vo in fours. Bodl. Ashm. A 40.

2nd A/cs. fol. 15, 3,000, price 15d.

14. TILLY, WILLIAM. The sins and vices of men's lives, the chief cause of their ignorance, and corrupt opinions in religion. A sermon preach'd before the University of Oxford at St. Mary's on Sunday december the 11th. 1709. By William Tilly [etc.]. London, printed for Anthony Peisley bookseller in Oxford, and are to be sold by J. Knapton and H. Clements booksellers in St. Paul's Church-yard London, 1710.

4to. Bodl. G. Pamph. 38(7).

Hearne, iv, p. 164. Arthur Charlett, as Pro-Vice-Chancellor, 'suppressed' the book when it was first issued with an Oxford imprint. It evidently was printed, as Hearne said, 'at the Theatre'.

15*. TRIGLANDUS, THEODORUS. Theodori Triglandii j.u.d. & professoris Paedia juris, sive examen Institutionum nova arte & methodo concinnatum, ita ut locis difficilioribus vice commentarii inservire possit. Continuato indice titulorum adjecto. Accedunt huic editioni index titulorum alphabeticus & catalogus Vett. JCC ordine chronologico. Oxoniae, e Th. Sh., MDCCX.

12mo. Imp. 5 Sept. 1710. Bodl. 8° V 44 Jur.

2nd A/cs. fol. 17, 750, price 16d. (Edited by Anthony Hall.)

16. WHALEY, NATHANIEL. The gradation of sin both in principles and practice. A sermon preach'd before the University of Oxford at St Mary's on the xxxth of January 1709/10. Wherein one of Mr Hoadly's arguments against the doctrine of non-resistance of the supreme power is occasionally considered. By Nathaniel Whaley [etc.]. Oxford, printed at the Theater for Anth. Peisley: and are to be sold by Jam. Knapton, Hen. Clements, and J. Morphew, booksellers in London, 1710. Price 2d.

8vo in fours. Imp. 22 Feb. 1709/10. Bodl. 8° K 103 Linc.

17. (— 2nd edition (1710): Madan 1710:18. No copy traced.)

18. WHEATLY, CHARLES. The Church of England man's companion; or a rational illustration of the harmony, excellency, and usefulness of the Book of Common Prayer &c. Wherein all the rubricks, prayers, rites and ceremonies &c. are explain'd, vindicated, and compar'd with the ancient liturgies and practices of the primitive Church [&c.]. Oxford, printed at the Theater for Anth. Peisley, and are to be sold by J. Knapton, H. Clements and J. Morphew, booksellers in London. 1710.

8vo. Imp. 20 June 1710. Bodl. 8° L 145 Th.

1711

1. BATTELY, JOHN. Antiquitates Rutupinae. authore Joanne Battely, S.T.P. archidiacono Cantuarensi. Opus posthumum. Oxoniae, e Th. Sh., A.D. MDCCXI.

8vo. Bodl. 8° K 30 Art.

2. BISSE, THOMAS. Jehoshaphat's charge. A sermon preach'd at the assizes held at Oxford July 12. 1711. by the Right Honourable Mr. Justice Powell and Mr. Baron Dormer. By T. Bisse [etc.]. Publish'd at the request of the High-Sheriff and Grand Jury. Oxford, printed at the Theatre for Henry Clements, and are to be sold by Hen. Clements bookseller at the Half Moon in St. Paul's Church yard London, 1711. Price 3*d*.

    8vo in fours. Bodl. Vet. A 4 e. 1382(5).

3. EDWARDS, JONATHAN. The doctrine of original sin as it was always held in the Catholick Church, and particularly in the Church of England, asserted and vindicated from the exceptions and cavils of the Reverend Dr. Daniel Whitby. By Jonathan Edwards [etc.]. Oxford, printed at the Theater, for Hen. Clements, and are to be sold by Henry Clements, bookseller at the Half Moon in St. Paul's Church-yard London. MDCCXI.

    8vo. Bodl. 8° K 98 Linc.

4. GRABE, JOHANN ERNST. An essay on two Arabick manuscripts of the Bodlejan Library, and that ancient book, call'd the Doctrine of the Apostles, which is said to be extant in them; wherein Mr Whiston's mistakes about both are plainly prov'd by John Ernest Grabe, D.D. Oxford, printed at the Theater for Henry Clements, bookseller at the Half-Moon in St Paul's Church Yard London. 1711.

    8vo in fours. Bodl. G. Pamph. 946(1).

5. HOWELL, WILLIAM. The doctrine of the Trinity prov'd from Scripture. A sermon preach'd to the University of Oxford, at St. Mary's, on Sunday, May 13. 1711. By the author of the collection entituled The Common-Prayer-Book the Best Companion, &c. Oxford, printed at the Theatre for Anth. Peisley, and are to be sold by James Knapton, Hen. Clements and J. Morphew booksellers in London. 1711. Price 3*d*.

    8vo in fours. Bodl. 8° I 99(11) Th.

6. LELAND, JOHN. The Itinerary of John Leland the Antiquary. Vol. the second . . . To which is prefix'd Mr Leland's Naenia upon the death of Sir Thomas Wyat, and at the end are annex'd (1) An account of several antiquities in and about the University of Oxford (2) A Latin oration spoken before King Henry VII at Cambridge (3) Dr. Plot's account of an intended journey through England and Wales. Oxford, printed at the Theater for the Publisher. MDCCXI.

— Vol. the third . . . To which is added Antoninus's Itinerary through Britain, with various readings and Dr. Robert Talbot's annotations on it.

— Vol. the fourth, in two parts. The first part publish'd from the original, the second from Mr. Burton's transcript in the Bodleian Library. By Thomas Hearne M.A. With an appendix and an account of some antiquities found in York-shire.

— Vol. the fifth . . . To which is prefix'd Mr. W. Vallants's account of several parts of Hartford-shire: and at the end is subjoyn'd a letter concerning some antiquities between Windsor and Oxford.

— Vol. the sixth . . . To which are annex'd a letter to the Publisher containing an account of some observations relating to the antiquities and natural history of England; and an essay towards the recovery of the courses of the four great Roman ways.

— Vol. the seventh, in two parts. The first part publish'd from the original in the Bodleian Library, the second from Mr. Stone's transcript in the library of Robert

Davies of Lhannerch in Denbigh-shire Esquire . . . To which is subjoyn'd an appendix; and at the beginning is prefix'd a letter from the Reverend Dr. White Kennett, Dean of Peterborough, to the Publisher concerning a passage in the preface to the IVth. Volume, with the Publisher's answer, and a discourse concerning the Saxon word Æstel.

8vo in fours. Bodl. Mus. Bibl. II 15.
The first volume was issued in 1710, the last in 1712.

7. LUPTON, WILLIAM. The resurrection of the same body. A sermon preach'd before the University of Oxford at St Mary's, on Easter Monday, Apr. 2. 1711. By Will. Lupton [etc.]. Oxford, printed at the Theatre for John Wilmot, and are to be sold by James Knapton and J. Morphew, booksellers in London.

8vo in fours. Bodl. G. Pamph. 999(31).

8*. OXFORD, UNIVERSITY. [List of books 'sub prelo' at the Sheldonian Theatre.] Two issues.

B.M. Cup. 645.e.5(5).
2nd A/cs. fol. 22.

9*. OXFORD, UNIVERSITY. Prohibition by the Vice-Chancellor to disperse or own Medley No. 41 and other libellous pamphlets. Dated 27 July 1711.

Broadside. Bodl. G. Pamph. 1686(13).
2nd A/cs. fol. 22, 'Composeing and Printing a Programma'.

10. PLATO, XENOPHON, PLUTARCH, LUCIAN. Πλατωνος και Ξενοφωντος Συμποσια. Πλουταρχου Συμποσιον επτα σοφων. Λουκιανου Συμποσιον η Λαπιθαι. Εκ Θεατρου εν Οξονια, ετει αψια.

8vo in fours. Bodl. 8° F 43 Jur.

11. ROGERS, FRANCIS. Orationes ex poetis Latinis excerptae. Argumenta singulis praefixa sunt, quae causam cujusque & summam rei gestae occasione explicant. Vol. I. Oxoniae, e Th. Sh., MDCCXI.

8vo. Bodl. Crynes 917.

12. [THWAITES, EDWARD.] Grammatica Anglo-Saxonica ex Hickesiano Linguarum Septentrionalium Thesauro excerpta. Oxoniae, e Th. Sh. A.D. MDCCXI.

8vo in fours. Bodl. 8° G 175 Art.
Attributed to Thwaites by Elizabeth Elstob in the preface to her *Rudiments of Grammar for the English-Saxon Tongue* (1715).

13. TRAPP, JOSEPH. Praelectiones poeticae in Schola Naturalis Philosophiae Oxon. habitae. Authore Josepho Trapp [etc.] Praelectore Publico. Lecturae poeticae; a viro insignissimo D. Henrico Birkhead . . . fundatae. Volumen primum. Oxonii, e Th. Sh., impensis Bernardi Lintott, bibliopolae Londinensis, MDCCXI.

8vo. Bodl. 8° G 177 8 Art.
Entered in Stationers' Reg. by Bernard Lintot, 27 Jan. 1710/11. Volumes 2 and 3 were printed in London.

14. VELLEIUS PATERCULUS. M. Velleii Paterculi quae supersunt: cum variis lectionibus optimarum editionum; doctorum virorum conjecturis et castigationibus et indice locupletissimo. Accedit annotationum libellus. Oxoniae, e Th. Sh., Ann. Dom. MDCCXI. Prostant apud Joan. Wilmot bibliopolam Oxon qui distrahit etiam exemplaria Longini et Dionysii Periegetae cum Eustathii commentariis.

8vo. Bodl. 8° S 205 Art.
2nd A/cs. fol. 24ᵛ, dues paid by John Hudson.

15. WELLS, EDWARD. An help for the more easy and clear understanding of the Holy Scriptures: being St Paul's Epistle to the Romans, explain'd after the following method [etc., as in the Specimen, 1709]. By Ed. Wells [etc.]. Oxford, printed at the Theater, for James Knapton at the Crown in S. Paul's Church-Yard, London, 1711.
4to. Bodl. FF 25 b(1) Th.
2nd A/cs. fols. 7ᵛ, 30ᵛ, 40 copies accepted as dues.

16. [WELLS, EDWARD.] A second part of an help to the more easy and clear understanding of the Holy Scriptures: being St Paul's Epistle to the Romans, explain'd [etc.]. Oxford, printed at the Theater for James Knapton at the Crown in S. Paul's Church-Yard, London, 1711.
4to. Imp. 15 Aug. 1711. Bodl. FF 25 b(2) Th.

1712

1. BISSE, THOMAS. A sermon preach'd before the University of Oxford on Whitsunday 1712. By Thomas Bisse [etc.]. Publish'd at the request of the Vice-Chancellor and many others. Oxford, printed at the Theater for Henry Clements, and are to be sold by H. Clements bookseller, at the Half Moon in St. Pauls Church-yard London. 1712.
8vo in fours. Bodl. 8° I 99(6) Th.

2. CLARENDON, EDWARD HYDE, EARL OF. The History of the Rebellion [etc.]. Volume I. Part I. Oxford, printed at the Theater, An. Dom. MDCCXII.
8vo. Imp. 29 Apr. 1702. Printer to the University.
The three volumes, in six parts bound separately, are all dated 1712. D.O. 20 Apr. 1711: Mr. Baskett's proposal for printing the Lord Clarendon in octavo accepted.
2nd A/cs. fol. 30ᵛ, dues.

3. DORRINGTON, THEOPHILUS. The worship of God recommended, in a sermon preach'd before the University of Oxford at St Mary's April 8th. 1711 with an epistle in defence of the Universities. By Theophilus Dorrington [etc.]. Oxford, printed at the Theatre for Edward Whistler, and are to be sold by Hen. Clements at the Half Moon, and Rich. Wilkin at the King's Head, booksellers in St Paul's Church yard, London, 1712. Price 3d.
8vo in fours. Bodl. 8° I 99(14) Th.

4. DUPORTE, JAMES. Δαβιδης εμμετρος, sive Metaphrasis Libri Psalmorum Graecis versibus contexta. Per Jacobum Duportum [etc.]. In usum scholarum. Oxonii, e Th. Sh. impensis Jonae Bowyer ad insigne Rosae juxta porticum occidentalem S. Pauli Londini. 1712.
12mo in sixes. Bodl. Ps. Gr. 1712 f. 1.

5. HOWELL, WILLIAM. Peace and unity recommended. A sermon preach'd before the University of Oxford at St Mary's on Sunday, Aug. 17th. 1712. By the author of a collection intitled, The Common Prayer Book the Best Companion. &c. Oxford, printed at the Theatre, for Anthony Peisley: and are to be sold by J. Knapton, H. Clements, and J. Morphew, booksellers in London, 1712. Price threepence.
8vo in fours. Imp. 19 Aug. 1712. Bodl. 8° I 99(12) Th.

6. [HUDSON, JOHN.] Geographiae veteris scriptores Graeci minores. Accedunt geographica Arabica &c. Vol. III. Oxoniae, e Th. Sh., MDCCXII.
8vo in fours. Bodl. 8° S 203 Art.

7. — Geographiae veteris scriptores Graeci minores. Cum dissertatione in Dionysium, annotationibus &c. Vol. IV. Oxoniae, e Th. Sh., MDCCXII.
8vo in fours. Bodl. 8° S 204 Art.
2nd A/cs. fol. 24ᵛ, dues. The previous volumes were issued in 1698 and 1700.

8. HUMFREYS, THOMAS. The divine authority of the New Testament prov'd and vindicated, in a sermon preach'd before the University of Oxford at St Mary's, Septemb. 30th. 1711. By T. Humfreys [etc.]. Oxford, printed at the Theatre, for Anthony Peisley: and are to be sold by J. Knapton, H. Clements, and J. Morphew, booksellers in London, 1711. Price threepence.
8vo in fours. Bodl. 8° I 99(13) Th.

9. IBBETSON, RICHARD. The divinity of our blessed Saviour prov'd from Scripture and antiquity. A sermon preach'd before the University of Oxford at St. Mary's, on the Epiphany, Jan. 6th. 1711/12. In which Mr Whiston's attempt to revive the Arian heresy is considered. By Richard Ibbetson [etc.]. Oxford, printed at the Theater for Anthony Peisley: and are to be sold by J. Knapton, H. Clements, and J. Morphew, booksellers in London, 1712. Price sixpence.
8vo in fours. Bodl. 8° I 99(10) Th.

10. — 2nd edition, 1712. Bodl. G. Pamph. 23(3).

11. LELAND, JOHN. The Itinerary of John Leland the Antiquary. Vol. the eighth, in two parts. The first part published from the original in the Bodleian Library, the second from Mr. Stone's transcript in the library of Robert Davies of Lhannerch in Denbigh-shire Esquire. By Thomas Hearne, M.A. To which are prefix'd a Discourse concerning the Stunsfield tesselated pavement, and an Account of the custom of the mannor of Woodstock; and at the end is subjoyn'd a Letter to Sir Christopher Wren Knt. occasion'd by several antiquities lately discovered near Bishops-Gate London, with William Fitz-Stephen's description of that city. Oxford, printed at the Theater for the Publisher, MDCCXII.
8vo in fours. Bodl. Mus. Bibl. II 23.
Previous volumes were issued in 1710 and 1711. 2nd A/cs. fol. 30ᵛ dues for two parts of 'Mr. Hearns Lelands Collections'.

12. LELAND, JOHN. Proposals for printing by subscription, from the original MSS. in the Bodlejan Library, the Collectanea of John Leland the Antiquary by Thomas Hearne [etc.].
Fol. s. sh. B.M. Harl. 5932(13).

13. MARSHALL, BENJAMIN. Tabulae chronologicae continentes tum sacra tum profana maxime notatu digna a creatione mundi, usque ad Christi nativitatem. Quod ad sacra attinet ea nobis suppeditarunt SS. Scripturae & Josephus [etc.]. Hasce tabulas in ordinem redegit, & hic una exhibuit Ben. Marshall [etc.]. Oxonii, e Th. Sh. 1712.

— Tabula II continens res maxime notatu dignas in historia tum sacra, tum profana, ab anno ante aeram vulgarem Domini 1200, usque ad annum ante eandem aeram 500 [etc.]. Oxonii, e Th. Sh. 1712.
Each table consists of two folded broadsides. Bodl. Mason B 221(1).
2nd A/cs. fols. 30, 33ᵛ, dues.

14. MARSHALL, BENJAMIN. Chronological tables in which are contain'd not only all the chief things of sacred history from the creation of the world 'till Christ's time, but also all other the most remarkeable things of those times that are recorded in any of the antient writers now extant [etc.]. All these tables were compiled, and are here represented together by Benjamin Marshall [etc.]. Printed at the Theater in Oxford. 1712.

— Table II. [From 1200 B.C. to 500 B.C. Imprint as above.]
  Each table consists of two folded broadsides. Bodl. Mason B 221(2).
  2nd A/cs. fols. 30ᵛ and 33ᵛ, dues.

15. MILNES, JAMES. Sectionum conicarum elementa nova methodo demonstrata. Authore Jacobo Milnes [etc.]. Editio secunda emendata, plurimisque in locis aucta & illustrata. Oxoniae, e Th. Sh. MDCCXII. Impensis Anth. Peisley, bibliop.
  8vo in fours. Imp. 2 Aug. 1712. Bodl. 8° K 135 Linc.
  2nd A/cs. fol. 23ᵛ, dues. The first edition was of 1702.

16. MOERIS, ATTICIST, AND MARTIN, GREGORY. Μοιριδος Αττικιστου Λεξεις Αττικων και Ελληνων κατα στοιχειον. Εκ Θεατρου ἐν Οξονια. ἐν τῷ ἔτει αψιβ΄.
  [In the same volume:] Gregorius Martinus Ad Adolphum Metkerchum pro veteri et vera Graecarum literarum pronunciatione. E bibliotheca cl. v. Joannis Seldeni. Oxoniae, e Th. Sh., MDCCXII.
  8vo in fours. Bodl. 8° S 206(1) Art. Inscribed 'Ex dono editoris J. H.'
  2nd A/cs. fol. 24ᵛ, dues paid by John Hudson.

17*. OXFORD, UNIVERSITY. A programma about University discipline dated 22 Sept. 1712.
  Broadside. Bodl. G.A. Oxon. b. 19(34).
  2nd A/cs. fol. 24.

18. TALBOT, WILLIAM, BISHOP OF OXFORD. Articles of visitation and enquiry concerning matters ecclesiastical; exhibited to the minister, church-wardens, and side-men of every parish in the Diocese of Oxford, at the triennial visitation of the Right Reverend Father in God William by divine permission Lord Bishop of Oxford. Oxford, printed in the year 1712.
  4to. 4 pp. Lincoln Coll. o.6.29(22).
  Perhaps printed by Leonard Lichfield.

1713

1. ARCHER, EDMUND. A sermon preach'd at the Parish Church of St Martin October the 21st. 1712. at the anniversary meeting of the Mayor, aldermen, and other trustees, for the charity schools of the City of Oxford. By Edmund Archer [etc.]. Oxford, printed at the Theatre for Henry Clements; and are to be sold by H. Clements bookseller, at the Half-moon in St Paul's Church-yard. London. 1713. Price three pence.
  8vo. Imp. 27 Oct. 1712. Bodl. Bliss B 147(11).

2. ATHANASIUS, SAINT. St Athanasius's four orations against the Arians, and his oration against the Gentiles. Translated from the original by Mr Samuel Parker. In two volumes. To which the translator has prefixed observations for the better

application of St Athanasius's reasoning: together with a few queries recommended to Mr Whiston's consideration, and a confutation of his impious doctrines in a table of references from Mr Whiston's Treatises to the orations aforesaid. Oxford, printed at the Theatre for Henry Clements, at the Half-Moon, in St Paul's Church-Yard, London, 1713.

8vo. Bodl. 8° D 106 Th.
2nd A/cs. fol. 30ᵛ, dues.

3. BISSE, THOMAS. A sermon preach'd before the University of Oxford on Act-Sunday July 12. 1713. By Thomas Bisse [etc.]. Publish'd at the request of Mr Vice-Chancellor. Oxford, printed at the Theatre for Henry Clements at the Half Moon in St Paul's Church-yard, London. MDCCXIII.

8vo in fours. Imp. 13 July 1713. Bodl. G. Pamph. 1000(20).

4. COTES, DIGBY. The duty and happiness of delighting in God. A sermon preach'd before the University of Oxford at St Mary's Dec. 27. 1713. by Digby Cotes [etc.]. Publish'd at the request of Mr Vice-Chancellor. Oxford, printed for Stephen Fletcher bookseller: and are to be sold by A. Churchil, J. Knapton, W. Taylor, H. Clements, and J. Morphew booksellers in London. 1713. Price three pence.

8vo in fours. Bodl. 8° C 732(8) Linc.
On typographical grounds attributable to the University's press.

5. CROFT, WILLIAM. Dr. Croft's Exercise perform'd in the Theatre at Oxford, July 10 1713.

Fol. single sheet. Bodl. MS. Ballard xlvii, 103.

6. DINGLEY, WILLIAM. Cathedral service decent and useful. A sermon preach'd before the University of Oxford at St Mary's on Cecilia's Day, 1713. By W. Dingley [etc.]. Publish'd at the request of the lovers of church-music. Oxford, printed for Anthony Peisley: and are to be sold by J. Knapton, H. Clements, and J. Morphew, booksellers in London. MDCCXIII. Price three pence.

8vo in fours. Imp. 7 Dec. 1713. Bodl. 8° S 239(9) Th.
Attributable to the University's press on typographical grounds.

7. DODWELL, HENRY. Henrici Dodwelli De parma equestri Woodwardiana dissertatio. Accedit Thomae Neli Dialogus inter Reginam Elizabetham & Robertum Dudleium, Comitem Leycestriae & Academiae Oxoniensis Cancellarium, in quo de Academiae aedificiis praeclare agitur. Recensuit ediditque Tho. Hearne, A.M. Oxoniensis, qui & Dodwelli operum editorum catalogum praemisit. Oxonii, e Th. Sh., MDCCXIII. impensis editoris.

8vo in fours. Bodl. Mus. Bibl. II 43.
Hearne, iv, pp. 135–8.

8. Author of the Whole DUTY OF MAN. The ladies calling in two parts. By the Author of the Whole Duty of Man &c. The ninth impression. Oxford, printed at the Theater MDCCXIII.

8vo in fours. Bodl. 26520 e. 358.

9. Author of the Whole DUTY OF MAN. The government of the tongue. By the Author of the Whole Duty of Man &c. The sixth impression. Oxford, printed at the Theater 1713.

8vo in fours. Imp. 24 Jan. 1675. Bodl. 1419 e. 20.

10. Author of the Whole DUTY OF MAN. The lively oracles given to us: or the Christian's birth-right and duty, in the custody of the holy Scripture. By the Author of the Whole Duty of Man &c. At the Theater in Oxford, 1713.

8vo in fours. Imp. 10 June 1678. Bodl. 109 e. 11.

11. EYRE, RICHARD. The blessing of peace. A sermon preach'd at the Cathedral Church of Sarum, July 7. 1713. the Day of Thanksgiving for the Peace. By Rich. Eyre [etc.]. Publish'd at the request of the Mayor and Corporation of the city of New Sarum; and of the gentlemen, that heard it. Oxford, printed at the Theater, for Stephen Fletcher, bookseller; and are to be sold by John Morphew near Stationers Hall, London, 1713.

8vo. Imp. 22 July 1713. Bodl. Pamph 310(21).

12. — 2nd edition, Oxford, 1713. Bodl. 12 Θ 1777(14).

13. GARDYNER, JAMES. Concio habita in solenni conventu cleri Londinensis ad Collegium Sionense, iv Kal. Maias MDCCXIII. Per Jacobum Gardynerum [etc.]. Oxonii, e Th. Sh. Prostat venalis apud Hen. Clements, sub signo Lunae Falcatae in Coemeterio Paulino, Lond. 1713.

4to. Imp. 17 Sept. 1713. Bodl. F 2. 1 (1) Linc.

14. (Kennett, Basil. Romae antiquae notitia. Has a copper-engraving of the Sheldonian Theatre on the title-page but a London imprint, and its types are not those used in Oxford.)

15. MARSHALL, BENJAMIN. Tabulae chronologicae. Tabula III continens res maxime notatu dignas [etc.] ab anno ante aeram vulgarem Domini 500, usque ad annum ante eandem aeram 1; una cum appendice, quam v. infra. Oxonii, e Th. Sh. 1713.

— Tabula IV, seu appendicis continuatio. Oxonii, e Th. Sh. 1713.

Each table consists of two folded broadsides. Imp. 16 Oct. 1713. Bodl. Mason B 221(1).

16. MARSHALL, BENJAMIN. Chronological tables. Table III and Appendix [etc.]. Printed at the Theater in Oxford, 1713. Table IV [imprint as above].

Each table consists of two folded broadsides. Imp. 16 Oct. 1713. Bodl. Mason B 221(2).

17. NEWTON, RICHARD. A sermon preach'd before the Queen in the Royal Chappel at Windsor on Thursday November the 5th. 1713. by Richard Newton [etc.]. Publish'd by Her Majesty's special command. Oxford: printed for Stephen Fletcher bookseller in Oxford, and George Strahan at the Golden Ball in Cornhil, London. MDCCXIII.

4to. Bodl. C 8. 40(4) Linc. Attributable to the University's press on typographical grounds.

18*. OXFORD, UNIVERSITY. Academiae Oxoniensis Comitia philologica in Theatro Sheldoniano decimo die Julii A.D. 1713. celebrata in honorem serenissimae reginae Annae Pacificae. Oxonii, e Typographeo Clarendoniano, An. Dom. MDCCXIII.

Fol. Bodl. F 3. 8 Jur.

2nd A/cs. fol. 31, 400, price 3s. 4d.; fol. 31ᵛ. 2nd impression, 300. The first book to bear the imprint of the Clarendon Press.

19*. OXFORD, UNIVERSITY. Ordo Comitiorum philologicorum.
Fol. single sheet. Printer to the University.
2nd A/cs. fol. 31, 'Working at press Ord: Com: and Dr Croffts Exercise at three several times'.

20*. (Oxford, University. A supplement to the list of Oxford graduates. 8vo. Madan 1713:34. No copy traced.)

21*. OXFORD, UNIVERSITY. Books to be had of Stephen Richardson at the Theater-Press by any gentleman of the University at the following rates until the end of Michaelmas Term. [Dated:] 25 Aug. 1713.
Fol. s. sh. B.M. Harl. 5932(7).

22. WELCHMAN, EDWARD. XXXIX Articuli Ecclesiae Anglicanae textibus e Sacra Scriptura depromptis confirmati, brevibusque notis illustrati. Adjectis insuper nominibus auctorum locisque in quibus doctrina in Articulis contenta fusius explicatur. In usum juventutis academicae. Auctore Edwardo Welchman [etc.]. Oxoniae, e Th. Sh. Ann. Dom. MDCCXIII.
8vo in fours. Imp. 28 Aug. 1712. Bodl. 8° M 1(3) Linc.

23. [WELCHMAN, EDWARD.] Concentus veterum sive appendix ad XXXIX Articulos Ecclesiae Anglicanae in qua ejusdem Ecclesiae doctrina Patrum antiquissimorum testimoniis confirmatur. Oxoniae, e Th. Sh. MDCCXIII.
8vo in fours. Bodl. 8° M 1 Linc.
Preface by Edward Welchman. 2nd A/cs. fol. 30ᵛ, dues paid by Mr Hall (i.e. Anthony Hall of Queen's College).

24. WELLS, EDWARD. An help for the more easy and clear understanding of the Holy Scriptures: being St Paul's Epistle to the Hebrews explain'd after the following method [etc., as in the Specimen of 1709]. Oxford, printed at the Theater, for James Knapton at the Crown in S. Paul's Church-Yard, London, 1713.
4to. Imp. 29 July 1713. Magdalen Coll. d.6.7.

25. WELLS, EDWARD. Remarks on Dr Clarke's Introduction to his scripture doctrin of the Trinity. By Edward Wells [etc.]. Oxford, printed at the Theatre for Anthony Peisley, and are to be sold by James Knapton, Henry Clements, William Taylor, and John Morphew booksellers in London, MDCCXIII. Price one shilling.
8vo in fours. Imp. 25 July 1713. Bodl. 8° S 233(2) Th.

26. WELLS, EDWARD. A letter to the Reverend Dr Clarke, Rector of St James's Westminster, in answer to his letter to Dr Wells. By Edward Wells [etc.]. Oxford, printed at the Theatre for Anthony Peisley, and are to be sold by James Knapton, Henry Clements, William Taylor, and John Morphew booksellers in London, MDCCXIII.
8vo in fours. Imp. 11 Dec. 1713. Bodl. 8° S 233(3) Th.
2nd A/cs. fol. 30ᵛ, dues.

27. YOUNG, EDWARD. A poem on the last day. By Edward Young [etc.]. Printed at the Theatre for Edward Whistler, MDCCXIII.
8vo in fours. Imp. 19 May 1713. Bodl. 8° I 102 Th.

28. — 2nd edition, as above, 1713. Bodl. 52 Θ 1111.

1714

1. DUKE, RICHARD. Fifteen sermons preach'd on several occasions. by Richard Duke [etc.]. Oxford, printed at the Theatre, for Anth. Peisley bookseller: and are to be sold by J. Churchill, J. Knapton, W. Taylor, H. Clements, W. Meadows, and J. Morphew booksellers in London, 1714.
8vo. Imp. 17 Sept. 1713. Bodl. 8° Z 136 Th.
2nd A/cs. 37ᵛ, dues.

2. GAGNIER, JEAN. [Prospectus and specimen] Concordantiae SS. Bibliorum Veteris Testamenti Graecae, secundum literarum Graecarum ordinem, cum vocibus Hebraeis Graecibus respondentibus, inversa methodo Kircheriana, digestae et concinnatae. Opus a cl. viro Henrico Savilio olim adornatum: nunc demum, adjectis, praeter LXXII Seniorum versionem, aliorum quoque interpretum, Aquilae scilicet, Symmachi & Theodotionis, nec non quinti, sexti, & septimi editionum longe pluribus locis quam antea, ex Origenis Exaplis, quae supersunt, a D. Bernardo de Montfaucon nuper editis, auctum & locupletatum, opera et studio Johannis Gagnier, A.M.
Oxoniae, e Th. Sh., MDCCXIV.
Fol. 4 pp. B.M. Harl. 5929, No. 324.

3. GRABE, JOHANN ERNST. Spicilegium SS. Patrum, [etc., as in the edition of 1698] Tomus I sive Seculum I. Editio altera, priore auctior & emendatior. Oxoniae, e Th. Sh. MDCCXIV. Impensis J. Bowyer & H. Clements, bibliopolarum Londinensium.
8vo in fours. Bodl. 8° L 162, 163 Th.
2nd A/cs. 37ᵛ, dues. Hearne, iv, pp. 326–7. Promoted by Atterbury.

4. HOMER. Ομηρου Ιλιας. Εκ Θεατρου ἐν Οξονια εν τῷ ετει αψιδ'. Impensis J. Bowyer & H. Clements, bibliopolarum Londinensium. 1714.
8vo fours. Imp. 19 Oct. 1713. Bodl. 8° L 165 Th.
2nd A/cs. 37ᵛ, dues. Hearne, iv, pp. 326–7. Promoted by Atterbury. Done by Fairfax, Fenton, and Stevens.

5*. LILY, WILLIAM. A short introduction of grammar [as in the edition of 1709. Followed by Brevissima institutio etc.]. Oxford, at the Theater. 1714.
8vo. Bodl. Bliss B 150.
2nd A/cs. 38, 2,000. 12d. each. All sold to Peisley and Fletcher.

6*. MAUNDRELL, HENRY. A journey from Aleppo to Jerusalem at Easter, A.D. 1697. The third edition, to which is now added an account of the author's Journey to the banks of the Euphrates at Beer, and to the County [sic] of Mesopotamia. By Henry Maundrell [etc.]. Oxford, printed at the Theater, An. Dom. MDCCXIV.
8vo fours. Imp. 8 Apr. 1703. Bodl. 55 b. 123.
2nd A/cs. 40, in part. A reissue of the second edition (1707) with added sheets.

7*. OXFORD, UNIVERSITY. Pietas Universitatis in obitum serenissimae Reginae Annae et gratulatio in augustissimi Regis Georgii inaugurationem. Oxonii, e Typographeo Clarendoniano, An. Dom. MDCCXIV.
Fol. Bodl. M 6. 6(2) Art.
2nd A/cs. 39, 400. 163 given away, 200 sold to Peisley, 37 to Baskett.

7*a. OXFORD, UNIVERSITY. [Notice] At a general meeting of the Vice-Chancellor, Heads of Houses, and Proctors of the University of Oxford, at the Apodyterium of the Convocation-House, on Wednesday Aug. 4. 1714. Whereas a letter addressed to Mr. Mayor . . .

4to single leaf. Bodl. Hearne's diary 51. Fol. 45e.
Printed in Hearne, iv, p. 390.

8*. OXFORD, UNIVERSITY. [Arrangements for the funeral of Dr John Radcliffe] At a general meeting of the Vice-Chancellor, Heads of Houses, and Proctors of the University of Oxford, at the Apodyterium of the Convocation-House on Saturday, Nov. 27. 1714 . . .

Fol. single leaf. Bodl. MS. Top. Oxon. 643(3).
2nd A/cs. 42, Hearne v, pp. 1–3.

9*. OXFORD, UNIVERSITY. [Gallery in St Peter's Church.] Advertisement. At a meeting of the Vice-Chancellor, Heads of Houses and Proctors of the University of Oxford, on Monday Feb. 8. 1713/14. . . .

8vo single leaf. Bodl. Hearne's diary 49, p. 131a.
2nd A/cs. 42. Printed in Hearne iv, p. 314.

10*. OXFORD, UNIVERSITY. Orders and statutes of the Ashmolean Museum. (in Latin:) Bodl. G.A. Oxon. b. 19(66). (in English:) Bodl. G.A. Oxon. b. 15(261). Dated 13 Dec. 1714.

Broadside.
2nd A/cs. 46, 40 of each.

11. RYE, GEORGE. The supremacy of the Crown and the power of the Church asserted and adjusted. A sermon preach'd before the University of Oxford, at St Mary's, on Sunday Jan. 17. 1713/14. By George Rye [etc.]. Printed at the Theatre, for Anth. Peisley bookseller: and are to be sold by J. Churchill, J. Knapton, W. Taylor, H. Clements, W. Meadows, and J. Morphew booksellers in London.

8vo fours. Bodl. 8° M 237(3) Th.

12. [WELCHMAN, EDWARD.] XXXIX Articuli Ecclesiae Anglicanae, textibus e sacra Scriptura depromptis confirmati, brevibusque notis illustrati. Adjectis insuper nominibus auctorum locisque in quibus doctrina in Articulis contenta fusius explicatur. In usum juventutis academicae. Auctore Edvardo Welchman [etc.]. Editio secunda auctior & emendatior, cui accedit appendix de doctrina Patrum. Oxonii, e Typographeo Clarendoniano, ann. Dom. MDCCXIV.

8vo fours. Imp. 28 Aug. 1712. Bodl. 8° Rawl. 1073.

13. [WELCHMAN, EDWARD.] Concentus veterum, sive Appendix ad XXXIX Articulos Ecclesiae Anglicanae, in qua ejusdem Ecclesiae doctrina Patrum antiquissimorum testimoniis confirmatur. Editio altera emendatior. Oxoniae, e Typographeo Clarendoniano MDCCXIV.

8vo fours. Bodl. Pamph. 312(12).

14. WELLS, EDWARD. An help for the more easy and clear understanding of the Holy Scriptures: being St Paul's two Epistles to the Corinthians, explained after the following method, viz. I. The original Greek text amended according to the best and most antient readings, II. The common English translation render'd more agreeable to the original, III. A paraphrase, wherein not only the difficult expressions and passages are explain'd, but also the design of the Apostle, and the method

used by him in prosecuting his design, are set forth by proper divisions into sections and paragraphs; and withall are exhibited on one view by a synopsis subjoin'd to the end of the Epistle. IV. Short annotations, relating (as occasion requires) to the several particulars afore-mentioned. By Ed. Wells [etc.]. Oxford, printed at the Theater, for James Knapton at the Crown in S. Paul's Church-Yard, London. 1714. 4to. Imp. 11 May 1714. Bodl. 101 d. 695(2).

15. WHEATLY, CHARLES. The Church of England man's companion; or a rational illustration of the harmony, excellency, and usefulness of the Book of Common Prayer, etc. wherein all the rubricks, prayers, rites and ceremonies, etc. are explain'd and vindicated, and compar'd with the ancient liturgies, and the practices of the primitive church. To which is prefix'd an introductory discourse, shewing the lawfulness and necessity of a national precompos'd liturgy. By Charles Wheatly [etc.]. The second edition with large additions. Oxford, printed at the Theater, for Anth. Peisly bookseller: and are to be sold by A. Churchill, J. Knapton, W. Taylor, H. Clements, and J. Morphew, booksellers in London. 1714.

8vo. Imp. 1 Feb. 1714. Bodl. 1 b. 159.
2nd A/cs. 37ᵛ, dues.

1715

1. ACTS OF THE APOSTLES. Acta Apostolorum Graeco-Latine, litteris majusculis. e codice Laudiano, characteribus uncialibus exarato, & in Bibliotheca Bodlejano adservato, descripsit ediditque Tho. Hearnius [etc.]. qui & Symbolum Apostolorum ex eodem codice subjunxit. Oxonii, e Th. Sh., MDCCXV. sumptibus editoris.

8vo fours. Bodl. Ashm. F 12.
2nd A/cs. 51ᵛ, dues. Inscribed: Maii 24° MDCCXVI Museo Ashmoliano dono dedit Editor. 120 printed.

2. ÆLFRIC, ABBOT. [Proposals] The English Saxon homilies of Ælfric arch-bishop of Canterbury . . . Now first printed and translated into the language of the present times by Elizabeth Elstob. Printed at the Theatre in Oxford An. Dom. MDCCXV.

Fol. 4 pp. B.M. MS. Lansd. 373, fols. 88–9.
Thirty-six pages of this work, with no title-page, are in the B.M. inscribed 'These sheets, all that were printed of Mrs. Elstob's Homiliarium, were purchased at the Sale of Herbert Croft's Library. See Nichols, *Lit. Anec.* ii, p. 44.' B.M. 695.1.8.

3. AESCHINES AND DEMOSTHENES. Αισχινου ο κατα Κτησιφωντος και Δημοσθενους ο περι στεφανου λογος. Interpretationem Latinam, et vocum difficiliorum explicationem adjecerunt P. Foulkes J. Freind [etc.]. Editio secunda. Oxonii e Typographeo Clarendoniano An. Dom. MDCCXV impensis Stephani Fletcher, prostant venales apud J. Knapton, R. Knaplock, G. Taylor, H. Clements & G. Innys bibliopolas Londinenses.

8vo fours. Imp. 24 Dec. 1695. Bodl. Auct. S 6. 21.
2nd A/cs. 51ᵛ, dues.

4. [CATCOTT, A. S.] The poem of Musaeus, on the loves of Hero and Leander, paraphras'd in English heroick verse. Oxford, printed at the Theater for Anthony Peisley bookseller: and are to be sold by James Knapton, William Taylor, Henry

Clement, William Meadows, and John Morphew, booksellers in London. 1715. Price six pence.
8vo fours. Bodl. Bliss B 153(1).
Dedication by Alexander Stopford Catcott.

5. CHAMBRES, CHARLES. Religion and vertue the sure way to human favour and esteem. In a sermon preach'd at Hertford, March the 11th. 1714/15. at the solemnity of the Hertford-School-Feast. By Charles Chambres [etc.]. Oxford, printed for Anthony Peisley bookseller: and are to be sold by J. Knapton, W. Taylor, H. Clement, W. Meadows, and J. Morphew booksellers in London. 1715.
8vo fours. Imp. 26 March 1715.
Perhaps printed by Lichfield.

6. CICERO. Proposals for printing by subscription a new edition of Marcus Tullius Cicero, by Thomas Hearne [etc.]. (Dated 12 July 1715.)
Fol. 4 pp. with specimen leaf. Bodl. MS. Rawl. D. 732 (180–1).
Hearne, v, pp. 62, 63.

7. CLEMENT OF ALEXANDRIA. [Greek title.] Clementis Alexandrini opera, quae extant recognita & illustrata per Johannem Potterum, Episcopum Oxoniensem. Oxonii, e Th. Sh., A.D. MDCCXV. sumptibus Georgii Mortlock, bibliopolae Londiniensis.
Fol. 2 vol. Imp. 23 Aug. 1715. Bodl. A 7. 9. 10 Th.

8. EUCLID. Euclidis Elementorum libri priores sex, item undecimus & duodecimus. Ex versione Latina Frederici Commandini. Quibus accedunt trigonometriae planae & sphaericae elementa. Item tractatus de natura & arithmetica logarithmorum. In usum juventutis academicae. Oxonii, e Th. Sh. impensis Henr. Clements bibliopolae Oxoniensis. MDCCXV.
8vo. Imp. 25 March 1715. Bodl. Bliss B 151.
2nd A/cs. 45ᵛ, dues. The second edition of a book first printed in 1701. Edited by J. Keill (D.N.B.).

9. IVIE, EDWARD. Epicteti Enchiridion versibus adumbratum, per Edwardum Ivie [etc.]. Oxoniae, e Th. Sh., MDCCXV. impensis H. Clements, ad insigne Lunae Falcatae in Coemeterio D. Pauli, Londini.
8vo fours. Imp. 25 March 1715. B.M. 674.c.15.
2nd A/cs. 45ᵛ, dues.

10. KEILL, JOHN. Introductio ad veram physicam, seu lectiones physicae habitae in Schola Naturalis Philosophiae Academiae Oxoniensis An. Dom. 1700. Quibus accedunt theorematum Hugeniorum de vi centrifuga & motu circulari demon-strationes. Authore Joanne Keill. Editio tertia. Oxoniae, e Th. Sh., impensis Hen. Clements, ad insigne Lunae Falcatae in Coemeterio D. Pauli Londini, An. Dom. MDCCXV.
8vo. Imp. 14 Feb. 1701/2 Bodl. 8° Y 510 BS.
2nd A/cs. 51ᵛ, dues. Previous editions were of 1702 and 1705.

11. [KEILL, JOHN.] Trigonometriae planae & sphaericae elementa. Item de natura et arithmetica logarithmorum tractatus brevis. Oxoniae, e Th. Sh. impensis Henr. Clements bibliopolae Oxoniensis. 1715.
8vo. Bodl. 8° T 15 Jur.
A separate issue of appendices to the Euclid, above No. 8.

12. LELAND, JOHN. Joannis Lelandi antiquarii de rebus Britannicis Collectanea. Ex autographis descripsit ediditque Tho. Hearnius [etc.] qui & appendicem subjecit, totumque opus (in vi. volumina distributum) notis & indice adornavit. Oxonii, e Th. Sh. MDCCXV. Sumptibus Editoris.
  8vo fours. Bodl. Mus. Bibl. II 44-9.
  2nd A/cs. 45ᵛ, dues.

13. MORISON, ROBERT. Historia plantarum [etc.]. [Reissue of Vols. i and ii with 8 new preliminary pages.] Oxoniae, e Th. Sh. et prostant Londini apud Paulum & Isaacum Vaillant. MDCCXV.
  Fol. Bodl. Sherard 732.

13a. — Vol. iii. Four preliminary pages reprinted. Includes the original title-page of 1699. Imprint as above.
  Bodl. Sherard 733.

14*. OXFORD, UNIVERSITY. Exequiae clarissimo Johanni Radcliffe M.D. ab Oxoniensi Academia solutae. Oxonii, e Typographeo Clarendoniano An. Dom. MDCCXV.
  Fol. Bodl. M 6 6 Art.
  2nd A/cs. 47, 200 small, 30 large. A notice of the funeral arrangements is prefixed. Hearne, v, p. 95.

15*. OXFORD, UNIVERSITY. [Letter of thanks to Radcliffe's executors.] Ornatissimis viris Georgio Beaumont, baronetto, Gulielmo Bromley, Thomae Slater, armigeris, & Antonio Keck, generoso, supremi testamenti Johannis Radcliffe M.D. curatoribus integerrimis . . . [subscribed] Academia Oxoniensis.
  Fol. s. sh. n.d. Bodl. MS. Ballard xlviii (125).
  MS. note: Univers. Oxon. Pridie Nonas Maii.

16*. OXFORD, UNIVERSITY. [Arrangements for Radcliffe's funeral.] A copy is bound with the Exequiae: Bodl. MS. Ballard xlviii (125).
  Fol. s. sh.
  2nd A/cs. 46, '1300 Programmas for Dr. Radcliffs Funeral'.

17*. OXFORD, UNIVERSITY. 'Dr. Radcliffs Pictures'.
  2nd A/cs. 44ᵛ, 46, 1,000, 4d. each.
  Presumably the engraving used as frontispiece to the Exequiae.

18*. OXFORD, UNIVERSITY. [Warning to rioters.] At a general meeting of the Vice-Chancellor, Heads of Houses, and Proctors of the University of Oxford, at the Apodyterium of the Convocation-House on Saturday June 4. 1715. Whereas on Saturday and Sunday last, late at night, a multitude of persons, to us unknown, did in a tumultuous and riotous manner, of which we had never seen an example in this place, assemble together in the publick streets . . .
  Fol. s. sh. Bodl. G.A. Oxon. b. 19, fol. 39.
  2nd A/cs. 46, 350.

19*. OXFORD, UNIVERSITY. [Thanksgiving Day.] At a general meeting of the Vice-Chancellor, Heads of Houses, and Proctors of the University of Oxford, at the Apodyterium of the Convocation-House, on July 25. 1715. Whereas Monday the first of August next, is appointed for a day of public thanksgiving for His Majesty's

happy accession to the Throne; least so just an occasion of rejoycing should be
turn'd into excess and tumult . . .

Broadside. Bodl. G.A. Oxon. b. 19, fol. 37.

2nd A/cs. 46, 300. Hearne, v, p. 83.

20*. (A 'Programma for habitts' was issued in 1715 (2nd A/cs. 46, 200 printed), but
no copy has been found.)

21. TRAPP, JOSEPH. Praelectiones poeticae in Schola Naturalis Philosophiae habitae.
Authore Josepho Trapp, A.M. Coll. Wadh. socio, & Praelectore Publico Lecturae
Poeticae a viro insignissimo D. Henrico Birkhead [etc.] in celeberrima Universitate
Oxoniensi nuper fundatae. Volumen secundum. Oxonii, e Th. Sh., impensis Henr.
Clements bibliopolae Londinensis, MDCCXV.

8vo. Bodl. 8º G 177, 8 Art.

2nd A/cs. 45ᵛ, dues. The first volume was issued in 1711, and the third in 1719.

22. WELLS, EDWARD. An help to the more easy and clear understanding of the
Holy Scriptures: being St Paul's Epistles to the Ephesians, Philippians, Colossians,
Timothy, Titus, and Philemon . . . [etc., as for Corinthians, 1714]. Oxford, printed
at the Theater for James Knapton at the Crown in S. Paul's Church-Yard, London,
1715.

4to. Imp. 7 Dec. 1714. Bodl. 101 d. 695(4).

2nd A/cs. 51ᵛ, dues.

23. WELLS, EDWARD. An help to the more easy and clear understanding of the
Holy Scriptures: being all the Epistles of St. Paul [etc.]. Oxford, printed at the
Theater for James Knapton at the Crown in S. Paul's Church-Yard, London. 1715.

4to. Imp. 7 Dec. 1714. Bodl. 101 d. 695(1).

24. WELLS, EDWARD. An help to the more easy and clear understanding of the
Holy Scriptures: being the Epistles of St James, St Peter, St John, and St Jude [etc.].
Oxford, printed at the Theater for James Knapton at the Crown in S. Paul's
Church-Yard, London. 1715.

4to. Imp. 1 July 1715. Bodl. 101 d. 695(6).

2nd A/cs. 51ᵛ, dues.

1716

1. ALFRED OF BEVERLEY. Aluredi Beverlacensis Annales, sive historia de gestis
regum Britanniae, libris ix. e codice pervetusto, calamo exarato, in bibliotheca viri
clarissimi Thomae Rawlinsoni armigeri descripsit ediditque Tho. Hearnius [etc.],
qui et praefatione, notis, atque indice illustravit. Oxonii, e Th. Sh., MDCCXVI.
sumptibus editoris.

8vo fours. Bodl. Douce HH 183.

2nd A/cs. 51ᵛ, dues. An Advertisement, dated 16 July 1716, gives the number
printed as 148 and the price as 12s. on large paper and 8s. on small: Bodl. MS. Rawl.
letters 39, fols. 88–9.

2. ARISTOTLE. [Greek title.] Aristotelis Ethicorum Nicomacheorum libri decem. Codicum MSS. collatione recogniti, & notis illustrati a Gulielmo Wilkinson [etc.]. Oxonii, e Th. Sh., MDCCXVI.

> 8vo fours. Imp. 23 Aug. 1714. Bodl. Radcl. e. 161.
> 2nd A/cs. 64ᵛ, dues.
> Letter from Wanley: Bodl. MS. Ballard xiii (130).

3. BION, MOSCHUS etc. Miscellaneous translations from Bion, Moschus, Ovid, and Mr. Addison, with an original poem on bowling. Oxford, printed for E. Whistler, bookseller: and are to be sold by R. Smith, J. Knapton, and J. Tonson, booksellers in London. MDCCXVI.

> 8vo fours. Bodl. Vet. A 4 e. 515.
> Perhaps printed by Lichfield.

4. CICERO. M. T. Ciceronis Liber de claris oratoribus, qui dicitur Brutus. Ad M. Brutum Orator. Ad C. Trebatium Topica. Oratoriae partitiones. Liber de Optimo genere oratorum. Cum interpretatione, ac notis, quas in usum serenissimi Delphini edidit Jacobus Proust, e Societate Jesu. Cum indice copioso. Juxta editionem novissimam Parisiensem. Oxonii, e Typographeo Clarendoniano, An. Dom. MDCCXVI. Impensis Stephani Fletcher bibliopolae.

> 8vo fours. Bodl. Radcl. d. 54.
> 2nd A/cs. 51ᵛ, dues.

5. CICERO. M. Tullius Cicero De officiis ad Marcum F. Ex MSS. recensuit Tho. Cockman [etc.]. Editio secunda. Oxoniae, e Th. Sh. 1716. Impensis Henrici Clements, & prostant venales apud Henr. Clements, ad insigne Lunae Falcatae in Caemeterio D. Pauli Londini.

> 8vo. Imp. 2 March 1694/5. Bodl. 90 b. 16.
> 2nd A/cs. 51ᵛ, dues.

6. CICERO. Cicero on Old Age, a dialogue. Oxford: printed at the Theatre. Anno Dom. 1716.

> 8vo fours. Imp. 5 June 1716. Bodl. G. Pamph. 2709(2).
> Preface signed by Samuel Hemming.

7. COTES, DIGBY, AND YOUNG, EDWARD. Orationes duae Codringtono sacrae in Collegio Omnium Animarum nuper habitae. Una a Digbeo Cotes, Oratore Publico, altera ab Edvardo Young [etc.]. Oxoniae, e Th. Sh., impensis Ant. Peisley, MDCCXVI.

> 8vo fours. Bodl. G.A. Oxon. 8° 61.

8. [GRABE, JOHANN ERNST.] Proposals for printing by subscription, in the University Press at Oxford, the two other parts of the Septuagint, whereby the whole will be rendered complete, as being taken from the Alexandrian manuscript, by the late learned and Reverend Dr. J. E. Grabe, with great additions and emendations by the same hand . . . [no imprint].

> Fol. s. sh. Bodl. MS. Rawl. J. 4° 2(247).
> Presumably issued in 1716, when Smalridge wrote on 17 May that he had seen the specimen: MS. Ballard vii fol. 48ᵛ. The volumes were printed in 1719 and 1720.

9. HOLE, MATTHEW. Addresses unto Heaven, the best security of the Church militant upon earth, together with the set times and seasons assign'd for her

deliverance. A sermon preach'd before the University of Oxford at St. Mary's on Act-Sunday, July the 8th 1716. By Matthew Hole [etc.]. Publish'd at the request of the Vice-Chancellor and other heads of Colleges. Oxford, printed at the Theater, for J. and S. Wilmot; and are to be sold by J. Knapton, W. Taylor, and J. Morphew, booksellers in London, 1716. Price four pence.

8vo fours. Imp. 16 July 1716. Bodl. G. Pamph. 1631(10).

10. LIVIUS FORO-JULIENSIS, TITUS. Titi Livii Foro-Juliensis Vita Henrici Quinti, regis Angliae. Accedit, sylloge epistolarum, a variis Angliae principibus scriptarum. E codicibus calamo exaratis descripsit ediditque Tho. Hearnius [etc.]. qui & appendicem notasque subjecit. Oxonii, e Th. Sh., MDCCXVI. sumptibus editoris.

8vo fours. Bodl. Mus. Bibl. II 53.

2nd A/cs. 51ᵛ, dues. Held up by order of the Vice-Chancellor: Hearne, v, p. 183.

11. NEWTON, RICHARD. A sermon preach'd at the consecration of Hart-Hall Chapell in Oxford. By R. Newton [etc.]. Oxford, printed for Stephen Fletcher bookseller in Oxford, and are to be sold by H. Clements at the Half-Moon in S. Paul's Church Yard, London. 1716. Price three pence.

8vo fours. Imp. 8 Dec. 1716. Bodl. 12 Θ 1780(10).

Perhaps printed by Lichfield.

12*. OXFORD, UNIVERSITY. Catalogus librorum qui die 17. Maii, A.D. 1716 in Theatro Sheldoniano sub prelo sunt.

Fol. s. sh. Bodl. fol. Θ 682(12).

2nd A/cs. 53. This is believed to be the latest of a series of lists compiled by Arthur Charlett to have survived.

13. ROPER, WILLIAM. Guilielmi Roperi Vita D. Thomae Mori equitis aurati, lingua Anglicana contexta. Accedunt Mori Epistola de scholasticis quibusdam Trojanos sese apellantibus; Academiae Oxoniensis Epistolae et orationes aliquam multae; anonymi Chronicon Godstovianum; et Fenestrarum depictarum ecclesiae parochialis de Fairford in agro Glocestriensi explicatio. E codicibus vetustis descripsit ediditque Tho. Hearnius [etc.]. qui et notas subjecit. Veneunt apud editorem. A.D. MDCCXVI.

8vo fours. Bodl. Allen e. 41.

2nd A/cs. 56ᵛ, dues. Hearne had been forbidden to use the University's imprint. An engraving with the legend 'Vad. Boum' supplies the place of printing. See MS. Rawl. letters 34, fol. 17. An advertisement of the book is in the same collection, vol. 39, fol. 89.

14. ROSS, JOHN. Joannis Rossi antiquarii Warwicensis Historia regum Angliae. E codice MS. in Bibliotheca Bodlejana descripsit, notisque et indice adornavit Tho. Hearnius [etc.]. Accedit Joannis Lelandi antiquarii Naenia in mortem Henrici Duddelegi equitis; cui praefigitur testimonium de Lelando amplum & praeclarum, hactenus ineditum. Oxonii, e Th. Sh., MDCCXVI. sumptibus editoris.

8vo fours. Bodl. Mus. Bibl. II. 51.

2nd A/cs. 51ᵛ, dues. An advertisement of the book, dated 10 Feb. 1715/16, is in B.M. Harl. 5929 (fol. 109).

15. TAYLOR, JOHN. The evil nature of rebellious principles and practices, and the fatal consequences of them. A sermon preach'd on the 30th of January 1715/16, being the fast for the martyrdom of King Charles I of blessed memory. By John

Taylor [etc.]. Oxford, printed for Stephen Fletcher bookseller in Oxford, and for
J. Knapton, and W. Taylor booksellers in London. 1716.

   8vo fours. Bodl. Mar. 848.

   Perhaps printed by Lichfield. Bodl. 8° 12 Θ 1777(15) seems to me to be equivalent.

16. WELLS, EDWARD. An help to the more easy and clear understanding of the
Holy Scriptures: being the Book of Daniel [etc.]. Before the Book of Daniel are
prefix'd 1. A general preface 2. A discourse concerning those prophecies of Daniel
which relate to the Four Kingdoms of the Gentiles, and the Kingdom of Christ and
his saints &c. 3. Four tables shewing the synchronism or correspondency of all the
prophecies of Daniel relating to the Four Kingdoms of the Gentiles, and the
Kingdom of Christ and his saints &c. 4. A chronological table of the more remarkable particulars relating to the Book of Daniel. 5. Some observations concerning the
chronology relating to the prophecy of the Twenty Weeks. After the Book of Daniel
are subjoin'd 1. A collection of the various readings of the LXX or Greek version of
Daniel 2. A view (or collection) of such passages and expressions in the Book of
Daniel, as are found likewise refer'd to in the New Testament, especially in the
Revelations of St. John. Oxford, printed at the Theater for James Knapton at the
Crown in S. Paul's Church-Yard, London. 1716.

   4to. Imp. 13 Feb. 1715/16. Bodl. 101 d. 695(8).

   2nd A/cs. 51ᵛ, dues. Pages 1–44 at the beginning of the book are set in types which
the Press did not own, and must have been printed elsewhere.

17*. WILKINS, DAVID. [Title in Coptic.] hoc est Novum Testamentum Aegyptium
vulgo Copticum ex MSS. Bodlejanis descripsit, cum Vaticanis et Parisiensibus contulit, et in Latinum sermonem convertit David Wilkins [etc.]. Oxonii, e Th. Sh.
typis et sumptibus Academiae, 1716.

   4to. Imp. xv Kal. Octobr. 1716.

   2nd A/cs. 52, 500. D.O. 17 Aug. 1715.

18. WORMIUS, CHRISTIAN. Arae Multiscii Schedae de Islandia. Accedit dissertatio
de Arae Multiscii vita & scriptis. Oxoniae, e Theatro Seldeniano. An. Dom.
MDCCXVI.

   8vo fours. Bodl. 12 Θ 1707.

   The text was printed for the Delegates in 1696. It is part of a work which was
never completed. On Feb. 15 1711 the Delegates ordered the printed sheets to be
sold for 6d. a set. It is unlikely that this edition was sanctioned by them, as
the imprint on the title-page (not set in Oxford types) is enough to show. For the
character of Christian Wormius see Hickes's letter, MS. Ballard xii (75).

1717

1. BIBLIOTHECA BIBLICA. Proposals for printing by subscription Bibliotheca
Biblica, being a commentary upon all the Books of the Old and New Testament. . . .

   4to. 8 pages. Bodl. fol. Θ 663(10).

   Probably of this year: Hearne, vi, pp. 116, 260. Five volumes, on the Pentateuch,
were printed in 1720–35.

2. CAMDEN, WILLIAM. Gulielmi Camdeni Annales rerum Anglicarum et Hiberni-
carum regnante Elizabetha. Tribus voluminibus comprehensi. E codice praeclaro
Smithiano, propria auctoris manu correcto, multisque magni momenti additionibus
locupletato, eruit ediditque Tho. Hearnius, qui & alium codicem e bibliotheca
Rawlinsoniana adhibuit. A.D. MDCC.XVII.
   3 vols. 8vo fours. Bodl. Douce HH 162–4.
   2nd A/cs. 56ᵛ, dues.

3. CATCOTT. A. S. The Court of Love, a vision from Chaucer. By Mr Catcott.
Oxford. printed at the Theater for Anthony Peisley bookseller: and are to be sold
by James Knapton, William Taylor, Henry Clements, William Meadows, and John
Morphew, booksellers in London. 1717. Price six pence.
   8vo fours. Bodl. Bliss B 153(2).

4. CICERO. M. T. Ciceronis De officiis, Cato Major, Laelius, Paradoxa, Somnium
Scipionis, ex optimis exemplaribus recensuit, selectisque variorum notis nonnullas
etiam suas adjecit Tho. Tooly [etc.]. Oxoniae, e Th. Sh. 1717. Prostant apud Joh.
& Sam. Wilmot bibliopol. Oxon.
   8vo fours. Imp. 14 Jan. 1716. Bodl. 8° F 38 Jur.
   2nd A/cs. 56ᵛ, dues.

5. CLARENDON, EDWARD HYDE, EARL OF. The History of the Rebellion and Civil
Wars in England [etc.]. Oxford, printed at the Theater, An. Dom. MDCCXVII.
   6 vols. 8vo. Imp. 29 Apr. 1702. Bodl. 22856 e. 80–85.
   D.O. 29 March 1716, 1650 to be printed for John Baskett, of which 150 for the
University. The 4th edition in 8vo. The Bodleian copy is illustrated with engravings
of portraits.

6. DOD, THOMAS. The rule of equity. A sermon preach'd at the assizes held at
Oxford, March 14. 1716/17. by the Right Honourable Mr. Justice Blencow and
Mr. Baron Montague. By Thomas Dod [etc.]. Oxford, printed at the Theatre for
Henry Clements, and are to be sold by Henry Clements, bookseller at the Half
Moon in St. Paul's Church Yard London, 1717.
   4to. Bodl. G. Pamph. 55(10).
   2nd A/cs. 57, dues.

7. [DRY, J.] Merton Walks, or the Oxford Beauties, a poem. Oxford, printed for
Edward Whistler bookseller, and are to be sold by J. Knapton, H. Clements, W.
Smith booksellers in London, 1717. Price six pence.
   8vo fours. Bodl. Vet. A 4 e. 369(1).
   Perhaps printed by Lichfield. The attribution is from the *Catalogue of the Library
of the Rev. Philip Bliss* (1858). Madan (1717:4) records two editions of the same year.

8. Author of the Whole DUTY OF MAN. The Ladies Calling [etc., as in 1713].
The tenth impression. Oxford, printed at the Theater, MDCCXVII.
   8vo fours. Bodl. Bliss B 154.
   2nd A/cs. 56ᵛ, dues.

9*. [FELL, JOHN.] Grammatica rationis, sive institutiones logicae. Oxonii, e Th.
Sh. Anno Dom. MDCCXVII.
   12mo sixes. Bodl. Vet. A 4 f. 891.
   2nd A/cs. 53, 58, 1,000; D.O. 29 March 1716 and 21 April 1721. The fourth
edition. Madan, *Oxford Books*, iii, No. 2974.

10. (Proposals for Gagnier's *Vindiciae Kircherianae*, published in 1718, were printed in 1717, according to 2nd A/cs. 57. No copy has been found.)

11. HIND, THOMAS. The divinity of our Saviour prov'd from the Scriptures of the Old and New Testaments. In a sermon preached before the University of Oxford at St Mary's, on Act-Sunday, July 7. 1717. together with some remarks on Dr. Clark's and Mr. Whiston's explication of the said Article. By Thomas Hind [etc.]. Published at the request of Mr. Vice-Chancellor. Oxford, printed at the Theater for Anthony Peisley: and are to be sold by J. Knapton, H. Clements, J. Morphew, and W. Meadows, booksellers in London. Price six pence.
 8vo fours. Imp. 18 July 1717. Bodl. 8° S 246(8) Th.

12. [HOLE, MATTHEW.] A.B. An antidote against the poison of some late pamphletts intituled I. The Protestant Dissenters hopes from the present Government freely declar'd. II. The Protestant Dissenters case represented and argued. III. A plain discovery of what the Dissenters would be at. IV. Two letters annext to the said pamphletts: The one, to the author of the Occasional Paper. The other, From a Dissenter to a Member of Parliament. V. Two letters from a person in London to a correspondent in Evesham, Worcestershire. VI. An Essay of comprehension answer'd. To which is added VII. A reply to two pamphletts more, the one Of Presbyterian loyalty; the other Of plain dealing. With some short advice to the Doctors in the Close. In several letters to a friend. Oxford, printed at the Theater for Edw. Whistler bookseller: and are to be sold by James Knapton, and William Smith, booksellers in London. 1717. Price one shilling.
 8vo fours. Bodl. 8° S 237(2) Th.
 2nd A/cs. 56ᵛ, dues.

13. HOLE, MATTHEW. The second part of the Antidote against the poison of the following pamphletts intituled I. The curse causeless. II. An useful ministry a valid one. III. Presbyterian ordination prov'd regular. IV. The state-anatomist against universities and pulpits. V. Considerations on the present state of Great Britain. VI. Reasons for visiting of the Universities. In several letters to a friend. By Matthew Hole [etc.]. Oxford, printed at the Theater for E. Whistler bookseller: and are to be sold by J. Knapton and H. Clements in St Paul's Church-Yard, and W. Smith at Bp. Beveridge's Head in Pater-Noster Row, booksellers in London. 1717. Price 1s.
 8vo fours. Imp. 24 May 1717. Bodl. 8° O 17(2) Linc.
 2nd A/cs. 56ᵛ, dues.

14. HOLE, MATTHEW. Practical discourses upon the Communion Service, prescrib'd in the liturgy of the Church of England. Volume V. By Matthew Hole [etc.]. Oxford, printed at the Theater for E. Whistler bookseller in Oxford; and are to be sold by J. Knapton, J. Tonson, H. Clements, and W. Smith, booksellers in London. 1717.
 8vo Imp. 6 Aug. 1717. Christ Church ZD.5.16.
 2nd A/cs. 64ᵛ, dues.

15. HUDDESFORD, WILLIAM. A congratulatory letter written from Oxford to the Right Honourable Joseph Addison, Esq; upon his being appointed one of His Majesty's Principal Secretaries of State. By W. Huddesford [etc.]. Oxford, printed at the Theater for E. Whistler bookseller in Oxford; and J. Knapton, J. Tonson, H. Clements, and W. Smith, booksellers in London. MDCCXVII.
 4to. Imp. 22 May 1717. Bodl. Gough Oxf. 137(1).

16. [JACKMAN, JOHN.] The rational and moral conduct of Mr Peirce examined: in remarks upon his sermon, entituled Presbyterian ordination prov'd regular. Wherein is also contained An Examination of the doctrinal part of his sermon, entituled, An useful ministry a valid one. To which is added Mr Chillingworth's Demonstration of the Apostolical institution of episcopacy. By a clergyman of the Church of England. The second edition. Oxford, printed at the Theater for E. Whistler bookseller: and are to be sold by J. Knapton, and H. Clements in St Paul's Church-yard, and by W. Smith at Bp. Beveridge's Head in Pater-Noster Row, booksellers in London. 1717. Price 1s.
8vo fours. Imp. 13 Apr. 1717. Bodl. 8° S 237(1) Th.
2nd A/cs. 56ᵛ, dues.

17. MUSAE ANGLICANAE. Musarum Anglicanarum analecta: sive poematum quorundam melioris notae, seu hactenus ineditorum, seu sparsim editorum. Vol. III. Oxon. e Typographeo Clarendoniano. impensis Ant. Peisley bibliopol. MDCCXVII.
12mo. Imp. 12 Mar. 1716. Bodl. 29696 f. 5.
2nd A/cs. 56ᵛ, dues.

18. PEARSE, ROBERT. The reasonableness, the ease, the pleasure of the Christian life. A discourse deliver'd in the parish church of Hartlebury in Worcester-shire, on the third Sunday in Lent, 1717. By Robert Pearse [etc.]. Oxford, printed at the Theater for Steph. Fletcher, and are to be sold by James Knapton, A. Bettesworth, J. Round, W. Mears booksellers in London: and Cornelius Crownfield, bookseller in Cambridge, where may be had Mr Pearse's sermon preach'd at St Martins in Oxford. Price six pence.
8vo fours. Imp. 31 May 1717. Bodl. 8° S 246 Th.

19. PEERS, RICHARD. The character of an honest Dissenter, in twelve marks: together with an illustration of each. By Richard Peers [etc.]. The third edition. To which is prefix'd an additional preface in answer to a letter occasion'd by the two former editions, and pretended to be wrote by a clergy-man; and a letter from a lay-man to the author. Oxford, printed for Stephen Fletcher, and are to be sold by J. Knapton, W. Mears, J. Round, booksellers in London, C. Crownfield in Cambridge, and H. Hammond bookseller in Bath. 1717. The preface may be had single by any person who had the Character before.
8vo fours. Imp. 23 Jan. 1716. Bodl. G. Pamph. 2895(1).

20. SMALRIDGE, GEORGE. The charge of George Lord Bishop of Bristol, at his primary visitation of his diocese, anno 1716. Published at the request of the clergy. Oxford, printed at the Theatre for Jonah Bowyer at the Rose in Ludgate-street, London.
4to. Bodl. G. Pamph. 38(3).

21. SMALRIDGE, GEORGE. Twelve sermons preach'd on several occasions by the Right Reverend Father in God George Lord Bishop of Bristol. Oxford, printed at the Theater for Jonah Bowyer at the Rose in Ludgate-street, London. MDCCXVII.
8vo fours. Imp. 11 Feb. 1716. Bodl. 8° S 242 Th.
2nd A/cs. 64ᵛ, dues.

22. STEPHENS, WILLIAM. The personality and divinity of the Holy Ghost prov'd from Scripture, and the ante-Nicene Fathers. A sermon preach'd before the University of Oxford, at St Mary's, on St Matthias-Day, Feb. 24th 1716/17. in which also

Mons. Le Clerc's charge on the Fathers, as holding the unity of the divine essence to be a specifical one, is shown to be groundless. By William Stephens [etc.]. Publish'd at the request of Mr Vice-Chancellour. Oxford, printed at the Theater for John and Sam. Wilmot booksellers; and are to be sold by J. Knapton, W. Taylor, W. Churchill, Jonas Brown, and John Morphew booksellers in London. 1717. Price 6d.

8vo fours. Imp. 18 July 1717. Bodl. 4° S 246 Th.

23. STIRLING, JAMES. Lineae tertii ordinis Newtonianae, sive Tractatus D. Neutoni de enumeratione linearum tertii ordinis. Cui subjungitur solutio trium problematum. Authore Jacobo Stirling [etc.]. Oxoniae, e Th. Sh., impensis Edwardi Whistler bibliopolae Oxoniensis, MDCCXVII.

8vo fours. Imp. 11 Apr. 1717. Bodl. 8° D 44 Jur.

2nd A/cs. 64ᵛ, dues.

24. STOCKWELL, JOSEPH. A sermon preach'd at Faringdon in the County of Berks, June 24th. 1717. on the occasion of opening a charity-school there. By Joseph Stockwell [etc.]. Oxford, printed at the Theater for Stephen Fletcher; and are to be sold by J. Knapton bookseller in London. Price four pence.

8vo fours. Imp. 2 Oct. 1717. Bodl. G. Pamph. 882(7).

25. WELLS, EDWARD. An help to the more easy and clear understanding of the Holy Scriptures: being the Revelation of St John the Divine [etc.]. To the whole is prefix'd a table of the synchronism of the visions or prophecies of the Seal'd Book, as also of the Open Little Book. By Edward Wells [etc.]. Oxford, printed at the Theater, for James Knapton at the Crown in S. Paul's Church-Yard, London. 1717.

4to. Imp. 27 Nov. 1716. Bodl. 101 d. 695(7).

2nd A/cs. 56ᵛ, dues.

1718

1. ABELARD AND HÉLOÏSE. Petri Abaelardi, Abbatis Ruyensis, et Heloissae, Abbatissae Paracletensis, Epistolae . . . ed. Richard Rawlinson. E. Curll & W. Taylor. Londini. 1718.

8vo. Bodl. 8° U 47 Jur.

According to Hearne (vi, p. 131), the 'first part' was printed at Oxford. Sheets A–M are set in types used at the Clarendon Press.

2. AESOP. Μύθων Αἰσωπείων συναγωγη. Fabularum Aesopicarum collectio, quotquot Graece reperiuntur. Accedit interpretatio Latina. Oxoniae, e Th. Sh. MDCCXVIII.

8vo fours. B.M. 637.i.2.

2nd A/cs. 64ᵛ, dues. Large paper copies have the imprint 'e Typographeo Clarendoniano': B.M. 672.g.3. The dedication is signed 'Mariani' (i.e. John Hudson).

3. CICERO. M. T. Ciceronis omnes qui ad artem oratoriam pertinent libri, tribus voluminibus comprehensi. Cum interpretatione ac notis, quas in usum serenissimi Delphini edidit Jacobus Proust, e Societate Jesu. Vol. I in quo continentur incerti auctoris, seu, ut doctis quibusdam videtur, Cornificii, Rhetoricorum ad C. Heren-

nium libri iv, Rhetorica, seu De inventione rhetorica libri ii. Oxonii, e Typographeo Clarendoniano An. Dom. MDCCXVIII. impensis Stephani Fletcher bibliopolae.

8vo fours. Imp. 12 Feb. 1717/18. Bodl. 29469 e. 16ª.

2nd A/cs. 51ᵛ, dues.

4*. GAGNIER, JEAN. Vindiciae Kircherianae, sive Animadversiones in Abrahami Trommii concordantias Graecas versionis vulgo dictae LXX. Interpretum. I. Defenduntur, ac vindicantur Conradi Kircheri Concordantiae Graecae adversus injustas Abr. Trommii accusationes. II. Ostenditur novam editionem Trommianam adhuc gravissimis defectibus, & vitiis laborare. III. Proponitur vera ac genuina methodus, qua meliores, accuratiores, & commodiores concordantiae Graecae versionis LXX Interpretum de novo & facilius concordantur. Auctore Johanne Gagnier, A.M. Oxonii, e Th. Sh., A.D. 1718.

8vo. Imp. 3 May 1718. Bodl. Bliss B 155.

2nd A/cs. 58, folio 100, 8vo 200. No copy of the edition in folio has been found. D.O. 3 May 1718.

5*. GASSENDI, PIETRO. Logica in quatuor partes distributa: cui praemittuntur libri duo, 1. De origine & varietate logicae. 2. De logicae fine. Authore v. cl. Petro Gassendo. Oxoniae, e Th. Sh., MDCCXVIII.

12mo sixes. Imp. 24 Dec. 1717. Bodl. 2642 f. 41.

2nd A/cs. 58, 750.

6. HARRISON, JOSEPH. A Scriptural exposition of the Church Catechism, divided into as many chapters as there are Sundays in the year, and containing all things which a Christian ought to know and believe to his soul's health. With an office for the Sacrament, and devotions for most other occasions of a Christian life collected out of the public liturgy. The second edition corrected, with additions to the devotional part. For the use of the parish of Cirencester. By Joseph Harrison [etc.]. Oxford, printed at the Theatre for A. Peisley, bookseller in Oxford, and are to be sold by H. Clements and W. Meadows, booksellers in London. 1718.

12mo sixes. Imp. 6 Mar. 1717. Bodl. Tanner 649.

2nd A/cs. 56ᵛ, dues. The first edition (1708) was printed in London.

7. HORACE. The Odes of Horace translated into English verse, by Henry Coxwell, Gent. Oxford, printed for the author, MDCCXVIII.

4to. Bodl. 4° P 12 Art.

8. JACKMAN, JOHN. Success no rule. Being the first part of a reply to Mr. Peirce's Defence of the Dissenting ministry and Presbyterian ordination. In vindication of a book entituled, the Rational and Moral Conduct of Mr. Peirce examin'd. By J. Jackman [etc.]. Oxford, printed at the Theater for Edw. Whistler: and are to be sold by J. Knapton, and H. Clements, booksellers in St. Paul's Church-Yard, London. 1718.

8vo fours. Imp. 19 Apr. 1718. Bodl. 8° O 17(1) Linc.

9. KEILL, JOHN. Introductio in veram astronomiam, seu lectiones astronomicae habitae in Schola Astronomica Academiae Oxoniensis. Authore Joanne Keill [etc.]. Oxoniae, e Th. Sh., impensis Hen. Clement, ad insigne Lunae Falcatae in Coemeterio D. Pauli Londini, An. Dom. MDCCXVIII.

8vo. Imp. 5 July 1718. Bodl. 8° D 46 Jur.

10. LONGINUS. [Greek title.] Dionysii Longini de Sublimitate libellus, cum praefatione de vita & scriptis Longini, notis, indicibus, & variis lectionibus. Editio

altera. Oxonii, e Th. Sh., Anno MDCCXVIII. Prostat apud Joh. & Sam. Wilmot
bibliopolas Oxon.

    8vo fours. Imp. 24 Oct. 1718. Bodl. Crynes 756.

    2nd A/cs. 64ᵛ, dues.

11. NEWLIN, THOMAS. The sinner enslav'd by false pretences. A sermon preach'd
before the University of Oxford at St Mary's March 30th 1718. By Thomas Newlin
[etc.]. Oxford, printed at the Theater, for Edw. Whistler: and are to be sold by
J. Knapton, and H. Clements booksellers in St Paul's Church-Yard, London. Price
three pence.

    8vo fours. Imp. 5 Apr. 1718. Bodl. 8° O 12(3) Linc.

12. PEERS, RICHARD. The character of an honest Dissenter, in twelve marks:
together with an illustration of each. By Richard Peers [etc.]. The fourth edition.
[etc., as in the 3rd edition of 1717].

    8vo fours. Imp. 23 Jan. 1716. Bodl. 1305 e. 48(1).

13. PHALARIS. [Greek title.] Phalaridis Agrigentinorum tyranni Epistolae. Ex MSS
recensuit, versione, annotationibus, & vita insuper authoris donavit Car. Boyle [etc.].
Oxonii e Th. Sh. An. Dom. MDCCXVIII. impensis Stephani Fletcher bibliopolae.

    8vo fours. Bodl. 90 b. 22.

14. POINTER, JOHN. Miscellanea in usum juventutis academicae: containing 1.
Characters of the classick authors, and some of our English writers: collected from
Kennet, Addison, Pope, Garth, Dryden, Rapin, &c. 2. Instructions for reading the
classick authors: drawn from Hales, Pearson, and Blackwall. 3. A chronology of the
classick authors: together with some short instructions for reading chronology.
4. A catalogue of the best classick authors, and other books of polite learning, and
their best editions. 5. Pagan mythology: collected out of Vossius, Macrobius,
Lampridius, Bochartus, Diod. Sic., Philostratus, Diogenes, Lucian, Plato, Plutarch,
&c. 6. Latin exercises; viz. themes, declamations, poems, philosophical epigrams
and orations. 7. A correction of several palpable mistakes made by some of our
English historians and other authors, as Daniel, Trussel, Temple, Brerewood,
Hearne, Ayliffe, Puffendorf, Heylin, Savage, Spon, Brown, Walker, Dacier, Rapin,
Vergil, Seneca, Tibullus, Paterculus, Sleidan, &c. By John Pointer [etc.]. Oxford,
printed at the Theater for Ant. Peisley, and are to be sold by Ja. Knapton, Hen.
Clements, Will. Taylor, and Will. Meadows booksellers in London. 1718.

    8vo fours. Imp. 30 Apr. 1718. Bodl. 8° O 13 Linc.

    2nd A/cs. 64ᵛ, dues.

15. [WELCHMAN, EDWARD.] XXXIX Articuli Ecclesiae Anglicanae, textibus e
sacra Scriptura depromptis confirmati, brevibusque notis illustrati. Adjectis insuper
nominibus auctorum locisque in quibus doctrina in Articulis contenta fusius
explicatur. In usum juventutis academicae. Auctore Edwardo Welchman [etc.].
Oxonii, e Th. Sh., Ann. Dom. MDCCXVIII.

    8vo fours. Imp. 28 Aug. 1712. Bodl. 8° Rawl. 182.

    2nd A/cs. 64ᵛ, dues.

16. WELLS, EDWARD. An help to the more easy and clear understanding of the
Holy Scriptures: being the Four Gospels and the Acts of the Apostles [etc.].
Oxford, printed at the Theater, for James Knapton at the Crown in S. Paul's
Church-Yard, London. 1718.

    4to. Imp. 5 May 1718. Bodl. FF 25(1) Th.

    2nd A/cs. 64ᵛ, dues.

1719

1. [AINSWORTH, THOMAS.] The validity of episcopal ordination and invalidity of any other, considered in three letters, between a presbyter of the Church of England, and a Dissenting teacher. Oxford, printed at the Theatre for Ant. Peisley bookseller in Oxford; and are to be sold by J. Knapton, H. Clement, W. Taylor, W. Meadows, and J. Morphew, booksellers in London. 1719. Price six pence.
8vo fours. Imp. 15 May 1719. Bodl. G. Pamph. 781(15).

2. ARISTIDES. Proposals for a new edition of the works of Aristides, in four volumes octavo now ready for the press.
8vo. 4 pp. n.d. Bodl. fol. Θ 663(8).
Issued in 1719: Hearne vii, p. 78. The book was published (in 4to) in 1722 and 1730.

3. Author of the Whole DUTY OF MAN. The art of contentment by the Author of the Whole Duty of Man etc. At the Theater in Oxford, MDCCXIX.
8vo fours. Imp. 24 Feb. 1675. Bodl. Antiq. e. E 1719/2.
2nd A/cs. 74ᵛ, dues. The 10th edition.

4. GIBSON, JOHN. The frequent service of God in publick, the way to long life, honour, and undoubted happiness: set forth in a sermon preached at the consecration of the new chapel in Queen's College in Oxford, on the First day of November 1719. Oxford, printed at the Theatre, and are to be sold by Ant. Peisley and S. Wilmot in Oxford: J. Smith in Exeter Exchange, London; and H. Hammond in Bath. 1719.
8vo fours. Imp. 17 Nov. 1719. Bodl. G. Pamph. 1003(24).
Hearne vii, p. 82: 'in 8vo & some in 4to'.

5. [GRABE, JOHANN ERNST.] Τῆς Παλαιας Διαθηκης κατα τους Εβδομηκοντα τομ. β'. Septuaginta Interpretum tomus secundus, continens Veteris Testamenti Libros historicos omnes, sive canonicos sive apocryphos; quos ex antiquissimo MS. codice Alexandrino accurate descriptos, ope aliorum exemplarium, ac priscorum scriptorum, praesertim vero Hexaplaris editionis Origenianae, emendavit atque supplevit v. cl. Joannes Ernestus Grabe Borussus S.T.P. ὁ μακαρίτης; summa cum cura editus. Oxonii, e Th. Sh. Prostant venales apud M. Smith, bibliop. in Cambio Exoniensi. Anno Christi MDCCXIX.
Fol. Imp. 15 July 1719. Bodl. P 3. 12(2) Th.
Edited by Francis Lee: Hearne, vi, p. 260.

6. [HOLE, MATTHEW.] A second letter to Mr. James Peirce occasioned by some farther reflections in another pamphlet, intitled, the Loyalty, Integrity, and Ingenuity of Churchmen, and Dissenters Compar'd. By the author of the first. Printed at Oxford, 1719.
8vo. Bodl. 1305 e. 47.
Perhaps printed by Lichfield.

7. JACKMAN, JOHN. Presbyterian ordination presumptuous, being the second part of a reply to Mr. Peirce's defence of the Dissenting ministry and Presbyterian ordination. In vindication of a book, entituled, The Rational and Moral Conduct of Mr. Peirce examin'd, &c. By John Jackman [etc.]. Oxford, printed at the Theater,

for Edw. Whistler: and are to be sold by J. Knapton bookseller in St. Paul's Church-Yard, London. 1719.

8vo fours. Imp. 13 Nov. 1719. Bodl. 8° M 17 Linc.

8*. (Oxford, University. According to the accounts of the Press, a 'Catalogue of books in the Press' was printed in 1719: 2nd A/cs. 65. No copy has been found.)

9. OXFORD, UNIVERSITY, QUEEN'S COLLEGE. The present state of the new buildings of Queens College in Oxford. With an ichnography of the whole, and cuts of the several parts of the said buildings engraved. [No imprint. Dated 20 Feb. 1718.]
   4to. Bodl. Gough Oxf. 143.

10. [RANDOLPH, H.] Chichlaeus.
    Fol. Bodl. C 2. 19(8).
    A Latin poem in praise of Archbishop Chichele. The Bodleian copy has no title-page. See the notes by J. Lewis in Bodl. MS. Rawl. J. fol. 4 (fols. 30 and 253).

11. SPROTT, THOMAS. Thomae Sprotti Chronica, e codice antiquo MSSto. in bibliotheca praenobilis adolescentis Dni. Edwardi Dering, de Surrenden Dering in agro Cantiano, Baronetti, descripsit ediditque Tho. Hearnius, qui & alia quaedam opuscula, e codicibus MSStis. authenticis a seipso itidem descripta, subjecit. Oxonii, e Th. Sh., MDCCXIX.
    8vo fours. Bodl. Douce HH 176.
    2nd A/cs. 64ᵛ, dues.

12. STEPHENS, WILLIAM. The Catholick doctrine concerning the union of the two natures in the one person of Christ stated and vindicated. A sermon preach'd at the triennial visitation of the Right Reverend Father in God, John, Lord Bishop of Oxford; held at Witney, on Tuesday, July 21. 1719. In which also Dr Bennet's late notion, of the total quiescence of the divine nature in our Saviour during his ministry is considered and examined. By William Stephens [etc.]. Publish'd at the request of his Lordship and the clergy. Oxford, printed at the Theatre for Sam. Wilmot: and are to be sold by Awn. Churchill, R. Sare, J. Knapton, W. Innys, and J. Morphew, booksellers in London. 1719.
    8vo fours. Imp. 2 Oct. 1719. Bodl. G. Pamph. 23(7).

13. TRAPP, JOSEPH. Praelectiones poeticae; in Schola Naturalis Philosophiae Oxon. habitae. Authore Josepho Trapp [etc., as in vol. ii, 1715]. Volumen tertium & ultimum. Oxonii, e Th. Sh., impensis Henr. Clements bibliopolae Londinensis, MDCCXIX.
    8vo. Bodl. 8° G 178 Art.

14. TRIVET, NICOLAS. Nicolai Triveti, Dominicani, Annales sex regum Angliae. E praestantissimo codice Glastoniensi nunc primum emendate edidit Antonius Hall [etc.]. Oxonii, e Th. Sh., MDCCXIX.
    8vo fours. Imp. 26 Mar. 1718. Bodl. 8° D 45 Jur.
    2nd A/cs. 64ᵛ, dues.

15. TROTT, NICOLAS. מפתה לשון הקדש Clavis linguae sanctae continens grammaticalem explicationem 564. versiculorum ex Libro Psalmorum, & 546. versiculorum ex caeteris libris Veteris Testamenti: in quibus omnes radices pure Hebraicae Veteris Testamenti, cum nonnullis radicibus Chaldaicis (occurrentibus tamen in libris Hebraicis) inveniuntur: & in hac Clave reserantur, & juxta grammaticas

regulas, resolvantur, & explicantur. Authore Nicolao Trotio. Oxonii, e Th. Sh. Prostant venales apud Benj. Cowse ad insigne Rosae Coronatae in Coemeterio Divi Pauli Londini. 1719.

Fol. Imp. 15 July 1719. Bodl. fol. BS 50.

16*. WALLIS, JOHN. A treatise concerning St. Matthias Day, misplaced in the Oxford Almanack for the year 1684 (being leap-year) at Feb. 24. In a letter from Dr. Wallis to Dr. John Fell late Lord Bishop of Oxford. Published from the original manuscript in the Savilian Study. Oxford, printed in the year MDCCXIX.

8vo fours. Imp. 17 Nov. 1719. Bodl. 8° O 35 Linc.
2nd A/cs. 67, 150 small, 100 large.

17. WASSE, JOSEPH. Reformed devotions, being a collection of the best hymns, prayers, and other spiritual exercises for all occasions, composed by divines of the Church of England and foreign ascetics, Laud, Featley, Duppa, Whitchcot, Wettinghal, Cosins, Hammond, Taylour, Bernard, Scot, Tillotson, Patrick, Kettlewel, Bennet, Th. a Kempis, Stanhop, Inet, Hickes, Nelson, Gothair &c. The whole corrected, & improv'd by Joseph Wasse [etc.]. Oxford, printed at the Theatre for Jo. and Sam. Wilmot, and are to be sold by Jam. Knapton. William Innys, William Churchill booksellers in London. 1719.

8vo. Imp. 29 Jan. 1718/19. Bodl. Bliss B 156.
2nd A/cs. 64ᵛ, dues.

18. WELLS, EDWARD. An help to the more easy and clear understanding of the Holy Scriptures: being the Gospel of St. Luke and the Acts of the Apostles [etc.]. Oxford, printed at the Theater for James Knapton at the Crown in S. Paul's Church-Yard, London. 1719.

4to. Imp. 5 June 1719. Bodl. FF 25(1^d) Th.
2nd A/cs. 64ᵛ, dues.

19. WELLS, EDWARD. An help to the more easy and clear understanding of the Holy Scriptures: being the Gospel of St. John [etc.]. Oxford, printed at the Theater for James Knapton at the Crown in S. Paul's Church-Yard, London. 1719.

4to. Imp. 2 Oct. 1719. Bodl. FF 25(1^e) Th.
2nd A/cs. 64ᵛ, dues.

20. WILLIAM OF NEWBURGH. Guilielmi Neubrigensis Historia sive Chronica rerum Anglicarum, libris quinque. E codice pervetusto in bibliotheca praenobilis domini Dni. Thomae Sebright, Baronetti, uberrimis additionibus locupletata, longeque emendatius quam antehac edita, studio et industria Thomae Hearnii, qui & praeter Joannis Picardi annotationes, suas etiam notas & spicilegium subjecit. Accedunt homiliae tres eidem Guilielmo a viris eruditis adscriptae, partim e codice praeclaro antedicto, partim e codice antiquo Lambethano nunc primum editae. Oxonii, e Th. Sh. MDCCXIX.

8vo fours. Bodl. Douce HH 158, 9.
2nd A/cs. 64ᵛ, dues.

1720

1. BIBLIOTHECA BIBLICA. Bibliotheca Biblica, being a commentary upon all the Books of the Old and New Testament gather'd out of the genuine writings of Fathers and ecclesiastical historians, and acts of Councils, down to the year of our

Lord 451, being that of the Fourth General Council; and lower as occasion may require. Comprehending the proper, allegorical or mystick, and moral import of the text, as delivered or illustrated in the writings and monuments aforesaid, in such a manner that generally where the sense of several commentators is the same, the words only of one, with the names of the rest, are cited, to avoid repetition; and after such texts as have been made use of by the ancients against any heresies, the denominations of the hereticks against whom they have been produc'd, are inserted. To which are added introductory discourses upon the authors and authentickness of the Books, the time of their being written, &c. extracted for the most part, out of the best authors that have writ upon those subjects. With notes and scholia at the bottom of the page. Also a table, shewing in what page or pages the several chapters and verses are to be found; a table of texts of Holy Scripture incidentally illustrated; an index of things and words; and a catalogue of infidels, hereticks and others, confuted or censur'd by the Fathers. Vol. I. On the Book of Genesis. Part. I. Oxford, printed at the Theater, for William and John Innys, at the Prince's Arms, at the West End of St. Paul's; London. 1720.

4to. Imp. 28 Oct. 1720. Bodl. OO 3 Th.

2. — The same. Vol. I. On the Book of Genesis. Part II. [Imprint as for Part I.] Bodl. OO 4 Th.

Hearne, vi, p. 260. These two volumes were edited by Francis Lee.

3. [CATHERALL, SAMUEL.] An essay on the Conflagration in blank verse [Engraving of the Clarendon Building]. Oxford, printed for Anthony Peisley; and are to be sold by James Knapton, William Meadows, and John Morphew, booksellers in London. MDCCXX. Price one shilling.

8vo fours. Imp. 10 Aug. 1719. Bodl. 8° E 32(2) Jur.

Hearne, vii, p. 282.

4. CLARENDON, EDWARD HYDE, EARL OF. The History of the Rebellion and Civil Wars in England [etc.]. Oxford, printed at the Theater, An. Dom. MDCCXX. 6 vols. 8vo.

2nd A/cs. 74ᵛ (1724), dues for two impressions. D.O. 29 May 1719 gave Baskett permission to print 2,000.

In the set at the Bodleian (22856 e. 1–6) Vol. i, Part i is dated 1721 and has a different imprint.

5. CURIOUS DISCOURSES. A collection of curious discourses, written by eminent antiquaries upon several heads in our English antiquities, and now first published by Thomas Hearne, M.A. Oxford, printed at the Theater, M.DCC.XX.

8vo fours. Bodl. Mus. Bibl. II 63.

2nd A/cs. 64ᵛ, dues.

6. Author of the Whole DUTY OF MAN. The ladies calling by the Author of the Whole Duty of Man, &c. The eleventh impression. Oxford, printed at the Theatre, MDCCXX.

8vo fours. Bodl. 1419 e. 3030.

7. ERNULPHUS, BISHOP. Textus Roffensis, accedunt, professionum antiquorum Angliae episcoporum formulae, de canonica obedientia archiepiscopis Cantuarensibus praestanda, et Leonardi Hutteni dissertatio, Anglice conscripta, de anti-

quitatibus Oxoniensibus. E codicibus MSS. descripsit ediditque Tho. Hearnius. Oxonii, e Th. Sh., M DCC XX.

> 8vo fours. Bodl. Mus. Bibl. II 66.
> 2nd A/cs. 64ᵛ, dues.

8. FENTON, THOMAS. Of speaking as the oracles of God. A sermon preached before the University of Oxford at St. Mary's on Sunday, Sept. 11. 1720. By Thomas Fenton [etc.]. Oxford, printed at the Theatre, for Steph. Fletcher bookseller; and are to be sold by J. Knapton, W. Meadows, and J. Morphew, booksellers in London. 1720. Price 4*d*.

> 8vo fours. Bodl. G. Pamph. 24ᵇ(4).

9. GRABE, JOHANN ERNST. [Greek title.] Septuaginta Interpretum tomus tertius, continens Veteris Testamenti Libros Propheticos omnes, sive canonicos sive apocryphos, summa cum cura editus. Oxonii, e Th. Sh. Prostant venales apud M. Smith, in vico vulgo vocato Pater-Noster-Rowe. Anno Christi M DCC XX.

> Fol. Imp. 10 Sept. 1720. Bodl. P 3. 12(1) Th.
> 2nd A/cs. 74ᵛ, dues. Edited by George Wigan: Hearne, viii, p. 15.

10. HOLDSWORTH, WINCH. A sermon preached before the University of Oxford at St. Mary's on Easter-Monday, 1719. In which the cavils, false reasonings, and false interpretations of Scripture of Mr. Lock and others, against the resurrection of the same body are examin'd and answer'd. By Winch Holdsworth [etc.]. Oxford, printed at the Theatre for Rich. Wilkin at the King's Head in St Paul's Church Yard. London. 1720.

> 8vo fours. Imp. [illegible.] Bodl. G. Pamph. 23(9).

11. JOSEPHUS. [Greek title.] Flavii Josephi opera quae reperiri potuerunt omnia. Ad codices fere omnes cum impressos tum manuscriptos diligenter recensuit, nova versione donavit, & notis illustravit Joannes Hudson [etc.]. Duobus voluminibus. Oxonii, e Th. Sh., MDCCXX.

> Fol. Imp. 7 Apr. 1720. Bodl. fol. BS 276, 7.
> 2nd A/cs. 64ᵛ, dues. B.M. MS. Add. 4163, No. 107.

12. NEWLIN, THOMAS. Eighteen sermons on several occasions. By Thomas Newlin [etc.]. Oxford, printed at the Theatre for Ant. Peisley bookseller; and are to be sold by J. Knapton, W. Meadows, and J. Morphew, booksellers in London. 1720.

> 8vo. Imp. 24 May 1720. Bodl. 8° Z 413 Th.
> 2nd A/cs. 64ᵛ, dues.

13. ROBERT DE AVESBURY. Historia de mirabilibus gestis Edvardi III; accedunt I. Libri Saxonici qui ad manus Joannis Joscelini venerunt: II. Nomina eorum qui scripserunt historiam gentis Anglorum; et ubi exstant per Joannem Joscelinum; E codice MSS descripsit ediditque Tho. Hearnius, qui & appendicem subnexit. Oxonii, e Th. Sh., M.DCC.XX.

> 8vo fours. Bodl. Mus. Bibl. II 67.
> 2nd A/cs. 64ᵛ, dues.

14. [THEOBALD, JOHN.] Albion, a poem. [Engraving of the Clarendon Building] Oxford, printed in the year MDCCXX.

> 8vo fours. Bodl. 280 i. 280.
> Dedication by John Theobald.

1721

1. AUGUSTINE, ST. D. Aurelii Augustini Hipponensis episcopi De haeresibus ad Quod-Vult-Deum, una cum Gennadii Massiliensis appendice. Edidit, notisque illustravit Edvardus Welchman [etc.]. Oxonii, e Th. Sh. MDCCXXI.
8vo fours. Imp. 8 Aug. 1721. Bodl. 8° Y 91 Jur.
2nd A/cs. 64ᵛ, dues.

2. CATHERALL, SAMUEL. An epistle humbly inscrib'd to the University of Oxford, occasion'd by the death of the Ld. Bishop of Durham. Written in imitation of Waller's style. By Sam. Catherall [etc.]. Oxford, printed at the Theatre for Anth. Peisley, and are to be sold by J. Knapton, W. Meadows, W. Taylor, and T. Combes, booksellers in London. 1721.
Fol. Imp. 27 Sept. 1721. Bodl. C 2. 19(9) Art.

3. CLARENDON, EDWARD HYDE, EARL OF. The History of the Rebellion and Civil Wars in England [etc.]. Vol. I. Part 1. Oxford, printed at the Theatre for J. Batley at the Dove in Pater-Noster-Row. 1721.
8vo. Bodl. 22856 e. 1.
A volume uniform with the edition of 1720 excepting the date and the title-page, which is set in types not used at Oxford.

4. COKER, THOMAS. The character and doom of false teachers. A sermon preach'd at the Cathedral Church of Sarum on Sunday Aug. 27. 1721. By Thomas Coker [etc.]. Publish'd in his own vindication from the aspersions of some, and at the request of others his auditors. Oxford, printed at the Theatre for Step. Fletcher bookseller; and are to be sold by J. Knapton, W. Meadows, and T. Combes, booksellers in London, and by Mr. Pope bookseller in Sarum. 1721.
8vo fours. Imp. 15 Sept. 1721. Bodl. G. Pamph. 1633(5).

5. COTES, DIGBY. Fifteen sermons preach'd on several occasions. By Digby Cotes [etc.]. Oxford, printed at the Theatre for Ant. Peisley bookseller; and are to be sold by J. Knapton, W. Meadows, and T. Combes, booksellers in London. 1721.
8vo Imp. 15 Sept. 1721. Bodl. 8° A 182 Linc.
2nd A/cs. 74ᵛ, dues.

6. DEMOSTHENES AND AESCHINES. Δημοσθενους και Αισχινου οι περι της παραπρεσβειας λογοι αντιδικοι. Cum Latina Hier. Wolfii versione, plurimis in locis emendata, necnon Budaei aliorumque notis. His accedunt in Demosthenis orationem Ulpiani scholia, aliaque anonymi cujusdam in Aeschinis orationem nunc primum edita, & indices praeterea necessarii. Oxonii, e Th. Sh. MDCCXXI. Impensis Ant. Peisley bibliop. Oxon. Prostat apud J. Knapton, W. Taylor, & W. Meadows bibliopolas Lond.
8vo fours. Imp. 3 Apr. 1721. Bodl. 8° E 33 Jur.
2nd A/cs. 64ᵛ, dues. Edited by H. Brooke: Hearne, vii, p. 337.

7. Author of the Whole DUTY OF MAN. The government of the tongue. By the author of the Whole Duty of Man, &c. The seventh impression. Oxford, printed at the Theater, 1721.
8vo fours. Imp. 24 Jan. 1675. Bodl. 1419 e. 170.
2nd A/cs. 74ᵛ, dues.

8*. GASTRELL, FRANCIS. The Bishop of Chester's Case, with relation to the Wardenship of Manchester. In which is shewn, that no other degrees but such as are taken in the University, can be deemed legal qualifications for any ecclesiastical preferment in England. Oxford, printed at the Theater, MDCCXXI.

Fol. Bodl. G. Pamph. 67(8).

2nd A/cs. 68, 70v, 100 large, 3,000 small, 1s. Hearne, ix, pp. 83–4.

9. GOOLE, JOHN. An answer to a scandalous pamphlet entitul'd The Present State of the Free-School at Witney in the County of Oxford, &c. By John Goole [etc.]. Oxford, printed for Stephen Fletcher, and are to be sold by J. Knapton and Will. Meadows, booksellers in London. 1721.

8vo fours. Imp. 14 June 1721. Bodl. G. Pamph. 902(8).

10. LUPTON, WILLIAM. The temporal advantages of religion. A sermon preach'd before the Right Reverend and Right Honourable Nathaniel Crewe Lord Bishop of Durham and Baron of Stene, in the chapel of Stene, July 2. 1721. being the anniversary of his consecration, his lordship having then been fifty years a bishop. By William Lupton [etc.]. Oxford, printed at the Theatre for Sam. Wilmot: and are to be sold by J. Knapton, W. Innys, R. Knaplock in St Paul's Church-Yard, and J. Roberts in Warwick-Lane, London. 1721.

8vo fours. Imp. 8 Aug. 1721. Bodl. G. Pamph. 1004(4).

11*. (Thomas Marshall's booklet on the Catechism of the Church of England, first published in 1678 (Madan, *Oxford Books*, iii, p. 373), was reprinted in this or the following year in an edition of 3,000, priced at 4s. a dozen of 14: 2nd A/cs. 68, 72, 76v.)

12*. MAUNDRELL, HENRY. A journey from Aleppo to Jerusalem at Easter A.D. 1697. The fourth edition, to which is now added an account of the author's journey to the banks of the Euphrates at Beer, and to the country of Mesopotamia. By Hen. Maundrell [etc.]. Oxford, printed at the Theater, An. Dom. MDCCXXI.

8vo fours. Imp. 8 Apr. 1703. Bodl. 8° F 135 Art.

2nd A/cs. 69, 50 large, 750 small. See 1703, 1707, 1714–15.

13. NEWLIN, THOMAS. God's gracious design in inflicting national judgments. A sermon preach'd before the University of Oxford at St Mary's on Friday, Dec. 16th. 1720. being the day appointed by His Majesty for a general fast and humiliation for obtaining pardon for our sins, and averting God's judgments; and particularly for beseeching God to preserve us from the plague with which several other countries are at this time visited. By Thomas Newlin [etc.]. Publish'd at the request of Mr. Vice-Chancellor. Oxford, printed at the Theater, for Stephen Fletcher bookseller; and are to be sold by J. Knapton, W. Meadows, and J. Morphew booksellers in London. 1721. Price four pence.

8vo fours. Bodl. Pamph. 364(3).

14. (A second edition of Newlin's sermon was printed in the same year, according to Madan, 1721:17. No copy found.)

15*. OXFORD, UNIVERSITY. Parecbolae sive excerpta e corpore statutorum Universitatis Oxoniensis. Accedunt Articuli religionis XXXIX. in Ecclesia Anglicana recepti: nec non Juramenta fidelitatis et suprematus. In usum juventutis academicae. Oxoniae, e Th. Sh. MDCCXXI.

8vo fours. Bodl. G.A. Oxon. 8° 318.

2nd A/cs. 69, 3,000.

16. PEARSE, ROBERT. The folly of complaints in a corrupt nation: the methods proper to remove them, and to procure prosperity and happiness. A sermon preach'd before the University of Oxford at St. Mary's, on Sunday in the afternoon, Novemb. 5. 1721. By Robert Pearse [etc.]. Oxford, printed at the Theater for Rich. Clements; and sold by James Knapton bookseller in London, 1721.

8vo fours. Imp. 6 Nov. 1721. Bodl. 994 e. 27(1).

17. ROGERS, JOHN. A sermon preach'd before the University of Oxford at St Mary's on Act-Sunday, July the 9th 1721. By John Rogers D.D. Publish'd at the request of Mr. Vice Chancellor. Oxford, printed at the Theater for Ant. Peisley: and are to be sold by Tho. Woodward, J. Knapton, and W. Meadows booksellers in London. 1721.

8vo fours. Bodl. 8° E 32(4) Jur.

18. WHEATLY, CHARLES. The schools of the Prophets. A sermon preach'd before the University of Oxford at St Mary's on Act-Sunday, MDCCXX. by Charles Wheatly [etc.]. Oxford, printed at the Theater for S. Wilmot: and are to be sold by J. Knapton, W. Innys, and J. Morphew, booksellers in London, 1721.

8vo fours. Imp. 1 July 1721. Bodl. G. Pamph. 24ᵇ(5).

1722

1. ARISTIDES. Aelii Aristidis Adrianensis Opera omnia Graece & Latine, in duo volumina distributa; cum notis & emendationibus Gul. Canteri, Tristani, Palmerii, T. Fabri, Spanhemii, Normanni, & Lamb. Bosii; adjunctis insuper veterum scholiis; et prolegomenis Sopatri Apamensis, ab erroribus plurimis repurgatis. Graeca, cum MSS. codicibus variis & praestantissimis collata, recensuit, & observationes suas adjecit Samuel Jebb. Oxonii, e Th. Sh., MDCCXXII.

4to. Imp. 26 Nov. 1720. Bodl. II 29 Art.
2nd A/cs. 74ᵛ, dues. Proposals were issued in 1719.

2. ASSER. Proposals for printing by subscription a new edition of Asser Menevensis De rebus gestis Ælfredi. By Francis Wise . . .

8vo 4 pp. n.d. Bodl. fol. Θ 663(1).
The year is uncertain.

3. ASSER. Annales rerum gestarum Ælfredi Magni, auctore Asserio Menevensi, recensuit Franciscus Wise [etc.]. Oxonii, A.D. MDCCXXII.

8vo fours. Imp. 18 Aug. 1722. Bodl. 8° C 88 Jur.
2nd A/cs. 64ᵛ, dues. Hearne, viii, pp. 30, 39.

4. BIBLIOTHECA BIBLICA. Bibliotheca Biblica [etc., as for vol. i of 1720]. Vol. II. on the Book of Exodus. Oxford, printed at the Theater for Charles Rivington, at the Bible and Crown, in St. Paul's Church-Yard; London. 1722.

4to. Imp. 24 Sept. 1722. Bodl. OO 5 Th.

5. [EYSTON, CHARLES.] The history and antiquities of Glastonbury. To which are added, (1) The endowment and orders of Sherington's chantry, founded in Saint Paul's Church, London. (2) Dr. Plot's letter to the Earl of Arlington concerning Thetford. To all which pieces (never before printed) a preface is prefix'd, and an

appendix subjoyn'd, by the publisher Thomas Hearne, M.A. Oxford, printed at the Theater, M.DCC.XXII.

8vo fours. Bodl. Mus. Bibl. II 73.

2nd A/cs. 64ᵛ, dues. Hearne, vii, pp. 39, 46, 59.

6. FORDUN, JOHN. Johannis de Fordun Scotichronicon genuinum, una cum ejusdem supplemento ac continuatione. E codicibus MSS. eruit ediditque Thomas Hearnius, qui et appendicem subjunxit, totumque opus (in quinque volumina distributum) praefatione atque indicibus adornavit. Oxonii, e Th. Sh., M.DCC.XXII.

8vo fours. 5 vols. Bodl. Mus. Bibl. II 68–72.

2nd A/cs. 64ᵛ, dues.

7. OPPIAN. Oppian's Halieuticks of the nature of fishes and fishing of the ancients in V Books. Translated from the Greek, with an account of Oppian's life and writings, and a catalogue of his fishes. Oxford, printed at the Theater, An. Dom. MDCCXXII.

8vo fours. Imp. 6 Feb. 1722. Bodl. 8° V 54 Jur.

2nd A/cs. 64ᵛ, dues. Dedication by John Jones.

8. OXFORD, UNIVERSITY. A true copy of the poll for Members of Parliament for the University of Oxford, taken March the 21st. 1721. digested into alphabetical order. Oxford, printed at the Clarendon Printing House. MDCCXXII.

4to. Bodl. G.A. Oxon. 4° 6(7).

Compiled and published by Joseph Bowles: Hearne, vii, p. 349.

9. POTTER, JOHN, BISHOP OF OXFORD. Articles of visitation and enquiry concerning matters ecclesiastical; exhibited to the minister, church-wardens, and side-men of every parish within the Diocese of Oxford, at the triennial visitation of the Right Reverend Father in God John by divine permission Lord Bishop of Oxford. Oxford, printed in the year 1722.

4to 4 pp. Lincoln College 0.6.29(23).

Perhaps printed by Leonard Lichfield.

10. PSEUDO-TERTULLIAN. Tertullian's Prescription against hereticks; and the Apologeticks of St. Theophilus of Antioch to Autolycus, against the malicious calumniators of the Christian religion, translated from their respective originals, with notes and preliminary dissertations. By Joseph Betty [etc.]. Oxford, printed at the Theatre for C. Rivington in St. Paul's Church-yard, and J. Clarke at the Bible under the Royal Exchange. MDCCXXII.

8vo fours. Imp. 15 May 1722. Bodl. 8° B 406 Linc.

2nd A/cs. 64ᵛ, dues. Hearne, vii, p. 221.

11. TRIVET, NICOLAS. Nicolai Triveti Annalium continuatio; ut et Adami Meri-muthensis Chronicon, cum ejusdem continuatione: quibus accedunt Joannis Bostoni Speculum Coenobitarum et Edmundi Boltoni Hypercritica. Omnia nunc primum edidit e codicibus manuscriptis Antonius Hallius, S.T.P. Oxonii, e Th. Sh. M.DCC.XXII.

8vo fours. Imp. 2 Aug. 1722. Bodl. 8° D 73 Jur.

2nd A/cs. 64ᵛ dues. The first part was published in 1719. Hearne, viii, p. 14.

12. VIDA, MARCUS HIERONYMUS. Marci Hieronymi Vidae, Cremonensis, Albae episcopi, Poematum, quae haud plane disjunxit a fabula, pars prima, continens De arte poetica libros tres, Bucolica, et Epistolam ad Joannem Matthaeum Gibertum. Edidit Thomas Tristram [etc.]. Oxonii, e Typographeo Clarendoniano. MDCCXXII.

8vo fours. Imp. 26 Oct. 1721. Bodl. Vet. A 4 d. 61.

2nd A/cs. 74ᵛ, dues for editions in 8vo and 12mo.

1723

1. ABU AL-FIDA. Ismael abu'l Feda, De vita, et rebus gestis Mohammedis, Moslemicae religionis auctoris, et imperii Saracenici fundatoris. Ex codice MSto. Pocockiano Bibliothecae Bodleianae textum Arabicum primus edidit, Latine vertit, praefatione, & notis illustravit Joannes Gagnier, A.M. Oxoniae, e Th. Sh. MDCCXXIII.

   Fol. Imp. 30 Apr. 1723. Bodl. N 2. 11 Th.
   2nd A/cs. 74^v, 83, dues.

2. [ALDRICH, HENRY.] Artis logicae compendium. Oxoniae, e Th. Sh., An. Dom. MDCCXXIII. Impensis A. Peisley, bibliop.
   12mo sixes. Imp. 1 Dec. 1703. Bodl. 2642 f. 14.
   2nd A/cs. 74^v, 83, dues, 'Dr. Aldrich's Logick'.

3. ARETAEUS CAPPADOX. [Greek title.] Aretaei Cappadocis, De causis et signis acutorum et diuturnorum morborum libri quatuor. Cum MSS. duobus, Harleyano, & Vaticano, contulit: novamque versionem dedit, Johannes Wigan [etc.]. Accedit, praefatio: dissertationes in Aretaeum: variae lectiones: notae, & emendationes: tractatus de Ionica Aretaei dialecto: quodque difficiliores hujus authoris voces exponit, lexicon. Oxoniae, e Typographeo Clarendoniano MDCCXXIII.
   Fol. Bodl. F 1. 1 Med.
   2nd A/cs. 80^v, dues. Hearne, viii, p. 294. The preliminary pages i–xxxiv and the appendices are set in types not used at Oxford. Four pages of corrected proof of the Greek text are bound in at the end of the Bodleian copy.

4. CICERO. M. T. Ciceronis de Oratore ad Q. fratrem dialogi, seu libri tres. Interpretatio ac notae, quas in usum serenissimi Delphini edidit Jacobus Proust, e Societate Jesu, hac editione auctae prodeunt & emendatae. Oxonii, e Typographeo Clarendoniano, An. Dom. MDCCXXIII. Impensis Stephani Fletcher bibliopolae.
   8vo fours. Imp. 8 Oct. 1714. Bodl. 29469 e. 2.
   2nd A/cs. 74^v, 80^v, dues. The first Oxford edition was of 1714.

5. EUCLID. Euclidis Elementorum libri priores sex, item undecimus & duodecimus [as in the edition of 1715]. Oxoniae. E Th. Sh. MDCCXXIII. Impensis Rich. Clements bibliop. Oxon. Prostat apud J. Knapton & C. Rivington bibliop. in Coemeterio D. Pauli Lond.
   8vo. Imp. 25 Mar. 1715. Bodl. 1831 e. 141.
   2nd A/cs. 74^v, 80^v, dues. The second edition.

6. HEMING, WALTER. Hemingi Chartularium ecclesiae Wigornensis. E codice MS. penes Richardum Graves, de Mickleton in agro Gloucestriensi, armigerum, descripsit ediditque Tho. Hearnius, qui & eam partem libri de Domesday, quae ad ecclesiam pertinet Wigornensem, aliaque ad operis (duobus voluminibus comprehensi) nitorem facientia, subnexuit. Oxonii, e Th. Sh. M.DCC.XXIII.
   8vo fours. Bodl. Mus. Bibl. II 74, 5.
   2nd A/cs. 64^v, dues.

7. IVIE, EDWARD. Epicteti Enchiridion Latinis versibus adumbratum. Editio secunda priori emendatior. Per Edvardum Ivie [etc.]. Oxoniae, e Th. Sh., MDCCXXIII. Impensis Steph. Fletcher, bibliopolae Oxoniensis.
   12mo. Imp. 25 Mar. 1715. Bodl. 90 c. 47.

8. [KEILL, JOHN.] Trigonometriae planae & sphaericae elementa. Item de natura et arithmetica logarithmorum tractatus brevis. Oxoniae, e Th. Sh. MDCCXXIII. Impensis Ric. Clements bibliop. Oxoniensis.

    8vo. Bodl. 1831 e. 141.

    The first edition was of 1715.

9. MILNES, JAMES. Sectionum conicarum elementa nova methodo demonstrata. Authore Jacobo Milnes [etc.]. Editio tertia nova & sexta parte auctior. Oxoniae, e Th. Sh., MDCCXXIII. Impensis Ant. Peisley bibliop. Oxon. Prostat apud J. Knapton, W. Taylor, & W. Meadows, bibliopolas Londinenses.

    8vo fours. Imp. 9 Sept. 1723. Bodl. 8° Godw. 484.

    Previous editions were of 1702 and 1712.

10. [NEWTON, RICHARD.] The proceedings of the Visitors of University College, with regard to the late disputed election of a Master, vindicated. Printed at the Theatre for Stephen Fletcher bookseller; and are to be sold by all the booksellers in Oxford, and by Jonah Bowyer, J. Knapton, W. Meadows, and T. Combes booksellers in London. 1723.

    Fol. Bodl. Fol. Θ 674(6).

    Some copies have matter added on the verso of the title-page: Bodl. Gough Oxf. 136. Hearne, viii, pp. 57, 58.

11. — A second edition was issued in this year.

    Bodl. J.J. Coll., 'Oxford' folder.

12*. OXFORD, UNIVERSITY. Praesidi clarissimo Sociisque ornatissimis Collegii Regalis Medicorum Londinensium S O Procancellarius, Doctores, Procuratores, & Magistri Universitatis Oxoniensis . . . [a letter in reply to one from the College of Physicians about qualifications in medicine].

    Fol. 4 pp. n.d. Bodl. G.A. Oxon. b. 19(29).

    2nd A/cs. 70 (1723).

13*. OXFORD, UNIVERSITY. At a general meeting of the Vice-Chancellor, Heads of Houses, and Proctors of the University of Oxford, at the Apodyterium of the Convocation-House, on September 30. 1723 [regulations as to money-dealings with minors and admission of young students to ale-houses].

    Broadside. Bodl. G.A. Oxon. b. 19.

    2nd A/cs. 70, printing 150: 'A programma for regulating divers disorders'.

14*. (An order concerning ale-house measures was printed for the University in this year: 2nd A/cs. 70.)

15. OXFORD, UNIVERSITY. CHRIST CHURCH. Carmina quadragesimalia ab Aedis Christi Oxon. alumnis composita et ab ejusdem Aedis baccalaureis determinantibus in Schola Naturalis Philosophiae publice recitata. Oxonii, e Th. Sh., MDCCXXIII.

    8vo fours. Imp. 13 June 1723. Bodl. 8° C 89 Jur.

    2nd A/cs. 64ᵛ, dues: 'Mr. East's Quadragesimal Verses'. Hearne, viii, p. 94. Dedication by C. Este.

16. VIDA, MARCUS HIERONYMUS. Marci Hieronymi Vidae Cremonensis, Albae episcopi, De arte poetica libri tres. Autoris vitam praemisit, & annotationes adjecit Tho. Tristram [etc.]. Editio secunda. Oxonii, e Typographeo Clarendoniano,

MDCCXXIII. Prostant venales apud Gul. & Joan. Innys bibliopol. Londinenses, Ant. Peisley & Steph. Kiblewhite bibliopol. Oxonienses.

12mo sixes. Imp. 28 Oct. 1721. Bodl. 8° E 68 Jur.

2nd A/cs. 74ᵛ, 80ᵛ, 86ᵛ, 92ᵛ. I have not found a copy of the first edition; but that of works by Vida of 1701 or 1722 was, perhaps, considered the first.

17. VIDA, MARCUS HIERONYMUS. Marci Hieronymi Vidae, Cremonensis, Albae episcopi, Poematum, quae haud plane disjunxit a Fabula, pars altera, continens Bombycum libros duos, Scacchiam ludum, et carmina diversi generis. Edidit Thomas Tristram [etc.]. Oxonii, e Typographeo Clarendoniano, MDCCXXIII.

8vo fours. Imp. 1 May 1722. Bodl. Vet. A 4 d. 62.

2nd A/cs. 74ᵛ, 80ᵛ, 86ᵛ, 92ᵛ. The first part of the book, Bombycum libri duo, has a separate title-page dated 1722. The previous volume was published in 1722. Hearne, viii, p. 71.

18. WELLS, EDWARD. An help for the more easy and clear understanding of the Holy Scriptures: being the twelve Lesser Prophets, explained [etc.]. By Edward Wells [etc.]. Oxford, printed at the Theater, 1723. And are to be sold by Will. Wells bookseller in Oxford: James Knapton at the Crown, and Jonah Bowyer at the Rose in St Paul's Church Yard, London.

4to. Imp. 6 Sept. 1723. Bodl. 1014 d. 1.

2nd A/cs. 74ᵛ, dues. Hearne, viii, pp. 73–4.

1724

1. BIBLIOTHECA BIBLICA. Bibliotheca Biblica [etc., as for Vol. i of 1720]. Vol. III. on the Book of Leviticus. Oxford, printed at the Theater for Charles Rivington, at the Bible and Crown, in St. Paul's Church-Yard; London. 1724.

4to. Imp. 6 Oct. 1724. Bodl. OO 6 Th.

2. GREEK ANTHOLOGY. Ἀνθολογια sive epigrammatum Graecorum ex Ἀνθολογία edita, MS. Bodleianâ, aliisque autoribus delectus in usum Scholae Westmonasteriensis. Oxoniae, e Typographeo Clarendoniano, MDCCXXIV.

8vo fours. Bodl. 8° Rawl. 193, 687.

2nd A/cs. 80ᵛ, dues, 'Mr Allen's Greek epigrams'. Hearne, viii, p. 56.

3. NOVATIAN. Novatiani presbyteri Romani Opera, quae extant, omnia, correctius longe quam usquam antehac edita notisque illustrata. Per Edvardum Welchman [etc.]. Oxonii, e Th. Sh., Prostant apud Ant. Peisley, bibliop. Oxon. J. Knapton, W. Meadows & S. Tooke, bibliop. Lond. MDCCXXIV.

8vo fours. Imp. 26 Feb. 1723. Bodl. Radcl. e. 188(1).

2nd A/cs. 74ᵛ, 80ᵛ, dues. Hearne, viii, p. 240.

4. ROBERT OF GLOUCESTER. Robert of Gloucester's Chronicle. Transcrib'd and now first publish'd from a MS. in the Harleyan Library by Thomas Hearne, M.A. To which is added, besides a glossary and other improvements, a continuation (by the author himself) of this Chronicle from a MS. in the Cottonian Library. In two volumes. Oxford, printed at the Theater, MDCCXXIV.

8vo fours. Bodl. Mus. Bibl. II 76.

2nd A/cs. 74ᵛ, dues.

5. SMALRIDGE, GEORGE. Sixty sermons preach'd on several occasions. By the Right Reverend Father in God George Smalridge [etc.]. Published from the originals. Oxford, printed at the Theater, MDCCXXIV.

Fol. Imp. 28 Oct. 1724. Bodl. B 6. 14 Th.

2nd A/cs. 80ᵛ, dues. The volume contains a royal privilege for sole printing and publishing granted to Mary Smalridge for 14 years, dated 19 Dec. 1724.

6. WELCHMAN, EDWARD. XXXIX Articuli Ecclesiae Anglicanae, textibus e Sacra Scriptura depromptis confirmati, brevibusque notis illustrati. adjectis insuper nominibus auctorum locisque in quibus doctrina in Articulis contenta fusius explicatur. In usum juventutis academicae. Auctore Edvardo Welchman [etc.]. Editio quarta auctior & emendatior, cui accedit appendix de doctrina Patrum. Oxonii, e Th. Sh. impensis Ant. Peisley, bibliop. Oxon. Prostant apud J. Knapton, W. Taylor, W. Meadows & S. Tooke, bibliop. Lond. MDCCXXIV.

[In the same volume, with signatures in the same series:] Concentus veterum, sive Appendix ad XXXIX Articulos Ecclesiae Anglicanae, in qua ejusdem Ecclesiae doctrina Patrum antiquissimorum testimoniis confirmatur. Editio quarta emendatior. Oxonii, e Th. Sh., Ann. Dom. MDCCXXIV.

8vo fours. Imp. 28 Aug. 1712. Bodl. 8° N 110 Th.

2nd A/cs. 80ᵛ, dues.

7. WELLS, EDWARD. An help to the more easy and clear understanding of the Holy Scriptures: being The Book of Genesis explain'd [etc.]. Hereto is prefix'd IV. A preface, at the end whereof are publish'd the Proposals for printing the four remaining Books of Moses. By Edward Wells [etc.]. Oxford, printed at the Theater, 1724. and sold by Will. Wells, bookseller in Oxford; and Ja. Knapton at the Crown in St. Paul's Church Yard, London.

4to. Imp. 22 Aug. 1724. Bodl. 4° AS 453(1).

2nd A/cs. 80ᵛ, dues.

1725

1. GREEK ANTHOLOGY. Ἀνθολογία δευτέρα, sive poematum Graecorum minorum delectus in usum Scholae regiae Westmonasteriensis. [Arms of Westminster School] Oxoniae, e Typ. Clar. sumptibus B. Barker, MDCCXXV.

8vo fours. Bodl. 8° C 707 Linc.

2nd A/cs. 86ᵛ, dues.

2. [COLLINS, THOMAS.] The Jewish philosophers encounter'd and confuted, in a sermon preach'd before the University of Oxford, by a late member of the said University. Oxford, printed in the year 1725.

8vo fours. Bodl. 124 e. 426(1).

Hearne, ix, p. 58.

3*. DOSITHEUS, ABBOT OF PANTOCRATOR. To the Vice-Chancellor, Doctors, and Proctors, and all other members of the University of Oxford. The humble petition of Dositheus Abbot of the Monastery Pantocrator on Mount Athos . . . [At foot, a recommendation from the Vice-Chancellor dated 2 July 1725.]

Broadside. Bodl. MS. Willis fol. LII(197).

2nd A/cs. 81, printing.

4. FELTON, HENRY. The resurrection of the same body, and its reunion to the
same soul; asserted in a sermon preached before the University of Oxford, at St
Mary's on Easter-Monday, 1725. in which Mr Lock's notions of personality and
identity are confuted. and the author of the Naked Gospel is answered. By Henry
Felton [etc.]. Oxford, printed at the Theatre, and are to be sold by Steph. Fletcher,
and Rich. Clements booksellers in Oxford; and Benj. Motte bookseller near the
Middle Temple-Gate in London.
   8vo fours. Imp. 6 May 1725. Bodl. G. Pamph. 18(7).

5. HEARNE, THOMAS. A letter containing an account of some antiquities between
Windsor and Oxford; with a list of the several pictures in the School-Gallery adjoyning to the Bodlejan Library. Written An. Dom. MDCCXVIII. Reprinted MDCCXX.
   8vo fours. Bodl. Mus. Bibl. II 13.

6. LANGTOFT, PETER. Peter Langtoft's Chronicle (as illustrated and improv'd by
Robert of Brunne) from the death of Cadwalader to the end of K. Edward the First's
reign. Transcrib'd and now first publish'd, from a MS. in the Inner-Temple Library
by Thomas Hearne, M.A. To which are added, besides a glossary and other curious
papers (1) a roll concerning Glastonbury Abbey, being a survey of all the estates
belonging to that house at the Dissolution, taken by King Henry the Eighth's order
and for his use. (2) An account of the Hospital of St. Mary Magdalen near Scroby in
Nottinghamshire, by John Slacke, Master of that hospital. (3) Two tracts by an
anonymous author; the first relating to Conquest in Somersetshire, the second
concerning Stone-henge. In two volumes. Oxford, printed at the Theater,
M.DCC.XXV.
   8vo fours. Bodl. Mus. Bibl. II 80(1).
   2nd A/cs. 86ᵛ, dues. Hearne, ix, p. 27.

7. OXFORD, UNIVERSITY. An order by the Vice-Chancellor to scavenge the streets.
   Broadside. Bodl. G.A. Oxon. b. 19(38).
   2nd A/cs. 81, printing 'a large advertisement'.

8. STUBBS, PHILIP. Farther advice to the Reverend the clergy of the peculiar
jurisdiction of St. Alban within the Diocese of London; given in the Court-
Consistorial held at the ninth general visitation of that Arch-deaconry. on April
29th. at St. Alban, Hertfordshire, and mutatis mutandis, on May 20th. at Winslow,
Buckinhamshire, 1725. By Philip Stubbs [etc.]. Published at the request of several of
the St. Alban clergy, and for the interest of their small augmentable livings. Oxford:
printed at the Theatre, for Richard Clements bookseller in Oxford, William and
John Innys booksellers at the Prince's Arms the West End of St. Paul's, and John
Penn at the Bible and Dove in Fleetstreet, London.
   8vo fours. Bodl. 8° Z 101(3) Jur.

9. VIDA. Marci Hieronymi Vidae, Cremonensis, Albae episcopi, Christiados libri
sex. Edidit Edvardus Owen [etc.]. Oxonii, e Typ. Clar., MDCCXXV.
   8vo fours. Imp. 29 Oct. 1725. Bodl. Vet. A 4 d. 63.
   2nd A/cs. 86ᵛ, dues.

10. WELLS, EDWARD. An help to the more easy and clear understanding of the
Holy Scriptures: being the Books of Exodus, Leviticus, Numbers and Deuteronomy
explain'd . . . Hereto is prefix'd IV. A preface, wherein is represented the order of
the Israelites encamping, as also of their marches. Likewise an account is given of
the sacred Books that are to be next publish'd, as to the terms and time, &c. By

Edward Wells [etc.]. Oxford, printed at the Theater, 1725. and sold by Will. Wells, bookseller in Oxford; and Ja. Knapton at the Crown in St Paul's Church Yard, London.

4to. Imp. 11 May 1725. Bodl. 4° AS 453(2).

2nd A/cs. 86ᵛ, dues.

11. WELLS, EDWARD. An help to the more easy and clear understanding of the Holy Scriptures: being the Books of Joshua, Judges and Ruth explain'd . . . By Edward Wells [etc.]. Oxford, printed at the Theater, 1725. and sold by Will. Wells bookseller in Oxford; and Ja. Knapton at the Crown in St Paul's Church Yard, London.

4to. Imp. 23 Dec. 1725. Bodl. 4° AS 454(2).

2nd A/cs. 86ᵛ, dues.

1726

1. AESCHINES AND DEMOSTHENES. Αισχινου ο κατα Κτησιφωντος και Δημο-σθενους ο περι στεφανου λογος. Interpretationem Latinam et vocum difficiliorum explicationem adjecerunt P. Foulkes, J. Freind Aedis Christi alumni. Editio quarta. Oxonii, e Typ. Clar. An. Dom. MDCCXXVI. Impensis Stephani Fletcher biblio-polae.

8vo fours. Imp. 24 Dec. 1695. Bodl. 90 b. 19.

2nd A/cs. 98ᵛ (1728), dues. Previous editions from the Press were dated 1696 and 1715.

2. BARBERINI, MAPHEO. Maphaei S.R.E. Card. Barberini postea Urbani PP. VIII Poemata. Praemissis quibusdam de vita auctoris & annotationibus adjectis. edidit Josephus Brown [etc.]. Oxonii, e Typ. Clar., MDCCXXVI.

8vo fours. Imp. 23 July 1726. Bodl. 8° B 421 Linc.

2nd A/cs. 92ᵛ, dues.

3. Author of the Whole DUTY OF MAN. Works of the learned and pious author of the Whole Duty of Man. Printed at the Theater in Oxford; and in London, by John Baskett, Printer to the King's Most Excellent Majesty. MDCCXXVI. [The Second part of the volume has another title-page:] The Second Part of the Works of the learned and pious author of the Whole Duty of Man. Oxford, printed at the Theater, MDCCXXVI.

Fol. Bodl. 141 c. 161.

2nd A/cs. 86ᵛ, dues, 'Second pt. of the Whole Duty of Man's Works'.

4. ISOCRATES. Ισοκρατους λογοι τινες In usum Scholae Wintoniensis Recensuit Phil. Fletcher e Coll. Nov. scholaris. Εκ Θεατρου ἐν Οξονια εν τῷ ετει ᾳψκϛ'.

8vo fours. Imp. 27 Oct. 1726. Bodl. Bliss B 160.

2nd A/cs. 92ᵛ, dues.

5. JOHN OF GLASTONBURY. Johannis confratris & monachi Glastoniensis, Chronica sive historia de rebus Glastoniensibus. E codice MS membraneo antiquo descripsit ediditque Tho. Hearnius. qui ex eodem codice historiolam de antiquitate & augmentatione vetustae Ecclesiae S. Mariae Glastoniensis praemisit, multaque

excerpta e Richardi Beere (Abbatis Glastoniensis) terrario hujus coenobii subjecit. Accedunt, quaedam, eodem spectantia, ex egregio MS. nobiscum communicato ab amicis eruditis Cantabrigiensibus, ut & appendix, in qua, inter alia, de S. Ignatii epistolarum Codice Mediceo, & de Johannis Dee, mathematici celeberrimi, vita atque scriptis agitur. Duobus voluminibus. Oxonii, e Th. Sh., M.DCC.XXVI.

8vo fours. Bodl. Mus. Bibl. II 82, 3.

2nd A/cs. 92ᵛ, dues.

6. MUSGRAVE, WILLIAM. De Arthritide primigenia regulari dissertatio. Auctore Gulielmo Musgrave Reg. Societ. utriusque Socio. Oxon. e Th. Sh., sumtibus Joan. March bibliopolae Exoniensis. Prostat apud Joan. Sprint ad insigne Campanae in vico Britannia Minore; Guil. & Joan. Innys in Coemeterio D Pauli ab occidente; & Joan. Osborne & T. Longman ad insigne Navis in Patris Nostri Aedium Serie, bibliopol Lond. MDCCXXVI.

8vo. Imp. 29 Apr. 1726. Bodl. 154 e. 80.

7. OXFORD, UNIVERSITY, CHRIST CHURCH. Liber precum Ecclesiae Cathedralis Christi Oxon. Litania, Ordo administrandae Coenae Domini, Catechismus, &c. Oxoniae, e Th. Sh., MDCCXXVI.

8vo fours. Bodl. Bliss B 163.

2nd A/cs. 92ᵛ, dues. Madan, *Oxford Books*, iii, No. 2474.

8. PETRA, SCANDALI. Liber dictus Petra Scandali, in quo continentur I. Historia initii schismatis inter duas ecclesias Orientalem sc. & Occidentalem; et quod ingentis hujus dissidii causa fuit Episcopi Romani ambitio, ut principatum suum amplificaret. II. Paraenesis, seu Adhortatio ad servos Domini, ut caveant a zizania, quam disseminant servi inimici in hisce Ecclesiis Orientalibus. Atque haec tum demum prodeunt e Graeco in Arabicum idioma translata, cura patris venerabilis Athanasii Patriarchae Antiocheni in urbe Halebo civitate a Deo custodita. anno aerae Christianae 1721. [Greek title page adds:] Additur Arabice, quae non extat in Graeco, تنبيه Tanbiah, i.e. Paraenesis seu Adhortatio &c. Item Tractatus Gabrielis Metropolitae Philadelphiae, De dissidiis ortis inter duas Ecclesias Orientalem sc. & Occidentalem de primatu Papae.

4to. Christ Church M.D. 7. 10. (The Bodleian copy, 8° B 420 Linc., lacks the Latin and Greek title-pages.)

2nd A/cs. 86ᵛ (1726), 'Dr. Mayow's Arabic Tract'.

9. STOCKWELL, JOSEPH. A sermon preach'd at St Helen's in Abingdon April 2d 1726, on the occasion of opening an organ: and a sermon preach'd before the University of Oxford at St Mary's on Rogation Sunday, May 15th 1726. By Joseph Stockwell. Oxford, printed at the Theatre for Sam. Wilmot; and are to be sold by Messieurs Knapton, R. Knaplock, D. Midwinter, J. Wyat, and J. Astley in St Paul's Church-Yard; Messieurs Innys in Ludgate-Street, J. Crockett in Fleet-Street, W. Mears without Temple-Bar, and J. Roberts in Warwick-Lane.

8vo fours. B.M. 4475.b.92.

10. TASSO, TORQUATO. Aminta favola boscareccia del Signor Torquato Tasso. Con alcune annotazioni, ed un elogio historico dell'autore. In Osford, nel Teatro Sceldoniano MDCCXXVI.

8vo fours. Imp. 7 Apr. 1726. Bodl. 8° B 422 Linc.

2nd A/cs. 86ᵛ, dues.

11. [Virgil (pseud.). Sibylla Capitolina, Publii Virgilii Maronis poemation; inter-pretatione et notis illustratum a S.L. [Device of a phoenix with motto: Vitam post funera reddit, engraved by B. Picart.] Oxonii, e Th. Sh., M.DCC.XXVI.

8vo. Bodl. 90 b. 10.

Attributed by Quérard and Brunet to Pierre Daudé. Apparently printed in France and probably published in Holland.]

12. WELLS, EDWARD. An help to the more easy and clear understanding of the Holy Scriptures; being the two Books of Samuel and the two Books of Kings explain'd . . . By Edward Wells [etc.]. Oxford, printed at the Theater, 1726, and sold by Will. Wells bookseller in Oxford; and James Knapton at the Crown in St Paul's Church Yard, London.

4to. Imp. 13 July 1726. Bodl. 4° AS 454(2).

2nd A/cs. 92ᵛ, dues. According to a note on p. 182, some sheets following it were printed at a different press (probably Lichfield's).

1727

1. ADAM DE DOMERHAM. Adami de Domerham Historia de rebus gestis Glastoni-ensibus e codice MS. perantiquo, in bibliotheca Collegii S. Trinitatis Cantabrigiae, descripsit primusque in lucem protulit Tho. Hearnius. Qui & (praeter alia, in quibus Dissertatio de inscriptione perveteri Romana, Cicestriae nuper reperta) Guilielmi Malmesburiensis librum De antiquitate ecclesiae Glastoniensis, et Edmundi Archeri excerpta aliquammulta satis egregia e registris Wellensibus, praemisit. Duobus voluminibus. Oxonii, e Th. Sh., M.DCC.XXVII.

8vo fours. Bodl. Mus. Bibl. II 84–5.

2nd A/cs. 92ᵛ, dues.

2. BRIDGE, WILLIAM. In obitum Georgii I. [An ode. n.p., n.d.]

Fol. s. sh. Bodl. Fol. Δ 755(8).

3. ELMHAM, THOMAS DE. Thomae de Elmham Vita & gesta Henrici Quinti, Anglorum regis. E codicibus MSS. vetustis descripsit, & primus luci publicae dedit Tho. Hearnius. Oxonii, e Th. Sh. M.DCC.XXVII.

8vo fours. Bodl. Mus. Bibl. II 86.

2nd A/cs. 98ᵛ, dues.

4. FELTON, HENRY. The common people taught to defend their Communion with the Church of England against the attempts and insinuations of popish emissarys. In a dialogue between a popish priest and a plain countryman. By Henry Felton [etc.]. Oxford, printed at the Theatre; and are to be sold by Stephen Fletcher and Richard Clements booksellers in Oxford; Benj. Motte bookseller near the Middle Temple-Gate in London; and by the booksellers in Leicester, Nottingham, Chesterfield, and Derby.

8vo fours. Imp. 11 May 1727. Bodl. G. Pamph. 794(9).

5*. OXFORD, UNIVERSITY. Pietas Universitatis Oxoniensis in obitum serenissimi regis Georgii I. et gratulatio in augustissimi regis Georgii II. inaugurationem. Oxonii, e Th. Sh., An. Dom. MDCCXXVII.

Fol. Bodl. H 9. 19 Art.

2nd A/cs. 94, 400 copies.

6*. Oxford, University. A catalogue of all graduats in Divinity, Law, and Physick: and of all Masters of Arts and Doctors of Musick: who have regularly proceeded or have been created in the University of Oxford, between October 10th. 1659. and October 10th. 1726. To which are added, the Proceeders between the 10th of October 1726 and the 10th of October 1727: likewise the Chancellors, High-Stewards, Vice-Chancellors and Proctors, from the year 1659 to 1727: also the Parliament men for the said University, from the year 1603, to 1727. Oxford, printed at the Theater MDCCXXVII.

8vo fours. Bodl. Gough Oxf. 35.
2nd A/cs. 101, 500 LP, 500 small.

7*. Oxford, University. [Diploma conferring the degree of Doctor of Divinity on Pierre-François Le Courayer and his letter acknowledging it. Dated 28 Aug. 1727.]

Fol. 4 pp. Bodl. G.A. Oxon. b. 19(50).
2nd A/cs. 99, printing.

8. Wells, Edward. An help to the more easy and clear understanding of the Holy Scriptures: being the Books of Chronicles, Ezra, Nehemiah and Esther explain'd . . . At the end of the Paraphrase is added IV. A brief continuation of the Jewish history from the times of the Old Testament to the times of the New Testament. Before the Paraphrase is plac'd, V. A preface to the reader, wherein notice is taken of the usefulness of the sections into which the Paraphrase is divided, for reading the sacred history in due order as to the series of time, wherein the several particulars were transacted. Also notice is given, what sacred Books are intended to be next printed, and of some improvements relating thereto. By Edward Wells [etc.]. Oxford, printed at the Theater, 1727. and sold by Will. Wells bookseller in Oxford; and J. Knapton at the Crown in St Paul's Church Yard, London.

4to. Imp. 22 Dec. 1726. Bodl. 4° AS 454(3).
2nd A/cs. 92ᵛ, dues.

9. Wells, Edward. An help to the more easy and clear understanding of the Holy Scriptures: being the Books of Job, Psalms, Proverbs, Ecclesiastes and Canticles explain'd . . . N.B. In the preface to Job it is put beyond all reasonable doubt, that Job liv'd, and his Book was written, after the coming of the Israelites out of Egypt. By Edward Wells [etc.]. [Imprint as in the preceding item.]

4to. Imp. 26 May 1727. Bodl. 4° AS 455(1).
2nd A/cs. 92ᵛ, dues.

10. Xenophon. Ξενοφῶντος Κύρου παιδείας βιβλία οκτω. Xenophontis de Cyri institutione libri octo. Graeca recognovit, cum codice MSto. Oxoniensi & omnibus fere libris editis contulit, plurimis in locis emendavit, versionem Latinam reformavit, observationibus suis, tabula geographica, binisque dissertationibus praemissis auxit & illustravit; notas H. Stephani, Leunclavii, Æ. Porti & Mureti recensitas & castigatas, variantium lectionum delectum, indicesque necessarios adjunxit Thomas Hutchinson A.M. E Th. Sh. MDCCXXVII.

4to. Imp. 13 Feb. 1726/7. Bodl. Radcl. c. 35.
2nd A/cs. 98ᵛ, dues.

11. Xenophon. Ξενοφῶντος Κυρου παιδειας βιβλια οκτω. Εκ Θεατρου εν Οξονια,

ετει αψκζ'. Prostant apud viduam Jonae Bowyer, ad insigne Rosae in vico vulgo dicto Pater-Noster-Row, Londini.

8vo fours. Bodl. Clar. Press 50 a. 67.

Apparently the text of Hutchinson's edition of the same year without the apparatus. There is no entry for it in the Accounts of the Press. The text is reset.

1728

1. ABELARD AND HÉLOÏSE. Petri Abaelardi, Abbatis Ruyensis et Heloissae, Abbatissae Paracletensis Epistolae a prioris editionis erroribus purgatae, & cum cod. MS. collatae cura Ricardi Rawlinson [etc.]. Oxonii, e Th. Sh. M.DCC.XXVIII. (Pretium 5s.)

8vo. Bodl. 1 a. 158.

Printed in types not used at Oxford. At the end is a list of books printed for H. Curll, over-against Catherine-Street in the Strand. The first edition was printed in 1718 for E. Curll and W. Taylor.

2. BIBLIOTHECA BIBLICA. Bibliotheca Biblica [etc., as for Vol. i of 1720]. Vol. iv on the Book of Numbers. Oxford, printed at the Theater for Charles Rivington, at the Bible and Crown in St. Paul's Church-Yard; London. 1728.

4to. Imp. 26 Feb. 1728. Bodl. OO 7 Th.

3. BLACK BOOK OF THE EXCHEQUER. Liber Niger Scaccarii e codice, calamo exarato, sibique ipsi a Richardo Gravesio Mickletoniensi donato, descripsit & nunc primus edidit Tho. Hearnius. qui & cum duobus aliis codicibus MSS. contulit. Wilhelmique etiam Worcestrii Annales rerum Anglicarum (antehac itidem ineditos) subjecit. Duobus voluminibus. Oxonii, e Th. Sh., M.DCC.XXVIII.

8vo fours. Bodl. Mus. Bibl. II 87–8.

2nd A/cs. 106ᵛ, dues. Hearne, x, p. 78.

4. FATIO DE DUILLIER, NICOLAS. Nicolai Fatii Duillierii Neutonus ecloga. [at foot:] Editio ab auctore recognita. Anno MDCCXXVIII pridie ante Paschatis diem.

8vo. 4 pp. Bodl. 4° Z 24 Art. (in a copy of the 3rd edition of Newton's *Principia*, 1726).

MS. note; Oxoniae ad Isin, E Theatro Sheldoniano.

5. HOOPER, GEORGE. De benedictione Patriarchae Jacobi Genes. xlix. Conjecturae [engraving of Adam digging] Oxonii, e Th. Sh. MDCCXXVIII.

4to. Imp. 2 Nov. 1728. Bodl. B 26. 80 Linc.

The preface by the editor, Thomas Hunt, explains that he completed the work left unfinished by the deceased Bishop of Bath and Wells. Hooper had the device engraved for the book.

6*. OXFORD, UNIVERSITY. An order for stage coaches to London, dated 23 Feb. 1727.

2nd A/cs. 99. Bodl. G.A. Oxon. b. 19(40).

7*. OXFORD, UNIVERSITY. A programma for regulating public houses, dated 28 May 1728.

2nd A/cs. 99. Bodl. G.A. Oxon. b. 19(41).

8*. PLATO. [Greek title.] Parmenides. sive de ideis et uno rerum omnium principio
Platonis dialogus. Studio Joh. Gul. Thomson [etc.]. Oxonii, e Th. Sh. MDCCXXVIII.
  8vo fours. Imp. 30 Aug. 1728. Bodl. 8° X 20 Art. BS.
  2nd A/cs. 102, 500 printed. D.O. 14 March 1726.

9. STUBBS, PHILIP. The divine right of prerogative royal. A sermon preach'd June
11th MDCCXXVIII in the Oratory of the Royal Hospital, Greenwich; on the first
anniversary of His Majesty King George IId's happy succession to the throne.
By Ph. Stubbs [etc.]. Made publick at the appointment of Sr John Jennings, the
most honoured Master and Governor thereof. Oxford, printed at the Theatre; and
sold by Rich. Clements bookseller in Oxon, and J. Roberts in Warwick-Lane, London.
  8vo fours. Bodl. 994 e. 7(3).

10. WELLS, EDWARD. An help to the more easy and clear understanding of the
Holy Scriptures: being the Books of Isaiah, Jeremiah, and Lamentations explain'd . . .
IV. At the beginning is a general discourse concerning the times, wherein prophesy'd
the Prophets, whose writings make up the last sixteen Books or parts of the Old
Testament. By the Revd. Dr Edward Wells. Oxford, printed at the Theater for
Will. Wells in Oxford; and sold by J. and J. Knapton, Ch. Rivington in St Paul's
Church Yard; J. Smith at Inigo Jones's Head in the Strand; and Jos. Hazard at the
Bible in Stationers' Court, London. 1728.
  4to. Imp. 13 Nov. 1727. Bodl. 4° AS 455(2) and 456(1).
  2nd A/cs. 113ᵛ, dues.

11. WELLS, EDWARD. An help to the more easy and clear understanding of the
Holy Scriptures: being the Book of Ezekiel explain'd . . . Hereto are also added
three draughts, viz. 1. A general draught of the courts of the Temple, 2. A particular draught of the Separate Place and Inner Court, 3. A draught of the Total
Oblation, and its several parts, viz. the Holy Portion, the Possession or Portion of
the City, and the Princes Portion. By the Revd. Dr. Edward Wells. [Imprint as in
the preceding item.]
  4to. Imp. 28 May 1728. Bodl. 4° AS 456(2).

12. WELLS, EDWARD. An help [etc.] . . . the Book of Daniel . . . The second
edition . . . [Title as in 1716. Imprint as in the two preceding items.]
  4to. Imp. 13 Feb. 1715/16. Bodl. 4° AS 456(3).

1729

1. AESCHYLUS, SOPHOCLES, AND EURIPIDES. Τρεις τραγῳδιαι, Αισχυλου Χοηφοροι,
Σοφοκλεους Ηλεκτρα, Ευριπιδου Ηλεκτρα. In usum Scholae regiae Westmonasteriensis [Arms of Westminster School] Oxoniae, e Typ. Clar. sumptibus B. Barker,
MDCCXXIX.
  8vo fours. Bodl. Rawl. 8° 696.

2. BURTON, JOHN. [Two sermons] Hophni & Phineas, sive impietas sacerdotum
publicae impietatis causa. Concio habita in Templo B. Mariae pro gradu S.T.B.
Jul. 19. 1729. a Joanne Burton [etc.]. Oxoniae, e Th. Sh., MDCCXXIX. Impensis
Viduae Fletcher. Prost. ven. apud J. Knapton, C. Rivington bibliopol. in Coemeterio
Paulino, & C. King in Aul. Westmonaster. & C. Crownfield, Cantabrig.

Heli; sive exemplum magistratus intempestiva lenitate peccantis. Concio habita in Templo B. Mariae coram Artium Baccalaureis determinantibus die Carnis-privii Feb. 10. 1729. A Joanne Burton [etc.]. [Imprint as above.]

4to. Imp. 12 Aug. 1729. Bodl. B 7. 20(7 and 8) Linc.
The two booklets have a single series of signatures.

3. CICERO. M. T. Ciceronis De officiis libri tres, Cato Major, Laelius, Paradoxa, Somnium Scipionis. Ex optimis exemplaribus recensuit, selectisque variorum notis nonnullas etiam suas adjecit Tho. Tooly [etc.]. Editio secunda. Oxoniae, e Th. Sh. 1729. Prostant venales apud Sam. Wilmot bibliopol. Oxon.

8vo fours. Imp. 24 Jan. 1716. Bodl. 90 b. 23.
The first edition was of 1716.

4. EVESHAM, MONK OF. Historia vitae et regni Ricardi II. Angliae regis, a monacho quodam de Evesham consignata. Accesserunt, praeter alia, Joannis Rossi Historiola de Comitibus Warwicensibus; Joannis Berebloci Commentarii de rebus gestis Oxoniae, ibidem commorante Elizabetha Regina; et D. Ricardi Wynni, baronetti, Narratio historica de Caroli, Wallii Principis, famulorum in Hispaniam itinere MDCXXIII. e codicibus MSS. nunc primus edidit Tho. Hearnius. Oxoniae, e Th. Sh. A.D. MDCCXXIX.

8vo fours. Bodl. Mus. Bibl. II 8° 89.
2nd A/cs. 106^v, dues. Hearne, x, pp. 89, 96, 268.

5. NEWLIN, THOMAS. The crime and punishment of Eli. A sermon preach'd at St Mary's in Oxford before the Honourable Mr Justice Price and Mr Justice Probyn at the assizes held there July the 17th 1729. By Thomas Newlin [etc.]. Publish'd at the request of the Judges. Oxford, printed at the Theater; and are to be sold by Richard Clements bookseller in Oxford. 1729.

8vo fours. Bodl. 100 aa. 12(10).

6*. OXFORD, UNIVERSITY. Parecbolae sive excerpta e corpore statutorum Universitatis Oxoniensis. Accedunt Articuli religionis XXXIX. in Ecclesia Anglicana recepti: nec non Juramenta fidelitatis & suprematus. In usum juventutis academicae. Oxoniae, e Th. Sh. MDCCXXIX.

8vo fours. Bodl. Gough Oxf. 20(1).
2nd A/cs. 109, 3,000 printed.

7*. (OXFORD, UNIVERSITY. 'A programma' [against spreading doctrines and books subversive of Christianity].
2nd A/cs. 107, 150 printed. [Hist. MSS. Comm., Portland vii, p. 468.])

8*. (Oxford, University. Order as to prices and size of bread.
2nd A/cs. 107. No copy found.)

9. STUBBS, PHILIP. The divine right of prerogative royal . . . [as in 1728] The second edition. [Imprint as in 1728 with the addition of John Penn in Westminster Hall.] 1729.

8vo fours. Bodl. 8° H 246 BS.
Hearne, x, p. 101.

10. STUBBS, PHILIP. More advice to the Reverend the clergy of the peculiar jurisdiction of St Alban in the diocese of London; given at a general visitation (both of the Hertfordshire and Buckinghamshire parts of it) in the Court Consistorial at St Alban's, May 23. MDCCXXIX. concerning 1. The faithfull discharge of their

sacred functions, 2. Their opinion of Woolston, the accuser of the brethren, 3. The proposal offer'd for augmenting the poorer livings amongst them. By Philip Stubbs [etc.]. Oxford, printed at the Theatre; for Richard Clements bookseller in Oxon; John Penn at the Bible and Dove in Fleet Street; and J. Roberts at the Oxford Arms in Warwick-Lane, London.

8vo fours. Bodl. G. Pamph. 1066(5).

His previous address to the same clergy was of 1725.

11. TROKELOWE. Johannis de Trokelowe Annales Edwardi II. Henrici de Blaneforde Chronica, et Edwardi II Vita a monacho quodam Malmesburiensi fuse enarrata. E codicibus MSS. nunc primus divulgavit Tho. Hearnius. qui &, praeter appendicem (in qua, inter alia, ordinationes Collegii Orielensis) monumenta quaedam vetera, ab Edmundo Archero communicata, subjunxit. Oxonii, e Th. Sh., A.D. MDCCXXIX.

8vo fours. Bodl. Mus. Bibl. II 90.

2nd A/cs. 113ᵛ, dues.

12. WELLS, EDWARD. An help for the right understanding of the several divine laws and covenants, whereby man has been oblig'd thro' the several ages of the world to guide himself in order to eternal salvation, wherein the most important points of religion are explain'd and set in a true light. Chiefly design'd for the benefit of young students in divinity, but very useful to be perused by all religious persons, in order to their right understanding of God's most gracious, as well as most just, dealings with all mankind from the creation to the end of the world. By the Revd. Dr. Edward Wells [etc.]. Oxford, printed at the Theater for Will. Wells bookseller in Oxford: and sold by Ja. Knapton, Ch. Rivington, in St Paul's Church-yard, and Jos. Hazard at the Bible in Stationers' Court, booksellers in London. 1729.

8vo fours. Imp. 6 Feb. 1728. Bodl. 141 j. 574.

1730

1. ARISTIDES. Aelii Aristidis Adrianensis Opera omnia Graece et Latine, in duo volumina distributa; cum notis & emendationibus Gul. Canteri, Tristani, Palmerii, T. Fabri, Spanhemii, Normanni, & Lamb. Bosii; adjunctis insuper veterum scholiis; et prolegomenis Sopatri Apameensis, ab erroribus ut plurimum repurgatis. Graeca, cum MSS. codicibus variis & praestantissimis collata, recensuit, & observationes suas adjecit Samuel Jebb, M.D. Tom. II. Oxonii, e Th. Sh., MDCCXXX. impensis Davidis Lyon.

4to. Bodl. I I 30 Art.

Vol. i was issued in 1722. The title-page of the Bodleian copy looks as though it were printed at a later date or elsewhere.

2. CAIUS (or KEY), THOMAS. Thomae Caii (Collegii Universitatis regnante Elizabetha Magistri) Vindiciae antiquitatis Academiae Oxoniensis contra Joannem Caiium, Cantabrigensem. In lucem ex autographo emisit Tho. Hearnius. Qui porro non tantum Antonii a Wood vitam, a seipso conscriptam, & Humphredi Humphreys (episcopi nuper Herefordiensis) De viris claris Cambro Britannicis Observationes, sed & Reliquias quasdam, ad familiam religiosissimam Ferrariorum, de Gidding

Parva in agro Huntingdoniensi, pertinentes, subnexuit. Duobus voluminibus. Oxonii, e Th. Sh., MDCCXXX.

    8vo fours. Bodl. Mus. Bibl. II 91, 2.

    2nd A/cs. 120^v, dues.

3. COXE, THOMAS C. A sermon preached at the assizes held at Bedford by the right Honourable Lord Chief Justice Eyre and the Honourable Mr Justice Denton, on Friday, July 17th, 1730. By Thomas Chamberlayne Coxe [etc.]. Published at the request of the High-Sheriff and gentlemen of the Grand Jury. Oxford, printed at the Theater; and are to be sold by Richard Clements bookseller in Oxford. 1730.

    8vo fours. Imp. 29 Aug. 1730. Bodl. G. Pamph. 910(14).

4. Author of the Whole DUTY OF MAN. The whole duty of man laid down in a plain and familiar way for the use of all, but especially the meanest reader. Divided into xvii chapters. One whereof being read over every Lord's Day, the whole may be read over thrice in the year. Necessary for all families. With private devotions for several occasions. Oxford, printed for John Eyre, and sold by Thomas Page and W. Mount, and the booksellers of London and Westminster 1730.

    12mo. Bodl. 1419 f. 50.

    The only edition of this work printed here.

5. GREY, RICHARD. The perpetuity of Christ's Church. A sermon preach'd at St. Mary's Leicester, August 20th, 1730. at the triennial visitation of the Right Reverend Father in God Richard Lord Bishop of Lincoln. By Richard Grey [etc.]. Oxford, printed at the Theatre for Sam. Wilmot, bookseller: and sold by J. and J. Knapton, R. Knaplock, and T. Astley in St. Paul's Church-Yard, S. Birt in Ave-Mary-Lane, and B. and C. Motte in Fleet-Street, London. 1730. Price six pence.

    8vo fours. Bodl. G. Pamph. 1005(10).

6. HARPER, JOHN. The natural efficacy of music to prepare the mind for good impressions. A sermon preach'd in the Cathedral-Church of Gloucester, at the anniversary meeting of the choirs of Gloucester, Worcester and Hereford, September 2. 1730. By John Harper [etc.]. Publish'd at the request of the Society. Oxford, printed at the Theatre for Richard Clements: and are to be sold by J. and J. Knapton, and Charles Rivington booksellers in St. Paul's Church-Yard, London.

    8vo fours. Bodl. G. Pamph. 39.

7. HEARNE, THOMAS. An advertisement announcing Caius as printed and Hemingford as now printing.

    8vo s. sh. Bodl. MS. Ballard xli, fol. 6.

8. HESIOD. Proposals for publishing by subscription the extant works of Hesiod in Greek and Latin, edited by Thomas Robinson.

    Fol. 4 pp. Bodl. AA 3 Jur.

    Hearne, x, p. 370. The book was published in 1737.

9. LONGINUS. [Greek title.] Dionysii Longini De sublimitate libellus, cum praefatione de vita & scriptis Longini, notis, indicibus, & variis lectionibus. Editio tertia. Oxoniae, e Th. Sh., anno MDCCXXX. Prostat apud Sa. Wilmot bibliopolam Oxon. Nicolaum Prevost & A. Vander-Haeck in vico vulgo vocato The Strand, & J. & J. Knapton in Coemeterio Paulino, Londini.

    8vo fours. Imp. 24 Oct. 1728. Bodl. Bliss B 162.

    Preface by the editor, J. H. (John Hudson). The earlier editions were of 1710 and 1718. 2nd A/cs. 113^v, dues.

10. ROBINSON, THOMAS. Youthful lusts inconsistent with the ministry. A sermon preach'd before the University of Oxford on St Stephen's Day 1729, in which the common translation of νεωτερικαὶ ἐπιθυμίαι is defended against Salmasius, Mr Thomas, &c. By Thomas Robinson [etc.]. Oxford, printed at the Theatre for Sam. Wilmot, bookseller: and sold by J. and J. Knapton, R. Knaplock, and T. Astley in St Paul's Church-Yard, S. Birt in Ave-Mary-Lane, and B. and C. Motte in Fleet-Street, London. 1730. Price six pence.

8vo fours. Bodl. G. Pamph. 105(9).

11. SALLUST. C. Sallustii Crispi Bellum Catilinarium, et Jugurthinum, ad ultimam Wassii editionem diligenter castigata, cum commentariis Johannis Min-Ellii. Oxonii, impensis Societatis Stationariorum. MDCCXXX.

12mo. Bodl. Gibson 20.

12. WELCHMAN, EDWARD. XXXIX Articuli Ecclesiae Anglicanae [etc., as in 1724]. Editio quinta. In usum juventutis academicae. Auctore Edvardo Welchman [etc.]. Oxonii, e Th. Sh., impensis Ant. Peisley bibliop. Oxon. Prostant apud J. and J. Knapton, W. Meadows, B. and C. Motte, bibliop. Lond. MDCCXXX.

8vo fours. Imp. 28 Aug. 1712. Bodl. 8° Rawl. 217.
2nd A/cs. 120ᵛ, dues. The previous editions were of 1713, 1714, 1718, and 1724.

13. WOODWARD, GEORGE. Poems on several occasions. By Mr. George Woodward. Printed at the Clarendon Printing-House MDCCXXX.

8vo fours. Bodl. 2799 e. 58.
Mentions (p. 131) a picture of Duns Scotus in the Printing-House.

1731

1. BENTIVOGLIO, ERCOLE. Les fantomes et le jaloux. Comedies Italiennes traduites en françois. A Oxford, MDCCXXXI.

8vo fours. Imp. 23 Oct. 1731. Bodl. 8° G 9 Art.
Preface by the translator, Jean Fabre.

2. BULKELEY, BENJAMIN. The insufficiency of human reason in matters of religion, and the consequent necessity of a revelation. A sermon preach'd before the University at St. Mary's in Oxford on Act Sunday 1731. By Benjamin Bulkeley [etc.]. Oxford, printed at the Theatre for Sam. Wilmot, bookseller: and sold by J. and J. Knapton, R. Knaplock, T. Astley, and J. Crownfield in St. Paul's Church-Yard, S. Bickerton near Temple-Barr, S. Birt in Ave-Mary-Lane, and B. Motte in Fleet-Street, London, 1731.

8vo fours. Bodl. 100 aa. 12(13).

3. CLARENDON, EDWARD HYDE, EARL OF. The History of the Rebellion [etc.]. Volume I. Part 2. Oxford, printed at the Theater, An. Dom. MDCCXXXI. [Illustrated with portraits.]

8vo. Imp. 29 Apr. 1702. Bodl. Clar. Press 31 a. 11.
Vols. ii and iii are also dated 1731: Vol. i, part i is dated 1732. 2nd A/cs. 134ᵛ, dues. For D.O., see Hearne, x, p. 75. £100 was received from Mount and Page, London booksellers, for the printing: V-C.'s Computus, 1732–3.

4. EUCLID. Euclidis Elementorum, libri priores sex, item undecimus & duodecimus. Ex versione Latina Federici Commandini. Quibus accedunt trigonometriae planae

& sphaericae elementa. Item tractatus de natura & arithmetica logarithmorum. In usum juventutis academicae. Oxoniae, e Th. Sh., MDCCXXXI. impensis Ric. Clements bibliop. Oxon. Prostat apud J. Knapton & C. Rivington bibliop. in Coemeterio D. Pauli Lond.

8vo. Imp. 25 March 1715. Printer to the University.

The third edition of John Keill's text. See 1715, 1723.

5. HEMINGFORD, WALTER. Walteri Hemingford, canonici de Gisseburne, Historia de rebus gestis Edvardi I. Edvardi II. & Edvardi III. Accedunt, inter alia, Edvardi III. historia per anonymum, Narratio de processu contra Reginaldum Peacockium, auctore Johanne Whethamstedio; Excerpta historica e Thomae Gascoignii Dictionario Theologico; Libellus de Caroli I. ab urbe Oxoniensi fuga sive discessu, Notitiaque Domorum religiosarum in dioecesi Batho-Wellensi. E codicibus MSS. nunc primus publicavit Tho. Hearnius. Duobus voluminibus. Oxonii, e Th. Sh., MDCCXXXI.

8vo fours. Bodl. Mus. Bibl. II 93, 4.

2nd A/cs. 127^v, dues.

6. [KEILL, JOHN.] Trigonometriae planae & sphaericae elementa [etc., as in 1715 and 1723]. Oxoniae, e Th. Sh. MDCCXXXI. Impensis Ric. Clements bibliop. Oxoniensis.

8vo.

Included in the volume of Euclid of the same year, but with its own title-page and series of signatures.

7. (Marshall, Thomas. The Catechism set forth in the Book of Common Prayer, briefly explained [etc., as in 1692].

The Delegates were charged in this year for an edition of 3,000 priced at 4s. a dozen of 14: 2nd A/cs. 122. This would be the 15th edition, the previous one being of 1721 or 1722. No copy has been traced.)

8. OXFORD, UNIVERSITY, QUEEN'S COLLEGE. The present state of the new buildings in Queens College in Oxford, with an ichnography of the whole, and cuts of the several parts of the said buildings engraved. [Dated 21 Dec. 1730.]

4to. Bodl. Gough Oxf. 143.

1732

1. CLARENDON, EDWARD HYDE, EARL OF. The History of the Rebellion [etc.]. Volume I, Part I. Oxford, printed at the Theater, An. Dom. MDCCXXXII. [Illustrated with portraits.]

8vo. Imp. 29 Apr. 1702. Bodl. Clar. Press 31 a. 10.

The five succeeding parts were dated in 1731. 2nd A/cs. 134^v, dues. Hearne, x, p. 75.

2. CLARENDON, EDWARD HYDE, EARL OF. The History of the Rebellion [etc.]. Volume the first. Oxford, printed at the Theater, An. Dom. MDCCXXXII. [Illustrated with portraits.]

Fol. Imp. 15 Sept. 1704. Bodl. 22856 b. 2.

2nd A/cs. 134^v, dues. Hearne, xi, p. 26. The volume contains the whole work, but has no other title-page.

3. FELTON, HENRY. The Christian faith asserted against Deists, Arians, and Socinians in eight sermons preach'd at the Lady Moyer's Lecture in the Cathedral-Church of St. Paul 1728, 1729. and since greatly enlarged: to which is prefixed a very large preface concerning the light and the law of nature, and the expediency and necessity of revelation. By Henry Felton [etc.]. Oxford, printed at the Theater and are to be sold by Mr Richardson Warehouse-Keeper there. MDCCXXXII. Price six shillings.

8vo. Imp. 2 Feb. 1731/2. Bodl. 8° A 5(14) Jur.

2nd A/cs. 149ᵛ, dues.

4*. MAUNDRELL, HENRY. A journey from Aleppo to Jerusalem at Easter A.D. 1697. The fifth edition, [etc.]. Oxford, printed at the Theater, An. Dom. MDCCXXXII.

8vo fours. Imp. 8 Apr. 1703. Bodl. Bliss B 163.

2nd A/cs. 127ᵛ, 129, 130, 1,000 small for Anthony Peisley, 50 LP for the University.

5. OTTERBOURNE, THOMAS, AND WHETHAMSTEDE, JOHN. Duo rerum Anglicarum scriptores veteres, viz. Thomas Otterbourne et Johannes Whethamstede, ab origine gentis Britannicae usque ad Edvardum IV. E codicibus MSS. antiquis nunc primus eruit Tho. Hearnius. Accedunt, inter alia, Liber de vita & miraculis Edvardi IVti. per Johannem Blakmannum; Statuta Hospitalis de Ewelme in agro Oxoniensi; litterae perplures de rebus gestis in partibus nostris septentrionalibus A.D. M.DXXIV. in quibus epistolae autographae perpaucae Margaretae, Scotorum reginae, Henrici nostri VIImi. filiae natu majoris; Francisci Godwyni Catalogus, hactenus ineditus, episcoporum Bathoniensium & Wellensium, Humphredique Humphreys Commentariolus de decanis Bangoriensibus & Asaphensibus. Duobus voluminibus. Oxonii, e Th. Sh., MDCCXXXII.

8vo fours. Bodl. Mus. Bibl. II 95, 6.

2nd A/cs. 134ᵛ, dues.

6. PANTING, MATTHEW. Religious vows. A sermon preach'd at the consecration of a chapel in Pembroke College in Oxford, on Monday, July 10. 1732. By M. Panting [etc.]. Oxford, printed at the Theater, MDCCXXXII.

4to. Imp. 9 Aug. 1732. Bodl. Bliss B 164.

1733

1*. ATTERBURY, FRANCIS. The late Bishop of Rochester's vindication of Bishop Smalridge, Dr. Aldrich, and himself from the scandalous reflections of Mr. Oldmixon, relating to the publication of Lord Clarendon's History. [Dated 26 Oct. 1731. Ends: Fr. Roffen. Printed at Paris MDCCXXXI.]

8vo. Bodl. G. Pamph. 2190(2).

2nd A/cs. 136, printing in 8vo and folio (1732–3). No copy in folio format has been found. Both may have been intended for binding with Clarendon's *History*, since the 8vo has only a half-title. It is a reprint of the pamphlet printed at Paris (Bodl. Mason I I 125 (20)). It was printed again as an appendix to Burton's *Genuine-ness of Lord Clarendon's History vindicated* (Oxford, 1744).

2. BRUCE, CHARLES, VISCOUNT. A catalogue of the books of the Right Honourable Charles Viscount Bruce of Ampthill (son and heir apparent of Thomas Earl of Ailesbury) and Baron Bruce of Whoreton, in his library at Totenham in the County of Wiltes. Oxford, printed at the Theater. MDCCXXXIII.

    4to. Bodl. C C 87 Art.

    2nd A/cs. 134ᵛ, dues.

3*. (Clarendon, Edward Hyde, Earl of. A history of the Rebellion [etc.].

    According to the Press Accounts, 100 copies in 8vo were printed for the University on large paper in 1732–3, presumably from the type of the edition of 1731–2, since there is no charge for composing. These are likely to have been the 'Masters' Edition' to which Bliss referred in a note to Wood's *Athenae*, iii, 1024.)

4. COCKMAN, THOMAS. The duty of not conforming to this world. A sermon preach'd before the University of Oxford, at St. Mary's on Act Sunday 1733. By Thomas Cockman [etc.]. Publish'd at the request of the Vice-Chancellor and Heads of Houses. Oxford, printed at the Theatre for Richard Clements, and for Thomas Osborn in Gray's Inn, London. 1733.

    8vo fours. Bodl. G. Pamph. 1005(14).

5. CONYBEARE, JOHN. Scripture difficulties consider'd. A sermon preach'd in the Cathedral Church of St. Peter Exon, on Thursday Aug. 31. 1732. at the anniversary meeting of the gentlemen educated at the Free-School there. By John Conybeare [etc.]. Publish'd at the request of the Stewards. Oxford, printed at the Theater for Sam. Wilmot: and are to be sold by J. J. and Paul Knapton, R. Knaplock, Will. Innys, T. Astley, J. Crownfield in St. Paul's Church-Yard, London. 1733.

    8vo fours. Bodl. G. Pamph. 39(7).

6. DUNSTABLE PRIORY. Chronicon sive Annales Prioratus de Dunstaple, una cum excerptis e chartulario ejusdem Prioratus. Thomas Hearnius e codicibus MSS. in Bibliotheca Harleiana descripsit, primusque vulgavit. Accedit appendix. Duobus tomis. Oxonii, e Th. Sh., MDCCXXXIII.

    8vo fours. Bodl. Mus. Bibl. II 97, 8.

7*. LE COURAYER, P.-F. Oratio habita in Theatro Sheldoniano apud Oxonienses a Petro Francisco Courayer S.T.P. quint. id. Julii MDCCXXXIII.

    4to. Bodl. 4° B 76(5) Jur.

    2nd A/cs. 136ᵛ, sold for 32s. a hundred, 138, printing 800.

8*. LILY, WILLIAM. A short introduction of grammar generally to be used [etc., followed by Brevissima institutio &c.]. Oxford, at the Theater. 1733.

    8vo. Bodl. 3058 e. 1.

    2nd A/cs. 137, printing 2,000. The previous edition was of 1714. This was the last edition from the University's press.

9*. OXFORD, UNIVERSITY. [Notice by the Vice-Chancellor about arrangements in the Sheldonian Theatre during the Act.] To the Reverend and Worshipful the Heads of the respective Colleges and Halls of the University of Oxford. Gentlemen, You are desired to signify to your societies, that during the approaching solemnity ... [Dated 4 July 1733].

    Fol. s. sh. Bodl. B 3. 15(3) Art. 2nd A/cs. 138, printing 500.

10*. OXFORD, UNIVERSITY. Ordo comitiorum philologicorum ... E Th. Sh., A.D. 1733.

    Broadside. Bodl. G.A. Oxon. b. 19(53).

    2nd A/cs. 138, printing 800.

11*. OXFORD, UNIVERSITY. Quaestiones discutiendae Oxonii An. Dom. 1733. Oxonii, e Typ. Clar. An. Dom. 1733.
  Broadside. Bodl. G.A. Oxon. b. 19(6ᶜ).
  2nd A/cs. 138, printing 1,500.

12*. (Oxford, University. [Advertisement of a Court Leet.]
  No copy found.
  2nd A/cs. 135, printing. I. G. Philip, 'The Court Leet of the University of Oxford', *Oxoniensia*, xv (Oxford, 1952), pp. 81–9.)

13. QUINTON, JOHN. A treatise of warm Bath water and of cures made lately at Bath in Somersetshire, plainly proving that it is more probable to cure diseases by drinking warm mineral waters, and bathing in them, than in cold mineral waters. By John Quinton, M.D. Volume I. Oxford, printed in the year MDCCXXXIII.
  4to. Bodl. Gough Somerset 39(8).
  Perhaps printed by Lichfield.

14. RANDOLPH, THOMAS. The advantages of publick education. A sermon preach'd in the Cathedral-Church at Canterbury, on Thursday, September 13. 1733. at the anniversary meeting of the gentlemen educated at the Kings-School there. By Tho. Randolph [etc.]. Publish'd at the request of the gentlemen there present. Oxford, printed at the Theatre for Mary Fletcher in the High-Street, Oxon; and sold by Mr King in Westminster Hall, Mr Rivington in St Paul's Church-Yard, Mr Thurlburn in Cambridge, and by the booksellers in Canterbury.
  8vo fours. Imp. 18 Dec. 1733. Bodl. 8° S 101(3) Jur.

15. SECKER, THOMAS. A sermon preach'd before the University of Oxford at St. Mary's, on Act Sunday in the afternoon, July 8. 1733. By Thomas Secker [etc.]. Publish'd at the request of the Vice-Chancellor and Heads of Houses. Oxford, printed at the Theatre for Samuel Wilmot, and are to be sold by Messieurs Knapton and Innys in Ludgate Street, T. Astley, and J. Crownfield in St. Paul's Church-Yard. London. 1733.
  8vo fours. Bodl. 994 d. 2(2).

16. — 2nd ed., 1733. Bodl. 100 e. 220 (1).

17. — 3rd ed., 1733. Bodl. G. Pamph. 1.

18. — 4th ed., 1733. Bodl. 100 e. 220 (2).

  A fifth edition was published in London, dated 1734.

19. STONE, EDWARD. The reasonableness, and excellency of Abraham's faith in offering up his son. A sermon preach'd before the University of Oxford, at St Mary's on Sunday, Decemb. 10. 1732. To which are added some remarks upon Mr. Chubb's Case of Abraham. By Edward Stone [etc.]. Oxford, printed at the Theatre for Richard Clements, and are to be sold by John, James, and Paul Knapton, and Charles Rivington, booksellers in Ludgate-Street, and St. Paul's Church Yard, London. 1733.
  8vo fours. Imp. 3 March 1732/3. Bodl. 100 aa. 12(14).

20. VIDA, MARCUS HIERONYMUS. Marci Hieronymi Vidae, Cremonensis, Albae episcopi, Hymni de rebus divinis. Oxonii, e Typ. Clar., MDCCXXXIII.
  8vo fours. Imp. 29 June 1733. Bodl. Vet. A 4 d. 64.
  2nd A/cs. 134ᵛ, 'Dr. Owen's last Vol. of Vida', dues. Earlier volumes of his poetry were dated 1722, 1723, and 1725.

1734

1*. OXFORD, UNIVERSITY. Epithalamia Oxoniensia. Oxonii, e Typ. Clar. MDCCXXXIV.

Fol. Bodl. H 1 19(1) Art.

2nd A/cs. 145, printing 500, of which 24 LP. Hearne, xi, pp. 304, 319. For the marriage of the Princess Anne to the Prince of Orange.

2. OXFORD, UNIVERSITY. An account of the Charity School in Oxford, maintain'd by the voluntary subscriptions of the Vice-Chancellor, Heads of Houses, and other members of the University for eight years: viz. from Michaelmas 1726. to Michaelmas 1734.

4to. Bodl. Gough Oxf. 138(14).

Without imprint, but evidently from the University Press. Gives a list of boys apprenticed in various trades.

3*. OXFORD, UNIVERSITY. An order by the Vice-Chancellor and Heads of Houses enjoining stricter discipline in the University. Dated 4 Jan. 1733/4.

Broadside. Bodl. G.A. Oxon. b. 19(48).

2nd A/cs. 143, printing.

4. PRIOR, MATTHEW. Solomon De mundi vanitate. Poema Matthaei Prior Arm. Latine redditum, per Guil. Dobson [etc.]. Oxoniae, e Th. Sh., MDCCXXXIV.

4to. Bodl. 85 e. 2.

2nd A/cs. 142ᵛ, dues.

5. QUINTON, JOHN. A treatise of warm Bath water, in which is more than two hundred cures made at Bath in Somersetshire, by bathing, pumping and drinking the water. With a philosophical account of the elements, subterraneous fires, and fermentations, of metals, minerals, &c. taken from Boyle, Sir Isaac Newton, Jones, Bassius, Guidott, Boerhaave, Miller, Lister, Cheney, Oliver, Wynter, Willis, Floyer and Barnard, Quincy, Sydenham, Lodwick Rowzee, and many others. By John Quinton, M.D. Volume II. Oxford, printed in the year MDCCXXXIV.

4to. B.M. 1166.i.5.

The first volume was published in 1733.

6. STONE, EDWARD. The reasonableness and excellency of Abraham's faith in offering up his son. A sermon [etc., as in 1733] . . . To which are added some remarks upon Mr. Chubb's Case of Abraham: and remarks upon his Case farther considered. By Edward Stone [etc.]. The second edition. Oxford, printed at the Theatre [etc., as in the first edition].

8vo fours. Imp. 3 Mar. 1732–3. Bodl. G. Pamph. 910(16).

7. STONE, EDWARD. Remarks on Mr. Chubb's Case of Abraham farther Consider'd in a letter to Mr. Chubb. By Edward Stone [etc.]. Oxford, printed at the Theatre for Richard Clements, and are to be sold by John, James, and Paul Knapton, and Charles Rivington, booksellers in Ludgate-Street, and St Paul's Church-Yard, London. 1734.

8vo fours. Bodl. G. Pamph. 910(17).

8. WELLS, EDWARD. A Commentary upon the Old Testament in four volumes. Volume I. containing Genesis, Exodus, Leviticus, Numbers, and Deuteronomy. By

Edward Wells [etc.]. Oxford: printed at the Theater; and sold by James, John, and Paul Knapton, at the Crown in Ludgate-Street, London. M.DCC.XXXIV.

4to. Bodl. 101 d. 690.

9–11. — Vols. ii, iii, and iv of the preceding work were published in this year. Bodl. 101 d. 691–3.

1735

1. BENEDICT, ABBOT OF PETERBOROUGH. Benedictus abbas Petroburgensis, De vita & gestis Henrici II. et Ricardi I. E codice MS. in Bibliotheca Harleiana descripsit, et nunc primus edidit Thomas Hearnius. Accesserunt alia. Duobus tomis. Oxonii, e Th. Sh., MDCCXXXV.

8vo fours. Bodl. Mus. Bibl. II 100.
2nd A/cs. 149ᵛ, dues.

2. BIBLIOTHECA BIBLICA. Bibliotheca Biblica, being a commentary upon all the Books of the Old and New Testament [etc., as in 1720]. Vol. V. on the Book of Deuteronomy. Oxford, printed at the Theater for Charles Rivington, at the Bible and Crown, in St. Paul's Church-Yard; London, 1735.

4to. Imp. 17 Dec. 1734. Bodl. OO 8 Th.
The last volume of this serial publication. Previous volumes were issued in 1720, 1722, 1724, and 1728. Hearne, xi, pp. 205, 438.

3. FELTON, HENRY. The Scripture doctrine of the Resurrection as it stood before the Law. A sermon preached before the University of Oxford, at St. Mary's, Nov. 24. 1734. By Henry Felton [etc.]. Oxford, printed at the Theater for Ben. Motte by the Middle Temple Gate London: and to be sold by R. Clements, Mrs. Fletcher and the booksellers in Oxford; by Simon Martin at Leicester; Will. Ward at Nottingham; and Job Bradley at Chesterfield.

8vo fours. Imp. 7 Jan. 1734. Bodl. G. Pamph. 2721(9).
2nd A/cs. 149ᵛ, dues. Hearne, xi, p. 254.

4. FOTHERGILL, GEORGE. The importance of religion to civil societies. A sermon preached at St. Mary's in Oxford, at the assizes before the Honourable Mr. Justice Fortescue-Aland, and Mr. Justice Lee; and before the University; on Thursday, March 6th. 1734/5. By George Fothergill [etc.]. Publish'd at the request of Mr. Vice-Chancellor and the Heads of Houses. Oxford, printed at the Theatre; and sold by Richard Clements bookseller in Oxford, and J. J. and P. Knapton in Ludgate-Street, C. Rivington in St. Paul's Church-Yard, and J. Roberts in Warwick-Lane, London. MDCCXXXV. Price six-pence.

8vo fours. Imp. 18 Mar. 1734–5. Bodl. G. Pamph. 1.
Hearne, xi, pp. 451–2.

5. — 2nd edition. Bodl. G. Pamph. 910(11).

6. HAYES, WILLIAM. Twelve ariettes or ballads, and two cantatas. Composed by William Hayes [etc.]. Oxford, printed in the year MDCCXXXV.

8vo. Bodl. Mus. 5 e. 99.
The music and words are engraved (probably in pewter). Doubtfully attributable to the University Press.

7. PRIOR, MATTHEW. Solomon De mundi vanitate. Poema Matthaei Prior Arm. Latine redditum, per Guil. Dobson [etc.]. Oxoniae, e Th. Sh., MDCCXXXV.

4to. Bodl. 85 e. 2.

2nd A/cs. 149ᵛ, dues. The second part of the work. The first was issued in 1734, and the third in 1736.

8. TOTTIE, JOHN. Ridicule, so far as it affects religion, consider'd and censur'd. A sermon preached before the University of Oxford, at St. Mary's, on Sunday, Dec. 8. 1734. By John Tottie [etc.]. Publish'd at the request of Mr. Vice-Chancellor and the Heads of Houses. Oxford, printed at the Theatre for Mary Fletcher; and sold by J. J. and P. Knapton in Ludgate-Street, C. Rivington in St. Paul's Church-Yard, London; W. Thurlbourn at Cambridge; and J. Leake at Bath. Price six-pence.

8vo fours. Imp. 2 April 1735. B.M. 693.e.15(4).

9. — 2nd edition. Bodl. G. Pamph. 666(7).

10. — 3rd edition. The third edition. Oxford, printed at the Theatre for Mary Fletcher bookseller in the High-street; and sold by J. and J. Rivington in St. Paul's Church-Yard, London; J. Mountfort at Worcester. Price 6d.

Bodl. Bliss B 166(1).

11. XENOPHON. [Anabasis and Agesilaus.]
(1) [Greek title.] Xenophontis De Cyri expeditione libri septem. Graeca recognovit, cum codicibus MStis. & omnibus fere libris editis contulit, plurimis in locis emendavit, versionem Latinam reformavit, observationibus suis, tabula geographica & dissertatione auxit & illustravit; notas H. Stephani, Leunclavii, Æ. Porti & Mureti, recensitas & castigatas, variantium lectionum delectum, indicesque necessarios adjunxit Thomas Hutchinson. Oxonii, e Th. Sh., MDCCXXXV.

4to. Imp. 28 Feb. 1734/5.
(2) [Greek title.] Xenophontis De Agesilao rege oratio. Graeca recognovit, cum Codice Msto. Harleiano & omnibus fere libris editis contulit [etc., as above].

4to. Imp. 7 April 1735. Bodl. 4° P 48 Jur.

The prefaces make it clear that the two books, though separately signed, were intended to make one volume. Hutchinson's edition of the *Cyropaedia*, in the same format, was published in 1727.

1736

1. [BURTON, JOHN.] S. Scripturae locorum quorundam versio metrica. sive exercitationum poeticarum quae pro disciplinae solennis ratione adolescentibus C. C. C. longae vacationis tempore praecipiuntur elaborandae delectus. Oxoniae, e Th. Sh. MDCCXXXVI.

8vo fours. Imp. 2 June 1736. Bodl. G. Pamph. 72(1).
Preface by John Burton. 2nd A/cs. 161ᵛ, dues.

2. [CAVE, WILLIAM.] Proposals for printing by subscription, a new edition of Scriptorum ecclesiasticorum historia literaria, autore Gulielmo Cave canonico Windesoriensi. With very large additions and emendations under the Doctor's own hand, [dated:] Oxon. Feb. 28. 1735–6.

Fol. 4 pp. Bodl. Dep. c. 233 (fol. 140).
The book was published: Vol. i in 1740, Vol. ii in 1743.

3. FOUQUET, NICOLAS. The counsels of wisdom. or a collection of such maxims of Solomon as are most necessary for the prudent conduct of life. With proper reflections upon them. Written originally in French by Monseigneur Fouquet, sometime Lord High Treasurer of France, in the reign of Lewis XIV. Done into English by a gentleman. With some account of the illustrious author. Vol. I. Oxford, printed at the Theater. MDCCXXXVI.

Vol. ii follows in the same series of signatures.

4to. Imp. 27 Apr. 1736. Bodl. C 3. 25 Linc.

2nd A/cs. 167^v, dues. Preface by J. Leake.

4. [LYE, EDWARD.] Proposals for publishing by subscription the Etymologicum Anglicanum of Francis Junius. [Dated 10 Sept. 1736.]

Fol. 4 pp. Bodl. MS. Rawl. J. fol. 4 (71–2).

Price 25s. small, 42s. LP. The book was published in 1743.

5*. OXFORD, UNIVERSITY. Gratulatio Academiae Oxoniensis in nuptias auspicatissimas illustrissimorum principum Frederici Principis Walliae et Augustae Principissae de Saxe-Gotha. Oxonii, e Typ. Clar. MDCCXXXVI.

Fol. Bodl. Pamph. 406(5).

2nd A/cs. 158, 24 LP, 476 small.

6*. OXFORD, UNIVERSITY. The catalogue of graduats &c. in the University of Oxford, continued from October 10. 1727. to October 10. 1735.

8vo. Bodl. Gough Oxf. 35(2).

2nd A/cs. 158, 'the Appendix to the Catalogue of Graduats', 500 LP, 500 small.

7. PRIOR, MATTHEW. Solomon de mundi vanitate. Poema Matthaei Prior arm. Latinae redditum. Per Guil. Dobson [etc.]. Oxoniae, e Th. Sh., MDCCXXXVI. [The third part.]

4to. Bodl. 85 e. 2.

2nd A/cs. 167^v, dues. Earlier parts were published in 1734 and 1735.

8. WISE, FRANCIS. Epistola ad v. cl. Joannem Masson de nummo Abgari regis. Oxoniae, e Th. Sh. MDCCXXXVI.

4to. Bodl. 4° M 28 Art.

1737

1. BANNER, RICHARD. The use and antiquity of musick in the service of God. A sermon preach'd in the Cathedral-Church at Worcester, Septemb. 14. 1737. at the annual meeting of the Three Choirs, Worcester, Gloucester and Hereford. By Richard Banner, B.D., Oxford, printed at the Theatre, 1737.

8vo fours. Imp. 24 Oct. 1737. Worcester Coll. D.10.4.1(13).

2. FELTON, HENRY. The Scripture doctrine of the Resurrection as it stood before the Law in the Books of Genesis and Job further asserted in two sermons preached before the University of Oxford, at St. Mary's, July 25. and November 23. 1736. By Henry Felton [etc.]. Oxford, printed at the Theatre for Ben. Motte by the Middle Temple Gate London: and to be sold by Mr Clements, Mr Fletcher and

the booksellers in Oxford; by Simon Martin at Leicester; Will. Ward at Nottingham; and Job Bradley at Chesterfield; and J. Hildyard at York.

8vo fours. Imp. 22 Feb. 1736-7. Bodl. 100 aa. 12(15).

3. FOTHERGILL, GEORGE. The danger of excesses in the pursuit of liberty. A sermon preach'd before the University of Oxford, at St. Mary's, on Monday, January 31. 1736-7. being the day appointed to be kept as the Day of the Martyrdom of King Charles the First. By George Fothergill [etc.]. Oxford, printed at the Theatre, and sold by Richard Clements bookseller: as also by Messieurs Knapton, Rivington, and Roberts in London; Mr. Thurlbourn in Cambridge, and Mr. Leake in Bath MDCCXXXVII. Price sixpence.

8vo fours. Imp. 24 Feb. 1736-7. Bodl. G. Pamph. 47(9).

4. HARTE, WALTER. The union and harmony of reason, morality, and revealed religion. A sermon preach'd before the University of Oxford at St. Mary's on Sunday, February 27. 1736-7. By Walter Harte [etc.]. Oxford, printed at the Theatre, for L. Gilliver and J. Clarke, at the Homer's-Head in Fleetstreet, London.

8vo fours. Imp. 30 Apr. 1737. Bodl. 100 aa. 12(16).

5. HESIOD. [Title in Greek.] Hesiodi Ascraei quae supersunt cum notis variorum. Edidit Thomas Robinson, S.T.P. Oxonii, e Th. Sh. MDCCXXXVII.

4to. Imp. 1 July 1737. Bodl. AA 3 Jur.

2nd A/cs. 180ᵛ, dues. The preliminary pages and prolegomena were printed in London by William Bowyer: Nichols, *Lit. An.* ii, p. 104. Proposals, not dated, are bound in the Bodleian copy. They give a much longer Latin title, which was also transcribed by the editor for reference by Richard Rawlinson: Bodl. MS. Rawl. J. fol. 4(302a). Hearne, x, p. 370.

6. HOLLOWAY, BENJAMIN. The commemorative sacrifice. A sermon preached at the visitation holden at Woodstock, Friday, October 5th, 1736. by the Revd. George Rye, D.D. Arch-Deacon of Oxford. By Benjamin Holloway [etc.]. Printed at the request of Mr. Arch-Deacon and the clergy. Oxford: printed at the Theatre for Richard Clements, and sold by J. and P. Knapton in Ludgate-Street, C. Rivington in St. Paul's Church-Yard, and J. Roberts in Warwick-Lane, London, and by W. Thurlbourn in Cambridge.

8vo fours. Bodl. G. Pamph. 1006(15).

7*. (Oxford, University. A Catalogue of plants in the Physic Garden.
2nd A/cs. 162, printing. No copy found.)

8. STEPHENS, WILLIAM. Sermons on several subjects. By William Stephens [etc.]. Vol. I. Oxford, printed at the Theater. MDCCXXXVII.

9. — Vol. II [as above].
8vo Bodl. Godw. subt. 199, 200.
2nd A/cs. 167ᵛ, dues.

10. TASSONI, ALESSANDRO. La secchia rapita. Poema eroicomico del Sig. Alessandro Tassoni con le dichiarazioni del Sig. Gasparo Salviani accresciute, ed emendate dal Sig. Abate Marchioni. Volume primo. In Osford, nel Teatro Sceldoniano MDCCXXXVII.
[Volume secondo follows in the same series of signatures.]
8vo fours. Bodl. 8° Godw. 215.

1738

1. HUTCHINSON, THOMAS. The usual interpretation of δαιμονες and δαιμονια, in the New Testament, asserted in a sermon preach'd before the University of Oxford, at St. Mary's, on Sunday, March 5. 1737–8. By Thomas Hutchinson [etc.]. Oxford, printed at the Theatre, for Mr Clements, bookseller; and sold by Mess. Innys and Manby, Knapton, Rivington and Roberts in London; and by Mr Thurlbourn, in Cambridge. MDCCXXXVIII. Price, six-pence.

    8vo fours. Imp. 17 March 1737. Bodl. G. Pamph. 25(4).

2★. OXFORD, UNIVERSITY. Pietas Academiae Oxoniensis in obitum augustissimae et desideratissimae Reginae Carolinae. Oxonii, e Typ. Clar. An. Dom. MDCCXXXVIII.

    Fol. Bodl. Pamph. 408(12).

    2nd A/cs. 170, 24 LP, 400 small. 4s. 6d.

3★. OXFORD, UNIVERSITY. Catalogus impressorum librorum Bibliothecae Bodleianae in Academia Oxoniensi. Volumen primum. Oxonii, e Th. Sh. MDCCXXXVIII.

4★. — Volumen secundum [as above].

    Fol. Bodl. 2590 b. Oxf. 1c. 3–6.

    2nd A/cs. 100, 115, 122, 129, 136, 144, 151, 157, 169, 169^v, 300 LP, 500 small, £3. 3s. LP, £2. 5s. small.

5★. OXFORD, UNIVERSITY. An order by the Vice-Chancellor and Heads of Houses for maintenance of discipline in the University. Dated 11 Dec. 1738.

    Broadside. Bodl. G.A. Oxon. b. 19(54).

    2nd A/cs. 176.

6. PAYNE, THOMAS. A defence of church-musick. A sermon preach'd in the Cathedral-Church of Hereford at the anniversary meeting of the Three Choirs, Worcester, Glocester, and Hereford. On Wednesday September 6th. 1738. By Thomas Payne [etc.]. Publish'd at the request of the Society. Oxford, printed at the Theatre for James Fletcher bookseller in the Turle: and sold by Ch. Rivington, and J. Knapton in London; James Wild in Hereford; J. Mountfort in Worcester; and J. Price in Glocester. 1738. Price 6d.

    8vo fours. Imp. 14 Oct. 1738. Bodl. G. Pamph. 5(11).

7. PERROTT, HUMPHREY. A sermon preached at the Cathedral Church of Worcester at the Assizes, before the Honourable Mr. Justice Page and Mr. Justice Denton, on Sunday, July 16. 1738. By Humphrey Perrott [etc.]. Published at the request of the Grand Jury. Printed in Oxford.

    8vo fours. Worcester Coll. D.10.6(3).

    Perhaps printed by Lichfield.

8★. REINOLDS, JOHN. Census habitus nascente Christo. Joannis Reinoldii S.T.B. [etc.]. dissertatio Oxonii Academiae typis ac sumtu impressa. cIↄ Iↄcc xxxviii.

    4to. Imp. 27 March 1738. Bodl. G. Pamph. 160.

    2nd A/cs. 171, 500.

9. SHAW, THOMAS. Travels or observations relating to several parts of Barbary and the Levant. By Thomas Shaw [etc.]. Oxford, printed at the Theatre. MDCCXXXVIII.

    Fol. Imp. 25 Apr. 1738. Bodl. P 3. 3 Th.

    2nd A/cs. 167^v, dues.

10. SWINTON, JOHN. De lingua Etruriae regalis vernacula dissertatio. Authore Joanne Swinton [etc.]. Oxonii, e Th. Sh. MDCCXXXVIII.
4to. Imp. 23 Feb. 1737/8. Bodl. DD 75(3) Art.

11. TOVEY, D'BLOSSIERS. Anglia Judaica: or the history and antiquities of the Jews in England, collected from all our historians, both printed and manuscript, as also from the records in the Tower, and other publick repositories, by D'Blossiers Tovey [etc.]. Oxford, printed at the Theatre, and are to be sold by James Fletcher, bookseller in the Turl. MDCCXXXVIII.
4to. Bodl. 4° Rawl. 30.
2nd A/cs. 161ᵛ, dues.

12. WEBBER, FRANCIS. The Jewish dispensation consider'd and vindicated, with a view to the objections of unbelievers, and particularly of a late author called The Moral Philosopher. A sermon preach'd before the University of Oxford, at St. Mary's, on Sunday, October 23d. 1737. By Francis Webber. Oxford, printed at the Theatre for James Fletcher, bookseller in the Turle: and are to be sold by Charles Rivington, and J. Knapton, booksellers in London. 1738.
8vo fours. Imp. 12 Jan. 1738. Bodl. G. Pamph. 666(9).

13. WELCHMAN, EDWARD. XXXIX Articulae Ecclesiae Anglicanae textibus e Sacra Scriptura depromptis confirmati, brevibusque notis illustrati. Adjectis insuper nominibus auctorum locisque in quibus doctrina in Articulis contenta fusius explicatur. Editio sexta. In usum juventutis academicae. Auctore Edvardo Welchman. Oxonii, e Th. Sh., impensis Jacobi Fletcher bibliop. Oxon. Prostant apud Ch. Rivington bibl. Lond. & W. Thurlbourn, Cantab. 1738.
8vo fours. Imp. 28 Aug. 1712. Bodl. 1365 e. 5.

14. WISE, FRANCIS. A letter to Dr. Mead concerning some antiquities in Berkshire, particularly shewing that the White Horse, which gives the name to the Vale, is a monument of the West Saxons, made in memory of a great victory obtained over the Danes A.D. 871. Oxford, printed for Thomas Wood at the University Printing-House, MDCCXXXVIII.
4to. Bodl. G. Pamph. 52(7).

1739

1. CLEAVER, WILLIAM. The doctrine of a future state necessary to the welfare and support of civil government. A sermon preached at the assizes held at Warwick, by the Honourable Mr. Justice Page, on Wednesday, March 28. 1739. By William Cleaver A.M. Publish'd at the request of the High Sheriff and the gentlemen of the Grand Jury. Oxford, printed at the Theatre for James Fletcher bookseller in the Turle: and are to be sold by J. and P. Knapton in Ludgate-Street, and Charles Rivington in St. Paul's Church-Yard, London. 1739.
8vo fours. Imp. 17 Apr. 1739. Bodl. G. Pamph. 672(9).

2. EPICTETUS, CEBES, PRODICUS, THEOPHRASTUS. Epicteti Manuale, Cebetis Thebani Tabula, Prodici Hercules, et Theophrasti Characteres ethici, Graece et Latine, notis illustrati a Josepho Simpson, A.M. Oxonii, e Th. Sh., MDCCXXXIX.
8vo fours. Imp. 8 Aug. 1739. Bodl. Clar. Press 50 b. 46.

2nd A/cs. 174ᵛ, dues. Each of the texts has its own title-page, all but the first dated 1738. There is a single series of signatures.

3. HOLLOWAY, BENJAMIN. The nullity of repentance without faith in the redemption by Jesus Christ, proved from Holy Scripture in three sermons. By Benjamin Holloway, L.L.B. Oxford: printed at the Theatre for Richard Clements; and sold by Messieurs Knapton in Ludgate-Street, Mr Rivington in St. Paul's Church-Yard, and Mr Roberts in Warwick-Lane, London. 1739.
8vo fours. Imp. 20 March 1738–9. Bodl. 100 bb. 15(1).

4. HUNT, THOMAS. De antiquitate, elegantia, utilitate, linguae Arabicae, oratio habita Oxonii, in Schola Linguarum, vii Kalend. Augusti. MDCCXXXVIII. a Thoma Hunt [etc.]. Oxonii, e Th. Sh., impensis Ricardi Clements, bibliopol. Oxon. MDCCXXXIX.
4to. Imp. 23 May 1739. Bodl. G. Pamph. 52(11).

5. HUTCHINSON, THOMAS. The usual interpretation of δαιμονες [etc., as in 1738]. The second edition. [etc., as in 1738].
8vo fours. Imp. 17 March 1737. Bodl. 8° S 146 Jur.

6★. (Oxford, University. 'Advertisement to publish Census &c.'
No copy found. Presumably relates to the book by John Reinolds published by the Delegates in 1738.
2nd A/cs. 176.)

7★. (Oxford, University. 'Mr. Vice-Chancellor's Letter to the Heads of Houses.'
2nd A/cs. 176. No copy found.)

8★. (Oxford, University. 'Advertisement to prohibit cock-fighting &c.'
2nd A/cs. 176. No copy found.)

9★. (Oxford, University. 'A catalogue of the Books to be sold at the University Ware-House.'
2nd A/cs. 176. No copy found. A list of the kind was issued in 1713.)

10. RANDOLPH, THOMAS. An enquiry into the sufficiency of reason in matters of religion. A sermon preach'd before the University of Oxford, at St. Mary's, on Sunday, September 17th. 1738. By Thomas Randolph [etc.]. Oxford, printed at the Theatre for the Widow Fletcher in the High-Street: and sold by J. Knapton in Ludgate-Street; C. Rivington in St. Paul's Church-Yard, London; W. Thurlburn at Cambridge, and J. Leake at Bath.
8vo fours. Imp. 28 Feb. 1738/9. Bodl. 80 A 10 28 (2) Jur.

11. (Sprott, Thomas. The Warehouseman received poundage in this year 'For Sprott's Chronicon 26 sheets at 1s. 6d. per sheet': 2nd A/cs. 174ᵛ. Hearne's edition of 1719 was rated at 26 sheets. No edition dated 1739 can be found.)

12. TILLY, WILLIAM. A letter to a worthy ınd learned gentleman in the law, concerning some passages in the life and death of Mrs. Sarah Tilly, his near relation, lately deceased; with some account of her descent and family; written by William Tilly [etc.]. Oxford: printed at the Theatre, and are to be sold by Mr. Clements, Mr. Piesly, and Mr. Broughton, booksellers there.
4to. Bodl. 211 d. 7.
The letter is headed with a date in 1739, but typographical evidence favours a later date for the printing.

13. TRYPHIODORUS. The destruction of Troy. Being the sequel of the Iliad. Translated from the Greek of Tryphiodorus. With notes. By J. Merrick scholar of Trinity Coll. Oxford. Oxford, printed at the Theatre.

8vo fours. Imp. 26 Oct. 1739. Bodl. 8° A 1(18) Jur.

James Merrick took the B.A. degree in 1739. The Greek text and a Latin translation, also undated, were published in 1741.

14. WILDER, JOHN. The trial of the spirits: or a caution against enthusiasm, or religious delusion. In a sermon preached before the University of Oxford, August 5th. 1739. By John Wilder [etc.]. Oxford, printed at the Theatre for the author, and are to be sold at his house, and by Mr. Doe and Mr. Burrows, booksellers in Oxford. Price 4d.

8vo fours. Bodl. Vet. A 4 e. 426(6).

1740

1. ABU AL-FIDA. [The first 72 pages of an edition by Jean Gagnier of this author's Geography are in the Bodleian Library, catalogued with this date. According to Hearne (xi, p. 130), the work was in the press in 1732.]

Fol. Bodl. A 1. 12 Th. Seld.

2. BENTHAM, EDWARD. Reflections upon the nature and usefulness of logick as it has been commonly taught in the schools by Edward Bentham [etc.]. Oxford, printed at the Theatre; and sold by Mary Fletcher bookseller in Oxford, S. Birt in Ave-Mary Lane, J. Stagg in Westminster Hall, London, and W. Thurlborn in Cambridge. 1740.

8vo fours. Imp. 1 Feb. 1739–40. Bodl. 8° F 110(3) Art.

3. BISSE, THOMAS. A course of sermons on the Lords-Prayer preach'd at the Rolls. By the Revd. Thomas Bisse, D.D. [etc.]. Printed from the author's original manuscripts, and published by Thomas Bisse, A.M. [etc.].

8vo. Imp. 16 July 1740. Bodl. 8° A 7(46) Jur.

2nd A/cs. 185ᵛ, dues.

4. BOWLES, THOMAS. A compendious and rational institution of the Latin tongue, with a critical dissertation on the Roman classics in a chronological order. By Thomas Bowles, D.D. Oxford. Printed in the year MDCCXL.

8vo fours. Bodl. 305 f. 49.

5. CAVE, WILLIAM. Scriptorum ecclesiasticorum historia literaria. a Christo nato usque ad saeculum xiv. facili methodo digesta. Qua, de vita illorum ac rebus gestis, de secta, dogmatibus, elogio, stylo; de scriptis genuinis, dubiis, suppositiis, ineditis, deperditis, fragmentis; deque variis operum editionibus perspicue agitur. Accedunt scriptores gentiles, Christianae religionis oppugnatores; & cujusvis saeculi Breviarium. Additur ad finem cujusque saeculi conciliorum omnium, tum generalium tum particularium, historica notitia. Inseruntur suis locis veterum aliquot opuscula et fragmenta, tum Graeca tum Latina, hactenus inedita. Praemissa denique prolegomena, quibus plurima ad antiquitatis ecclesiasticae studium spectantia traduntur. Autore Guilielmo Cave [etc.]. Accedunt ab aliis manibus appendices duae, ab ineunte saeculo xiv. ad annum usque MDXVII. nunc in unam

congestae. Ad calcem vero operis ejusdem Cavei dissertationes tres, I. De scriptoribus ecclesiasticis incertae aetatis, II. De libris & officiis ecclesiasticorum Graecorum, III. Adversus Johannem Clericum, una cum Epistola Apologetica adversus iniquas ejusdem Clerici criminationes. Editio novissima, ab autore ipsomet ante obitum recognita & auctior facta. Volumen I. Oxonii, e Th. Sh., apud Josephum Pote bibliopolam Etonensem. MDCCXL.

Fol. Imp. 30 Oct. 1739. Bodl. P 3. 15 Th.

2nd A/cs. 180ᵛ, dues. The first edition was printed in London, Vol. i in 1688, Vol. ii in 1698.

6. HARTE, WALTER. The reasonableness and advantage of national humiliations, upon the approach of war. A sermon preached before the University of Oxford, at St. Mary's, on Wednesday, Jan. 9. 1739–40. being the day appointed by his Majesty for a general fast and humiliation, in order to obtain of Almighty God pardon for our sins, and to implore his blessing and assistance on our arms against Spain. By Walter Harte [etc.]. Oxford, printed at the Theatre for R. Gosling, and G. Hawkins in Fleetstreet, London.

8vo fours. Imp. 1 Feb. 1739–40. Bodl. G. Pamph. 671(8).

7. HUTCHINSON, THOMAS. The use and scope of the ceremonial law briefly represented in a sermon preach'd before the University of Oxford at St. Mary's, on Sunday July 1st. 1739. By Thomas Hutchinson [etc.]. Oxford, printed at the Theatre for Mr. Clements, bookseller; and sold by Mess. Innys and Manby, Knapton, Rivington and Roberts, in London; and by Mr. Thurlborn in Cambridge. MDCCXL.

8vo fours. Imp. 24 Nov. 1739. Bodl. 8° S 146(3) Jur.

8. MAUNDRELL, HENRY. A journey from Aleppo to Jerusalem at Easter A.D. 1697. The sixth edition, to which is now added an account of the author's journey to the banks of the Euphrates at Beer, and to the country of Mesopotamia. With an index to the whole work, not in any former edition. By Henry Maundrell [etc.]. Oxford, printed at the Theatre, for A. Peisley bookseller in Oxford, and W. Meadows bookseller in Cornhill, London. MDCCXL.

8vo fours. Imp. 8 Apr. 1703. Bodl. 8° K 140 Linc.

2nd A/cs. 180ᵛ, dues. The Delegates took the opportunity to have 24 copies printed on large paper as presents and for sale: ibid. 182. The book was first printed in 1703, and again in 1707, 1715, 1721, and 1732.

9*. OXFORD, UNIVERSITY. Parecbolae sive excerpta e corpore statutorum Universitatis Oxoniensis. Accedunt Articuli religionis XXXIX. in Ecclesia Anglicana recepti: nec non Juramenta Fidelitatis et Suprematus. In usum juventutis academicae. Oxonii, e Th. Sh. MDCCXL.

8vo fours. Bodl. Vet. A 4 f. 1426.

2nd A/cs. 182, 3,000.

10. OXFORD, UNIVERSITY. An account of the Charity School in Oxford . . . [as in 1734].

4to. Bodl. Gough Oxf. 138(15a).

11. SKEELER, THOMAS. Fourteen sermons on several occasions preached before the University at St. Mary's in Oxford. By Thomas Skeeler [etc.]. Oxford: printed at the Theatre, MDCCXL.

8vo. Imp. 19 Aug. 1740. Bodl. 994 e. 18.

2nd A/cs. 185ᵛ, dues.

1741

1. BROWN, RICHARD. The case of Naaman considered. A sermon preached before the University of Oxford, at St. Mary's, on Sunday, October 12. 1740. By Richard Brown [etc.]. Oxford, printed at the Theatre for Richard Clements, bookseller: and sold by C. Rivington, J. and P. Knapton, and J. Roberts, booksellers in London. MDCCXLI.

8vo fours. Imp. 25 Feb. 1740. Bodl. G. Pamph. 768(7).

2. BURTON, JOHN. A sermon preached before the University of Oxford at St. Mary's, on Wednesday, Febr. 4. 1740-1. being the day appointed for a general fast on the occasion of the present war. By John Burton [etc.]. Oxford, printed at the Theatre: and are to be sold by Mary Fletcher bookseller in Oxford; Mr. Rivington and Mr. Innys in London; Mr. Thurlbourn at Cambridge; and Mr. Pote at Eton.

8vo fours. Worcester Coll. D.10.5(11).

3. DILLENIUS, J. J. Historia muscorum in qua circiter sexcentae species veteres et novae ad sua genera relatae describuntur et iconibus genuinis illustrantur: cum appendice et indice synonymorum. Opera Jo. Jac. Dillenii [etc.]. Oxonii, e Th. Sh. MDCCXLI.

4to. Imp. 14 Dec. 1741. Bodl. Arch. Nat. Hist. K 30.
The subject is mosses.

4. SPRY, JOHN. The case of the ministerial maintenance stated. A sermon preached at the triennial visitation of the Right Reverend Father in God Thomas Lord Bishop of Sarum, held at St. Helen's Church in Abingdon: on Tuesday, July 14. 1741. By John Spry [etc.]. Published by the command of his Lordship. Oxford, printed at the Theatre for James Fletcher, bookseller: and are to be sold by Ch. Rivington, and J. Knapton in London; and Edw. Score in Exeter. 1741.

8vo fours. Bodl. G. Pamph. 671(6).

5. TRYPHIODORUS. [Title in Greek.] Tryphiodori Ilii excidium, cum metrica Nicodemi Frischlini versione, et selectis virorum doctorum notis: lacunas aliquot e codice MSto. explevit, et suas annotationes adjecit, Jacobus Merrick [etc.]. Oxonii, e Th. Sh.

8vo fours. Imp. 6 Oct. 1741. Bodl. 8° A 1 (18) Jur.
2nd A/cs. 190ᵛ, dues. The editor's English translation was published in 1739.

6. WILDER, JOHN. Fifteen sermons preach'd before the University of Oxford, on the following subjects [etc.]. By John Wilder [etc.]. Second volume. Oxford, printed at the Theatre for the author, and are to be had of him on the payment of five shillings, of whom also may be had some few of the first volume at five shillings, the whole subscription price. 1741.

8vo fours. Imp. 9 Mar. 1741. Bodl. Bliss B 170.
The title-page announces thirteen sermons. A previous volume of fifteen sermons by this author was printed by Lichfield in 1729. According to the Press Accounts (199ᵛ), printing of this second volume was finished in 1743.

7. XENOPHON. [Title in Greek.] Xenophontis Memorabilium Socratis dictorum libri iv, Graece & Latine. cum notis integris Ernesti, aliorumque selectis; nunc variis etiam novis observationibus adaucti & illustrati. Huic editioni accedunt

capitum, verborum & phrasium indices locupletissimi. Oxonii, e Th. Sh. impensis Jacobi Fletcher bibliopol. Oxon. Venales prostant Londini apud C. Rivington, J. & P. Knapton, R. Manby, J. Nourse; et Gul. Thurlbourn, Cantab. MDCCXLI.

8vo fours. Imp. 20 Apr. 1741. Bodl. Bliss B 171.

2nd A/cs. 185^v, dues. Edited by Bolton Simpson.

1742

1. ALLEN, THOMAS. Oxon. Nov. 19. 1742. Proposals for printing by subscription, at the University Press in Oxford; Archaeologia Universalis, sive Historia mundi sacra & profana . . . By Thomas Allen [etc., 6 sheets to be issued monthly].

Fol. s. sh. Bodl. MS. Rawl. J. fol. 2 (54).

The work, intended to be based largely on Prideaux's *Connection*, was not published.

2. BATTELY, JOHN. Proposals for printing by subscription the posthumous Latin works of Dr. John Battely late Archdeacon of Canterbury, viz. Antiquitates Rutupinae et Antiquitates Sti. Edmundi Burgi ad annum 1272 perductae.

4to 4 pp. Bodl. MS. Rawl. J 4° 6(214).

A note by Richard Rawlinson (ibid., fol. 213) dates this in 1742. The book was published in 1745. Further proposals were issued in 1743.

3. CONINGESBY, GEORGE. A sermon preached before the Worshipful the Mayor, and Corporation of the City of Hereford, in the parish church of St. Peter, on Monday, Oct. 4. 1742. being the day of the Mayor's admission to office. Publish'd at the united request of Mr. Mayor and the gentlemen then present. By George Coningesby [etc.]. Oxford, printed for James Fletcher in the Turle; and sold by J. Knapton and J. Rivington in St. Paul's Church-Yard, London; and E. Wilde and J. Hunt at Hereford.

8vo fours. Bodl. G. Pamph. 74(7).

4. GAMBOLD, JOHN. Christianity tidings of joy. A sermon preach'd before the University of Oxford, at St. Mary's, on Sunday, Decemb. 27. 1741. By John Gambold [etc.]. Publish'd at the request of Mr. Vice-Chancellor. Oxford, printed at the Theatre for Edward Broughton bookseller: and are to be sold by Messieurs Knapton at the Crown in Ludgate-street, London.

8vo fours. Bodl. G. Pamph. 672(14).

5. [HOLMES, WILLIAM.] The country parson's advice to his parishioners of the younger sort. explaining what they are to believe and do, in order to be saved. Oxford: printed at the Theatre. MDCCXLII.

12mo sixes. Bodl. 8° T 134 Th.

6. NEW TESTAMENT IN GREEK. Η Καινη Διαθηκη, Novum Testamentum Graecum. Textu per omnia Milliano, cum divisione pericoparum et interpunctione J. A. Bengelii. Oxonii: e Th. Sh. impensis E. Broughton bibliop. MDCCXLII.

2 vols. 8vo fours. Imp. 7 Oct. 1742. Bodl. N.T. Gr. 1742 f. 1, 2.

2nd A/cs. 195^v, dues. Darlow & Moule 4746.

7. WEBBER, FRANCIS. The case of authority consider'd as it respects religion, particularly the Christian. A sermon preach'd at St. Mary's in Oxford, at the assizes: before the Honourable Mr. Justice Abney, and before the University; on Thursday, July 29. 1742. By Francis Webber [etc.]. Oxford, printed at the Theatre for James Fletcher bookseller in the Turl; and are to be sold by J. Knapton and J. Rivington in London. 1742.

8vo fours. Bodl. G. Pamph. 672(13).

8. WISE, FRANCIS. Further observations upon the White Horse and other antiquities in Berkshire. With an account of Whiteleaf-Cross in Buckinghamshire. As also of the Red Horse in Warwickshire, and some other monuments of the same kind. By Francis Wise [etc.]. Oxford, printed for Thomas Wood at the University Printing-House. MDCCXLII.

4to. Bodl. G. Pamph. 78(5).

1743

1. BATTELY, JOHN. Oxford, May 2, 1743. Proposals for printing by subscription the posthumous Latin works of Dr. John Battely [etc., as in 1742].

4to 4 pp. Bodl. MS. Rawl. J 4° 6(216).

Differs in the specimen pages from the proposals issued in 1742. The book was published in 1745.

2. BURTON, JOHN. The principles of Christian loyalty. A sermon preach'd before the University of Oxford, at St. Mary's on Monday, Jan. 31. 1742-3. being the anniversary of the martyrdom of King Charles I. By John Burton [etc.]. Oxford, printed at the Theatre for Mary Fletcher, and sold by J. Rivington and M. Cooper in London, W. Thurlbourne in Cambridge, J. Pote in Eton, and J. Leake in Bath, booksellers.

8vo fours. Imp. 17 March 1742-3. Bodl. G. Pamph. 72(3).

3. CAVE, WILLIAM. Scriptorum ecclesiasticorum historia literaria [etc., as in 1740]. Volumen II. Oxonii, e Th. Sh., apud Josephum Pote bibliopolam Etonensem. MDCCXLIII.

Fol. Bodl. P 3 16 Th.

2nd A/cs. 200ᵛ, dues. Signatures †A –†L, †Z, near the end, were printed in London by Charles Ackers: D. F. McKenzie and J. C. Ross, *A Ledger of Charles Ackers* (Oxford, 1968), p. 169.

4. CLEAVER, WILLIAM. The time of our Saviour's coming consider'd as to its fitness and propriety. A sermon preach'd before the University of Oxford, at St. Mary's on Sunday, March 6. 1742-3. By William Cleaver, M.A. Oxford, printed at the Theatre for James Fletcher bookseller in the Turl; and are to be sold by J. Rivington in St. Paul's Church-Yard, and M. Cooper in Pater-Noster-Row, London.

8vo fours. Imp. 17 March 1742/3. Bodl. G. Pamph. 672(10).

5. DODWELL, WILLIAM. The eternity of future punishment asserted and vindicated. In answer to Mr Whiston's late treatise on that subject. In two sermons preached before the University of Oxford on Sunday, March 21. 1743. By William

Dodwell [etc.]. Oxford, printed at the Theatre for James Fletcher bookseller in the Turl, and sold by S. Birt in Ave-Mary Lane, London. 1743.

8vo fours. Imp. 18 July 1743. Bodl. 8º P 119 Linc.

6. HOLE, WILLIAM. A sermon preached in the parish-church of Werrington, Devon, at the consecration of that church on Wednesday, Septemb. 7. 1743. By William Hole, Fellow of Exeter College in Oxford, and chaplain to the Lord Bishop of Exeter. Published by order of his Lordship, and at the desire of some gentlemen who were present. Oxford, printed at the Theatre for James Fletcher in the Turl, and are to be sold by S. Birt and J. Rivington booksellers in London, and E. Score at Exeter. 1743.

8vo fours. Imp. 28 Nov. 1743. Bodl. G. Pamph. 768(5).

7. HOMER. Ομηρου Ιλιας. Homeri Ilias, Graece. Editio altera. Oxonii, e Th. Sh., 1743. Impensis A. Peisley & J. Fletcher, bibliop. Oxon. Prostat apud W. Meadows & J. Rivington, bibliop. Lond.

8vo fours. Imp. 19 Oct. 1713. B.M. 52.i.3.

2nd A/cs. 199ᵛ. D.O. 11 Feb. 1741; *First Minute Book*, p. 53. The previous edition was of 1714.

8. HUNT, THOMAS. A dissertation on Proverbs vii, 22, 23. being a specimen of critical dissertations on the Proverbs of Solomon: addressed to the students of Arabic and other oriental languages, in the University of Oxford. By Thomas Hunt [etc.]. Oxford, printed at the Theater, for R. Clements; and sold by J. and P. Knapton in Ludgate-Street, J. Rivington in St. Paul's Church-Yard, and J. Roberts in Warwick-Lane, London. 1743.

4to. Bodl. G. Pamph. 90(2).

9. JUNIUS, FRANCIS. Francisci Junii Francisci filii Etymologicum Anglicanum ex autographo descripsit & accessionibus permultis auctum edidit Edwardus Lye [etc.]. Praemittuntur vita auctoris et grammatica Anglo-Saxonica. Oxonii, e Th. Sh., MDCCXLIII.

Fol. Imp. 9 June 1743. Bodl. Douce I subt. 9.

2nd A/cs. 199ᵛ.

10. [——]. Reflections on the natural foundation of the high antiquity of government, arts, and sciences in Egypt. Oxford, printed at the Theatre for James Fletcher in the Turl, and sold by Mrs. Cooper in Pater-Noster-Row, London, 1743.

8vo fours. Bodl. G. Pamph. 2064(2).

1744

1. BENTHAM, EDWARD. The connection between irreligion and immorality. A sermon preach'd at St. Mary's in Oxford, at the assizes: before the Honourable Mr. Justice Dennison and Mr. Serjeant Birch, and before the University on March 1. 1743–4. By Edward Bentham [etc.]. Oxford, printed at the Theatre for James Fletcher in the Turl, and sold by John Rivington in St. Paul's Church-Yard, London. 1744.

8vo fours. Imp. 12 March 1743–4. Bodl. G. Pamph. 887(5).

2. BIBLE (OLD TESTAMENT) IN HEBREW. Proposals for publishing a Hebrew Bible without points edited by Nathaniel Forster, in a new type provided by the

University. 350 on small paper and a few on large. Price, small, £1. 10s., large 2½ gns. Specimen page in Caslon's Pica Hebrew.

4to. Imp. 26 Sept. 1744. Bodl. MS. Rawl. J 4° 6(293).

The book was published in 1750.

3. BURTON, JOHN. The genuineness of Lord Clarendon's History of the Rebellion printed at Oxford vindicated. Mr. Oldmixon's slander confuted. The true state of the case represented. By John Burton B.D. Fellow of Eton College. Oxford, printed at the Theatre for James Fletcher bookseller in the Turl, and sold by M. Cooper in Pater-Noster-Row, London. 1744.

8vo. Bodl. Clar. Press 31 b. 42.

2nd A/cs. 204ᵛ, dues.

4. BURTON, JOHN. The folly and wickedness of misplacing our trust and confidence. A sermon preached before the University of Oxford, at St. Mary's, on Wednesday, April 9. 1744. being the day appointed for a general fast. By John Burton B.D. Fellow of Eton College [etc.]. Oxford, printed at the Theatre for James Fletcher bookseller in the Turl, and sold by M. Cooper in Pater-Noster-Row, London. 1744.

8vo fours. Bodl. G. Pamph. 72(5).

5. DODWELL, WILLIAM. The desireableness of the Christian faith illustrated and applied. A sermon preached at the triennial visitation of the Right Reverend Father in God Thomas Lord Bishop of Sarum, held at Reading on Thursday, August 30th. 1744. By William Dodwell [etc.]. Published at the request of his Lordship. Oxford, printed at the Theatre for James Fletcher bookseller in the Turl, and sold by M. Cooper in Pater-Noster-Row, London. 1744.

8vo fours. Imp. 15 Sept. 1744. Bodl. 8° P 119(2) Linc.

6. EDEN, ROBERT. Jurisprudentia philologica, sive Elementa juris civilis, secundum methodum et seriem Institutionum Justiniani, in brevem & facilem ordinem redacta, notis classicis, & historicis, nec non parallelis juris Anglicani locis, illustrata. Quibus accessit prooemium de jure civili Romanorum ante Justinianum, et de libris juris civilis Romanorum per Justinianum compositis. In usum juventutis academicae. Per Robertum Eden [etc.]. Oxonii, e Theatro Sheldoniano MDCCXLIV.

4to. Imp. 6 March 1743-4. Bodl. CC 53 Art.

2nd A/cs. 200ᵛ, dues.

7. FOTHERGILL, GEORGE. The danger of excesses in the pursuit of liberty. A sermon [etc., as in the edition of 1737]. The second edition. Oxford, printed at the Theatre, and sold by Richard Clements bookseller: as also by Messieurs Knapton, Rivington, and Roberts in London; Mr. Thurlbourn in Cambridge, and Mr. Leake in Bath MDCCXLIV. Price sixpence.

8vo fours. Imp. 24 Feb. 1736-7. Bodl. G. Pamph. 666(14).

8. HUNTER, JOHN. Aditus ad templum, or the path-way to church: being a preparative for a more solemn devotion at the publick worship of God in the church. A new-year's gift to the parishioners of Hampton-Poyle and South-Weston in the county of Oxford. By their rector, John Hunter [etc.]. Oxford: printed for the author. 1744.

8vo fours. Bodl. G. Pamph. 2865(1).

9. MERRICK, JAMES. A dissertation on Proverbs Chap. ix. v. 1, 2, 3, 4, 5, 6. Wisdom hath builded her house &c. Containing occasional remarks on other passages in sacred and profane writers. By James Merrick [etc.]. Oxford, printed at

the Theatre, and sold by John Rivington in St. Paul's Church-Yard, S. Birt in Ave-Mary Lane, London; W. Thurlbourn at Cambridge; R. Clements and J. Fletcher at Oxford; J. Newbery at Reading. 1744. Price one shilling.

4to. Bodl. Bliss B 414(1).

10*. (Oxford, University. A 'Catal[ogue]' of Books to be sold' was printed this year and charged to the Delegates. No copy has been found.

2nd A/cs. 201.)

11. PLUTARCH. Πλουταρχου Δημοσθενης και Κικερων. Plutarchi Demosthenis et Ciceronis vitae parallelae, nunc primum separatim editae. Graeca recensuit, Latine reddidit, notis illustravit, Philippus Barton [etc.]. Oxonii, e Typ. Clar. A.D. MDCCXLIV.

8vo fours. Imp. 8 Oct. 1743. Bodl. Radcl. e. 252.

12*. SHAKESPEARE. The works of Shakespear. in six volumes. Carefully revised and corrected by former editions, and adorned with sculptures designed and executed by the best hands. Oxford: printed at the Theatre, MDCCXLIV.

Each volume has its own title-page: The works of Mr. William Shakespear. Volume the . . . consisting of . . . Oxford: printed at the Theatre [date]. The first and second consist of comedies, the third and fourth of historical plays, the fifth and sixth of tragedies. The first four are dated 1743.

6 vols. 4to. Bodl. DD 44–49 Art.

2nd A/cs. 202, printing 600. Hanmer's edition.

13. SPRY, JOHN. The influence of education justified, with regard to the profession of Christianity. A sermon preached before the University of Oxford, at St. Mary's, May 8. 1744. By John Spry [etc.]. Oxford, printed at the Theatre for James Fletcher bookseller in the Turl, and sold by M. Cooper in Pater-Noster-Row, London. 1744.

8vo fours. Imp. 4 June 1744. Bodl. G. Pamph. 666(12).

1745

1. BATTELY, JOHN. Joannis Battelyi S.T.P. Archidiaconi Cantuarensis Opera posthuma. viz. Antiquitates Rutupinae et Antiquitates S. Edmundi Burgi ad annum 1272 perductae. Oxonii, e Th. Sh., A.D. MDCCXLV.

4to. Imp. 3 Dec. 1745. Bodl. 4° B 78 Jur.

Proposals were issued in 1742 and 1743.

2. BENTHAM, EDWARD. An introduction to moral philosophy. By Edward Bentham [etc.]. Oxford, printed at the Theatre, MDCCXLV. for James Fletcher in the Turl, and sold by M. Senex in London and W. Thurlborn in Cambridge. Price 1s. 6d.

8vo fours. Imp. 8 Apr. 1745. Bodl. G. Pamph. 767(1).

2nd A/cs. 205ᵛ, dues.

3. [BENTHAM, EDWARD.] Associatio Ciceroniana, sive cohortatio ad rempub. tuendam. [Arms of the University and City.] Oxonii MDCCXLV.

8vo 8 pages. Bodl. G. Pamph. 2704(4).

4. DALTON, JOHN. Two sermons preached before the University of Oxford, at St. Mary's, on Sept. 15th, and Oct. 20th, 1745. and now published for the use of

the younger students in the two Universities. By John Dalton [etc.]. Oxford, printed at the Theatre for Richard Clements: and sold by Mr Rivington in St. Paul's Church-Yard, Mr Dodsley in Pall-Mall, London; Mr Thurlbourn in Cambridge; Mr Leak in Bath. MDCCXLV. Price one shilling.

4to. Imp. 24 Oct. 1745. Bodl. G. Pamph. 2230(3).

5. DODWELL, WILLIAM. The nature, procedure, extent, value, and effects of a rational faith considered. in two sermons preach'd before the University of Oxford, on March 11. and June 24. 1744. By William Dodwell [etc.]. Oxford, printed for James Fletcher in the Turl; and sold by Sam. Birt in Ave Marie Lane, and J. Rivington in St. Paul's Church-Yard, London. MCCXLV [sic].

8vo fours. Imp. 15 June 1745. Bodl. 8° P 119(3) Linc.

6. DODWELL, WILLIAM. The practical influence of the doctrine of the Holy Trinity represented. A sermon preached before the University of Oxford, on Trinity Sunday, June 9th 1745. By William Dodwell [etc. imprint as in the preceding item].

8vo fours. Imp. 24 June 1745. Bodl. 8° P 119(4) Linc.

7. [——]. A mechanical enquiry into the nature, causes, seat, and cure of the diabetes, with an explication of the most remarkable symptoms. Oxford, printed at the Theatre for James Fletcher in the Turl; and sold by M. Cooper in Pater-Noster-Row, London, Ben. Hickey in Bristol, and J. Leake at Bath. 1745.

8vo fours. Bodl. G. Pamph. 77(3).

The imprint, identical with that of No. 15 following, suggests that George Randolph was the author.

8. FOTHERGILL, GEORGE. The importance of religion to civil societies. A sermon [as in the 2nd ed. of 1735]. The third edition corrected. Oxford, printed at the Theatre for Richard Clements: and sold by Mr. Knapton in Ludgate-Street, Mr. Clark under the Royal Exchange, Mr. Rivington in St. Paul's Church-Yard, London; Mr. Thurlbourn in Cambridge, and Mr. Leake in Bath. MDCCXLV.

8vo fours. Imp. 18 March 1734-5. Bodl. G. Pamph. 666(13).

9. — (A 4th edition, of the same year, of which no copy has been found, is reported: Madan 1745:23.)

10. FOTHERGILL, GEORGE. The unsuccessfulness of repeated fasts consider'd and apply'd. A sermon preach'd before the University of Oxford, at St. Mary's, on Wednesday, January 9. 1744-5. being the day appointed by His Majesty's proclamation to be kept as a general fast. By George Fothergill [etc.]. Oxford, printed at the Theatre, for Richard Clements: and sold by Mr. Knapton in Ludgate-Street, Mr. Clark under the Royal Exchange, Mr. Rivington in St. Paul's Church Yard, London; Mr. Thurlbourn in Cambridge, and Mr. Leake in Bath. MDCCXLV.

8vo fours. Imp. 23 Jan. 1744-5. Bodl. G. Pamph. 666(15).

11. HORBERY, MATTHEW. The inspiration of the moral parts of Scripture asserted. A sermon preached at the triennial visitation of the Right Reverend Father in God, Richard, Lord Bishop of Lichfield and Coventry, held at the Cathedral-Church in Lichfield, on Wednesday, August 29. 1744. in which the sentiments of Mons. Le-Clerc, and Dr. Sykes are considered. By Matthew Horbery [etc.]. Published at the request of his Lordship and the clergy. Oxford, printed at the Theatre for James Fletcher in the Turl, and sold by J. and J. Knapton in Ludgate-Street; S. Birt in Ave-Maria-Lane; J. Rivington in St. Paul's Church-Yard; and R. Bailye at Lichfield. 1745.

8vo fours. Imp. 18 Jan. 1744-5. Bodl. G. Pamph. 664.

12. [LANGBAINE, GERARD.] Ethices compendium in usum juventutis academicae auctius & emendatius editum. Cui accedit methodus argumentandi Aristotelica. Oxonii, impensis Edvardi Broughton bibliopolae. MDCCXLV.

12mo sixes. Imp. 14 Feb. 1744–5. Bodl. Bliss B 174.

2nd A/cs. 205ᵛ, dues. Bodl. Bliss B 175, with a similar title, was not, I think, printed at the University Press. Edited by Edward Bentham.

13. LELAND, JOHN. The itinerary of John Leland the antiquary. In nine volumes. The second edition: collated and improved from the original MS. With the addition also of a general index. Oxford: printed at the Theatre; for James Fletcher, bookseller in the Turl, and Joseph Pote, bookseller at Eton. MDCCXLV.

[The nine title-pages of Hearne's edition of 1710–12 are reprinted at the beginnings of the volumes, all dated 1744.]

8vo fours. Imp. 28 Sept. 1745. Bodl. Mus. Bibl. II 33–37.

2nd A/cs. 210ᵛ, dues.

14. PLATO. Πλατωνος Διαλογοι ε'. Platonis Dialogi v. Recensuit, notisque illustra vit Nath. Forster [etc.]. Oxonii, e Typ. Clar., impensis Jac. Fletcher bibliopolae. MDCCXLV.

8vo fours. Imp. 10 Apr. 1745. Bodl. 8º A 8(27) Jur.

3rd A/cs. p. 2, dues. Contains Amatores, Euthyphro, Apologia, Crito, Phaedo.

15. RANDOLPH, GEORGE. An enquiry into the medicinal virtues of Bristol water: and the indications of cure which it answers. By George Randolph M.D. [etc.]. Oxford, printed at the Theatre, MDCCXLV. for James Fletcher in the Turl; and sold by M. Cooper in Pater Noster Row, London, B. Hickey in Bristol, and J. Leake in Bath.

8vo fours. Imp. 24 Apr. 1745. Bodl. G. Pamph. 77(2).

16. ROSS, JOHN. Joannis Rossi antiquarii Warwicensis Historia regum Angliae. E codice MS. in Bibliotheca Bodlejana descripsit, notisque & indice adornavit Tho. Hearnius, A.M. Oxoniensis. Accedit Joannis Lelandi antiquarii Naenia in mortem Henrici Duddlegi equitis; cui praefigitur Testimonium de Lelando amplum & praeclarum, hactenus ineditum. Editio secunda. E Th. Sh.; impensis Jac. Fletcher bibliop. Oxon. & J. Pote Etonensis.

8vo fours. Bodl. Mus. Bibl. II 37. Forms part of the ninth volume of Leland's Itinerary, but has separate signatures and pagination.

2nd A/cs. 210ᵛ, dues.

17. SPRY, JOHN. The duty of Christian confidence in times of danger to the Church of Christ. A sermon preached before the University of Oxford, at St. Mary's, October 13. 1745. on occasion of the present Rebellion. By John Spry [etc.]. Oxford, printed for James Fletcher in the Turl, and sold by J. Knapton and J. Rivington in St. Paul's Church-Yard, London.

8vo fours. Imp. 21 Oct. 1745. Bodl. Bliss B 145(15).

18. STRADA, FAMIANO. Famiani Stradae Prolusiones academicae. Oxonii, e Th.Sh., impensis Jac. Fletcher bibliopolae. MDCCXLV.

8vo fours. Imp. 9 Apr. 1745. Bodl. 296945 e. 1.

3rd A/cs. p. 2, dues.

19. XENOPHON. [Greek title.] Xenophontis de Cyri expedition libri septem. Graeca recognovit, cum codicibus MStis. & omnibus fere libris editis contulit,

plurimis in locis emendavit, versionem Latinam reformavit, observationibus suis, tabula geographica & indice geographico auxit & illustravit; notas H. Stephani, Leunclavii, Æ. Porti & Mureti recensitas & castigatas, & variantium lectionum delectum, adjunxit Thomas Hutchinson. Editio secunda. Oxonii, e Typ. Clar., impensis Jac. Fletcher bibliopolae MDCCXLV.

8vo fours. Imp. 28 Feb. 1744-5. Bodl. 2354 e. 16.
3rd A/cs. p. 2, dues. The first edition was of 1735.

1746

1. BENTHAM, EDWARD. An introduction to moral philosophy. By Edward Bentham [etc.]. The second edition. Oxford, printed at the Theater, MDCCXLVI. for James Fletcher in the Turl; and sold by Sam. Birt and M. Senex in London; and in Cambridge. Price 1s. 6d.

8vo fours. Imp. 8 Apr. 1745. Bodl. G. Pamph. 211(2).
2nd A/cs. 210ᵛ, dues. The first edition was published in 1745.

2. BURTON, JOHN. Principles of religion the only sufficient restraint from wickedness. A sermon preach'd at the assizes before the Honourable Sr. Thomas Abney, and Mr. Serjeant Willes, and before the University of Oxford, at St. Mary's, Aug. 7. 1746. By John Burton B.D. [etc.]. Oxford, printed at the Theatre for James Fletcher in the Turl, and sold by J. and J. Rivington in St. Paul's Church-Yard, London. MDCCXLVI.

8vo fours. Imp. 1 Oct. 1746. Bodl. Bliss B 145(16).

3. BURTON, JOHN. The expostulation and advice of Samuel to the men of Israel applied. A sermon preach'd before the University of Oxford, at St. Mary's, Oct. 9. 1746. being the day appointed to be kept as a general thanksgiving to Almighty God for the suppression of the late Rebellion. By John Burton B.D. [etc. imprint as in the preceding entry].

8vo fours. Imp. 30 Oct. 1746. Bodl. Bliss B 145(17).
The signatures continue the series of the preceding sermon.

4. CICERO. M. T. Ciceronis sententiae duae de iis honore augendis, qui periculum vitae adierunt Reipub. causa. Oxonii MDCCXLVI.

4to. Bodl. 90 b. 20.
Preface by Edward Bentham.

5. CORNEILLE, PIERRE. Les chef-d'oeuvres [sic] de P. Corneille. Savoir Le Cid, Horace, Cinna, Polyeucte, Pompee, Rodogune. Avec le jugement des savans a la suite de chaque piece. Nouvelle edition. A Oxford, chez James Fletcher. MDCCXLVI.

8vo fours. Bodl. 8° Godw. 216.
3rd A/cs. p. 2, dues. Only the title-page is without accents. No earlier edition at Oxford can be traced.

6. FORSTER, NATHANIEL. Popery destructive of the evidence of Christianity. A sermon preached before the University of Oxford, at St. Mary's, on Wednesday, Novemb. 5. 1746. By Nathaniel Forster [etc.]. Oxford, printed at the Theatre for James Fletcher in the Turl; and sold by J. and J. Rivington in St. Paul's Church-Yard, London.

8vo fours. Imp. 8 Nov. 1746. Bodl. G. Pamph. 85(11).

7. [HAMPTON, JAMES(?).] Reflections on ancient and modern history. Oxford, printed for James Fletcher in the Turl; and sold by J. and J. Rivington in St. Paul's Church-Yard, R. Dodsley in Pall-Mall, and M. Cooper in Pater-Noster-Row, London. MDCCXLVI. Price one shilling.

    4to. Bodl. Vet. A 4 d. 262(1).

8. HUNT, THOMAS. Proposals for printing by subscription, Abdollatiphi Historiae Ægypti compendium: quod, sexaginta abhinc annis, ab Edvardo Pocockio, clarissimi Edvardi filio, [etc.] ex lingua Arabica in Latinam versum, nunc primum utraque edidit, notisque illustravit Thomas Hunt [etc.].

    4to 8 pages. Bodl. MS. Rawl. letters 96(245).

    The book was not published.

9. LIVY. Appendix Liviana, continens I. Selectas codicum MSS. & editionum anti-quarum lectiones, praecipuas variorum emendationes, & supplementa lacunarum in iis T. Livii qui supersunt libris. II. J. Freinshemii supplementorum libros x. in locum Decadis secundae Livianae deperditae. In usum juventutis academicae. Oxonii, e Typ. Clar., impensis Jac. Fletcher bibliopolae. MDCCXLVI.

    12mo sixes. Imp. 4 Apr. 1746. Bodl. 90 c. 45.

    2nd A/cs. 210ᵛ, dues.

10. (MARSHALL, THOMAS. [The Catechism in the Book of Common Prayer briefly explained . . . An edition of 3,000 was printed this year. No copy has been found.] 2nd A/cs. 212.)

11. [Meusnier de Querlon. Les soupers de Daphne et les dortoirs de Lacedemone. Anecdotes grecques. A Oxfort MCCXLVI.

    The imprint is false: Quérard, *La France littéraire*, vi (1834), p. 99.]

12. PARKER, WILLIAM. The nature and reasonableness of the inward call and outward mission to the holy ministry consider'd. A sermon preach'd before the Right Reverend Father in God Thomas Lord Bishop of Oxford, at the ordination held at Christ-Church, on Sunday, March 2. 1745–6. By William Parker [etc.]. Published by request. Oxford, printed at the Theatre for James Fletcher in the Turl, and sold by J. and J. Rivington in St. Paul's Church-Yard, London. MDCCXLVI.

    8vo fours. Imp. 9 Apr. 1746. Bodl. G. Pamph. 85(7).

13. SHAW, THOMAS. A supplement to a book entitled Travels, or Observations, &c. wherein some objections, lately made against it, are fully considered and answered: with several additional remarks and dissertations. By Thomas Shaw [etc.]. Oxford, printed at the Theatre. MDCCXLVI.

    Fol. Imp. 3 March 1745–6. Bodl. P 3 4 Th.

    2nd A/cs. 210ᵛ, dues.

14. SWINTON, JOHN. De priscis Romanorum literis dissertatio. Autore Joanne Swinton [etc.]. Oxonii, e Th. Sh. MDCCXLVI.

    4to. Imp. 7 Nov. 1746. Bodl. Auct. V 2 inf. II 22(2).

    The bill for the printing, in the amount of £2. 6s., dated in July 1750, is in Bodl. MS. Auct. V 2 inf. II 22*, fol. 16.

15. SWINTON, JOHN. De primigenio Etruscorum alphabeto dissertatio. Autore Joanne Swinton [etc.]. Oxonii, e Th. Sh. MDCCXLVI. [The first 8 pages. No more was printed.]

    4to. Imp. 7 Nov. 1746. Bodl. Auct. V 2 inf. II 22(1).

16. THUCYDIDES, PLATO, LYSIAS. Θουκυδιδου Πλατωνος και Λυσιου επιταφιοι. Εκ Θεατρου ἐν Οξονια, Ετει αψμς'.

8vo fours. Imp. 28 May 1746. B.M. 1090.1.3(1).

2nd A/cs. 214ᵛ, dues. Edited by Edward Bentham.

1747

1. BROWN, RICHARD. Job's expectation of a resurrection considered. A sermon preached before the University of Oxford, at St. Mary's on Sunday October 19. Oct. 26. 1746. and Febr. 22. 1746-7. By Richard Brown [etc.]. Oxford, printed at the Theatre for Richard Clements, bookseller. And sold by J. and J. Rivington, booksellers in St. Paul's Church-Yard, London. 1747.

8vo fours. Imp. 17 March 1746-7. Bodl. G. Pamph. 1634(5).

2. COSTARD, GEORGE. Some observations tending to illustrate the Book of Job, and in particular the words I know that my Redeemer liveth, &c. Job xix, 25. By G. Costard [etc.]. Oxford, printed at the Theatre for R. Clements; and sold by J. and P. Knapton in Ludgate-Street, J. and J. Rivington in St. Paul's Church-Yard, and M. Cooper in Pater-Noster-Row, London. 1747.

8vo fours. Bodl. 8° G. Pamph. 893(3).

3. EUCLID. Euclidis Elementorum libri priores sex, item undecimus & duodecimus. Ex versione Latina Frederici Commandini. Quibus accedunt Trigonometriae planae & sphaericae elementa. Item Tractatus de natura & arithmetica logarithmorum. In usum juventutis academicae. Editio quinta, auctior & emendatior. Oxoniae, e Th. Sh. MDCCXLVII. Impensis Ric. Clements bibliop. Oxon. Prostat apud J. & J. Knapton, S. Birt, & J. & J. Rivington, bibliop. London.

8vo Imp. 25 March 1715. Bodl. 8° F 250 BS.

2nd A/cs. 214ᵛ, dues. The 5th edition of John Keill's Euclid, first published in 1715.

4. FOTHERGILL, GEORGE. The duty of giving thanks for national deliverances. A sermon preach'd at St. Martin's in Oxford, before the Mayor and Corporation, on Thursday, October 9th, 1746. being the day appointed to be kept as a general thanksgiving to Almighty God, for the suppression of the late Rebellion. By George Fothergill [etc.]. Publish'd at the request of the Mayor, Bayliffs, and Commonalty of the City. Oxford, printed at the Theatre for Richard Clements: and sold by Mr Knapton in Ludgate-Street, Mr Clark under the Royal-Exchange, Mr Rivington in St. Paul's Church-Yard, London; Mr Thurlbourn in Cambridge, and Mr Leake in Bath.

8vo fours. Imp. 14 Nov. 1746. Bodl. G. Pamph. 761.

5. HURLY, JAMES. A sermon preached at the Visitation of the Reverend George Atwood, B.D. Archdeacon of Taunton, held at St. Mary Magdalen's in Taunton, on Thursday, June 19. 1746. By James Hurly [etc.]. Oxford, printed at the Theatre for James Fletcher in the Turl: and sold by S. Birt in Ave-Mary-Lane, London; and S. Chaulklin in Taunton. MDCCXLVII.

8vo fours. Bodl. 1243 e. 222.

6. HUTCHINS, RICHARD. Elucidatio sexti capituli Evangelii secundum Johannem in solenni praelectione habita in Schola Theologica Oxon, pro gradu Doctoris in Theologia. A Ric. Hutchins, S.T.B. Colleg. Lincoln. socio. MDCCXLVII. Oxonii: veneunt apud J. and J. Fletcher, et D. Prince et J. Cooke.

8vo fours. Bodl. 8° R 136(2) Th.

The style of printing and the names of the booksellers suggest a date a good deal later than 1747.

7. KENNICOTT, BENJAMIN. Two dissertations: the first on the Tree of Life in Paradise, with some observations on the Creation and Fall of Man; the second on the oblations of Cain and Abel. By Benjamin Kennicott [etc.]. Oxford, printed at the Theatre for the author: and sold by Mr. Clements in Oxford; Mr. Birt and Mess. Rivington, in London; Mr. Thurlbourn in Cambridge; Mr. Leake in Bath; and Mr. Score, in Exeter. MDCCXLVII.

8vo fours. Imp. 2 March 1746–7. Bodl. G. Pamph. 79(1).

2nd A/cs. 214^v, dues.

8. — A second edition, with an appendix. Bodl. 8° F 122(1) BS.

3rd A/cs. p. 2, dues.

9. KENNICOTT, BENJAMIN. A poem on the recovery of Mrs. Eliz. Courtenay from her late dangerous illness: humbly inscribed to Kellond Courtenay of Painsford, Esq.; and his lady. Written in the year 1743. The second edition. [Woodcut of the Theatre.] MDCCXLVII.

8vo fours. Bodl. G. Pamph. 766.

10*. OXFORD, UNIVERSITY. The catalogue of graduats &c. in the University of Oxford, continued from October 10. 1735. to October 10. 1747.

8vo fours. Bodl. Gough Oxf. 35(3).

3rd A/cs. p. 5, printing 1,000.

11. OXFORD, UNIVERSITY. An account of the Charity School in Oxford . . . [as in 1734 and 1740].

4to. Bodl. Gough Oxf. 138(15b).

12. PAULDEN, THOMAS. An account of the taking and surrendering of Pontefract Castle, and of the surprisal of General Rainsborough in his quarters at Doncaster, anno 1648. Written upon the occasion of Prince Eugene's surprising M. Villeroy at Cremona. In a letter to a friend. By Captain Thomas Paulden. Oxford, printed at the Theatre: and sold by R. Clements and S. Parker. And by J. and J. Rivington in St. Paul's Church-Yard, London. MDCCXLVII.

8vo fours. Bodl. Gough York 36(9).

13. WOOD, JOHN. Choir Gaure, vulgarly called Stonehenge on Salisbury Plain, described, restored, and explained; in a letter to the Right Honourable Edward late Earl of Oxford, and Earl Mortimer. By John Wood, architect. Oxford, printed at the Theatre in the year 1747. and sold by C. Hitch in Pater-Noster-Row; and S. Birt in Ave-Mary-Lane, London; by J. Leake in Bath; and by B. Collier in Salisbury.

8vo fours. Bodl. Gough Wilts. 26.

3rd A/cs. p. 14, dues.

1748

1. BEAR, JOHN. De primaevorum patrum auctoritate. Concio, coram Academia Oxoniensi pro gradu Baccalaureatus in Sacra Theologia, olim habita. A Johanne Bear [etc.]. Oxonii, e Th. Sh., impensis Jacobi Fletcher, bibliop. MDCCXLVIII.
8vo fours. Bodl. G. Pamph. 85(6).

2. BENTHAM, EDWARD. A letter to a young gentleman. By a tutor, and fellow of a college in Oxford. Printed in the year MDCCXLVIII.
8vo fours. Bodl. G. Pamph. 88(2).

3. BION AND MOSCHUS. [Title in Greek.] Bionis Smyrnaei, et Moschi Syracusani, quae supersunt. Notis Johannis Heskin [etc.]. Oxonii, e Typ. Clar., prostant venales apud Johan. Barrett, bibliop. MDCCXLVIII.
8vo fours. Imp. 27 Oct. 1748. Bodl. Godw. 368.
3rd A/cs. p. 14, dues.

4. (Bowles, J. Aristarchus. A book so entitled, 'privately printed', is entered in the Catalogue of the Library of Dr. Philip Bliss (1858) among books printed at Oxford.)

5. [BURTON, JOHN.] Epistolae, altera peregrinantis, altera rusticantis. Oxonii, e Th. Sh., impensis J. Fletcher. MDCCXLVIII.
4to. Bodl. G. Pamph. 88(1).

6. [COSTARD, GEORGE.] A further account of the rise and progress of astronomy amongst the antients, in three letters to Martin Folkes, Esq; President of the Royal Society. By the author of the first. Oxford, printed at the Theatre for Richard Clements: and sold by Mr. Tho. Osborne at Gray's-Inn, Mr Birt in Ave-Maria-Lane, and Mess J. and J. Rivington in St. Paul's Church-Yard, booksellers in London. MDCCXLVIII.
8vo fours. Bodl. G. Pamph. 893(2).
3rd A/cs. p. 2, dues. A letter to Martin Folkes, Esq., on the same subject, also anonymous, was printed in London in 1746.

7. HUNT, THOMAS. De usu dialectorum orientalium, ac praecipue Arabicae, in Hebraico Codice interpretando, oratio habita Oxonii, in Schola Linguarum, vii. Kalend. Martii, MDCCXLVIII. A Thoma Hunt [etc.]. Oxonii, e Th. Sh., impensis Ricardi Clements, bibliopol. Oxon. MDCCXLVIII.
4to. Imp. 5 Dec. 1748. Bodl. G. Pamph. 90(1).

8. IBBETSON, JAMES. De miraculis in Ecclesia Christiana. Concio ad Academiam Oxoniensem, pro gradu baccalaureatus in S. Theologia habita in ecclesia B. Mariae, Junii ix. A.D. MDCCXLVIII. A Jacobo Ibbetson S.T.B. [etc.]. Oxonii, e Th. Sh., impensis Jacobi Fletcher, bibliopol. Prostant apud J. & J. Rivington, Londoni. MDCCXLVIII.
8vo fours. Imp. 11 June 1748. Bodl. 1 a. 146.

9*. (Oxford, University. The Press charged for printing 150 copies of 'a Programma' this year: 3rd A/cs. p. 3. I have not found a copy, but the text is transcribed in Bodl. MS. Top. Oxon. e. 145, pp. 7-8. By ordering 'all persons to attend in the Common Hall, at the usual hours of Dinner and Supper' it caused the trouble at Queen's College. See below, No. 12.)

10*. (Oxford, University. 100 copies of an 'Advertisement of Books to be sold' were printed this year, probably like the one issued in 1713.)

11. OXFORD, UNIVERSITY, CHRIST CHURCH. Carmina quadragesimalia ab Aedis Christi Oxon. alumnis composita et ab ejusdem Aedis baccalaureis determinantibus in Schola Naturalis Philosophiae publice recitata. Volumen secundum. Oxonii, e Th. Sh., MDCCXLVIII.

    8vo fours. Imp. 16 July 1747. Bodl. 8° C 89* Jur.

    3rd A/cs. p. 14, dues. The first volume was printed in 1723.

12. OXFORD, UNIVERSITY, QUEEN'S COLLEGE. The case of Queen's College Oxford in regard to some late irregularities of its younger members.

    Fol. 4 pages. Bodl. MS. Willis 45 (237b).

    Refers to an attempted secession by undergraduates: J. R. Magrath, *The Queen's College* (1921), ii, p. 111.

13. PARKER, WILLIAM. The natural effect, and religious improvement of extra-ordinary divine judgments, and of solemn fasts instituted in remembrance of them. A sermon preached before the Right Honourable the Lord-Mayor, the Aldermen, and Citizens of London, at the Cathedral-Church of St. Paul, on Friday, Sept. 2. 1748. being the anniversary fast appointed for the dreadful fire in London in the year 1666. By William Parker [etc.]. Oxford, printed at the Theatre for James Fletcher in the Turl, and sold by J. and J. Rivington in St. Paul's Church-Yard, London. MDCCXLVIII.

    4to. Imp. 26 Sept. 1748. Bodl. G. Pamph. 90(16).

14. TOTTIE, JOHN. The pernicious effects of an intemperate indulgence in sensual pleasures. A sermon preached before the University of Oxford, at St. Mary's, on Sunday, March 13. 1747–8. By John Tottie [etc.]. Published at the request of Mr. Vice-Chancellor and the Heads of Houses. Oxford, printed at the Theatre for Mary Fletcher bookseller in the High-Street; and sold by J. and J. Rivington in St. Paul's Church-Yard; W. Sandby in Fleet-Street, London; and J. Mountfort at Worcester.

    8vo fours. Imp. 2 May 1748. Bodl. Bliss B 145(6).

15. WHITING, CHARLES. De doctorum auctoritate in rebus sacris. Concio coram Academia Oxoniensi, in Aede B. Mariae Virginis, habita ineunte termino Idibus Jan. A.D. MDCCXLVIII. A Carolo Whiting, S.T.B. [etc.]. Oxonii, e Th. Sh., impensis Jacobi Fletcher, bibliopol. Prostant apud J. & J. Rivington, Londoni. MDCCXLVIII.

    8vo fours. Bodl. 8° M 248(18) BS.

1749

1. BILSTONE, JOHN. Thirteen sermons preached before the University of Oxford. By John Bilstone [etc.]. Oxford: printed for the author. MDCCXLIX.

    8vo fours. Bodl. 8° F 114 BS.

    Apparently, but not certainly, from the University Press.

2. BURTON, JOHN. The principles of Christian loyalty. A sermon [etc., as in 1743]. The second edition. Oxford, printed at the Theatre for James Fletcher in the Turl: and sold by J. and J. Rivington in St. Paul's Church-Yard, London, MDCCXLIX.

    8vo fours. Imp. 17 March 1742–3. Bodl. G. Pamph. 788(3).

3. [FORSTER, NATHANIEL.] A dissertation upon the account suppos'd to have been given of Jesus Christ by Josephus. Being an attempt to shew that this celebrated passage, some slight corruptions only excepted, may reasonably be esteemed genuine. Oxford, printed at the Theatre for James Fletcher in the Turl, and sold by J. and J. Rivington in St. Paul's Church-Yard, London. MDCCXLIX.

8vo fours. Imp. 18 Jan. 1748–9. Bodl. Douce I 131.

4. FOTHERGILL, THOMAS. The desireableness of peace, and the duty of a nation upon the recovery of it. A sermon preach'd before the University of Oxford at St. Mary's, on Tuesday, April 25. 1749. being the day appointed to be kept as a General Thanksgiving to Almighty God for the Peace. By Thomas Fothergill [etc.]. Publish'd at the request of Mr. Vice-Chancellor and the Heads of Houses. Oxford, printed at the Theatre for Richard Clements, and sold by J. and J. Rivington in St. Paul's Church-Yard, London. MDCCXLIX.

8vo fours. Imp. 2 May 1749. Bodl. G. Pamph. 1009(8).

5. HANDEL ORATORIOS. Samson: an oratorio as performed at the Theatre in Oxford. Printed in the year MDCCXLIX.

Esther: an oratorio as performed at the Theatre. Printed in the year MDCCXLIX. The Sacred Oratorio. As performed at the Theatre in Oxford. Printed in the year MDCCXLIX.

8vo fours. Bodl. Vet. A 4 e. 128.
Three booklets, giving only the words.

6. HORBERY, MATTHEW. The Athanasian Creed defended and explain'd. A sermon preach'd in the parish-church of Eccleshall on Trinity-Sunday, by Matthew Horbery [etc.]. Publish'd at the desire of several who heard it. Oxford, printed at the Theatre for James Fletcher in the Turl, and sold by J. and J. Rivington in St. Paul's Church-Yard, London. MDCCXLIX.

8vo fours. Imp. 8 March 1748. Bodl. G. Pamph. 1009(18).

7. LEWIS, WILLIAM. Oratio in Theatro Sheldoniano habita Idibus Aprilis, MDCCXLIX, die dedicationis Bibliothecae Radclivianae. A Guilielmo Lewis M.D. [etc.]. Oxonii, e Theatro Sh. impensis Jacobi Fletcher, bibliopol. Oxon. MDCCXLIX.

4to. Imp. 1 May 1749. Bodl. G. Pamph. 117(5).

8. — A second edition was printed in the same year: Bodl. Gough Oxf. 90.

9. MAUNDRELL, HENRY. A journey from Aleppo to Jerusalem . . . The seventh edition . . . [as in the sixth edition of 1740]. Oxford, printed at the Theatre, for W. Meadows bookseller in Cornhill, London. MDCCXLIX.

8vo fours. Imp. 8 Apr. 1703. Bodl. Douce M 650.
3rd A/cs. p. 14, dues; p. 17, printing 50 LP. Fifty copies on large paper were printed for the Delegates.

10. MORES, EDWARD ROWE. Nomina et insignia gentilitia nobilium equitumque sub Edoardo Primo rege militantium. Accedunt classes exercitus Edoardi Tertii regis Caletem obsidentis. Edidit Edoardus Rowe Mores. E Th. Sh. MDCCXLViiii.

4to. Imp. 18 Aug. 1749. Bodl. 4° AS 494.

11*. (Oxford, University. 'A programma at opening Dr. Radcliffe's Library.' See *Bodleian Quarterly Record,* i (1917), p. 169. No copy found.
3rd A/cs. p. 15, printing 200.)

12*. OXFORD, UNIVERSITY. Orders and statutes of the Ashmolean Museum.
22 May 1749.
  Broadside. Bodl. G.A. Oxon. b. 19(67).

13. PARKER, WILLIAM. [Half-title:] The expediency of the miraculous powers of
the Christian Fathers: and The inexpediency of those that are claim'd by the Church
of Rome, consider'd. [Title:] The expediency of some divine interpositions, during
the first ages of the Christian Fathers, consider'd. A sermon preached in His
Majesty's chapel at Whitehall, May 7. 1749. being the Sunday after Ascension-Day.
And before the University of Oxford, at St. Mary's, on Sunday, July 2. 1749. By
William Parker [etc.]. Publish'd by request. Oxford, printed at the Theatre for
James Fletcher in the Turl, and sold by J. and J. Rivington in St. Paul's Church-
Yard, London MDCCXLIX.
  [2nd. title:] The supposal of the continuance of divine interpositions, during the
first ages of the Christian Fathers, proved to be no sanction, or ground of credit to
the pretended miracles of the Church of Rome. A sermon preached in His Majesty's
chapel at Whitehall, on Whitsunday, May 14. 1749. And before the University of
Oxford at St. Mary's on Sunday, July 9. 1749. being Act-Sunday. By William
Parker [etc. Imprint as above].
  8vo fours. Imp. 21 Aug. 1749. Printer to the University.
  The signatures are consecutive.

14. XENOPHON. [Title in Greek.] Xenophontis Memorabilium Socratis dictorum
libri iv. Cum notis H. Stephani, Leunclavii, Æ. Porti, & Ernesti. Recensuit, suisque
annotationibus auxit Bolton Simpson [etc.]. Editio secunda. Oxonii, e Th. Sh.,
impensis Jacobi Fletcher, bibliopol. Oxon. MDCCXLIX.
  8vo fours. Imp. 20 Apr. 1741. Bodl. 8º P 170(1) Linc.
  3rd A/cs. p. 26, dues. The first edition was of 1741.

1750

1. (Aldrich, Henry. Artis logicae compendium. An edition of the book first
printed in 1703. No copy found.
  3rd A/cs. p. 26, dues.)

2. BARTON, PHILIP. The edification of the church of Christ. A sermon preached in
Lambeth-Chapel at the consecration of the Right Reverend Father in God Thomas
Lord Bishop of Norwich, on Sunday, Dec. 3. 1749. By Philip Barton [etc.]. Published
by request of His Grace the Lord Arch-Bishop of Canterbury. Oxford, printed at
the Theatre for Richard Clements; and sold by William Sandby, bookseller in
Fleet-Street, London. MDCCL.
  8vo fours. Bodl. G. Pamph. 90(19).

3. [BEARE, WILLIAM.] Turnus and Drances: being an attempt to shew, who the
two real persons were, that Virgil intended to represent under those two characters.
Oxford, printed for W. Owen near Temple-Bar, London; and Sackville Parker,
Oxford. MDCCL.
  8vo fours. Imp. 13 Feb. 1749. Bodl. G. Pamph. 902(3).

4. BENTHAM, EDWARD. A sermon preached before the Honourable House of Commons at St. Margaret's, Westminster, on Tuesday, January 30. 1749–50. being the anniversary of the martyrdom of King Charles I. By Edward Bentham [etc.]. Oxford, printed at the Theatre for James Fletcher in the Turl; and sold by J. and J. Rivington in St. Paul's Church-Yard, London. MDCCL.

    8vo fours. Bodl. G. Pamph. 90(12).

5. BIBLE (O.T.) IN HEBREW. Biblia Hebraica sine punctis. Accurante Nath. Forster [etc.]. Oxonii, e Typ. Clar., typis et sumtibus academicis. MDCCL.

    4to. Imp. 7 Feb. 1749. Bodl. Opp. adds. 4° V 264^{ab}.

    3rd A/cs. p. 26, dues. Despite the imprint the work was not paid for by the University, but it bought Hebrew type from Caslon specially for this book.

6. [BUCKLER, BENJAMIN.] Οἶνος κρίθινος, a dissertation concerning the origin and antiquity of barley wine. Oxford, printed at the Theatre for James Fletcher in the Turl: and sold by J. and J. Rivington in St. Paul's Church-Yard, London. MDCCL.

    4to. Bodl. G. Pamph. 159(2).

    3rd A/cs. p. 26, dues. Attributed by some to Samuel Rolleston.

7. [BURTON, JOHN.] Epistola critica ad J. Gul. Thompson Graece conscripta. Elogium memoriae sacrum Joh. Rogers S.T.P. Oxonii, e Th. Sh., impensis J. Fletcher. MDCCL.

    8vo fours. Bodl. 90 b. 14.

8. CLEAVER, WILLIAM. The expediency and advantage of an early education in piety and virtue. A sermon preached before the University of Oxford, at St. Mary's, on Sunday, Novemb. 12. 1749. By William Cleaver [etc.]. Published at the request of Mr. Vice-Chancellor. Oxford, printed at the Theatre for Richard Clements; and sold by J. and J. Rivington in St. Paul's Church-Yard, London. MDCCL.

    8vo fours. Bodl. Bliss B 145(21).

9. COLLINS, WILLIAM. The passions, an ode. Written by Mr. Collins. Set to musick by Dr. Hayes. Performed at the Theatre in Oxford, July 2. 1750.

    4to. Trinity Coll., Cambridge, Roths. 660. (Possibly printed elsewhere.)

10. [COSTARD, GEORGE.] Two dissertations, I. containing an enquiry into the meaning of the word kesitah, mentioned in Job, chap. 42. vers. 11. in which it is endeavoured to be proved, that though it more probably there stands for the name of a coin, yet that there is no reason for supposing it stamped with any figure at all, and therefore not with that of a lamb in particular. II. On the signification of the word Hermes. In which is explained the origin of the custom among the Greeks of erecting stones called Hermai; together with some other particulars, relating to the mythology of that people. Oxford, printed at the Theatre for Richard Clements: and sold by J. and J. Rivington, booksellers in St. Paul's Church-Yard, London. MDCCL.

    8vo fours. Bodl. G. Pamph. 106(4).

    Dedication by G. Costard.

11. DODWELL, WILLIAM. The nature extent and support of human laws considered. A sermon preached at the assizes held at Oxford, by the Honourable Mr. Baron Clarke and Mr. Justice Foster, on Thursday, March 8. 1749. By William Dodwell [etc.]. Published at the request of the Vice-Chancellor and the Heads of Houses. Oxford, printed at the Theatre for James Fletcher in the Turl: and sold by

Sam. Birt in Ave Mary Lane, and by J. and J. Rivington in St. Paul's Church-Yard, London. MDCCL.
  8vo fours. Bodl. Bliss B 172(5).

12. GRONOVIUS, J. F. Joanni Frederici Gronovii notae in Terentium. Oxonii, e Th. Sh. impensis Jac. Fletcher, bibliop. MDCCL.
  8vo fours. Imp. 10 Nov. 1749. Bodl. Clar. Press 58 c. 22.
  3rd A/cs. p. 26, dues.

13. HOMER. Ομηρου Οδυσσεια. Homeri Odyssea Graece. Editio altera. Oxonii, e Th. Sh. 1750. Impensis R. Clements, J. Fletcher & S. Parker, bibliop. Oxon. Prostat apud W. Meadows & J. and J. Rivington, bibliop. Lond.
  8vo fours. Imp. 4 Dec. 1705. Bodl. 292 h. 17.
  3rd A/cs. p. 26, dues.

14. KALMÁR, GEORGE. Q. D. O. M. B. F. F. Q. E. V. Dissertatio critico-philologico-theologica in Isa. vii:14=Matth. i:23. Cui accedunt v. animadversiones criticae succincte institutae. Prooemii loco praemittitur progymnasma criticum. Auctore Georgio Kalmar Hungaro. Oxonii, e Th. Sh., MDCCL.
  4to. Imp. 17 July 1750. Bodl. G. Pamph. 160(2).
  3rd A/cs. p. 26, dues.

15. MILTON, JOHN. Paradisus amissus. Poema Joannis Miltoni, Latine redditum a Guilielmo Dobson [etc.]. Oxonii, e Th. Sh., MDCCL.
  4to. Imp. 12 March 1749–50. Bodl. 4° BS 574.
  3rd A/cs. p. 26, dues.

16*. NEW TESTAMENT. Sacrorum Evangeliorum versio Gothica ex Codice Argenteo emendata atque suppleta, cum interpretatione Latina & annotationibus Erici Benzelii non ita pridem Archiepiscopi Upsaliensis. Edidit, observationes suas adjecit, et grammaticam Gothicam praemisit Edwardus Lye, A.M. Oxonii, e Typ. Clar., MDCCL.
  4to. Imp. 19 Feb. 1749. Bodl. Clar. Press 1 f. 42.
  3rd A/cs. pp. 5, 17, 29, printing 300 LP.

17*. (Oxford, University. 'A programma at the Commemoration of the benefactors of the University.' No copy found.
  3rd A/cs. p. 27, printing 200.)

18*. (Oxford, University. 'An advertisement about the riot at the assizes.' No copy found.
  3rd A/cs. p. 27, printing 150.)

19*. (Oxford, University. 'An advertisement about insulting the Proctors.' No copy found.
  3rd A/cs. p. 27, printing 150.)

20. PARKER, WILLIAM. [Half-title] Two sermons on the Mosaick history of the Fall. [Title] The Mosaick history of the Fall consider'd. A sermon preached in His Majesty's Chapel at Whitehall, on Sunday, May 6. 1750. and before the University of Oxford, at St. Mary's on Friday June 29. 1750. being the Festival of St. Peter. By William Parker [etc.]. Oxford, printed at the Theatre for James Fletcher in the Turl, and sold by J. and J. Rivington in St. Paul's Church-Yard, London, MDCCL.
  [Second title] The Mosaick history of the Fall consider'd. A sermon preached in

His Majesty's Chapel at Whitehall, on Sunday, May 13. 1750. and before the University of Oxford, at St. Mary's, on Sunday, July 1. 1750. By William Parker [etc., as for the first sermon].

8vo fours. Imp. 5 Sept. 1750. Bodl. G. Pamph. 91(5 and 6).

21. POPE, ALEXANDER. This day are published proposals for printing by subscription, Pope's Essay on Man, translated into Latin from Mr. Warburton's edition. By John Sayer [etc. Dated: Oxford, Nov. 19. 1750].

Fol. s. sh. Bodl. MS. Rawl. J fol. 5(5ᵇ).

22. RUSSELL, RICHARD. De tabe glandulari, sive de usu aquae marinae in morbis glandularum dissertatio. Auctore Ricardo Russell, M.D. E Th. Sh., prostant venales apud Jacobum Fletcher, Oxon. & J. and J. Rivington, Lond. MDCCL.

8vo fours. Imp. 4 July 1749. Bodl. 8° P 131 Linc.
3rd A/cs. p. 26, dues.

23. SWINTON, JOHN. Metilia: sive de quinario gentis Metiliae, e nummis vetustis caeteroquin minimum notae, dissertatio. A Joanne Swinton [etc.]. Oxonii, e Th. Sh., impensis Jacobi Fletcher, bibliopol. Oxon. MDCCL.

4to. Imp. 30 Aug. 1749. Bodl. BD Diss. S 229(7).

24. SWINTON, JOHN. Inscriptiones Citieae: sive in binas inscriptiones Phoenicias, inter rudera Citii nuper repertas, conjecturae. Accedit de nummis quibusdam Samaritanis & Phoeniciis, vel insolitam prae se literaturam ferentibus, vel in lucem hactenus non editis, dissertatio. Autore Joanne Swinton [etc.]. Oxonii e Th. Sh., typis academicis, MDCCL. Prostant apud Jacobum Fletcher, bibliopolam. Oxoniensem.

4to. Imp. 1 June 1750. Bodl. BD Diss. S 229(8).

25. WATSON, GEORGE. Christ the light of the world. A sermon preached before the University of Oxford, at St. Peter's, on Saturday, October 28. 1749. By George Watson [etc.]. Published by request. Oxford, printed at the Theatre for Sackville Parker, and sold by Mr Cooper at the Globe in Pater-Noster-Row, London. MDCCL.

4to. Imp. 23 Dec. 1749. Bodl. 101 h. 76(3).

26. WEBBER, FRANCIS. A sermon preached in Lambeth-Chapel at the consecration of the Right Reverend Father in God John Lord Bishop of Bristol, on Sunday, Dec. 23. 1750. By Francis Webber [etc.]. Published by order of the Lord Arch-Bishop of Canterbury. Oxford, printed at the Theatre for James Fletcher in the Turl, and sold by J. and J. Rivington in St. Paul's Church-Yard, London. MDCCL.

8vo fours. Bodl. G. Pamph. 887(18).

27. WILMOT, GEORGE. A sermon preached at the Cathedral Church of Worcester, at the Lent-Assizes, April 1, 1750, before the Hon. Mr. Baron Clerke. By George Wilmot [etc.]. The second edition. Oxford, printed for R. Baldwin Jun. at the Rose in Pater-noster Row, London. Price six-pence.

8vo fours. Bodl. G. Pamph. 97(13).
Doubtfully ascribable to the University Press.

28. [WISE, FRANCIS.] Nummorum antiquorum scriniis Bodleianis reconditorum catalogus cum commentario tabulis aeneis et appendice. Oxonii e Th. Sh., A.D. MDCCL.

Fol. Bodl. Gough Oxf. 95.
3rd A/cs. p. 38, dues.

29. XENOPHON. [Title in Greek.] Xenophontis Oeconomicus. Huic editioni accessere variae lectiones & notae quaedam breves ex H. Stephano, Leunclavio, aliisque collectae. Oxonii, e Typ. Clar., impensis Ricardi Clements, bibliopolae. MDCCL.
    8vo fours. Imp. 10 March 1749. Bodl. 8° Z 26 Art.

1751

1. CONYBEARE, JOHN. A sermon preached before the House of Lords, in the Abby-Church of Westminster on Tuesday, June 11. 1751. being the anniversary of His Majesty's accession to the Throne. By John Lord Bishop of Bristol. Oxford, printed at the Theatre for James Fletcher in the Turl, and sold by J. and J. Rivington in St. Paul's Church-Yard, London; Ben. Hickey in Bristol; and J. Leake in Bath. MDCCLI.
    4to. Bodl. G. Pamph. 69.

2. DRYDEN, JOHN. Alexandri festum, sive Vis musicae, ode, quam numeris solutis cecinit, & St. Ceciliae dicavit Johannes Dryden poetarum princeps, et quam paululum immutavit, sive emendavit Johannes Hughes poeta lyricus, & celeberrimus, Latine reddita. Oxonii, e Typ. Clar., impensis Jacobi Fletcher bibliopolae. Prostant apud J. & J. Rivington, London. MDCCLI.
    4to. Bodl. I I 33 Art.

3. HOLLOWAY, BENJAMIN. Remarks on Dr Sharp's pieces on the Elohim and Berith. Among which, in shewing the absolute unfitness of the Arabic tongue to give a root to the divine name Elohim, some account is given of the Chaldee, Syriac, Samaritan, and Arabic dialects; shewiing them to be all anciently one language: as also what that language was: with a word on the Hebrew and Samaritan alphabets, proving that those alphabets could not have been chang'd, the one for the other, in copying the Hebrew Scriptures, after the Babylonish captivity, as hath been pretended. By Benjamin Holloway [etc.]. Oxford, printed at the Theatre. MDCCLI.
    8vo fours. Bodl. 104 e. 5.

4. HOLLOWAY, BENJAMIN. Originals physical and theological sacred and profane. Or an Essay towards a discovery of the first descriptive ideas in things, by discovery of the simple or primary roots in words; as the same were, from the beginning, rightly applied by believers; and afterwards perverted by infidels, in which some hundreds of Hebrew words are traced to their first themata; and their original, as well as their derived or deflected reasons and meanings, shewn; according to the order in which they do occur in Leusden's Compendium Biblicum as far as to the 12th Chapter of Exodus. By Benjamin Holloway [etc.]. Oxford, printed at the Theatre. MDCCLI.
    2 vols. 8vo. Imp. 8 May 1750. Bodl. 8° P 123, 4 Linc.
    3rd A/cs. p. 38, dues.

5*. OXFORD, UNIVERSITY. Epicedia Oxoniensia in obitum celsissimi et desideratissimi Frederici Principis Walliae. Oxonii, e Typ. Clar., An. Dom. MDCCLI.
    Fol. Bodl. H 4. 1 Art.
    3rd A/cs. p. 41, printing 400 small and 24 LP.

6*. OXFORD, UNIVERSITY. [Rules and fees for the use of books in the Ashmolean Museum. Dated 6 Nov. 1751.]

Fol. s. sh. Bodl. Gough Oxf. 101(4).

3rd A/cs. p. 51, printing.

7. [THOMPSON, WILLIAM.] Gondibert and Birtha. A tragedy. Oxford, printed at the Theatre, MDCCL.

8vo fours. Bodl. Malone B 217.

The sheets are signed 2S–3K. See under 1757.

8. WARTON, THOMAS. Ode for music as performed at the Theatre in Oxford on the second of July, 1751. being the anniversary appointed by the late Lord Crew, Bishop of Durham, for the commemoration of benefactors to the University. By Thomas Warton [etc.]. Set to music by Dr. Hayes, Professor of Music. Oxford, printed for R. Clements and J. Barrett; W. Thurlbourn in Cambridge; and R. Dodsley, in Pall-Mall, London.

4to. Bodl. *MS. Mus. d. 70(1).

The music is handwritten.

9. (Weales, T. Proposals for a translation of Longinus.

Madan: 1751:17. Not found. The Bodleian copy is missing. The book was not published.)

10. WEBBER, FRANCIS. The Jewish dispensation consider'd and vindicated [etc., as in 1738]. The second edition. Oxford, printed for James Fletcher in the Turl, and sold by J. and J. Rivington in St. Paul's Church-Yard, London. MDCCLI.

8vo fours. Imp. 12 January 1738. Bodl. G. Pamph. 887(16).

11. WHITFIELD, HENRY. The possibility of a resurrection illustrated by analogy. A sermon preach'd before the University of Oxford, at St. Mary's, on Monday, April 16. 1750. by Henry Whitfield [etc.]. Oxford, printed at the Theatre: and sold by Mrs. Fletcher bookseller in the High-Street. MDCCLI.

8vo fours. Imp. 3 July 1751. Bodl. G. Pamph. 887(9).

12. [WILMOT, GEORGE.] Grammatica Hebraea sive methodus brevis discendi linguam sanctam sine punctis Masoreticis. Oxonii, e Typ. Clar., impensis Jacobi Fletcher bibliopolae. Prostant apud J. and J. Rivington, Lond. MDCCLI.

8vo fours. Bodl. G. Pamph. 106(5).

1752

1. ARISTOTLE AND PLETHO. Ἀριστοτέλους περι αρετων καὶ κακων. Πληθωνος περι αρετων. Recensuit Edvardus Fawconer [etc.]. Oxonii, e Th. Sh., impensis Jacobi Fletcher, bibliopolae. Prostant apud J. and J. Rivington, Lond. MDCCLII.

8vo fours. Bodl. 8º F 24 BS.

3rd A/cs. p. 50, dues.

2. CONYBEARE, JOHN. A sermon preach'd in the Cathedral-Church of Bristol, on Thursday, Sept. 5. 1751. at the anniversary meeting of the Sons of the Clergy. By John Lord Bishop of Bristol. Published at the request of that society. Oxford, printed at the Theatre for James Fletcher in the Turl; and sold by J. and J. Rivington in

St. Paul's Church-Yard, London; Ben Hickey in Bristol; and J. Leake in Bath. MDCCLII.

    4to. Bodl. G. Pamph. 69(3).

3. COSTARD, GEORGE. Dissertationes II critico-sacrae: quarum prima explicatur Ezek. xiii, 18. Vae quae consuunt pulvillos sub omni cubito manus: & faciunt cervicalia sub capite universae aetatis ad capiendas animas. Vulg. Altera vero 2 Reg. x. 22. Dixitque his qui erant super vestes, proferte vestimenta universis servis Baal, et protulerunt eis vestes. Vulg. Auctore Georgio Costard, A.M. Oxonii, e Th. Sh., impensis Richardi Clements, bibliopol. Oxon. Prostant apud R. Baldwin Jun. in vico vulgo dicto Pater-Noster-Row, London. MDCCLII.

    8vo fours. Bodl. G. Pamph. 106(3).

4. DODWELL, WILLIAM. The importance of the Christian faith illustrated in the explanation of St. Paul's wish of being accursed for his brethren. A sermon preach'd before the University of Oxford, on Sunday, January 26. 1752. By William Dodwell [etc.]. Printed at the request of the Vice-Chancellor and the Heads of Houses. Oxford, printed at the Theatre for James Fletcher in the Turl, and sold by S. Birt in Ave-Mary-Lane, and J. and J. Rivington in St. Paul's Church-Yard, London. MDCCLII.

    8vo fours. Bodl. 8° M 241(11) BS.

5. HAWKINS, WILLIAM. A sermon preach'd before the University of Oxford, at St. Mary's, on Thursday, January 30. 1752. being the anniversary of the martyrdom of King Charles I. By William Hawkins [etc.]. Published at the request of the Vice-Chancellor and the Heads of Houses. Oxford, printed at the Theatre for Sackville Parker bookseller at Oxford; J. and J. Rivington in St. Paul's Church-Yard, and W. Owen, at Temple-Bar, Lond. MDCCLII.

    8vo fours. Imp. 15 Feb. 1752. Bodl. G. Pamph. 97(9).

6. HODGES, WALTER. The Christian plan, exhibited in the interpretation of Elohim: with observations upon a few other matters and expressions, relative to the same subject. By Walter Hodges [etc.]. Oxford, printed at the Theatre for James Fletcher in the Turl; John Whiston and B. White, in Fleet-Street, London. MDCCLII.

    4to. Bodl. OO 60 Th.
    3rd A/cs. p. 50, dues.

7. JENNER, THOMAS. Charity and compassion towards men the occasion of thanksgivings to God. A sermon preached at St. Swithin's in Worcester, on Friday, Aug. 23. 1751. being the anniversary meeting of the Governors of the Worcester Infirmary. By Thomas Jenner [etc.]. Published for the benefit of the charity. Oxford, printed at the Theatre; and sold by S. Parker, bookseller in Oxford; and by J. and J. Rivington in St. Paul's Church-Yard, and W. Sandby in Fleet-Street, London. MDCCLII.

    8vo fours. Imp. 23 May 1752. Bodl. G. Pamph. 1630(5).

8. (Kall, ——. 'Dissertation on Hebrew points &c.'
    Not found.
    3rd A/cs. p. 50, dues.)

9*. (Oxford, University. 'Programma at the Commemoration of the benefactors to the University.'
    Not found.
    3rd A/cs. p. 51, printing.)

10. PENROSE, FRANCIS. A treatise on electricity: wherein its various phaenomena are accounted for, and the cause of the attraction and gravitation of solids assigned. To which is added, a short account, how the electrical effluvia act upon the animal frame, and in what disorders the same may probably be applied with success, and in what not. By Francis Penrose surgeon at Bicester. Oxford, printed at the Theatre for Sackville Parker, bookseller at Oxford, and W. Owen, at Homer's Head, Temple-Bar, London. MDCCLII.

8vo fours. Bodl. G. Pamph. 2832(1).

11. PLATO. [Title in Greek.] Platonis dialogi V. Recensuit, notisque illustravit Nath. Forster [etc.]. Editio secunda. Oxonii, e Typ. Clar., impensis Jac. Fletcher bibliopolae. MDCCLII.

8vo fours. Imp. 10 Apr. 1745. Bodl. 2912 d. 29.
3rd A/cs. p. 50, dues. The first edition was of 1745.

12. POPE, ALEXANDER. De homine. Poema Alexandri Popii quatuor epistolis conscriptum, a Johanne Sayer, A.M. Latine redditum. Oxonii, e Th. Sh., impensis Jacobi Fletcher bibliopolae. Prostant apud J. and J. Rivington, M. Cooper, & W. Owen, London. MDCCLII.

4to. Bodl. Vet. A 5 d. 360(2).
Contains only Epistola tertia.

13. RANDOLPH, THOMAS. Party-zeal censur'd. in a sermon preach'd before the University of Oxford, at St. Mary's, on Sunday, January 19. 1752. By Thomas Randolph [etc.]. Published at the request of the Vice-Chancellor and the Heads of Houses. Oxford, printed at the Theatre for James Fletcher in the Turl, and sold by J. and J. Rivington in St. Paul's Church-Yard, London; J. Smith in Canterbury. MDCCLII.

8vo fours. Imp. 7 Feb. 1752. 8° M 239(15) BS.

14. ROTHERAM, JOHN. The force of the argument for the truth of Christianity drawn from a collective view of prophecy, in three parts. I. A brief state of the argument. II. A defence and further illustration of the argument. III. A brief state of the question, whether prophecies or miracles afford stronger evidence for the truth of Christianity. Occasion'd by Dr. Middleton's Examination of the Lord Bishop of London's discourses. By the Rev. Mr. John Rotheram [etc.]. Oxford, printed at the Theatre for Richard Clements: and sold by J. and J. Rivington in St. Paul's Church-Yard, London. MDCCLII. (Pr. 1s. 6d.).

8vo fours. Imp. 20 Feb. 1752. Bodl. G. Pamph. 891(3).
3rd A/cs. p. 50, dues, 'Mr. Graham's Defence of Christianity' (the author was in the West Indies).

15. SWINTON, JOHN. Inscriptiones Citieae: sive in binas alias inscriptiones Phoenicias, inter rudera Citii nuper repertas, conjecturae. Accedit de nummis quibusdam Samaritanis et Phoeniciis dissertatio secunda.

4to. Bodl. Auct. V 2 inf. II 22.
It lacks preliminary pages and ends incomplete at p. 70.

16. THEOPHRASTUS. Proposals for printing by subscription, 4,000 copies of the Characters of Theophrastus, with a strictly literal translation of the Greek into Latin, according to the specimen hereto annexed; and with notes and observations on the text in English: for the benefit of Hertford College. By R. Newton [etc.]. Oxford printed: and this specimen to be had of R. Clements and J. Fletcher,

booksellers in Oxford; and J. and J. Rivington, in St. Paul's Church-Yard; and W. Owen, at Homer's Head near Temple Bar; and R. Dodsley in Pall-Mall, London. At which places subscriptions are taken in. Price of the specimen six-pence. [Money would be returned if the book were not printed by New Year's Day, 1753.]

    8vo. Bodl. Gough Oxf. 120(7).

    The book was published in 1754.

17. [TYRWHITT, THOMAS.] Translations in verse. Mr. Pope's Messiah, Mr. Philips's Splendid Shilling in Latin; the Eighth Isthmian of Pindar in English. Oxford, printed at the Theatre for James Fletcher, and sold by J. and J. Rivington in St. Paul's Church-Yard, London. MDCCLII.

    4to. Bodl. II 33(7) Art.

1753

1. [COMINGS, FOWLER.] The printed Hebrew text of the Old Testament vindicated. An answer to Mr. Kennicott's Dissertation in two parts. Wherein all the texts produc'd by that author in favour of corruptions are re-examin'd and vindicated. To which are prefix'd some general observations on the insufficiency of those helps by which he endeavours to correct the Hebrew text. Oxford, printed at the Theatre for James Fletcher in the Turl, and sold by J. and J. Rivington in St. Paul's Church-Yard, London MDCCLIII.

    8vo fours. Bodl. G. Pamph. 248.

    3rd A/cs. p. 62, dues. Preface signed by Fowler Comings.

2. FOTHERGILL, GEORGE. The reasons and necessity of publick worship. A sermon preached at St. Mary's in Oxford, at the assizes before the Honourable Mr. Justice Gundry, and before the University, on Thursday, March 8. 1753. By George Fothergill [etc.]. Published at the request of the High-Sheriff and the Grand Jury. Oxford, printed at the Theatre for Richard Clements: and sold by J. and J. Rivington in St. Paul's Church-Yard, London; W. Thurlbourne in Cambridge, and J. Leake at Bath. MDCCLIII.

    8vo fours. Imp. 13 March 1753. Bodl. G. Pamph. 97(8).

3. FOTHERGILL, GEORGE. The delay of success to repeated fasts consider'd and apply'd. A sermon preached before the University of Oxford, at St. Mary's on Wednesday, January 9. 1744-5. being the sixth general fast appointed to be kept on occasion of the war. By George Fothergill [etc.]. The second edition. [Imprint as the preceding.]

    8vo fours. Imp. 23 Jan. 1744-5. Bodl. 994 e. 168(2).

4. FOTHERGILL, THOMAS. The reasonableness and uses of commemorating King Charles's martyrdom. A sermon preached before the University of Oxford, at St. Mary's, on Thursday, January 30. 1753. By Thomas Fothergill [etc.]. Oxford, printed at the Theatre for Richard Clements; and sold by J. and J. Rivington in St. Paul's Church-Yard, London. MDCCLIII.

    8vo fours. Imp. 17 Feb. 1753. Bodl. G. Pamph. 97(10).

5. HOLLOWAY. BENJAMIN. Letter and spirit; or annotations upon the Holy Scriptures according to both. By Benjamin Holloway [etc.]. Oxford, printed at the theatre, MDCCLIII.

8vo. Imp. 30 May 1752. Bodl. 8° F 179 BS.

3rd A/cs. p. 62, dues.

6. HORNE, GEORGE. A fair, candid, and impartial state of the case between Sir Isaac Newton and Mr. Hutchinson. In which is shewn, how far a system of physics is capable of mathematical demonstration; and consequently, what regard Mr. Hutchinson's claim may deserve to have paid it. By George Horne [etc.]. Oxford, printed at the Theatre for S. Parker, bookseller: and sold by R. Baldwin, in London; and Mess. Merrill and Matthews, in Cambridge. 1753. Price 1s. 6d.

8vo fours. Bodl. G. Pamph. 2064(9).

3rd A/cs. p. 62, dues.

7. KENNICOTT, BENJAMIN. The state of the printed Hebrew text of the Old Testament considered. A dissertation in two parts. Part the First compares 1 Chron. xi with 2 Sam. v and xxiii; and Part the Second contains observations on seventy Hebrew MSS., with an extract of mistakes and various readings. By Benjamin Kennicott [etc.]. Oxford, printed at the Theatre: and sold by Mr. Clements and Mr. Fletcher in Oxford; Mr. Birt, Mess. Rivington and Mr. Dodsley, in London; Mr. Thurlbourn and Mr. Merril, in Cambridge; Mr. Leake in Bath; and Mr. Score, in Exeter. MDCCLIII.

8vo fours. Imp. 17 May 1751. Bodl. 8° F 123 BS.

3rd A/cs. p. 62, dues.

8. LOWTH, ROBERT. De sacra poesi Hebraeorum. Praelectiones academicae Oxonii habitae a Roberto Lowth [etc.]. Subjicitur metricae Harianae brevis confutatio: et oratio Crewiana. Oxonii, e Typ. Clar. MDCCLIII.

4to. Imp. 1 Feb. 1753. Bodl. CC 55 Th.

3rd A/cs. p. 62, dues.

9. MARKHAM, WILLIAM. A sermon preached in Lambeth-Chapel, at the consecration of the Right Reverend Father in God James Lord Bishop of Gloucester on Sunday, Dec. 10. 1752. By William Markham [etc.]. Published by order of the Lord Arch-Bishop of Canterbury. Oxford, printed at the Theatre for James Fletcher in the Turl, and sold by J. and J. Rivington in St. Paul's Church-Yard, London. MDCCLIII.

4to. Bodl. I I 53(5) Th.

10. PENROSE, FRANCIS. An essay on magnetism: or an endeavour to explain the various properties and effects of the loadstone: together with the causes of the same. By Francis Penrose, surgeon at Bicester, Oxfordshire. Oxford, printed at the Theatre for Sackville Parker, bookseller at Oxford, and W. Owen, at Homer's Head, Temple-Bar, London. MDCCLIII.

8vo fours. Bodl. G. Pamph. 2832(2).

11*. POTTER, JOHN. The theological works of the most Reverend Dr. John Potter, late Lord Arch-Bishop of Canterbury, containing his sermons, charges, Discourse on Church-Government and divinity-lectures. In three volumes. Vol. I. Oxford, printed at the Theatre, MDCCLIII.

8vo. Bodl. Vet. A 5 e. 5049(1).

3rd A/cs. p. 65, printing 300 small and 200 LP.

12*. POTTER, JOHN. The theological works [etc., as above]. Vol. II. . . . MDCCLIII.
8vo. Bodl. Vet. A 5 e. 5049(2).
3rd A/cs. pp. 65, 77, printing 300 LP.

13. RANDOLPH, HERBERT. A sermon preached at the parish-church of Deal, October 15th, 1752. By Herbert Randolph [etc.]. Published at the request of the Mayor and Corporation. Oxford, printed at the Theatre for James Fletcher in the Turl, and sold by J. and J. Rivington in St. Paul's Church-Yard, London; and T. Smith in Canterbury. MDCCLIII.
8vo fours. Imp. 16 Dec. 1752. Bodl. 8° M 239(16) BS.

14. [RANDOLPH, THOMAS.] A vindication of the doctrine of the Trinity from the exceptions of a late pamphlet entitled An Essay on Spirit &c. By a divine of the Church of England. Part I. Oxford, printed at the Theatre for James Fletcher in the Turl, and sold by J. and J. Rivington in St. Paul's Church-Yard, London. MDCCLIII.
8vo fours. Bodl. 1243 e. 89.
3rd A/cs. p. 62, dues.
— Part II. MDCCLIII.
Imp. 16 June 1753. Bodl. 1243 e. 89.

15. ROTHERAM, JOHN. The force of the argument for the truth of Christianity [etc., as in the edition of 1752]. The second edition. Oxford, printed at the Theatre for Richard Clements: and sold by R. Baldwyn in Pater-Noster-Row, London. MDCLIII [sic]. (Pr. 1s. 6d.)
8vo fours. Imp. 20 Feb. 1752. Bodl. 124 e. 23.

16. RUSSELL, RICHARD. A dissertation concerning the use of sea water in diseases of the glands, &c. To which is added an epistolary dissertation to R. Frewin M.D. by Richard Russell [etc.]. Oxford, printed at the Theatre: and sold by James Fletcher in the Turl, and J. and J. Rivington in St. Paul's Church-Yard, London. MDCCLIII.
8vo. Imp. 4 Apr. 1753. Bodl. Vet. A 5 d. 84.
3rd A/cs. p. 74, dues.

1754

1. ALCOCK, THOMAS. The law not made for a righteous man. An assise sermon preached in the Cathedral-Church of St. Peter, Exon, on Tuesday, March 19, 1754. Published at the request of the High-Sheriff &c. By Thomas Alcock [etc.]. Oxford: printed at the Theatre, for Richard Clements; and sold by R. Baldwin at the Rose in Pater-noster-Row, London; and Theoph. Rose bookseller in Plymouth. MDCCLIV.
8vo fours. Imp. 1 May 1754. Bodl. G. Pamph. 97(11).

2. DODWELL, WILLIAM. The nature, mischiefs, and remedy of superstition illustrated. In two sermons preached before the University of Oxford, on Sunday, Feb. 17. 1754. By William Dodwell [etc.]. Published at the request of Mr. Vice-Chancellor and the Heads of Houses. Oxford, printed at the Theatre for James Fletcher in the

Turl; and sold by S. Birt in Ave-Mary Lane, and J. and J. Rivington in St. Paul's Church-Yard, London.

8vo fours. Bodl. Bliss B 172(7).

3rd A/cs. p. 74, dues.

3. HOLLOWAY, BENJAMIN. The primaevity and preeminence of the sacred Hebrew, above all other languages vindicated from the repeated attempts of the Reverend Dr. Hunt to level it with the Arabic, and other oriental dialects; in a letter to a friend. With a word in the preface to Dr. Shuckford. By Benjamin Holloway, LL.B. Oxford, printed at the Theatre for S. Parker, and E. Withers, bookseller, at the Seven Stars in Fleetstreet, London. 1754.

8vo fours. Bodl. 8° M 251(5) BS.

3rd A/cs. p. 74, dues.

4. OXFORD, COUNTY. A copy of the poll for the knights of the shire for the County of Oxford, taken at Oxford on the 17th of April 1754, from the check-books of the clerks of Lord Wenman and Sir James Dashwood Bart. containing not only the names of the freeholders, their place of abode and freehold, but also the freehold on which they voted, and the occupier of it. Candidates: Right Hon. Lord Viscount Wenman, Sir James Dashwood, Bart. Right Hon. Lord Viscount Parker, Sir Edward Turner Bart. Oxford, printed at the Theatre, and sold by M. Cooper at the Globe in Pater-Noster-Row, London; by the booksellers in Oxford, Charles Micklewright printer in Reading, and the news carriers in Oxfordshire, Berkshire and Gloucestershire. 1754. Price 1s. 6d.

4to. Bodl. G.A. Oxon. 4° 6(4).

3rd A/cs. p. 74, dues.

5. OXFORD, COUNTY. The poll of the freeholders of Oxfordshire, taken at Oxford, on the 17th, 18th, 19th, 20th, 22d, and 23d. of April 1754. Thomas Blackall, Esq; High-Sheriff. Candidates. Right Honourable Lord Viscount Wenman. Sir James Dashwood, Bart. Right Honourable Lord Viscount Parker. Sir Edward Turner, Bart. Oxford, printed at the Theatre, 1754.

4to. Bodl. Gough Oxf. 91(5).

6*. OXFORD, UNIVERSITY. [Order from the Vice-Chancellor to Heads of Houses to keep college gates shut during the Oxfordshire election.] Whereas there is great reason to apprehend that the intermixing of gownsmen in the great concourse expected in this county election . . . [Dated 15 April 1754].

Fol. s. sh. Bodl. Gough Oxf. 101(3).

3rd A/cs. p. 75, 'a Program. at the Elections of Kts. of the Shire'.

7*. OXFORD, UNIVERSITY. [Order by the Vice-Chancellor and Heads of Houses against inoculating with smallpox.] Whereas the long continuance and contagion of the small pox: from which by God's blessing we seem at length to be freed, [entreats regular physicians and requires and enjoins surgeons and apothecaries not to inoculate].

Fol. s. sh. Bodl. G.A. Oxon. 4° 6(21).

3rd A/cs. p. 75, 'a Program. concerning Inoculating'. The Bodleian copy is cropped and no date appears.

8*. OXFORD, UNIVERSITY. [A 'Programma for commemorating the benefactors to the University'.] 24 June 1754.

Bodl. G.A. Oxon. b. 19(73a).

3rd A/cs. p. 75.

9. PARKER, WILLIAM. [Half-title:] Two discourses before the University of Oxford: in which are contained remarks upon some passages in the writings of the late Lord Viscount Bolingbroke. [Title:] The nature, evidences, and importance of truth considered. A sermon preached before the University of Oxford, at St. Mary's, on St. Andrew's Day, 1754. By William Parker [etc.]. Published at the request of the Vice-Chancellor, and Heads of Houses. Oxford, printed at the Theatre for James Fletcher in the Turl; and sold by R. Baldwin at the Rose in Pater-noster-Row, London. MDCCLIV.
   8vo fours. Bodl. G. Pamph. 97(6).

10. — The nature [etc.] . . . at St. Mary's on Advent Sunday, December 1, 1754. [Imprint as above.]
   8vo fours. Bodl. G. Pamph. 97(7).

11*. POTTER, JOHN. Opera theologica Reverendissimi Patris Johannis Potter S.T.P. nuper Archiepiscopi Cantuarensis. Vol. III. Oxonii, e Th. Sh., MDCCLIV.
   8vo. Bodl. Vet. A 5 e. 5049.
   3rd A/cs. pp. 65, 77, printing 300 small and 200 LP. The two previous volumes (in English) were published in 1753.

12. [RANDOLPH, THOMAS.] A vindication of the doctrine of the Trinity [etc., as in 1753]. Part III. Oxford, printed at the Theatre for James Fletcher in the Turl, and sold by J. and J. Rivington in St. Paul's Church-Yard, London; and by Mr. Smith at Canterbury.
   8vo fours. Bodl. 1243 e. 89.
   3rd A/cs. pp. 62, 74, dues.

13. ROTHERAM, JOHN. A sketch of the one great argument, formed from the several concurring evidences, for the truth of Christianity. By the Rev. John Rotheram [etc.]. Oxford, printed at the Theatre for Richard Clements: and sold by R. Baldwin in Pater-noster-row, London. MDCLIV [sic]. (Pr. 1s.).
   8vo. Imp. 15 Nov. 1753. Bodl. 124 e. 21.
   3rd A/cs. p. 74, dues.

14. SHARP, WILLIAM. A sermon preach'd before the University of Oxford, at St. Mary's, on Act Sunday in the forenoon, July 7. 1754. By William Sharp [etc.]. Publish'd at the request of the Vice-Chancellor and Heads of Houses. Oxford, printed at the Theatre for James Fletcher in the Turl; and sold by J. and J. Rivington in St. Paul's Church-Yard, London. MDCCLIV.
   8vo fours. Bodl. G. Pamph. 1010(12).

15. SKINNER, WILLIAM. A sermon preached at the Great Sessions at Brecon, on Saturday, March 30. 1754. before the Honorable John Hervey Esq. one of His Majesty's Justices of the Great Session for the Brecon circuit. By William Skinner [etc.]. Published at the request of Mr. High-Sheriff, and the gentlemen of the Grand-Jury. Oxford, printed at the Theatre for James Fletcher in the Turl; and sold by J. and J. Rivington in St. Paul's Church-Yard, London. MDCCLIV.
   8vo fours. B.M. 225.g.8(4).

16. THEOPHRASTUS. The characters of Theophrastus, with a strictly literal translation of the Greek into Latin, and with notes and observations on the text in English: for the benefit of Hertford College. By the late R. Newton D.D. and Principal. Oxford, printed: and to be had of R. Clements and J. Fletcher, booksellers

in Oxford; and of J. and J. Rivington, in St. Paul's Church-Yard; and W. Owen, at Homer's Head, near Temple Bar; and R. Dodsley, in Pall-Mall, London. MDCCLIV.

8vo. Imp. 1 May 1754. Bodl. Godw. 370.

3rd A/cs. p. 74, dues.

17. XENOPHON. Ξενοφωντος Λογος εις Αγησιλαον, Ιερων, η Τυραννικος, Λακεδαιμονιων πολιτεια, Αθηναιων πολιτεια, και Ποροι, η περι Προσοδων, Graece & Latine. Recensuit Bolton Simpson [etc.]. Oxonii, e Typ. Clar. impensis Jacobi Fletcher, Oxon. et Londini, Georgii Hawkins, bibliop. MDCCLIV.

8vo fours. Bodl. 8° A 6 (13) Jur.

3rd A/cs. p. 86, dues. *Agesilaus* has a separate title-page and an imprimatur dated 17 May 1754.

1755

1. ALCOCK, THOMAS. The nature and obligation of oaths. An assise sermon preached in the Cathedral-Church of St. Peter, Exon, on Wednesday, Aug. 7. 1754. Published at the request of the Right Reverend the Lord Bishop and mr. High-Sheriff. By Thomas Alcock [etc.]. Oxford, printed at the Theatre for Richard Clements; and sold by R. Baldwin at the Rose in Pater-noster-Row, London; and Theoph. Rhodes bookseller in Plymouth. MDCCLV.

8vo fours. Imp. 25 Feb. 1755. Bodl. G. Pamph. 97(12).

3rd A/cs. p. 124, dues.

2. BARTON, PHILIP. The antiquity and holiness of places set apart for publick worship. A sermon preached at the consecration of St. George's Chapel, in the parish of Portsea, near Portsmouth in the County of Southampton, on Tuesday, Sept. 17. 1754. By Philip Barton [etc.]. Oxford, printed at the Theatre, for Richard Clements; and sold by William Sandby in Fleet-street, London, and James Wilkinson in Portsmouth. MDCCLV.

8vo fours. Imp. 17 Nov. 1754. Bodl. G. Pamph. 97(16).

3. (Battely, John. Antiquitates Rutupinae. [According to the Press Accounts, an edition was printed in this year. No copy has been found. The book was first printed in 1745.]

3rd A/cs. p. 86, dues.)

4. [BENTHAM, EDWARD.] Reflexions upon logick. The second edition. Oxford, printed at the Theatre for James Fletcher in the Turl; and sold by J. and J. Rivington in St. Paul's Church-Yard, London. MDCCLV.

8vo fours. Bodl. G. Pamph. 212(5).

3rd A/cs. p. 124, dues. The first edition was of 1740. The dedication is by Edward Bentham.

5. BOURCHIER, ROGER. A catalogue of books to be sold on —— the — day of February, 1755, and the following days, at a room belonging to Mr —— in the parish of —— Oxford. Being a collection late belonging to Roger Bourchier, of Worcester College, deceased.

8vo. Bodl. Mus. Bibl. III 8° 135(4).

3rd A/cs. p. 124, 'Catal. of Books for Auction', dues.

6. BURTON, JOHN. *Τοῦ δεινὸς νοσοῦντος καὶ περὶ τῶν νοσούντων μελετήματα.* Oxonii, e Th. Sh., impensis Jacobi Fletcher, bibliop. Prostant apud J. & J. Rivington, Lond. MDCCLV.

8vo fours. Bodl. 8° C 114(2) BS. Accents as in the original.

7. DODWELL, WILLIAM. The equal and impartial discharge of justice, with respect both to the guilty and the innocent, recommended. A sermon preached at St. Mary's in Oxford, at the assizes, before the Honourable Mr. Justice Foster, and Baron Smythe, on Wednesday, July 16. 1755. By William Dodwell [etc.]. Published at the request of the Judges, the High-Sheriff, and the Vice-Chancellor. Oxford, printed at the Theatre for James Fletcher in the Turl; and sold by J. and J. Rivington in St. Paul's Church-Yard, London. MDCCLV.

8vo fours. Bodl. G. Pamph. 65(1).
3rd A/cs. p. 124, dues.

8. HIND, RICHARD. The abuse of miraculous powers in the church of Corinth considered. A sermon preached before the University of Oxford, at Christ Church, on Sunday, Feb. 2. 1755. By Richard Hind [etc.]. Published at the request of the Vice-Chancellor and Heads of Houses. Oxford, printed at the Theatre for James Fletcher in the Turl; and sold by J. and J. Rivington in St. Paul's Church-Yard, London. MDCCLV.

8vo fours. Bodl. G. Pamph. 97(15).
3rd A/cs. p. 124, dues.

9. HORNE, GEORGE. Christ and the Holy Ghost the supporters of the spiritual life. And repentance the forerunner of faith. Two sermons preached before the University of Oxford, the former at St. Mary's on Sunday, April 13. the latter in St. Mary Magdalen College Chapel, on St. John Baptist Day, 1755. By George Horne, [etc.]. Oxford, printed at the Theatre for S. Parker; and sold by J. Rivington in St. Paul's Church-Yard, and E. Withers at the Seven-Stars in Fleet-Street, London.

8vo fours. Bodl. G. Pamph. 275(8).
3rd A/cs. p. 124, dues.

10. HUDDESFORD, GEORGE. A proper reply to a pamphlet, entitled, A Defence of the Rector and Fellows of Exeter College, &c. By George Huddesford, D.D., Vice-Chancellor of the University of Oxford. Oxford, printed at the Theatre for Richard Clements; and sold by J. and J. Rivington in St. Paul's Church-Yard, London. MDCCLV.

4to. Bodl. Gough Oxf. 91(7).
3rd A/cs. p. 124, dues.

11. JAGO, RICHARD. The causes of impenitence consider'd: as well in the case of extraordinary warnings, as under the general laws of Providence, and Grace. A sermon preached at Harbury in Warwickshire, May 4. 1755. on occasion of a conversation said to have pass'd between one of the inhabitants, and an apparition, in the church-yard belonging to that place. By Richard Jago [etc.]. Oxford, printed at the Theatre for the benefit of the Free-School at Harbury; and sold by R. Baldwin, R. and J. Dodsley, and E. Withers in London; Mr. Clements and Mr. Fletcher at Oxford, Mr. Leake at Bath, Mr. Lacy at Northampton, Mr. Hopkinson and Mr. Keating at Stratford, Mr. Warren at Birmingham, and Mr. Harris at Glocester. MDCCLV.

8vo fours. Imp. 27 May 1755. Bodl. G. Pamph. 2136(8).
3rd A/cs. p. 124, dues.

12. KING, WILLIAM. Doctor King's Apology: or, vindication of himself from the several matters charged on him by the society of informers. Oxford, printed at the Theatre for S. Parker, bookseller; and sold by W. Owen near Temple-Bar, London. MDCCLV.

4to. Bodl. Gough Oxf. 81(10).

13. KING, WILLIAM. [As above] The second edition. Oxford [etc., as above].

4to. Bodl. Gough Oxf. 81(11).

14. (King, William. [According to the Press accounts, there was a third edition in the same year, but no copy of it has been found.]

3rd A/cs. p. 98, dues for three editions.)

15. [LE MARCHANT DE L'HYVREUSE, WILLIAM. Appendixes to his Histoire de l'erection originelle de l'avancement & augmentation du havre de la ville de St. Pierre Port a Guernesey. Charters of Henry VIII and Elizabeth I.

4to. Bodl. Gough Islands 3.

3rd A/cs. p. 86, 'Charters to the Isles of Jersey and Guernsey' dues. The text, dated 'a Longworth, Bark-shire', and signed by William Le Marchant de l'Hyvreuse, was printed elsewhere.]

16. NEWTON, JOSEPH. A prudent enforcement of the penal laws against immorality and profaneness recommended; in a sermon preached at the assizes held at Reading, Berks, by the Honourable Mr. Justice Birch, and Mr. Baron Adams, on Tuesday, March 4, 1755. Published at the request of the High-Sheriff-Representative, of the gentlemen of the of the [sic] Grand-Jury, and of other gentlemen then present. By Joseph Newton [etc.]. Oxford, printed for Richard Clements: and sold by Rich. Baldwin, at the Rose in Pater-noster-Row, London. 1755.

8vo fours. Bodl. G. Pamph. 2136(9).

3rd A/cs. p. 124, dues.

17. OXFORD, COUNTY. Informations and other papers relating to the treasonable verses found at Oxford, July 17. 1754. Oxford printed; [sic] and sold by Daniel Prince. And by J. and J. Rivington in St. Paul's Church-Yard, London. 1755.

8vo fours. Bodl. Gough Oxf. 39(16*).

3rd A/cs. p. 124, dues.

18*. OXFORD, UNIVERSITY. [A Broadside, for regulating Proceedings in the Chancellor's Court.] 6 Jan. 1755.

Broadside. Bodl. G.A. Oxon. b. 19(74).

3rd A/cs. p. 87, printing 100.

19*. OXFORD, UNIVERSITY. ['A Programma at the Commemorating the Publick Benefactors, 30 June 1755'.]

4to. Bodl. G.A. Oxon. b. 19(75).

3rd A/cs. p. 87, printing 100.

20. PARKER, WILLIAM. The true intention, publick use and importance of academick education considered. A sermon preached before the University of Oxford, at St. Mary's, on Act-Sunday, July 13, 1755. By William Parker [etc.]. Published at the request of the Vice-Chancellor, and Heads of Houses. Oxford, printed at the Theatre for James Fletcher in the Turl; and sold by R. Baldwin at the Rose in Pater-noster-Row, London. MDCCLV.

4to. Bodl. G. Pamph. 69(11).

3rd A/cs. p. 124, dues.

21. PARRY, RICHARD. The Scripture account of the Lords-Supper. The substance of three sermons preached at Market-Harborough in the County of Leicester. 1755. By Richard Parry [etc.]. Oxford, printed at the Theatre for James Fletcher in the Turl; and sold by R. Dodsley in Pall-Mall, London. MDCCLV.
  8vo fours. Imp. 30 Oct. 1755. Bodl. 100 aa. 58(1).
  3rd A/cs. p. 98, dues.

22. PATTEN, THOMAS. The Christian apology. A sermon preached before the University of Oxford, at St. Mary's, on Act-Sunday in the afternoon, July 13, 1755. By Thomas Patten [etc.]. Published at the request of the Vice-Chancellor, and other Heads of Houses. Oxford, printed at the Theatre for S. Parker, Mess. Rivingtons in St. Paul's Church-Yard, and Mess. Newtons in Manchester. MDCCLV.
  8vo fours. Bodl. G. Pamph. 65(1).

23. PATTEN, THOMAS. [As above.] The second edition. Printed [etc., as above].
  8vo fours. Bodl. G. Pamph. 275(9).
  3rd A/cs. p. 98, dues.

24. PERIAM, GEORGE. The means of redressing, and the duty of forgiving injuries consider'd. A sermon preached at the assizes, held for the County of Bucks, at Buckingham, before the Honourable Mr. Justice Clive, and Mr. Justice Birch, on Tuesday, July 8, 1755. By George Periam [etc.]. Publish'd at the request of the High-Sheriff, and Grand-Jury. Oxford, printed at the Theatre for James Fletcher in the Turl; and sold by J. and J. Rivington in St. Paul's Church-Yard, London. MDCCLV.
  8vo fours. Imp. 16 Sept. 1755. Bodl. 994 e. 1.
  3rd A/cs. p. 124, dues.

25. POWNEY, RICHARD. Ad honorabilem ornatissimumque virum Robertum Trevoro-Hampdenium Ricardi Pownei epistola paraenetica. Oxonii e Th. Sh. MDCCLV.
  Fol. 4 pp. Bodl. G.A. fol. A 240(2).

26. RANDOLPH, THOMAS. The certainty of a future state asserted and vindicated against the exceptions of the late Lord Bolingbroke: in a sermon preached at St. Mary's in Oxford, at the assizes, held there by the Honourable Mr. Justice Birch, and Mr. Baron Adams, on Thursday, March 6. 1755. By Thomas Randolph [etc.]. Published at the request of the Vice-Chancellor, and Heads of Houses. Oxford, printed at the Theatre for James Fletcher in the Turl; and sold by J. and J. Rivington in St. Paul's Church-Yard, London. MDCCLV.
  8vo fours. Bodl. G. Pamph. 65(2).
  3rd A/cs. p. 124, dues.

27. SHARP, WILLIAM. National prosperity the joint product of just government and dutiful subjection. A sermon preach'd before the University of Oxford, at St. Mary's, on Sunday, June 22, 1755, being the anniversary thanksgiving for His Majesty's happy accession to the Throne. By William Sharp [etc.]. Publish'd at the request of the Vice-Chancellor, and Heads of Houses. Oxford, printed at the Theatre for James Fletcher in the Turl; and sold by J. and J. Rivington in St. Paul's Church-Yard, London. MDCCLV.
  8vo fours. Bodl. G. Pamph. 1010(19).
  3rd A/cs. p. 124, dues.

28. SHARP, WILLIAM. The amiableness and advantage of making suitable provision for the education and employment of poor children. A sermon preach'd at the parish-church of S. Martin in the City of Oxford, on Sunday, Sept. 28. 1755, being the annual meeting for the encouragement of the charity-schools within that city. By William Sharp [etc.]. Published by request. Oxford, printed at the Theatre for James Fletcher in the Turl; and sold by J. and J. Rivington in St. Paul's Church-Yard, London. MDCCLV.

    8vo fours. Bodl. G. Pamph. 1010(20).
    3rd A/cs. p. 124, dues.

29. SPEED, JOHN. De aqua marina commentarius. Authore J. Speed M.D. Oxonii, e Th. Sh. impensis Ricardi Clements, bibliopolae. Prostat apud R. Baldwin in Pater-noster-Row, London. MDCCLV.

    4to Bodl. G. Pamph. 159(3).
    3rd A/cs. p. 86, dues.

30. [WATSON, GEORGE.] A seasonable admonition to the Church of England. A sermon preached before the University of Oxford, at St. Mary's, on the twenty ninth of May, 1751. Oxford, printed at the Theatre for Sackville Parker, and E. Withers at the Seven-Stars, near Temple-Bar. MDCCLV. Price one shilling.

    4to. Imp. 12 March 1755. Bodl. 101 h. 76(4).
    3rd A/cs. p. 86, dues.

1756

1. ALCOCK, THOMAS. A sermon on the late earthquakes, more particularly that at Lisbon; part whereof was preached December 31. 1755, and the other part February 4. 1756. in the parish church of St. Andrew, Plymouth: wherein the subject is considered both in a philosophical and religious light. By Thomas Alcock [etc.]. Oxford, printed at the Theatre for Richard Clements; and sold by R. Baldwin at the Rose in Pater-noster-Row, London; and Theophilus Rhodes, bookseller in Plymouth. MDCCLVI.

    8vo fours. Bodl. 8° M 241(1) BS.
    3rd A/cs. p. 124, dues.

2. BILSTONE, JOHN. Grace considered in it's operations on the understanding, the will, and the affections. A sermon preached before the University of Oxford, at St. Mary's, on Sunday, October 5. 1755. By John Bilstone [etc.]. Oxford, printed at the Theatre for Richard Clements: and sold by J. Rivington, in St. Paul's Church-Yard, London. MDCCLVI.

    8vo fours. Imp. 28 July 1756. Bodl. 8° M 241(5) BS.
    3rd A/cs. p. 124, dues.

3. BLACKSTONE, WILLIAM. An analysis of the laws of England. Oxford, printed at the Clarendon Press. MDCCLVI.

    8vo. Bodl. Vet. A 5 e. 2034.
    3rd A/cs. p. 98, dues.

4. BLAKE, EDWARD. Religion, and it's temporal promises consider'd. in a sermon preached before the University of Oxford, at St. Mary's Church, on Act-Sunday,

July 11. 1756. By Edward Blake [etc.]. Published at the request of the Vice-Chancellor and Heads of Houses. Oxford, printed at the Theatre for James Fletcher in the Turl; and sold by J. Rivington and J. Fletcher in Pater-Noster-Row, London. MDCCLVI.

> 8vo fours. Bodl. G. Pamph. 65(12).
> 3rd A/cs. p. 124, dues.

5. BURTON, JOHN. De fundamentalibus dissertatio theologica. Sive concio ad clerum Londinensem habita in ecclesia S. Elphegi, Maii 11. 1756. A Johanne Burton [etc.]. Oxonii, e Th. Sh. Prostat apud Jacobum Fletcher, Oxon. Jac. Rivington & Jac. Fletcher, in vico Pater-noster-row, Londini. MDCCLVI.

> 8vo fours. Imp. 21 June 1756. Bodl. 8° C 114(3) BS.
> 3rd A/cs. p. 98, dues.

6. DODWELL, WILLIAM. The doctrine of the divine visitation by earthquakes illustrated, confirmed, and applied. In two sermons preached on the fast-day and the preceding Sunday. By William Dodwell [etc.]. Oxford, printed at the Theatre for James Fletcher in the Turl; and sold by Messrs. Rivington and Fletcher, booksellers, in Pater-Noster-Row, London.

> 8vo fours. Imp. 12 March 1756. Bodl. G. Pamph. 788(6).
> 3rd A/cs. p. 124, dues.

7. EURIPIDES. [Title in Greek.] Euripidis Hippolytus ex MSS. Bibliothecae Regiae Parisiensis emendatus. Variis lectionibus & notis editoris accessere viri clarissimi Jeremiae Markland emendationes. Oxoniae, e Typ. Clar. Prostant apud J. Fletcher, & R. Clements; Londini apud T. Wilcox. MDCCLVI.

> 4to Imp. 30 Dec. 1755. Bodl. XX 156 Art.
> 3rd A/cs. p. 122, dues. Edited by Samuel Musgrave.

8. FOTHERGILL, GEORGE. The proper improvement of divine judgments. A sermon preached before the Mayor and Corporation, at St. Martin's in Oxford, on Friday, February 6. 1756. being the day appointed to be kept as a fast, on account of the present important situation of publick affairs, and particularly on occasion of many dreadful earthquakes at Lisbon and other places. By George Fothergill [etc.]. Printed at the request of the Mayor, Recorder, Aldermen, and Assistants of the City. Oxford, printed at the Theatre for Richard Clements: and sold by Mr. John Rivington in St. Paul's Church-Yard, London; Mr. Thurlbourn in Cambridge, and Mr. Leake in Bath. MDCCLVI.

> 8vo fours. Imp. 13 Feb. 1756. Bodl. 8° M 241(14) BS.
> 3rd A/cs. p. 124, dues.

9. GRIFFITH, THOMAS. The use and extent of reason in matters of religion. A sermon preached before the University of Oxford at St. Mary's, on Tuesday in Whitsun-week, June 8. 1756. By Thomas Griffith [etc.]. Printed at the request of the Vice-Chancellor and Heads of Houses. Oxford, printed at the Theatre for S. Parker; and sold by J. Rivington in St. Paul's Church-Yard, London. MDCCLVI.

> 8vo fours. Bodl. G. Pamph. 788(8).
> 3rd A/cs. p. 124, dues.

10. HALL, CHARLES. The Gospel credibility defended against the objection of its decrease by length of time. in a sermon preached before the University of Oxford, at St. Mary's Church, on Sunday, July iv. MDCCLVI. By Charles Hall [etc.].

Oxford, printed at the Theatre for James Fletcher in the Turl; and sold by J. Rivington and J. Fletcher in Pater-noster-Row, London. MDCCLVI.

8vo fours. Bodl. G. Pamph. 65(11).

3rd A/cs. p. 124, dues.

11. HAWKINS, WILLIAM. The reasonableness of our belief in the doctrines of Christianity asserted. Two sermons preached before the University of Oxford at St. Mary's on Sunday, Oct. 12. 1755. By William Hawkins [etc.]. Published at the request of the Vice-Chancellor and Heads of Houses. Oxford, printed at the Theatre for S. Parker, and sold by J. Rivington in St. Paul's Church-Yard; and S. Farley at Bristol. MDCCLVI.

8vo fours. Univ. Libr., Cambridge, Syn. 5.75.14^{13}.

3rd A/cs. p. 124, dues.

12. HODGES, WALTER. Strictures upon some passages in Dr. Sharp's Cherubim. To which is subjoin'd a short reply to certain reviewers, by way of postscript. By the author of Elihu, and the Christian Plan. Oxford, printed at the Theatre, and sold by J. Fletcher in the Turl, and E. Withers at the Seven-Stars, Fleet-street, London. MDCCLVI. Price six-pence.

8vo fours. Bodl. 125 e. 6(1).

3rd A/cs. p. 124, dues.

13. HORNE, GEORGE. The Almighty glorified in judgment. A sermon preached before the University of Oxford on Sunday, Feb. 15. 1756. Preached also before the Mayor and Corporation of the City of Oxford, and at several other places, on occasion of the late earthquakes and public fast. By George Horne [etc.]. Oxford, printed at the Theatre for S. Parker; and sold by E. Withers at Seven-Stars in Fleet-Street, London.

8vo fours. Bodl. G. Pamph. 65(8).

3rd A/cs. p. 124, dues.

14. HORNE, GEORGE. Apology for certain gentlemen in the University of Oxford aspersed in a late anonymous pamphlet. With a short postscript concerning another pamphlet lately published by the Rev. Mr. Heathcote. By George Horne [etc.]. Oxford; printed at the Theatre for S. Parker; and sold by J. Rivington in St. Paul's Church-Yard, and E. Withers at the Seven-Stars in Fleet-Street, London. MDCCLVI.

8vo fours. Bodl. G. Pamph. 275(10).

3rd A/cs. p. 98, dues.

15. HUDDESFORD, GEORGE. Observations relating to the Delegates of the Press: with an account of their succession from their original appointment. Oxford, printed at the Theatre, 1756.

4to. Bodl. MS. Top. Oxon. d. 387(1).

3rd A/cs. p. 98, dues. The author's name is given at the end. Dated 10 Sept. 1756.

16. JONES, WILLIAM. The Catholic doctrine of a Trinity proved by above an hundred short and clear arguments, expressed in the terms of the Holy Scripture, compared after a manner entirely new and digested under the four following titles 1. The Divinity of Christ. 2. The Divinity of the Holy Ghost. 3. The Plurality of Persons. 4. The Trinity in Unity. With a few reflections, occasionally interspersed, upon some of the Arian writers, particularly Dr. S. Clark. To which is also prefixed a discourse to the reader on the necessity of faith in the true God, and upon diversity of opinion. By the Reverend William Jones [etc.]. Oxford, printed at the Theatre for

S. Parker; and sold by J. Rivington and J. Fletcher in Pater-noster-Row, and
E. Withers at the Seven Stars, near Temple-Bar, London.

  8vo fours. Imp. 21 May 1756. Bodl. 101 f. 340.

  3rd A/cs. p. 110, dues.

17*. OXFORD, UNIVERSITY. Parecbolae sive excerpta e corpore statutorum Universitatis Oxoniensis. Accedunt Articuli religionis XXXIX. in ecclesia Anglicana
recepti: nec non Juramenta fidelitatis & suprematus. In usum juventutis academicae.
Oxonii, e Th. Sh. MDCCLVI.

  8vo fours. Bodl. Bliss B 191.

  3rd A/cs. p. 101, printing 3,000.

18*. OXFORD, UNIVERSITY. Order of speakers in the Theater in honour of the
Countess of Pomfret, and in commemoration of the other benefactors of the
University according to the institution of Lord Crewe. Tuesday, July 6.

  4to s. sh. Bodl. G.A. Oxon. b. 19(76).

  3rd A/cs. p. 99 (1756), printing 350.

19. PATTEN, THOMAS. St. Peter's Christian apology as set forth in a sermon on
I Pet. iii, 15, 16. lately published at the request of the Vice-Chancellor of the
University of Oxford and other Heads of Houses, by Thomas Patten [etc.]; farther
illustrated and maintained against the misrepresentations and objections of the
Rev. Mr. Ralph Heathcote Preacher Assistant at Lincoln's Inn. By the author of
the sermon. Oxford, printed at the Theatre for S. Parker and R. Clements, Oxford;
J. Rivington in St. Paul's Church-Yard, Messrs. Rivington and Fletcher in Pater-
Noster-Row, London; and Messrs. Newton in Manchester. MDCCLVI.

  8vo fours. Bodl. 8° F 26 Th. BS.

  3rd A/cs. p. 124, dues.

20. SKINNER, WILLIAM. A sermon preached at the Great Sessions at Brecon, on
Saturday, March 30. 1754. before the Honourable John Hervey Esq. one of His
Majesty's justices of the Great Session for the Brecon Circuit. By William Skinner
[etc.]. Published at the request of Mr. High-Sheriff and Gentlemen of the Grand
Jury. Oxford, printed at the Theatre for James Fletcher in the Turl; and sold by
J. and J. Rivington in St. Paul's Church-Yard, London. MDCCLVI.

  8vo fours. B.M. 225.g.8(4).

21. SPRY, JOHN. A sermon preached in Lambeth Chapel at the consecration of the
Right Reverend Fathers in God, John, Lord Bishop of Bristol, and John, Lord
Bishop of Bangor, on Sunday, July 4. 1756. By John Spry [etc.]. Published, at the
command of H.G. the Lord Archbishop of Canterbury, and the Reverend the
Bishops in commission for the consecration. Oxford, printed at the Theatre for
James Fletcher in the Turl; and sold by J. Rivington and J. Fletcher in Pater-noster-
Row, London.

  8vo fours. Bodl. 100 aa. 54(12).

  3rd A/cs. p. 124, dues.

22. THOMPSON, WILLIAM. Gratitude. a poem on the Countess of Pomfret's benefaction to the University of Oxford. By William Thompson [etc.]. Oxford, printed
at the Theatre. MDCCLVI.

  4to. Bodl. Gough Oxf. 142(10).

23. WATKINS, R. A sermon preached on the fast-day, at Clifton Campvill in
Staffordshire, Febr. 6. 1756. By R. Watkins, M.A. Oxford, printed and sold by

James Fletcher in the Turl, and J. Whiston and B. White in Fleet-Street, London.
MDCCLVI.

8vo fours. B.M. 225.g.1(20).

24. WATSON, GEORGE. Aaron's intercession, and Korah's rebellion considered. A
sermon preached before the University of Oxford; now printed with what the
author judged some seasonable additions; and humbly recommended, at this time
of visitation, to the attention of the public. By George Watson [etc.]. Oxford,
printed at the Theatre for Sack. Parker, and R. Clements in Oxford; and E. Withers,
at the Seven-Stars, near Temple Bar, London.

8vo fours. Imp. 25 Feb. 1756. Bodl. 8° X 100(4) Th.
3rd A/cs. p. 124, dues.

1757

1. ALSOP AND OTHERS. Fabularum Aesopiarum libri quinque. Oxonii, e Typ. Clar.
impensis Jac. Fletcher bibliopolae. Prostant apud J. Rivington et J. Fletcher,
bibliopolae Lond. MDCCLVII.

8vo fours. Bodl. 2905 e. 71.
3rd A/cs. p. 110, dues.

2. BARTON, PHILIP. Firmitas prophetici sermonis. Concio pro termino habita in
aede B. Mariae Virginis coram Academia Oxoniensi, quinto kalendas Maii anno
Redemptionis MDCCLVI. A Philippo Barton [etc.]. Vice-Cancellarii et Coll.
Praefectorum jussu impressa. Oxonii, e Typ. Clar., MDCCLVII.

8vo fours. Imp. 24 Jan. 1757. Bodl. 8° C 114(5) BS.
3rd A/cs. p. 124, dues.

3. [BLACKSTONE, WILLIAM.] An analysis of the laws of England. The second
edition. Oxford, printed at the Clarendon Press. MDCCLVII.

8vo. Bodl. 8° F 228 BS.
3rd A/cs. p. 110, dues. The first edition was of the previous year.

4. [BURTON, JOHN.] Sacerdos paroecialis rusticus. Oxonii, e Th. Sh., impensis
Jacob. Fletcher bibliop. Oxon. Prostat apud J. Rivington & J. Fletcher bibliop.
Lond. MDCCLVII.

8vo fours. Bodl. G. Pamph. 107(14).
3rd A/cs. p. 124. Preface by Johannes Burton de Maplederham in Com. Oxon.
vicarius.

5. DERHAM, WILLIAM. A catalogue of books; being the library of the Revd.
William Derham, D.D. President of St. John's College, Oxford; lately deceased . . .
which will begin to be sold cheap, (the prices printed in the catalogue) on Tuesday,
October, 18. 1757. by Daniel Prince, bookseller, near the Clarendon Printing
House, Oxford.

8vo. Bodl. 2593 e. 27.
3rd A/cs. p. 122.

6. FOTHERGILL, GEORGE. The condition of man's life a constant call to industry.
A sermon preached before the University of Oxford, at St. Mary's Church, on

Sunday, June 19. 1757. By George Fothergill [etc.]. Published at the request of Mr. Vice-Chancellor and the Heads of Houses. Oxford, printed at the Theatre, for Daniel Prince: and sold by Mr. John Rivington in St. Paul's Church-Yard, London; Mr. Thurlbourn in Cambridge, and Mr. Leake in Bath. MDCCLVII.

8vo fours. Imp. 27 June 1757. Bodl. G. Pamph. 788(9).

3rd A/cs. p. 124, dues.

7. FOTHERGILL, THOMAS. The qualifications and advantages of religious trust in times of danger. A sermon preached before the Mayor and Corporation, at St. Martin's in Oxford, on Friday, February 11. 1757. being the day appointed by royal proclamation to be kept as a general fast. By Thomas Fothergill [etc.]. Published at the request of the Mayor, Recorder, Aldermen, and Assistants of the City. Oxford, printed at the Theatre for Daniel Prince; and sold by John Rivington in St. Paul's Church-Yard, London. MDCCLVII.

8vo fours. Imp. 18 Feb. 1757. Bodl. G. Pamph. 1011(25).

3rd A/cs. p. 124.

8. — 2nd edition. Bodl. Vet. A 5 e. 531(4).

9. GRIFFITH, THOMAS. The difficulties and due discharge of the ministerial office in the present age. A sermon preach'd before the University of Oxford, at St. Mary's, on Sunday, November 27. 1757. By Thomas Griffith [etc.]. Published at the request of Mr. Vice-Chancellor and the Heads of Houses. Oxford, printed at the Theatre, for S. Parker: and sold by Mr. J. Rivington in St. Paul's Church-Yard, and Mr. A. Millar in the Strand, London. MDCCLVII.

8vo fours. Imp. 5 Dec. 1757. Bodl. G. Pamph. 1011(17).

3rd A/cs. p. 124, dues.

10. HOOPER, GEORGE. The works of the Right Reverend Father in God, George Hooper, D.D. late Bishop of Bath and Wells. Oxford, printed at the Theatre for James Fletcher in the Turl; and sold by J. Rivington and J. Fletcher in Pater-Noster-Row, London. MDCCLVII.

Fol. Imp. 25 July 1753. Bodl. P 4. 15 Th.

3rd A/cs. p. 122, dues. Edited by Thomas Hunt.

11. KENNICOTT, BENJAMIN. Christian fortitude. A sermon preached before the University of Oxford, at St. Mary's Church, on St. Paul's Day, Jan. 25. 1757. By Benjamin Kennicott [etc.]. Oxford, printed at the Theatre; and sold by J. Fletcher and D. Prince, in Oxford; and by R. and J. Dodsley, J. Rivington, J. Rivington and J. Fletcher, and R. Griffiths, in London. MDCCLVII.

4to. Bodl. G. Pamph. 112(11).

3rd A/cs. p. 124, dues.

12. KENNICOTT, BENJAMIN. [As above] . . . Kennicott [etc.]. Second edition, with a list of the falshoods in a late pamphlet called Remarks on this sermon. [Imprint as above.]

8vo fours. Bodl. 8° F 122(4) BS.

3rd A/cs. p. 124, dues.

13. PATTEN, THOMAS. The sufficiency of the external evidence of the Gospel farther supported against the Reply of the Reverend Mr. Heathcote to St. Peter's Christian Apology, written in defence of a sermon entitled the Christian Apology, lately published at Oxford, at the request of the Vice-Chancellor and Heads of

Houses; by Thomas Patten [etc.]. Oxford, printed at the Theatre for S. Parker: and sold by J. Rivington in St. Paul's Church-Yard, Messrs. Rivington and Fletcher in Pater-noster Row, London: and Messrs. Newton in Manchester. 1757.

8vo fours. Bodl. G. Pamph. 275(11).

3rd A/cs. p. 110, dues.

14. SNOWDON, JAMES. The duty of fasting with its appendages briefly considered. A sermon preached at the parish church of St. Peter's, in the East, in Oxford, on Friday, Febr. 11. 1757. being the day appointed by royal proclamation to be kept as a general fast. By James Snowdon [etc.]. Oxford, printed at the Theatre for James Fletcher in the Turl; and sold by J. Rivington and J. Fletcher in Pater-noster Row, London. MDCCLVII.

8vo fours. Imp. 17 Apr. 1757. Bodl. G. Pamph. 1011(30).

3rd A/cs. p. 124, dues.

15. THOMPSON, WILLIAM. Poems on several occasions, to which is added Gondibert and Birtha, a tragedy. By William Thompson [etc.]. Oxford, printed at the Theatre, MDCCLVII.

8vo fours. Bodl. 2799 e. 2.

3rd A/cs. p. 122, dues. Signed [A]–2A. In the same series of signatures are two other books with title-pages: 2B–2R, Poems on several occasions. By William Thompson [etc.]. Tome the second. Oxford, printed at the Theatre, MDCCLI, and 2S–3K, Gondibert and Birtha. A tragedy. Oxford, printed at the Theatre, MDCCLI.

1758

1. ALLEN, JOHN. The two-fold evidence of adoption. A sermon preached before the University of Oxford, at St. Mary's Church, on Monday in Whitsun-Week, May 15. 1758. By John Allen [etc.]. Oxford, printed at the University Press for Daniel Prince, and sold by Sackville Parker. Also by E. Withers at the Seven-Stars in Fleet-Street; and J. Rivington and J. Fletcher at the Oxford Theatre in Pater-noster-Row, London. MDCCLVIII.

8vo fours. Imp. 12 June 1758. B.M. 4474.d.2.

2. BLACKSTONE, WILLIAM. A discourse on the study of the law; being an intro-ductory lecture, read in the Public Schools, October xiv, M.DCC.LVIII, by William Blackstone, Esq; D.C.L. barrister at law, and Vinerian Professor of the Laws of England in the University of Oxford. Published by direction of the Vice-Chancellor, the Heads of Houses and Proctors. Oxford, printed at the Clarendon Press. M.DCC.LVIII.

4to. Bodl. G. Pamph. 116(1).

3. — 2nd edition. Oxford, printed at the Clarendon Press. M.DCC.LVIII.

4to. Bodl. Vet. A 5 d. 121.

3rd A/cs. p. 142, dues. 1,000 of each.

4. BLACKSTONE, WILLIAM. An analysis of the laws of England. The third edition; to which is prefixed an Introductory discourse on the law. By William Blackstone [etc.]. Oxford, printed at the Clarendon Press. MDCCLVIII.

8vo. Bodl. 8° F 229 BS.

3rd A/cs. p. 133, dues. 1,000.

5. BURTON, JOHN. De linguae Graecae institutione dissertatio. Epistola ad Edv. Bentham S.T.P. Oxonii ex Typ. Clar. Prostant apud J. Fletcher bibliop. Oxon. & J. Rivington & J. Fletcher, Lond. MDCCLVIII.

8vo fours. Bodl. 8° C 114(6) BS.
3rd A/cs. p. 133, dues. 500.

6. BURTON, JOHN. Pentalogia, sive tragoediarum Graecarum delectus. Σοφοκλεους Οιδιπους Τυραννος, Οιδιπους επι Κολωνω, Αντιγονη. Ευριπιδου Φοινισσαι. Αισχυλου Επτα επι Θηβαις [sic]. Oxonii, ex Typ. Clar. Prostant apud J. Fletcher, bibliop. Oxon. & J. Rivington & J. Fletcher, Lond. MDCCLVIII.

8vo fours. Imp. 29 Sept. 1757. Bodl. 8° A 7(49) Jur.
3rd A/cs. p. 122, dues.

7. DODWELL, WILLIAM. The false witness reproved. A sermon preached at St. Mary's in Oxford, at the assizes, before the Honourable Mr. Justice Bathurst and Mr. Justice Noel, on Friday, March 3. 1758. By William Dodwell [etc.]. Printed at the request of the Judges, the Vice-Chancellor, and the Heads of Houses. Oxford, printed at the Theatre for James Fletcher in the Turl; and sold by J. Rivington and J. Fletcher in Pater-noster-Row, London. MDCCLVIII.

8vo fours. Bodl. G. Pamph. 778(13).
3rd A/cs. p. 132, dues. 500.

8. [FOSTER, MICHAEL.] The case of the King against Alexander Broadfoot, at the Sessions of Oyer and Terminer and Goal [sic] Delivery held for the City of Bristol and County of the same City, on the 30th of August, 1743. Oxford, printed at the Clarendon Press. MDCCLVIII.

4to. Bodl. G. Pamph. 116(4).
3rd A/cs. p. 132, dues. 500.

9. FOTHERGILL, GEORGE. The violence of man subservient to the will of God. A sermon preached before the University of Oxford, at St. Mary's Church, on Friday, February 17. 1758. being a day appointed by royal proclamation to be kept as a general fast, on occasion of the present war against France. By George Fothergill [etc.]. Published at the request of Mr. Vice-Chancellor and the Heads of Houses. Oxford, printed at the University Press for Daniel Prince; and sold by Mr. Rivington in St. Paul's Church-Yard, London, Mr. Thurlbourn in Cambridge, and Mr. Leake in Bath. MDCCLVIII.

8vo fours. Imp. 27 Feb. 1758. Bodl. G. Pamph. 107(5).
3rd A/cs. p. 142, dues. 1,000.

10. FOTHERGILL, GEORGE. The duty, objects, and offices of the love of our country. A sermon preached before the Honourable House of Commons, at St. Margaret's, Westminster, on Monday. May 29. 1758. being the anniversary day of thanksgiving for the Restoration of King Charles the Second. By George Fothergill [etc.]. Oxford, printed at the University Press for Daniel Prince; and sold by Mr. Rivington in St. Paul's Church-Yard, London, Mr. Thurlbourn in Cambridge, and Mr. Leake in Bath. MDCCLVIII.

8vo fours. Bodl. G. Pamph. 778(14).

10a. — The same in quarto format.
Bodl. G. Pamph. 112(10).
3rd A/cs. p. 132, dues. 750 and 400.

11. FOTHERGILL, GEORGE. The proper improvement of divine judgments [as in 1756]. The second edition. Oxford, printed at the Theatre for Daniel Prince; and sold by Mr. John Rivington in St. Paul's Church-Yard, London; Mr. Thurlbourn in Cambridge, and Mr. Leake in Bath. MDCCLVIII.

8vo fours. Imp. 13 Feb. 1756. Bodl. 994 e. 168(5).
3rd A/cs. p. 132, dues.

12. FOTHERGILL, GEORGE. The danger of excesses in the pursuit of liberty [as in 1737 and 1744]. The third edition. Oxford, printed at the University Press, for Daniel Prince; and sold by Mr. Rivington in St. Paul's Church-Yard, London, Mr. Thurlbourn in Cambridge, and Mr. Leake in Bath. MDCCLVIII.

8vo fours. Imp. 24 Feb. 1736-7. Bodl. 994 e. 168(3).
3rd A/cs. p. 132, dues. 500.

13. FOTHERGILL, GEORGE. The duty of giving thanks for national deliverances. A sermon preached before the Mayor and Corporation at St. Martin's in Oxford, on Thursday, October 9th 1746. being the day appointed to be kept as a general thanksgiving for the suppression of the late Rebellion. By George Fothergill [etc.]. Published at the request of the Mayor, Bayliffs, and Commonalty of the City. The second edition. Oxford, printed at the University Press for Daniel Prince; and sold by Mr. Rivington in St. Paul's Church-Yard, London, Mr. Thurlbourn in Cambridge, and Mr. Leake in Bath. Mdcclviii.

8vo fours. Imp. 14 Nov. 1746. Bodl. 994 e. 168(4).
3rd A/cs. p. 132, dues. 400.

14. HOMER. Ομηρου Ιλιας. Homeri Ilias Graece. Editio tertia. Oxonii, e Th. Sh. Impensis Jac. Fletcher, bibliopolae. Prostant apud J. Rivington & J. Fletcher, bibliopolas Lond. MDCCLVIII.

8vo fours. Imp. 19 Oct. 1713. B.M. 11315.h.8.
3rd A/cs. pp. 122, 132, dues. 1,000. The previous editions were of 1714 and 1743.

15. JOHN CHRYSOSTOM. De orando Deum. Ιωαννου του Χρυσοστομου Περι προσευχης λογοι δυο. In usum alumnorum Collegii Wintoniensis. Oxonii, e Typ. Clar. MDCCLVIII.

12mo sixes. Bodl. G. Pamph. 2866(3).
3rd A/cs. p. 132, dues. 500.

16. JONES, WILLIAM. The Catholic doctrine of a Trinity proved [as in 1756]. Second edition. Oxford, printed at the Theatre for S. Parker: and sold by J. Rivington and J. Fletcher in Pater-noster-Row; and E. Withers at the Seven Stars, near Temple-Bar, London. MDCCLVIII.

12mo sixes. Imp. 21 May 1756. B.M. 4225.c.37.
3rd A/cs. p. 133, dues. 1,000. The first edition was of 1756.

17. LATES, DAVID F. Regulae generales legendi linguam sanctam sine punctis Masoreticis. breviter, & methodice in usum tyronum propositae, & in ordine alphabetico expressae. A Davido Francisco Lates, linguarum Italicae, Gallicae, Hispanae, Lusitanae, Hebraicae et in musica magistro &c. qui in Acad. Taurin. & in Collegio Jesuitano annos xxii studiis operam dedit; & hasce linguas permissione Vice-Cancellarii in Universitate Oxon. docet. Oxonii, e Th. Sh., MDCCLVIII.

8vo fours. Bodl. Opp. adds. 4° IV 362(4).
3rd A/cs. p. 124, dues.

18*. MENELAUS. Menelai Sphaericorum libri iii. quos olim, collatis MSS. Hebraeis & Arabicis, typis exprimendos curavit vir cl. Ed. Halleius, LL.D. R.S.S. & Geometriae Professor Laud. [*sic*] Oxoniensis. Praefationem addidit G. Costard, A.M. Oxonii, sumptibus academicis MDCCLVIII.

8vo fours. Christ Church U.5.5.23(2).

3rd A/cs. p. 135, printing title and preface. The text, notes, and Latin translation were printed in 1714.

19*. OXFORD, UNIVERSITY. [Papers relating to the benefaction of Charles Viner: extracts from his will; resolutions of the Delegates; statutes for the benefaction.]

Bodl. Gough Oxf. 96.

3rd A/cs. p. 132, dues.

20*. OXFORD, UNIVERSITY. Books printed at the University-Press in Oxford. Sold by Daniel Prince, Warehouse-Keeper to the University; and by Mr. Thomas Payne, bookseller, in Castle-Street, near St. Martin's Church, London . . .

Fol. s. sh. Bodl. MS. Top. Oxon. d. 387(13).

3rd A/cs. p. 149, printing.

21. SNOWDON, JAMES. The genuine fear of God the best foundation of private and national happiness. A sermon preached at the parish church of St. Peter's, in the East, in Oxford, on Friday, Febr. 17. 1758. being the day appointed by royal proclamation to be kept as a general fast. By James Snowdon [etc.]. Oxford, printed at the Theatre for James Fletcher in the Turl, and sold by J. Rivington and J. Fletcher in Pater-noster-Row, London. MDCCLVIII.

8vo fours. Imp. 25 Feb. 1758. Bodl. 994 e. 40.

3rd A/cs. p. 132, dues. 500.

22. [VIVIAN, JOHN.] A poem on the Pomfret statues. To which is added another on Laura's grave. Oxford, printed for Daniel Prince, MDCCLVIII.

4to Bodl. G. Pamph. 115(6).

3rd A/cs. p. 133, dues. 250. A manuscript note gives the author's name.

23. WEBBER, FRANCIS. The government of the heart. A sermon preached before the University of Oxford, at St. Peter's, on Sunday, February 26. 1758. By Francis Webber [etc.]. Published at the request of Mr. Vice-Chancellor, and the Heads of Houses. Oxford, printed at the Theatre for James Fletcher in the Turl; and sold by J. Rivington and J. Fletcher in Pater-noster-Row, London. MDCCLVIII.

8vo fours. Imp. 2 March 1758. Bodl. G. Pamph. 107(8).

3rd A/cs. p. 132, dues for 500 8vo and 200 4to.

24. [WISE, FRANCIS.] Some enquiries concerning the first inhabitants, languages, religion, learning, and letters of Europe. By a member of the Society of Antiquaries in London. Oxford, printed at the Theatre for J. Fletcher, S. Parker, D. Prince, booksellers in Oxford, and Messrs. Rivington and Fletcher in Pater-noster-Row, London. MDCCLVIII.

4to. Bodl. 4° BS 668.

3rd A/cs. p. 133, dues. 500.

1759

1. ARISTOTLE. Ἀριστοτέλους Τέχνης ῥητορικῆς βιβλία τρια. Ἐκ Θεάτρου ἐν Ὀξονια, Ἐτει αψνθ'.
   8vo fours. Imp. 12 Jan. 1759. Bodl. 8° A 263 BS.
   3rd A/cs. p. 142, dues. 500. Edited by G. Holwell.

2. BILSTONE, JOHN. Provision for eternity the best use we can make of a short and uncertain life. A sermon preached at St. Martin's Church in the City of Oxford, before the Mayor and Corporation, on Sunday November the 4th, 1759, being the day of the interment of Thomas Rowney, Esq; one of their late worthy representatives in Parliament. By John Bilstone [etc.]. Published at the request of the Mayor and Corporation and other auditors. Oxford, printed for S. Parker in the High-Street: and sold by D. Prince in Oxford; and J. Rivington in St. Paul's Church Yard.
   8vo fours. Bodl. Gough Oxf. 128(2).
   3rd A/cs. p. 133, dues. 250.

3. BLACKSTONE, WILLIAM. An analysis of the laws of England to which is prefixed An introductory discourse on the study of the law. By William Blackstone, Esq. [etc.]. The fourth edition. Oxford, printed at the Clarendon Press. M.DCC.LIX.
   4to. Bodl. 35 a. 36.
   3rd A/cs. p. 142, dues. 1,000.

4. BLACKSTONE, WILLIAM. A treatise on the law of descents in fee-simple. By William Blackstone [etc.]. Oxford, at the Clarendon Press. MDCCLIX.
   8vo. Imp. 31 Oct. 1759. Bodl. G. Pamph. 210(7).
   3rd A/cs. p. 158, dues. 1,000.

5. BLACKSTONE, WILLIAM. The Great Charter and Charter of the Forest, with other authentic instruments: to which is prefixed an introductory discourse, containing the history of the charters. By William Blackstone [etc.]. Oxford, at the Clarendon Press. M.DCC.LIX.
   4to. Imp. 7 July 1759 (by the Chancellor). Bodl. fol. Godwyn 279.
   3rd A/cs. p. 143, dues.

6. BUCKLER, BENJAMIN. The alliance of religion and learning considered: preached before the Right Honourable John Earl of Westmorland Chancellor, and the University of Oxford, at St. Mary's, on Act Sunday, viii July M.Dcc.Lix. Published by his Lordship's Command. By Benjamin Buckler [etc.]. Oxford, at the Clarendon Printing House. M.Dcc.Lix. For J. Fletcher in the Turl, and sold by Mess. Rivington and Fletcher in Paternoster Row, London.
   4to. Imp. 10 July 1759 (by the Chancellor). Printer to the University. 8vo. Imp. as above. Bodl. G. Pamph. 778(15).
   3rd A/cs. p. 143, dues. 4to 100, 8vo 750.

7. BURTON, JOHN. Samuel triplici nomine laudatus, propheta, populi Israelitici judex, scholarum propheticarum rector. Conciones duae habitae in Templo B.V.M. Oxon. coram baccalaureis determinantibus. A Johanne Burton [etc.]. Oxonii, ex Typ. Clar. Prostant apud J. Fletcher, bibliop. Oxon. & J. Rivington & J. Fletcher, Londin. MDCCLIX.
   8vo fours. Bodl. G. Pamph. 107(13).
   3rd A/cs. p. 142, dues. 750.

8. [CHANDLER, RICHARD.] *Τα σωζομενα των ελεγειακων και τινων των λυρικων ποιητων. Προστιθενται και σχολια τινα. Οξονια αψν'θ'.*
8vo. Imp. 28 June 1759. Bodl. 8° Godw. 373.
3rd A/cs. p. 142, dues. 500. A manuscript note gives the name of the editor.

9. CLARENDON, EDWARD, EARL OF. The life of Edward Earl of Clarendon, Lord High Chancellor of England, and Chancellor of the University of Oxford, containing I. An account of the Chancellor's life from his birth to the Restoration in 1660. II. A continuation of the same, and of his History of the Grand Rebellion, from the Restoration to his banishment in 1667. Written by himself. Printed from his original manuscripts given to the University of Oxford by the heirs of the late Earl of Clarendon. Oxford, at the Clarendon Printing-House. M.DCC.LIX.

10. — The same in 8vo, 3 volumes. Bodl. Clar. Press 31 b. 42–44.
3rd A/cs. p. 142, dues. 2,000 of each, 250 of each LP.

11. EPICTETUS. *To του Επικτήτου ἐγχειρίδιον.* Oxonii, e Typ. Clar. impensis Dan. Prince. MDCCLIX.
12mo sixes. Bodl. 29062 f. 12.

12. FOTHERGILL, GEORGE. Nine sermons upon several occasions. By George Fothergill [etc.]. Oxford, printed at the University Press, for Daniel Prince; and sold by Mr. Rivington in St. Paul's Church-Yard London, Mr. Thurlbourn in Cambridge, and Mr. Leake in Bath. MDCCLIX.
8vo title-page and contents only. Bodl. 994 e. 168(7).

13. FOTHERGILL, GEORGE. The reasons and necessity of public worship [as in 1753]. The second edition. Oxford, printed at the University Press, for Daniel Prince; and sold by Mr. Rivington in St. Paul's Church-Yard, London, Mr. Thurlbourn in Cambridge, and Mr. Leake in Bath. MDCCLIX.
8vo fours. Imp. 13 March 1753. Bodl. 100 w. 287(16).
3rd A/cs. p. 142, dues.

14. FOTHERGILL, GEORGE. The importance of religion to civil societies [as in 1735 and 1745]. The fourth edition. Oxford [imprint as above].
8vo fours. Imp. 18 March 1734–5. Bodl. 994 e. 168(7).
3rd A/cs. p. 142, dues.

15. HANDEL, GEORGE FREDERICK. [Editions of Samson, Esther, and the Messiah. Only one found.] Messiah, or the sacred oratorio. As performed at the Theatre in Oxford. Printed in the year MDCCLIX. [The words only.]
4to. B.M. 3128.e.35.
3rd A/cs. p. 143, dues. 500 of each.

16. ([Holmes, William.] The country clergyman's advice to his parishioners, as in 1742.
12mo. No copy found.
3rd A/cs. p. 158, dues. 6,000.)

17. JOHNSON, SAMUEL. Two satires by Samuel Johnson, A.M. Oxford, at the Clarendon Printing House. MDCCLIX.
8vo. Bodl. Arch. A e. 109, and, with a different ornament on the title-page, Arch. A e. 75.
3rd A/cs. p. 143, dues. 250.

18. KENNICOTT, BENJAMIN. The state of the printed text of the Old Testament considered. Dissertation the second. Wherein the Samaritan copy of the Pentateuch is vindicated: the printed copies of the Chaldee paraphrase are proved to be corrupted: the sentiments of the Jews on the Hebrew text are ascertained: an account is given of all the Hebrew MSS. now known; and also a particular catalogue of CX Hebrew MSS. in Oxford, Cambridge and the British Museum. By Benjamin Kennicott [etc.]. Oxford, printed at the Theatre: and sold by Messrs. Fletcher and Prince, in Oxford; John Rivington, Dodsley, Rivington and Fletcher, and Griffiths, in London. MDCCLIX.

8vo fours. Imp. 31 Oct. 1758. Bodl. 8° F 124 BS.

3rd A/cs. p. 158, dues. 750.

19. NEVE, TIMOTHY. The comparative blessings of Christianity. A sermon preached before the Right Honourable John Earl of Westmorland Chancellor, and the University of Oxford, at St. Mary's on Act Sunday, viii July M.DCC.LIX. Published by his Lordship's command. By Timothy Neve [etc.]. Oxford, at the Clarendon Printing House. M.DCC.LIX. for S. Parker, and sold by J. Rivington and J. Fletcher in Pater-noster-Row, and C. Bathurst in Fleetstreet, London.

4to. Bodl. G. Pamph. 2708(8).

3rd A/cs. p. 143, dues. 150.

20. — The same in 8vo. B.M. 4473.b.21.

3rd A/cs. p. 143, dues. 500.

21*. OXFORD, UNIVERSITY. Opinions of counsel on the statutes [relating to the Vinerian benefaction].

Fol. Bodl. Gough Oxf. 96(55, 61).

3rd A/cs. p. 142, dues.

22*. OXFORD, UNIVERSITY. A pocket companion for Oxford: or, Guide through the University, containing an accurate description of the public edifices, the buildings in each of the colleges; the gardens, statues, busts, pictures; the hieroglyphics at Magdalen College, and all other curiosities in the University. With an historical account of the foundation of the colleges, their history and present state [etc.]. A new edition, corrected and much enlarged. Oxford, for Daniel Prince, near the Clarendon Printing-House; John Rivington, in St. Paul's Church-Yard and R. Baldwin, in Pater-noster-Row, London. 1759.

12mo sixes. Bodl. Bliss B 180(1).

3rd A/cs. p. 133, dues. 2,000.

23. PARKER, WILLIAM. The Scripture doctrine of predestination stated and explained. Two discourses preached before the University of Oxford at St. Mary's, on Sunday, June 18. 1758. By William Parker [etc.]. Published at the request of the Vice-Chancellor and Heads of Houses. Oxford, printed at the Theatre for James Fletcher in the Turl; and sold by J. Rivington and J. Fletcher, and R. Baldwin in Pater-noster-Row, London. MDCCLIX.

8vo fours. B.M. 4473.b.35(3).

24. PATTEN, THOMAS. The opposition between the Gospel of Jesus Christ and what is called the religion of nature. A sermon preached before the University of Oxford, at St. Mary's, on Sunday, 1 July M.DCC.LIX. By Thomas Patten [etc.]. Published by request. Oxford, at the Clarendon Printing House, for S. Parker, and

Dan. Prince, in Oxford; John Rivington, J. Rivington and J. Fletcher, in London; and W. Newton in Manchester. M.DCC.LIX.

8vo fours. Bodl. 8° F 26(6) Th. BS.

3rd A/cs. p. 158, dues. 500.

25. XENOPHON. [Title in Greek.] Xenophontis Memorabilium Socratis dictorum libri iv. Cum notis Stephani, Leunclavii, Æ. Porti & Ernesti. Recensuit, suisque annotationibus auxit Bolton Simpson [etc.]. Editio tertia auctior. Oxonii, e Th. Sh. Impensis Jacobi Fletcher, bibliopol. Oxon. et J. Rivington & J. Fletcher, Lond. MDCCLIX.

[followed in the same volume by] Ξενοφωντος Σωκρατους Απολογια προς τους δικαστας. Xenophontis Socratica defensio ad judices. Oxonii, e Th. Sh. MDCCLIX.

8vo fours. Imp. 20 Apr. 1741. Bodl. 29168 e. 24.

3rd A/cs. p. 142, dues. 1,250. Previous editions were of 1741 and 1749.

1760

1. ARISTOTLE. Αριστοτελους Περι ποιητικης. Οξονια. Ετει αψ′ξ′.

12mo sixes. Imp. 22 Jan. 1760. Bodl. Godw. subt. 42.

3rd A/cs. p. 158, dues. 500.

2. ARISTOTLE. [Title in Greek.] Aristotelis De poetica liber, Graece et Latine, cum notis. Oxonii, e Typ. Clar. MDCCLX.

8vo fours. Imp. 24 Apr. 1760. Bodl. Radcl. d. 87.

3rd A/cs. p. 159, dues. 750. Edited by W. Parsons (Madan).

3. BURTON, JOHN. University politics. Or, the study of a Christian, gentleman, scholar, set forth in three sermons on the King's inauguration before the University of Oxford, at St. Mary's Church. By John Burton [etc.]. Oxford, printed for J. Fletcher in the Turl, and sold by Hen. Payne in Pater-noster-Row, London. MDCCLX.

8vo fours. Imp. 15 Oct. 1760. Bodl. G. Pamph. 111(1).

3rd A/cs. p. 172, dues. 500.

4. CLARENDON, EDWARD HYDE, EARL OF. The life of Edward Earl of Clarendon [as in 1759]. Volume the first [second]. Oxford, at the Clarendon Printing-House. MDCCLX.

8vo. 2 vols. Bodl. 22855 d. 2,3.

3rd A/cs. p. 143, dues. 750. The second 8vo edition.

5. [Corneille, Pierre and Thomas. Les chef-d'œuvres [sic] dramatiques de Messieurs Corneille, avec le jugement des sçavans à la suite de chaque pièce. Tome premier [second]. A Oxford, M.DCC.LX.

12mo. Bodl. 38688 f. 179–181.

The types are decidedly French and were not available at Oxford. Émile Picot, *Bibliographie Cornélienne* (Paris, 1876), No. 669.]

6. DODWELL, WILLIAM. The doctrine of a particular Providence stated, confirmed, defended and applied. In two sermons preached before the University of Oxford, at St. Mary's, on Sunday April 20. 1760. By William Dodwell [etc.]. Printed at the

request of the Vice-Chancellor and Heads of Houses. Oxford, printed for James Fletcher in the Turl, and sold by Hen. Payne in Pater-noster-Row, London. MDCCLX.

8vo fours. Imp. 15 Oct. 1760. Bodl. G. Pamph. 111(2).
3rd A/cs. p. 159, dues. 500.

7. FALCON, THOMAS. Gratitude for divine mercies, the special duty of Britons. A sermon preached at St. Michael's Church in Bridge Town, Barbados, before His Excellency Charles Pinfold Esq; on Thursday, February 7th, 1760. being the day appointed for a public thanksgiving to Almighty God, for the many signal successes lately vouchsafed to His Majesty's arms by sea and land. By Thomas Falcon [etc.]. Published at His Excellency's request. Oxford, printed at the University Press, sold by Daniel Prince, and by William Sandby in Fleet-Street, London. MDCCLX.

8vo fours. Imp. 11 June 1760. Bodl. 22863 e. 64.
3rd A/cs. p. 159, dues. 300.

8. FOTHERGILL, THOMAS. The qualifications and advantages of religious trust in times of danger [as in 1757]. The second edition. [Imprint as in 1757.]

8vo fours. Imp. 18 Feb. 1757. Bodl. Vet. A 5 e. 531(4).

9. GRIFFITH, THOMAS. The evils arising from misapply'd curiosity. A sermon preached before the University of Oxford, at St. Mary's, on Sunday March 9. 1760. By Thomas Griffith [etc.]. Published at the request of the Vice-Chancellor and Heads of Houses. Oxford, printed at the Theatre for S. Parker; and sold by J. Rivington in St. Paul's Church-Yard, London. MDCCLX.

8vo fours. Imp. 20 March 1760. Bodl. G. Pamph. 111(3).
3rd A/cs. p. 159, dues. 500.

10*. HYDE, THOMAS. Historia religionis veterum Persarum, eorumque Magorum. [as in 1700].

[Half-title:] Veterum Persarum et Parthorum et Medorum religionis historia. Autor est Thomas Hyde [etc.]. Editio secunda. Oxonii, e Typ. Clar., MDCCLX.

4to. Bodl. EE 129 Art.
3rd A/cs. p. 161, printing 500.

11. LHUYD, EDWARD. Edvardi Luidii apud Oxonienses Cimeliarchae Ashmoliani Lithophylacii Britannici ichnographia. Sive lapidum aliorumque fossilium Britannicorum singulari figura insignium, quotquot hactenus vel ipse invenit vel ab amicis accepit, distributio classica: scrinii sui lapidarii repertorium cum locis singulorum natalibus exhibens. Additis rariorum aliquot figuris aere incisis; cum epistolis ad clarissimos viros de quibusdam circa marina fossilia & stirpes minerales praesertim notandis. Editio altera: novis quorundam speciminum iconibus aucta. Subjicitur authoris praelectio de stellis marinis, &c. Oxonii, e Typ. Clar. Prostant apud bibliopolas Oxonienses; J. Rivington in Coemeterio Paulino; J. Whiston & B. White in Fleetstreet, Londini. MDCCLX.

8vo fours. Imp. 13 May 1760. Bodl. Gough Oxf. 35.
3rd A/cs. p. 158, dues. 300. The first edition was printed in London in 1699. This one was edited by William Huddesford, who added a preface.

12. [Pas, Manasses de, Marquis de Feuquières. Phantasiologie . . . 'A Oxfort, et se trouve a Paris, chez Cuissart, libraire à l'Ange Gardien, sur le Quai de Gesvres. M.DCC.LX.

24to. Bodl. 265 k. 156.
The Oxford imprint is manifestly false.]

13. RANDOLPH, THOMAS. Christ the lord of glory. A sermon preached before the University of Oxford at St. Mary's Dec. 9. 1759. with several additions confirming and enforcing the same doctrine. By Thomas Randolph [etc.]. Oxford, printed for J. Fletcher in the Turl, and sold by Hen. Payne in Pater-noster-Row, London. 1760.

8vo fours. Imp. 11 Feb. 1760. Bodl. G. Pamph. 909(3).
3rd A/cs. p. 158, dues. 500.

14. SCROPE, JOHN. Charity better than knowledge: a sermon preached at the visitation held at Lacock in Wiltshire, May 23. 1760. By John Scrope [etc.]. Published at the request of the clergy and other gentlemen who heard it. Oxford, printed at the Theatre; sold by J. Fletcher and D. Prince in Oxford; and J. Rivington in St. Paul's Church-Yard, London.

8vo fours. Imp. 9 June 1760. Bodl. G. Pamph. 909(2).
3rd A/cs. p. 159, dues. 500.

15. STILLINGFLEET, JAMES. The Christian ministry and stewardship. A sermon preached before the University of Oxford at St. Mary's, on Sunday, June 8. 1760. By James Stillingfleet [etc.]. Published at the request of Mr. Vice-Chancellor and the Heads of Houses. Oxford, at the Clarendon Printing House. Sold by James Fletcher, S. Parker, and D. Prince in Oxford, by John Rivington in London; by J. Leake and W. Frederick in Bath; and H. Lewis in Worcester. MDCCLX.

8vo fours. Imp. 27 June 1760. Bodl. 100 aa. 12(20 and 21).
3rd A/cs. p. 159, dues. 500.

16. SWANNE, GILBERT. The advantages of the Jews under their dispensation set forth, and the use they made of them considered. Two sermons preached before the University of Oxford at St. Mary's, on Sunday, April 27th, and Sunday, May 4th, 1760. By Gilbert Swanne [etc.]. Oxford, at the Clarendon Printing House. 1760. Sold by Daniel Prince; and John Rivington in St. Paul's Church-Yard, London.

8vo fours. Imp. 25 Sept. 1760. Bodl. 100 aa. 12(19).
3rd A/cs. p. 172, dues. 500.

17. THOMPSON, WILLIAM. Garden inscriptions. By William Thompson [etc.]. Oxford, printed at the Clarendon Press M.DC.LX [sic].

8vo fours. Bodl. Vet. A 5 e. 3918.

18. TROUGHEAR, THOMAS. A short account and defence of the Athanasian Creed, with reference to the doctrine of the Trinity, in letters occasionally written to his friends by Thomas Troughear [etc.]. Oxford printed at the Clarendon Press MDCCLX. Sold by Daniel Prince in Oxford; and John Rivington in St. Paul's Church-Yard, London.

8vo fours. Imp. 12 March 1760. Bodl. Clar. Press 1 e. 21.
3rd A/cs. p. 159, dues. 250.

1761

1. ABINGDON, 2ND EARL OF. [Act of Parliament for vesting his estates in trustees, 1732.]

Fol. Bodl. L. Eng. C 13 c. 3.
3rd A/cs. p. 172, dues. 25.

1a. — (Particulars of valuation of the estates.
No copy found.
3rd A/cs. p. 172, dues. 500.)

2. BILSTONE, JOHN. The nature and excellency of Christian zeal considered. A sermon preached before the University of Oxford. By John Bilstone [etc.]. Published at the request of many who heard it. Oxford, printed at the Theatre for D. Prince, bookseller. MDCCLXI.
8vo fours. All Souls Coll. LX.1.7.e.
3rd A/cs. p. 173, dues. 500.

3. BLACKSTONE, WILLIAM. [A circular notice about his appointing deputies to deliver his lectures. Begins:] The Vinerian professor is extremely concerned . . .
Fol. s. sh. Bodl. Gough Oxf. 96.
3rd A/cs. p. 173, dues.

4. BRAY, THOMAS. The evidence of prophecy superior to the evidence of miracles, only in a restrained and limited sense. A sermon preached before the University of Oxford, on February 2. 1760. By Thomas Bray [etc.]. Oxford, printed at the Theatre for James Fletcher, and sold by Mess. Payne and Cropley in Pater-noster-Row, London. MDCCLXI.
8vo fours. Imp. 17 Feb. 1761. Bodl. 994 e. 124(8).
3rd A/cs. p. 172, dues. 600.

5. BURTON, JOHN. De praxeos theologicae abusibus. Concio ad Academiam Oxoniensem habita in Templo B. Mariae, Jun. 3. 1760. A Johanne Burton [etc.]. Oxoniae, e Th. Sh. Prostat apud J. Fletcher, bibliop. Oxon & J. Fletcher, in Coemeterio Paulino, Lond. MDCCLXI.
8vo fours. Bodl. 1419 e. 137.
3rd A/cs. p. 173, dues. 500.

6. BURTON, JOHN. Opuscula miscellanea theologica Johannis Burton [etc.]. Hophni & Phinees, sive impietas sacerdotum publicae impietatis causa. Concio habita in Templo B. Mariae, pro gradu S.T.B. Jul. 17. 1729. A Johanne Burton [etc.]. Editio secunda. Oxoniae. E Th. Sh. Prostant apud J. Fletcher, bibliop. Oxon. & J. Fletcher in Coemeterio Paulino, Lond. MDCCLXI.
8vo fours. Bodl. 1419 e. 137(1).
3rd A/cs. p. 186, dues. 500. The first edition was of 1729.

7. BURTON, JOHN. Heli: sive exemplum magistratus impestiva lenitate peccantis. Concio habita in Templo B. Mariae, coram artium baccalaureis determinantibus die Cinerum Feb. 10. 1725. A Johanne Burton [etc.]. Editio secunda. Oxoniae, e Th. Sh. MDCCLXI.
8vo fours. Bodl. 1419 e. 137(2).
3rd A/cs. p. 186, dues. 500. The signatures follow on those of the preceding. The first edition was of 1729.

8. CLARENDON, EDWARD HYDE, EARL OF. The life of Edward Earl of Clarendon [as in 1759]. In three volumes. The third edition. Oxford, at the Clarendon Printing-House. MDCCLXI.
8vo. Bodl. 210 n. 440-442.
3rd A/cs. p. 159, dues. 1,000. The third edition in 8vo.

9. EUTHELIUS. Religion represented in a true light. By Euthelius. Oxford, at the Clarendon Printing House. MDCCLXI.

4to. Imp. 18 June 1760. B.M. 11632.g.79.

3rd A/cs. p. 172, dues. 300. Preface dated at Little Rissington.

10. FOTHERGILL, GEORGE. Sermons on several subjects and occasions by George Fothergill [etc.]. Published from the author's original MSS, by Thomas Fothergill [etc.]. Oxford: at the Clarendon-Press, MDCCLXI. Printed for Daniel Prince. Sold by John Rivington, in St. Paul's Church-Yard, London; Mess. Thurlbourn and Woodyer at Cambridge; Mr. Leake at Bath; Mr. Score at Exeter; and Mr. Hinxman at York.

8vo. Imp. 5 Aug. 1761. Bodl. 8° Godw. 769.

3rd A/cs. p. 172, dues. 750.

11. GIBSON, EDMUND. Codex juris ecclesiastici Anglicani: or, the statutes, con-stitutions, canons, rubricks and articles of the Church of England, methodically digested under their proper heads. With a commentary, historical and juridical. Before it, is an introductory discourse, concerning the present state of the power, discipline and laws of the Church of England; and after it, an appendix of instru-ments, ancient and modern. By Edmund Gibson [etc.]. The second edition, revised and improved with large additions by the author. Oxford, at the Clarendon Press. MDCCLXI.

Fol. Bodl. 2 vols. Σ 10 56, 7.

3rd A/cs. pp. 158, 173, dues. 500.

12. GREENWOOD, WILLIAM. A paraphrastical exposition of the fifteenth chapter of the first Epistle of St. Paul to the Corinthians: with some critical notes. By William Greenwood, D.D. The second edition with some alterations, and the addition of an allegory prefix'd, and a postscript of remarks. Oxford, at the Clarendon-Press. MDCCLXI. Sold by Dan. Prince: also by B. Dod, at the Bible and Key in Ave-Mary-Lane, London, H. Keating in Warwick, and S. Aris in Birmingham.

8vo. Trinity Coll., Cambridge, I.3.35.

3rd A/cs. p. 173, dues. 300. The first edition was printed at Warwick in 1759.

13. HITCHCOCK, THOMAS. The mutual connexion between faith, virtue and knowledge. A sermon preached before the University of Oxford, at St. Mary's, on Act-Sunday, July 12. 1761. By Thomas Hitchcock [etc.]. Published at the request of Mr. Vice-Chancellor, and the Heads of Houses. Oxford, printed at the Theatre for James Fletcher in the Turl; and sold by James Fletcher in St. Paul's Church-Yard, London.

8vo fours. Bodl. G. Pamph. 111(13).

3rd A/cs., p. 173, dues. 500.

14. — 2nd edition. Bodl. G. Pamph. 1012(6).

15. HORNE, GEORGE. The Christian king. A sermon preached before the University of Oxford, at St. Mary's on Friday, January 30. 1761, being the day appointed to be observed as the day of the martyrdom of King Charles I. By George Horne [etc.]. Oxford, printed for S. Parker, and sold by John Rivington in St. Paul's Church-Yard, London, and W. Mercer in Maidstone. MDCCLXI.

8vo fours. Imp. 16 Feb. 1761. Bodl. G. Pamph. 111(12).

3rd A/cs. p. 172, dues. 500.

16. HORNE, GEORGE. Works wrought through faith a condition of our justification. A sermon preached before the University of Oxford, at St. Mary's, on Sunday, June 7. 1761. By George Horne [etc.]. Published at the request of Mr. Vice-Chancellor. Oxford, printed at the Clarendon-Press for S. Parker, and sold by J. Rivington in St. Paul's Church-Yard, London.

    8vo fours. Bodl. G. Pamph. 2721(10).

    3rd A/cs. p. 173, dues. 500.

17. HUDDESFORD, WILLIAM. Catalogus librorum manuscriptorum viri clarissimi Antonii a Wood. being a minute catalogue of each particular contained in the manuscript collections of Antony a Wood deposited in the Ashmolean Museum at Oxford. By William Huddesford [etc.]. Oxford, printed at the Clarendon-Press. Sold by the Oxford booksellers, and by J. Fletcher in St. Paul's Church-Yard, London. MDCCLXI.

    8vo fours. Imp. 27 Oct. 1761. Bodl. Gough Oxf. 70.

    3rd A/cs. p. 172, dues. 500.

18*. OXFORD, UNIVERSITY. Pietas Universitatis Oxoniensis in obitum serenissimi regis Georgii II. et gratulatio in augustissimi regis Georgii III. inaugurationem. Oxonii, e Typ. Clar. MDCCLXI.

    Fol. Bodl. H 4. 1(2) Art.

    3rd A/cs. p. 175, printing 750 (50 LP).

19*. OXFORD, UNIVERSITY. Epithalamia Oxoniensia, sive gratulationes in augustissimi regis Georgii III. et illustrissimae principissae Sophiae Charlottae nuptias auspicatissimas. Oxonii, e Typ. Clar. MDCCLXI.

    Fol. Bodl. H 4. 1(3) Art.

    3rd A/cs. p. 189, printing 75 fine and 675 ordinary paper.

20*. OXFORD, UNIVERSITY. The catalogue of graduates &c. in the University of Oxford, continued from October 10. 1747. to October 10. 1760.

    8vo fours. Bodl. Gough Oxf. 35.

    3rd A/cs. p. 175, printing 750. A supplement to the volume issued in 1747.

21. RAWLINS, JOHN. The Scripture prophecies consider'd—and compar'd with the oracles of the heathens. A sermon preached before the University of Oxford, at St. Mary's, on Sunday, Aug. 2. 1761. By John Rawlins [etc.]. Oxford, printed at the Theatre for James Fletcher in the Turl; and sold by J. Fletcher in St. Paul's Church-yard, London.

    8vo fours. Imp. 4 Aug. 1761. Bodl. G. Pamph. 1649(6).

    3rd A/cs. p. 173, dues. 500.

22. SCROPE, JOHN. An enquiry concerning the Sacrament of the Lord's Supper. Wherein this Sacrament in general is first considered, and afterwards the manner in which it is administered in the Church of England. With an appendix containing some observations on a book entitled A Plain Account of the Nature & End of the Sacrament of the Lord's Supper. By John Scrope [etc.]. Oxford, at the Clarendon Printing-House. Sold by D. Prince and J. Fletcher in Oxford, J. Rivington in St. Paul's Church-Yard, London, Mr. Frederick in Bath, Mr. Easton and Mr. Collins in Salisbury. MDCCLXI.

    12mo sixes. Imp. 15 Oct. 1760. Bodl. 8° F 50 BS.

    3rd A/cs. p. 172, dues. 1,000. A reply to Hoadly.

23. SIMPSON, JOSEPH. Religion and learning mutually assistant to each other. A sermon preached before the University of Oxford, at St. Mary's, on Act-Sunday, July 12. 1761. By Joseph Simpson [etc.]. Published at the request of the Vice-Chancellor, and Heads of Houses. Oxford, at the Clarendon-Press. MDCCLXI. Sold by D. Prince; and G. Hawkins in Fleet-Street, London; Ed. Baker at Tunbridge Wells, B. Collins at Salisbury, and J. Noyes at Andover.

    8vo fours. Bodl. G. Pamph. 2721(13).

    3rd A/cs. p. 173, dues. 500.

24. — 2nd edition.

    8vo fours. Printer to the University.

25. — 3rd edition.

    8vo fours. Bodl. 100 aa. 12(22).

26. (Sprat, Thomas. Visitation discourse, 1695. No copy found: one included in the Catalogue of the British Museum was destroyed during the War.

    Madan 1761:9.)

27. WORTHINGTON, WILLIAM. The use, value, and improvement of various readings shewn and illustrated, in a sermon preached before the University of Oxford, at St. Mary's, on Sunday, Oct. 18. 1761. By William Worthington [etc.]. Published at the request of the Vice-Chancellor, and Heads of Houses. With additions. Oxford, printed at the Theatre: and sold by J. Fletcher in the Turl, Oxford; and J. Fletcher in St. Paul's Church-yard, London.

    8vo fours. Bodl. G. Pamph. 887(2).

    3rd A/cs. p. 186, dues. 500.

1762

1. BENTHAM, EDWARD. Advice to a young man of fortune and rank, upon his coming to the University. Oxford, printed at the Theatre. Sold by J. Fletcher, in the Turl, Oxford; and J. Fletcher, in St. Paul's Church-Yard, London.

    8vo fours. Bodl. Gough Oxf. 44(5).

    3rd A/cs. p. 187 (1762), dues. 750.

2. BLACKSTONE, WILLIAM. Law tracts, in two volumes, by William Blackstone, Esq. Vol. I [II]. Oxford, at the Clarendon Press. M.DCC.LXII.

    8vo. Bodl. 35 a. 34,5.

    3rd A/cs. p. 187, dues. 1,000.

3. BLACKSTONE, WILLIAM. An analysis of the laws of England. To which is pre-fixed an introductory discourse on the study of the law. By William Blackstone [etc.]. The fifth edition. Oxford, printed at the Clarendon Press. M.DCC.LXII.

    8vo. Bodl. 35 a. 42.

    3rd A/cs. p. 187, dues. 1,000.

4. BURTON, JOHN. Two sermons preached at St. Mary's before the University of Oxford, Feb. 11. 1757. and Mar. 12. 1762. being the days appointed for general fasting and humiliation, &c. By John Burton [etc.]. Oxford: printed at the Theatre

for J. Fletcher in the Turl, Oxon, and sold by J. Fletcher in St. Paul's Church-Yard, London. 1762.

8vo fours. Imp. 23 March 1762. Bodl. G. Pamph. 819(5).

3rd A/cs. p. 186, dues.

5. (A catalogue of books.

Not identified.

3rd A/cs. p. 187 (1762), dues. 500.)

6. (Cherokees. [——] An enquiry into the origin of the Cherokees, in a letter to a Member of Parliament . . . Oxford, 1762.

8vo. Not found. Copies reported at the Library of Congress and the New York Public Library in the *National Union Catalogue*, Vol. 160, p. 470.

3rd A/cs. p. 201. Mentioned in Joseph Sabin, *A Bibliography of Works relating to America*, Vol. iii (New York, 1870), p. 568.)

7. CLEAVER, WILLIAM. An inquiry into the true character of David King of Israel. A sermon preached before the University of Oxford, at St. Mary's, on Sunday, Jan. 24. 1762. in which the exceptions of a late writer to the conduct of David on some occasions are obviated. By William Cleaver [etc.]. Oxford, printed at the Clarendon-Press for D. Prince; and sold by J. Rivington in St. Paul's Church-Yard, London.

8vo fours. Imp. 4 Feb. 1762. Bodl. Bliss B 145(12).

3rd A/cs. p. 186, dues. 500.

8. F., J. Vita M. Tullii Ciceronis litteraria. Oxonii, e Typ. Clar., impensis Dan. Prince, Oxon. et Joan. Rivington, bibliop. Londini. MDCCLXII.

8vo fours. B.M. T.862(3).

3rd A/cs. p. 187, dues. 500. The dedication is by J. F.

9. FOSTER, MICHAEL. A report of some proceedings on the Commission of Oyer and Terminer and Goal [*sic*] Delivery for the trial of the rebels in the year 1746 in the County of Surry, and of other Crown cases. To which are added discourses upon a few branches of the Crown law. Oxford, at the Clarendon-Press. M.DCC.LXII. Sold by M. Withers in Fleetstreet and T. Osborne in Gray's Inn, London; and by D. Prince at Oxford.

Fol. Bodl. L 3. 16 Jur.

3rd A/cs. p. 186, dues.

10. FOTHERGILL, THOMAS. Religion and learning capable of being rendered mutually serviceable, or mutually prejudicial, to each other. A sermon preached before the University of Oxford, at St. Mary's, on Act-Sunday, July 11. 1762. By Thomas Fothergill [etc.]. Published at the request of Mr. Vice-Chancellor and the Heads of Houses. Oxford, printed at the Theatre for Daniel Prince: and sold by John Rivington in St. Paul's Church-Yard, London. MDCCLXII.

8vo fours. Imp. 22 July 1762. Bodl. G. Pamph. 1012(14).

3rd A/cs. p. 187, dues. 500.

11. (Hall, Joseph. Joseph. Exoniensis Henochismus.

No copy found.

3rd A/cs. p. 187, dues. 150.)

12*. HEATH, BENJAMIN. Notae sive lectiones ad tragicorum Graecorum veterum

Aeschyli Sophoclis Euripidis quae supersunt dramata deperditorumque reliquias. Auctore Benjamino Heath. Oxonii, e Typ. Clar. MDCCLXII.

    4to. Imp. 18 Dec. 1760. Bodl. EE 127 Art.

    3rd A/cs. p. 189, printing 300 fine, 200 ordinary paper.

13. JONES, WILLIAM. An essay on the first principles of natural philosophy: wherein the use of natural means, or second causes, in the oeconomy of the material world, is demonstrated from reason, experiments of various kinds, and the testimony of antiquity. In four books. By the Reverend William Jones, late of University College, Oxford; and author of The Catholic Doctrine of the Trinity. Oxford, printed at the Clarendon Printing-house. Sold by S. Parker, and D. Prince in Oxford; J. Rivington in St. Paul's Church-Yard, London; and W. Watson in Capel Street, Dublin. MDCCLXII.

    4to. Bodl. 198 h. 48.

    3rd A/cs. p. 186, dues. 750.

14*. OXFORD, UNIVERSITY. Gratulatio solennis Universitatis Oxoniensis ob celsissimum Georgium Fred. Aug. Walliae Principem Georgio III. et Charlottae reginae auspicatissime natum. Oxonii, e Typ. Clar. MDCCLXII.

    Fol. Bodl. H 4. 1(4) Art.

    3rd A/cs. p. 203, printing 100 fine, 400 ordinary paper.

15. PATTEN, THOMAS. King David vindicated from a late misrepresentation of his character. In a letter to His Grace the Archbishop of Canterbury. By Thomas Patten [etc.]. Oxford: at the Clarendon-Press. MDCCLXII. Printed for Daniel Prince. Sold by S. Parker in Oxford; and by John Rivington in St. Paul's Church-Yard, London.

    8vo. Imp. 22 Feb. 1762. Bodl. Clar. Press 1 b. 160.

    3rd A/cs. p. 186, dues. 400.

16. RANDOLPH, THOMAS. The use of reason in matters of religion stated and explain'd in a sermon preached before the University of Oxford, at St. Peter's in the East on Sunday, Mar. 7. 1762. By Thomas Randolph [etc.]. Published at the request of the Vice-Chancellor and Heads of Houses. Oxford, printed at the Theatre; and sold by J. Fletcher, in the Turl, Oxford; and J. Fletcher in St. Paul's Church-yard, London.

    8vo fours. Imp. 22 March 1762. Bodl. G. Pamph. 1012(10).

    3rd A/cs. p. 186, dues. 500.

17. (Troughear, Thomas. Legacy to his parishioners.

    No copy found.

    3rd A/cs. p. 186, dues. 250.)

1763

1. (A catalogue of books. Not identified.

    3rd A/cs. p. 200, dues. 500.)

2*. CHANDLER, RICHARD. Marmora Oxoniensia. Oxonii. e Typ. Clar. Impensis Academiae. MDCCLXIII.

    Fol. Imp. (by the Chancellor) 6 July 1763. Bodl. 17573 a. 1.

    3rd A/cs. pp. 204, 217, printing 750.

3. CLARENDON, HENRY HYDE, 2ND EARL OF. The state letters of Henry Earl of Clarendon Lord Lieutenant of Ireland during the reign of K. James the Second: and his Lordship's diary for the years 1687, 1688, 1689, 1690. From the originals in the possession of Richard Powney, Esq. With an appendix from Archbishop Sancroft's manuscripts in the Bodleian Library. Oxford, at the Clarendon Press. M.DCC.LXIII. Sold by J. Stephens at the Temple-Gate, Fleetstreet; A. Millar in the Strand; R. and J. Dodsley in Pall-Mall; J. Rivington in St. Paul's Church-Yard, London: and Daniel Prince in Oxford.

2 vols. 4to. Bodl. 4° Godw. 44, 45.
3rd A/cs. p. 200, dues. 500. Edited by John Douglas.

4. DOBSON, JOHN. Chronological annals of the war: from its beginning to the Present time. In two parts. Part I. containing from April 2. 1755, to the end of 1760. Part II. from the beginning of 1761. to the signing of the preliminaries of the peace. With an introductory preface to each part, a conclusion, and a general index to the whole. By Mr. Dobson. Oxford, at the Clarendon Press. MDCCLXIII. Sold by Daniel Prince: by John Rivington in St. Paul's Church-Yard, R. and J. Dodsley in Pall-Mall, and J. Walters at Charing-Cross, London.

8vo. Bodl. 2287 e. 7.
3rd A/cs. p. 200, dues. 500.

5. DURELL, DAVID. The Hebrew text of the parallel prophecies of Jacob and Moses relating to the Twelve Tribes; with a translation and notes: and the various lections of near forty MSS. To which are added I°. the Samaritan-Arabic version of those passages, and part of another Arabic version made from the Samaritan text; neither of which have been before printed: II°. a map of the Land of Promise; and III°. an appendix containing four dissertations on the subject of these prophecies. By David Durell [etc.]. Oxford: printed at the Clarendon Press. MDCCLXIII.

4to. Imp. 14 Jan. 1763. Bodl. G. Pamph. 121(1).
3rd A/cs. p. 201, dues.

6. DURELL, DAVID. Three dissertations: the first on the character of the patriarch Abraham; the second on the principal objections made to the Mosaic institution; and the third on the changes, improvements, and duration of that institution. By D. Durell [etc.]. Printed at the Clarendon Press in Oxford. MDCCLXIII.

4to. Imp. 14 Jan. 1763. Bodl. G. Pamph. 2819(7).

7. (Valuation of an estate at Frilsham. No copy found.
3rd A/cs. p. 200, dues. 250.)

8. GREENWOOD, WILLIAM. Some essays on the Creation with a paraphrastical exposition on the first chapter of Genesis. By William Greenwood, D.D. Oxford, at the Clarendon-Press MDCCLXIII. Sold by Dan. Prince: also John Rivington at the Bible and Crown in St. Paul's Church-Yard, London; H. Keating in Warwick; and S. Aris in Birmingham.

8vo fours. Univ. Libr., Cambridge, 8.31.33².
3rd A/cs. p. 215, dues. 300.

9. JAGO, RICHARD. The nature, and grounds of a Christian's happiness in, and after death. A sermon preached at Snitterfield in Warwickshire, Sunday, [March] 20. 1763. On occasion of the death of the Right Hon. the Lady Anne Countess of Coventry, on Feb. 14. 1763. and in the 90th year of her age. By the Rev. Richard

Jago [etc.]. Oxford, printed at the Theatre for J. Fletcher in the Turl; and sold by J. Fletcher and Co. in St. Paul's Church-Yard, London. MDCCLXIII.

8vo fours. Imp. 12 July 1763. B.M. 1415.f.16.

3rd A/cs. p. 200, dues. 500.

10. JEFFERSON, JACOB. The blessing of peace and the means of preserving it. A sermon preached before the University of Oxford, at St. Mary's, on Thursday, May 5. M.DCC.LXIII. being the day appointed for a general thanksgiving to Almighty God for the peace. By Jacob Jefferson [etc.]. Oxford: at the Clarendon Press MDCCLXIII. Sold by Daniel Prince. And by John Rivington in St. Paul's Church-Yard, and John Robson in New Bond-Street, London.

8vo fours. Imp. 9 May 1763. Bodl. G. Pamph. 1012(20).

3rd A/cs. p. 200, dues. 750.

11. LOWTH, ROBERT. De sacra poesi Hebraeorum. Praelectiones academicae Oxonii habitae a Roberto Lowth [etc.]. Subjicitur metricae Harianae brevis confutatio: et Oratio Creweiana. Editio altera, emendatior. Oxonii, e Typ. Clar. MDCCLXIII.

8vo. Imp. 1 Feb. 1753. Bodl. Opp. adds. 4° V 261.

3rd A/cs. p. 200, dues. 750. The first edition was of 1753.

12. MERRICK, JAMES. Poems on sacred subjects: viz. the Benedicite paraphrased. The Lord's Prayer paraphrased. The Nunc Dimittis paraphrased. Balaam's blessing on Israel. Numbers, xxiv. v. 5, 6, 7, 8, 9. A hymn. The trials of virtue. The ignorance of man. Verses written originally in Persian. Matthew xi. 28. Come unto me all ye that labour. By James Merrick [etc.]. Oxford, at the Clarendon Press. MDCCLXIII. Sold by R. and J. Dodsley, in Pall-Mall, London.

4to. Bodl. Bliss B 414(2).

3rd A/cs. p. 200, dues. 500.

13. MICHAELIS, JOANNES D. Johannis Davidis Michaelis, philos. profess. ord. et Societatis Regiae Scientiarum Goettingensis collegae, in Roberti Lowth Praelectiones de sacra poesi Hebraeorum notae et epimetra. Ex Goettingensi editione praelectionum. Oxonii, e Typ. Clar. MDCCLXIII.

8vo fours. Bodl. 8° Godw. 713.

3rd A/cs. p. 200, dues. 500.

14*. NEW TESTAMENT IN GREEK. H $K\alpha\iota\nu\eta$ $\Delta\iota\alpha\theta\eta\kappa\eta$. Novum Testamentum. Juxta exemplar Millianum. Typis Joannis Baskerville. Oxonii: e Typ. Clar. MDCCLXIII. Sumptibus Academiae.

4to. Bodl. Clar. Press 1 f. 43. 8vo fours. Bodl. N.T.Gr. 1763 d. 1.

3rd A/cs. p. 203, printing 500 in quarto, 2,000 in 8vo.

15*. OXFORD, UNIVERSITY. At a meeting of the Vice-Chancellor, Heads of Houses, and Proctors of the University of Oxford, on the 30th day of March in the year of Our Lord 1763 . . . [Dealings in money with undergraduates and minors.]

Folio s. sh. Bodl. G.A. Oxon. b. 19(141).

16*. OXFORD, UNIVERSITY. [Programma and notices for the Encaenia.]

Some are in Bodl. G.A. Oxon. b. 19(142, 145, 146–7).

3rd A/cs. p. 206, printing.

17. TOTTIE, JOHN. The folly and guilt of satirical slander. A sermon preached before the University of Oxford, at Christ Church, on Sunday, February 20. 1763.

By John Tottie [etc.]. Published by request of the Vice-Chancellor and Heads of Houses. Oxford, printed at the Theatre for James Fletcher in the Turl; and sold by W. Sandby in Fleetstreet, and J. Fletcher in St. Paul's Church-Yard, London.

4to. Imp. 24 March 1763. Printer to the University. The same in 8vo fours. Bodl. G. Pamph. 127(9).

3rd A/cs. p. 200, dues. 750.

18. WEARE, THOMAS. The necessity, and means, of religious knowledge: a sermon preached before the University of Oxford, at St. Mary's, on Sunday morning, Jan. 30. 1763. By Thomas Weare [etc.]. Oxford: at the Clarendon Press. M.DCC.LXIII. Sold by Dan. Prince. And by John Rivington in St. Paul's Church-Yard, London. Price 6d.

8vo fours. Imp. 17 May 1763. Bodl. 8° M 248(14) BS.

3rd A/cs. p. 200, dues. 250.

1764

1. BENTHAM, EDWARD. De studiis theologicis. Praelectio habita in Schola Theologica Oxon. Ab Edvardo Bentham [etc.]. Oxonii, e Typ. Clar, MDCCLXIV.

8vo fours. Bodl. G. Pamph. 127(10).

3rd A/cs. p. 227, dues. 500.

2. BENTHAM, EDWARD. [Notice.] Christ Church, Oxford: July 3. 1764. Edward Bentham, Regius Professor of Divinity, proposes to give gratis a course of instruction . . .

4to. s. sh. Bodl. G.A. Oxon. b. 19(152).

3*. BURTON, JOHN. Occasional sermons preached before the University of Oxford, on publick days appointed for fasts and thanksgivings. By John Burton [etc.]. Oxford, printed at the Clarendon Press. MDCCLXIV.

[Title of Vol. ii:] Sermons preached on publick occasions, by John Burton [etc.]. Vol. II. Oxford, printed at the Clarendon Press. MDCCLXVI.

8vo. Imp. 26 May 1764. Bodl. Godw. subt. 146,7.

3rd A/cs. p. 217, printing 500.

4. [BURTON, JOHN.] The present state of navigation of the Thames considered; and certain regulations proposed. By a Commissioner. Oxford: printed for Daniel Prince. Sold by John Rivington in St. Paul's Church-Yard, London. MDCCLXIV.

8vo fours. Bodl. G. Pamph. 138(2).

3rd A/cs. p. 215, dues. 500.

5. FOTHERGILL, THOMAS. Religion and learning capable of being rendered mutually serviceable . . . [as in 1762]. The second edition. Oxford, printed at the Theatre for Daniel Prince: and sold by John Rivington in St. Paul's Church-Yard, London. MDCCLXIV.

8vo fours. Imp. 22 July 1762. Bodl. 100 aa. 12(23).

3rd A/cs. p. 215, dues. 250.

6*. (Oxford, University. Notice of a Convocation to elect a deputy Vinerian professor.

No copy found.

3rd A/cs. p. 230, printing 50.)

7. OXFORD, UNIVERSITY. A pocket companion for Oxford: or, a guide through the University. Containing an accurate description of the public edifices, the buildings in each of the colleges, the gardens, statues, busts, pictures, the hieroglyphicks at Magdalen College, and all other curiosities in the University. With an historical account of the foundation of the colleges, their history and present state. To which is prefix'd, correct lists of the Chancellors, University-Stewards, Vice-Chancellors, professors, lecturers, &c. With perspective views of Radcliffe's Library, Magdalen College New Building, New College from the garden, Peckwater Square, and the inner quadrangle of All Souls College. A new edition, corrected and much enlarged. Oxford, printed for Daniel Prince near the Clarendon Printing-House; John Rivington, in St. Paul's Church-Yard, and R. Baldwin, in Pater-noster-Row, London. 1764.

    12mo sixes. Bodl. G.A. Oxon. 16° 43.
    3rd A/cs. p. 214, dues. 2,000.

8. (Potter, John. Charge to the clergy of his diocese . . .
    No copy found.
    3rd A/cs. p. 214, dues. 250.)

9. RAWLINS, JOHN. The plan of divine revelation justified in answer to the objections of unbelievers. A sermon preached before the University of Oxford, at Christ Church on Christmas-Day, 1763. By John Rawlins [etc.]. Oxford, printed at the Theatre for James Fletcher in the Turl; and sold by J. Fletcher in St. Paul's Church-Yard, London.

    8vo fours. Imp. 17 Jan. 1764. Bodl. G. Pamph. 127(8).
    3rd A/cs. p. 214, dues. 500.

10. WEARE, THOMAS. Gratitude to God, for the Restoration, and its consequent blessings: a sermon preached before the University of Oxford, at St. Mary's, on the 29th of May, 1764. By Thomas Weare [etc.]. Oxford: at the Clarendon Press. M.DCC.LXIV. Sold by Dan. Prince. And by John Rivington in St. Paul's Church-Yard, London. (Price six-pence.)

    8vo fours. Imp. 6 Sept. 1764. Bodl. 8° H 246(9) BS.
    3rd A/cs. p. 215, dues. 200.

11. WHITE, JOHN. The usefulness and abuses of philosophy in matters of religion. A sermon preached at the visitation of the Right Reverend William Lord Bishop of Gloucester, holden at Stroud-Water, on Wednesday, May 30. 1764. By John White [etc.]. Published by desire of the Bishop. Oxford, at the Clarendon-Press. MDCCLXIV. Sold by Daniel Prince. By John Rivington in St. Paul's Church-Yard, London; and by A. Williams in West-Gate-Street, Gloucester.

    8vo fours. Imp. 26 July 1764. Bodl. 8° M 248(17) BS.
    3rd A/cs. p. 215, dues. 500.

12. [WISE, FRANCIS.] The history and chronology of the fabulous ages considered. Particularly with regard to the two ancient deities Bacchus and Hercules. By a Member of the Society of Antiquaries in London. Oxford, printed at the Theatre. MDCCLXIV.

    4to. Bodl. 4° BS 668(2).
    3rd A/cs. p. 214, dues. 120. The initials F. W. R. L. are set at the end.

1765

1. ANSALDUS, C. I. Casti Innocentis Ansaldi O.P. Placentini in Reg. Taurin. Athen. S.T. prof. De Romana tutelarium deorum in oppugnationibus urbium evocatione liber singularis. Editio quarta. Oxonii, e Typ. Clar. MDCCLXV. Prostat apud Danielem Prince, bibliop. Oxonii; & Paulum Vaillant, & Thomam Payne. Londini.
   8vo fours. Bodl. G. Pamph. 166(1).
   3rd A/cs. p. 226, dues. 250.

2. BLACKSTONE, WILLIAM. Commentaries on the laws of England. Book the first. By William Blackstone, Esq. Vinerian Professor of Law, and Solicitor-General to Her Majesty. Oxford, printed at the Clarendon Press. M.DCC.LXV.
   4to. Bodl. AA 81 Jur. Seld.
   3rd A/cs. p. 227, dues. 1,500.

3. [BUCKLER, BENJAMIN.] Stemmata Chicheleana: or, a general account of some of the families derived from Thomas Chichele, of Higham-Ferrers in the County of Northampton; all whose descendants are held to be entitled to fellowships in All Souls College, Oxford; by virtue of their consanguinity to Archbishop Chichele, the founder. Oxford, at the Clarendon Press, MDCCLXV.
   4to. Bodl. GG 83 Art.
   3rd A/cs. p. 238, dues. 500.

4. FOTHERGILL, GEORGE. Sermons on several subjects and occasions. In two volumes. By George Fothergill [etc.]. Volume the first. Oxford: at the Clarendon Press. MDCCLXV. Sold by Daniel Prince. Also by John Rivington, in St. Paul's Church-Yard, London; Mess. Thurlbourn and Woodyer at Cambridge; Mr. Leake at Bath; Mr. Score at Exeter; and Mr. Hinxman at York.
   8vo. Bodl. 100 bb. 175 (Vol. i only).
   3rd A/cs. p. 226, dues, 600. Vol. ii, 500.

5. — The second edition [Imprint as above].
   8vo. Bodl. 100 bb. 176 (Vol. ii only).

6. (Homer. The Iliad in Greek.
   No copy found.
   3rd A/cs. p. 226, dues. 750. The 4th edition at Oxford. The previous one was of 1758.)

7. KENNICOTT, BENJAMIN. A sermon preached before the University of Oxford at St. Mary's Church, on Sunday, May 19. 1765: by Benjamin Kennicott [etc.]. Published by request of Mr. Vice-Chancellor and the Heads of Houses. With notes on the sermon; on Psalms 48 and 89; and on some late reflections of the Lord Bishop of Gloucester. Oxford printed, at the Theatre: and sold by Messrs. Fletcher and Prince, in Oxford; and by Messrs. Rivington, Payne, Dodsley, and Fletcher, in London. MDCCLXV.
   8vo fours. Bodl. G. Pamph. 126.
   3rd A/cs. p. 239, dues. 500.

8. [LOWTH, ROBERT.] A letter to the Right Reverend author of the Divine Legation of Moses Demonstrated: in answer to the Appendix to the fifth volume of

that work. With an appendix containing a former literary correspondence by a late professor in the University of Oxford. Oxford printed, at the Clarendon Printing-House; and sold by A. Miller and J. Dodsley in London. MDCCLXV.

8vo fours. Imp. 24 Sept. 1765. Bodl. G. Pamph. 128(1).

3rd A/cs. p. 239, dues. 500.

9. OXFORD, CITY. Account of the Gray-Coat School in Oxford, maintained by the voluntary subscriptions of the Vice-Chancellor, Heads of Houses, and other members of the University, for six years: viz. from Michaelmas 1759 to Michaelmas 1765.

4to. Bodl. Gough Oxf. 138(17).

10*. (Oxford, University. The statutes, case, and opinion of Mr. Wilbraham [on the power to grant leases].

No copy found.

3rd A/cs. p. 230, printing 50.)

11. (Parliament, Road Acts. Two Acts of Parliament for repair of the road between Nuffield and Wallingford.

No copy found.

3rd A/cs. p. 226, dues. 250.)

12. PLATO. Platonis dialogi V. Recensuit, notisque illustravit Nath. Forster [etc.]. Editio tertia. Oxonii, e Typ. Clar., impensis Jac. Fletcher bibliopolae. MDCCLXV.

8vo fours. Imp. 10 Apr. 1745. Bodl. 290 j. 47.

3rd A/cs. p. 215, dues. 1,250. Previous editions were dated 1745 and 1752.

13. SHAW, THOMAS. The use and office, with some instances of the weakness and imperfection, of reason in matters of religion. A sermon preached at the triennial visitation of the Rev. the Dean and Chapter at the Cathedral Church of Lichfield, on Saturday, April the 20th. 1765. By Thomas Shaw [etc.]. Published at the request of the Dean, Prebendaries, and clergy. Oxford: at the Clarendon Press, MDCCLXV. Sold by Daniel Prince. Also by John Rivington in St. Paul's Church-Yard, London.

8vo fours. Imp. 15 June 1765. B.M. 4474.3.98.

3rd A/cs. p. 226, dues. 750.

1766

1. ANTHOLOGIA GRAECA. Anthologiae Graecae a Constantino Cephala conditae libri tres. Ad editionem Lipsiensem Joannis Jacobi Reiske expressi. Accedunt interpretatio Latina, poetarum anthologicorum notitia, indices necessarii. Oxonii. E Typ. Clar. Prostant venales apud Jacobum Fletcher, Oxonii: J. Nourse, P. Vaillant, et J. Fletcher, Londini. MDCCLXVI.

8vo fours. B.M. 166.l.4.

3rd A/cs. p. 239, dues. Edited by Thomas Warton, the younger.

2. BEVER, THOMAS. A Discourse on the study of jurisprudence and the civil law; being an introduction to a course of lectures: by Thomas Bever [etc.]. Oxford, printed at the Clarendon Press. M.DCC.LXVI. Sold by Daniel Prince, at Oxford; and by Benjamin White at Horace's Head, Fleetstreet, London.

4to. Imp. 20 March 1766. Bodl. G. Pamph. 156(2).

3rd A/cs. p. 239, dues. 500.

3. BLACKSTONE, WILLIAM. Commentaries on the laws of England. Book the second. By William Blackstone [etc.]. Oxford, printed at the Clarendon Press. M.DCC.LXVI.
    4to. Bodl. AA 82 Jur. Seld.
    3rd A/cs. p. 238, dues. 1,500.

4. BLACKSTONE, WILLIAM. Commentaries on the laws of England. Book the first. By William Blackstone [etc.]. The second edition. Oxford, printed at the Clarendon Press, M.DCC.LXVI.
    4to. B.M. 17.b.2.
    3rd A/cs. p. 250, dues. 1,500.

5*. BURTON, JOHN. Sermons preached on publick occasions, by John Burton [etc.]. Oxford, printed at the Clarendon Press. MDCCLXVI.
    8vo. Imp. 26 May 1764. Bodl. Godw. subt. 147.
    3rd A/cs. p. 241, printing 500. A sequel to the volume printed in 1764.

6. (Catalogue. A catalogue of books.
    Not identified.
    3rd A/cs. p. 239, dues. 500.)

7. FOTHERGILL, GEORGE. The present impunity of wicked men no argument against the justice of God's government. Illustrated in two sermons. By George Fothergill [etc.]. Oxford: at the Clarendon Press, MDCCLXVI. Sold by Daniel Prince. Also by John Rivington, in St. Paul's Church-Yard, London; Mess. Thurlbourn and Woodyer at Cambridge; Mr. Leake at Bath; Mr. Score at Exeter; and Mr. Hinxman at York.
    8vo. Bodl. 994 e. 168(8).

8. [MICKLE, WILLIAM JULIUS.] Pollio: an elegiac ode. Written in the wood near R—— Castle, 1762. Oxford, at the Clarendon Press. Sold by D. Prince: and by T. Payne, at the Mews-Gate, London. MDCCLXVI. (Price one shilling.)
    4to. Bodl. G. Pamph. 2818(14).
    3rd A/cs. p. 239, dues. 500. Halkett and Laing, *Dictionary of Anonymous and Pseudonymous English Literature*.

9. NEVE, TIMOTHY. Animadversions upon Mr. Phillips's History of the Life of Cardinal Pole. By Timothy Neve [etc.]. Oxford, at the Clarendon Press. MDCCLXVI. Sold by Dan. Prince, at Oxford; and by J. Robson, bookseller to her Royal Highness the Princess Dowager of Wales, in New-Bond-Street, London.
    8vo. Imp. 1 Nov. 1765. Bodl. 8° P 135 Linc.
    3rd A/cs. p. 238, dues. 500.

10*. (Oxford, University. [Jobbing work.]
Form of a petition to Parliament for Botley Causeway.
    No copy found.
    3rd A/cs. p. 254, printing 100.
Notice of a Convocation to appoint a delegacy for letting the Bible Press.
Order to prevent fireworks on 5 November.
Notice of a Convocation to elect Curators of the Theatre.
Report of the Delegacy for the Printing-House lease.
Notice of the election of a Vinerian Professor.
Another for a Vinerian Fellow.
Notice of the election of a Poetry Professor and a Vinerian Scholar.

Agreement of Heads of Houses as to refectories and cooks of colleges.
Programma about coffee-houses and phaetons.
Notice to Convocation of a statute against phaetons.

No copies of these found.

3rd A/cs. pp. 242, 243, 254.)

11. RANDOLPH, THOMAS. Jephtha's vow considered. A sermon preached before the University of Oxford, at St. Mary's, on Sunday, June 8. 1766. With an appendix containing a dissertation on Lev. xxvi, 28, 29. and on the nature and kinds of vows under the Mosaical law. By Thomas Randolph [etc.]. Oxford, printed at the Theatre; for J. Fletcher, in the Turl, and sold by J. Fletcher and Co. in St. Paul's Church-yard, London. MDCCLXVI.

8vo. Imp. 20 Oct. 1766. Bodl. 8° M 239(18) BS.

3rd A/cs. p. 250, dues. 500.

12. RAWLINS, JOHN. The connexion between religion and government, and the usefulness of both to civil society. A sermon preached in the Cathedral Church of Worcester, on Sunday, July 13th, 1766. at the assizes held by the Honourable His Majesty's Justices, Sir Henry Gould, and Sir Richard Aston, knights. By John Rawlins [etc.]. Published at the request of the High Sheriff and Grand Jury. Oxford, printed at the Theatre for James Fletcher in the Turl; and sold by J. Fletcher and Co. in St. Paul's Church-Yard, London, and S. Gamidge in Worcester.

8vo fours. B.M. 4474.bbb.103.

3rd A/cs. p. 239, dues. 500.

13. [SELIS, NICOLAS-JOSEPH.] L'Inoculation du bon sens. Oxfort: chez Dan. Prince. MDCCLXVI.

8vo fours. Bodl. G. Pamph. 2911(8).

3rd A/cs. p. 239, dues. 250. Quérard, Dict. des ouvrages anonymes.

14. TOTTIE, JOHN. Two charges delivered to the clergy of the Diocese of Worcester, in the years 1763 and 1766; being designed as preservatives against the sophistical arts of the Papists, and the delusions of Methodists. By John Tottie [etc.]. Published at the request of the clergy. Oxford, printed at the Theatre; and sold by J. Fletcher, in the Turl, Oxford; J. Fletcher and Co. in St. Paul's Church-yard, London; and S. Gamidge at Worcester. MDCCLXVI.

8vo. Bodl. 13025 e. 54(13).

3rd A/cs. p. 239, dues. 500.

15. [TYRWHITT, THOMAS.] Proceedings and debates in the House of Commons, in 1620 and 1621. Collected by a Member of that House. And now published from his manuscript, in the Library of Queen's College, Oxford. With an appendix: in which some passages are illustrated from other manuscripts. In two volumes. Vol. I [II]. Oxford: at the Clarendon Press. MDCCLXVI. Sold by Daniel Prince, at Oxford; and by J. Rivington, in St. Paul's Church-Yard, and J. Robson in New Bond Street, London.

8vo. Bodl. 8° F 225, 226 BS.

3rd A/cs. p. 239, dues. 750.

16. [TYRWHITT, THOMAS.] Observations and conjectures upon some passages of Shakespeare. Oxford, at the Clarendon Press. MDCCLXVI. Sold by Dan. Prince, at Oxford; by J. Rivington, in St. Paul's Church-yard, and T. Payne, near the Mews-Gate, St. Martin's, London.

8vo fours. Bodl. Malone 142.

3rd A/cs. p. 239, dues. 40. Nichols, Lit. An. v, p. 16.

1767

1. (Blackstone, William. Commentaries on the laws of England. [Book the second. 2nd edition.]
   No copy found.
   3rd A/cs. p. 250, dues. 1,000.)

2*. BURTON, JOHN. Opuscula miscellanea theologica Johannis Burton, [etc.]. Oxonii, e Typ. Clar. Apud Jac. Fletcher.
   8vo. Bodl. 1419 e. 137.
   3rd A/cs. pp. 229, 241, printing 500. Reprints of his sermons with an added title-page and list of contents.

3. CLARENDON, EDWARD, EARL OF. State papers collected by Edward, Earl of Clarendon, commencing from the year MDCXXI. containing the materials from which his History of the Rebellion is composed, and the authorities on which the truth of his relation is founded. Volume the first. Oxford, printed at the Clarendon Printing-House. MDCCLXVII.
   Fol. Bodl. I 3 13 Jur.
   3rd A/cs. p. 238, dues. 500 ordinary, 150 LP.

4. — [The same in 3 volumes 8vo.]
   B.M. 808.k.14–16.
   3rd A/cs. p. 238, dues. 500 ordinary, 250 LP.

5. HYDE, THOMAS. Syntagma dissertationum quas olim auctor doctissimus Thomas Hyde S.T.P. separatim edidit. Accesserunt nonnulla ejusdem opuscula hactenus inedita; necnon de ejus vita scriptisque προλεγομενα. Cum appendice de lingua Sinensi, aliisque linguis orientalibus una cum quampluribus tabulis aeneis quibus earum characteres exhibentur. Omnia diligenter recognita a Gregorio Sharpe [etc.]. Volumen primum [secundum]. Oxonii, e Typ. Clar. MDCCLXVII.
   4to. Imp. 20 May [no year]. Bodl. EE 130,1 Art.
   3rd A/cs. p. 251, dues. Part was printed in London.

6. OXFORD, COUNTY. An Act for repairing and widening the road from the west end of Thames Street, in the City of Oxford, over Botley Causeway, to the turnpike road near Fifield, in the County of Berks. Oxford; printed at the Clarendon Press. M.DCC.LXVII.
   8vo fours. Bodl. Gough Oxf. 138(25).
   3rd A/cs. p. 250, dues. 250.

7*. (Oxford, University. [Jobbing work.]
   Notices of a Convocation—
      of Heads of Houses for relief of the poor;
      for Mr. Long's lawsuit.
      to seal the nomination of a High Steward.
      for Dr. Frewin's will.
      for the election of a yeoman bedel.
   No copies found.
   3rd A/cs. pp. 242, 243, printing.)

8. (Prince, Daniel. Catalogue of his books for sale.
No copy found.
3rd A/cs. p. 250, dues. 500.)

9. STATIUS. The Thebaid of Statius, translated into English verse, with notes and observations; and a dissertation upon the whole by way of preface. Oxford, printed at the Clarendon Press. MDCCLXVII.
2 vols. 8vo. Bodl. 298 f. 53,4.
3rd A/cs. p. 250, dues. Preface by W. L. Lewis.

10. WEARE, THOMAS. Trust in God, in time of scarcity, recommended. A sermon preached before the University of Oxford, at St. Peter's, on Sunday, April 5. 1767. By Thomas Weare [etc.]. Oxford: printed for Daniel Prince; and sold by John Rivington in St. Paul's Church-Yard, London. (Price six-pence.)
8vo fours. Imp. 25 June 1767. Bodl. 8° X 100(1) Th.
3rd A/cs. p. 251, dues. 250.

1768

1. [BENTHAM, EDWARD.] Τῶν παλαιῶν, Θουκυδιδου, Λυσιου, Πλατωνος, Ξενοφωντος, επιταφιοι. Εν Οξονια, ετει αψξή. [On the verso:] Funeral eulogies upon military men from Thucydides, Lysias, Plato, Xenophon, in the original Greek. To which are added extracts from Cicero. With observations and notes in English. The second edition. Oxford, at the Theatre. 1768.
8vo fours. Bodl. 290 j. 44.
3rd A/cs. p. 262, dues. 1,250. The first edition was of 1746.

2. BLACKSTONE, WILLIAM. Commentaries on the Laws of England. Book the third. Oxford, printed at the Clarendon Press. M.DCC.LXVIII.
4to. Bodl. AA 83 Jur. Seld.
3rd A/cs. p. 262, dues. 3,500.

3. BLACKSTONE, WILLIAM. Commentaries on the laws of England. Book the first. By William Blackstone [etc.]. The third edition. Oxford, printed at the Clarendon Press. M.DCC.LXVIII.
4to. Bodl. 35 e. 15.
3rd A/cs. p. 250, dues. 1,500.

4. — Book the second. The third edition. M.DCC.LXVIII.
4to. Bodl. 35 e. 16.
3rd A/cs. p. 250, dues. 1,000.

5. BURTON, JOHN. Johannis Burton ad amicum epistola: sive commentariolus Thomae Secker Archiep. Cantuar. memoriae sacer. Oxonii, e Typ. Clar. MDCCLXVIII.
8vo fours. Imp. 25 Nov. 1768. Bodl. G. Pamph. 134(3).
3rd A/cs. p. 274, dues. 500.

6. C., W. Remarks upon the Reverend Mr. Whitefield's letter to the Vice-Chancellor of the University of Oxford; in a letter to the Rev. Mr. Whitefield. By a late member of the University of Oxford. Oxford; printed at the Theatre; for

J. Fletcher in the Turl; and sold by J. Fletcher and Co. in St. Paul's Church-Yard, London. MDCCLXVIII.

    8vo fours. Bodl. Gough Oxf. 61(5).

    3rd A/cs. p. 262, dues. 500.

7. HOWARD, MIDDLETON. The conquest of Quebec: a poem. By Middleton Howard [etc.]. Oxford: printed at the Theatre: for J. Fletcher in the Turl, and sold by J. Fletcher and Co. in St. Paul's Church-Yard, London. MMCCLXVIII [*sic*].

    4to. Bodl. G. Pamph. 1705(5).

    3rd A/cs. p. 274, dues. 500.

8. MUSELLI, PHILIP. Philippi Muselli ad Reverendissimum praesulem Robertum Lowth Oxoniae episcopum. Carmen votivum. Oxonii, e Typ. Clar. M.DCC.LXVIII.

    4to. Bodleian Opp. adds. 4° V 91.

    The poem is in Hebrew.

9. NOWELL, THOMAS. An answer to a pamphlet entitled Pietas Oxoniensis, or a Full and Impartial Account of the Expulsion of Six Students from St. Edmund-Hall, Oxford. In a letter to the author. By Thomas Nowell [etc.]. Oxford, at the Clarendon-Press. MDCCLXVIII. Sold by Daniel Prince. And by John Rivington in St. Paul's Churchyard, London.

    8vo. Imp. 19 Oct. 1768. Bodl. Gough Oxf. 62(5).

    3rd A/cs. p. 262, dues. 1,000.

10*. OXFORD, UNIVERSITY. Corpus statutorum Universitatis Oxoniensis: sive Pandectes constitutionum academicarum, e libris publicis et regestis universitatis consarcinatus. Oxonii, e Typ. Clar., MDCCLXVIII.

    4to. Delegates' records.

    3rd A/cs. p. 265, printing 500.

11. OXFORD, UNIVERSITY. An authentic copy of the poll for members to serve in the ensuing Parliament for the University of Oxford. Taken March xxiii. MDCCLXVIII. Candidates Sir Roger Newdigate, Bart. LL.D., George Hay, Esq; LL.D., Francis Page, Esq; LL.D., Charles Jenkinson, Esq; M.A. By permission of the Vice-Chancellor. Oxford; at the Clarendon-Press. MDCCLXVIII. Sold by Dan. Prince. And by J. Rivington and Thomas Payne in London.

    4to. Bodl. G.A. Oxon. 4° 6(5).

    3rd A/cs. p. 262, dues. 1,250.

12*. OXFORD, UNIVERSITY. A specimen of the several sorts of printing-types belonging to the University of Oxford at the Clarendon Printing-House. MDCCLXVIII.

    8vo fours. All Souls 1.Z.I.25(4).

    3rd A/cs. p. 297, printing 150. Not issued until 1770.

13*. (Oxford, University. [Jobbing work.]

Notice of a Convocation to elect a Keeper of the Archives.

A new statute to be proposed in Convocation.

Form of a petition to Parliament for the removal of East Gate.

Notice of the election of a new Member in the room of Sir W. Bagot.

Notice of two annual prizes established by the Chancellor.

Notice of the election of University Members.

Two new statutes for stated delegacies.

    No copies found.

    3rd A/cs. pp. 266–7, printing.)

14. PLUTARCH. [Title in Greek.] id est, Plutarchi Chaeronensis liber de regum atque imperatorum scite dictis, quae Apophthegmata nuncupantur. Recensuit & ornavit Stephanus Pemberton [etc.]. Oxonii, e Typ. Clar. MDCCLXVIII.
    8vo. Imp. 23 Nov. 1767. Bodl. 8° P 47 Linc.
    3rd A/cs. p. 274, dues. 750.

15. (Prince, Daniel. Catalogue of his books for sale.
    No copy found.
    3rd A/cs. p. 262, dues. 500.)

16. RANDOLPH, THOMAS. The witness of the spirit. A sermon preached before the University of Oxford. By Thomas Randolph [etc.]. Oxford: printed at the Theatre; for J. Fletcher in the Turl, and sold by J. Fletcher and Co. in St. Paul's Church-Yard, London. MDCCLXVIII.
    8vo fours. Imp. 17 March 1768. Bodl. G. Pamph. 778(20).
    3rd A/cs. p. 262, dues. 500.

17. RANDOLPH, THOMAS. The doctrine of justification by faith explained in a sermon preached before the University of Oxford, at St. Mary's, on Sunday, July 3. 1768. By Thomas Randolph [etc.]. Oxford, printed at the Theatre; for J. Fletcher in the Turl, and sold by J. Fletcher and Co. in St. Paul's Church-Yard, London. MDCCLXVIII.
    8vo fours. Imp. 10 Aug. 1768. Bodl. G. Pamph. 2708(4).
    3rd A/cs. p. 262, dues. 500.

18. RAWLINS, JOHN. The principles of infidelity and faith consider'd in a comparative view. Two discourses preached before the University of Oxford, at St. Mary's in the morning and St. Peter's in the afternoon, on the first Sunday in Lent; March 21. 1768. By John Rawlins [etc.]. Oxford: printed at the Theatre; for J. Fletcher in the Turl, and sold by J. Fletcher and Co. in St. Paul's Church-Yard, London. MDCCLXVIII.
    8vo fours. Imp. 22 March 1768. Bodl. 994 e. 420.
    3rd A/cs. p. 262, dues. 500.

19. [THEODORUS PRODROMUS.] Γαλεωμυομαχια. Οξονια. Ετει αψξη.
    4to. Bodl. Vet. A 5 d. 221.
    Attributable to the Press on typographical grounds.

1769

1. BLACKSTONE, WILLIAM. Commentaries on the laws of England. Book the fourth. By William Blackstone [etc.]. Oxford, printed at the Clarendon Press. M.DCC.LXIX.
    4to. Bodl. AA 84 Jur. Seld.
    3rd A/cs. p. 274, dues. 3,500.

2. BOULTER, HUGH. Letters written by His Excellency Hugh Boulter, D.D., Lord Primate of all Ireland, &c. to several ministers of state in England, and some others. Containing, an account of the most interesting transactions which passed in Ireland from 1731 to 1738. Volume the first. Oxford, at the Clarendon Press. Sold by

D. Prince. Sold also by R. Horsfield in Ludgate-Street, London; and by George Faulkner in Dublin. M.DCC.LXIX.

    8vo. Bodl. 8° P 37 Linc.

    3rd A/cs. p. 289, dues. 500. 'At the expense of Dr. Wall of Christ Church'.

3. (Fabellarum delectus Graec.

    No copy found.

    3rd A/cs. p. 275, dues. 500.)

4. FRAMPTON, MATTHEW. A sermon preached before the University of Oxford, at St. Mary's on Act Sunday, July ix. M.DCC.LXIX. By Matthew Frampton [etc.]. Published at the request of the Vice-Chancellor and Heads of Houses. Oxford, at the Clarendon Press. M.DCC.LXIX. Sold by Daniel Prince. By Benjamin White, in London; and by Mr. Frederick and Mr. Leake in Bath. (Price one shilling.)

    4to. Imp. 26 July 1769. Bodl. 4° D 4(19) Th.

    3rd A/cs. p. 275, dues. 1,000.

5. HAWKINS, WILLIAM. The pretences of enthusiasts, considered and confuted: a sermon preached before the University of Oxford, at St. Mary's, on Sunday, June 26. 1768. By William Hawkins [etc.]. Published by desire. Oxford, printed at the Clarendon-Press, for Dan. Prince; and sold by J. Rivington, in St. Paul's Church-Yard, London. M.DCC.LXIX.

    8vo fours. Imp. 28 Jan. 1769. Univ. Libr., Cambridge, Syn. 5.76.29⁵.

    3rd A/cs. p. 274, dues. 300.

6. HAWKINS, WILLIAM. The pretences of enthusiasts, as grounded in the Articles of the Church, considered, and refuted: a sermon preached before the University of Oxford, at St. Mary's, on Sunday, August 6. 1769. By William Hawkins [etc.]. Published by desire. Oxford, printed at the Clarendon-Press. For Dan. Prince; and sold by J. Rivington in St. Paul's Church-Yard, London. M.DCC.LXIX.

    8vo fours. Imp. 2 Oct. 1769. Bodl. G. Pamph. 1639(5).

7. HORNE, GEORGE. Considerations on the life and death of St. John the Baptist. By George Horne [etc.]. Oxford; printed at the Clarendon-Press. For S. Parker, in Oxford; sold by J. and F. Rivington in St. Paul's Church-Yard, and T. Cadell (successor to Mr. Millar), in the Strand, London. MDCCLXIX.

    8vo fours. Imp. 5 Jan. 1769. Bodl. 101 f. 623.

    3rd A/cs. p. 275, dues. 500.

8. JACOTIUS, DESIDERIUS. Desiderii Jacotii Vandoperani De philosophorum doctrina libellus ex Cicerone. Oxonii, e Typ. Clar. Impensis Dan. Prince. M.DCC. LXIX.

    8vo fours. Bodl. G. Pamph. 194.

    3rd A/cs. p. 274, dues. 500.

9. NOWELL, THOMAS. An answer to a pamphlet entitled Pietas Oxoniensis [as in 1768]. The second edition, with large additions, and a postscript, occasioned by the Reply of the same author. Oxford, at the Clarendon-Press, MDCCLXIX. Sold by Daniel Prince. And by John Rivington in St. Paul's Church-yard, London.

    8vo. Imp. 5 Jan. 1769. Bodl. G. Pamph. 130(3).

    3rd A/cs. p. 274, dues. 500.

10. OXFORD, UNIVERSITY. Bishop Barlow's State of the case, whether any books may be lent out of Sir Thomas Bodley's Library? [Dated Feb. 1769.]

    Fol. s. sh. Bodl. Gough Oxf. 96(11).

11. (Oxford, University. [Jobbing work.]
Notice of conference of degrees on Baron Leuchstat and Prof. Seyberth (56)
Notice of a Convocation to seal a petition to Parliament for a canal from Coventry
   to Oxford (56)
Form of the petition as above (60)
Second notice of a Convocation to seal the petition (56)
Notice of a Convocation to alter the hours of the Bodleian Library (50)
Order as to the altered hours (100)
Notice of a Convocation about Bledington inclosure (56)
Notice of a Convocation about Marcus Wolfe and Dr. Kennicott's request (56)
Inhibition of Marcus Wolfe (100)
List of the University's books (100)
Extract of a letter from Sir R. Newdigate (56)
Notice of a Convocation about Dr. Kennicott's request to borrow MSS. from the
   Bodleian (56)
Notice to ascertain the expense of cleaning the streets (100)
Notice of a Convocation for an address to the King (56)
Notice of a Convocation for sealing the address (56)
Notice of a letter for Sir R. Newdigate about opposition in the House of Lords to
   the canal (56)
New notice of the Chancellor's prize (56)
Notice of Dr. Fothergill's benefaction (56)
New notice of the last day for delivery of the verses on public infirmaries (56)
Notice of a Convocation to consider the matriculation of Mr. Seager.
   No copies of these found.
   3rd A/cs. pp. 279–81.)

12. PARKER, WILLIAM. The pleasures of gratitude and benevolence improved by
church-musick. A sermon preached at the anniversary meeting of the three choirs
of Gloucester, Worcester, and Hereford, in the cathedral church at Hereford, on
Wednesday, Sept. 12. 1753. By William Parker [etc.]. Published at the request of
the audience. The second edition. Oxford: printed at the Theatre; for J. Fletcher in
the Turl; and sold by R. Baldwin, at the Rose in Pater-noster-Row; and James
Wilde in Hereford. MDCCLXIX.
   8vo fours. Bodl. G. Pamph. 130(6).
   3rd A/cs. p. 262, dues. 250.

13. PARLIAMENT, ROAD ACT. An Act of Parliament for repairing the highways
from Counters Bridge, in the County of Middlesex, through Brentford and Hounslow
to the Powder Mills in the road to Staines, and to Cranford Bridge, in the same
County; and for repairing, turning, or altering the highway leading to the said
road through Sion Lane and Isleworth, to a gate on the south side of Tedington
Field; and also the highway leading out of the said great road near Smallberry Green
turnpike, to the George in the town of Isleworth aforesaid; and for lighting and
watering part of the said highways. Oxford: printed at the Clarendon Press
M.DCC.LXIX.
   8vo. Bodl. G.A. Middlesex 8° 133.
   3rd A/cs. p. 275, dues. 400. 'For Mr. James Clitherow'.

14. PARLIAMENT, ROAD ACT. An Act of Parliament to continue and render more
effective three Acts for repairing the highways between Tyburn and Uxbridge, in
the County of Middlesex; and for amending the road leading from Brent Bridge

over Hanwell Heath, through the parishes of Hanwell, New Brentford, and Ealing, to the Great Western Road in the said County; and for lighting, watching, and watering the highway between Tyburn and Kensington Gravel Pits. Oxford: printed at the Clarendon Press. M.DCC.LXIX.

8vo. B.M. 883.k.19.

3rd A/cs. p. 275, dues. 400. 'For Mr. Clitherow'. Folding map by P. Fourdrinier.

1770

1. ADEE, SWITHIN. Oratio anniversaria a Gulielmo Harveio instituta in theatro Collegii Medicorum Londinensium habita festo Sancti Lucae Oct. xviii. A.D. MDCCLXIX. Oxonii, e Typ. Clar. Prostant apud Dan. Prince; & Benj. White, Lond. MDCCLXX.

4to. Bodl. G. Pamph. 159.

3rd A/cs. p. 289, dues. 250. Dedication by Swithinus Adee. Following the Oratio, and in the same series of signatures and page-numbers is Meadus. Poema grati animi testimonium editum A.D. MDCCLV. iterumque A.D. MDCCLXIX.

2. APOLLONIUS PERGAEUS. Apollonii Pergaei Inclinationum libri duo. Restituebat Samuel Horsley, R.S.S. Oxonii, e Typ. Clar. M.DCC.LXX. Prostant venales apud Dan. Prince, Oxonii. J. Rivington, J. Nourse, P. Elmsley, & B. White, Londini. J. Woodyer, Cantabrigiae.

4to. Bodl. HH 24 Art.

3rd A/cs. p. 289, dues. 250.

3. AUHAD AL-DIN AL-NASAFI. [Title in Arabic.] Carmen Arabicum sive verba doctoris Audeddini Alnasaphi de religionis Sonniticae principiis numero vincta. Nec non Persicum. Nimirum doctoris Saadi Shirazitae operis Pomarium dicti initium, ubi de Deo T.O.M. Edidit ac Latine vertit J. Uri. Oxonii, e Typ. Clar., MDCCLXX.

4to. Bodl. 4° BS 875.

4. BLACKSTONE, WILLIAM. Commentaries on the laws of England. By William Blackstone [etc.]. Book the first [second, third]. The fourth edition. Oxford, printed at the Clarendon Press. M.DCC.LXX.

4to. All Souls Coll. 2 g 27, 3 a 122.

3rd A/cs. p. 336, dues. 3,000.

5. BOULTER, HUGH. Letters [about the state of Ireland, as in 1769]. Volume the second. [Imprint as in vol. i, but dated M.DCC.LXX].

8vo. Bodl. 8° P 37 Linc.

6. CHARLETON, RICE. An inquiry into the efficacy of warm bathing in palsies. By R. Charleton [etc.]. Oxford; at the Clarendon Press MDCCLXX. Sold by Daniel Prince in Oxford, by Benjamin White in London; and by Mr. Frederick and Mr. Lake [sic] in Bath.

8vo fours. Bodl. 8° C 133 BS.

3rd A/cs. p. 289, dues. 500.

7. ([——]. Considerations on the Corn Trade.
Not identified.

3rd A/cs. p. 289, dues. 300.)

8. KENNICOTT, BENJAMIN. The ten annual accounts of the collation of Hebrew MSS. of the Old Testament; begun in 1760, and completed in 1769: by Benjamin Kennicott [etc.]. Oxford. Sold by Mr. Fletcher and Prince, in Oxford; Mr. Woodyer in Cambridge; Mr. Rivington, Payne, Dodsley, and Fletcher, in London. MDCCLXX.

  8vo fours. Bodl. 8° Z 438(4) Th.
  3rd A/cs. p. 289, dues. 500.

9. LELAND, JOHN. The itinerary of John Leland the antiquary, in nine volumes. Published by Mr. Thomas Hearne. The third edition: printed from Mr. Hearne's corrected copy in the Bodleian Library. Oxford: printed at the Theatre; for James Fletcher, in the Turl, and Joseph Pote, at Eton College. MDCCLXX.

  8vo. Bodl. Mus. Bibl. II 38–42.
  3rd A/cs. p. 289, dues. 500. The title-pages of the volumes of the first edition are reprinted in each volume, the first dated 1768, the others 1769.

10*. LISTER, MARTIN. Martini Lister, M.D. Historiae sive synopsis methodicae conchyliorum et tabularum anatomicarum editio altera. Recensuit et indicibus auxit Gulielmus Huddesford [etc.]. Oxonii, e Typ. Clar. MDCCLXX.

  Fol. Bodl. Lister 49.
  3rd A/cs. p. 293, printing 300. First printed in London in 1685.

11*. OXFORD, UNIVERSITY. Litania et Ordo administrandae coenae Domini. Oxonii, e Typ. Clar. MDCCLXX.

  8vo fours. Bodl. C.P. Lat. 1770 e. 1.
  3rd A/cs. p. 293, printing 250.

12*. OXFORD, UNIVERSITY. Registrum privilegiorum almae Universitatis Oxoniensis. Oxonii, e Typ. Clar. MDCCLXX.

  4to. Bodl. G.A. Oxon. 4° 260.
  3rd A/cs. p. 293, printing 64. It contains two charters and an Act of Parliament.

13*. (Oxford, University. [Jobbing work.]
Notice of a Convocation to relieve the Vaudois.
Mr. Blayney's letter to the Delegates (of the Press) (160).
Mr. Majendi's petition for the Vaudois.
Form of a new statute for the Bodleian Library (60 and 80).
Notice of a new delegacy for cleaning the streets (6?).
First directions for junior academic dress (48).
Notice of a Convocation about Mr. Godwyn's will (60 and 60).
Notice of a Convocation with a letter from the Archbishop recommending American divines for degrees.
Form of a new statute De habitu (60).
Alphabets and figures for cataloguing Mr. Godwyn's books.
Notice of a Convocation to seal leases (60).
Notice of a Convocation to decide whether it has power to make a new statute De habitu (60).
Counsel's opinion on the above (60).
Answers to the three queries (60).
Notice of a Convocation to elect a lecturer of St. Giles's (60).
Statute De habitu as passed (60).

  No copies found.
  3rd A/cs. pp. 295–7, printing.)

14*. OXFORD, UNIVERSITY, UNIVERSITY PRESS. A specimen of the several sorts of printing types belonging to the University of Oxford at the Clarendon Printing-House. MDCCLXVIII.

8vo fours. All Souls Coll., 1.Z.1.25(4).

3rd A/cs. p. 297, printing 150. The last page is dated 29 September 1770.

15. OXFORD, UNIVERSITY, WORCESTER COLLEGE. Liber precum et psalmorum.

Worcester Coll. RR W7.

3rd A/cs. p. 289. dues. 150.

16. RAWLINS, JOHN. True compassion exemplified in the institution of publick infirmaries. A sermon preached in the Cathedral Church of Worcester, July 26, 1770. being the anniversary meeting of the Governors of the Worcester Infirmary. By John Rawlins [etc.]. Published at the request of the Governors. Oxford, printed for James Fletcher in the Turl, and sold by J. Rivington in St. Paul's Church-Yard, London. MDCCLXX.

8vo fours. Bodl. G. Pamph. 1639(11).

3rd A/cs. p. 289, dues. 500.

17*. THEOCRITUS. Theocriti Syracusii quae supersunt. Cum scholiis Graecis auctioribus, emendationibus et animadversionibus in scholia editoris et Johannis Toupii, glossis selectis ineditis, indicibus amplissimis. Praemittuntur editoris dissertatio de bucolicis Graecorum, vita Theocriti a Josua Barnesio scripta, cum nonnullis aliis auctariis. Accedunt editoris et variorum notae perpetuae, epistola Johannis Toupii de Syracusiis, ejusdem addenda in Theocritum, necnon collationes quindecim codicum. Edidit Thomas Warton [etc.]. Tomus primus [secundus]. Oxonii, e Typ. Clar. MDCCLXX.

4to. Bodl. I I 9, 10 Art.

3rd A/cs. p. 293, printing.

1771

1. ALDRICH, HENRY. Artis logicae compendium: E Th. Sh., An. Dom. MDCCLXXI. Impensis J. Fletcher, bibliop.

12mo. sixes. B.M. G.19401.

3rd A/cs. p. 309, dues. 750.

2. BENTHAM, EDWARD. Reflexions upon the study of divinity. To which are subjoined Heads of a course of lectures. By Edward Bentham [etc.]. Oxford, printed at the Clarendon-Press. Sold by Mess. Fletcher, Prince and Bliss, Oxford; B. White, London. MDCCLXXI.

8vo fours. Bodl. G. Pamph. 1087(1).

3rd A/cs. p. 309, dues. 750.

3. BENTHAM, EDWARD. De vita et moribus Johannis Burtoni, S.T.P. Etonensis. Epistola Edvardi Bentham, S.T.P.R. ad Reverendum admodum Robertum Lowth, S.T.P. Episcopum Oxoniensem. Oxonii: e Typ. Clar. MDCCLXXI. Prostat apud Fletcher, Prince, Bliss. Londini, apud White.

8vo fours. Bodl. 8° T 302 BS.

3rd A/cs. p. 309, dues. 500.

4. BLACKSTONE, WILLIAM. An analysis of the laws of England. By William Blackstone [etc.]. The sixth edition. Oxford, printed at the Clarendon Press. M.DCC.
LXXI.
  8vo. B.M. 6146.bbb.19.
  3rd A/cs. p. 309, dues. 1,000. 'At Daniel Prince's expense'.

5. BLACKSTONE, WILLIAM. Tracts chiefly relating to the antiquities and laws of
England. By William Blackstone [etc.]. The third edition. Oxford, printed at the
Clarendon Press. MDCCLXXI.
  4to. Bodl. Vet. A 5 d. 141.
  3rd A/cs. p. 309, dues. 1,000.

6. BURTON, JOHN. Opuscula miscellanea metrico-prosaica Johannis Burtoni [etc.].
Oxonii, e Typ. Clar. Apud Jac. Fletcher. MDCCLXXI.
  2 vols. 8vo fours. Bod. 296946 d. 1–2.
  3rd A/cs. p. 309, dues. 500.

7. EURIPIDES. Τετραλογια, sive tragoediarum delectus ex Euripide. Nempe, Medea,
Hippolytus, Iphigenia in Aulide, et in Tauride. Oxonii, e Typ. Clar., impensis Dan.
Prince. MDCCLXXI.
  8vo fours. Bodl. 2927 e. 22.
  3rd A/cs. p. 309, dues. 500.

8. HOPKINS, JOHN. An attempt to restore the true reading and rendering of the last
verse of the 4th Chapter of Nehemiah. A discourse preached before the University
of Oxford, at St. Mary's, on Sunday, Sept. 29. 1771. By John Hopkins [etc.].
Oxford, printed at the Clarendon-Press. For Dan. Prince; and sold by J. & F.
Rivington, in St. Paul's Church-yard, London. MDCCLXXI.
  8vo fours. Imp. 30 Sept. 1771. Bodl. G. Pamph. 778(21).

9*. HORNSBY, THOMAS. [A memorial for Convocation requesting it to authorize
the Delegates of the Press to lend money for equipping the University's Observatory.] Dated 5 Feb. 1771.
  4to. Bodl. Gough Oxf. 90(9).
  3rd A/cs. p. 316, printing 100.

10. (Hutchins, [Richard?]. Three sermons.
  Not found.
  3rd A/cs. p. 309, dues. 500.)

11. LOWTH, ROBERT. A sermon preached before the Governors of the Radcliffe
Infirmary at St. Mary's Church in Oxford, on Wednesday, July 3. 1771. By the
Right Reverend Robert Lord Bishop of Oxford. Published at the request of the
Governors. To which is annexed an account of the establishment of the Infirmary.
Oxford: printed at the Clarendon Press. M.DCC.LXXI. Sold for the benefit of the
Infirmary by J. and J. Fletcher, and D. Prince in Oxford; J. Dodsley and T. Cadell
in London.
  4to. Imp. 16 Sept. 1771. Bodl. G. Pamph. 1749(13).
  3rd A/cs. p. 323, dues. 1,500.

12*. OXFORD, UNIVERSITY. Parecbolae sive excerpta e corpore statutorum Universitatis Oxoniensis. Accedunt Articuli religionis XXXIX. in Ecclesia Anglicana

recepti: nec non Juramenta fidelitatis et suprematus. In usum juventutis Academicae. Oxonii, e Typ. Clar. MDCCLXXI.

 8vo fours. Bodl. Gough Oxf. 21.

 3rd A/cs. p. 313, printing 3,000.

13*. (Oxford, University. [Jobbing work.]

Notice of a Convocation to invest the endowment of the Radcliffe Infirmary in the Funds. (56)

Form for claiming drawback of duty on paper (A copy is inserted in the Minutes of the Delegates of the Press).

Heads of a Bill for repair of Magdalen Bridge and reprint as altered (100 and 80).

Notice that members of Convocation may inspect the Bill (56).

Notice of a Convocation for a letter of thanks to the King of Denmark (56).

Advertisement requesting corrections for the Catalogue of Graduates.

Notice of a Convocation to seal the Bill for improvements in paving (56).

Notice of the subject for the Chancellor's prize (100).

Rules as to chaplains at the Radcliffe Infirmary (60).

Notice of a Convocation to secure Mr. Carte's papers (60).

Notice of a Convocation for nominating supervisors of the market (60).

Notice to colleges and halls to provide chaplains for the Radcliffe Infirmary (60).

Notice of a Convocation to elect a Praelector of Poetry (60).

 No copies found.

 3rd A/cs. pp. 315–17.)

14. PLATO. [Title in Greek.] Platonis Dialogi iii. Quibus praefiguntur Olympiodori vita Platonis et Albini in dialogos Platonis introductio. Opera et studio Guil. Etwall [etc.]. Oxonii, e Typ. Clar., impensis J. & J. Fletcher bibliopolarum. MDCCLXXI.

 8vo fours. Bodl. Clar. Press 50 a. 46.

 3rd A/cs. p. 309, dues. 1,500.

15. RANDOLPH, THOMAS. The reasonableness of requiring subscription to articles of religion for persons to be admitted to holy orders or a cure of souls, vindicated in a charge delivered to the clergy of the Diocese of Oxford, in the year 1771. By Thomas Randolph [etc.]. Published at the united request of the clergy. Oxford, printed at the Clarendon-Press for J. and J. Fletcher; and sold by Mess. Rivington, St. Paul's Church-Yard, London.

 8vo fours. Imp. 14 Nov. 1771. Bodl. 8° M 239(19) BS.

 3rd A/cs. p. 323, dues. 500.

16*. SHAKESPEARE. The works of Shakespear. In six volumes. The second edition. Oxford: printed at the Clarendon Press. MDCCLXXI.

 4to. Bodl. Clar. Press 41 a. 16–21.

 3rd A/cs. pp. 293, 313, printing 500. Volumes 4, 5, 6 are dated in 1770. A reprint with additions of Hanmer's edition of 1743–4.

17. URI, JOHANNES. Epistolae Turcicae et narrationes Persicae, editae ac Latine conversae a Joh. Ury. Accedit appendix de literarum apud Persas inter se permutatione. Oxonii, e Typ. Clar. MDCCLXXI.

 4to. Bodl. G. Pamph. 167(5).

18. [An edition of Ouvrages classiques de l'élégant poète Mr. Arouet, fameux sous
le nom de Voltaire, has an imprint 'A Oxford, pour les Académiciens. MDCCLXXI'.
Émile Weller, *Dictionnaire des ouvrages français portant de fausses indications des lieux
d'impression et des imprimeurs* (Leipzig, 1864), p. 189, ascribes it to Paris with a query.]

1772

1. DURELL, DAVID. Critical remarks on the Books of Job, Proverbs, Psalms,
Ecclesiastes, and Canticles. By D. Durell [etc.]. Oxford: printed at the Clarendon
Press. MDCCLXXII.
   4to. Imp. 14 Feb. 1772. Bodl. Clar. Press 1 f. 44.
   3rd A/cs. p. 323, dues. 500.

2. HOMER. Ομηρου Ιλιας. Homeri Ilias Graece. Editio altera. Oxonii, e Th. Sh.,
1772. Impensis J. & J. Fletcher, bibliop. Oxon. Prostat apud J. Rivington, Lond.
J. Ginger, Westmonast. J. Pote, Eton. & Jos. Burdon, Winton.
   8vo fours. Imp. 19 Oct. 1713. Brasenose Coll. Σ C.3.6.
   3rd A/cs. p. 323, dues. 1,000.

3. [HUDDESFORD, WILLIAM, ed.] The lives of those eminent antiquaries John
Leland, Thomas Hearne, and Anthony a Wood; with an authentick account of their
respective writings and publications, from original papers. In which are occasionally
inserted memoirs relating to many eminent persons and various parts of literature.
Also, several engravings of antiquity, never before published. In two volumes.
Vol. i. Oxford: printed at the Clarendon Press, for J. and J. Fletcher in the Turl, and
Joseph Pote, at Eton College. MDCCLXXII.
   8vo fours. Bodl. Mus. Bibl. II 103.
   3rd A/cs. p. 323, dues. 750. According to Madan, Huddesford was the editor.

4. [JONES, WILLIAM.] Poems consisting chiefly of translations from the Asiatick
languages. To which are added two essays, I. on the poetry of the Eastern nations.
II. on the arts commonly called imitative. Oxford, at the Clarendon-Press.
MDCCLXXII. Sold by Peter Elmsly, in the Strand, London; and Dan. Prince, at
Oxford.
   8vo fours. Bodl. 3967 e. 2.
   3rd A/cs. p. 336, dues. 750. See *D.N.B.*

5*. OXFORD, UNIVERSITY. A catalogue of all graduates in divinity, law, and
physick; and of all Masters of Arts and Doctors of Musick, who have regularly proceeded or been created in the University of Oxford, between October 10, 1659. and
October 10, 1770. To which are added, the Chancellors, High-Stewards, Vice-
Chancellors and Proctors, from the year 1659 to 1770. Also the Burgesses for the
University, from the year 1603 to 1770. Oxford: printed at the Clarendon Press, in
the year MDCCLXXII.
   8vo. Bodl. G.A. Oxon. 8° 335.
   3rd A/cs. pp. 326, 339, printing 500.

6*. (Oxford, University. [Jobbing work.]
Notice of a Convocation to confer degrees on Messrs. Banks and Solander.
Notice of a Convocation for a letter of thanks to the King for the Journals of the

House of Lords and House of Commons (56).
Reasons against the Nullum tempus Bill (500).
Notice of a Convocation to elect a Vinerian scholar (60).
History and state of the 39 Articles (204).
Notice of the Chancellor's prize for 1772 (100).
Notice of a Convocation to hear a report on Mr. Carte's papers (60).
Advertisements of Lister's Synopsis in Latin and French (250).
Form of a statute to forbid undergraduates to keep servants, horses, and dogs (60).
The same, as amended (60).
The same, as passed (500).
Programma for enjoining order in the Theatre at the Encaenia (100).
Notice of the election of a Chancellor (600).
Reprint of the new statute for the Bodleian Library (250).

No copies found.
3rd A/cs. pp. 327–30.)

7. OXFORD, UNIVERSITY, BRASENOSE COLLEGE. Statuta Aulae regiae et Collegii de Brasenose in Oxonio. Subjiciuntur excerpta ex compositionibus et testamentis benefactorum et alia quaedam notatu digna ad idem collegium pertinentia. A.D. MDCCLXXII.
8vo fours. Bodl. G.A. Oxon. 8° 30.

8. RAWLINS, JOHN. A dissertation upon heretical opinions, giving a short distinctive view of the principal errors, which have prevailed in all the several ages of the Church, and shewing that there are no reasonable objections against the truth of Christianity, nor any grounds for the false pretences of popery or infidelity. By John Rawlins [etc.]. Oxford: at the Clarendon Press, M.DCC.LXXII.
8vo fours. Bodl. Vet. A 5 e. 2049.

9*. ROBINSON, ROBERT. Indices tres vocum fere omnium quae occurrunt, I. in Dionysii Longini Commentario de sublimitate, et in ejusdem fragmentis. II. in Eunapii libro de vitis philosophorum et sophistarum. III. in Hieroclis Commentario in Pythagorae Aurea carmina. Concinnavit Robertus Robinson. Oxonii, e Typ. Clar., MDCCLXXII.
8vo fours. Bodl. 304 e. 179.
3rd A/cs. pp. 313, 339, printing 500.

10. TOTTIE, JOHN. A charge relative to the Articles of the Church of England, delivered to the clergy of the Archdeaconry of Worcester in the year MDCCLXXII. and published at their request. By John Tottie [etc.]. Oxford, printed at the Clarendon-Press; for J. and J. Fletcher in the Turl; and sold by Mess. Rivington in St. Paul's Church-Yard, London, and Mess. Merril at Cambridge.
8vo fours. Imp. 9 May 1772. Bodl. G. Pamph. 202(1).
3rd A/cs. pp. 323, 336, dues. 750.

11. XENOPHON. [Title in Greek.] Xenophontis Memorabilium Socratis dictorum libri iv. Cum notis Stephani, Leunclavii, Æ. Porti & Ernesti. Recensuit, suisque annotationibus auxit Bolton Simpson [etc.]. Editio quarta, emendatior. Cui accessere notulae quaedam non prius editae. Oxonii, e Th. Sh. impensis J. and J. Fletcher, bibliopol. Oxon. et Joannis Rivington, Lond. MDCCLXXII.
8vo fours. Bodl. 8° E 269 BS.
3rd A/cs. p. 309, dues. 1,250. Previous editions were of 1741, 1749, and 1759.

12. XENOPHON. Ξενοφωντος Κυρου παιδειας βιβλια οκτω. Oxonii, e Typ. Clar.,
M.DCC.LXXII.

8vo fours. Bodl. 2354 e. 7.
3rd A/cs. p. 323, dues. 500.

13. XENOPHON. Ξενοφωντος Κυρου αναβασεως βιβλια επτα. Oxonii, e Typ. Clar.,
M.DCC.LXXII.

8vo fours. Bodl. 2354 e. 22.

1773

1. ALLEN, JOHN. Associations against the established Church indefensible. A
sermon preached before the University of Oxford at St. Mary's on Monday,
February 24. 1772. By John Allen [etc.]. Oxford: printed at the Clarendon Press.
Sold by S. Parker and D. Prince; and J. Rivington in St. Paul's Church-yard, London.
M.DCC.LXXIII.

8vo fours. Bodl. 100 aa. 13(4).

2. BLACKSTONE, WILLIAM. Commentaries on the laws of England In four Books.
By William Blackstone, Esq. Solicitor General to Her Majesty. The fifth edition.
Oxford, at the Clarendon Press, MDCCLXXIII. Printed for William Strahan,
Thomas Cadell, and Daniel Prince.

8vo. Univ. Libr., Cambridge, Ant. c.28.573–6.
3rd A/cs. p. 361, dues. 3,000.

3. CLARENDON, EDWARD, EARL OF. State papers collected by Edward, Earl of
Clarendon. Volume the second. Oxford: at the Clarendon-Press. MDCCLXXIII.

Fol. Bodl. I 3. 14 Jur.
3rd A/cs. p. 336, dues. 500 small, 150 LP.

4. COOKE, JOHN. The unlawfulness of private revenge. A sermon preached at the
assizes at Winchester, before the Honourable Mr. Baron Adams, and Mr. Justice
Ashurst, on Tuesday, July 27. 1773. By John Cooke, [etc.]. Published at the request
of the judges, the High-Sheriff, and the gentlemen of the Grand-Jury. Oxford: at the
Clarendon Press, M.DCC.LXXIII. Sold by Sackville Parker and Daniel Prince; by
John and Francis Rivington, in London; by John Burdon at Winchester; and E.
Easton at Salisbury.

8vo fours. Bodl. 100 r. 283(1).

5. GRIFFITH, THOMAS. A sermon preached before the University of Oxford, at
St. Mary's, on Act Sunday, July the 11th. 1773. By Thomas Griffith [etc.]. Published at the request of the Vice-Chancellor and Heads of Houses. Oxford: printed
at the Clarendon Press. Sold by Daniel Prince; and by J. Rivington in St. Paul's
Church-Yard, London. MDCCLXXIII.

8vo fours. Bodl. 100 aa. 13(5).
3rd A/cs. p. 336, dues. 500.

6. GRIFFITH, THOMAS. The difficulties and due discharge of the ministerial office
in the present age. A sermon preached before the University of Oxford, at St. Mary's,
on Sunday, November 27, 1757. By Thomas Griffith [etc.]. Published at the request

of Mr. Vice-Chancellor and the Heads of Houses. The second edition. Oxford: printed at the Clarendon Press. Sold by Daniel Prince; and by J. Rivington in St. Paul's Church-Yard, London. MDCCLXXIII.

8vo fours. Imp. 5 Dec. 1757. B.M. 4475.aaa.48.

7. GRIFFITH, THOMAS. The evils arising from misapply'd curiosity. A sermon preached before the University of Oxford, at St. Mary's, on Sunday, March 9, 1760. By Thomas Griffith [etc.]. Published at the request of Mr. Vice-Chancellor and the Heads of Houses. The second edition. Oxford: printed at the Clarendon Press. Sold by Daniel Prince; and by J. Rivington, in St. Paul's Church-Yard, London. MDCCLXXIII.

8vo fours. Imp. 20 March 1760. B.M. 4473.e.10(7).

8. GRIFFITH, THOMAS. The use and extent of reason in matters of religion. A sermon preached before the University of Oxford at St. Mary's, on Tuesday in Whitsun-week, June 8, 1756. By Thomas Griffith [etc.]. Published at the request of Mr. Vice-Chancellor and the Heads of Houses. The second edition. Oxford: printed at the Clarendon Press. Sold by Daniel Prince; and by J. Rivington, in St. Paul's Church-Yard, London. MDCCLXXIII.

8vo fours. B.M. 225.g.5(10).

9. HAWKINS, THOMAS. The origin of the English drama, illustrated in its various species, viz. mystery, morality, tragedy, and comedy, by specimens from our earliest writers: with explanatory notes by Thomas Hawkins [etc.]. Volume the first [second, third]. Oxford, printed at the Clarendon-Press, for S. Leacroft, Charing Cross, London. And sold by D. Prince at Oxford, and J. Woodyer at Cambridge. M.DCC.LXX.III.

12mo eights. Bodl. 8° Q 139–41 Linc.

10. HAWKINS, WILLIAM. The principle of the confessional considered and confuted, by the substance of two sermons preached before the University of Oxford in the years 1772 and 1773. By William Hawkins [etc.]. Oxford: printed at the Clarendon Press. Sold by Daniel Prince; and by J. Rivington, St. Paul's Church-Yard, London. MDCCLXXIII.

8vo. Imp. 1 Aug. 1773. Pembroke College M I b(3).

11. HORNE, GEORGE. The influence of Christianity on civil society. A sermon preached at St. Mary's, in Oxford, at the assizes: before the Honourable Mr. Justice Nares, and Mr. Baron Eyre; and before the University; on Thursday, March 4, 1773. By George Horne [etc.]. Published at the request of the judges. Oxford: at the Clarendon Press. M.DCC.LXXIII. Sold by Daniel Prince; and by John and Francis Rivington, London.

8vo fours. Imp. 17 March 1773. Bodl. 8° M 239(3) BS.
3rd A/cs. p. 336, dues. 500.

12. MARKHAM, WILLIAM. A Sermon preached at St. Mary's Church in Oxford, on Tuesday, July 6, 1773. on occasion of the anniversary meeting of the governors of the Radcliffe Infirmary: by William Lord Bishop of Chester. Published at the request of the governors for the benefit of the charity. Oxford: printed at the Clarendon Press. M.DCC.LXXIII.

4to. Imp. (by the Chancellor) 8 Nov. 1773. Bodl. G. Pamph. 519(3).
3rd A/cs. p. 349, dues. 750.

13*. OXFORD, UNIVERSITY. Ode at the Encaenia, held at Oxford, July 1773, for the reception of the Right Honourable Frederic Lord North, Chancellor of the

University. The words by Dr Wheeler; set to musick by Dr Hayes. Oxford, at the Clarendon Press. M.DCC.LXXIII. Sold by Daniel Prince.

4to. Bodl. Gough Oxf. 90(27).
Words only.

14*. OXFORD, UNIVERSITY. [Jobbing work.]
Notice of a Convocation to seal bonds for the new market.
Notice and form of a new subscription at matriculation.
Form of the new intended statute (10).
Notice of the Chancellor's prize 1773 (200).
Notice of a Convocation to propose a new statute Tit. II, III with an explanation.
Notice of a Convocation on the statute.
Case on the statute (60).
Explanation of the postscript to the case (60).
Notice of a Convocation with a form of new statute.
Notice of a Convocation to elect a curate for Llanganfeling.
Programma on an insult to the Proctors.
Orders to be observed during Commemoration and the Chancellor's visit.
Orders to be observed during the sermon.
List of speakers in the Theatre (300).
Notice of a Convocation to authorize the Vinerian Professor to lecture by deputy.
Notice of a Convocation to consider a proposal to lend £2,000 on the new market.

The above, in so far as they relate to subscription to the Articles at matriculation, are in Bodl. G.A. Oxon. b. 17.

3rd A/cs. pp. 340–3.

15. RANDOLPH, THOMAS. The excellency of the Jewish law vindicated. In two sermons preached before the University of Oxford, at St. Mary's. To which is added an appendix: and also a short comment on Psal. cix. and lv. wherein they are shown not to be imprecatory but prophetical. By Thomas Randolph [etc.]. Oxford: printed for J. and J. Fletcher in the Turle; and sold by J. and F. Rivington, in St. Paul's Church-Yard, London; and Messrs. Merril at Cambridge. M.DCC.LXXIII.

8vo fours. Imp. 22 March 1773. Bodl. 8° M 239(20) BS.
3rd A/cs. p. 336, dues. 500.

16. WHITFIELD, HENRY. A sermon preached before the University of Oxford, in St. Mary's Church, on Act Sunday, July the 11th. 1773. By Herny [sic] Whitfield [etc.]. Published at the request of the Vice-Chancellor, and the Heads of Houses. Oxford: printed At the Clarendon Press. Sold by Daniel Prince; and by John Pridden, No. 100, Fleetstreet, London. MDCCLXXIII.

4to. Imp. 13 July 1773. Bodl. 994 d. 2(6).
3rd A/cs. p. 336, dues. 500.

1774

1. BENTHAM, EDWARD. Reflexions upon the study of divinity. [as in 1771] The second edition. Oxford. Printed at the Clarendon-Press. Sold by Mess. Fletcher, Prince and Bliss, Oxford; B. White, London. MDCCLXXIV.

8vo fours. Bodl. G. Pamph. 908(2).
3rd A/cs. p. 349, dues. 1,000.

2. BINGHAM, GEORGE. A vindication of the doctrine and liturgy of the Church of England occasioned by the Apology of Theophilus Lindsey, M.A. on resigning the vicarage of Catterick, Yorkshire, by George Bingham [etc.]. Oxford, at the Clarendon Press. MDCCLXXIV. Sold by Daniel Prince; and by John and Francis Rivington in St. Paul's Church-Yard, London.
  8vo fours. Bodl. 8° Y 310(4) BS.
  3rd A/cs. p. 349, dues. 500.

3. CHANDLER, RICHARD. Inscriptiones antiquae, pleraeque nondum editae: in Asia Minori et Graecia, praesertim Athenis, collectae. Cum appendice. Exscripsit ediditque Ricardus Chandler [etc.]. Oxonii, e Typ. Clar. MDCCLXXIV. Prostant apud J. Dodsley, Jac. Robson, et Tho. Cadell, Londini; et Dan. Prince, Oxonii.
  Fol. Imp. 7 March 1774. Bodl. A 5 15 Art.
  3rd A/cs. p. 349, dues. 250.

4. HARIRI. Abi Mohammed Alcasim vulgo dicti Hariri eloquentiae Arabicae principis quinquagesimus consessus Basrensis e codice manuscripto Bibliothecae Bodleianae Latine conversus a Joh. Ury. Accedunt dialogi Persico-Anglici. Oxonii, e Typ. Clar. MDCCLXXIV.
  4to. Bodl. 4° AS 147.

5. HORBERY, MATTHEW. Eighteen sermons on important subjects. By Matthew Horbery [etc.]. Published from the original manuscripts by Jeoffry Snelsum [etc.]. Oxford: at the Clarendon-Press, MDCCLXXIV. Sold by Daniel Prince; and by John and Francis Rivington, and Thomas Cadell, in London.
  8vo. Bodl. 8° D 173 BS.
  3rd A/cs. p. 349, dues. 750.

6*. (Oxford, University. [Jobbing work.]
Notice of a Convocation to augment the salary of the Keeper of the Museum (60).
Form of discommoning James Kemp (150).
Notice of the Chancellor's prizes (120).
Quaestiones logicae in Parvisiis (440).
Quaestiones in Augustinibus (200).
Form of discommoning Mr. Wynne.
List of University books for Mr. Elmsly (300).
Statute De habitu (200).
Programma to preserve order in the Theatre on 5 July.
Notice of a Convocation to allow the Vinerian Professor to lecture by deputy.
  No copies found.
  3rd A/cs. pp. 352–5.)

7. PYE, HENRY JAMES. Faringdon Hill. A poem in two books. Oxford: printed for Daniel Prince; and sold by J. Wilkie at No. 71 St. Paul's Church-Yard, London. MDCCLXXIV.
  4to. Bodl. Gough Berks. 3(28).
  3rd A/cs. p. 349, dues. 250.

8. [RANDOLPH, THOMAS.] Answer to a pamphlet entituled Considerations on the Propriety of Requiring a Subscription to the Articles of Faith. Oxford. At the Clarendon Press. Printed for J. and J. Fletcher in the Turle; and sold by Mess. Rivington, in St. Paul's Church-yard, London. MDCCLXXIV.

8vo fours. Bodl. 8° M 248 BS. Inscribed 'From the author Dns. Randolph, Pres. C.C.C.'

3rd A/cs. p. 349, dues. 500.

9. [WARTON, THOMAS.] Mons Catharinae, prope Wintoniam. Poema. Editio tertia emendatior. Oxonii, e Typ. Clar. MDCCLXXIV.

4to. Bodl. G. Pamph. 498(5).

The previous editions were not printed here.

1775

1. BLACKSTONE, WILLIAM. Commentaries on the laws of England. in four books. By William Blackstone [etc.]. The seventh edition. Oxford, at the Clarendon Press, MDCCLXXV. Printed for William Strahan, Thomas Cadell, and Daniel Prince.

8vo. Bodl. 35 a. 37–40.

3rd A/cs. p. 409, dues. 3,000.

2. BLAYNEY, BENJAMIN. A dissertation by way of inquiry into the true import and application of the vision related Dan. IX. ver. 20. to the end, usually called, Daniel's Prophecy of Seventy Weeks. With some occasional remarks on the very learned J. D. Michaelis's letters to Sir John Pringle on the same subject. By Benjamin Blayney [etc.]. Oxford: at the Clarendon Press. MDCCLXXV.

4to. Imp. 22 Oct. 1774. Bodl. XX 46(5) Th.

3rd A/cs. p. 361, dues. 500.

3. [BUCKLER, BENJAMIN.] A supplement to Stemmata Chicheleana; containing corrections, and very large additions to the tables of descents from Thomas Chichele, of Higham-Ferrers in the County of Northampton; all whose descendants are held to be entitled to fellowships in All Souls College, Oxford; by virtue of their consanguinity to Arch-Bishop Chichele, the founder. Oxford, at the Clarendon Press MDCCLXXV.

4to. Bodl. GG 84 Art.

3rd A/cs. p. 361, dues. 450.

4. CHANDLER, RICHARD. Travels in Asia Minor: or an account of a tour made at the expense of the Society of Dilettanti. By Richard Chandler [etc.]. Oxford: printed at the Clarendon Press. M.DCC.LXX.V. Sold by J. Dodsley, J. Robson, T. Cadell, P. Elmsly, and G. Robinson, London; and by D. Prince, Oxford.

4to. Bodl. AS 513.

3rd A/cs. p. 361, dues. 500.

5. HOMER. The beauties of Homer selected from the Iliad. By William Holwell [etc.]. Oxford: printed for J. and J. Fletcher in the Turle: and sold by J. and J. Rivington in St. Paul's Church-yard, London. MDCCLXXV.

8vo. Bodl. 8° Q 138 Linc.

3rd A/cs. p. 361, dues. 750. Extracts in Greek. The corresponding English versions were published in 1776.

6. HORNE, GEORGE. Christ the object of religious adoration; and therefore very God. A sermon preached before the University of Oxford, at St. Mary's, on Sunday,

May 14, 1775. By George Horne [etc.]. Oxford: at the Clarendon Press. M.DCC. LXXV. Sold by Daniel Prince; and by John and Francis Rivington, London.

8vo fours. Imp. 26 May 1775. Bodl. 8° M 239(4) BS.

3rd A/cs. p. 361, dues. 500.

7. HORNE, GEORGE. The providence of God manifested in the fall of empires. A sermon preached at St. Mary's, in Oxford, at the assizes: before the Honourable Mr. Baron Eyre, and Mr. Baron Hotham; and before the University; on Thursday, July 27. 1775. By George Horne [etc.]. Oxford: at the Clarendon Press. M.DCC. LXXV. Sold by Daniel Prince; and by John and Francis Rivington, London.

8vo fours. Imp. 16 Oct. 1775. Bodl. 8° M 239(5) BS.

3rd A/cs. p. 377, dues. 500.

8. HUNT, THOMAS. Observations on the Book of Proverbs; in two sermons: by Thomas Hunt [etc.]. Oxford, printed at the Clarendon Press: sold by D. Prince; and J. Rivington, London. MDCCLXXV.

4to. Bodl. XX 46(4) Th.

3rd A/cs. p. 361, dues. 500.

9*. LACROZE, MATURINUS V. Lexicon Aegyptiaco-Latinum, ex veteribus illius linguae monumentis summo studio collectum et elaboratum a Maturino Veyssiere Lacroze, quod in compendium redegit, ita ut nullae voces Aegyptiacae, nullaeque earum significationes omitterentur, Christianus Scholtz [etc.]. Notulas quasdam, et indices, adjecit Carolus Gotofredus Woide. Oxonii: e Typ. Clar. MDCCLXXV.

4to. Bodl. FF 38 Jur.

3rd A/cs. pp. 351, 365, printing 250.

10. LOWTH, ROBERT. De sacra poesi Hebraeorum. Praelectiones academicae Oxonii habitae a Roberto Lowth [etc.]. Subjicitur metricae Harianae brevis confutatio: et oratio Creweiana. Editio tertia emendatior. Oxonii, e Typ. Clar. MDCCLXXV.

8vo. Imp. 1 Feb. 1753. Bodl. Opp. adds. 4° V 262.

3rd A/cs. p. 361, dues. 750. The previous editions were of 1753 and 1763.

11. NICOLL, RICHARD. False pretensions to science pointed out, and true knowledge recommended. A sermon preached before the University of Oxford, at St. Mary's, on Act Sunday, July 9, 1775. By Richard Nicoll [etc.]. Published at the request of the Vice-Chancellor, and Heads of Houses. Oxford: at the Clarendon Press. MDCCLXXV. Sold by J. and J. Fletcher; by John & Francis Rivington, London; and Thomas and John Merrill, Cambridge.

8vo fours. Imp. 3 Aug. 1775. Bodl. 100 aa. 13(6).

3rd A/cs. p. 361, dues. 500.

12*. OXFORD, UNIVERSITY, UNIVERSITY PRESS. [A supplement to the specimen of type dated 1768 and issued in 1770. Heading on fol. 1ʳ:] New letters purchased in the years 1771, 1772, 1773, 1774.

8vo fours. All Souls Coll. in LZ 125.

3rd A/cs. p. 368, printing.

13*. (Oxford, University. [Jobbing Work.]

Notice of electing burgesses.

Notice of a Convocation to seal an answer to a bill in Chancery.

A proposal to build an Episcopal church in Edinburgh (66).

Mr. Fawconer's memoir about an edition of Strabo.

Notice of the Chancellor's prizes (120).
Notice of a Convocation to confer the degree of D.C.L. on Mr. Johnson.
The same, on Mr. Nikitin and Mr. Suveroff.
Notice of a Convocation to continue the Vinerian Professor for a year.
Notice of a Convocation to elect a Vinerian Scholar.

No copies found.
3rd A/cs. pp. 366–9.)

14. RANDOLPH, THOMAS. A vindication of the worship of the Son and the Holy
Ghost against the exceptions of Mr. Theophilus Lindsey from Scripture and antiquity, being a supplement to a treatise formerly published and entitled A Vindication of the Doctrine of the Trinity. By Thomas Randolph [etc.]. Oxford: printed by
J. and J. Fletcher in the Turle: and sold by J. and F. Rivington, in St. Paul's Church-
Yard, London: T. and J. Merrill, at Cambridge, and J. Smith in Canterbury. 1775.
8vo fours. Imp. 14 Feb. 1775. Bodl. 8° Y 313(2) BS.
3rd A/cs. p. 361, dues. 500.

15. TRAPP, JOSEPH. Explanatory notes upon the four Gospels: in a new method.
For the use of all, but especially the unlearned English reader. In two parts. To
which are prefixed, three discourses relating to both parts; of which an account is
given in the preface. By Joseph Trapp [etc.]. The second edition, corrected. Oxford:
printed for Daniel Prince: and sold by J. Rivington, St. Paul's Church-Yard, London.
MDCCLXXV.
8vo. Bodl. 1016 e. 7.
3rd A/cs. p. 361, dues. 500.

1776

1. [BENTHAM, EDWARD.] De tumultibus Americanis deque eorum concitatoribus
meditatio senilis. Oxonii: e Typ. Clar. Apud J. Fletcher, & D. Prince; B. White,
Londini. MDCCLXXVI.
8vo. Bodl. 8° C 114(6) BS.
3rd A/cs. p. 377, dues. 750.

2. CHANDLER, RICHARD. Travels in Greece: or an account of a tour made at the
expense of the Society of Dilettanti. By Richard Chandler [etc.]. Oxford: printed at
the Clarendon Press. M.DCC.LXX.VI.
4to. Bodl. 4° BS 163.
3rd A/cs. p. 377, dues. 500.

3. HOMER. Extracts from Mr. Pope's translation corresponding with The Beauties
of Homer selected from the Iliad. By William Holwell [etc.]. Oxford: printed for
J. and J. Fletcher in the Turle: and sold by J. and J. Rivington in St. Paul's Church-
yard, London. MDCCLXXVI.
8vo. Bodl. 2931 e. 63.
3rd A/cs. p. 377, dues. 750.

4. HORNE, GEORGE. A commentary on the Book of Psalms, in which the literal, or
historical sense, as they relate to King David, and the people of Israel, is illustrated;
and their application to Messiah, to the Church, and to individuals, as members

thereof, is pointed out: with a view to making the use of the psalter pleasing and profitable to all orders and degrees of Christians. Volume the first [second]. By George Horne [etc.]. Oxford: at the Clarendon Press. MDCCLXXVI. Sold by Daniel Prince; and by John Rivington, T. Payne, T. Cadell, and G. Robinson, London.

2 vols. 4to. Bodl. OO 54, 5 Th.

3rd A/cs. p. 377, dues. 500.

5. HORNE, GEORGE. Christ the object of religious adoration [as in 1775]. The second edition. Oxford: at the Clarendon Press. M.DCC.LXX.VI.

8vo fours. Imp. 26 May 1775. B.M. 4473.e.10(8).

3rd A/cs. p. 377, dues. 250.

6. KENNICOTT, BENJAMIN. Vetus Testamentum Hebraicum, cum variis lectionibus. Edidit Benjaminus Kennicott [etc.]. Tomus primus. Oxonii, e Typ. Clar. MDCCLXXVI.

Fol. Bodl. Z 2. 16 Th.

3rd A/cs. p. 377, dues. 650.

7. LUCIAN. [Title in Greek.] Luciani Samosatensis quomodo historia conscribenda sit. Edidit ac notis illustravit Franciscus Riollay A.M. Oxonii, e Typ. Clar. Impensis J. & J. Fletcher bibliop. Oxon. MDCCLXXVI.

8vo fours. Bodl. 8° Q 107 Linc.

3rd A/cs. p. 377, dues. 1,000.

8. MAURICE, THOMAS. Netherby: a poem. By Mr. Maurice of University College, Oxford. Oxford: at the Clarendon Press. MDCCLXXVI. Sold by J. and J. Fletcher and D. Prince; by G. Kearsley, Fleetstreet, and W. Shropshire, New-Bond-Street, London.

4to. Bodl. I I 33(16) Art.

3rd A/cs. p. 377, dues. 500.

9. [NAPLETON, JOHN.] Elementa logicae. Subjicitur appendix de usu logicae: et conspectus Organi Aristotelis. Editio altera. Oxonii, e Typ. Clar. impensis Dan. Prince. M.DCC.LXXVI.

8vo fours. Bodl. 8° Q 112 Linc.

3rd A/cs. p. 377, dues. 500.

10*. (Oxford, University. [Jobbing work.]
Notice of a Convocation to address His Majesty on the American Rebellion.
Form of discommoning Leonard Wood.
Notice of a Convocation to give the degree of D.C.L. to Mr. Foster.
The same, to elect a Curator of the Theatre.
Notice of the Chancellor's prizes (150).
Notice to elect a squire bedel *vice* Walker.
Notice of a Convocation to relieve Church of England clergy in North America.
Notice of a Convocation to give £200 to rebuild the Physick Garden house and
    library.
Notice of a Convocation to elect a Public Orator.
The same to elect a Vinerian Fellow.
The same to elect a Vinerian Scholar.
A programma to preserve order in the Theatre on 4 July.
Notice of a proposal to accept rent for South Petherwin.

No copies found.
3rd A/cs. pp. 381–5.)

11. WARNEFORD, JOHN. Sermons on several subjects and occasions. by John Warneford [etc.]. Volume the first [second]. Oxford: at the Clarendon Press MDCCLXXVI. Sold by J. and J. Fletcher, and D. Prince, Oxford; Mess. Rivington, in London; and T. and J. Merrill in Cambridge.
    2 vols. 8vo. Bodl. 8° Q 145, 6.
    3rd A/cs. p. 377, dues. 1,000.

12. WHITE, JOSEPH. De utilitate linguae Arabicae, in studiis theologicis, oratio; habita Oxonii, in Schola Linguarum, vii Id. Aprilis, MDCCLXXV: auctore Josepho White [etc.]. Oxonii, e Typ. Clar. MDCCLXXVI.
    4to. Bodl. G. Pamph. 160(7).

1777

1*. APOLLONIUS RHODIUS. Apollonii Rhodii Argonauticorum libri quatuor. Edidit, nova fere interpretatione illustravit, priorum editorum notas praecipuas selegit, Sanctamandi nunquam prius editis nonnullas suas adjecit, necnon indices tres addidit, Joannes Shaw [etc.]. Tomus primus [secundus]. Oxonii, e Typ. Clar. MDCCLXXVII.
    2 vols. 4to. Printer to the University.
    3rd A/cs. pp. 351, 365, 380, 397, printing 250 LP.

2. CHELSUM, JAMES. The character of the laws of England considered. A sermon preached on Thursday, March 6, 1777, in St. Mary's Church, Oxford, at the assizes, before the Honourable Mr. Baron Eyre and Mr. Baron Perryn, and before the University. By James Chelsum [etc.]. Published at the request of the Judges. Oxford: printed for Daniel Prince. Sold also by J. F. and C. Rivington, in St. Paul's Church-Yard; T. Payne and Son, at the Mews-Gate; and J. Robson and Co., New Bond-street, London. MDCCLXXVII.
    4to. Imp. 22 March 1777. Bodl. 994 d. 2(7).
    3rd A/cs. p. 393, dues. 400.

3. [CLEAVER, WILLIAM.] Decretum Lacedaemoniorum contra Timotheum Milesium, e codd. msstis. Oxoniensibus, cum commentario. Oxonii, M.DCC.LXXVII.
    8vo fours. Bodl. 8° S 165 Linc.
    3rd A/cs. p. 409, dues. 250.

4. COOPER, MYLES. National humiliation and repentance recommended, and the causes of the present rebellion in America assigned. in a sermon preached before the University of Oxford, on Friday, December 13. 1776. being the day appointed by proclamation for a general fast. By Myles Cooper, LL.D., President of King's College, New York; and fellow of Queen's College, Oxford. Published at the request of the Vice Chancellor and Heads of Houses. Oxford: at the Clarendon Press. Sold by J. and J. Fletcher, S. Parker, and D. Prince. By J. F. and C. Rivington in St.

Paul's Church-Yard; J. Robson in New Bond-street; and J. Pridden, in Fleet-street, London. And by J. Woodyer at Cambridge. MDCCLXXVII.

4to. Imp. 24 Dec. 1776. Bodl. 4° D 4(16) Th.
3rd A/cs. p. 393, dues. 1,000.

5. HOLMES, ROBERT. The resurrection of the body, deduced from the Resurrection of Christ, and illustrated from his Transfiguration. A sermon preached before the University of Oxford, at St. Mary's, on Easter-Monday, March 31, 1777. By Robert Holmes [etc.]. Oxford: printed for Daniel Prince; and sold by Mess. Rivington in St. Paul's Church-Yard, London. MDCCLXXVII.

4to. Bodl. 4° E 27(3) Th.
3rd A/cs. p. 393, dues. 250.

6. [HORNE, GEORGE.] A letter to Adam Smith LL.D. on the life, death, and philosophy of his friend David Hume Esq. By one of the people called Christians. Oxford: at the Clarendon Press. 1777. Sold by Daniel Prince; and by J. F. and C. Rivington, G. Robinson, and T. Payne and Son, London.

8vo. Bodl. 12 ϴ 822.

7. — The second edition. Bodl. 8° A 370(3) BS.

8. — The third edition. Bodl. 26683 f. 1.

3rd A/cs. p. 393, dues. First and second editions 500, third 250.

9. HORNE, GEORGE. Considerations on the life of St. John the Baptist. By George Horne [etc.]. The second edition. Oxford: at the Clarendon Press. MDCCLXXVII. Sold by Daniel Prince; and G. Robinson, London.

8vo fours. Bodl. 8° Q 185 Linc.
3rd A/cs. p. 393, dues. 500. The first edition was of 1769.

10. KENNICOTT, BENJAMIN. Benjamini Kennicotti Epistola ad celeberrimum Professorem Joannem Davidem Michaelis; de censura primi tomi Bibliorum Hebraicorum nuper editi, in Bibliotheca ejus Orientali, Parte XI. Oxonii; prostat venalis apud Rivington, Londini. MDCCLXXVII.

8vo fours. Bodl. 104 e. 2.
3rd A/cs. p. 393, dues. 500.

11. LOWTH, ROBERT. The life of William of Wykeham, Bishop of Winchester. Collected from records, registers, manuscripts, and other authentic evidences: by Robert Lowth, D.D., now Lord Bishop of Oxford. The third edition, corrected. Oxford, at the Clarendon Press, MDCCLXXVII. Sold by D. Prince: and by J. Dodsley and T. Cadell, London.

8vo Imp. 11 Jan. 1777. Bodl. 8° Q 88 Linc.
3rd A/cs. p. 393, dues. 500.

12*. (Oxford, University. [Jobbing work.])
Notice of the Chancellor's prizes.
Notice of a Convocation to authorize the spending of £300 on building the botanical professor's house and library.
Form of discommoning Jonathan Thatcher, a barber (150).
Notice of a Convocation to elect a Vinerian Professor, and a Keeper of the Archives, and to consider Sir Robert Chandler's letter.
The same, to elect a Vinerian Fellow.
The same, to elect a Vinerian Scholar.

A programma to preserve order in the Theatre on 3 July.
Order of performances in the Theatre on 3 July.

No copies found.
3rd A/cs. pp. 399–403.)

13. [——]. A panegyrical essay, or a few serious arguments, irrefragably proving that the present times are of all times there ever were, the most heroic, wise, and virtuous: with some occasional encomiums on a late apology for the life and writings of David Hume, Esq. Oxford: printed for Daniel Prince, and sold by J. Bew, in Pater-noster row. and Messrs. Payne, at the Mews Gate, London. MDCCLXXVII.
4to. B.M. 115.h.21.
3rd A/cs. p. 393, dues. 250.

14. RANDOLPH, THOMAS. A letter to the remarker on the Layman's Scriptural Confutation. Wherein the divinity of the Son of God is farther vindicated against the remarker's exceptions. To which is added, an appendix, taking some notice of Mr. Lindsey's sequel. By Thomas Randolph [etc.]. Oxford, at the Clarendon Press. MDCCLXXVII.
8vo fours. Imp. 24 Oct. 1776. Bodl. G. Pamph. 170(3).
3rd A/cs. p. 393, dues. 500.

15. RANDOLPH, THOMAS. The proof of the truth of the Christian religion, drawn from its successful propagation, considered and enforced, in two sermons lately preached before the University of Oxford. By Thomas Randolph [etc.]. Oxford: printed at the Clarendon Press, for J. and J. Fletcher in the Turle; and sold by Messrs. Rivington, in St. Paul's Church-Yard, London. MDCCLXXVII.
8vo fours. Imp. 18 Nov. 1777. Bodl. 8° V 166 Th.
3rd A/cs. p. 409, dues. 500.

16. RICHARDSON, JOHN. A dictionary, Persian, Arabic and English. By John Richardson, Esq. F.S.A. of the Middle Temple, and of Wadham College, Oxford. To which is prefixed a dissertation on the languages, literature, and manners of eastern nations. Oxford: printed at the Clarendon Press. Sold by J. Murray, No. 32, Fleetstreet, London; and by D. Prince, Oxford. MDCCLXXVII.
Fol. Bodl. I 3. 6 Art.
This is Vol. i. The second vol. is dated 1780.
3rd A/cs. p. 433, dues. 1,000.

17. RICHARDSON, JOHN. A dissertation on the languages, literature, and manners of the eastern nations. (Originally prefixed to a Dictionary Persian, Arabic, and English.) By John Richardson [etc.]. Oxford: printed at the Clarendon Press. Sold by J. Murray, No. 32, Fleet-street, London; and by D. Prince, Oxford. MDCCLXXVII.
8vo. Bodl. 8° Rawl. 676.

1778

1*. ABULCASIS. Abulcasis de Chirurgia. Arabice et Latine. Tomus primus [secundus]. Cura Johannis Channing, natu et civitate Londoniensis. Oxonii: e Typ. Clar. MDCCLXXVIII.
2 vols. 4to. Bodl. I I 23,4 Art.
3rd A/cs. pp. 351, 365, 380, 397, 413, printing 350.

2. BLACKSTONE, WILLIAM. Commentaries on the laws of England. In four books. By William Blackstone [etc.]. The eighth edition. Oxford. At the Clarendon Press, MDCCLXXVIII. Printed for William Strahan, Thomas Cadell, and Daniel Prince.
    8vo. Bodl. 8° Q 113–116 Linc.
    3rd A/cs. p. 409, dues. 3,000.

3. BURGESS, THOMAS. Observationes in Sophoclis Oedipum Tyrannum, Oedipum Coloneum, Antigonam: Euripidis Phoenissas, Aeschyli Septem contra Thebas. Auctore T. Burgess, e C.C.C. Oxonii: e Typ. Clar. Apud J. & J. Fletcher. MDCCLXXVIII.
    8vo fours. B.M. 995.g.21(2).

4. BUTLER, JOHN. A sermon preached at St. Mary's Church in Oxford, on Thursday, July 2, 1778. on occasion of the anniversary meeting of the Governors of the Radcliffe Infirmary: by John Lord Bishop of Oxford. Published at the request of the Governors, for the benefit of the charity. Oxford: printed at the Clarendon Press. MDCCLXXVIII. Sold at the Infirmary; also by J. and J. Fletcher, D. Prince and J. Cooke in Oxford; J. F. and C. Rivington, and T. Cadell in London.
    4to. Imp. 25 Sept. 1778. Bodl. 4° D 4(11) Th.
    3rd A/cs. p. 421, dues. 500.

5. CHELSUM, JAMES. Remarks on the two last chapters of Mr. Gibbon's History of the Decline and Fall of the Roman Empire. By James Chelsum [etc.]. The second edition, greatly enlarged. Oxford; printed at the Clarendon Press; and sold by D. Prince in Oxford; and by T. Payne and Son, Mews Gate; and J. Robson and Co. New Bond-Street, London. MDCCLXXVIII.
    8vo fours. Imp. 3 Jan. 1778. Bodl. 8° Q 147 Linc.
    3rd A/cs. p. 409, dues. 500.

6. COSTARD, GEORGE. A letter to Nathaniel Brassey Halhead, Esquire, Containing some remarks on his preface to the Code of Gentoo Laws lately published. By George Costard [etc.]. Oxford: at the Clarendon Press. MDCCLXXVIII. Sold by Daniel Prince; and by J. F. and C. Rivington, in London.
    8vo fours. Bodl. 24717 e. 11(2).
    3rd A/cs. p. 409, dues. 250.

7*. EURIPIDES. Εὐριπίδου τα σωζομενα. Euripidis quae extant omnia. Tragoedias superstites ad fidem veterum editionum codicumque MSS. cum aliorum, tum praecipue Bibliothecae Regiae Parisiensis recensuit: fragmenta tragoediarum deperditarum collegit: varias lectiones insigniores notasque perpetuas subjecit; interpretationem Latinam secundum probatissimas lectiones reformavit Samuel Musgrave M.A. Accedunt scholia Graeca in septem priores tragoedias ex optimis et locupletissimis editionibus recusa. Vol. I [II etc.]. Oxonii, e Typ. Clar. MDCCLXXVIII.
    4 vols. 4to. Bodl. I I 11–14 Art.
    3rd A/cs. pp. 351, 365, 380, 397, 413, printing 500.

8. HOLMES, ROBERT. Alfred. An ode. With six sonnets. By Robert Holmes [etc.]. Oxford: at the Clarendon Press. Printed for Daniel Prince; and sold by Mess. Rivington, in St. Paul's Church-Yard, London. MDCCLXXVIII.
    4to. Bodl. I I 35(19) Art.

9*. LONGINUS. Dionysii Longini quae supersunt Graece et Latine. Recensuit,

notasque suas atque animadversiones adjecit Joannes Toupius. Accedunt emendationes Davidis Ruhnkenii. Oxonii, e Typ. Clar. MDCCLXXVIII.

> 4to. Bodl. 29111 c. 1.
> 3rd A/cs. pp. 380, 397, printing 500 (100 LP).

10*.The same in 8vo. Bodl. Clar. Press 58 a. 87.

> 3rd A/cs. p. 413, printing 1,500 and 500 LP.

11*. NEW TESTAMENT IN SYRIAC. Sacrorum Evangeliorum versio Syriaca
Philoxeniana ex Codd. MSS. Ridleianis in bibliotheca Coll. Nov. Oxon. repositis
nunc primum edita: cum interpretatione et annotationibus Josephi White [etc.].
Tomus primus [secundus]. Oxonii. E Typ. Clar., MDCCLXXVIII.

> 2 vols. 4to. Bodl. Clar. Press 1 f. 61, 62.
> 3rd A/cs. pp. 365, 380, 413, printing 250.

12*. (Oxford, University. [Jobbing work.]
Composing 1½ sheets of Mr. Swinton's dissertation on the Coptick language.
Notice of a Convocation for Mr. Inglis's degree.
Notice of a Convocation to confer a degree on Mr. Burgh.
The same, on Mr. Gwatkin.
Programma to preserve order in the Theatre on 3 July.
Form of discommoning Allan Mackinnon, ladies' hairdresser.

> No copies found.
> 3rd A/cs. pp. 414–17.)

13. PYE, HENRY JAMES. Faringdon Hill. A poem. In two books. The second edition,
with odes, elegies and miscellaneous pieces. By Henry James Pye, Esq; Oxford:
printed for Daniel Prince; and sold by J. F. and C. Rivington, St. Paul's Church-
Yard, London. MDCCLXXVIII.

> 8vo fours. Bodl. G. Pamph. 179.
> 3rd A/cs. p. 409, dues. 500.

14. RICHARDSON, JOHN. A dissertation on the languages, literature and manners
of eastern nations. Originally prefixed to a Dictionary, Persian, Arabic, and English.
The second edition, to which is added, Part II. containing additional observations,
together with further remarks on A New Analysis of Ancient Mythology: in
answer to an Apology, addressed to the author, by Jacob Bryant, Esq. By John
Richardson [etc.]. Oxford: printed at the Clarendon Press. Sold by J. Murray, No.
32, Fleetstreet, London; and by D. Prince, Oxford. MDCCLXXVIII.

> 8vo. Bodl. Douce R 508.

15*. SCHOLTZ, CHRISTIAN. Christiani Scholtz, Berolin. Marchici, Aulae Regiae
Borussicae a concionibus sacris, et ecclesiae reformatae cathedralis Berolinensis
pastoris; grammatica Aegyptiaca utriusque dialecti: quam breviavit, illustravit,
edidit, Carolus Gotofredus Woide, S.A.S. Oxonii: e Typ. Clar. MDCCLXXVIII.

> 4to. Bodl. Clar. Press 66 a. 12.
> 3rd A/cs. pp. 380, 397, printing 250.

16. TOWNSON, THOMAS. Discourses on the four Gospels, chiefly with regard to
the peculiar design of each, and the order and place in which they were written.
To which is added, an inquiry concerning the hours of St. John, of the Romans,
and of some other nations of antiquity. By Thomas Townson [etc.]. Oxford: at the
Clarendon Press. MDCCLXXVIII.

> 4to. Imp. 10 Nov. 1777. Bodl. OO 58 Th.
> 3rd A/cs. p. 409, dues. 500.

1779

1*. APOLLONIUS RHODIUS. Apollonii Rhodii Argonauticorum libri quatuor Priorum editorum et interpretum notis selectis accedunt Ruhnkenii, Piersoni, Georgii d'Arnaud necnon Joannis Toupii animadversiones. Edidit nova fere interpretatione suisque nonnullis annotationibus illustravit, indices tres addidit Joannes Shaw [etc.]. Editio secunda. Oxonii, e Typ. Clar. MDCCLXXIX.

8vo fours. Bodl. Clar. Press 54 b. 1.

3rd A/cs. pp. 397, 413, 426, printing 1,500 (500 LP).

2. BAGOT, LEWIS. A sermon preached at St. Mary's Church in Oxford, on Thursday, July 1, 1779. on occasion of the anniversary meeting of the Governors of the Radcliffe Infirmary: by Lewis Bagot [etc.]. Published at the request of the Governors for the benefit of the charity. Oxford: printed at the Clarendon Press M.DCC.LXXIX. Sold at the Infirmary; also by D. Prince and J. Cooke, J. and J. Fletcher, in Oxford; J. F. and C. Rivington in London.

4to. Bodl. 4° D 4(3) Th.

3rd A/cs. p. 433, dues. 500.

3. BURTON, JOHN. Πενταλογια, sive tragoediarum Graecarum delectus: cum adnotatione Johannis Burton. Editio altera. Cui observationes, indicemque Graecum longe auctiorem et emendatiorem, adjecit Thomas Burgess, A.B. e C.C.C. Tom. I. Oxonii: e Typ. Clar. apud J. & J. Fletcher. MDCCLXXIX.

8vo fours. Bodl. Clar. Press 54 a. 9.

The first edition was published in 1758.

4. HOLMES, ROBERT. The resurrection of the body, deduced from the Resurrection of Christ, and illustrated from his Transfiguration. A sermon preached before the University of Oxford, at St. Mary's on Easter-Monday, March 31, 1777. By Robert Holmes [etc.]. The second edition. Oxford: printed for Daniel Prince and J. Cooke, and sold by Mess. Rivington in St. Paul's Church-Yard, London. MDCCLXXIX.

8vo fours. Bodl. 100 aa. 13(8).

5*. (Oxford, University. [Jobbing work.]

Notice of Mr. Curtis's resignation of the lectureship of St. Giles's.

Notice of a Convocation to elect a new lecturer at St. Giles's.

Notice of a Convocation to confer a degree on Lord Lewisham.

Notice of altering the time of sermons (200).

Notice of altering the time of Bodley's speech.

Notice of a Convocation to confer a degree on Mr. Townson.

Notice of the Chancellor's prizes (120).

Extracts from Mr. Bampton's will (60).

Notice of a Convocation to petition the House of Commons against the Dissenter's Bill.

Copies of the Dissenter's Bill.

Petition to the House of Commons (350).

A request to colleges to apply for a new Paving Act.

Notice of a Convocation to elect to the living of Hanlipp.

A programma to preserve order in the Theatre on 2 July.

Notice for Gentlemen to meet for care of lighting and paving.

Notice of a Convocation to give £200 to Government in the present exigency.
Mr. Woide's proposals for printing fragments of the New Testament in the
   Ægyptian dialect
   No copies found.
   3rd A/cs. pp. 427–9.)

6. RANDOLPH, JOHN. A sermon preached at the ordination held at Christ Church,
Nov. 21, 1779. by John Lord Bishop of Oxford. Published at his Lordship's request.
By John Randolph [etc.]. Oxford. Printed for J. and J. Fletcher in the Turle; and
Mess. Rivington in St. Paul's Church-Yard, London. MDCCLXXIX.
   4to. Imp. 8 Dec. 1779. Bodl. G. Pamph. 519(18).
   3rd A/cs. p. 433, dues. 500.

7. WESTON, PHIPPS. Christian bishops and pastors the salt of the earth. A sermon
preached at the consecration of the Right Reverend Thomas by divine permission
Bishop of Lincoln; on Trinity Sunday, 1779. in the chapel at Lambeth; and published by command of His Grace the Arch-Bishop of Canterbury. By Phipps Weston
[etc.]. Oxford: at the Clarendon Press. MDCCLXXIX.
   4to. Bodl. Vet. A 5 d. 785.

1780

1*. ARISTOTLE. [Title in Greek.] Aristotelis De poetica liber ex versione Theodori
Goulstoni. Lectionis varietatem e codd. iv Bibliothecae Mediceae, verborum
indicem et observationes suas adjunxit T. Winstanley [etc.]. Oxonii, E Typ. Clar.
MDCCLXXX.
   8vo fours. Bodl. Clar. Press 50 b. 3.
   3rd A/cs. p. 438, printing 1,500 (500 LP).

2. BAGOT, LEWIS. Twelve discourses on the prophecies concerning the first establishment and subsequent history of Christianity, preached in Lincoln's-Inn-Chapel,
at the Lecture of the Right Rev. William Warburton, late Lord Bishop of Gloucester.
By Lewis Bagot [etc.]. Oxford: printed for J. and J. Fletcher, D. Prince and J. Cooke;
J. F. and C. Rivington, and T. Cadell, London. MDCCLXXX.
   8vo. Imp. 2 Feb. 1780. Bodl. 8° Q 72 Linc.
   3rd A/cs. p. 433, dues. 750.

3. BANDINEL, JAMES. Eight sermons preached before the University of Oxford, in
the year 1780, at the lecture founded by the late Rev. and pious John Bampton,
M.A. Canon of Salisbury. To which is added, a vindication of St. Paul from the
charge of wishing himself accursed, a sermon preached before the University, on
Sunday, March 14 [sic], 1778. By James Bandinel [etc.]. Oxford: printed for D. Prince
and J. Cooke, J. and J. Fletcher; J. F. and C. Rivington, and T. Cadell, London.
MDCCLXXX.
   8vo. Imp. 6 March 1780. Bodl. Clar. Press 1 b. 170.
   3rd A/cs. p. 433, dues. 524.

4*. CAESAR, JULIUS. C. Julii Caesaris et aliorum De bellis Gallico, Civili, Pompeiano,
Alexandrino, Africano et Hispaniensi commentarii juxta editionem Oudendor-

pii. Accedunt tabulae et index geographicus auctiores. Oxonii, e Typ. Clar. MDCCLXXX.

8vo. Bodl. 8° C 54 BS.

3rd A/cs. p. 438, printing 1,500.

5*. HOMER. *Ομηρου Ιλιας συν τοις σχολιοις ψευδεπιγραφοις Διδυμου. Τμημα πρωτον* [δευτερον]. *Εν Οξονια, αψ'π'.*

2 vols. 8vo fours. Bodl. 2931 d. 38, 39.

3rd A/cs. p. 438, printing 2,000 (500 LP). Edited by Thomas Hind.

6*. HOMER. Index vocabulorum in Homeri Iliade atque Odyssea caeterisque quotquot extant poematis. Studio M. Wolfgangi Seberi Sulina. Editio nova auctior et emendatior. Oxonii, ex Typ. Clar. MDCCLXXX.

8vo fours. Bodl. Monro d. 5.

3rd A/cs. p. 438, printing 2,000 (500 LP).

7. KENNICOTT, BENJAMIN. Vetus Testamentum Hebraicum; cum variis lectionibus. Edidit Benjaminus Kennicott [etc.]. Tomus secundus. Oxonii, e Typ. Clar. MDCCLXXX.

Fol. Bodl. Z 2. 17 Th.

3rd A/cs. p. 433, dues. 650. The first volume was published in 1776.

8*. (Oxford, University. [Jobbing work.]

Notice of Congregations in Michaelmas term (100).

Notice of a Convocation to appoint a delegacy to consider the expiry of the lease of the Bible Press.

Notice of a Convocation to give £100 to the Society for Propagating the Gospel in Foreign Parts.

Notice of a Convocation to raise a fund for the Bodleian Library.

A request to preserve order in the Musick Room.

Notice of Congregations in Hilary term.

Form of a statute for raising a fund for the Bodleian Library.

Notice of a Convocation to present to the living of Weston under Wetherby.

Notice of a Convocation to pass the Bodleian statute.

New statute for the Bodleian Library (500).

Report of the Delegates on the proposal of Messrs. Hamilton and Jackson to print Bibles (80).

Notice of a Convocation to confer the degree of M.A. on Mr. Richardson.

Notice of the Chancellor's prizes (120).

Request to each college to send a deputy to apply for a new Paving Act.

Notice of a meeting of the deputies for lighting and paving.

Mr. White's grammatical analysis of the Hebrew (150).

Request to relieve the sufferers by fire at Drayton.

Notice of Congregations in Act term.

Notice of a Convocation to elect a clinical professor (100).

Programma to preserve order in the Theatre on 4 July.

Notice of a Convocation to petition Parliament for an altered assessment to the pound rate.

Notice of a rehearsal of the prize composition.

Notice of a Convocation to elect burgesses for the University.

No copies found.

3rd A/cs. pp. 439–43.)

9. RICHARDSON, JOHN. A dictionary English, Persian and Arabic by John Richardson [etc.]. Vol. II. Oxford: printed at the Clarendon Press. Sold by J. Murray, No. 32, Fleetstreet, London; and by Daniel Prince, Oxford. MDCCLXXX.

Fol. Bodl. I 3. 7 Art.

The first volume was published in 1777.

10. WALL, JOHN. Medical tracts by the late John Wall, M.D. of Worcester. Collected and republished by Martin Wall, M.D. Oxford, printed: sold by D. Prince and J. Cooke, Oxford; and T. Cadell, London. MDCCLXXX.

8vo fours. Imp. 17 Jan. 1780. Bodl. 8° F 168 BS.

3rd A/cs. p. 433, dues. 500.

11*. WHITE, JOSEPH. A specimen of the civil and military institutes of Timour, or Tamerlane: a work written originally by that celebrated conqueror in the Mogul language, and since translated into Persian. Now first rendered from the Persian into English, from a MS. in the possession of William Hunter, M.D., F.R.S. Physician in Ordinary to the Queen. With other pieces. By Joseph White [etc.]. Oxford: at the Clarendon Press. MDCCLXXX. Sold by P. Elmsly in London; D. Prince and J. Cooke in Oxford.

4to. Bodl. G. Pamph. 1813(10).

3rd A/cs. p. 438, printing 300.

12. XENOPHON. [Title in Greek.] Xenophontis Memorabilium Socratis dictorum libri iv. Cum notis H. Stephani, Leunclavii, Æ. Porti & Ernesti. Recensuit, suisque annotationibus auxit Bolton Simpson [etc.]. Editio quinta emendatior, cui accessere adnotationes quaedam non prius editae. Oxonii, e Th. Sh. Impensis J. & J. Fletcher, bibliopol. Oxon. J. F. & C. Rivington, Lond. MDCCLXXX.

8vo fours. Bodl. 290 i. 180.

3rd A/cs. p. 433, dues. 1,250. Previous editions were of 1741, 1749, 1759, and 1772. Presumably this was the edition that Jonathan Edwards was preparing in 1775: B.M. MS. Add. 42561, fol. 53.

Index

Years following A are those of publications listed in the Appendix. U stands for University of Oxford, V.-C. for Vice-Chancellor, Delegate for Delegate of the Press, Bp. for Bishop.

— Greek type by, 380–3

BASKETT, John, Stationer, 166–76

— Bibles, his monopoly of printing, 167–8

— — quality of his, 173

— Clarendon Building, contributes to the cost of, 169, 199, 279

— Clarendon's *History* sold wholesale by, 153, 165–6

— — editions of, printed for him, 166–7, A 1707, 1712, 1717, 1720

— Duty of Man's *Works* partly printed by, 320

— financial difficulties, in, 173–5

— King's Printer, 167–8, 332

— lessee of the Oxford Bible Press, 168–76, 321

— *Oxford Almanack* sold wholesale by, 167

— paper supplied to the Press by, 166–7, 173, 214, 216

— Stationers' Company, his agreements with, 168–9, 175–6

Baskett, Mark, 352–4

— Robert, 176, 321, 352

— Thomas, 176, 321, 352

Baskett v. The University of Cambridge, 329, 345–7

Bate, Julius, 307

Bateman, Christopher, bookseller, 183, 184

Battely, John, A 1711, 1742, 1743, 1745, 1755

Battersby, Robert, 81

Bear, John, A 1748

Beare, William, A 1750

Beaver, Herbert, 146

Beckford, family of, paper-makers, 167, 215

bedels, esquire, Laud wishes to employ in the Press, 34–5

— of law also architypographi, 31–2

— staff of one mended, 6

Bellinger, John, 105

Benedict, Abbot of Peterborough, A 1735

Bennett, Thomas, of Christ Church, corrector and editor, 48, 220

— — fails election as architypographus, 51, 64

— Thomas, bookseller, 221, 258

— — Clarendon's *History* sold wholesale by, 152, 153, 154, 164–5

— — complains of Oxford books sold cheap abroad, 183

— — his death regretted, 161

Benson, Thomas, A 1690, 1701

Bentham, Edward, advice to young men by, 289, A 1748, 1762

— American Revolution, on the, A 1776

— anti-Jacobite writings by, 288, A 1745

— Burton, his *Life* of, A 1771

— King, William, lampooned by, 289

— logic, on, A 1740, 1755

— moral philosophy, on, A 1745, 1746

— sermons, A 1744, 1750

— theological writings, A 1764, 1771, 1774

Bentivoglio, Ercole, A 1731

Bentley, Richard, advocates a learned press at Cambridge, 158

— Malalas, his comments on, 227

— offensive references to, 268

— Phalaris, on, 262

Benzelius, Erik, 298–301, 311

Bernard, Edward, ancient mathematicians, his work on, 88, 240, 241, 242

— *Catalogi* of MSS. nominally edited by, 245, A 1694, 1697

— comparative linguistic studies of, 120, 243, 310

— Coptic dictionary given to, for publication, 293

— — verses by, 293

— Delegate, 140

— Euclid, proposes an edition of, 128, 161, 240, A 1694

— Fell's Greek Testament criticized by, 81

— Josephus, his unfinished edition of, 88–9, A 1694

Bettenham, James, printer, 377

Bever, Thomas, A 1766

Beveridge, William, Bp., 39 Articles, on the, A 1710

— *Synodicon* compiled by, see *Synodicon*

BIBLE. *See also* New Testament, Pentateuch, Psalms, Septuagint

— *Polyglot*, the London, 41–2

— *Hebrew* (Old Testament), 307, ed. Forster, 310, A 1744, 1750

— — Kennicott's variorum, 410–13, A 1776, 1780

— *Greek*, 63

— *Latin*, monopoly of printing, 59

— *English*, Genevan Version printed at Cambridge, 28

— Authorized Version, America, sale in, xxx, 354

— annotated, proposed by Fell, 60, 86

— Baskett, printed by, 167–76

— — prices raised by, 171

— Blayney's revision, 358–60

— Cambridge, printed at, 28, 29, 72, 357–60

— capital letters sparingly used in, 360

— Crown copyright in, 347–51

— drawback of paper-duty on, 217, 341

— errors in, 169–72, 359

— Fell's desire to print, 59–60, 68, 101

— — edition of (1675), 71, 72

rules, brass and tin, 210
Runic, type for, 125
Ruskin, John, *Lectures on Art* by, 368
Russell, Richard, on sea water, 313, A 1750, 1753
Russian, grammar of, 210, 243–6
— script cut in wood, 229
— type for, 210
Rye, George, sermon, A 1714

Sacheverell, Henry, sermons, 222, 283, A 1702
Sacra Congregatio de Propaganda Fide, 127, 135
St. Aldates, Bible Press moved to, 198
St. Amand, James, 334, 396–7
St. Frideswide's fair, books sold at, 17
sale of publications, difficulty of, 61, 70, 151, 160–1, 181–3, 274
— Charlett's attention to, 177
— Fell's attempts to stimulate, 62, 131–2, 177
— University Press, books of, in modern times, xxv, xxvi, xxx
Sallust, ed. Ayerst, A 1701
— Stationers' Company, printed for the, 313, A 1730
Salvini, Antonio, 224
Samaritan Pentateuch, 410, 412
— script, type for, 126
Sancroft, William, Archbishop, 115
Sanderson, Robert, Bp., book on logic by, 25
Sanderus, *Bibliotheca Belgica* by, 247
Sandius, Christopher, 116
Savage, Henry, engraver, 129
Savile, Sir Henry, Warden of Merton College, 239
— Greek type given by, 25, 30, 381
Sawbridge, George, Stationer, 72
'scabbarding' of lines of type, 209
Scaliger, Joseph, A 1700
Schardam, P. J., 401
'Scheduled Books', the, 28, 59, 159
Scheffer, Johann, 128
Scholtz, Christian, 313, 400, A 1778
school books, monopoly of printing, *see* Stationers of London
— printed by Fell in 1672, 59, 68, 70
— printed at Oxford and sold by Parker and Guy, 96
— University, seldom published by, in the 18th century, 219
— — published by, in modern times, xxvii
Schools Money, surplus of, devoted to printing, 32, 34, 37, 43
— Blackstone's estimate of the amount of, due to the Press, 32

— payments of, for printing, 37, 55, 341–4
science at Oxford, Plot's account of, 90–1
'Sclavonian', type named, 243
Scolar, John, printer, 12–13, 14, 15
Scotland, Bible-printing in, law as to, 351
— Bibles and prayer-books printed in, and sold in England, 349–50
— King's Printer in, 168, 175, 349
Scott, Robert, bookseller, 47–9, 73
scribes in Oxford in early times, 2, 3
Scrope, John, A 1761
— — sermon, A 1760
— Richard, 364
sea water, cures by, 313–14
Seale, William, bookbinder, 216
Seaman, William, 43
Secker, Thomas, Archbishop, 300, 334, 358, 410
— sermon, A 1733
Secretary to the Delegates, first appointment of, xxiv
Selden, John, 41, 77, 84, 86, 119, 393
Sélis, N.-J., A 1766
Septuagint, the, Aristeas on, 222
— Fell's desire to print, 63
— ed. Grabe, *see* Grabe
Serenus, 242
sermons, censured, 284–5, A 1695
— cost of printing, 283
— multitude of, printed at the Press, 283
— Oxford, preached at, character of, 284–6
Shakespeare's plays, ed. Hanmer, 301–5, 408, A 1744, 1771
Sharp, William, sermons, A 1754, 1755
Sharpe, Gregory, 395–6
Shaw, John, *Argonautica* edited by, 403–4, A 1777, 1779
— Thomas, *Travels* of, A 1738, 1746
— — sermon, A 1765
— William, secretary to the Earl of Clarendon, 231
Sheldon, Gilbert, Archbishop, 46, 55, 60
Sheldonian Theatre, the, arrangements for printing in, 46–7, 198
— Bibles printed in, by London Stationers, 96–7
— compositors' frames made for, 47
— device, publisher's, of the U, showing the, 46, 129, 201
— — counterfeit, 116
— endowment for repair of, *see* Theatre Money
— first book printed in, 49, 142
— imprint in Oxford books, as, 66, 199–200
— last use of, for printing, 198